RUNNING

Microsoft®
Word 2000

Charles Rubin

Microsoft Press

PUBLISHED BY
Microsoft Press
A Division of Microsoft Corporation
One Microsoft Way
Redmond, Washington 98052-6399

Library of Congress Cataloging-in-Publication Data
Rubin, Charles, 1953-
    Running Microsoft Word 2000 / Charles L. Rubin.
        p. cm.
    Includes index.
    ISBN 1-57231-943-7
    1. Microsoft Word. 2. Word processing. I. Title.   II. Title:
Running Microsoft Word two thousand.
Z52.5.M52R83 1999   IN PROCESS
652.5'5369--dc21   98-50600
                                CIP

Printed and bound in the United States of America.

1 2 3 4 5 6 7 8 9 QMQM   4 3 2 1 0 9

Distributed in Canada by ITP Nelson, a division of Thomson Canada Limited.

A CIP catalogue record for this book is available from the British Library.

Microsoft Press books are available through booksellers and distributors worldwide. For further information about international editions, contact your local Microsoft Corporation office or contact Microsoft Press International directly at fax (425) 936-7329. Visit our Web site at mspress.microsoft.com.

For Microsoft Press
Acquisitions Editor: Christey Bahn
Project Editor: Sandra Haynes

For nSight, Inc.
Project Manager: Peter Whitmer
Manuscript Editor: Joseph Gustaitis
Technical Editor: Alison Fields

For Sara and Dan—
my loves, my joys, my reasons.

CHAPTERS AT A GLANCE

TABLE OF CONTENTS

Part V   Data Handling and Automation Tools   581

Chapter 26   Using Mail Merge 583

Acknowledgments

T his book has been the greatest single challenge I have faced in more than fifteen years of writing, and I am grateful to many people who made it possible.

At the top of my list is Claudette Moore of Moore Literary Agency— my friend, sounding board, inspirer of brainstorms, and agent par excellence. As you foresaw all along, Claudette, things really did work out.

I would next like to thank Douglas Hergert, whose generosity and profound knowledge of Visual Basic made Chapter 29 possible. Malcolm Lowe created the best of the graphical examples in this book and helped resolve some knotty graphics-related problems. Thanks also to Morgan Linton, who survived a number of system crashes and other problems while helping me understand Word's new Web-related features.

Among the cheerful and hard-working people at Microsoft Press, I would especially like to thank Kim Fryer and Sandra Haynes. Thanks to Kim for this tremendous opportunity, and thanks to Sandra for making things happen.

I would also like to thank a number of people at nSight, Inc., who turned my manuscript into the finished product you see here. I'm particularly grateful to Alison Fields, the technical editor, who worked tirelessly through a couple of beta versions and numerous hardware and software problems to keep the book accurate and complete. Thanks also to Joseph Gustaitis, the copy editor, who made many things clearer; Rebecca Merz, who supervised the layout, and to Peter Whitmer, who patiently held together the entire production team during a project whose length and complexity would have sent other people screaming for the door.

Charles Rubin

Introduction

Microsoft Word has evolved over the years from a typical word processing program into a document management powerhouse. You can use Word to create documents that combine text with graphics, sounds, or multimedia objects, and you can publish those documents on paper, on the World Wide Web (Web), via e-mail, fax, or other electronic media. Word was the first word processing program that was widely known for its ease of use, and Word 2000 extends this tradition by making more document-processing power more accessible for users at all levels.

Whether you've been using Word since the early 80s or you're new to it today; whether you're writing a memo, creating a Web site, or producing a book-length corporate report; this book will help you understand how Word can deliver better-looking, more effective documents quickly and easily.

How This Book Is Organized

Word is a big program with hundreds of different features. This book will familiarize you with all of them. To make the material as accessible as possible, I have divided Word's feature sets into 38 different chapters in seven parts. Here's how the book is organized.

Part I – Word Basics

Chapters 1 through 8 are a quick introduction to Word's most important editing, formatting, file management, Help, and customization features. If you're new to Word, these chapters will show you how to do most of the things you'll want to do most of the time, and how to get more information about any of them.

Part II – Writing and Editing Tools

Chapters 9 through 13 explain features that make text entry, editing, and document navigation faster or easier. In these chapters, you'll learn about the spelling and grammar checkers, automatic hyphenation, finding and replacing text, sorting, organizing with outlines, and using templates or wizards to speed document creation.

Part III – Formatting Tools

When you're ready to produce a finished document, Chapters 14 through 18 will show you how to use special formatting features in Word. You'll learn about styles, Web page themes, tables, special paragraph and document format options, sections, and tools that automatically create proper formats for envelopes and labels.

Part IV – Graphics, Page Design, and Publishing Tools

While Word lacks some of the features of stand-alone publishing programs such as FrameMaker or QuarkXpress, it does a fine job of producing professional-looking documents for many small business, corporate, and individual projects. Chapters 19 through 25 explain how to incorporate colorful graphics, digital pictures, or other objects in your documents. You'll also learn how to design pleasing formats for publications ranging from resumes to newsletters to training manuals; how to manage documents containing hundreds of pages; and how Word can easily generate indexes, cross-references, tables of contents, and other professional document features.

Part V – Data Handling and Automation Tools

Chapters 26 through 30 will show you how to insert information automatically, calculate information in documents, or automate any Word operation or group of operations. You'll also learn how to use Word to create printed or electronic forms that make it easy to gather information from others.

Part VI – Web and Internet Tools

With corporate intranets and personal Web sites sprouting like weeds, Web publishing has become the easiest way to present graphically rich information to a wide audience. Word includes powerful yet easy-to-use tools for accessing the Internet and for creating and publishing Web pages. In Chapters 31 through 33, you'll find out how to go online from inside Word and how to create and publish exciting Web pages that include colorful graphics, sounds, movies, and animation. And if you're already familiar with HTML programming, you'll find a new suite of tools you can use to easily create Web-based forms.

Part VII – Collaboration Tools

Word is the standard word processor for offices everywhere. Word 2000 includes a variety of collaboration tools you can use to easily share documents with others on a company network. You can route a document to a group of reviewers, consolidate comments from several reviewers into one document, or convert files to or from Word's document format. Chapters 34 through 38 will show you how.

Appendix – Installing and Running Word

Word 2000 has a host of new installation modes and features. The Appendix will show you how to install Word, add new features, remove features, and use Word's self-repairing tools. You'll also find out about some of Word's network administration features that can make your life a lot easier if you're running Word on a company network.

Tips, Notes, and Other Goodies

Throughout the book, you'll find some notes, tips, and margin icons that draw your attention to specific features in Word.

- **Tips** offer advice about how to better use a feature, or how to overcome a potential problem you may have when you use one.

 TIP

> To edit header or footer text, double-click it. *See "Using Headers and Footers" on page 320 for details.*

- **Notes** offer additional information about things that happen when you use certain features, or warn you about minor problems or limits of functionality.

NOTE

> The Outline view command is on the extended portion of the View menu, but if you choose this command frequently, Word will add it to the short version of the menu.

- **Warnings** call your attention to severe consequences—such as deleting information or causing major formatting changes—that can arise from using a particular feature.

WARNING

> Don't save a document when Shrink to Fit is turned on. If you do, Word will save it at the reduced size, so all the fonts in the document will be smaller than they were before. You'll have to reformat all the text to restore it to its normal size.

- **See Also** notes in the margin direct you to other resources you can use to learn more about a feature or an area of Word's operations.

SEE ALSO

For more information about using Outline view, see Chapter 12, "Working with Outlines."

- **On The Web** elements direct you to Web-based resources you can visit to get more information or download additional Word accessories.

ON THE WEB

Choose Office On The Web from the Help menu to check for new sounds and video clips available from the Microsoft Office Web site.

- **New** is a margin icon that highlights features that are new or significantly changed in Word 2000. It helps older Word hands locate new features quickly.

Assumptions and Conventions

This book will show you how to get the most out of Word, but it's not a one-stop guide to using a computer. Although you'll find some very basic information about managing windows, menus and dialog boxes in Chapter 2, this book generally assumes that you are familiar with Microsoft Windows, and with such terms as *window, mouse, pointing, clicking,* and *dragging*. If you don't know what any of these terms means, choose the Help command from the Start menu (the button labeled Start in the lower-left corner of your screen), click the Contents tab in the Windows Help dialog box, and explore the information you find there.

About the Instructions

As this is a how-to book, there are lots of step-by-step examples and detailed instructions. Here's how I will let you know what to do at each step:

- When I want you to hold down the Ctrl or Alt key along with another key or two, I list the keys together with plus signs linking them, as in, "Press Ctrl+X to cut the text from the document."

- I will always tell you to *press* a key on your keyboard, but to *click* or *double-click* the mouse button. (Double-clicking means clicking the mouse button twice in rapid succession.)

- When I want you to hold down the Shift key and then click the mouse button, I'll ask you to *Shift-click*.

- When I want you to hold down the mouse button and move the pointer across text or objects, I'll ask you to *drag*.

- When you are supposed to type text into a document, the text you are supposed to type appears in italic type, as in "Type *Murchison Report* and press the Enter key." I also use italic type to refer to text you have already typed, as in "Select *obnoxious* on the first line and press Ctrl+X."

You're On Your Way

With Word 2000 and this book, you have the tools you need to create better documents with less work than ever. To get started, just turn the page.

PART I

Word Basics

Microsoft Word 2000 at a Glance

Microsoft Word 2000 is a powerful program with hundreds of features. This book will show you how to use those features, but to begin, it's best to get an overall idea of what Word is and how it works. Once you have a general idea of the features available in Word, you'll find it easier to see how each feature fits into the program's overall context.

Microsoft Word is one of the world's leading word processing programs, and that's not by accident. Word was the first word processing program that combined a broad range of powerful editing, formatting, and publishing features with an interface that a novice could learn in minutes. Over the past 15 years, Word has evolved with a new interface, new intelligence, and new features that help you create any document more quickly and easily.

Word Processing, Word Style

Any word processor can store text in documents and allow you to print that text on paper, but Word does far more than that. Computer networks and raw computing power have grown over the years, so the definition of "document" has expanded, and Word has improved along with it. Word is now a full-featured text, graphics, World Wide Web page creation, and document-processing program.

What Word Does

With Word, you can create just about any kind of document you want and publish it electronically on paper. Word's key capabilities can be divided into a handful of categories.

Text Editing

You can enter text by typing with your keyboard, and you can also insert selections of text or whole files into a document. Word has many features that make correcting, editing, and changing your text as easy as possible. For example, AutoText completes words or phrases that you use frequently whenever you type just the first few letters. AutoCorrect fixes common typing, spelling, and grammatical mistakes automatically so you don't have to bother with them.

Text Formatting

You can set the spacing, alignment, or indentations of text, and you can also choose the font, font size, and style of type used to display it. You can define styles that contain several text format settings and apply them all at once, or use themes to give Web pages a coordinated look with a customized set of styles, graphics, and a background. You can arrange text in tables, add headers and footers, position footnotes and endnotes, and add captions or text boxes to graphics or tables.

Graphics

Word has a built-in set of tools you can use to create shapes, lines, boxes, ovals, captions, and other simple graphics. You can also select from dozens of predefined shapes or clip art images and insert these into documents. You can import graphics from most other Microsoft Windows applications into a Word document, and you can use Word's Photo Editor to view and modify digital photographs and other electronic images.

Desktop Publishing

Word has special publishing tools you can use to arrange text and graphics on a page for just about any publishing project, from signs to newsletters to books and magazines. For example, you can lay text out in multiple columns, add graphics, wrap text around display quotations or graphics, make alternating headers and footers (for facing-pages layouts), create indexes, cross-references, and tables of contents. Word includes a number of predesigned templates for different publication formats, and you can easily modify them for your own uses (or create your own).

Data Management and Automation

Word has a built-in mail merge feature that pulls data from a database file and creates form letters or mailing labels. The same basic capability makes it possible for you to include the contents of any database field anywhere in a document, and you can set Word to update fields automatically when you print. You can also create macros to automate procedures, so you can complete several tasks with just a couple of keystrokes; or create entire programs in Microsoft Visual Basic for Applications that can run automatically when Word is started.

Web Publishing

A newly enhanced suite of Web publishing tools in Word 2000 makes it easy to publish your Word documents on the Web with exactly the formatting you want. You can use Word to create complex Web pages that include forms, tables, Microsoft Excel worksheets, graphics, video clips, sounds, animations, and other components. A new Script Editor even allows you to create and include HTML scripts in your Web pages. You can access Web-based resources from within Word and you can include hypertext links in any document.

Collaboration

Document creation is a team effort in many companies, and Word includes several features that make it easier to manage the process. You can add text or spoken comments, keep track of different versions and revisions, and automatically route a document to a group of reviewers. You can also add reviewer comments to a Web page, or schedule conferences with Microsoft NetMeeting.

Integration

Word supports Microsoft's Object Linking and Embedding (OLE), so it can share data and capabilities with any other program that supports OLE. Since Word is part of Microsoft Office, it can easily share data with Microsoft Excel, Microsoft PowerPoint, Microsoft Access, icrosoft Outlook, and also with Microsoft Internet Explorer. Here are some examples:

■ Go to a Web page from within a Word document (Word launches Internet Explorer as the Web browser when you do this.)

■ View Web pages you create in Word using Internet Explorer

■ Insert Excel spreadsheets into Word documents and have them automatically updated whenever you change the figures in Excel

■ Insert Access fields into Word documents and have them up-dated automatically when the data changes in Access

■ Use addresses from an Access database to generate form letters in Word

■ Use Web page layout themes in Access forms

■ Use the same spelling dictionaries to check spelling in Word, Excel, PowerPoint, Outlook, and Access so that when you enter words in one custom dictionary, they are available to every Office program

■ E-mail Word documents from inside Word, using Outlook's mail-box profile

■ Insert PowerPoint slides or slide shows into a Word document

Customization

Word can be completely adapted to the way you work. For example, you can do any of the following:

■ Create, edit, or delete menus, menu commands, toolbars, and toolbar buttons

■ Hide, move, or rearrange toolbars

- Create or change keyboard shortcuts for any Word operation

- Create or change the templates from which new documents are made

- Select an alternate language for Word's spelling and grammar checking features

- Change the language used for the entire interface

- Change Word's units of measurement from inches to centimeters or from points to picas

- Add new fonts

Automation

Finally, Word has lots of intelligent features that help automate document creation. AutoCorrect and AutoText were mentioned earlier, but there are more. AutoFormat reformats text as you type, creating bulleted or numbered lists automatically, or replacing Web addresses with active hypertext links, for example. Word's adaptive menus and toolbars move frequently used commands and buttons to a more prominent place, so they're easier to find. And wizards make it easy to create letters, newsletters, Web pages, and other kinds of documents.

How Word Works

Each program has its own working style and terminology, and Word is no different. Let's look at some basic Word terms and concepts.

Documents

Each Word document can contain text as well as objects such as graphics, sounds, fields, hyperlinks or shortcuts to other documents, and even video clips. You can save documents as Web pages and add HTML scripts to them, too. Figure 1-1 at the top of the next page shows a sample document that contains hyperlinks and graphics as well as text.

FIGURE 1-1.

Word documents can contain text, graphics, hyperlinks, and data fields.

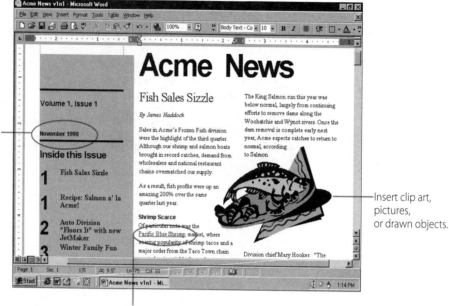

Insert fields to calculate and present information.

Insert clip art, pictures, or drawn objects.

Insert hyperlinks to Web pages or other documents.

Document Views

Word lets you view documents in four different ways.

? SEE ALSO

For more information about using views, see Chapter 6.

- The Web Layout and Print Layout views show how a document will look when printed or when viewed on the Web. You can also use these two views to insert graphics, text boxes, images, sounds, video, and text to create professional-looking publications and Web pages. Print Layout view is the default view in Word.

- Normal view lets you focus on the text in your document.

- Outline view shows the document as an outline so you can easily reorganize it.

- In addition, you can zoom (magnify or reduce) a document's contents to make it easier to read or to fit more of the document onto your screen.

Characters

Each letter of text you place in a document is called a character. You can format each character individually, but more often you'll format text by word, line, or paragraph. You can change each letter's font, style (bold or underline, for example), font size, position, spacing, or color. Figure 1-2 shows an example of a few different fonts, sizes, and styles. You can also add special text effects such as flashing or marquee lights for Web pages or e-mail documents.

Paragraphs

Documents are divided into paragraphs. You can set the indentation, alignment, tab stops, and line spacing of each paragraph individually if you like. You can also enhance paragraphs with borders or a shaded background, or format them as bullet points, numbered lists, or outlines.

Pages

Printed documents are divided into pages. Word's page formatting options let you control the placement of margins, headers, footers, footnotes, line numbers, multiple columns, and other page elements.

FIGURE 1-2.

By dividing a page into three sections, you can apply three sets of page formatting options on the same page, such as the single and three-column layouts shown here.

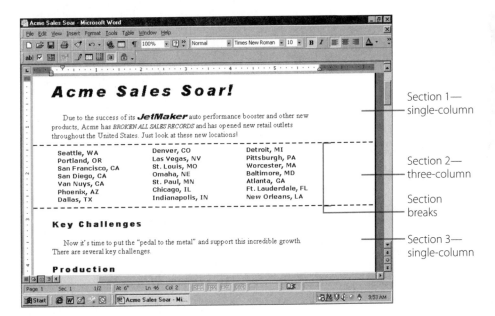

Sections

In complex documents, you may want to use more than one group of page format settings. For example, you might want to use different header or footer text on different groups of pages in a document, or create pages that include both single-column and multiple-column formats. In this case, you divide the document into sections as shown in Figure 1-2. Each section has its own page format settings.

Templates

Word uses templates to store document formatting information, keyboard shortcuts, custom menus or toolbars, and other information. Every new document is based on a template. Word comes with dozens of predesigned templates for various types of documents, including memos, letters, reports, resumes, newsletters, and legal pleadings. You can modify these templates or create new ones of your own.

Styles and Themes

There are dozens of formatting options in Word, so the program uses styles and themes to make it easier to apply a group of formatting options all at once.

Styles can contain both character and paragraph formatting options. Each document template has a default style collection (or style sheet), but you can add, remove, or change styles, and you can copy styles from one document template to another. Figure 1-3 shows how a style applies several format settings to the name at the top of a resume.

FIGURE 1-3.

You can create named format styles in Word that store different font, size, style, and paragraph format options.

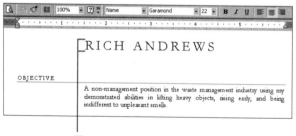

The name on this resume is formatted by using the Name style (Garamond, 22 point, all caps, expanded spacing, centered).

Themes are collections of styles that coordinate with one another so as to produce a unified look for a Web page or other electronic document. Themes contain character and paragraph styles, backgrounds, and graphics for Web pages or e-mail messages. Word comes equipped with dozens of predesigned themes that you can use.

What's New in Word 2000

Microsoft has added dozens of new features to Word 2000. Some are designed to make life easier for network administrators who must oversee a large population of Word users, but most of these features are designed to improve the individual user's experience.

Installation

Word has several new installation features that make life easier for individual users:

- **Intelligent Install** Office 2000 automatically determines the best installation profile for your computer based on which programs are already installed and used.

- **Install on Demand** Rather than installing every single template, theme, and other file, Word installs a few of them and then offers to install others when you try to use them. This feature saves a lot of hard disk space.

- **Office Profile Wizard** This new program stores your custom Word preferences and allows you to back them up and restore them. This feature is especially helpful when you switch to another networked computer or when you transfer Word to a laptop.

Self-Diagnosis and Repair

Word and other Office applications now automatically scan their own files for problems and repair them. The following Wizards and commands perform these functions:

- **Office Tune-Up Wizard** This wizard automatically searches for problems when you start Word and then offers to fix them. It checks for corrupted file or registry information, missing files that are required by Office programs, and various other problems. Then it tells you where to locate the files if you need to install them.

- **Office Clean-Up Wizard** This detects previous versions of Office and offers to remove all of the files of any previous versions.

- **Detect and Repair** This new command on the Help menu locates and fixes problems with non-critical Word files such as fonts and templates.

- **Improved Virus Checking** Macro developers can now add digital signatures to sign their macros to prevent Word's macro virus alert from popping up each time anyone opens a document that includes macros.

Personal Productivity

Word has several features to help increase your productivity:

- **New Open and Save As dialog boxes** These display 50 percent more files than previous versions of Word. A new Places bar offers one-click access to those folders you view most, and it includes a History icon that keeps track of the last 20 to 50 documents that you worked on. A new, browser-like Back arrow button returns you to the last location you visited.

- **Adaptive Menus and Toolbars** Menus and toolbars now show only the frequently used commands when first opened. Word automatically adds or deletes commands or buttons from the frequently used set depending on which you use most.

- **Individual Documents in Taskbar** The Windows taskbar now shows a button for each Word document you open, so you can activate documents from there as well as from the Window menu.

- **Office Assistant** The Assistant is much easier to hide or show. The Assistant character is no longer in a separate window (it just floats on your screen), and you can turn the Assistant off completely if you like.

- **Collect and Copy** The Clipboard can store up to a dozen different items. A new Clipboard toolbar shows the Clipboard's contents and allows you to paste them individually or as a group.

- **Print Zoom** New options in the Print dialog box allow Word to scale documents automatically to fit more than one on a page or to match international paper formats.

Editing and Formatting

Word's industry-leading editing and formatting capabilities just keep getting better. New features include these:

- **Click and Type** You can use Word's new Click and Type feature in Print Layout or Web Layout view to set or change tabs or the text alignment in a document by simply double-clicking anywhere in a blank line. For example, if you double-click at the right edge of a blank line, Word right-aligns the text you insert.

- **Improved Tables and Table Tool** Word can now create nested tables, floating tables, side-by-side tables, and integrated header rows in tables. You can also use the Table tool to draw a table around existing text.

- **Improved AutoCorrect** This labor-saving feature now uses the spelling dictionary to spot and correct any misspelled word.

- **Smarter Spelling Checks** A larger spelling dictionary results in fewer false alarms.

Graphics

You'll find an improved Clip Art Gallery (CAG) that has a browser-like interface plus new artwork, sounds, and animated graphics. You can leave the CAG open on your screen while editing a document, and from it, you can drag clips into a document. The CAG also includes new advanced searching tools. For example, you can select a money-related image and search for more images like it. You can also create custom categories for clip art, sounds, or animated graphics.

Collaboration

Microsoft has integrated its latest collaboration technologies into Word and other Office products. You can schedule and participate in NetMeetings while working in Word, and you can now use Word to create and maintain threaded network discussions in Web documents. You can also add or switch automatic signatures in e-mail documents you create with Word.

HTML Support

Recognizing the growing importance of Web pages in corporate intranets as well as on public Web sites, Microsoft has significantly expanded Word's HTML features.

- **Save As Web Page** Word will save any document as a Web page and publish it on a server all in the same operation. When you save a Web page, Word creates a folder for all of its supporting files.

- **Edit HTML Documents** When you view an HTML document in Internet Explorer and click the Edit button, Office opens the Office application that was originally used to create it. You can also view the HTML source code rather than the document's formatted contents by selecting the HTML Source command from the View menu.

■ **Web Page Preview** You can now preview a document in a Web browser before saving it.

■ **Easier Hyperlinks** The controls for updating and managing hyperlinks have been greatly improved. It's now much easier to create hyperlinks to document bookmarks, other files, Web pages, and even e-mail documents. Word can now update links automatically whenever you save a page, if you like.

■ **Graphics** You can now add graphics such as bullets and horizontal lines, and you can use the Picture command on the Insert menu to add other image files. Default color and fill settings are now stored with documents, and Word automatically groups overlapping graphics.

■ **Themes** Just as a style is a collection of text formatting options, a theme is a coordinated collection of Web page formatting options that includes styles, a background color or pattern, and graphical bullets and horizontal lines. Word comes with dozens of themes that you can apply to any Web page.

■ **Round-Trip Word Features** Special Word document formats are now maintained when you save a document as a Web page and open it for editing in Word from a browser. Even though the document was converted to HTML format for the Web, it opens as a standard document in Word so you can see and change its original formatting.

■ **Subscription and Notification** You can set up Word to notify you whenever any published Web page has been updated.

■ **HTML Scripting** A new Script Editor allows you to create and insert HTML scripts into Web pages.

Programming and Security Features

Microsoft Office comes with the much-improved version 6 of Visual Basic for Applications (VBA), and there are other new features that smooth the way for advanced macro and application developers.

■ **VBA Version 6** VBA is now on par, feature-wise, with the Microsoft Visual Basic language.

■ **Shared Add-in Architecture** You can create integrated solutions that include any Microsoft Office product by inserting ActiveX controls.

- **Automatic Virus Checks** Integrated, automatic virus checks can be incorporated into any Visual Basic for Applications macro, and there's a new virus-checking API for Word's Open dialog box so developers can add automatic virus checking for any document as it is opened.

- **Digital Signatures** You can digitally sign macros to ensure that they are free of viruses.

Network Administration

Microsoft has reduced the cost-of-ownership overhead for network administrators. New features include the following:

- **Install on First Use** Network administrators can set up Office so that specific features or programs are not installed until a user tries to access them.

- **Custom Installation Wizard** The next-generation Network Installation Wizard is the main tool for customizing Office product installations for users on your network.

- **Office Profile Wizard** This program allows network administrators to change Word's default settings or to back up and restore Office 2000.

- **Selective interface disabling** You can disable specific features of Word for individual users.

- **Template Manager** This new utility makes it easy to manage corporate document templates and install them so they're available in every user's New dialog box.

- **Customize Answer Wizard** You can extend Word's Help system with custom files and Help content, or you can customize alerts with hyperlinks to Microsoft Web sites or your own corporate Web site.

Now that you have a general idea of how Word works and what's new in Word 2000, let's dig into the program itself, starting in Chapter 2.

Getting Started

The best way to begin learning a new program is to start it up and poke around in it. You might open up menus to see what kinds of commands Microsoft Word has to offer and how they're organized; you might check out the features of its document window and you'll probably want to try a few commands to see what they do. In this chapter, you'll learn how to start Word and find your way around the Word document window.

Starting Word

 SEE ALSO

For help installing Word, see the Appendix "Installing and Running Word," on page 879.

Once you have Microsoft Office 2000 installed on your computer, there are several different ways to start Word.

Using the Start Menu to Open Word

You will probably have more than one option for starting Word from your Microsoft Windows Start menu. These options will depend on how Word was installed, but you can do at least one of the following:

- Choose Programs from the Start menu and then choose Microsoft Word.

- Choose New Office Document from the Start menu, click the General tab at the top of the New Office Document dialog box, and then double-click the Blank Document icon.

- Choose Open Office Document from the Start menu and then navigate to and open a Word document you created previously.

Using the Desktop to Open Word

There are four ways to open Word directly from the Windows desktop. Again, your computer may not offer all of these options, but you can use at least one of them:

- Click the Word icon on the Office toolbar.

- Open a disk or folder and double-click a Word document icon to open Word along with that document.

- Double-click a shortcut for Word on your desktop.

- Open the Microsoft Office applications folder (located in C:\Program Files\Microsoft Office\Office on your hard disk) and then double-click the Word program icon there.

TIP

To make a Word shortcut on your desktop, right-click the original Word program icon inside the Office folder and choose Create Shortcut from the pop-up menu. Then, drag the shortcut onto your desktop.

Working in the Document Window

The document window can change considerably as you work, but the basic controls and features are always the same whenever you have a document open. When you open Word without selecting a particular document to open, Word automatically opens a new document as shown in Figure 2-1.

FIGURE 2-1.

Your Word documents may change, but the document window controls remain the same.

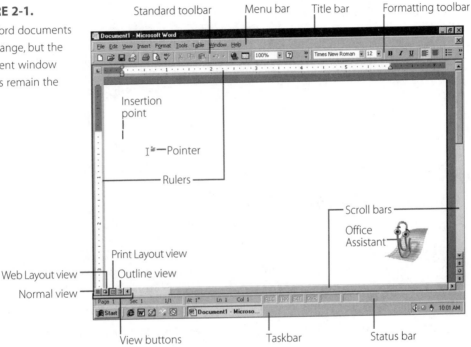

Standard toolbar   Menu bar   Title bar   Formatting toolbar

Insertion point

I≛—Pointer

Rulers

Scroll bars

Office Assistant

Web Layout view

Print Layout view

Outline view

Normal view

View buttons   Taskbar   Status bar

The Title Bar

For more information on managing multiple windows, see "Managing Windows," on page 30.

The title bar at the top of the screen identifies the program as well as the document name. You might have several different Microsoft Word documents open at once, but the title bar tells you which document you're viewing. You use the application control menu or the window control buttons to close or resize the window.

> When you have more than one document open, click the Close button on the title bar to close the current document. If you have only one document open (or no documents open), clicking the title bar's Close button exits Word itself.

Other Views Available in Word

By default, Word starts every new document in Print Layout view, but there are three other views you can use to work with documents. Each has its own advantages; your choice will depend on the task at hand. Chapter 6 explains these views in detail, but here's a quick rundown:

■ Outline view displays your document as an outline. *See Chapter 12, "Working with Outlines," for instructions on using Outline view.*

■ Web Layout view is used for creating Web pages. *See Chapter 32, "Creating Web Pages," for more information.*

■ Normal view shows the document text, but not any graphics, page breaks, or special page formatting such as multiple columns. This view is best when you want to focus on the text in a document.

To select a different view, use the View menu or click the buttons at the lower left corner of the document window.

The Menu Bar

The menu bar contains the menus and commands you'll use to work with Word. *See "Using Menus" on page 24.*

When you have only one document open, the Close button appears at the right end of the menu bar—you can click it to close the document window without exiting Word. *See "Managing Windows" on page 30.*

You can also move or resize the menu bar, or turn it into a floating palette. *See "Moving, Resizing, or Floating a Toolbar" on page 21.*

Toolbars

Toolbars contain buttons and menus that you can use to select common commands. Word has nearly two dozen different toolbars that you can display, but you'll typically display only two or three of them at a time. *See "Hiding and Displaying Toolbars" on page 158.* When you first open Word, for example, the Standard and Formatting toolbars are "docked" beneath the Menu bar as in Figure 2-1 on the previous page.

 NOTE

Word 2000 has adaptive toolbars in which the buttons on view can change according to the commands you use most. As a result, the toolbars on your screen may not look the same as those illustrated in this book. *For more information, see "About Adaptive Toolbars" on page 22.*

■ To use a toolbar button, just click it.

■ To use the drop-down boxes, click the number or name shown in the box and type a new one, or click the arrow button next to the box to open it and then choose another option.

For example, you can change plain text to bold by clicking the Bold button, or you can increase the size of text by clicking the *12* in the Font Size box and typing *14*, or by clicking the arrow button next to it and choosing *14* from the Font Size list.

Expanding a Toolbar

Usually, there isn't enough room to display all of the buttons on a toolbar. To see more of the buttons, click the More Buttons button as shown in Figure 2-2. You'll see a palette of other buttons, and you can click them to use them.

FIGURE 2-2.

The Standard and Formatting toolbars are docked at the top of the document window. Click the More Buttons button at a toolbar's right edge to see more tools.

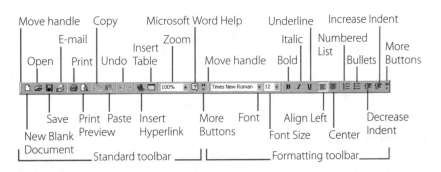

When a toolbar is already showing all of its buttons, the More Buttons palette is empty.

Moving, Resizing, or Floating a Toolbar

If you don't like the position of a toolbar or you want to display more of its buttons at all times, you can move or resize the toolbar or make it float by dragging the Move handle at the toolbar's left edge. When you point to the Move handle, you'll see the Move pointer like this:

You can also move the menu bar or make it float by using the same technique you use to move a toolbar.

- To move a docked toolbar above or below others, drag its Move handle up or down.

- To resize a docked toolbar, drag its Move handle to the left or right.

- To make a toolbar float, drag its Move handle down into the document window. The toolbar becomes a floating palette:

- To move a floating toolbar, drag its title bar.

- To resize a floating toolbar, drag its bottom or right edge.

- To re-dock a floating toolbar, drag its title bar to the top, left, right, or bottom of the document window until it docks.

- To close a floating toolbar, click its Close button.

 TIP

Double-click any toolbar to dock it at the top of the screen.

 **SEE ALSO**

You can create new toolbars or customize the buttons on existing toolbars. For more information, see "Customizing Toolbars" on page 158.

About Adaptive Toolbars

In Word 2000, the toolbars are adaptive. In other words, if you frequently use a button that isn't on a toolbar, Word automatically adds it to the toolbar. If there are other buttons on the toolbar that you never use, Word eventually moves them to the More Buttons palette.

The Ruler

The ruler shows the width of your text, as well as any indents or tabs. You can click or drag in it to set indents and tabs; Chapter 5 explains how. You can also display a vertical ruler at the left side of the document in Print Layout view.

The Insertion Point and Pointer

 SEE ALSO

These document controls are slightly different in Normal view. See "Normal View" on page 111 for more information.

The insertion point is a blinking vertical line at the upper left corner of a new document, as shown in Figure 2-1 on page 19. The mouse pointer is displayed as an I-beam when it's inside the document window. When you want to move the insertion point to any other place in your document's text, move the pointer to the new location and click.

SEE ALSO

For more information about paragraph marks, see "Editing Text" on page 63.

To begin entering text, just start typing. Text always appears at the insertion point's location. Word's default text entry method is Insert mode, so when you move the insertion point to the left of an existing word and begin typing, for example, the word to the right is moved to make room for the new text. A document's text always ends after the last character you type, whether it's a period, a letter, or a paragraph marker that you insert by pressing the Enter key.

NOTE

> You can't click or enter text outside of the text area in a document—in margins or beyond the end of the text, for example.

Scroll Bars

Scroll bars are one of the main ways to navigate through a document. The vertical scroll bar at the right moves you up and down through a document.

The vertical scroll bar also includes special buttons to help you navigate more quickly. *See "Scrolling" on page 56 and "Splitting a Window" on page 117.* The horizontal scroll bar at the bottom moves you right and left through a document.

You can use the four view buttons at the left side of the horizontal scroll bar to change the document view. *See "Using Views" on page 108.*

The Status Bar and Taskbar

The status bar below the horizontal scroll bar shows you information about the document you're viewing and your location within it. It contains buttons that activate various text entry modes and buttons that turn on macro recording or document change tracking. There is also a book icon that starts up Word's spelling and grammar checker.

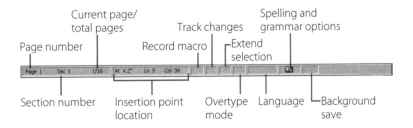

SEE ALSO

Choose Help from the Start menu to learn more about the Windows taskbar.

The taskbar appears at the bottom of your screen whenever you run Microsoft Windows. It includes the Start menu, buttons for each of the programs or Office documents that you have open, and icons you can use to display controls for various Windows settings.

Using Menus

Most of the time, you'll use menus to control Word. As with toolbars, the menus in the menu bar are adaptive.

Opening a Menu

You can open a menu in the menu bar with the mouse or by using the keyboard.

- To open a menu with the mouse, click the menu name.

- To open a menu with the keyboard, press Alt to activate the menu bar and then press the letter underlined in the menu name. For example, to open the File menu, you would press Alt and then F (Alt+F).

Using Adaptive Menus

Word 2000 has new adaptive menus that reduce screen clutter and re-design themselves as you work. When you first open a menu, you'll see a short list of commands with a double arrowhead at the bottom.

Expand button

 NOTE

Since Word's menus adapt by moving commands from the expanded version of the menu to the short version shown above, your short menus may look different from the ones illustrated in this book.

If you click the Expand button at the bottom or simply leave the menu open a few seconds, it expands and adds all of the other commands normally listed on it. The newly added commands are shown in a different shade so you can distinguish them from those on the short menu. Compare the example on the previous page with the expanded version shown in Figure 2-4 on the next page.

When you choose a command that isn't normally on the short menu, Word adds it to the menu so you don't have to expand the menu to find it again.

> You can personalize menus by rearranging commands, adding or removing commands, adding or removing menus, or creating whole new menus if you want. *See "Changing Menus" on page 163.*

Choosing Commands

You can choose commands with either the keyboard or the mouse. Along with commands, most of Word's menus contain submenus that offer more commands, as shown in Figure 2-3. A submenu is identified by an arrow icon next to its name. Click a submenu name to display the submenu and choose one of its commands.

FIGURE 2-3.

Many Word menus contain submenus.

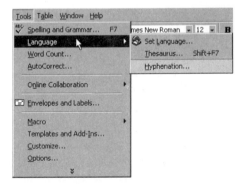

Choosing Commands with the Mouse

To choose a command with the mouse, open the menu and then click the command you want to choose. To choose a command on a submenu, open the menu, point to the submenu name to open it, and then choose the command.

TIP

SEE ALSO

To see the shortcuts for all Word actions, see "Shortcut Key" in the Help index, or see "Using the Index" on page 46 for details. You can also use the Customize dialog box; see "Changing Keyboard Shortcuts," page 172.

To close a menu without choosing a command, click outside the menu or press the Esc key.

Using Keyboard Shortcuts

If you prefer to choose commands with the keyboard, Word gives you several different ways to do that. The fastest method is to type the keyboard shortcut for the command you want. Some of the commands on Word's menus have keyboard shortcuts listed next to them, as shown in Figure 2-4, but most of the commands in Word have shortcut keys assigned to them even if they're not shown on a menu.

FIGURE 2-4.

Many of Word's common commands have keyboard shortcuts, which appear next to the command names on menus.

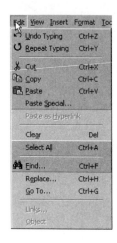

To choose a command with shortcut keys, press and hold the Ctrl key and then press the shortcut's letter key. For example, to choose the Select All command, press Ctrl+A.

NOTE

You can use either upper or lower case when typing letters in shortcut commands. When the Shift key is required, the shortcut will indicate this, or it will use a keyboard symbol that can be produced only by holding down the Shift key, such as + or *.

Activating the Menu Bar with the Alt Key

If you don't remember the shortcut keys for a particular command, you can use the Alt key and other keys to manipulate the menus from the keyboard. When you press the Alt key, Word activates the menu bar so that you can use other keys to open menus and choose commands.

1 Press the Alt key. Word outlines the File menu name to show that the menu bar is active, like this:

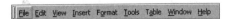

2 Press the key for the underlined letter in the name of the menu you want. Word will open the menu.

3 Press the key for the underlined letter in the name of the command you want.

For example, to open a document from your hard disk (the Open command from the File menu), you would press Alt, then F, and then O.

On the other hand, if you're more comfortable using the arrow keys on your keyboard, you can use these to access menu commands as well:

1 Press the Alt key to activate the menu bar.

2 Press the Left or Right arrow keys (Tab or Shift+Tab also work) to select a menu name. As you move from one menu to the next, the menu name is highlighted to show that the menu is selected.

3 Press the Down arrow key to open the selected menu and continue pressing it until the command you want is selected.

4 Press Enter to choose the command.

Using Shortcut Menus

In addition to the menus at the top of the screen, you can display shortcut menus as you work by pressing the right mouse button or pressing Shift+F10. Once the menu is open, just click a command to choose it.

The commands you see on the shortcut menu depend on which part of the screen you're pointing to when you right-click with the mouse. The menu in Figure 2-5 on the next page appears when you click text that is underlined in red (which means it's misspelled). Try right-clicking in the menu bar, in the document window, or on the book icon in the status bar to check out different shortcut menus.

FIGURE 2-5.

Shortcut menus appear when you right-click areas of the screen. They save time by putting useful commands at your fingertips.

Using Dialog Boxes

When you choose a menu command that has an ellipsis (…) after it, you'll see a dialog box that presents more options, so you can tell Word more specifically how you want a task to be done. Figure 2-6 shows the Print dialog box.

FIGURE 2-6.

Dialog boxes appear when Word needs more information in order to complete a command.

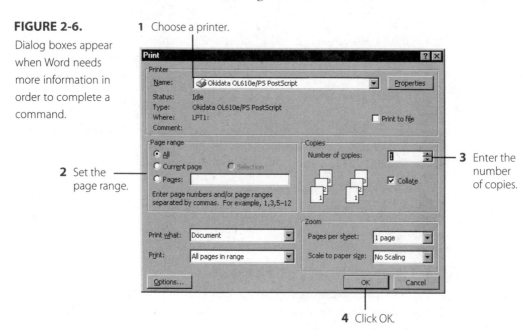

1 Choose a printer.

2 Set the page range.

3 Enter the number of copies.

4 Click OK.

To use a dialog box, specify the options you want using the buttons, lists, or data entry boxes; then click the OK button or press the Enter key to complete the command and close the dialog box.

Choosing Options within a Dialog Box

Once you're inside a dialog box, you might find several different types of options. Table 2-1 shows you how to select each type of option.

TABLE 2-1.   Setting Dialog Box Options

To set this option...	Do this...
Button	Click to complete or cancel the command or to open another dialog box.
Radio button	Click to select one of a group of options. The selected button has a black dot in it.
Check box	Click to toggle on (checked) or off (cleared).
List	Click the list name and type in another value or name, or click the list's arrow button to display the list and choose an option.
Data box	Click and type a name or value, or use the arrow buttons to set the value.
Tab	Click to display another group of options.

TIP

You can scroll quickly though any list in Word by typing the first few letters of the name of the option you want.

TIP

You can usually enter data in more precise increments by typing them in rather than by using arrow buttons. For example, the margin boxes in the Page Setup dialog box let you change the margin value in 1/10-inch increments, but if you type in a value , you can specify values in hundredths of inches, such as *1.15*.

Applying Dialog Box Options

Once you have chosen the options you want in a dialog box, click the OK button to complete the command and close the dialog box. In a few cases (such as the Style dialog box), the dialog box has an Apply button that allows you to apply groups of options without closing the dialog box, and there's a separate Close button to actually close the dialog box.

Canceling a Dialog Box

To close a dialog box without making any changes, do any one of the following:

- Click the Cancel button.

- Click the Close button (the X) at the right edge of the title bar.

- Press the Esc key.

Dialog Box Shortcuts

As with most Windows programs, you can use keyboard shortcuts to navigate within Word dialog boxes:

- Press the Tab key to move from one option to the next or press Shift+Tab to move from an option to the previous option.

- When an option is selected, press one of the arrow keys to change it.

- Press Alt and the underlined letter in an option or tab name to select it.

- Press Enter instead of clicking the OK button to complete the command and close the dialog box.

Managing Windows

You can have more than a dozen different document windows open at the same time in Word, each of which can be managed separately. Only one document is active at a time. In Word 2000, each document has its own activation button in the Windows taskbar.

The exact number of documents you can have open at once is limited by your computer's available memory.

The document window is often maximized, or set to the largest possible size on your monitor, but you can resize or move it if you like using the Application Control menu and the window control buttons in the window's title bar, as shown in Figure 2-7 at the top of the next page.

FIGURE 2-7.

Use the Application Control menu or the control buttons at the right edge of the window title bar to resize or close a window.

Application Control menu

Maximize Close
Minimize Word

Close window

When a maximized window has been reset to a smaller size, the Maximize button becomes the Restore button, like this:

Restore

Once you have minimized a window, you must click the window's button in the taskbar to open it again.

Table 2-2 shows the easiest way to adjust a document window.

TABLE 2-2. Ways to Move, Close, or Resize a Document Window

Task	Button or Command
Close one of several open windows.	Click the Close button.
Close the only open window.	Click the Close button in the window's menu bar.
Exit Word when only one document is open.	Click the Close button in the window's title bar.
Hide the window.	Click the Minimize button.
Maximize the window.	Click the Maximize button.
Set the window to a smaller preset size.	Click the Restore button.
Resize a window manually.	Click the Restore button and then drag a window edge, or choose Size from the Application Control menu and press arrow keys.
Move a window.	Drag the title bar. Or, click the Restore button, choose Move from the Application Control menu, and then press arrow keys.

I

Word Basics

Switching to a Different Document

Whenever a document is open, its name appears at the bottom of the Window menu as in Figure 2-8. Choose a document name from the Window menu or click the document's button in the Windows taskbar to activate that document.

FIGURE 2-8.

Every open document appears on the Window menu.

Each document has an underlined number in front of its name on the Window menu. Press the Alt key and then W, and then a document's number to activate that document.

Other Ways to Change the Word Screen

Word offers lots of other ways to change the way it presents document information. In Chapter 6, you'll learn how to:

- Split a document window into two panes
- Open more than one window, each window showing the same document
- Arrange multiple document windows on the screen so you can see them all at once

In Chapter 8, you'll learn how to:

- Hide or show the menu bar, taskbars, or the status bar
- Add, remove, or change the contents of taskbars
- Change the list of commands shown on any menu
- Change the ruler measurements to centimeters, points, or picas

Exiting Word

When you're finished using Word for the day, choose Exit from the File menu in order to close the program. You can also click the Close button in the window title bar if you have only one document open.

Clicking the Close button on the active document's menu bar closes only the active document.

If you haven't saved changes to any open documents, Word will ask you if you want to save the changes to each one.

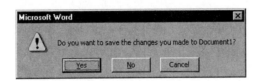

Click the Yes button to save the changes to each document as Word closes it.

The Office Assistant will display program alerts like this when you have the Assistant showing. *See Chapter 3, "Getting Help," for details.*

? SEE ALSO
For full details about saving documents, see "Saving Documents" on page 137.

Now that you know your way around Word's document window, you're ready to learn how to work with documents.

Getting Help

Microsoft Word is a powerful program, and you'll probably need to master only a small percentage of its features for day-to-day use. Occasionally, however, you'll want to learn about a more sophisticated feature or perhaps search for a more convenient way to complete a task. Word offers extensive online Help resources that can explain how to use any feature.

Using the Office Assistant

Your first introduction to Word's online Help is likely to be the Office Assistant, an animated character that pops up on the screen shortly after you start Word. Using a speech balloon, the Assistant provides daily tips for using Word, suggestions for better ways to handle specific tasks as you work, and alert messages. You can also use it to search for answers to questions you may have.

You can choose among several different Assistant characters, and each one has a name. The character in Figure 3-1 is "Clippit."

FIGURE 3-1.

The Office Assistant watches as you work and suggests easier ways to perform tasks.

> **NOTE**
>
> You'll see many of the other Assistant characters in other examples in this book.

SEE ALSO

To find out how to change the Assistant character or how to turn it off, see "Setting Assistant Options" on page 41.

For many of us, however, the very best thing about the new Assistant in Word 2000 is that you can control its behavior much better than you could in previous Word versions. In fact, you can even turn it off completely.

Managing the Assistant's Balloon

Normally, the speech balloon is hidden—it appears automatically when the Assistant has a suggestion, and you can display it whenever you want to search the Help system. There are four ways to display the balloon when you need it:

- Click the Assistant.

- Press F1.

- Click the Help button in the Standard toolbar.

 —— Help button

- Choose Microsoft Word Help from the Help menu.

To put the balloon away, click anywhere outside of it.

If you find the Assistant distracting, there are various ways to control its behavior or to turn it off completely. You can also choose a different Assistant character if you want to. *See "Setting Assistant Options" on page 41.*

Searching for Answers with the Assistant

When you summon the Assistant to ask for help, the balloon contains a search box where you can enter a question, like this:

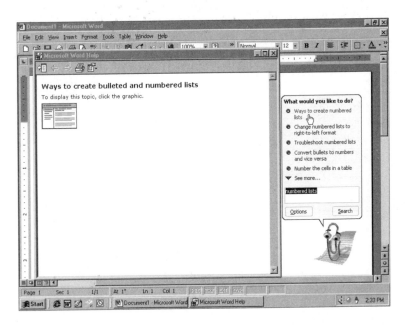

To search for answers, follow these steps:

1 Click the Assistant.

2 Type a topic name or a question in the search box. For example, you might type *numbered lists* or *How do I add a numbered list?*

3 Click the Search button. The Assistant's balloon will display a list of appropriate topics:

 TIP

> You can type in a question of up to 255 characters. Word doesn't care whether you use proper capitalization or punctuation!

4 The Assistant can display up to a dozen topics. Click the See More option at the bottom of the balloon to see the other topics that match your request, if you don't see the topic you need.

5 Click a topic to read about it. The Help window opens so you can view the topic as shown in Figure 3-2 on the next page.

6 Click the graphic in the Help window to see a list of topics related to numbered lists.

 TIP

> The Help window opens on top of your document in Word. You can minimize or resize the window as you can any other window.

FIGURE 3-2.

When you click a topic in the Assistant's list, the Help window opens.

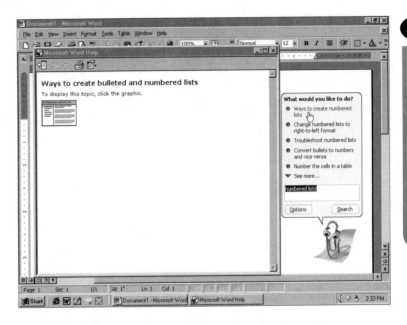

If you want to see help for another one of the topics listed in the Assistant's balloon, just click it. If you don't see the topic you want, click outside the Help window to display the Assistant's list again, and click another topic there or type a new question in the Search box. The Assistant will display another list of topics.

 TIP

> You can use the Help window without using the Assistant first, and you can use the Help window to search for help in other ways. *See "Working with Help Topics" on page 47.*

Using Tips

The Assistant can display a new daily tip each time you start Word, and it offers others throughout the day. The daily tip appears automatically, but other tips announce themselves with a light bulb icon. Here's the icon as it looks above Rocky, another of the Assistant characters:

Click the light bulb to see the tip.

> If the Assistant is hidden, the light bulb icon appears next to the Help button in the Standard toolbar, and you can click it there to display the tip. *See "Hiding or Turning off the Assistant" below.*

Hiding or Turning off the Assistant

As you gain experience with Word, you may find that the Assistant is a distraction. If you don't want the Assistant on your screen at all times, you can either hide it or turn it off completely.

Hiding the Assistant

There are two ways to hide the Assistant:

- Right-click the Assistant and choose Hide from the shortcut menu.

- Choose Hide the Office Assistant from the Help menu.

You can reveal a hidden assistant by choosing Show Office Assistant from the Help menu.

Turning the Assistant Off

To turn the Assistant off completely, follow these steps:

1 Click the Assistant to display its balloon.

2 Click the Options button in the balloon. You'll see the Office Assistant dialog box with the Options tab selected, as in Figure 3-3.

3 Clear the Use The Office Assistant check box at the top of the list.

Word without the Assistant

Turning off the Assistant doesn't mean that you can't get help using Word—you just use other ways to get it.

When the Assistant is turned off (not just hidden):

- Word displays program alert messages in standard alert boxes like the one shown on page 33 at the end of Chapter 2.

- Pressing F1 or choosing Microsoft Word Help from the Help menu displays the Help window.

- Daily tips and ongoing suggestions will not appear.

Many experienced Word users prefer to work without the Assistant.

FIGURE 3-3.

You can set options to control the Office Assistant's behavior.

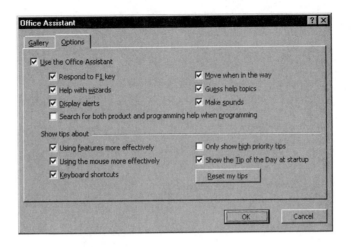

4 Click the OK button.

To turn the Assistant back on at any time, choose Show Office Assistant from the Help menu.

Setting Assistant Options

The dialog box shown in Figure 3-3 has two groups of options that control how the Assistant behaves and which tips are displayed. Table 3-1 describes the Assistant behavior options.

TABLE 3–1. Office Assistant Behavior Options

Option Name	Description
Use The Office Assistant	Turns the Assistant on or off.
Respond To F1 Key	When this check box is cleared, pressing F1 displays the Help window.
Help With Wizards	Assistant automatically offers help on using a wizard whenever you open one.
Display Alerts	Assistant's balloon displays program alerts.
Search For Both Product And Programming Help When Programming	Assistant searches both Word and Visual Basic help files when you work on a macro or VB program.
Move When In The Way	Assistant moves aside to avoid blocking the Help window or text you're editing.
Guess Help Topics	Assistant offers a list of topics about the task you're performing when you open its balloon.
Make Sounds	Turns on sound effects.

Resetting Tips

The Assistant presents an entire catalog of tips in sequential order so you don't see the same tip twice in a row. Clicking the Reset My Tips button tells the Assistant to restart the sequence so that it will begin again with the tip you saw when you ran Word for the first time.

Changing the Assistant Character

Word offers a variety of Assistant characters so that you won't get tired of the same face every day. Each character also has a unique set of movements and sound effects, and you can watch each character do its stuff before deciding on one. Follow these steps to change the Assistant character:

1   Click the Assistant and then click the Options button in its balloon.

2   Click the Gallery tab in the Office Assistant dialog box. You'll see the options as shown in Figure 3-4 on the next page.

3   Click the Next or Back buttons to see and hear a different character.

4   Click the OK button to choose the displayed character.

Save Time and Do More with the Assistant Shortcut Menu

Instead of clicking the Option button inside the Assistant's balloon, you can manage the assistant with a shortcut menu. Just right-click the Assistant to display the menu, which will look like this:

Using the commands on this menu, you can hide the Assistant, display its options, choose a different Assistant, or animate the Assistant.

When you choose the Animate! command, the Assistant goes into a short, animated routine that's great for a little comic relief now and then. The Animate! command can be accessed only through the Assistant Shortcut menu.

FIGURE 3-4.

There are many differ-
ent Assistant charac-
ters to choose from on
the Gallery tab in the
Office Assistant dialog
box.

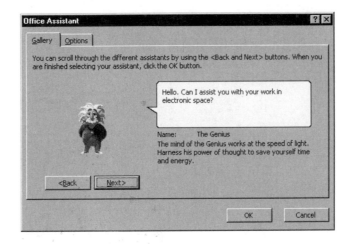

Using the Help Window

The Help window displays help topics and text, and it offers alternative ways to search for them. You can type a question in the same
manner as you would in the Assistant's balloon, but you can also
search by browsing a list of topics or by using an index.

Opening the Help Window Directly

Whenever the Assistant is turned off, the commands you would use to
display the Assistant's balloon will open the Help window instead. You
can do one of the following:

- Click the Help button on the Standard toolbar.

- Press F1.

- Choose Microsoft Word Help from the Help menu.

When you display the Help window without using the Assistant, you'll
see the Help window illustrated in Figure 3-2 on page 39. When you
click the Show button at the top of the Help window, however, you'll
see the expanded version shown in Figure 3-5 on the next page.

You can use the expanded Help window to browse a Help topic
library, enter a question, or search the Help index.

FIGURE 3-5.

Use the Help window to locate help by browsing topics, typing a question, or searching an index.

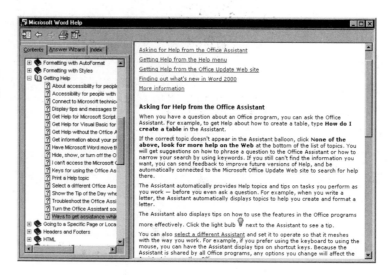

Searching the Topic List

❓ SEE ALSO

For details about navigating within a help topic, see "Working with Help Topics" on page 47.

The Contents tab shows topics organized into "books" that cover broad functional areas such as formatting and editing. To find help using the topic list:

1   Open the Help window and click the Contents tab.

2   Double-click a book (or click the plus sign next to it) to display a list of the topics the "book" contains, as in Figure 3-5.

3   Click a topic to view it. You'll see the topic information at the right side of the Help window.

Using the Answer Wizard

By using the Answer Wizard tab, you can search the help system for every topic that contains a particular word or phrase, as shown in Figure 3-6 on the next page.

To use the Answer Wizard:

1   Click the Answer Wizard tab.

2   Type a word or phrase in the What Would You Like To Do? box. Although the instruction in the box says to type a question, you need only enter the main keywords that describe what you want to know about, such as "number lists" or "format paragraphs."

FIGURE 3-6.

Use the Answer Wizard in the Help window to find help by typing a question.

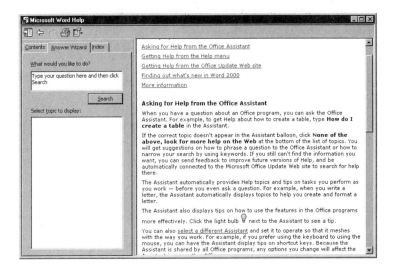

3 Click the Search button or press the Enter key. Word searches for topics related to your question and then displays them in the list at the bottom:

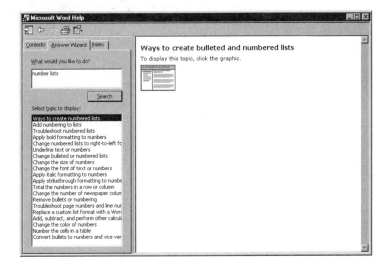

4 Click a topic to display it.

If you don't get the information that you want, reword your question or phrase and search again.

> ## Finding the Most Useful Information Faster
>
> When you type questions, words, or phrases into the Answer Wizard or into the Assistant's balloon, Word scans your entry for keywords that are associated with Help topics. With a question such as "How do I find a file?" for example, Word will zero in on "find" and "file" and then list topics that include those keywords (or variations of them, such as "finding," "found," or "files").
>
> If you browse the keyword list on the Help window's Index tab, you'll get a sense of the keywords that Word recognizes. You can then use just those keywords instead of entering a question. By using keywords, you don't have to waste time phrasing your question as a "How do I..." sentence.
>
> If Word fails to locate the topic you want, try using a synonym for it. For example, you might try "enter" as a synonym for "type."

Using the Index

To see an index of topics like the one shown in Figure 3-7, click the Index tab.

FIGURE 3-7.

Use the Index tab in the Help window to search for help topics by typing a keyword or by selecting one from a list.

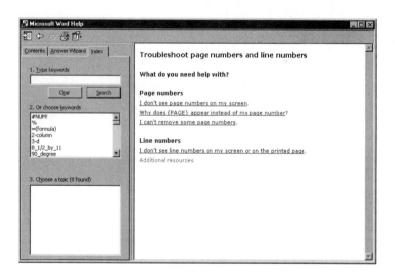

The Index tab allows you to search Word's Help system by specific keywords:

1 Type one or more keywords into the Type Keywords box at the top. A list of closely related keywords will appear in the Or Choose Keywords list.

2 Double-click a word in the Or Choose Keywords list or click the Search button. In either case, a list of topics will appear in the Choose A Topic list at the bottom, and the text of the first topic will be displayed in the area at the right.

3 Click a different topic to display it.

Elsewhere in this book you will be referred to specific topics in the Help system index. To locate them, type the topic name into the Type Keywords box and then click the Search button.

Working with Help Topics

When you display a Help topic, its text appears at the right side of the Help window. The topic appears in a scrolling window, so you can scroll down to read more of it. Underlined text (shown in a different color on your screen) indicates a hyperlink to another topic. Click the hyperlink to display that topic.

In many cases, the topic you display will simply explain how to complete an operation by listing numbered steps. If a topic is fairly broad, however, you're likely to see a list of hyperlinks to more specific subtopics.

Clicking a Show Me button (if the topic includes one) tells Word to move your mouse pointer through the steps of the procedure and display comments about each step as it goes along.

There may also be a Web button. When you click this button, Word navigates you to the Office On The Web site (provided that you have Internet access) where it then locates more information about the topic.

Using Help Window Buttons and Menus

The buttons at the top of the Help window let you navigate the Help system, change the size of the Help window, or print Help topics.

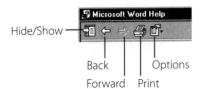

Here's how to use these buttons:

- Click the Hide button to hide the tabs in the Help window and display only the topic text.

- Click the Back or Forward buttons to jump to the previous or next Help topic.

- Click the Print button to print the Help topic.

- Click the Options button to display the Options menu, which looks like this:

The Options menu contains commands that duplicate the Hide, Back, Forward, and Print buttons, but it also contains four more commands:

- The Home button returns you to the home page of a Web site if you're viewing Help information on the Web.

- The Stop command cancels a search, leaving the topic you were viewing before the search displayed in the window.

- The Refresh command tells Word to display the topic again. Use it if the screen doesn't redraw itself completely as you move from one help topic to another.

- The Internet Options command opens a dialog box where you can set such Internet options as the address of the home page that opens with your Internet browser. *For more information about the Internet Options dialog box, open your Internet browser and consult its online help system.*

Getting Descriptions While You Work

Word can also help you get assistance as you work, without resorting to the Help window or the Assistant. You can get descriptions of items in the document window, on menus, in toolbars, or in dialog boxes using ScreenTips or the What's This? command.

Using the What's This? Command

The What's This? command on the Help menu provides short descriptions of any menu command, window feature, document format, or dialog box option.

Here's how to learn about a window control, toolbar button, menu, or format option in a document:

1   Choose What's This? from the Help menu or press Shift+F1. You'll see a question mark icon appear next to your mouse pointer.

2   Point to anything on the screen that you want to know more about and click. Word displays information about that item, as shown in Figure 3-8.

FIGURE 3-8.

With the What's This? command, you can click any item to read a description.

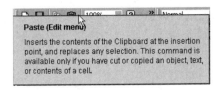

3   Choose What's This? from the Help menu a second time to close the description and return to your current task.

You can also use What's This? to display formatting information about characters and paragraphs. See "Viewing Character and Paragraph Formats" on page 273 for more information.

Using What's This? in Dialog Boxes

The menu bar is disabled when dialog boxes are open, so you can't use the What's This? command as described above to learn about a dialog box option. But don't despair. To get a description of an option

within a dialog box, click the Help button in the dialog box itself—
it's a question mark at the right end of the title bar—and then click
any dialog box option.

> You can also right-click any dialog box option and choose the What's This?
> command from the pop-up menu to see a description of that option.

Using ScreenTips

ScreenTips are pop-up labels for the tools and buttons in the document window. Whenever you point to a tool or button for more than
one second, you'll see a small yellow label like the one in the illustra-
tion below:

Changing or Hiding ScreenTips

If you don't like ScreenTips, you can turn them off. On the other
hand, you can also add keyboard shortcuts to ScreenTips, if you like.

To turn ScreenTips off:

1   Choose Customize from the Tools menu.

2   Click the Options tab.

3   Clear the Show ScreenTips On Toolbars check box.

To display keyboard shortcuts in ScreenTips, select the Show Shortcut
Keys In ScreenTips option, which is also located on the Options tab in
the Customize dialog box.

Getting Help from Microsoft's Web Site

Microsoft has lots of additional resources on the World Wide Web,
from general information about the company to tips, technical support,
and free programs that you can download to enhance your use of
Word. You can also send feedback to Microsoft if you like.

If you have an Internet connection, choosing Office On The Web from
the Help menu takes you directly to a Web site where you can search
for further information about many of Word's features.

Getting Help with WordPerfect

If you're switching to Word from WordPerfect, you'll find a special resource that will help ease your transition. To access WordPerfect help, choose WordPerfect Help from the Help menu. You'll see the WordPerfect Help dialog box, as shown in Figure 3-9.

 NOTE

> WordPerfect Help is not part of a typical Word installation. To use it, you must install it from the Office CD. *See the Appendix for more information.*

FIGURE 3-9.

Use the WordPerfect Help dialog box for help in converting WordPerfect commands to Word commands.

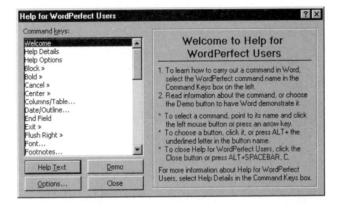

Click an item in the Command Keys list to see help about it at the right. If you click the Demo button, Word will show you how to perform the operation by moving your mouse pointer automatically and explaining each step along the way. To view help text on the screen as you work, click the Help Text button.

To learn more about WordPerfect Help, click and read the Help Details and Help Options topics, or click the Help button in the dialog box's title bar and then click an option.

You'll find the Help resources incredibly useful as you proceed further into your exploration of Word. In Chapter 4, we'll look at Word's basic text editing features.

Word Basics

I

CHAPTER 4

Editing Text

Microsoft Word has powerful features for formatting and document publishing, but most people use it for entering and editing text. Once you enter text in a document, you can add to it, rearrange it, delete it, or copy it. In this chapter, you'll learn how to insert, select, and rearrange text, as well as how to navigate from one place to another in a document.

Entering Text

You can enter text into any document open on your screen. To see how this works, create a short sample file that you'll use throughout this chapter:

1 Start Word if necessary, or if Word is already running, choose New from the File menu and press Enter to create a new document.

2 Type the following paragraph without pressing the Enter key:

Acme is pleased to introduce the JetMaker automotive performance booster. The JetMaker dramatically increases acceleration and top speed in virtually any vehicle and requires no professional expertise to install.

Never press the Enter key to end lines within a paragraph. This causes uneven line breaks and other problems when you format the text.

To refresh your memory about the insertion point, see "Working in the Document Window" on page 19.

As you type, Word moves the insertion point from the end of one line to the beginning of the next or moves words to the next line when they're too long to fit on the existing line. If you make a typo, press the Backspace key to back up to the mistake and then type the correct version.

3 Press the Enter key twice. Word ends the paragraph and moves the insertion point down two lines.

Word can automatically add space before or after a paragraph. *See "Changing Line Spacing" on page 95.*

4 Type the following paragraph:

Thanks to its easily adaptable design, the JetMaker can be mounted on a vehicle's roof, load bed, or rear deck. The attachment straps are as simple to use as an ordinary tie-down belt, and the unit has a self-contained power source to avoid straining your vehicle's electrical system.

Your document should now look like the sample shown in Figure 4-1 at the top of the next page.

FIGURE 4-1.

Word automatically wraps text from one line to the next as you type; you don't have to press the Enter key to begin a new line.

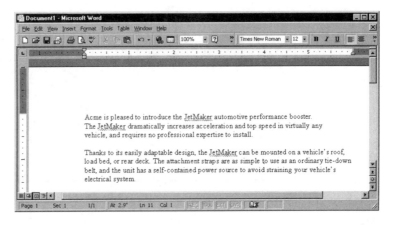

SEE ALSO

For more information about the spelling checker, see "Checking Spelling and Grammar" on page 190.

Don't be alarmed by the wavy red lines under the JetMaker name. Word is simply identifying a word that is not found in its built-in spelling dictionary so you can be sure to check the spelling during final proofreading.

Leave the sample paragraphs on your screen. You'll use them again.

Inserting Text

The blinking insertion point in your document shows you where text will appear when you enter it. You can move the insertion point by pointing and clicking to insert text wherever you like. For example, click in the space to the left of the word "pleased" in the first line of the first paragraph, and type *very* and add a space. The word is inserted.

SEE ALSO

To learn how to display Word's invisible formatting characters, see "Displaying Nonprinting Characters" on page 86.

Breaking a Line Before the Right Margin

Word wraps lines within a paragraph by adding a "soft" return to the right end of each line. If you reformat or edit your text so the line endings change, the soft returns change along with them, which prevents improper line breaks.

Sometimes, though, you'll want to break a line within a paragraph without starting a new paragraph. To do this, press Shift+Enter. Word inserts a "hard" return character and ends the current line, no matter how short the line is. When you display nonprinting characters in Word, hard return characters have a special symbol, while soft returns are invisible. A hard return, however, does not end a paragraph.

Insert Mode vs. Overtype Mode

By default, Word enters text in Insert mode so that when you add a word in
the middle of a line of text, the text to the right of the new word moves
ahead. However, you can also operate Word in Overtype mode, so that what
you type replaces any text that's in the way rather than pushing it to the right.
To set Overtype mode, double-click the shaded OVR button in the status bar,
or choose Options from the Tools menu, click the Edit tab, and then select the
Overtype Mode check box.

Typing is the most common way to enter text into a document, but it's not
the only way. You can also enter text by pasting it or by using a command on
the Insert menu. *See "Cutting, Copying, and Pasting" on page 64 for more
information.*

Navigating in a Document

As you fill a document with text or graphics, you'll want to move around
the document and view different parts of your creation. The document
window's scroll bars are the most obvious way to navigate through a
document, but you can also use the keyboard, some special navigation
buttons, and the Go To command.

You can also navigate in a document with the Document Map. *See "Using the
Document Map" on page 113.*

Scrolling

Scroll bars and buttons are the most common way to move through a
document. Each scroll bar has a scroll box and arrow buttons at each end,
but you can also scroll using the keyboard. Figure 4-2 shows the controls
in the horizontal scroll bar.

FIGURE 4-2.

The scroll bars in the
document window.

Scroll button   Scroll box   Scroll button

Scrolling with the Mouse

You can use the mouse in several ways to scroll with a scroll bar, depending on how far you want to move in your document.

- To scroll in small increments, click the scroll button at either end of the scroll bar. To scroll quickly, hold down the mouse button as you click the scroll button.

- To scroll up or down one screen at a time, click anywhere in the vertical scroll bar above or below the scroll box.

- To scroll proportionally through a document, drag the scroll box up or down. For example, to scroll to the middle of a document, drag the scroll box to the middle of the scroll bar. As you drag the scroll box, a label appears and reports the current page number:

Scrolling does not move the insertion point. You must remember to click in the document after scrolling when you want to enter text at the new location. If you forget, Word will automatically scroll back to the insertion point when you begin typing.

Navigating with Browse Buttons

With the browse buttons at the bottom of the vertical scroll bar, you can scroll to specific places in your document. Unlike using the scroll bars, clicking browse buttons scrolls your document and moves the insertion point at the same time.

—Browse Up
—Select Browse Object
—Browse Down

Normally, the Browse Up and Browse Down buttons are set so you move to the next and previous document page when you click them, but you can use the Select Browse Object button to change this setting. When you click the Select Browse Object button, you'll see the Browse Object palette, which allows you to determine where the browse buttons take you when you click them. See Figure 4-3.

FIGURE 4-3.

The Browse Object palette.

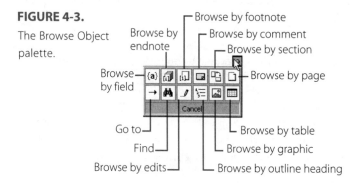

Point to any button to see its description at the bottom of the palette. Click a button to set it as the browse option. When you choose a browse option other than Browse By Page, the browse buttons turn blue to indicate that you've set a special option.

The browse buttons are handy when you're focusing on one type of information, such as reviewer comments or footnotes, and you want to jump quickly from one to the next.

> If you can't remember which browse option you have set, just point to one of the browse buttons and wait for the ScreenTip to tell you.

Navigating with the Keyboard

When you use the keyboard to navigate, you scroll through the document and move the insertion point at the same time. Table 4-1 shows keys and key combinations you can use.

> Word always places the insertion point at the beginning of a document when you open it. To return quickly to the last place you edited in the document when it was open previously, press Shift+F5.

TABLE 4-1. Keyboard Navigation Shortcuts

Press These Keys...	To Jump Here...
Up or Down arrow	Up or down one line
Left or Right arrow	Left or right one character
Ctrl+Left Arrow or Ctrl+Right Arrow	Left or right one word
Home or End	The beginning or end of the current line
Ctrl+Home or Ctrl+End	The beginning or end of the document
Page Up or Page Down	Up or down one screen
Ctrl+Page Up or Ctrl+Page Down	Up or down one document page
Shift+F5	The last place you edited your document

Navigating with the Go To Command

When you want to jump to a particular place in your document, the Go To command can often take you there much more quickly than scrolling. The Go To command locates document features. You can use it to jump to a particular page, footnote, graphic, reviewer comment, or other item in your document. To use the Go To command, follow these steps:

1 Choose Go To from the Edit menu or press Ctrl+G to display the Find and Replace dialog box with the Go To tab selected, as in Figure 4-4.

FIGURE 4-4.

Use the Go To command to navigate to specific pages, comments, bookmarks, or other items in your document.

2 Select the type of item you want to go to.

3 If you know the exact number of the page, comment, or other item you want to see, enter the item number.

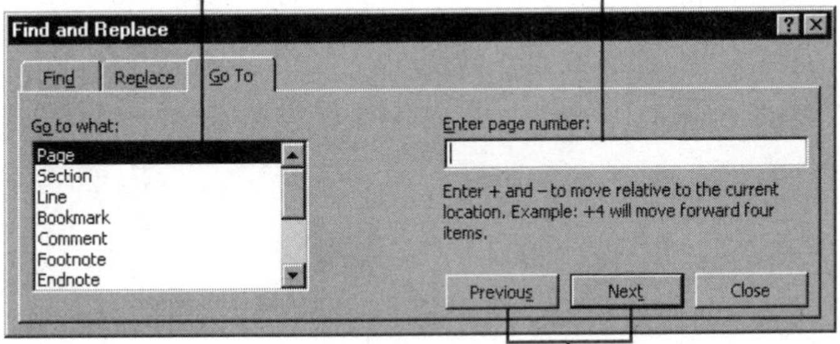

4 Click Next or Previous to navigate forward or backward.

5 Click the Close button to put away the dialog box.

You can also navigate by searching for text with the Find command. *For more information, see "Finding Text" on page 179.*

When you use the Go To command, Word sets the Browse Up and Browse Down buttons to go to the next and previous occurrence of the document element you're looking for. *See "Navigating with Browse Buttons" on page 57.*

Selecting Text

After you enter text in your document, you might want to edit it or change its formatting. Either way, the first step is to select the text you want to change. By selecting, you tell Word which text you want to work on. There are several ways to select text.

Selecting by Dragging

Pointing and dragging is the most intuitive way to select text. You can select anything from a single character to your entire document this way. Try it by selecting some text in your sample document.

1   Point to the space to the left of the word *dramatically* in the first paragraph of your sample document.

2   Hold down the mouse button, drag across the line to the space to the right of *acceleration*, and then release the mouse button. A dark selection highlight appears as you drag, and it remains to show the area that you selected after you release the mouse button, as in Figure 4-5. You can always tell which text is selected by looking for this selection highlight.

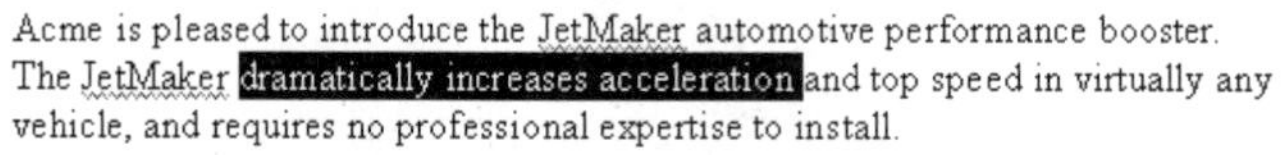

FIGURE 4-5.

You must select text to edit or format it.

Acme is pleased to introduce the JetMaker automotive performance booster. The JetMaker dramatically increases acceleration and top speed in virtually any vehicle, and requires no professional expertise to install.

You can drag up and down as well as across to select lines, paragraphs, or the whole document. When you drag to the top or bottom of a document window, the document scrolls automatically to extend your selection.

To cancel a selection, click anywhere outside the selection highlight.

⭐ **TIP**

You can change Word's selection method so it automatically selects an entire word when you drag. To change the selection method, choose Options from the Tools menu, click the Edit tab, and then select the When Selecting, Automatically Select Entire Word check box.

Selecting by Clicking

Word offers some mouse-click shortcuts that help you select specific text areas more quickly. You can click inside your document's text or select whole lines, paragraphs, or the document by clicking in the left margin. Table 4-2 shows how to select different parts of text by clicking.

TABLE 4-2. Options for Selecting Text with Mouse Clicks

To Select This Text...	Click This...
One word	Double-click a word
One sentence	Press the Ctrl key and click in the sentence
One paragraph	Triple-click in the paragraph
One line	Click next to the line in the left margin
The entire document	Triple-click in the left margin or hold down the Ctrl key and click in the left margin

You can also combine clicking and dragging to speed up your selections. For example, click in the left margin to select a line, hold down the mouse button, and drag up or down to select other lines.

Selecting with the Keyboard

If you prefer not to use the mouse, Word has keyboard alternatives for all of its commands, including selecting. Refer to Table 4-1 on page 59 to see other keyboard navigation shortcuts. To select with the keyboard:

1 Use the arrow keys to move the pointer to the beginning of the selection.

2 Hold down the Shift key while using the arrow keys to move the pointer to the end of the selection.

⭐ **TIP**

Hold down the Shift key and an arrow key to select and scroll quickly.

3 Release the Shift key.

Selecting Large Areas Quickly

To select large parts of a document quickly, you can hold down the Shift key while using other keyboard navigation shortcuts. For example:

- To select the current paragraph, press Alt+Shift and either the Up or Down arrow key.

- To select everything on the screen, move the insertion point to the top of the screen and press Shift+Page Down.

- To select from the insertion point to the beginning or end of a line, press Shift+Home or Shift+End.

Press Ctrl+A to select the whole document.

Shift-Clicking and Other Selection Nuances

You can speed up text selections by Shift-clicking or holding down the Shift key as you click the mouse. Shift-clicking is particularly handy when you want to enlarge an existing selection, or when you want to select large areas of text that span several screens.

To extend the current selection, hold down the Shift key and click anywhere beyond the end of the current selection. The selection highlight will extend to the place where you clicked, like this:

Insertion point location   End of original selection

Acme is pleased to introduce the JetMaker automotive performance booster. The JetMaker dramatically increases acceleration and top speed in virtually any vehicle, and requires no professional expertise to install.

End of extended selection

Compare this extended selection with the one in Figure 4-5 on page 60.

When it extends a selection, Word assumes you want to extend the selection between the insertion point's original position and the place where you Shift-click. To extend a selection properly, be sure to click past the *end* of the current selection rather than in front of or above the insertion point's original position. If you Shift-click above, you remove the original selection and select new text from the insertion point to the new click location.

To create a new selection, click at the beginning of the text you want to select, scroll the document, if necessary, and then Shift-click at the end of the text you want to select.

Editing Text

The text you enter into your document is usually just the raw material for your finished product. As you refine what you've written, you'll want to use other editing controls in Word to replace, delete, or rearrange your text.

Typing to Replace a Selection

To replace a word or phrase, select it and then type the replacement. For example:

1 Double-click the word *straining* at the end of the second paragraph of your sample text.

2 Type *overloading*. This text automatically replaces the selection, and the selection highlight disappears.

Word is preset to replace selected text when you type. To turn this option off, choose Options from the Tools menu, click the Edit tab, and clear the Typing Replaces Selection box. When typing does not replace a selection, you must select text, delete it, and then enter the replacement.

Deleting Text

You can use either the Backspace or Delete key to delete text, or you can remove text by cutting it to the Clipboard. *For a definition and explanation of the Clipboard, see "Cutting, Copying, and Pasting" on page 64.*

■ To delete text immediately to the left of the insertion point, press the Backspace key. The insertion point will back up and remove text as it goes.

Press Ctrl+Backspace to back up and delete a word at a time.

■ To delete several words, lines, or paragraphs, select the text and then press the Backspace or Delete key.

Word Basics

Moving Text with Drag and Drop

The simplest way to rearrange text in your document is to "drag and drop"—select text with the mouse and drag it to its new location. Try it in your sample document:

1 Select *load bed* and the comma and space after it in the second paragraph.

2 Point to any part of the selection highlight and hold down the mouse button.

3 Drag the text to the space in front of *roof*.

4 Release the mouse button. The text moves.

> If you have more than one document open and both are visible on your screen, you can use drag-and-drop editing to move text from one document to another.

Cutting, Copying, and Pasting

Drag-and-drop editing is fine for relocating text short distances, but with Cut, Copy, and Paste you can move text or graphics large distances between documents or make copies of text rather than moving the original copy.

> You can also use Cut, Copy, and Paste to move or copy graphics, reviewer comments, hyperlinks, footnotes, or endnotes.

Basic Cutting, Copying, and Pasting

To cut text or a graphic, select the text or graphic in your document and choose Cut from the Edit menu, press Ctrl+X, or click the Cut button on the Standard toolbar. The text or graphic disappears from your document and is placed on the Clipboard.

To copy text or a graphic, select the text or graphic in your document and choose Copy from the Edit menu, press Ctrl+C, or click the Copy button on the Standard toolbar. The selected text or graphic remains in your document, but a copy is placed on the Clipboard.

> You can copy by dragging and dropping, too. Just hold down the Ctrl key as you drag, and you'll place a copy of the selected text in the new location.

To paste text or graphics, move the insertion point to the place where you want the pasted item to appear, and then choose Paste from the Edit menu, press Ctrl+V, or click the Paste button on the Standard toolbar. *For information about pasting copies of text you have just typed, see "Using the Repeat Command" on page 72.*

 ## Using Word's New Clipboard

When you cut, copy, or paste text in your documents, Word uses a special area of memory called the Clipboard. In older versions of Word, the Clipboard stored only one cut or copied item at a time, so any new item you cut or copied would replace its previous contents. In Microsoft Word 2000, the Clipboard can store up to 12 cut or copied items, and there's a handy toolbar for selecting, pasting, or clearing its contents.

When you add more than one item to the Clipboard, the Clipboard toolbar opens, and you see buttons for each of the copied items, as in Figure 4-6.

FIGURE 4-6.

Word's new Clipboard can store and paste as many as 12 items at a time.

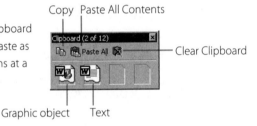

You can use the toolbar to copy new items, paste any or all of the items stored on the Clipboard, or erase the Clipboard. The button style used for each item stored on the Clipboard shows whether it's text or a graphic.

 You can display or hide the Clipboard toolbar by right-clicking in any toolbar and selecting Clipboard on the shortcut menu.

You can use the toolbar to copy new items, paste any or all of the items stored on the Clipboard, or erase the Clipboard. The button style used for each item stored on the Clipboard shows whether it's text or a graphic.

Items are added to the Clipboard in the order you cut or copy them, and you can paste any or all of them from there.

- To see the contents of an item, point to the button and wait for the ScreenTip to appear.

- To paste an item, move the insertion point to the location where you want the text to appear and click the item's button on the Clipboard toolbar.

- To paste all items on the Clipboard in the order in which they were copied, click the Paste All button.

- To clear the Clipboard, click the Clear Clipboard button.

- To put the Clipboard toolbar away, click the Close button on the right edge of its title bar.

Using the Paste Special Command

The normal Paste commands you use with the Clipboard and the Edit menu place exact duplicates of text you cut or copied wherever the insertion point is located. With the Paste Special command, however, you can paste text or other objects into a document with special instructions about how they are formatted.

You can also paste information from another document into your document as a shortcut or hyperlink that automatically navigates you to the original document.

Pasting Information and Shortcuts

(?) SEE ALSO

For information about pasting linked objects, see "Linking with Paste Special" on page xxx. For more information about pasting hyperlinks, see "Copying and Pasting a Hyperlink" on page 780.

With the Paste Special dialog box, you can determine the format of information pasted into your document. To use the Paste Special command:

1 Cut or copy text, a graphic, or another document object from the current document or another document to the Clipboard.

2 Move the insertion point to the place where you want to insert the cut or copied item.

3 Choose Paste Special from the Edit menu. You'll see the Paste Special dialog box, as in Figure 4-7.

FIGURE 4-7.

Use the Paste Special command to control how information is pasted into your documents.

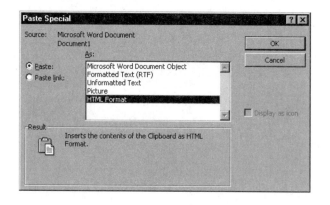

4 Click an option in the As list to determine the format of the pasted item. The options will depend on the type of item you last copied or cut. If you cut a picture, for example, you'll have options about the picture file format that is used when the item is pasted into your document. The Result area at the bottom of the dialog box explains what happens when you paste an item using each of the options.

5 Click the OK button to paste the information.

Using Document Scraps

Document scraps are another way to copy and paste information in your documents. Unlike Clipboard contents, document scraps are individual documents that contain text you've copied. You create a document scrap by dragging text from your document onto the Windows desktop, and you can insert document scraps into documents by dragging them from the Windows desktop to a location in a document. Since the scraps are documents themselves, you can open, view, and edit them in Word, and you can reuse them whenever you want. Document scraps are a great way to save standard paragraphs for contracts or other lengthy text entries that you use frequently.

Creating a Document Scrap

To create a document scrap, select the text in your document and then drag the selection to the Windows desktop. The scrap will be created as a document, as in Figure 4-8.

FIGURE 4-8.

Drag a selection from your document to the Windows desktop to create a document scrap.

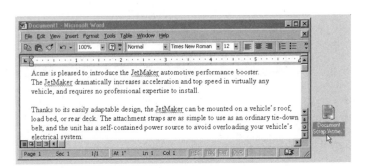

You must drag to the desktop to create a scrap, so the desktop must be visible. If the Word window is maximized on your screen, you'll need to resize it so that part of the desktop is visible.

Word adds the beginning of the scrap's text to the document name to help you distinguish one scrap from another.

> Although you must drag a scrap to the Windows desktop to create it, you're free to move scraps into a folder. If you use a lot of scraps, create a Scraps folder to store and organize all of your scraps in one place rather than cluttering your desktop.

Pasting a Document Scrap

To paste a document scrap, just drag the scrap from the desktop (or the folder where you've stored it) into your document and release the mouse button. A ghost insertion point appears in your document when you drag the scrap into it so you can see exactly where the scrap's text will appear when you release the mouse button.

Using the Spike

The Spike is another tool that allows you to accumulate text cut from various places in your document and then paste all of the cuttings in one place.

The Spike vs. the Clipboard Toolbar

At first blush, the Spike appears to duplicate the gather-and-paste function of the Clipboard toolbar, but the two features aren't exactly the same. Table 4-3 shows the differences.

TABLE 4-3. Differences Between the Clipboard and the Spike

Feature	Clipboard	Spike
Type of information stored	Text or graphics	Text only
Cut or copy items to it?	Cut or copy	Cut only
Paste individual items from it?	Yes—Paste any item or all of them at once	No—Paste entire contents
Item storage limit?	Yes—12 items	No
Requires mouse or keyboard?	Requires mouse to select and paste items	Requires keyboard

For example, suppose you initially list a group of 15 employee names in a paragraph, like this:

October Employees of the Month

Acme recognizes the following employees for outstanding service during the month of October: Bob Albertson, Tom Arnett, Sheila Boardman, Will Chu, Laurie Coleman, Mike French, Leslie Gibbons, Julian Guerrero, Larry O'Leary, Frances Oatman, Luann Park, Al Stapley, Mo Steinberg, Melissa Tran, and Billie Zender.

Upon further reflection, you decide the names would look better in a separate list, like this:

October Employees of the Month

Bob Albertson
Tom Arnett
Sheila Boardman
Will Chu
Laurie Coleman
Mike French
Leslie Gibbons
Julian Guerrero
Larry O'Leary
Frances Oatman
Luann Park
Al Stapley
Mo Steinberg
Melissa Tran
Billie Zender

The Clipboard won't hold all 15 names, so you might use the Spike to move the information from the paragraph to the list more quickly than you could do it by cutting and pasting each name individually.

Cutting to the Spike

To cut anything to the Spike, select it and press Ctrl+F3. The text is removed from your document and placed on the Spike. You can add any number of text selections to the Spike and they'll be maintained there in the order in which you cut them. To turn the group of names into a list, for example, you could cut each name (without the comma after it) to the Spike in order.

> **NOTE**

Like the Clipboard, information on the Spike is stored only as long as you have Word running.

Pasting the Spike

When you paste a group of items from the Spike, each item is placed on its own line in your document. So, in our example, pasting the 15 names from the Spike would automatically put them in a list.

There are two ways to paste the Spike's contents. You can paste and clear the Spike, or paste and retain the spiked text for further uses.

To paste text and clear the Spike, place the insertion point where you want the spiked text to appear and press Ctrl+Shift+F3.

To paste text without clearing the spike:

1 Display the AutoCorrect dialog box by going to the Insert menu, choosing AutoText, and then choosing AutoText from the submenu.

2 Choose Spike in the Enter AutoText Entries Here list. You'll see the contents of the Spike in the Preview box below, like this:

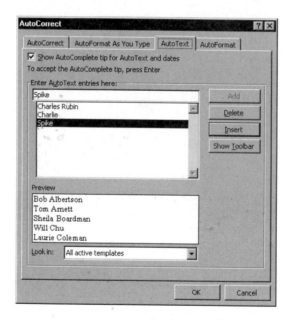

3 Press the Enter key or click the Insert button to paste the Spike's contents without clearing them.

 TIP

You can also clear the Spike by selecting it in the AutoCorrect dialog box and clicking the Delete button. To display the AutoCorrect dialog box quickly, choose AutoCorrect from the Tools menu.

Undoing, Redoing, and Repeating Changes

Sometimes you'll make a change to your text and then regret it. Fortunately, Word remembers every change you make to a document during a given session and lets you undo any number of them—even if you made them hours ago—as long as you don't exit the program. You can undo typing as well as formatting changes. Word also has a Redo command that redoes changes you've previously undone, and you can repeat the previous change when you want to apply a text or formatting change to more than one place in your document.

Using Undo and Redo

You'll find an Undo command at the top of the Edit menu (Ctrl+Z is the keyboard shortcut), and there are also Undo and Redo buttons on the Standard toolbar, as shown in Figure 4-9.

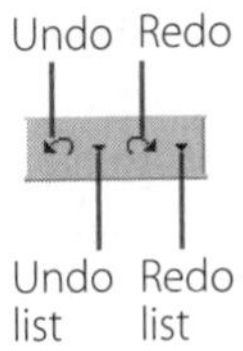

FIGURE 4-9.

Use the Undo or Redo buttons to cancel or redo previous changes.

Undo Redo

Undo Redo
list   list

Choose Undo from the Edit menu, press Ctrl+Z, or click the Undo button to undo the last action you took.

Immediately after you undo an action, the Redo command appears below the Undo command on the Edit menu. To redo your last change (essentially "undoing the Undo"), choose Redo from the Edit menu, press Ctrl+Y, or click the Redo button on the toolbar. To try these commands in your sample document, follow these steps:

1 Select the word *virtually* in the first paragraph of your sample document.

2 Press the Backspace key to delete it.

3 Press Ctrl+Z to undo your change. The deleted word returns.

4 Press Ctrl+Y to redo your change. Word deletes *virtually* again.

> **NOTE**

As you work, the Undo and Redo command names change on the Edit menu to show what will happen when you choose them. If you've been entering text, for example, the command name reads Undo Typing.

You can undo and redo actions as many times as you like, but the Redo command is only active immediately after you use the Undo command.

Undoing Multiple Changes

Rather than using the Edit menu or keyboard shortcuts to reverse changes one at a time, you can also use the Undo and Redo lists to deal with several changes at once. To use one of these lists, click the arrow button next to the Undo or Redo button on the Standard toolbar. You'll see a list of previous actions you can undo or redo, as shown here:

Click the most recent action to undo or redo it, or drag the pointer or scroll down the menu to select and change several actions. The comment at the bottom of the list shows how many actions you will undo or redo.

 **TIP**

Pressing Ctrl+Z or Ctrl+Y repeatedly also backs Word up through changes in the order you made them.

Using the Repeat Command

The Redo command shares space on the Edit menu with the Repeat command. When you haven't just undone something, the Repeat command allows you to repeat the last bit of typing you did or the last formatting change you made. This is handy when you want to add text or apply a format change in more than one place.

For example, suppose you're preparing a new sales report, and you know you'll want the same subheadings under each of five main headings (one for each sales region, perhaps). You might enter all the main headings first, and then type the first group of subheadings, as shown in the figure at the top of the next page.

To enter the same group of subheadings under each of the other main headings, move the insertion point below each heading and press Ctrl+Y or choose Repeat Typing from the Edit menu.

Eastern Region

Sales

Manufacturing

Payroll

Purchasing

Management/

Saving a Document

You'll learn about all of Word's file management features in Chapter 7, but if you have been following along in this chapter, you now have a document open on your screen. To save the sample document:

1 Choose Save from the File menu, press Ctrl+S, or click the Save button on the Standard toolbar. You'll see the Save As dialog box, as shown in Figure 4-10.

FIGURE 4-10.
Use the Save As dialog box to save new documents.

2 Choose a location.

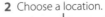

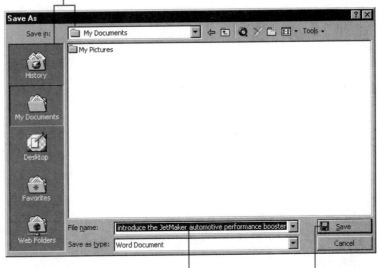

3 Word suggests the first line of text in the document as its name. Type *My Text Sample* to replace the suggestion.

4 Press Enter or click the Save button.

NOTE

> Be sure to remember the name and location of the folder where you save the file so you can find it again easily the next time you need to open it.

What Else Can Word Do?

This chapter barely scratches the surface of Word's powerful text handling features. In Parts III and VII you'll learn about a variety of other text manipulation options, including spelling and grammar checks, automatic typing and corrections, form letter processing, footnotes, headers and footers, and collaborative document editing, and organizing documents with outlines.

Once you get text into a document, you'll want to format it. In Chapter 5 we'll look at Word's basic formatting features.

Using Basic Formatting Tools

Microsoft Word offers dozens of ways to change the appearance of text on your screen and in your printed documents. You can apply formatting options to individual characters (letters), to paragraphs, to sections of a document, or to the whole document. In this chapter, you'll learn about common formatting options you'll use all the time. Part III of this book, "Formatting Tools," covers Word's advanced formatting features.

Formatting with Word

Word offers several different ways to apply formatting options. You can use keyboard shortcuts; buttons or menus in the Formatting toolbar; or commands on the Format menu to make text look exactly the way you want it. You can also format with styles. *For more information about formatting with styles, see Chapter 15, "Using Styles and Themes."*

NOTE

> Word always tries to show you the formatting your document will have when printed on paper, but there are limitations. See Chapter 6 to find out how you can preview your document or look at it in a different way for a more accurate picture of how your printouts will look.

Word allows you to format documents at five levels: by the character, by the paragraph, by document section, by page, and by document. *For information about section formatting, see "Using Sections" on page 317.* Figure 5-1 shows these format levels at work.

FIGURE 5-1.
You can apply formatting at five different levels in your documents.

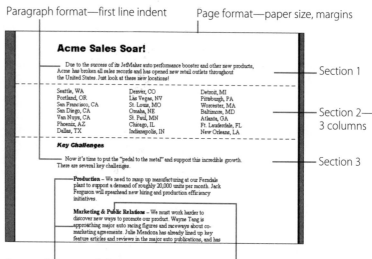

Paragraph format—first line indent   Page format—paper size, margins

Section 1

Section 2—3 columns

Section 3

Paragraph format—left and right indents   Character format—bold

You can apply any formatting option to existing text by selecting the text first and then choosing the option or by choosing the formatting option first and then typing.

- To select existing characters, multiple paragraphs, or sections, drag across them to select them. Then choose formatting options.

■ To format a single paragraph or section, click anywhere in it and then choose formatting options.

■ To format a document, choose formatting options in the Page Setup dialog box.

 **TIP**

Use styles to store and apply several character or paragraph formatting options at once. *See Chapter 15 for details.*

Formatting Characters

Character formatting options include the font (typeface) used, the font size, the style of type (such as bold, italic, or underline), and character spacing or position. You can set character formats with keyboard commands, with the Font dialog box, or by applying a style. Most of the formatting options you'll use frequently are also located on the Formatting toolbar, as shown in Figure 5-2.

FIGURE 5-2.

Click a button on the Formatting toolbar to apply a format.

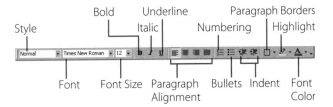

 NOTE

The toolbar in Figure 5-2 has been resized to show its buttons more clearly. If you use formatting buttons frequently, you can resize your Formatting toolbar by dragging the Move/Resize handle at its left edge.

Changing the Text Style

One of the most common formatting choices is to make a word, phrase, or document heading boldface. Try it:

1 Open a new document in Word.

2 Type *This is a bold statement*.

3 Select the word *bold*.

4 Click the Bold button on the Formatting toolbar or press Ctrl+B. The word is now formatted in the bold type style, and the Bold button is highlighted on the Formatting toolbar to show that this style is set.

5 Click outside of the selection highlight to eliminate it so you can see the bold type in its natural state, like this:

This is a **bold** statement.

If you like, you can apply more than one style. For example, clicking the Bold and Italic buttons with the same text selected makes the text both bold and italic. Figure 5-3 shows examples of various styles and combinations.

FIGURE 5-3.

You can combine character styles to create lots of interesting typographical effects.

Plain text
Italic text
Underlined text
Bold Italic text
Shadow text
SMALL CAPS TEXT WITH INITIAL CAPITAL LETTERS
~~Strikethrough text~~
Italic text expanded 3 points
SMALL CAPS BOLD EXPANDED BY 1 POINT
Outlined bold text

 TIP

Each formatting button is a toggle: click it once to set that format, and click it again to remove the format.

Changing Font Characteristics

The default font in Word is 12-point Times New Roman, but Microsoft Windows comes with more than 150 fonts, and you can add more—you can install about 1000 different fonts in Windows (disk space and memory permitting). The standard font collection includes fonts for every purpose, from business to school, from formal to frivolous. In addition, you can change the size, color, or position of your text or add a colored highlight to it. Fonts are a great way to add personality to your documents.

Changing the Font

You can change the font with the Font menu in the Formatting toolbar or with the Font dialog box shown in Figure 5-5. Like other format options, you can set a different font for existing text by selecting the text first, or you can choose a new font before you begin typing. To use the Font menu, follow these steps:

1 Click the Font menu's down-arrow button to display the font menu, like this:

 Microsoft Word 2000's Font menu lists each font's name in that font so you can see just how text will look.

2 Click the name of the font you want to use.

You may have to scroll through the menu to find the font you want. However, Word puts the names of recently used fonts at the top of the menu so you don't have to scroll to find them.

 TIP

> Type the first few letters of a font name and the menu will automatically scroll to that name.

If you know the name of the font you want to use, you can enter it on the Font menu: click the current name, type the new font's name, and press Enter. Naturally, you must spell the font name correctly or Word won't know which font you mean.

Serif vs. Sans-Serif Fonts

There are two basic font styles: serif and sans serif.

> Serif fonts have "feet" on them, like the h, i, l, t, and f characters in this sentence.

> Sans serif fonts don't have feet, like the characters in this sentence.

Serif fonts are best for body text, because the feet on the characters make them easier to read. Sans-serif fonts are best for titles and headings.

It's fine to use both serif and sans serif fonts in the same document, but don't get carried away with more than one font of each type. If you need to vary the look of type beyond having the two fonts, use font sizes or styles to do it.

Changing the Font Size

When you add document titles or headings, you may want to use a larger size of type to make them stand out. You can change the font size with the Size menu in the Formatting toolbar, or by using the Font Size dialog box. *For more details see "Using the Font Dialog Box" later in this chapter.* To change the font size with the Size menu, follow these steps:

1   Click the Size menu's arrow button to display the size menu, like this:

2   Click a size to select it.

As with the Font list, you may have to scroll through the menu to see the size you want. If you don't like the sizes shown on the list, you can use any font size by clicking the number shown on the Size menu and then typing a different number. You can even specify incremental sizes such as 11.5.

Press Ctrl+] to increase the font size one point, and Ctrl+[to decrease it one point. The font size change applies to the word where the insertion point is located, unless you have text selected.

Changing the Font Color

For more information about setting a custom color, see "Changing the Fill Color" on page 428.

If you're tired of looking at black text or you want to use colored text in World Wide Web pages, e-mail messages, or printouts, you can use a different color. To apply a text color, follow these steps:

1 Select the text you want to color.

2 Click the Font Color button on the Formatting toolbar to apply the color shown below the letter on the button, or click the arrow button next to it to display the Font Color palette and choose a different color there.

To choose from an even larger selection of colors, click the More Colors command at the bottom of the Font Color palette.

If you don't see the Font Color button or any other formatting button referred to in this chapter, click the More Buttons button at the end of the Formatting toolbar to display it.

To remove a text color, select the text and display the Font Color palette and then choose either Black or Automatic.

Highlighting Characters

Word has a built-in highlighter you can use to add bright highlighting to text. Follow these steps to use the Highlight tool:

1 Click the Highlight button on the Formatting toolbar to highlight with the color shown below the letter on the button. If you want a different color, click the arrow button next to the Highlight button to display the color palette and then select a different color.

2 When you select the Highlight button, the button is highlighted and the I-beam pointer in your document has a highlighter attached to it.

3 Select the text you want to highlight and then release the mouse button. The text is highlighted, as shown on the following page.

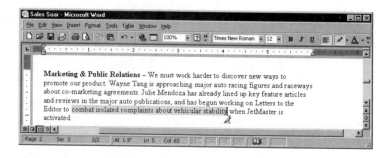

The Highlight tool remains active until you click it again, so you can move the pointer around and highlight text throughout a document.

To remove a highlight, select the highlighted text and click the Highlight button.

Changing the Case

The Change Case command on the Format menu makes it easy to apply, remove, or change capitalization. To use it, follow these steps:

1 Select the text you want to change.

2 Choose Change Case from the Format menu. You'll see the Change Case dialog box, as shown in Figure 5-4.

FIGURE 5-4.

Use the Change Case dialog box to change text capitalization instead of retyping.

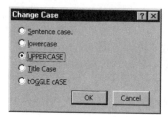

Each option's name shows how the text will appear. The Sentence Case option capitalizes only the first word in a sentence, while the Toggle Case option reverses the case for all of the selected text, changing uppercase to lowercase and vice versa.

3 Click one of the options and then click the OK button.

 TIP

For details about the Change Case options, click the Help button in the upper right corner of the dialog box and then click the option you want to know about, or right-click an option and choose the What's This? command on the pop-up menu.

TIP

If you're using a bidirectional operating system (such as Arabic or Hebrew) and have installed a Microsoft Language Pack, you can also change the direction of your text for languages that run from right to left. *See the Appendix, "Installing and Running Word," for more information.*

Word Basics

Using the Font Dialog Box

For the most common character formatting chores, you'll use the Formatting toolbar or keyboard shortcuts, but for maximum flexibility and convenience, use the Font dialog box. As you can see in Figure 5-5, the Font dialog box offers the style, font, size, and color options discussed earlier, and also gives you some more formatting choices.

Here's the basic procedure for opening and using the Font dialog box:

1 Select the text you want to reformat (if you don't, the options you choose will apply to the text you type next).

2 Choose Font from the Format menu or press Ctrl+D to display the Font dialog box. The dialog box appears with the Font tab selected, as in Figure 5-5.

FIGURE 5-5.

The Font dialog box offers all character formatting options in one handy place.

3 Choose the font, style, size, color, and effects. Your choices appear on sample text in the Preview box.

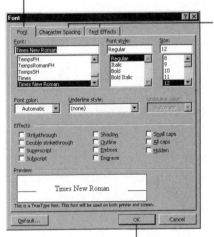

4 Click tabs, and choose Character Spacing or Text Effects options.

5 Click here to apply the changes.

Now let's take a closer look at the Font dialog box options, one tab at a time.

SEE ALSO

For more information about fonts or for special character formatting options such as drop caps, bullets, or numbered lists, see Chapter 14, "Formatting Special Characters and Paragraphs."

Font Options

The Font, Style, and Size lists show the options in these categories. Click the option you want to select. If necessary, scroll through the list until you see the option you want, or double-click in the current selection box and type the name or value of the option you want.

The Font Color, Underline Style, and Underline Color options are limited to what's on each list. (The Underline Color option is available only when you have selected an underline style.) Click one of these options to see the list of choices, and then click the option you want. Notice that the Underline list offers more than a dozen different underline styles, instead of the single underline you apply when you click the Underline button in the Formatting toolbar.

The Effects options on the Font tab are available only in this dialog box. Try choosing different effects and notice how they look in the Preview box.

 TIP

There are keyboard shortcuts for many of the options in the Font dialog box. For example, to create subscript or superscript text, select the text, and then press Ctrl+= or Ctrl++. Look up "Shortcut keys" in the Help system index for a complete list of shortcuts.

Character Spacing Options

When you click the Character Spacing tab in the Font dialog box, you'll see the options shown in Figure 5-6. Use these options to change the position of characters or to adjust their size more precisely. The Preview box shows the effect of your choices on sample type.

FIGURE 5-6.

Use Character Spacing options to adjust the size, horizontal spacing, or vertical position of text.

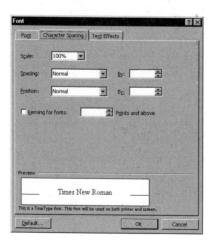

The Scale option lets you set the size of text by a percentage of its normal size. Normal size is 100%, but you can choose other options from the list or you can enter an alternate scale percentage if you don't see it on the list.

The Spacing options let you adjust the space between characters in the selected text. The Normal option is the default, but you can choose Expanded or Condensed spacing to increase or decrease the spacing. If you choose the Expanded or Condensed option, Word suggests a space value in the By box. Click the By box to enter a different value, or use the arrow buttons to increase or decrease the value incrementally.

 TIP

> Increase the space between characters and use small caps instead of lower-case letters in a heading or title to create a more elegant look.

The Position options let you adjust the text's position on the line. You can raise (superscript) or lower (subscript) text so that it's higher or lower than the text around it on the same line. As with the Spacing options, you can also set the precise amount by which the text is raised or lowered.

To turn kerning on, select the Kerning For Fonts check box. With kerning on, Word automatically adjusts the spacing between characters to compensate for differences in character shapes, as in Figure 5-7.

FIGURE 5-7.

With kerning, you can adjust the spacing between individual characters.

Very nicely done.

Kerned

Very nicely done.

Not kerned

When kerning is on, you can tell Word which text to kern and not kern by its size. Kerning doesn't make much difference on small type sizes, so you can use the Points And Above box to set the size below which Word will not kern type.

 TIP

> Select an initial capital letter and the letter next to it to adjust the kerning between those two letters only.

Text Effects Options

The Text Effects tab offers a list of options that make your text stand out by blinking in various ways. These options are useful only in documents that you will distribute to other Word users electronically on your network or via e-mail—they aren't supported in Web documents. Try selecting each of the Animations options in turn. The Preview box shows you how text will be animated.

Removing Character Formatting

If you change your mind about a character formatting option, there are three easy ways to remove it:

- Choose Undo from the Edit menu or click the Undo tool immediately after applying the formatting option.

- Choose the option you applied—along with any others listed above it—from the Undo tool's list of recent actions.

- Select the text and then click the same formatting button or type the command's keyboard shortcut. Applying a format to text that already has it will remove the existing format.

Displaying Nonprinting Characters

Along with the characters you type, Word inserts nonprinting characters in order to format your document properly. For example, each paragraph ends with an invisible paragraph marker. It's not always easy to spot extra spaces, tabs, or paragraph endings in a document, but you can see all of them when you display their nonprinting characters. Figure 5-8 shows some of Word's nonprinting characters, although you can create others when you insert fields or other objects.

FIGURE 5-8.

Word adds invisible (or nonprinting) characters to your document as you type. You can reveal them if you want.

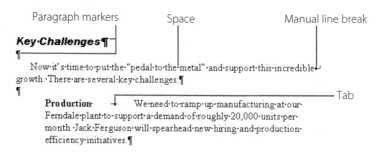

To hide or show nonprinting characters, click the Show/Hide button in the Standard toolbar (it looks like the paragraph marker in Figure 5-8) or press Ctrl+* (Ctrl+Shift+8).

Showing Nonprinting Characters at All Times

Nonprinting characters can help you see exactly how your document is formatted. Here's how to set Word so it shows these characters by default in every document:

1 Choose Options from the Tools menu to display the View tab in the Options dialog box, like this:

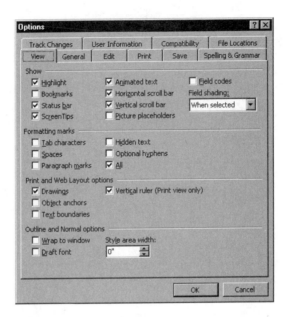

2 Select the check boxes in the Formatting Marks area to choose which characters you want displayed in your documents.

3 Press Enter or click OK.

Explore the other options on the View tab. You can hide scroll bars or the Status Bar, for example.

Formatting Paragraphs

Paragraph formatting options include indents, tabs, text alignment, and line spacing. You can set indents and tabs with the Ruler, click buttons in the Formatting toolbar to set the text alignment or indents, or use the Paragraph dialog box to handle all paragraph formatting tasks at once.

Since paragraph formatting options work only on whole paragraphs, you only need to click anywhere inside a paragraph to select it. To apply formatting to more than one paragraph, however, you'll have to select at least part of every paragraph you intend to change, or press Ctrl+A to select the entire document.

When formatting, it sometimes helps to display paragraph markers so you can tell where one paragraph ends and the next one begins. *See "Displaying Nonprinting Characters" earlier in this chapter.*

Setting Indents and Tabs with the Ruler

The Ruler at the top of the document window shows you the width of your text lines and any tabs or indents you have set. The ruler is set for inch measurements by default. If you don't see the ruler at the top of your document window, choose Ruler from the View menu.

You can change the ruler measurements to centimeters, points, or picas by choosing Options from the Tools menu, clicking the General tab, and selecting a different option on the Measurement Units list.

As you can see in Figure 5-9, the ruler has two areas: the white area represents the text area of your document, and the shaded area represents the page margins. You can adjust indents by dragging the indent markers anywhere in the ruler—even into the margin areas. *For details about setting page margins, see "Formatting Pages" on page 100.*

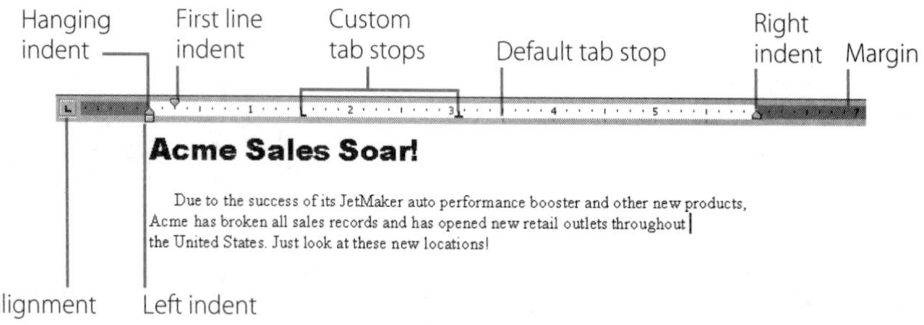

FIGURE 5-9.
The Ruler shows the width of text in a document, and you can use it to set tabs or indents for the selected paragraph.

Hanging indent — First line indent Custom tab stops Default tab stop Right indent Margin

Acme Sales Soar!

Due to the success of its JetMaker auto performance booster and other new products, Acme has broken all sales records and has opened new retail outlets throughout the United States. Just look at these new locations!

Tab alignment   Left indent

Margin sizes are controlled with the Page Setup dialog box. Double-click the shaded area of the ruler to display this dialog box.

Setting Indents

The Ruler's four indent markers represent the types of indents you can use in a paragraph, and each marker's position shows the indent settings for the current paragraph. To set indents, drag a marker to a different place on the ruler. Figure 5-10 shows paragraph indents at work.

FIGURE 5-10.

Use indents to set off a paragraph from others or to create a visual break at the beginning of each paragraph.

The ruler shows indents and tab stops
for the second paragraph in this example.

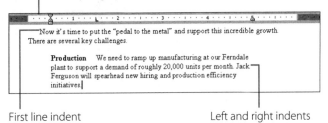

First line indent   Left and right indents

Try selecting a paragraph and dragging these controls to see how they work. Each of the four indent markers has a different effect on your text.

The Right Indent marker indents all the text in the paragraph from the right margin.

If you have trouble dragging the appropriate indent marker, point to one and wait for the ScreenTip to appear so you're sure you have the right marker for the job. If you click in the Ruler itself by mistake, a tab stop will appear. Delete the tab stop by dragging it down into the document. *See "Setting Tabs with the Ruler," on page 91, for more information about tabs.*

The Left Indent marker indents all of the text in the paragraph from the left margin. If the paragraph also contains a first line indent, the First Line Indent marker moves along with the Left Indent marker so that the first line remains at a different indent level from the rest of the paragraph.

The First Line Indent marker indents only the first line of a paragraph. You can use this marker to create regular indents or hanging indents. A hanging indent is indented less than the other lines in the paragraph, like this:

Production   We need to ramp up manufacturing at our Ferndale plant to support a demand of roughly 20,000 units per month. Jack Ferguson will spearhead new hiring and production efficiency initiatives.

Why Not Indent With Tabs or Spaces?

In the old typewriter days, you could indent a paragraph by pressing the Tab key or by hitting the Spacebar a few times. But when you use Word, there's a big difference between indenting with tabs or spaces and using indent controls.

In Word, pressing the Tab key or the Spacebar inserts a group of spaces into a line. When you press the Tab key to indent the first line of a paragraph in a new document, for example, you are beginning the line with five space characters. This causes two problems:

- You must remember to press the Tab key at the beginning of every paragraph to indent consistently.

- If you later merge the paragraph into the one above it, Word will move the tab or extra spaces along with it, like this:

> Manufacturing output picked up considerably in the fourth quarter. We brought the Eastwood plant fully online and began producing 4,000 units per month with one shift per day. Eastwood's utility usage also looks promising| The Ferndale plant has been working two shifts a day with approximately 200 man-hours per week in overtime since September. With the opening of the Eastwood facility, we should be able to eliminate nearly all of the overtime and return to a saner 8-hour daily production schedule.

You must then delete the tab to create the proper space between the two sentences.

On the other hand, when you set an indent you are telling Word to begin the paragraph at a particular position on the line. This has two advantages:

- You can easily merge the paragraph snugly with the one above it, because there aren't any extra tab or space characters in it.

- Word will indent every paragraph you type automatically, because the indent setting is carried forward with the other paragraph format settings each time you press the Enter key.

Use Word's indent controls whenever possible to save time and ensure format consistency. Save tabs for positioning text on individual lines or in columns.

To set a hanging indent with the First Line Indent marker, drag it to the left of the Left Indent marker.

The Hanging Indent marker also creates a hanging indent—it indents every line in the paragraph except the first line. To set a hanging indent with this marker, drag it to the right of the First Line Indent marker.

> **Hanging Indents vs. Left Indents**
>
> At first glance, a hanging indent may look like a left indent in a different location, so you might think that there's no difference between using the Left Indent and the Hanging Indent marker. But there is:
>
> - When you move the Left Indent marker, the First Line Indent marker moves with it, so the relationship between the first line's indent and the rest of the paragraph is maintained.
>
> - When you move the Hanging Indent marker, the First Line Indent marker stays put, so the relationship between the first line's indent and the rest of the paragraph changes.
>
> If you're not using a first line indent in your paragraph, you can use the Left Indent marker to create a hanging indent. But to be on the safe side, get in the habit of using the Hanging Indent marker every time you want to create a hanging indent.

Removing Indents

To remove left and right indents, drag the appropriate indent marker back to the edge of the white text area in the ruler. To remove a first line or hanging indent, drag the First Line Indent marker until it lines up directly above the Left Indent marker.

Setting Tabs with the Ruler

You use the ruler to determine the location of tab stops, and Word allows you to see, add, or delete tab stops by clicking and dragging there.

By default, Word documents have tab stops at every half-inch mark on the ruler. These default tab stops are indicated with gray tickmarks in the bottom edge of the ruler. When you set a custom tab stop, Word inserts a bolder tab mark in the ruler.

You can use five different tab stop alignments, and the Tab Alignment button indicates what sort of tab it is. Text and numbers align to each kind of tab stop in a different way, as you can see in Figure 5-11 on the next page. The Bar tab in line five in Figure 5-11 inserts a vertical bar. Bar tabs are used in legal documents.

⭐ TIP

You can change the default tab stops by using the Tabs dialog box. *See "Using the Tabs Dialog Box" on page 97.*

FIGURE 5-11.

You can use five different tab alignments, and each has its own distinctive marker on the ruler.

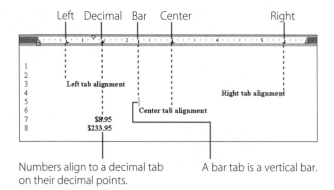

Numbers align to a decimal tab on their decimal points.

A bar tab is a vertical bar.

SEE ALSO

To learn how to apply line numbers as shown in Figure 5-11, see "Adding Line Numbers" on page 286.

■ To choose the alignment for a new tab, click the Tab Alignment button at the left edge of the ruler to cycle through the various tab types. The button itself shows the alignment you have selected.

■ To set a tab, click in the ruler where you want it to appear. Word inserts a tab marker and deletes the default tab stops between your new tab stop and the left margin. (If it didn't, you wouldn't be able to press the Tab key once to jump to the new tab stop.)

■ To move a tab, drag it sideways in the ruler.

■ To remove a tab, drag the tab marker down into your document and then release the mouse button.

 TIP

To remove all custom tab stops at once, press Ctrl+Shift+N.

Why Won't That Formatting Option Work?

When you apply a formatting option, Word is very precise in understanding exactly what is selected in your document. Sometimes this precision makes it seem as if a format option you've chosen isn't working. For example, if you have one character selected in a paragraph when you apply a paragraph formatting option, Word ignores your command because it can't apply a paragraph format to a single character. At other times, you may set a tab stop and then find it's gone when you move the insertion point to another paragraph. It's easy to think that Word is trying to frustrate you at times like this, but Word is only following its selection rules. Table 5-1 on the next page shows exactly how Word applies formatting options when you select various parts of your document.

Pay attention to what is selected when you choose formatting options and you'll always get the result you expect.

TABLE 5-1. **Word Applies Different Format Options Depending on What You Select**

You Select By...	Word Applies...
Moving the insertion point into a paragraph	Paragraph formatting options to that paragraph and to any new paragraphs you create by pressing the Enter key at the end of that paragraph, but not to other existing paragraphs
Selecting one or more characters in a paragraph	Character formatting options to the selected text, but not paragraph formatting options
Selecting all of one paragraph and part of another	Paragraph formatting options to both paragraphs

Using the Indent and Alignment Buttons

For setting quick indent and alignment options in a paragraph, use the indent and alignment buttons on the Formatting toolbar, as shown in Figure 5-12. A close look at the indent and alignment buttons gives you a pretty good idea of how they work.

FIGURE 5-12.

Click the Alignment or Indent buttons on the Formatting toolbar to quickly set paragraph indents or alignments.

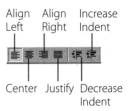

Align Left   Align Right   Increase Indent

Center   Justify   Decrease Indent

? SEE ALSO

You can be more precise or creative with indents by using the Ruler (see page 88) or the Paragraph dialog box (see page 94).

The four alignment buttons set left, center, right, and justified alignment for the selected paragraph. Click a button to change the alignment of the selected paragraph. The highlighted button shows which alignment option is set. The two indent buttons shown in Figure 5-12 change the indent for the left edge of the selected paragraph. You can move a paragraph's left edge to the left or right, depending on which button you click. Each time you click one of these buttons, Word changes the indent by half an inch.

Instead of clicking the Indent buttons, you can accomplish the same indenting tasks by pressing Ctrl+M (to indent to the left) or Shift+Ctrl+M (to indent to the right). If you're working in Print Layout or Web Layout view, you can set tabs or the alignment for a new paragraph with the Click and Type feature. *For more information on the Click and Type feature, see "Click and Type in Web or Print Layout Views" on page 109.*

Using the Paragraph Dialog Box

The Paragraph dialog box brings together all of the alignment, tab, and indent settings discussed so far. It also adds other options to control the line spacing and page breaks in paragraphs. When you choose Paragraph from the Format menu, you'll see the Paragraph dialog box as shown in Figure 5-13.

The specific settings you'll see when you open the Paragraph dialog box will vary depending on the indent, alignment, and spacing options set for the paragraph you have selected at the time.

FIGURE 5-13.

You can be more precise in setting indents and line spacing with the Paragraph dialog box.

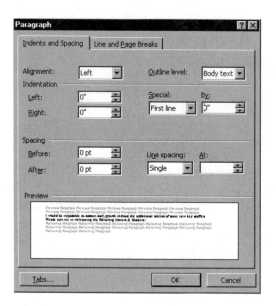

SEE ALSO

For details on using the Tabs dialog box, see "Using the Tabs Dialog Box" on page 97.

Paragraph format options come in the two groups that are indicated by the tabs in this dialog box. You can also access the Tabs dialog box by clicking the Tabs button at the bottom.

As you enter various indent and spacing options, the Preview box at the bottom shows how your changes will look in your document; the paragraph in bold shows the effects of your changes.

Setting Text Alignment and Indents

When you select the Indents and Spacing tab (as in Figure 5-13), you can customize options for the alignment, indents, line spacing, or space above or below the selected paragraph.

> The Paragraph dialog box is the only place in Word where you can specify line spacing options.

To set the text alignment, choose one of the four options from the Alignment list.

> Outline Level settings apply only when you're working in Outline view. *See Chapter 12, "Working with Outlines," for details.*

To set left and right indents, type the indent sizes into the Left and Right boxes, or the click the arrow buttons to select values.

To set hanging or first line indents, choose an indent type from the Special list and then enter a value or use the arrow buttons to set the indent size in the By box.

Changing Line Spacing

The Spacing options in the Paragraph dialog box allow you to tell Word how much space to leave before and after a paragraph and between lines.

To add space before or after a paragraph, enter a value in the Before or After box by typing the value or by using the arrow buttons.

> Use Before and After paragraph spacing instead of pressing the Enter key twice to separate paragraphs in your document.

To set the spacing between lines in the paragraph, choose a preset option from the Line Spacing list. If you choose At Least or Exactly from the Line Spacing list, you can enter a value in one-point increments in the By box at the right. If you choose Multiple from the Line Spacing list, you can specify spacing in half-line increments.

Word Basics

Setting Line and Page Breaks

To control how paragraphs are broken between pages, click the Line And Page Breaks tab in the Paragraph dialog box. Figure 5-14 shows these options.

FIGURE 5-14.

Use the Line And Page Breaks tab in the Paragraph dialog box to control hyphenation as well as paragraph breaks between pages.

? SEE ALSO

For more information about page breaks, see "Setting Page Breaks," page 104.

- Widow/Orphan Control tells Word not to break a paragraph between document pages if it will mean leaving either a widow or an orphan. A first line of a paragraph that is alone at the bottom of a page is known in publishing as an orphan. A last line of a paragraph left alone at the top of a page is known as a widow.

- Keep Lines Together tells Word not to break the paragraph between pages.

- Keep With Next tells Word not to place a page break between the current paragraph and the one that follows it.

- Page Break Before tells Word to insert a manual page break before the paragraph.

- Suppress Line Numbers tells Word not to print line numbers in the paragraph. This option applies only if automatic line numbering is set. *See "Adding Line Numbers" on page 286 for details.*

- Don't Hyphenate tells Word not to hyphenate words when breaking lines within a paragraph. This option applies only if automatic hyphenation is on. *See "Hyphenating Text" on page 210 for details.*

Using the Tabs Dialog Box

Tabs automatically indent the insertion point to specific places in the ruler when you press the Tab key. You can set tabs by clicking or dragging in the ruler as shown on page 92, but when you use the Tabs dialog box, you can specify tabs with numeric values, set or clear several tabs at once, and add special tab leader characters.

To display the Tabs dialog box, choose Tabs from the Format menu. You'll see the dialog box shown in Figure 5-15.

FIGURE 5-15.

Use the Tabs dialog box to specify numeric positions for tab stops or to set a group of tab stops all at once.

1 Enter a numeric value for ruler position.

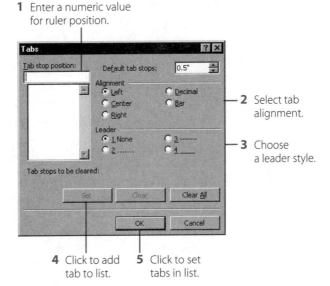

2 Select tab alignment.

3 Choose a leader style.

4 Click to add tab to list.

5 Click to set tabs in list.

You can add, change, or clear tab stops by specifying positions or choosing options in the Tabs dialog box. You can set several tabs at a time. Click the OK button or press the Enter key to apply your hanges.

■ To set a custom tab stop, type a ruler location (down to 100th of an inch) in the Tab Stop Position box and then click the Set button. The custom tab stop is added to the Tab Stop Position list below. You can add tab stops one after the other this way, as long as you know the locations you want.

■ To clear a tab stop, select it in the Tab Stop Position list and click the Clear button. The tab stop's location disappears from the Tab Stop Position list and appears in the Tab Stops To Be Cleared area. You can select and clear several stops this way.

■ To clear all custom tab stops, click the Clear All button.

■ To change a custom tab's alignment or add a leader character, select the tab in the Tab Stop Position list and then click one of the Alignment or Leader buttons to the right. Figure 5-16 shows how you might use tab leaders in a document.

Acme/Ferndale Telephone List

Name	Extension
Albertson, Jim	3345
Chu, Jennifer	3349
Gardener, Ellen	3381
Ferguson, Jack	3329

■ To change the spacing of the default tab stops, enter a different value or click the arrow buttons in the Default Tab Stops box.

After you click the OK button or press the Enter key, Word creates the tab stops and they appear in the ruler. If any tab's position, alignment, or leader isn't exactly right, you can drag it to the right location or double-click it to reopen the Tabs dialog box and change it there.

Copying Paragraph Formats

The best way to maintain consistency in paragraph formats throughout your document is to use styles *(see Chapter 15)*, but, in a pinch, the Format Painter makes it easy to copy one paragraph's styles and apply them to other paragraphs. You'll find the Format Painter button on the Standard toolbar (click the More Buttons button to find this button if it's not on your Formatting toolbar):

Format Painter

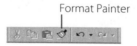

To use it, follow these steps:

1 Click in the paragraph whose format you want to copy.

2 Click the Format Painter button. Word adds an animated paint-brush to the I-beam pointer.

3 Select the paragraph or paragraphs where you want the format copied.

If you click the Format Painter button and then change your mind, you can cancel the paste operation by pressing Esc or clicking the button a second time.

> Keyboard shortcuts for the Format Painter are Ctrl+Shift+C (to copy a format) and Ctrl+Shift+V (to paste a format).

To copy a format to more than one location in a document, double-click the Format Painter button and then click wherever you want the format applied. When you're done, click the Format Painter again to turn it off.

Formatting with Built-In Styles

As we've seen, there are lots of formatting options for characters and paragraphs. Styles are groups of format settings that are given names and that you can apply all at once. Chapter 15, "Using Styles and Themes," covers styles in detail, but it's easy to format text with a style without knowing much at all about them.

Every document comes with a group of styles already defined for it. You can see these by clicking the Style list button in the Formatting toolbar, as in Figure 5-17.

FIGURE 5-17.

Use the Style list in the Formatting toolbar to apply format styles in your document.

Follow these steps to apply a style with the Style menu:

1 Select the text you want to format with the style.

2 Click the arrow button next to the Style menu.

3 Click a style to apply it to the selected text.

> If you know the name of the style you want, click the name in the Style menu, type the style name, and press Enter to apply it.

You don't have to use styles, but they make it much easier to standardize and apply the formatting in your documents.

Formatting Pages

To finish up with basic formatting techniques, let's look at the basics of formatting pages. Most of the time, you'll use just a couple of options in the Page Setup dialog box to handle page formatting.

Using the Page Setup Dialog Box

To display the Page Setup dialog box, choose Page Setup from the File menu. You'll see the dialog box shown in Figure 5-18.

> Double-click in the dark gray (margin) areas of the Ruler to display the Page Setup dialog box.

FIGURE 5-18.

Use the Page Setup dialog box to set margins and other page-level formatting options for your documents.

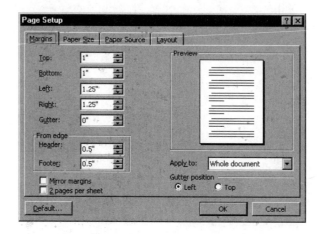

You can choose options on four different tabs in this dialog box, and click the OK button to apply those options.

As you try out various options in the Page Setup dialog box, you'll see how your changes will look in the Preview area at the right.

Choosing Where to Apply Page Format Settings

With the Apply To list, select the part of your document to which Word will apply Page Setup options. This choice applies to every option in the Page Setup dialog box, not just to those on the current tab. This list may contain the following choices:

- Whole Document (the default) sets the same margins for the whole document.

- This Point Forward applies the settings from the insertion point on.

- Selected Text applies the settings only to the selected paragraphs when you have one or more paragraphs selected in your document.

If your document contains more than one section, the Apply To list contains two other options:

SEE ALSO

For more information about sections and how to use them, see Chapter 16, "Formatting Pages and Sections."

- This Section applies the margin settings only to the current document section.

- Selected Sections applies the margin settings only to the section or sections you have selected.

Setting Default Page Setup Options

Each Word template comes preset with specific Page Setup options. However, when you change the options here, you can set them as the new defaults for the template you're using. Here's how to do this:

1 Choose Page Setup options on any of the four tabs.

2 Click the Default button in the lower left corner of the Page Setup dialog box. Word will ask you to confirm that you want to reset the document template's defaults.

NOTE

> Every document in Word is based on a template. *For more information about templates, see Chapter 13, "Using Templates and Wizards."*

3 Click Yes.

Setting Margins

If you don't see the options shown in Figure 5-18 when you open the Page Setup dialog box, click the Margins tab. You can use these options to set left, right, top, and bottom margin widths for an entire document, or you can apply the settings to only selected parts of a document.

To set margins, click the arrow buttons on the Top, Bottom, Left, or Right box to increase or decrease the current value shown, or select the value in any data box and type a new one.

To create wider or narrower margins for just one page, select the text on that page, choose new margin settings, and choose the Selected Text option on the Apply To list in the Page Setup dialog box.

By setting margins wider in certain parts of your document, you can more easily accommodate large graphics or tables.

You can also adjust margins in Print Preview mode. *See "Previewing Documents," on page 122.*

Setting the Paper Size

For more information about using sections as well as the Gutter Position and other options in the Page Setup dialog box, see Chapter 16.

The Paper Size tab in the Page Setup dialog box allows you to choose the type of paper on which you'll be printing and the way text is oriented on the page:

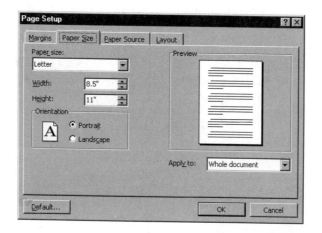

If you're using a standard paper size, choose it from the Paper Size list in the upper-left corner. You'll see the Height and Width dimensions change according to the paper size you choose. To set a custom paper size, choose Custom from the Paper Size list and then click the arrow buttons or type values in the Width and Height boxes to set it.

Setting the Page Orientation

Click the Portrait or Landscape button in the Orientation section. The Preview area shows the difference between them. By default, Word assumes you'll print down the tall (Portrait) dimension of the page, but you might switch to wide (Landscape) orientation when you want to print items such as extra-wide tables or three-fold brochure layouts.

Choosing the Paper Source

On the Paper Source tab, you can choose paper sources for the first document page and for all of its other pages. If you have a printer with more than one input tray, for example, you might choose a tray containing letterhead for the first page of a document, and a tray containing plain paper or second sheet paper for the other document pages. The Paper Source options look like this:

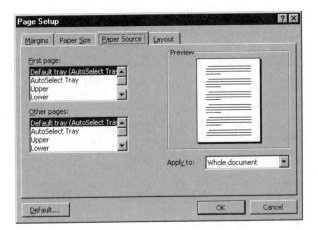

Choose a paper source option from each list, or—if you're printing the entire document on the same paper—leave the settings on Default Tray.

Page Layout Options

The options on the Page Layout tab are for more advanced formatting with sections, headers and footers, borders, endnotes, and line numbers. We'll cover them elsewhere in this book. *For information about using endnotes in your document, see "Inserting Footnotes and Endnotes" on page 231. For more about using line numbers, see "Adding Line Numbers" on page 286. For more about formatting headers and footers, see "Using Headers and Footers" on page 320.*

Setting Page Breaks

Based on the margins you set for your document, Word divides the document into pages for printing. In Print Layout view, you see a gap between two pages like this:

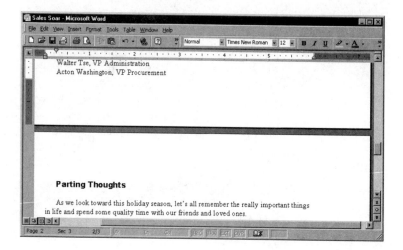

When you work in Normal view, Word identifies page breaks with a dotted line. You can't insert a page break in Web Layout view, and breaks aren't shown in Outline view.

 TIP

> You can also view page breaks in Print Preview mode. *See Chapter 6, "Viewing, Previewing, and Printing Documents," for details.*

To break a page in a different place, add a manual page break:

1   Move the insertion point to the first line of the new page to be started after the break.

 NOTE

> Word inserts a new page break immediately to the right of the insertion point. If the insertion point is in the middle of a word when you insert a break, the word and the line it's on will be divided between two pages.

2   Press Ctrl+Enter. Word adds the manual page break above the insertion point.

To remove a manual page break, place the insertion point at the beginning of the line below the break and press the Backspace key, or click in the left margin next to the break to select it and then press the Backspace or Delete key.

When you format sections or when you work with columns, you can also specify breaks to determine how and when these format elements are divided. *See Chapter 16, "Formatting Pages and Sections," for more information.*

More Formatting Options

Word has many more formatting options besides those discussed in this chapter. For more information about additional formatting features, see Part III, "Formatting Tools." To learn about Word's extensive page layout and graphics capabilities, see Part IV, "Graphics, Page Design, and Publishing Tools." And if you're planning to format and publish documents for viewing on the Web, check out Part VI, "Web and Internet Tools."

For now, let's move on to more basics. Chapter 6 explains how to print Word documents or view them in different ways.

CHAPTER 6

Viewing, Previewing, and Printing Documents

Microsoft Word offers four different document views to suit your needs when editing, formatting, organizing, or publishing your work. Other window tools allow you to split the document window, to open new windows for the same document, and to magnify or reduce the contents of a document. The different views and window tools help you work more efficiently and get a more accurate picture of how your documents will look when either printed or viewed on the World Wide Web. In this chapter you'll learn about the different document views and how to preview and print documents.

Using Views

Word offers four different views of a document, and each is tailored for a different editing or publishing task.

- Print Layout view lets you work with formatted columns, page breaks, headers, and everything else in your document as it will appear when printed. In Word 2000, this is the default document view.

- Web Layout view allows you to work with text and graphics on a page with a colored background, sounds, movies, and other Web features.

- Normal view works best when you're concentrating primarily on your document's text.

- Outline view displays your document as an outline so you can easily view and reorganize its contents.

Selecting a View

To select a view, choose its name from the top of the View menu. Or, if you prefer, you can select a view by clicking the appropriate button at the left end of the horizontal scroll bar.

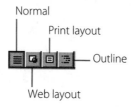

Normal
Print layout
— Outline
Web layout

 NOTE

> The Outline view command is on the extended portion of the View menu, but if you choose this command frequently, Word will add it to the short version of the menu.

Print Layout View

Print Layout view shows the text of the document as it will look when printed, with columns, graphics, margins, page breaks, headers, and footers. Figure 6-1 shows an example.

FIGURE 6-1.

Print Layout view shows documents as they will appear when printed, with margins, page breaks, and multi-column layouts.

Left Margin control

Indent controls

Indent control

Right Margin control

Bottom Margin control

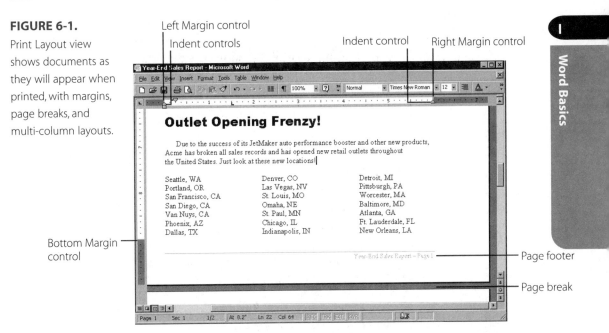

Page footer

Page break

Click and Type in Web or Print Layout Views

Word normally aligns the insertion point according to the paragraph alignment or tab stops that you previously set. But when you're working with a single-column layout in Web Layout or Print Layout view, you can use the new Click and Type feature in Word 2000 to add text and align it at the same time:

1 Point to any blank line or empty document area and double-click. Word places the insertion point there and sets a tab stop or changes the alignment setting for the text you type. The pointer even changes to show the text alignment, like this:

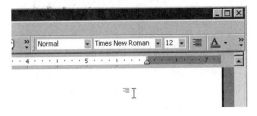

2 Type the text you want to enter.

3 Press Enter to finish entering text and return to your document's normal paragraph alignment.

Click and Type doesn't work in layouts with more than one column.

You can select, edit, or move text or graphics in this view just as you can in Normal view, but this view shows the text in its actual size in proportion to the size of each printed page. This view shows a vertical ruler as well as the horizontal one you see in Normal view. You can adjust the page margins by dragging markers at the ends of the two rulers.

To edit header or footer text, double-click it. *See "Using Headers and Footers" on page 320 for details.*

You can also adjust the page margins for the entire document in Print Layout view. Just point to the left, right, top, or bottom margin control in a ruler and drag it to a new location. Notice that when you point to the margin control, the pointer changes to a double arrow.

When you drag the margin control, a dotted line extends from the margin control across your document so you can see exactly where the margin will be.

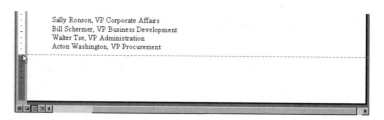

To reset margins in only one section or page of a document, use the Page Setup dialog box. *See "Formatting Pages" on page 100.*

Web Layout View

For more information about creating Web pages, see Chapter 32, "Creating Web Pages," and Chapter 33, "Using Advanced Web Features."

The Web Layout view shows your document as it will appear on a Web site—you can see colored backgrounds and the document is shown as one long page without breaks. Figure 6-2 shows an example.

FIGURE 6-2.

In Web Layout view, you can create and edit Web pages by combining text, graphics, and other elements on the page.

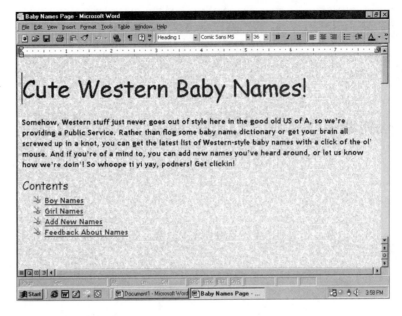

Normal View

As you can see in Figure 6-3, Normal view shows the text in a document alone. Page and section breaks are shown with dotted lines, and you can't really tell how your text looks in relationship to the page margins. Character and paragraph formats are shown as they will appear in print, but if you have formatted text in multiple columns, this view shows the text in just one column.

FIGURE 6-3.

The Normal view does not display format options such as multiple columns.

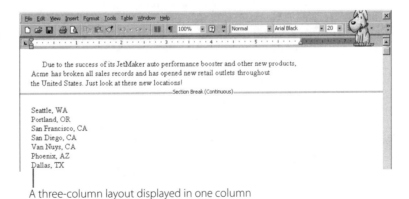

A three-column layout displayed in one column

NOTE

Notice that Figure 6-3 shows another of the Assistant characters (in the upper right corner). This one is called Rocky.

Outline View

Word has a built-in outline processor that allows you to work with documents in an outline format. To work with an outline, you switch to Outline view. As you can see in Figure 6-4, Outline view converts every heading, title, or line of text into an outline heading.

FIGURE 6-4.

In Outline view you can drag document headings to reorganize your document.

Headings with gray underlines have text beneath them.

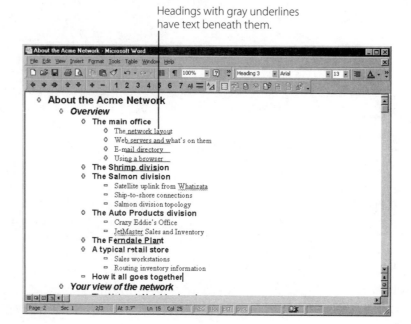

SEE ALSO

For more information about using Outline view, see Chapter 12, "Working with Outlines."

In Outline view, you can open headings to see the text contained in them, or you can drag headings to rearrange text. You'll also use Outline view when creating master documents and subdocuments. *See Chapter 24, "Using Master Documents."*

Using Window Tools

Each document view lets you work with the information in your document in different ways, but Word doesn't stop there. You can also change the way the document window is displayed. You can do the following:

- Use the Document Map to jump quickly to other sections of your document.

- Display the document's contents in Full Screen mode without showing the document window's menus, toolbars, scroll bars, or other controls.

- Split the document window into two panes so you can see two parts of your document at once.

- Zoom in or out of the document view to magnify or reduce its contents.

- Open additional windows on the same document.

- Arrange multiple windows on your screen to see several at once.

Using the Document Map

SEE ALSO

For more information about applying styles, see "Formatting with Built-In Styles" on page 99. For complete information about styles, see Chapter 15, "Using Styles and Themes."

The built-in styles you get with each Word document include Heading styles for document headings, and if you have used them to format your document, you can use the Document Map as a navigation tool to quickly see how your document is organized.

The Document Map appears in a pane at the left side of the screen, as seen in Figure 6-5. The map shows each heading in your document. You can quickly navigate to a part of the document by clicking on its heading in the map. When you're working on a long document, it's much faster to navigate with the Document Map than it is to scroll through the document itself. The Document Map is also a quick way to check the heading and subheading structure of your document.

NOTE

The Document Map is blank if there are no Heading style headings in your document.

Displaying the Document Map

To display the Document Map, click the Document Map button in the Standard toolbar as shown in Figure 6-5, or choose Document Map from the View menu.

FIGURE 6-5.

The Document Map shows your document's headings. Navigate to a heading by clicking it.

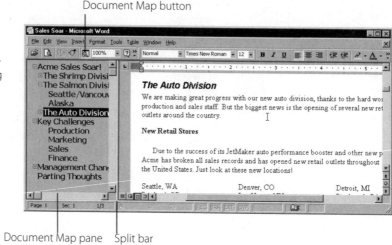

Document Map button

Document Map pane   Split bar

When Word shows the Document Map, it splits the document window into two panes. As you can see in Figure 6-5, the Document Map pane has its own vertical scroll bar.

Navigating with the Map

To navigate to a different part of your document, click the map heading you want to jump to—Word will scroll through the document to that heading and move the insertion point, too. If you don't see the heading you want, scroll up or down through the map until you do.

Adjusting the Map Pane

If the map pane is too wide or too narrow, drag the split bar to the left or right. If you make the map too narrow, you'll obscure some of the text in the map headings, but you can point to any partially hidden heading and the full heading will appear, like this:

Hiding and Showing Headings

You can also change the map by hiding or showing headings. Notice the plus and minus boxes next to some headings in Figure 6-5. A plus box indicates that there are more subheadings under the heading. Click the plus box to display the headings under it.

The example in Figure 6-5 shows just three heading levels, but you can show more of them. Right-click inside the Document Map, and you'll see the Document Map shortcut menu, like this:

Choose a different heading level to reveal more or fewer headings. You can also use this menu to expand or collapse the selected heading or to put the Document Map away.

 TIP

> You can reformat the Document Map text by modifying the Document Map style in the Style dialog box. *For more information, see "Modifying Styles" on page 307.*

Closing the Document Map

There are several ways to close the Document Map:

- Click the Document Map button.

- Choose Document Map from the View menu.

- Right-click in the map and choose Document Map from the shortcut menu.

- Double-click the split bar in the document window.

Using Full Screen Mode

Full Screen mode spreads the contents of your document across the entire screen and eliminates the toolbars, menu bar, status bar, and even the Windows taskbar, as shown in Figure 6-6. To show a document in Full Screen mode, choose Full Screen from the View menu.

FIGURE 6-6.

Full Screen mode hides the menu bar, scroll bars, and other window controls.

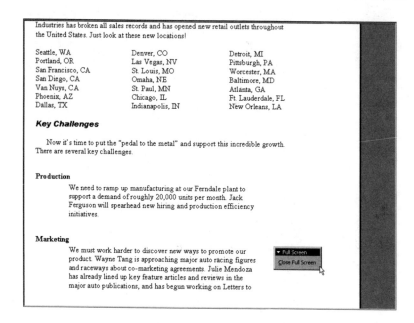

Many experienced Word users prefer to work in Full Screen mode because more of a document is visible. You can still edit, format, and navigate in the document when using Full Screen mode, but you have to access the controls a little differently.

 NOTE

You can't use Full Screen mode when the Document Map is displayed.

To navigate in the document, use the navigation keys on your keyboard or the wheel on your mouse (if you have an IntelliMouse pointing device).

TIP

You can return the status bar or the vertical or horizontal scroll bars to Full Screen view by choosing Options from the Tools menu and selecting the Status Bar, Vertical Scroll bar, or Horizontal Scroll Bar check boxes on the View tab.

To choose a command from the menu bar, point to the top of the document and the menu bar will appear. Or you can press the Alt key to display the menu bar and then select a command with the keyboard or the mouse. You can also right-click to display a shortcut menu and choose a command from it, or you can type any command's keyboard shortcut.

TIP

> You can use any document view while in Full Screen mode. Just turn on Full Screen mode and then select the view you want with the View menu.

To exit Full Screen mode, click the Close Full Screen command on the Full Screen palette and you'll return to the standard document window.

Splitting a Window

When you're working with a long document, it can be helpful to view two parts of it at the same time. With Word you can split the document window into separate, independently scrolling panes, and you can adjust the sizes of these panes.

There are two ways to split the document window:

- Drag the split box from the top of the vertical scroll bar
- Choose Split from the Window menu

Using the Split Box

The split box appears at the top of the vertical scroll bar, like this:

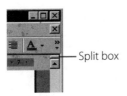
Split box

To split the window, drag the split box down into the document, and release the mouse button when the bar is where you want it. The window will split into two panes, as in Figure 6-7 on the next page.

FIGURE 6-7.

By splitting the document window, you can view two different parts of the document at once or see two different views of it.

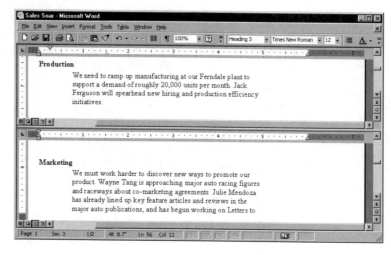

You can scroll through each pane independently to view two different parts of the document.

> The insertion point can be in only one pane at a time. Before editing text in a pane, click in that pane.

To resize the panes, drag the split bar up or down.

Using the Window Menu

To split the window with the Window menu, follow these steps:

1 Choose Split from the Window menu. The split bar appears in the middle of the document window.

2 Drag the split bar up or down or press the Up or Down arrow keys to move it.

3 Click or press the Enter key to fix the location and create the two window panes.

Removing a Split Window

To remove the split bar and return to a single-pane view, double-click the split bar or choose Remove Split from the Window menu. When you remove a split, Word displays the document at the position of the insertion point. To save navigation time, make sure to click inside the pane that contains the part of the document you want to see before removing the split.

Zooming In or Out of Documents

In addition to presenting your information in various views, you can enlarge or reduce your document's contents with zoom controls. For example, you might magnify the document to avoid eyestrain or to view small details in graphics. On the other hand, you might reduce the document to fit more of it on the screen.

You can zoom in or out of a document with the Zoom menu in the Standard toolbar or by choosing Zoom from the View menu. When you zoom, you specify a magnification percentage for the document's contents: actual size is 100%, for example.

NOTE

> Zooming changes only your *view* of the document, not the size of text or graphics that will be printed or displayed on the Web.

Using the Zoom Menu

The Standard toolbar has a Zoom menu, like this:

Zoom menu

You can select one of Word's built-in settings or use any zoom percentage between 10 and 500.

NOTE

> You may have to click the More Buttons button on the Standard toolbar to see the Zoom menu.

To choose another preset zoom level, click the arrow next to the Zoom menu and choose a different value from the drop-down menu. To zoom to a percentage not listed on the menu:

1 Select the current percentage shown.

2 Type a new value—it's not necessary to add the percent sign after it.

3 Press Enter. Word zooms in or out of the document and shows the new setting in the Zoom menu.

Using the Zoom Dialog Box

If you use the Zoom dialog box, you have more options for displaying your document, and you can preview zoom settings.

1 Choose Zoom from the View menu. You'll see the Zoom dialog box, as shown in Figure 6-8.

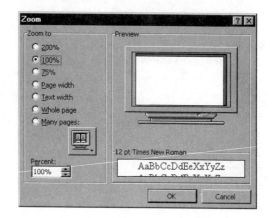

2 Click one of the buttons to select a preset percentage, or use the Percent control to enter a different percentage by either clicking the arrows or selecting the value and typing a new one. You can see a preview of the zoom size at the right.

When you're in Print Layout view, you can click the Whole Page or Many Pages options to reduce the document to the point where you can see entire pages. If you choose the Many Pages option, click the button below it to select the number of pages you want to view at once.

3 Click OK to apply the zoom setting and close the dialog box.

To return to the default 100% zoom setting, just use the same procedure detailed above.

Making a New Window

If the panes in a split document window are too small for your purposes, you can open an entirely new window onto the same document. It can be handy to have two windows open on the same document at once.

For example, you might display the outline of a document in one window and the full text in another (as in Figure 6-9), or display the Print Layout view in one window and the Normal view in another.

FIGURE 6-9.

By opening two windows of the same document, you can set a different view for each window.

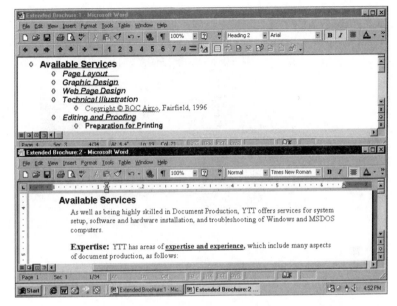

To open a second window of a document, click in it to make it the active document and then choose New Window from the Window menu. Word opens a new window of the same document and adds a colon and a window number after the document name, as in Figure 6-9. Each window is listed separately on the Window menu.

 NOTE

In Word 2000, each document window is represented separately on the Windows taskbar, and each has its own menu bar, toolbars, and status bar, as shown in Figure 6-9.

Arranging Multiple Windows

It's not uncommon to have several different document windows open at once. You can move or resize these windows manually to see more than one at a time (as in Figure 6-9), but Word can also arrange all of your document windows automatically.

To arrange all of your document windows, choose Arrange All from the Window menu. The windows will be resized and arranged to fill your screen, as shown in Figure 6-10.

FIGURE 6-10.

Choose Arrange All from the Window menu to resize all open document windows and arrange them on the screen side by side.

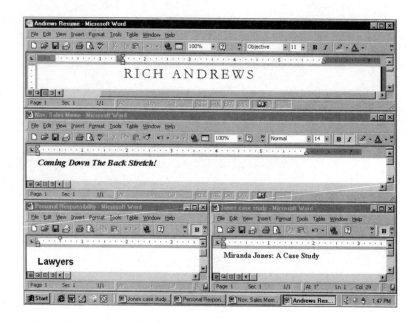

To return any document to full size, click the Maximize button in the document's window.

Previewing Documents

Print Preview shows your document's pages just as they will appear when they are printed. Choose Print Preview from the File menu to display this view, as shown in Figure 6-11 on the next page.

The main purpose of Print Preview is to check your document's formatting before you print. You can set the magnification in this mode, and you can use the window scroll bars or keyboard navigation keys to navigate in the window. You can also use the Print Preview mode to adjust the page margins.

FIGURE 6-11.

Print Preview shows your document as it will look when printed. It's the best way to do a quick final check before printing.

Click the zoom pointer to view an area at its actual size.

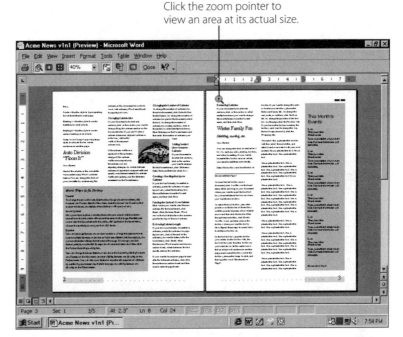

Zooming to Actual Size

In the Print Preview mode, the zoom pointer replaces the standard pointer. When you want to look more closely at text or formatting, click in an area of the reduced document to magnify it to actual size. Click again and the document will be reduced again.

Using the Print Preview Toolbar

When you display Print Preview mode, the standard toolbars in the document window are replaced with the Print Preview toolbar:

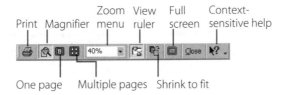

Print Magnifier Zoom menu View ruler Full screen Context-sensitive help

One page Multiple pages Shrink to fit

- The Print button prints the document without displaying the Print dialog box. *See "Printing Documents" on page 125 for more information about this dialog box.*

- The Magnifier button toggles the mouse pointer between the magnifier and the normal pointer. The Magnifier button is on by default, so the mouse pointer is a magnifier as shown in Figure 6-11. When you turn the Magnifier button off, the pointer is an I-beam, and you can select or edit text in the document.

- The One Page button tells Word to display one page at a time in Preview mode. Clicking the Multiple Pages button opens a palette where you can choose the number of pages you want to display on the screen.

? SEE ALSO

For instructions about using the Zoom menu, see "Using the Zoom Menu" on page 119.

- The Zoom menu works just like the Zoom menu in the Standard toolbar, except that it includes other options to zoom by the amount of the page you want to see, like this:

? SEE ALSO

For information about adjusting margins with the horizontal and vertical rulers, see "Print Layout View" on page 108 earlier in this chapter.

- The View Ruler button displays horizontal and vertical rulers at the sides of the document. When these rulers are visible, you can use them to set the page margins or indents, just as you can in Print Layout view. Hiding the rulers leaves a little more screen space for the document.

When the last page of your document contains only one or two lines of text, you can use the Shrink To Fit button to remove this final page. Shrink to Fit will automatically reduce the size of the text to fit entirely on the previous pages. Choose another zoom setting to cancel the shrinkage.

Don't save a document when Shrink to Fit is turned on. If you do, Word will save it at the reduced size, so all the fonts in the document will be smaller than they were before. You'll have to reformat all the text to restore it to its normal size.

- The Full Screen button presents the previewed document at maximum size on your screen. Unlike the Full Screen mode (covered on page 116 earlier in this chapter), you can still see the Print Preview toolbar in Full Screen mode when you use this button.

- The Close button cancels Print Preview mode, closes the Print Preview toolbar, and returns you to the previous document view.

- The Context-Sensitive Help button works like the What's This? command on the Help menu. When you click this button, the pointer turns into a question mark, and you can then click any feature of the Preview screen to get a description of it.

SEE ALSO

For more information about the What's This? command, see "Using the What's This? Command" on page 49.

SEE ALSO

For details about setting indents and tabs in rulers, see "Formatting Paragraphs" on page 87.

Adjusting Indents, Tabs, and Margins

You can use the rulers in Print Preview mode to set paragraph indents or tabs just as you can in the Normal or Print Layout views. To set indents, simply drag the appropriate indent marker to its new location. Click the Tab Alignment button and then click in the ruler to set a tab stop.

To set a new page margin in Print Preview mode, follow these steps:

1 Point to the gray margin control between the white and dark gray section at the end of a ruler. The pointer changes to a double arrow.

2 Drag the margin control and release the mouse button to reset the margin.

Printing Documents

Once your document looks the way you want, you're ready to print it. To print a document, follow these steps:

1 Choose Print from the File menu or press Ctrl+P. You'll see the Print dialog box, as shown in Figure 6-12 at the top of the next page.

NOTE

The options in the Print dialog box apply only to the current document. *See "Using Advanced Printing Options" on page 127 for information about options that apply to every document you print.*

FIGURE 6-12.
Select printing options
and print your docu-
ment with the Print
dialog box.

2 Choose an alternate
printer if one is available.

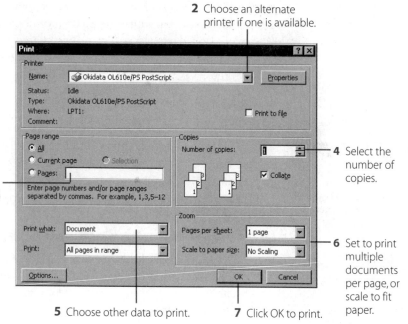

3 Set the range
of pages to be
printed.

4 Select the
number of
copies.

6 Set to print
multiple
documents
per page, or
scale to fit
paper.

5 Choose other data to print.

7 Click OK to print.

To print your document without checking the options in the Print dialog box,
click the Print button in the Standard or Print Preview toolbar.

You can also use Word to print envelopes and labels. *See "Creating Envelopes
and Labels" in Chapter 18 for more information.*

Now let's look at the options you can choose for printing the current
document.

Setting Printing Options

The Print dialog box shown in Figure 6-12 contains all of the options
you'll normally need to use when printing. Table 6-1 describes these
options. You can also set advanced options from inside the Print dialog box, and you can change your printer's characteristics as well.

You can specify ranges of pages (3-6, for example) or groups of individual
pages (1,3,5) in the Page Range box.

TABLE 6-1. Options in the Print Dialog Box

Option Name	Description
Name list	Choose an alternate printer if one is available.
Properties button	Displays printer properties. See page 129.
Print To File	Print the formatted document to a file on your disk.
Page Range	Choose All to print the entire document, or enter numeric ranges to print certain pages.
Copies	Enter the number of copies to be printed.
Collate	Collate each document when printing multiple copies (one complete document copy at a time) or clear to print copies a page at a time (copies of page 1, copies of page 2, etc.).
Print What	Select type of data to print from the document—document properties, styles, reviewer comments, or other data.
Print	Print only Even or Odd pages from the document or All pages.
Pages Per Sheet	Print multiple copies of the document on one sheet of paper, such as nametags or business cards.
Scale To Paper Size	Automatically zoom the document's contents to fit on various sizes of paper.
Options	Display more advanced printing options.

Using Advanced Printing Options

When you click the Options button at the bottom of the Print dialog box, you'll see a whole range of additional options you can choose when printing, as shown in Figure 6-13 on the next page. Few of these options will matter to you during basic printing jobs, but many of them are mentioned later in the book, and you'll be referred back here for information about them.

TIP

You can also display these options by choosing Options from the Tools menu and clicking the Print tab.

FIGURE 6-13.

Click the Options button in the Print dialog box to set options that affect all printing jobs.

Most of these options are global—they affect every document you will print from this point on, not just the current document. Table 6-2 explains the global options.

If you're printing data onto a preprinted form, you can tell Word to print only data (rather than borders or graphics) from a document. Select the check box under Options For Current Document Only.

TABLE 6-2. Global Printer Options You See When You Click the Options Button in the Print Dialog Box

Option Name	Description
Draft Output	Speeds printing with minimum formatting on some printers.
Update Fields	Updates contents of fields in document before printing.
Update Links	Updates contents of link in document before printing.
Allow A4/Letter Paper Resizing	Resizes documents to fit on A4 (8.24" x 11.7") paper.
Background Printing	Prints document quickly to a memory buffer so you can continue working during printing.

(continued)

TABLE 6-1. *continued*

Option Name	Description
Print PostScript Over Text	Obeys PostScript commands before printing document text. (For PostScript experts only.)
Reverse Print Order	Prints document from last page to first. This is useful for printers that output pages face up.
Document Properties	Prints document properties at end of text.
Field Codes	Prints field codes at end of text when the document contains fields.
Comments	Prints reviewer comments at end of text when the document contains them.
Hidden Text	Prints hidden text such as index entries or cross-references.
Graphics	Prints graphics when the document contains them (option is on by default).
Default Tray	Selects the paper tray normally used when printing.

Setting Printer Properties

When you click the Properties button in the Print dialog box, you'll see options that control the way your printer works and the way in which Word prints document information on each page, as shown in Figure 6-14.

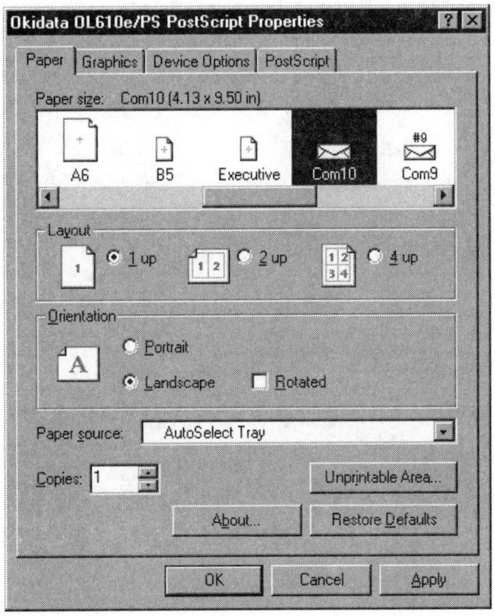

FIGURE 6-14.

You can display and set these output options for your printer by clicking the Properties button in the Print dialog box.

As with advanced printing options, you can safely ignore these options most of the time. Nevertheless, it helps to have information about them when you need it, and you'll be referred back to this section later in the book.

The Properties options are exclusive to the printer you have selected at the time. These options affect your printer's behavior with all documents. There are four tabs containing lots of different options:

- Paper options set the paper size, layout, orientation, paper source, and number of copies.

- Graphics options control the resolution and sizing of printed information.

- Device options control print enhancement features of your printer.

- PostScript options control the way your printer interprets PostScript commands, if in fact it does interpret them.

Consult your printer's manual for more information about how these options affect printing.

If you reset several options on a tab and want to return everything to the way it was originally, click the Restore Default button and then click OK.

Monitoring and Controlling Printing

When you send one or more print jobs to your printer and have Background Printing turned on, Word sends each job to the Windows print queue. You can tell when the queue is at work because you'll see a printer icon at the right end of the Windows taskbar, like this:

Printer icon

To check on the progress of a printing job, double-click the printer icon. You'll see the print queue window, as shown in Figure 6-15.

FIGURE 6-15.

You can view or re-schedule pending print jobs in the Print Queue window.

Title bar shows the printer status.

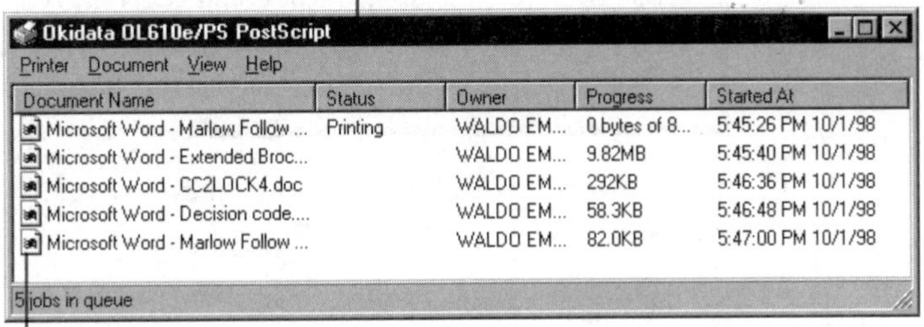

Drag documents up or down to reprioritize.

The print queue window lists each document that hasn't yet been printed by your printer. You'll see the document name, printing status, owner, printing progress, and the date and time the print job was started. You can drag the dividing lines between the columns to resize them if you like. In addition, the window name indicates whether or not printing is paused.

When you have more than one document in the queue, the documents are printed in order from top to bottom. You can rearrange the queue by selecting a document and dragging it up or down in the list. For example, you might drag a high-priority print job to the top of the print queue so that it prints sooner. No matter which way you rearrange the queue, however, the job that's currently printing will finish first unless you cancel it.

To pause or cancel printing, you use the Printer and Document menus at the top of the print queue window.

- To pause printing for a document, select the document and choose Pause Printing from the Document menu.

- To resume paused printing of a document, select that document and choose Resume Printing from the Document menu.

- To cancel printing for one document, choose Cancel Printing from the Document menu.

- To pause or resume all printing, choose Pause Printing or Resume Printing from the Printer menu.

- To empty the entire print queue, choose Purge Print Jobs from the Printer menu.

⚠ WARNING

> When you use the Pause Printing command in the print queue window, you take your printer out of action. You must choose Resume Printing from the Printer menu before the printer will print anything.

You can resize or close the print queue window using its window controls.

So far we've explored Word's basic features with just one document open on the screen. In Chapter 7, you'll learn how to save documents, open stored documents, and create new documents.

CHAPTER 7

Managing Files

As you create documents in Microsoft Word, you'll want to save them so you can open them again or share them with others. You can save documents in a variety of formats that let you use them with other programs or display them on the World Wide Web, and you can easily find and open any document that you have saved. In this chapter, you'll learn all about how to manage files with Word.

How Word Handles Documents

For information about converting files, see Chapter 38, "Importing, Exporting, and Converting Documents."

You will normally store documents in Word's native file type (.doc). Word 2000 uses the same native file type as Word 97 and Word 98 for the Macintosh, but other programs and previous versions of Word use different file types. To facilitate file sharing with users of other programs or older versions of Word, you can save documents in other file types. Word will automatically convert and open many other file types when you open documents, too:

- Word can save files for various versions of WordPerfect, Microsoft Works, Microsoft Windows Write, HTML, and a handful of different text formats. It can also save files in the native file types for older versions of Microsoft Word for Windows and MS-DOS.

- Word can open files from various versions of WordPerfect, Microsoft Works, Windows Write, Microsoft Excel worksheets, and various text formats. It can also open files in native file types for older versions of Microsoft Word for Windows and MS-DOS.

About Templates

Another file type that is available when you save documents is a document template. A template opens as a new, untitled document, but it already contains text, formatting, graphics, or other items.

> Every new document you create in Word is based on a template. *For more information about using templates, see Chapter 13, "Using Templates and Wizards."*

You'll use templates to store document layouts, text, custom toolbars or menu commands, and other information so you can start new documents that are already customized and use them repeatedly for different projects.

Creating New Documents

There are two ways to create new documents. If you press Ctrl+N, you'll create a new document using Word's default Blank Document template.

If you want to choose the type of new document, follow these steps:

1 Choose New from the File menu to display the New dialog box as shown in Figure 7-1. Once inside the New dialog box, you'll see the following:

FIGURE 7-1.

Use the New dialog box to choose the type of new document you want to create.

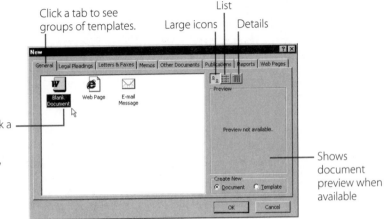

Click a tab to see groups of templates.

List

Large icons

Details

Double-click a document template to open a new document.

Shows document preview when available

 SEE ALSO

For a definition of a wizard, see "Using Document Wizards" on the next page.

2 Select a document template or wizard. Click the tabs to see dozens of predesigned templates and wizards you can use.

The Document type is selected automatically to create a new Word document. To create a new template instead, click the Template button.

3 Click the OK button. The new document appears on your screen.

 TIP

> You can change the view of the document list by clicking one of the View buttons above the Preview area.

Choosing a Document Template

Every new document you create is based on a template, and the Blank Document template on the General tab is selected by default. This template creates a standard blank document, the same as you see when you start Word.

If you prefer, you can use one of Word's other predesigned document templates to begin a new document. Click one of the tabs in the New dialog box to see a variety of templates containing predesigned formats and content for letters, faxes, memos, reports, and other types of documents. Try opening each of them to see what they have to offer.

Word Basics

There are dozens of document templates on the Microsoft Office CD-ROM, but you may not see all of them in the New dialog box because they're not installed. For more information about installing additional templates in Word, see the Appendix. In addition, Microsoft periodically adds new templates to the Office Web site. To see the latest goodies, choose Office On The Web from the Help menu.

Choosing the Document Type

By default, Word creates a new document. If you would prefer to create a new template, click the Template button in the Create New area.

When you create a new document, Word will offer to save it in Word's standard file type (.doc). When you create a new template, Word will offer to save it in the Templates folder inside the Windows\Application Data\Microsoft folder with the template file type (.dot).

Changing the View

Initially, you'll see templates displayed as large icons in the New dialog box. However, you can click one of the other view buttons as shown in Figure 7-1 to view templates in other ways.

Using Document Wizards

Calendar
Wizard

Rather than opening a document template, you can use one of the document wizards in Word. Wizards automatically create a formatted document based on your answers to a series of questions. The icons for wizards have a magic wand in them.

When you open a wizard, you're asked a series of questions. After you answer each question by typing information or choosing an option, click the Next button. When the wizard is finished, click the Finish or Done button, and Word will create the document according to your specifications.

To cancel a wizard before you finish, click the Cancel button or the Close box on the wizard's dialog box.

Take a look at the document wizards located on some of the tabs in the New dialog box to see what they have to offer. As with templates, there may be other wizards available to you that aren't yet installed. *See the Appendix for more information about installing additional wizards.*

Saving Documents

Saving a document is the most important task you can perform in Word, because if you don't save your documents, all the work you have done will vanish.

Opening and Saving Files with Windows 95

Word's Open and Save As dialog boxes work basically the same way under either Windows 95 or Windows 98, but some of the features are implemented differently. For example, there are separate buttons for different file views in Windows 95 rather than the Views menu you see when you run Word under Windows 98.

This chapter describes the Open and Save As dialog boxes as they work under Windows 98. For information about the features of the Save As and Open dialog boxes you see when running under Windows 95, click the Help button in the upper right corner of the dialog box and then click the feature you want to learn more about.

Saving a Document for the First Time

The procedure for saving a new document is simple:

1 Choose Save from the File menu or press Ctrl+S. You'll see the Save As dialog box, as shown in Figure 7-2.

FIGURE 7-2.

You can save documents or perform other file management tasks with the Save As dialog box.

2   Type a name for the new file in the File Name box. (Word suggests the text from the first paragraph in the document, which is handy if your first paragraph is also the document's title.)

? SEE ALSO

For more information on changing file locations, see "Changing File Locations and Views" on page 145.

3   Select a location for the file with the Save In list. The main area (or *file list*) shows all of the files at the current location. The Save In list box above the file list shows the name of current location, and if you like you can use the list box to navigate to another location. *See "Navigating to Other Locations" on page 145 later in this chapter for details.*

The Places bar at the left shows disk locations you frequently use. If you like, click one of the icons there to select a location.

4   Click the arrow button next to the Save As Type box to display the Save As Type list and choose a file type, if necessary. (Word automatically selects the Word Document type in this example because the document being saved is a standard document, rather than a template or another file type.)

5   Click Save or press Enter to save the file.

★ TIP

> You can use as many as 255 characters (including spaces) in a file name in Word, but you can't use slash marks and a few other characters because Microsoft Windows uses them to identify file locations. If you try to save a file and you see a message telling you that Word can't locate the directory, you have probably used an improper character in your file name.

Saving an Existing Document

When you save an existing document, Word already knows the document's name and location, and you can save it without using the Save As dialog box. Just press Ctrl+S or choose Save from the File menu. Word saves the changes without displaying the Save As dialog box.

★ TIP

> Save your documents early and often—every 15 minutes at least—to store your changes safely. This way, you won't lose hours of work if there's a power failure or a problem with your computer.

Saving with a Different Name, File Type, or Location

Sometimes you'll want to save an existing file under a different name or save it as a different file type or in a different location. For example, you may want to save a copy of your document as a WordPerfect file so you can share it with someone who uses that program, or save a copy of your file to a network server.

To save a file with a different name, file type, or location, use the Save As command:

1   Choose Save As from the File menu or press F12. Word displays the Save As dialog box as shown in Figure 7-2, except that the file's current name and location are showing.

2   Choose a different file type, location, or enter a different name for the file.

3   Press Enter or click the Save button.

TIP

Click the arrow button to display the File Name list. You'll see a list of recently used file names, and you can choose one of those if you like.

Replacing an Existing File

Sometimes you'll want to completely replace an existing file. For example, you may have decided to rewrite the document from scratch in a new document, and now you want to save the new document with the same name, type, and location as the existing one. When you click the Save button or press Enter to save the file, Word asks you to confirm that you want to replace the current version of the file, like this:

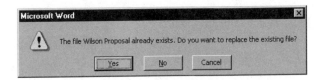

Click Yes to replace the existing file.

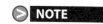 **NOTE**

The file save warning (and other warning messages) will appear as a standard message box when the Assistant is turned off. When the Assistant is on, the warning pops up in the Assistant's speech bubble. *For more information about how the Assistant affects the display of warning messages, see "Word Without the Assistant" on page 40.*

Securing a File with a Password

If you want to prevent unauthorized users from viewing a file, you can set a password for it:

1   Choose Save As from the File menu and name the file, if necessary.

2   Click the Tools button and choose General Options from the menu that appears. You'll see the Save Options dialog box, like this:

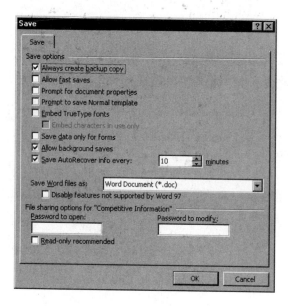

In the File Sharing Options area at the bottom of the dialog box, you can enter one or two passwords:

- When you enter a password in the Password To Open box, you make it necessary to have a password in order to open the file.

- When you enter a password in the Password To Modify box, you prevent anyone without a password from modifying the file. Anyone, however, can open the file as a Read Only document.

- If you enter a password in both of the password boxes, the user will need one password to open the file and a second password to open a modifiable version of the file.

If you check the Read-Only Recommended check box, Word will suggest, but not require, that the file be opened as a Read Only document.

3 Enter one or two passwords to protect the file.

4 Click OK to close the Save Options dialog box.

5 Retype one or both passwords in the Confirm box and click OK.

6 Click Save to save the file with those passwords.

You can also display the Save options by choosing Options from the Tools menu in Word's menu bar and clicking the Save tab in the Options dialog box.

Using Other Save Options

With the exception of passwords, every other option you apply in the Save Options dialog box applies to every document you save.

After you have changed a file's options you must save the file to store the changes—even if you haven't edited the file itself.

Protecting Files with Backups and AutoRecover

Sometimes a file can be corrupted at the moment it's saved—a power surge at precisely the wrong moment can make the file unreadable. To help prevent such mishaps, Word can automatically create a second, backup copy of each file you save. You can also have Word automatically save file recovery information at regular intervals as you work.

To make automatic backup files, click the Always Create Backup Copy check box. Backup files are saved in the same folder as the original. The backup copy will have the same name with "Backup Of" in front of it, and the backup file type will be .wbk rather than Word's normal .doc. Word can't make automatic backups when the Allow Fast Saves option is selected.

By default, Word's AutoSave feature automatically stores unsaved changes to a file at certain intervals, and its AutoRecover feature attempts to restore that information after a crash. To turn off AutoSave, clear the Save AutoRecover Info Every: check box. To change AutoSave

Word Basics

options, make sure that the Save AutoRecover Info Every check box is selected and then set the interval at which you want this information saved. If Word or your computer crashes, AutoRecover will attempt to restore unsaved information from the files you were working on.

WARNING

AutoRecover saves only unsaved information. Don't use this as a substitute for saving your files in the normal way.

Other Save Options

The other options in the Save Options dialog box are covered in Table 7-1.

SEE ALSO

For more information about other commands on the Tools menu in the Save As dialog box, see "Managing Files with the Tools Menu" on page 149.

TABLE 7-1. General File Saving Options in Word

Option Name	Description
Allow Fast Saves	Word saves only changes to a document, which is faster, but makes the file larger than necessary when you edit and save frequently.
Prompt For Document Properties	Opens the document's Properties dialog box when you save it the first time, so you can enter this information. *(See "Viewing Properties" on page 156).*
Prompt To Save Normal Template	Word prompts you to save any changes to styles or page formatting to the Normal document template.
Embed TrueType Fonts	Embeds any special font used to create text in the document, so other users needn't have them installed to view your document properly.
Embed Characters In Use Only	Embeds specific characters from a special font.
Save Data Only For Forms	Saves data from an online form as Text Only file in a tab-delimited format so you can use it in a database.
Allow Background Saves	Saves files in the background so you can work on other tasks at the same time.
Save Word Files As	Sets the default file type used when saving documents.
Disable Features Not Supported By Word 97	Saves files without special Word 2000 features that aren't supported in Word 97.

Opening Files

? SEE ALSO

For more information about converting files from other formats, see Chapter 38, "Importing, Exporting, and Converting Documents."

Word can open native Word 2000 or Word 97 files as well as text files in various formats, including WordPerfect files, Microsoft Excel files, HTML files, Microsoft Works files, and others. Word will open and convert any of these file types automatically. You can have as many documents open on your screen as your computer's available memory allows.

You can double-click any Word-compatible file on your Windows Desktop to open the file automatically, but when you're inside Word, you use the Open command. To open a file from inside Word, follow these steps:

1 Press Ctrl+O or choose Open from the File menu to display the Open dialog box, as shown in Figure 7-3. The file list shows the contents of the current folder.

FIGURE 7-3.

Use the Open dialog box to navigate to disk locations and select files to open.

2 Click a Places icon or use the Look In menu to view a location.

Search the web   Delete selected file or folder
Up one level   Create new folder
Previous location   Views menu

3 Double-click a file or folder to open it, or select it and click Open.

Places bar

Tool menu

Open

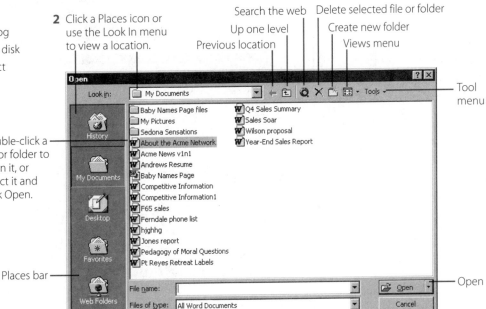

TIP

You can open more than one file at a time by selecting them all before clicking the Open button. Just drag across the files you want to open, or hold down Shift and click the first and last file in the group. To select files at different places in the list, hold down the Ctrl key and click each file name.

Word Basics

How Does Word Decide Which Is the Current Folder?

The current folder you see in the Open or Save As dialog box is the last folder from which you opened a file or to which you saved a file. If you have just started Word, the current folder is a preset location, such as the My Documents folder.

If you open or save most of your documents in the same folder, you can change the default location for documents so Word will always start at this location when you open or save files. To reset the default location for your Word documents, you use the Tools menu in Word's menu bar:

1 Choose Options from the Tools menu to display the Options dialog box.

2 Click the File Locations tab. You'll see a list of document types and default locations, like this:

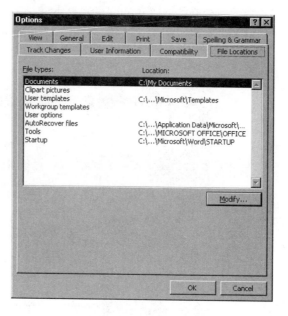

3 Select the Documents file type and click the Modify button. You'll see a file navigation box like the ones in the Open and Save As dialog boxes.

4 Navigate to and select the folder you want, so its name appears in the Folder Name box at the bottom.

5 Click the OK button.

6 Check that the folder location shown for Document files is correct.

7 Click the OK button to close the Options dialog box.

Reverting to the Last Saved Version of a Document

If you open a document, make changes, and then decide you don't want the changes after all, you can close the document without saving those changes and then open it again. But there's an easier way: try to open the file a second time. You'll see a message asking if you want to revert to the last saved version of the file. Click the Yes button, and Word will close the current document and open the last saved version of it.

Opening Files as Copies or in a Browser

When you click the Open button in the Open dialog box, Word opens a standard, editable document. But there's an arrow button next to the Open button (as shown in Figure 7-3 on page 143), and when you click this button you can choose other file opening options.

- Choose Open Read-Only to open the file and prevent changes to it.

- Choose Open As Copy to have Word make a copy of the file and open the copy, so you can make changes without touching the original.

- Choose Open In Browser to view a Web page document in Internet Explorer or another browser. This option is available only when you have selected a Web page document.

Changing File Locations and Views

The Save As and Open dialog boxes have several controls you can use to view other folders or disks, select a different file location, and change the way files are listed.

Navigating to Other Locations

There's a toolbar containing buttons and menus at the top of both the Save As and Open dialog boxes, as shown in Figures 7-2 and 7-3. You can point to most of these for a second to see ScreenTips that identify them, but here's a rundown.

Using the Look In and Save In Lists

The Look In or Save In list box shows the name of the current folder or disk that you're viewing. Click the arrow button next it to display the Look In or Save In list, which shows each of the disk drives or other storage locations on your computer.

Select another storage location from the list (another disk on your computer, perhaps) by clicking it. The list of files and folders below will change to show the new location's contents.

Using the Navigation Buttons

Three of the buttons in the Open or Save As dialog box are quick ways to navigate through your disk.

- The left arrow immediately to the right of the Look In or Save In box takes you back to the location you last viewed, just as it would in a browser.

- The Up One Level button jumps you up one level in the storage hierarchy, from a folder up to the disk or folder that contains it, for example.

 TIP

> If your disk contains several levels of folders, or folders inside folders, you can lose your way. To orient yourself quickly, display the Look In or Save In list to see the pathway from the current folder all the way up to the Windows desktop.

- The Search the Web button launches your Web browser and takes you to Microsoft's search page, where you can search for a Web document and then open it in Internet Explorer.

Using the Places Bar

 SEE ALSO

For more information on accessing the Web from Word, see Chapter 31, "Using Word to Access the Internet."

The Places bar at the left side of the dialog box gives you another way to navigate quickly to frequently used files or folders. Click an icon to see that location's contents in the file list.

■ History lists the last 20 to 50 documents and folders you opened.

 TIP

> You can adjust the number of documents maintained in the History location by using the Internet settings control in the Control Panels folder, which is accessed from the Windows start menu. *For more information, see "Resetting the Address List" on page 741.*

■ My Documents is the default save location in Word, unless you've changed it.

■ Desktop jumps you to the Windows desktop.

■ Favorites is a folder to which you can easily add files or folders you know you'll want to use frequently. *(See "Managing Files with the Tools Menu" on page 149.)*

 SEE ALSO

For more information about the Web Folders location, see "Publishing Web Pages" on page 781.

■ Web Folders is a special location where you can save collections of Web pages you want to publish on a Web server.

Changing the File View

You can view a location's contents in four different ways and even change the way files are sorted with the View menu. When you click the Views button at the top of the Open or Save As dialog box, you'll see the Views menu like this:

■ The List view is normally selected, as shown in Figures 7-2 and 7-3.

■ Choose the Details command to list files with sizes, file types, and modification dates, as shown in the figure at the top of the next page.

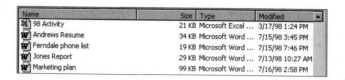

You can resize the columns in Detail view by dragging the dividing lines that run between their headings.

■ Choose the Properties command to display much more detailed information about each file, like this:

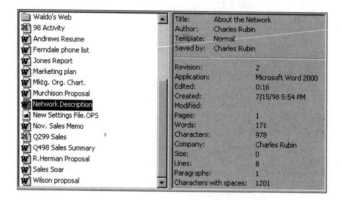

■ Choose the Preview command to display a preview of the selected document in the Open dialog box, like this:

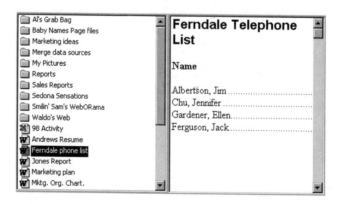

■ Click the Arrange Icons command to choose a different sorting order for items in the list. You can arrange files by name, type, size, or modification date.

Accessing FTP Sites

SEE ALSO

For more information about opening FTP files with Word's Open dialog box, see "Opening Files from FTP Servers" on page 747.

FTP sites are file servers on the Internet from which you can retrieve files. You use FTP servers by *transferring* files from them rather than merely *viewing* the information contained in files that are stored on them (as you do on the Web). If you have access to the Internet or to a corporate network, you can use Word and your Web browser to open files from an FTP server.

Managing Files with the Tools Menu

When you click the Tools button in the Open or Save As dialog box, you'll see the Tools menu.

The Tools menu in the Open dialog box looks like this:

There are a few different commands on the Tools menu in the Save As dialog box, and we'll explore the differences a little later. First let's look at the commands that both Tools menus have in common.

Using Common File Management Commands

You can handle most standard file management operations with commands on the Tools menu. Just select a file in the list and then choose a command from the Tools menu:

- To delete a selected file, choose Delete.

- To rename a selected file, choose Rename. Word will display a blinking insertion point next to the file's name, and you can type the replacement name. Press Enter when you're finished.

Word Basics

SEE ALSO

For more information about using properties, see "Using Document Properties" on page 156 at the end of this chapter.

SEE ALSO

For more information about printing documents, see "Printing Documents" on page 125.

■ To put a shortcut to the file in the Favorites folder, choose Add To Favorites. You can add shortcuts for files or folders to the Favorite Places folder, and then find them easily by clicking the Favorites button in the Places bar.

■ Choose the Properties command to display the selected file or folder's properties. This is the same as choosing Properties from the File menu when the document is open on your screen.

Printing From the Tools Menu

When you're in the Open dialog box, you can select and print one or more documents without having to open them. Choose the Print command from the Tools menu to print the document.

Mapping a Network Drive to Your Desktop

The Map Network Drive command on the Tools menu lets you add a network disk or directory location to your Windows desktop so it appears as another disk drive. This is useful when you frequently save or open documents from that network location, because it saves you having to navigate with the Network Neighborhood icon on your desktop each time. To map a network drive to your desktop, follow these steps:

1 Choose Map Network Drive from the Tools menu. You'll see a dialog box like this:

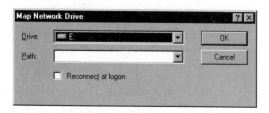

2 Designate a letter by which the drive will be known on your desktop by choosing a letter from the Drive menu.

3 Enter the path name for that network drive in the Path box. Ask your network administrator for help if you don't know the path name.

4 Click the Reconnect At Logon check box if you want this network drive on your desktop each time you log on to the network.

5 Click OK.

Using Shortcut Menus

You can use the same shortcut menus in Word's Open or Save As dialog boxes as you can use when you work with files on the Windows desktop. There are two different shortcut menus, depending on whether you click a file (or folder) or in a blank area of the file list. Many of the commands on these menus are the same as file management commands covered earlier under "Managing Files with the Tools Menu," and the others are self-explanatory. Try right-clicking files or in blank areas of the Open or Save As dialog boxes to explore these commands on your own.

Finding Files

The file list in the Open dialog box shows you all the files in a folder or disk, but you may forget the name and location of a particular file. Fortunately, Word allows you to search for files right inside the Open dialog box.

Essentially, using Find options changes the list of files you see in the Open dialog box's file list. Rather than displaying all the contents of a particular location, using the Find options instructs Word to list only the files that match your search criteria, and you can then select and open the file you want.

Performing a Simple Find

The Find dialog box offers many ways to search for a file, but most of the time you'll search for a file by name. To find a file by name, follow these steps:

1 Choose Find from the Tools menu. Word displays the Find dialog box as in Figure 7-4 on the next page.

FIGURE 7-4.

Use the Find dialog box to search for files from inside the Open dialog box.

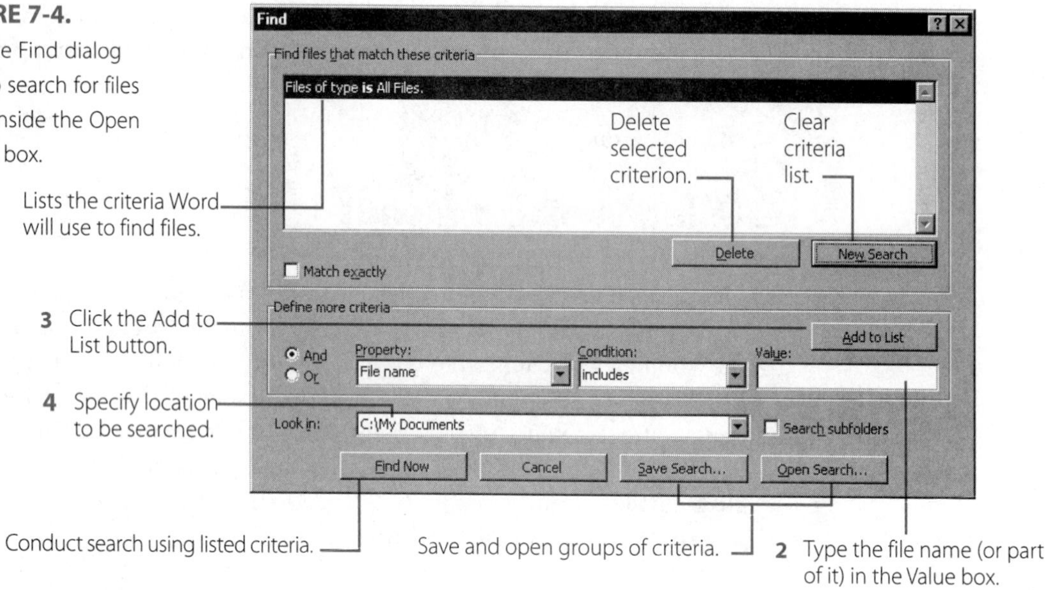

Lists the criteria Word will use to find files.

Delete selected criterion.

Clear criteria list.

3 Click the Add to List button.

4 Specify location to be searched.

Conduct search using listed criteria.

Save and open groups of criteria.

2 Type the file name (or part of it) in the Value box.

SEE ALSO

The Find dialog box shown above is for finding files only. To learn about searching for text within a document, see "Finding and Replacing Text" on page 178.

5 If you want Word to display the folders that contain each file found in the location you're searching and to show each folder's path back up to the Desktop, click the Search Subfolders check box. *(For more information, see step 7 under "Using Find Options for Advanced Searches" on page 152.)*

6 Click Find Now. Word will search that location for files containing the text in the Value box and then display all files containing that text in the Open dialog box list.

Using Find Options for Advanced Searches

You can have Word search according to several criteria. To do this, define one criterion at a time and add it to the list at the top of the Find dialog box. The Find dialog box always opens with at least one criterion already listed: the option set in the Files Of Type list in the Open dialog box. If you have already entered a file name in the Open dialog box, the file name will be listed as a second criterion. Follow these steps to add a new criterion:

1 Choose an option from the Property list. This list contains many different data types for which Word can search. Often you search for file names, but you could also search by the name of the document's author, by the date modified, or by many other

properties. As you select different properties, the selection options on the Condition list change, because only certain conditions apply to each property.

2   Choose an option from the Condition list. This option defines how Word matches your search value with the property you have chosen. For example, if you choose File Name as the Property, you can choose whether found files must begin with, end with, or simply contain the text you specify in the Value box.

3   Enter text or numbers in the Value box. Word finds all files whose names or other conditions match or include the value you type. The search is normally not case sensitive—typing "sales" will find files whose names contain "Sales" or "sales." You need not enter a complete name or phrase, but the more specific you are, the more precisely Word will search.

4   Choose whether to add the criterion to the list as an additional or alternative criterion. When you click And, Word *must* match this criterion along with others in the list of criteria. If you click Or, Word *may* match this criterion instead of others in the list.

5   Click the Add To List button to add your new criterion to the list. You can add as many criteria as you like to the list.

6   Select a location to search with the Look In menu.

7   If you want Word to display the folders that contain each file found in the location you're searching and to show each folder's path back up to the Desktop, click the Search Subfolders check box.

8   Click the Find Now button.

Word locates the files and displays them in the file list of the Open dialog box, like this:

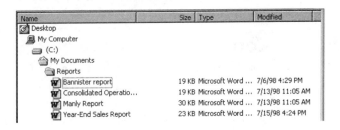

In the example, the Search Subfolders option was selected in the Find dialog box, so the file list shows not only the found files but their path back to the desktop.

Table 7-2 summarizes these and other options in the Find dialog box.

TABLE 7-2. Options in the Find Dialog Box

Find Option	Description
Match Exactly	Finds the exact combination of uppercase and lowercase letters you specify in the Value box, except in file names. (Word always finds all forms of file names.)
Delete	Deletes the selected search criterion.
New Search	Clears all added criteria from the list except the one created by the settings in the Open dialog box.
Property	Defines the type of file information Word locates.
Condition	Defines the way Word applies the Value data to the Property.
Value	Defines the specific text or number you want Word to match.
And	Adds this criterion to others: Word must match them all.
Or	Specifies that this criterion can be satisfied instead of others.
Add To List	Adds the new criterion you specify to the list of criteria.
Look In	Defines the location where Word searches.
Search Subfolders	Displays path from files to the desktop.

? SEE ALSO

For more information about document properties, see "Using Document Properties" on page 156.

Combining and Resetting Search Criteria

You don't have to reinvent the wheel each time you conduct a new search. If many of your existing criteria will still be helpful in the new search, you can delete the others individually. Simply select the unwanted criteria in the list in the Find dialog box and click the Delete button. You can then add new criteria to those that remain in the list. To clear all of the criteria and start over, click the New Search button.

Word Basics

Saving and Reusing Searches

If you have spent a lot of time crafting an especially precise search and there's a chance you might use it again; you should name the search and save it. This way, you can reuse the same set of criteria by choosing the search name from a menu.

To name a search, click the Save Search button. You'll see a dialog box where you can name and save the search.

To reuse a saved search, click the Open Search button. You'll see a list of named searches in the Open Search dialog box, like this:

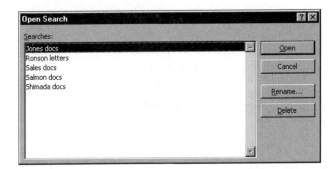

Select the search name and click Open. The Find dialog box will now contain those search criteria. You can also use the Open Search dialog box to rename or delete saved searches.

Modifying a Saved Search

To change the criteria in a saved search, follow these steps:

1 Open the search with the Open Search button.

2 Choose Find from the Tools menu to display the Find dialog box.

3 Add or delete search criteria.

4 Click the Save Search button, enter the same name as the previous search, and click OK. Word will ask if you want to replace the existing search.

5 Click Yes.

Using Document Properties

❓ SEE ALSO

For more information about using fields, see Chapter 27, "Using Fields."

Each document you create has properties—a collection of information about the document. You can use properties to search for documents, and you can also use them to insert data into documents with fields.

There are two types of properties:

- General facts and statistics about the document, such as the file name, size, modification date, number of pages, or the number of minutes you've spent working on the document. Word calculates these automatically.

- User-specified properties, which can include keywords describing the document; the document title, author name, and subject; a summary of the document's contents; and a variety of custom properties you can create.

Viewing Properties

To view your document's properties, choose Properties from the File menu. You'll see a dialog box like the one in Figure 7-5.

FIGURE 7-5.

Use the Properties dialog box to add or view information about your document.

Properties are grouped on five tabs. Click any tab to view the properties on it. As you explore the tabs, you'll see that the General, Statistics, and Contents tabs contain information supplied by Word and the Summary and Custom tabs have blanks where you can add properties yourself.

In Chapter 8, you'll learn how to customize Word's commands and toolbars to suit your individual preferences.

Customizing Toolbars, Menus, and Commands

As you gain experience with Microsoft Word, you'll develop your own personal work style. You'll find that you use some tools and commands constantly and others hardly at all. With Word, you can customize toolbars, menus, and keyboard shortcuts to match your work style. You can create a keyboard shortcut or toolbar button for any command, remove menus you don't use, add new commands to menus, and create whole new menus of your own.

You can customize Word in two ways:

■ Change the way you interact with Word by modifying toolbars, menus, and keyboard shortcuts. These changes are stored in the specific document or document template you're using. *For more information about templates, see Chapter 13, "Using Templates and Wizards."*

■ Set global options to change the way Word always performs dozens of program operations—from automatically creating backup files to ignoring words in uppercase letters during spelling checks. These are called global options because they affect every document you work on rather than one document or template.

In this chapter you'll learn how to customize toolbars, menus, and commands. You'll find Word's global options by choosing Options from the Tools menu. Many specific options are mentioned throughout this book, but you can find out more about any option by clicking the Help button in the upper right corner of the Options dialog box and then clicking any option to see a description of it.

Customizing Toolbars

Word's creators have designed the toolbars, menus, and keyboard shortcuts in ways that work best for most people most of the time. In Word 2000 the toolbars change as Word learns more about which buttons and toolbars are your favorites. Still, you may want a specific collection of toolbars displayed each time you open a document, or you may want to add, remove, or rearrange the buttons on them. Word makes it easy to do this.

Hiding and Displaying Toolbars

When you first start Word, you'll see the Standard and Formatting toolbars in the same row at the top of your screen, but there are many more toolbars than that. Word has nearly two dozen different toolbars you can display or hide at any time. Figure 8-1 shows most of them.

There are two quick ways to display or hide a toolbar:

- Choose Toolbars from the View menu and then choose the toolbar name from the submenu.

- Right-click any toolbar and choose the toolbar name from the shortcut menu.

Customize Tools for Different Projects

Since changes to Word's toolbars, menus, and commands affect a particular document template, you can create a whole gallery of templates with buttons and commands that help you work more efficiently on different projects. In a template for a simple memo, for example, you might remove the Table menu. In a template for newsletters, you might have Word automatically display the Drawing toolbar. And if others frequently use your computer, you might leave the Normal template's toolbar and command options unchanged so other users will see the standard Word screen they expect to see when they create a new document.

FIGURE 8-1.

You can add nearly two dozen toolbars to the document window. They can be docked at the edges of the window or they can float on the screen.

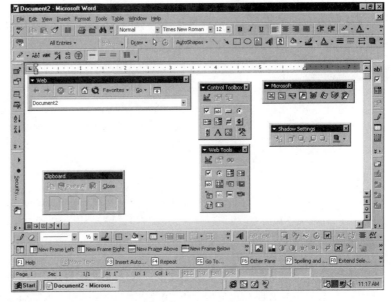

Word Basics

The toolbar menu contains 16 of the most popular toolbars. To see the complete list of toolbars and select others to display, follow these steps:

1 Choose Customize from the Tools menu or choose the Customize command from the bottom of a toolbar shortcut menu.

2 Click the Toolbars tab in the Customize dialog box.

3 Select a toolbar's check box to display it, or clear a toolbar's check box to hide it.

4 Click the Close button.

Moving or Resizing a Toolbar

When Word adds a new toolbar to your screen, it may anchor or "dock" it to the top or bottom of the document window, or it may allow it to float inside the window. You can change the position or size of any toolbar with its Move handle.

Move handle ——

■ To move a toolbar, drag the Move handle. As you drag the handle to another location, you'll see a dotted outline that shows where the toolbar will appear when you release the mouse button. You can drag a toolbar to a window edge to dock it or drag a toolbar inside the document window to make it float. Drag a floating toolbar by its title.

> You can move the menu bar by dragging it as well, but you can't resize it.

- To resize a docked toolbar, drag its Move handle to the left or right.

- To resize a floating toolbar, drag one of its edges.

When you resize a docked toolbar, Word automatically adds buttons to and deletes buttons from the More Buttons palette as the space on the toolbar becomes larger or smaller.

Creating a Custom Toolbar

If you don't like the makeup of the existing toolbars, design a toolbar of your own. You can add buttons or menus for any command you want, including those that don't currently appear on any toolbar. To create a custom toolbar, follow these steps:

1 Right-click a toolbar and choose the Customize command from the shortcut menu. You'll see the options shown in Figure 8-2.

FIGURE 8-2.

Use the Customize dialog box to create new toolbars and add or remove buttons.

> By removing and rearranging buttons, you can consolidate two or more tool-bars into one so there's more space for the document on your screen. However, you may be better off creating a new toolbar that contains only the buttons you want and then hiding the unwanted toolbars.

2 Click the New button. Word displays the New Toolbar dialog box:

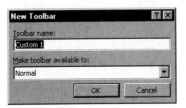

3 Type a name for the toolbar and then choose either the current document or the current template as the storage location for the new toolbar.

4 Click OK. Word creates a new, empty toolbar with the name you gave it and adds the toolbar's name to the list in the Customize dialog box.

5 Add new buttons as described under "Adding Buttons" on page 162.

Deleting or Renaming a Custom Toolbar

You can also use the Customize dialog box to delete or rename a custom toolbar.

1 Right-click a toolbar and choose the Customize command from the shortcut menu.

2 Click the Toolbars tab.

3 Select the custom toolbar in the Toolbars list.

4 Click the Delete or Rename button and enter a new name for the toolbar if necessary.

> Word won't let you delete or rename any of its predefined toolbars. However, you can add or remove buttons until they're customized to your liking.

Adding, Removing, and Rearranging Buttons

You can customize predefined or custom toolbars by adding, removing, or rearranging the buttons on them. In fact, if you have created a custom toolbar, it won't contain any buttons until you add them.

Adding Buttons

Each predefined toolbar has a More Buttons palette. It contains additional buttons that are defined for that toolbar but can't be displayed in the space available on the toolbar itself. When you use a button from the More Buttons palette, Word automatically adds it to the toolbar. However, you may want to add other buttons to predefined or custom toolbars.

You can easily add buttons to toolbars by dragging and dropping from a list in the Customize dialog box. You might want to add a previously deleted button to a different toolbar or add a new button that wasn't on any toolbar at all. To add a button, follow these steps:

1 Right-click a toolbar and choose the Customize command from the shortcut menu to display the Customize dialog box. (The dialog box is already open if you have just created a custom toolbar.)

2 Select a check box to display the toolbar you want to modify—if it isn't already selected. (You can't modify a toolbar that isn't displayed on the screen.)

3 Click the Commands tab. You'll see a list of commands and categories as shown in Figure 8-3.

FIGURE 8-3.

Drag any button to a toolbar to add it from the Commands tab in the Customize dialog box.

4 Select a command category in the Categories list.

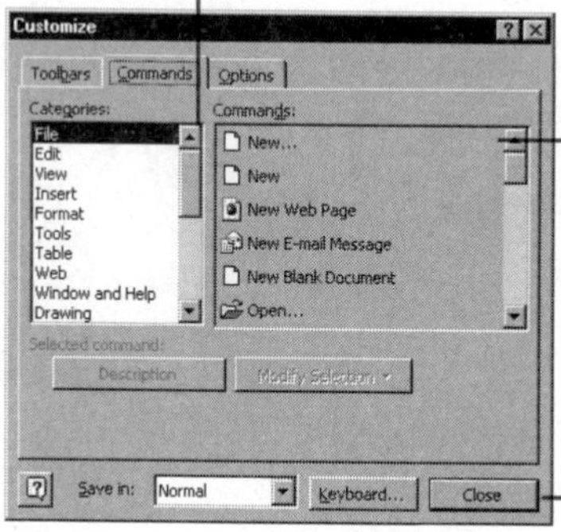

Drag a command to a toolbar.

Click Close when you're done.

5 Drag a command from the Commands list to the place on the toolbar where you want the new button to appear. As you do, you'll see a pointer that shows you exactly where the button will appear:

The I-beam pointer shows where the new button will appear.

6 Release the mouse button. The new button appears on the toolbar.

Moving or Deleting Buttons

Unlike many other customization options, the option of moving or deleting a button can be chosen without having to open the Customize dialog box. Just hold down the Alt key as you click and drag the button. Drag the button to a new location on the toolbar, or drag the button down into the document window. When you drag a button into the document window, Word places an X over it to show that it will be deleted when you release the mouse button.

If you have the Customize dialog box open, you can move or delete a button by dragging as well, but you don't have to hold down the Alt key to do it.

Restoring Default Toolbars

If you decide you would prefer to return to Word's standard configuration for any toolbar, you can easily do it:

1   Right-click a toolbar and choose the Customize command from the shortcut menu.

2   On the Toolbars tab, click the toolbar you want to reset.

3   Click the Reset button.

4   Click OK, and then click Close to close the Customize dialog box.

Changing Menus

By default, Word displays nine command menus, but you can add, remove, or change the contents or position of menus to suit the way you work. As with toolbars, you use the Customize dialog box to change menus, but you work mostly with the Commands tab. Figure 8-3 shows the Commands tab. To display the Commands tab, right-click in the menu bar, choose Customize from the bottom of the toolbar shortcut menu, and click the Commands tab in the Customize dialog box.

NOTE   Word 2000's new adaptive menus display only the most commonly used commands at first, and then expand to show all of their commands. *For more information, see "Using Adaptive Menus" on page 24.*

Adding and Removing Menus

By adding and removing menus, you can customize the menu bar so it contains only the menus you need. You can add a predefined menu or create a new menu of your own.

Creating a New Menu

If you don't like Word's menus, make one of your own. You can create any number of new menus and add them to the menu bar, as long as there is room. To create a new menu, follow these steps:

1 Right-click the menu bar and choose Customize from the shortcut menu to display the Customize dialog box, and then click the Commands tab if necessary.

2 Scroll to the bottom of the Categories list and choose the New Menu option.

3 Drag the New Menu command from the Commands list onto the menu bar. Word adds a menu called New Menu to the menu bar, and that menu is selected, like this:

| File Edit View Insert Format Tools Table Window Help New Menu |

4 Click the Modify Selection button in the Customize dialog box. You'll see the Modify Selection menu. (See Figure 8-5 for a sample of this menu; however, many of the commands on it are dimmed when you are working with a menu.)

5 Type a new name in the Name box on the Modify Selection menu.

6 Click outside the Modify Selection menu to put it away.

You can also display the Modify Selection menu by right-clicking a menu name on the menu bar when the Customize dialog box is open.

Adding a Menu to the Menu Bar

If you delete one of Word's predefined menus, you can always restore it. In addition, Word has two other predefined menus, Font and Work, that don't appear in the menu bar. To add a predefined menu to the menu bar, follow these steps:

1 Right-click the menu bar and choose Customize from the shortcut menu to display the Commands tab in the Customize dialog box.

2 Scroll down to the bottom of the Categories list and click Built-In Menus. You'll see a list of predefined menus you can add. (You'll need to scroll down to the bottom of this list to see the two additional menus that aren't visible.)

3 Drag the menu you want onto the menu bar. As with adding a button on a toolbar, an I-beam pointer shows you exactly where the new menu will appear. You can place it between two existing menus or at the right end of the menu bar if you like.

4 Release the mouse button and the menu is added.

Rearranging Menus

You can rearrange menus in the menu bar just as you rearrange toolbar buttons. Just hold down the Alt key and drag the menu name to another location. You can drag right or left to rearrange the order of menus in the menu bar, and you can even drag a menu onto a toolbar.

If you find your menu bar is getting crowded, however, you can use the same drag-and-drop technique to turn a menu into a submenu. To do this, follow these steps:

1 Hold down the Alt key and drag a menu name onto another menu. The destination menu opens.

2 Drag up or down to a specific place on the destination menu. Word displays a heavy black line that shows where the submenu will appear, as in Figure 8-4 on the next page.

3 Release the mouse button and the former menu becomes a submenu on the destination menu.

FIGURE 8-4.

Drag a menu onto another menu to turn it into a submenu.

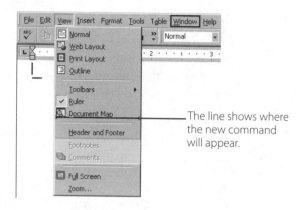

The line shows where the new command will appear.

Deleting a Menu

You can delete a menu by turning it into a submenu, as discussed under "Rearranging Menus" in the previous section, but you can also delete a menu entirely:

1 Hold down the Alt key and drag the menu down into the document window. You'll see an X icon over it to indicate that it will be deleted.

2 Release the mouse button to delete the menu.

 WARNING

> You can delete one of Word's predefined menus and add it again later, but if you delete a custom menu, it's gone for good.

Adding, Deleting, and Rearranging Commands

In addition to rearranging menus, you can also add, delete, or rearrange the commands on them. The technique is similar to the one you use when you work with toolbar buttons, except that you must open the Customize dialog box to do it.

To add a menu command, follow these steps:

1 Right-click the menu bar and choose Customize from the shortcut menu to display the Customize dialog box, and then click the Commands tab.

2 Select the All Commands category in the Categories list, and then drag the command you want from the list on the right onto a menu. When you drag the command to the menu, you'll see a heavy black line showing where it will be inserted. You can place the command anywhere on the menu.

3 Release the mouse button to lock the command in place.

To delete or rearrange a menu command, follow these steps:

1 Right-click the menu bar and choose Customize from the shortcut menu to display the Customize dialog box.

2 Click any menu to open it, and then drag the command. Drag up or down on the menu to rearrange the command or drag off the menu and into the document window to delete the command.

3 Release the mouse button to complete the change.

Changing Buttons and Commands

By default, every toolbar button is displayed as an icon, and many of Word's menu commands have icons next to them as well. You can add, remove, or change these icons if you like, and you can set other display options for menus and toolbars.

Adding or Changing Icons

By using the Modify Selection shortcut menu, you can change the icons used for specific buttons or commands, remove icons from buttons or commands, or add icons to commands. To add an icon to a command or change an existing icon, follow these steps:

1 Choose Customize from the Tools menu to open the Customize dialog box.

2 On the toolbar or menu, right-click the command or button whose icon you want to change. You'll see the Modify Selection menu, as shown in Figure 8-5 on the next page.

3 Choose Change Button Image from the menu. You'll see a palette of button images you can add.

4 Click an image in the palette.

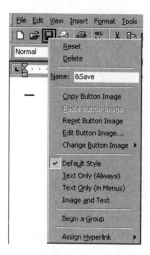

Copying or Pasting Icons

When the Customize dialog box is open, you can also use the Modify Selection menu to copy icons from one button or command to another.

1 Choose Customize from the Tools menu to open the Customize dialog box.

2 Right-click the button or command on its toolbar or menu to display the Modify Selection menu.

3 Choose Copy Button Image.

4 Right-click the destination button or command on its toolbar or menu.

5 Choose the Paste Button Image command from the Modify Selection menu.

Editing Icons

If you don't like any of the predefined button icons, you can alter them to create others with Word's built-in button editor. Modifying a button icon is especially handy when you have copied an icon onto another toolbar button—you can avoid confusion between the two buttons by modifying the copy so that it looks a little different than the original.

1 Choose Customize from the Tools menu to open the Customize dialog box.

2 Right-click the button or command whose icon you want to edit.

3 Choose the Edit Button Image command from the Modify Selection menu. You'll see the Button Editor, as in Figure 8-6.

The Button Editor's Picture area shows each screen pixel that makes up the icon, and the Preview area shows the image at actual size.

FIGURE 8-6.

Use the Button Editor to modify the icons used for buttons and menu commands.

4 Click a square to turn a pixel on or off, or

5 Select a color and then click a square in the picture to color it.

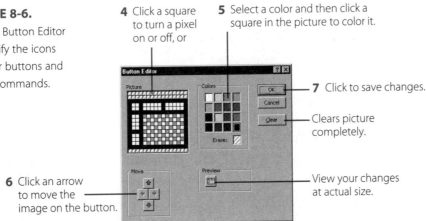

7 Click to save changes.

Clears picture completely.

6 Click an arrow to move the image on the button.

View your changes at actual size.

Hiding Icons

If the multitude of icons in Word makes it difficult to remember which is which, you can replace them with text:

1 Choose Customize from the Tools menu to open the Customize dialog box.

2 Right-click the toolbar button or menu command you want to change to open the Modify Selection menu.

3 Choose either the Text Only (Always) or Text Only (In Menus) command.

The Text Only (Always) command removes the icon from both toolbar buttons and menus and replaces button icons with the command name. The Text Only (In Menus) command deletes the icon only from menus, leaving toolbars alone.

The Text Only (Always) and Text Only (In Menus) commands aren't available if you have selected a button for which there is no replacement text.

Creating Groups

On Word menus and toolbars, commands and buttons are arranged in functional groups with dividing lines between them. You can use the Modify Selection menu to create a new group dividing line:

1 Choose Customize from the Tools menu to open the Customize dialog box.

2 Right-click the toolbar button or menu command you want to change.

3 Choose the Begin A Group command. Word inserts a group dividing line above or to the left of the item you selected.

Restoring Default Settings

You can get pretty carried away when fiddling with buttons, menus, and commands. To return a button, menu, or command to its standard display setting:

1 Choose Options from the Tools menu to open the Customize dialog box.

2 Right-click the button, menu, or command that you want to reset.

3 Choose Reset from the top of the Modify Selection menu.

? SEE ALSO

For more information about hyperlinks, see "Using Hyperlinks" on page 772.

Adding Hyperlinks to a Button

Not only can you assign a command and an icon to a button, but you can also assign a hyperlink so that clicking it opens another document or navigates you to a specific Web page. Here's how:

1 Choose Customize from the Tools menu to open the Customize dialog box.

2 Right-click the toolbar button you want to change to display the Modify Selection menu.

3 Choose the Open command from the Assign Hyperlink submenu. You'll see the Assign Hyperlink: Open dialog box, where you can select a document or location to open.

4 Enter the file or Web page name, or select a document or location from the list.

5 Click OK.

To remove a link, right-click the button and choose the Remove Link command from the Edit Hyperlink submenu.

⭐ TIP

If you've spent a lot of time customizing menus or toolbars, consider saving the document as a new template before restoring defaults. This way you can always return to your customized setup by creating a new document based on that template.

Changing Button and Menu Display Options

For easier identification, you can display buttons in a larger size or have Word display a ScreenTip showing each button's name when you point to it. You can also have Word animate menus when they open. To set or change these options, follow these steps:

1 Choose Customize from the Tools menu, and click the Options tab. You'll see a series of display options, as seen in Figure 8-7.

FIGURE 8-7.

Change menu and toolbar display options with the Options tab in the Customize dialog box.

2 Select any of the options to change button or menu display properties. Table 8-1 on the next page describes all of the options.

3 Click the Close button to apply your changes.

▶ NOTE

When you choose the Large Icons option for toolbars, fewer buttons will fit on a docked toolbar.

Try some of these options for yourself to see if they make Word easier on your eyes.

TABLE 8-1.   Toolbar and Menu Display Options

Option Name	Description
Standard And Formatting Toolbars Share One Row	Word docks these two toolbars side by side to save room in the document window.
Menus Show Recently Commands First	Seldom used commands are hidden on Used menus.
Show Full Menus After A Short Delay	Seldom used commands appear on menus when you wait a few seconds.
Reset My Usage Data	Resets frequent command and button tracking, as if you began using Word for the first time.
Large Icons	Displays larger icons on toolbars.
List Font Names In Their Font	Shows font names in their fonts on the Font menu.
Show ScreenTips On Toolbars	Adds ScreenTips to toolbar buttons when ScreenTips are turned on in the Help Options dialog box.
Show Shortcut Keys In ScreenTips	Adds keyboard shortcuts to ScreenTips for toolbar buttons.
Menu Animations	Selects menu to open and close animations.

(?) SEE ALSO

For more information about turning ScreenTips on and off, see "Using ScreenTips" on page 50.

Changing Keyboard Shortcuts

You see only a handful of keyboard shortcuts listed on Word's menus; but there are dozens of predefined shortcuts available, and you can change them or add new ones to suit your work style. As with toolbar and menu changes, shortcut changes affect only the current document template.

Viewing Shortcuts

All of the predefined shortcuts in Word are listed in the Help system index. To see them, follow these steps:

1   Display the Help window. *(See "Using the Help Window" on page 43 for instructions.)*

2   Click the Show button at the top of the Help window and then click the Index tab.

3 Type *shortcut* in the Type Keywords box and click the Search button. Word displays several dozen topics related to shortcuts in the Choose A Topic list.

4 Click a hyperlink in the list at the right to view groups of shortcut keys.

TIP

> You can print a complete list of shortcut keys for quick reference. View the "Print A List Of Shortcut Keys" topic in the Help window's topic list for instructions.

Adding, Changing, or Deleting Shortcuts

To make new shortcuts of your own or to change or delete existing ones, use the Customize dialog box.

Adding or Changing a Shortcut

To create a new keyboard shortcut, follow these steps:

1 Choose Customize from the Tools menu to display the Customize dialog box, and then click the Keyboard button at the bottom. You'll see the Customize Keyboard dialog box as shown in Figure 8-8.

FIGURE 8-8.

You can select or change a keyboard shortcut for any command in Word using the Keyboard tab in the Customize dialog box.

2 Choose a category.   **3** Select a command.   **6** Click to assign the shortcut— or to replace the existing shortcut, if there is one.

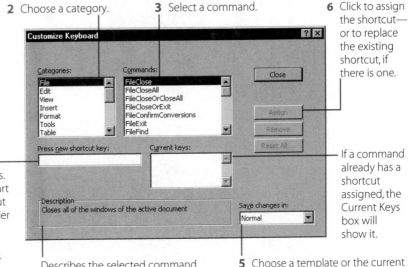

4 Press new shortcut keys. You must start each shortcut with a modifier key such as Ctrl, Alt, or a function key.

Describes the selected command.   **5** Choose a template or the current document as the storage location.

If a command already has a shortcut assigned, the Current Keys box will show it.

7 Click Close to put away the Customize Keyboard dialog box.

8 Click Close to put away the Customize dialog box.

Removing a Shortcut

Some commands have more than one shortcut, and you may want to remove one or more of them. Deleting an existing shortcut frees it up for use with another command.

Here's how to remove a shortcut:

1 Choose Customize from the Tools menu and click the Keyboard button.

2 Choose the command using the Categories and Commands lists in the Customize Keyboard dialog box. You'll see the currently assigned shortcut(s) in the Current Keys list.

3 Select the key combination you want to delete and click the Remove button.

4 Click Close.

5 Click Close to put away the Customize dialog box.

Beyond Shortcuts

You can assign a shortcut to choose any command in Word, but that's not the only way you can use keystrokes to work more quickly.

You can define macros that execute a whole series of commands when you press a couple of keys. *For more information, see Chapter 28, "Using Macros."*

You can define keystrokes that are automatically replaced with words or phrases by using the AutoCorrect options. *For more information, see "Using AutoCorrect" on page 204.*

Congratulations! You've made it through basic training. The rest of this book is devoted to showing you how to use Word's more advanced writing, editing, formatting, graphics, publishing, and data management tools. You'll also see how to use Word to access or publish documents on the Internet and the World Wide Web, and how it can help you collaborate with others on a network. Choose any topic you like, and you'll quickly see how much more productive you can be with Microsoft Word.

PART II

Writing and Editing Tools

Finding, Replacing, and Sorting Text

B esides typing, correcting, and arranging your text, you'll want to manipulate it in other ways. If the name of a product or a procedure changes, for example, you'll want to replace it everywhere in your document with the new name. You may want to sort text that's in a list. Or you may simply want to locate a particular spot in your document by searching for words or phrases. Microsoft Word makes it easy to do these things, and in this chapter you'll learn how.

Finding and Replacing Text

Finding text is one of the most common and efficient ways to navigate in a document. Rather than scrolling and scanning for the text, Word can jump directly to a specific word or phrase. Word can also replace what it finds. Word's Replace command can save you hours of word hunting and retyping by replacing words or phrases automatically.

Word's ability to find and replace text speeds up editing, but it is also useful for finding and replacing formatting options, special characters such as tabs or optional hyphens, and other elements in your document such as footnote markers, highlights, or frames. The more familiar you become with Word's finding and replacing capabilities, the easier it will be to polish your prose.

How Word Searches Documents

Unless you use special Find options (see "Using Find and Replace Options" on page 181), Word searches for all occurrences of the text you type. If you search for "bank" for example, Word will find and select that text not only as a separate word, but also as it appears in "banker," "Fairbanks," and "embankment." It also ignores case, finding "Banker" or "Banking" when you search for "bank."

TIP

> Be as specific as possible in searching, or else Word will find a lot of occurrences that you didn't mean to find. For example, if you're searching for "railway," enter the whole word. If you tell Word to search for "way," it will find "highway," "byway," and "passageway" as well as "railway."

When you use the Find or Replace command, you can search either your entire document or a selection within it. If you have any text selected when you choose the Find or Replace command, Word searches only that selection. Otherwise it searches the whole document.

By default, Word searches your document from the insertion point's location downward, scanning through the whole document until it returns to the insertion point's location. For example, if your insertion point is on page 2 of a 3-page document, Word will search from the insertion point to the end of page 3, and then from the beginning of page 1 back down to the insertion point.

In addition, you can set Word to search from the insertion point up, and you can have the search stopped when Word reaches the beginning or end of the document.

Finding Text

You use Word's Find command to locate and select words or phrases in your document. To find text, follow these steps:

1 Choose Find from the Edit menu, or press Ctrl+F. You'll see the Find and Replace dialog box as shown in Figure 9-1.

FIGURE 9-1.

Use the Find tab in the Find and Replace dialog box to search for text inside documents.

Type text or select text from previous find.

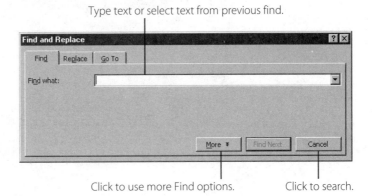

Click to use more Find options.   Click to search.

2 Click in the Find What box and type the text you want to locate. You can enter up to 255 characters.

 TIP

If you have searched for other text previously, it will be listed on the Find What list, and you can select it there to search for the same text again. *See "Reusing Old Searches" on page 184.*

3 Click the Find Next button. Word searches for the word or phrase and selects the text if it finds it. You can then click in the document to edit the text you want or click the Find Next button again to continue searching for other occurrences of the same word or phrase.

4 Click the Cancel button to close the Find and Replace dialog box.

TIP

You can drag the Find and Replace dialog box to another part of your screen if it's covering up the text Word has found.

II

Writing and Editing Tools

Replacing Text

When you replace text, you tell Word to find a particular word or phrase and replace it with another.

1 Choose Replace from the Edit menu, or press Ctrl+H. The Find and Replace dialog box appears, and the Replace tab is selected as in Figure 9-2.

FIGURE 9-2.

Use the Replace tab in the Find and Replace dialog box to locate and replace words or phrases.

2 Enter text to be found, or choose previous text.

3 Enter replacement text, or choose previous text.

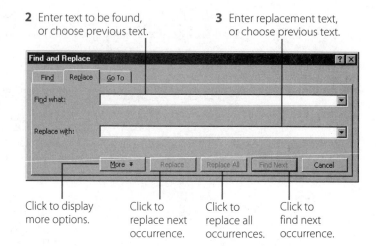

Click to display more options.

Click to replace next occurrence.

Click to replace all occurrences.

Click to find next occurrence.

4 Click Find Next.

 NOTE

Click Replace to replace the first occurrence of the found text automatically or click Replace All to replace all occurrences without reviewing them first.

Word searches for and selects the text you entered in the Find What box, like this:

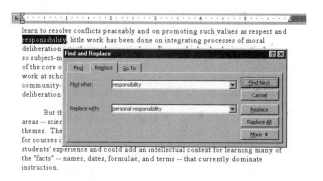

5   Click Replace to have Word replace this instance of the found text with your replacement, or Click Replace All to replace every occurrence of the found text with your replacement. If you replace just the current instance of found text, Word replaces the text and then finds the next occurrence.

6   Repeat steps 4 and 5 until Word has finished searching the document.

7   Click Cancel to close the Find and Replace dialog box.

Using Find and Replace Options

Figures 9-1 and 9-2 show the basic Find and Replace options, but you can make your searches much more specific. When you click the More button at the bottom of the Find and Replace dialog box, you'll see additional options and buttons where you can be more specific about what you're looking for and tell Word just how to search. Figure 9-3 shows the extra options on the Replace tab.

Click the Help button on the Find and Replace dialog box's upper-right corner and then click an option to see a brief description.

Writing and Editing Tools

FIGURE 9-3.
Click the More button on the Find and Replace dialog box to use more specific options for finding text, formats, or special characters.

1 Enter search text.   2 Enter replacement text.

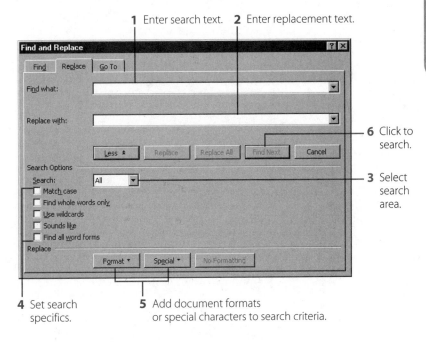

6 Click to search.

3 Select search area.

4 Set search specifics.

5 Add document formats or special characters to search criteria.

Here's what you can do with these options.

- **The Search list** Tells Word which portion of your document to search. The default here is All, meaning Word will search the whole document, starting at the insertion point. You can also choose Up or Down to search only from the insertion point to the start or end of the document.

 TIP

To search a portion of a document, select it before searching.

- **Match Case** Tells Word to exactly match the case of your entry in the Find What box. Normally, Word finds all forms of the text you enter, both upper, lower, and mixed case, but checking this option tells it to match your entry *exactly*.

- **Find Whole Words Only** Tells Word to ignore occurrences of a word you typed if they are only part of a word. For example, if you check this option when you're searching for "car," Word will ignore such words as "carpenter" or "scar." This is a very useful option when you're searching for a word that is contained within a lot of other words.

- **Use Wildcards** Tells Word to read *, ?, !, or other symbols as wildcards that replace one or more missing characters in a text string, rather than as text themselves. For example, searching for "sp*ll" will find words such as "spell" and "spill." *See "Searching with Wildcards or Special Characters" on page 184 for more on wildcards, or look up "wildcards" in the Help System Index.*

- **Sounds Like** This feature is the lifesaver for poor spellers. If you can't spell the word you're looking for, type it out as it sounds, and Word will try to match it with the actual word. For example, if you check the Sounds Like box and search for "opshuns," Word will find "options."

- **Find All Word Forms** Tells Word to locate and select any whole-word form of the text you type, such as adverbs and plurals. If you search for "run," for example, Word will find and select "running" and "runs," but not "Brunswick."

You can return to the basic Find and Replace dialog box by clicking the Less button.

Searching for Formats

By using the Format button at the bottom of the expanded Find and Replace dialog box, you can search for text solely based on its format characteristics.

1 Press Ctrl+F or Ctrl+H to display the Find and Replace dialog box, and click the More button to expand it if necessary.

2 Click the Format button. You'll see a menu of formatting options for which you can search, like this:

3 Choose a format type. You'll see a dialog box showing all the options for that format area (Fonts, Paragraphs, Language, Frame options, and so on). You can also ask Word to search for text that you previously highlighted with Word's Highlight button. *See "Highlighting Characters" on page 81.*

As you specify options with the Format menu, they are shown below the Find What box as additional criteria, as shown in Figure 9-4.

FIGURE 9-4.

As you add special search criteria, Word lists them below the Find What box.

You can add as many format options as you like. To change format options, reset them with the appropriate Format menu commands. To remove all of the formatting options from your search, click the No Formatting button on the Find and Replace dialog box.

4 Click Find or Replace to begin a search with the criteria you added.

Searching with Wildcards or Special Characters

You can also use wildcards to extend your searches or to have Word search for special characters such as paragraph marks, tab characters, graphics, or page breaks. Click the Special button on the Find and Replace dialog box and you'll see a menu of special characters you can use. As you choose them, they are added to the Find What dialog box.

Special characters help you locate format markers and other elements in a document. For example, if you wanted to find all the Tab characters in your document, you would choose "Tab Character" from the Special menu to add a special search character to the Find What dialog box.

? SEE ALSO

For more information about these options, search for "wildcards" in the Help System index.

Wildcards are invaluable when you want to find more than one word. To use them, select the Use Wildcards check box and then choose a wildcard character from the Special menu. (The Special menu's options change when you have the Use Wildcards option selected.)

For example, suppose you want to locate all of the words in your document that begin with "e" and end with "d." To do this, type *e* in the Find What box; select the Use Wildcards check box; choose 0 Or More Characters from the Special menu to add this wildcard character to the Find What box; and then type *d* so the Find What box entry reads *e*d*. When you click the Find Next button, Word will find such words as "end," "extend," "errand," and "England." Try viewing the Special menu with and without the Use Wildcards option selected, and experiment with various options to see how you can tailor your searches.

Reusing Old Searches

When you close the Find and Replace dialog box, it retains the last word or phrase for which you searched, as well as the options you chose for that search. As you search for new words or phrases or choose new options, the ones you previously entered are placed on the Find What and Replace With lists. To reuse an old search, just choose it from the Find What list.

When you exit Word, all of the remembered searches are erased.

Sorting Text

Any time you create a list of items in your document, you may add the items in a haphazard order and then later want to arrange them alphabetically. Fortunately, Word's Sort command makes it easy. Suppose you have a table that looks like this:

Third Quarter Sales Contest Winners

Division	Sales Rep	Sales Total
Shrimp	Ginny Calandini	$424,603
Salmon	Horst Heitzinger	$897,335
Auto	June Thomas	$124,417
Home & Garden	Lamont Russell	$756,310
Explosives	Buck Brawley	$194,577

You want to sort these items in ascending alphabetical order, from A to Z. To sort this list, you would do the following:

1   Select all the items in the list.

2   Choose Sort from the Table menu. You'll see the Sort Text dialog box, as shown in Figure 9-5.

FIGURE 9-5.

Use the Sort Text dialog box to sort text in tables or in ordinary paragraphs.

Choose sorting method.

Click to sort.

Choose data type.

Choose sort order.

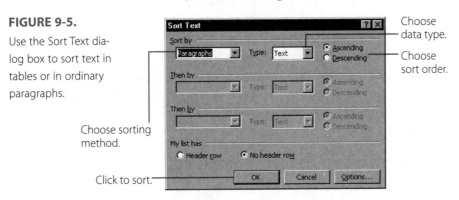

3   Select the sort options you want.

4   Click the OK button. The list is sorted, like this:

Third Quarter Sales Contest Winners

Division	Sales Rep	Sales Total
Auto	June Thomas	$124,417
Explosives	Buck Brawley	$194,577
Home & Garden	Lamont Russell	$756,310
Salmon	Horst Heitzinger	$897,335
Shrimp	Ginny Calandini	$424,603

Compare this with the previous table example.

II

Writing and Editing Tools

Using Sorting Options

By using the options in the Sort Text dialog box, you can tell Word exactly how to arrange your text. Here's how they work.

? SEE ALSO

For more information about using fields, see Chapter 27, "Using Fields."

- The Sort By list has options to sort text by paragraph, column number, or field number. When you choose Paragraph, Word sorts by the first letters in the first word of each paragraph you have selected. (In tables each row is a paragraph.) If you choose Field 1, Word will sort by the contents of that field.

- To change the way Word sorts data, you can choose the data type with the Type list. Text information is sorted alphabetically, while Number data is sorted numerically and Date data is sorted chronologically.

- The Ascending and Descending buttons tell Word how to arrange the sorted text. Ascending (which is the default setting) arranges text from A through Z, 0 through 9, or earlier to later dates. Descending order is the opposite.

- You can search on as many as three columns at a time. The two Then By lists allow you to specify how the second and third columns of information are sorted. However, it usually isn't necessary to use these.

Using Even More Sorting Options

To exercise even more control over your sorting activities, you can click the Options button in the Sort Text dialog box. You'll see the Sort Options dialog box, like this:

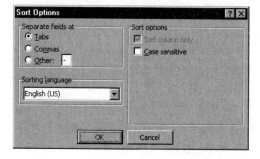

Here's how these options work:

For more information
about tables, see
Chapter 17.

- **The Separate Fields At option** Lets you specify how Word recognizes the fields (or columns). If you've used tabs to arrange text in columns, the Tabs option is automatically selected here. However, you can also separate text into columns with commas, hyphens, or other characters you can choose from the Other list. When you're sorting a table in a document, these options are dimmed because the columns are obvious.

- **The Sort Column Only check box** This is available only if you're working with a table in your document and you have a single column selected. By selecting the Sort Column Only check box, you tell Word to sort only the data in that column, leaving the data in the other columns alone. Normally you won't want to do this, because after such a sort the data from this column may no longer match the corresponding data in the other columns.

- **The Case Sensitive check box** Tells Word to distinguish between upper and lower case words when sorting. When you sort in the standard Ascending order, Word arranges lowercase versions of a word before uppercase versions of the same word.

As you familiarize yourself with finding and sorting options, you'll find it a faster and easier way to put the text you want where you want it.

II

Writing and Editing Tools

Using the Writing Tools

Microsoft Word contains a number of writing tools that make it easier to create letter-perfect documents. These writing tools can check spelling, grammar, and readability; help you find synonyms or antonyms; insert hyphens automatically; and even correct or add text automatically. Many of these tools are turned on when you first begin using Word. In this chapter you'll learn how to make the most of them.

Checking Spelling and Grammar

You can have Word check spelling and grammar as you work or at a specific time. Word can also mark spelling and grammar problems so they're easy to spot, and you can set other groups of options to customize spelling or grammar checks. For example, you can have Word ignore spelling in acronyms or in words that contain numbers.

How Word Checks Spelling and Grammar

Spelling and grammar checks help you spot glaring errors quickly, but they're no substitute for careful proofreading. You should always proofread documents before considering them final. A summary of how the spelling and grammar checkers work shows why.

How the Spelling Checker Works

? SEE ALSO

For information about using dictionaries with Word, see "Working with Dictionaries" on page 199.

The spelling checker scans your document or a selection of text and then compares the words in it with two or more built-in dictionaries. The Main Dictionary is a standard college-level dictionary in English or another language you select, while custom dictionaries contain words you add as you work. You can also buy and install custom dictionaries which contain predefined collections of technical or industry-specific terms.

When your text contains a word that isn't found in a dictionary, Word flags it as misspelled. As a result, Word will often flag a properly spelled word such as a proper name or technical term simply because it isn't in one of its dictionaries. When this happens, you have the option to add the word to the custom dictionary. As an alternative, you can instruct Word to ignore this misspelled word throughout your document.

In addition, the spelling checker will ignore properly spelled words that are wrong in context. For example, you might make a typo and write "ruining the show" instead of "running the show," but since both "ruining" and "running" are correctly spelled, Word won't mark them.

The spelling checker also checks for and flags repeated words in a document.

How the Grammar Checker Works

The grammar checker applies a set of grammatical and stylistic rules to your text, flagging text that violates those rules.

- Grammar rules cover specific mistakes, such as double negatives, run-on sentences, subject-verb agreement, passive sentences, and misused plurals or possessives.

■ Style rules evaluate your document's readability by checking for jargon, wordiness, cliches, and unclear language. In addition to choosing which rules are applied in style checks, you can also select one of several general writing styles for Word to use as a guide, such as technical, casual, or formal.

Finally, Word's spelling and grammar rules aren't written in stone. The grammar rules, in particular, are sometimes applied incorrectly to a particular context. You're always free to turn off specific rules or to tell Word to ignore various problems as they appear in your document.

Checking Spelling and Grammar Automatically

When you first start Word and begin working, you'll probably notice wavy red and green underlines popping up beneath certain words or sections of text. Figure 10-1 shows an example with both types of underlines.

FIGURE 10-1.

Word identifies spelling and grammar errors in your document. Right-click them to see suggested replacements or other correction options.

Spelling error

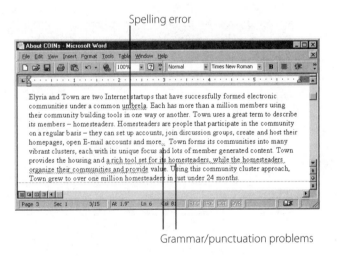

Grammar/punctuation problems

These are Word's spelling and grammar tools at work. The wavy red line underneath "umbrela" indicates that the word is misspelled. Wavy green lines flag an extra period in the middle of the paragraph and a punctuation problem toward the bottom of the paragraph.

⭐ **TIP**

You can tell Word to hide the wavy lines if you don't like them. *See "Using Spelling and Grammar Options" on page 195.*

II

Writing and Editing Tools

Correcting Spelling Errors

Just as Word can check spelling as you type, you can correct it on the fly as well. To correct a spelling error, right-click the wavy red underline. You'll see a shortcut menu as in Figure 10-2.

FIGURE 10-2.

Right-click a flagged error to see a menu of suggested replacements and other options.

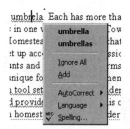

You can choose an alternate spelling or access Word's Spelling, AutoCorrect, or Language dialog boxes for more options. Table 10-1 explains the options.

TABLE 10-1.   Commands Available on the Shortcut Menu

Command	Description
Alternate word spelling	Select to replace the misspelled word in your document.
Ignore All	Ignore current and all other occurrences of this spelling.
Add	Add this spelling to a custom spelling dictionary.
AutoCorrect	Open the AutoCorrect dialog box to add this word to the list of words, if you mistype it frequently.
Language	Open the Language dialog box to set a different language for the word if it's a foreign term.
Spelling	Open the Spelling and Grammar dialog box for more options.

? SEE ALSO

For more information about AutoCorrect, see "Using AutoCorrect" on page 204. For more about the Language dialog box, see "Changing a Dictionary's Language" on page 201.

Using the Spelling and Grammar Dialog Box

When you want access to more spelling and grammar checking options, choose Spelling And Grammar from the Tools menu to open the Spelling And Grammar dialog box, as shown in Figure 10-3. If Word has not been checking your document as you type, opening this dialog box will start a spelling and grammar check.

 **TIP**

> Double-click the Spelling And Grammar Status icon on the status bar to locate the next spelling or grammar problem.

FIGURE 10-3.

When you check spelling and grammar from the Spelling And Grammar dialog box, you can make corrections inside the dialog box itself.

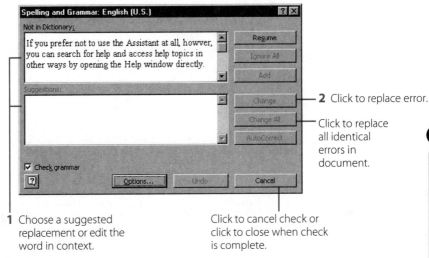

2 Click to replace error.

Click to replace all identical errors in document.

1 Choose a suggested replacement or edit the word in context.

Click to cancel check or click to close when check is complete.

The Not In Dictionary box at the top shows the error in context, and the Suggestions list at the bottom offers one or more solutions. You can edit the text in the Not In Dictionary box or select one of the suggestions from the list, and then click a button at the right to fix the problem. As you make a choice about how to handle each problem, Word resumes the check and displays the next problem it finds.

Resolving Spelling Problems

When Word displays a spelling error in the Spelling And Grammar dialog box (as in Figure 10-3), you have several options for handling it. Some of these options are the same as on the spelling shortcut menu, but you have others in this dialog box:

- Click Ignore All to skip over this occurrence of the problem and move on to the next problem.

 TIP

> You can create new custom dictionaries, edit them, or choose which custom dictionary will receive newly added words with the spelling options. *See "Working with Dictionaries" on page 199.*

II

Writing and Editing Tools

■ Click Change to accept the currently selected suggestion in the suggestion list or to use the text you have edited in the Not In Dictionary box. Word replaces the problem word in your document with the suggested word or with the edited text.

■ Click Change All to replace all occurrences of the problem with the one you've selected in the dialog box.

■ Clear the Check Grammar check box to stop grammar checking, so you can concentrate on spelling problems.

■ Click Options to display the spelling and grammar options. *See "Using Spelling and Grammar Options" on page 195 for more information.*

■ Click Undo to cancel the last correction you applied.

Resolving Grammar Problems

When Word locates a grammar or style problem, the Spelling And Grammar dialog box looks a little different, as in Figure 10-4.

FIGURE 10-4.

When you're working with a grammar problem in the Spelling And Grammar dialog box, Word offers suggested rewrites.

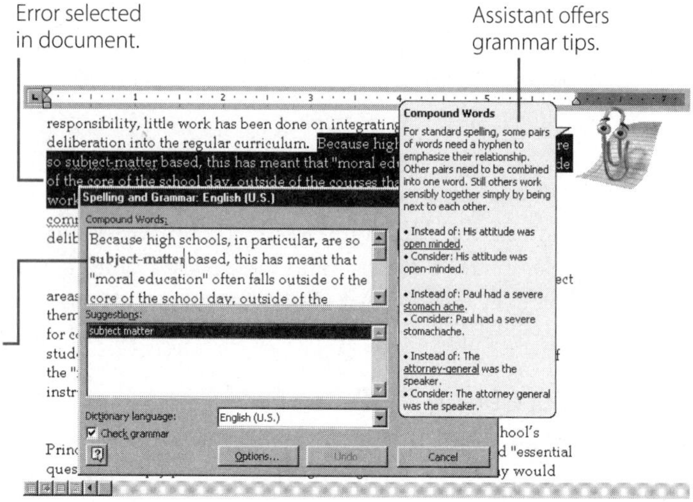

Error selected in document.

Assistant offers grammar tips.

Error in context

Rather than a list of suggested spellings, the Suggestion List shows one or more rewritten versions of your text that are grammatically correct. If you have the Assistant on (the Clippit character is shown in Figure 10-4), it offers general advice on how to avoid this kind of grammar problem.

As with spelling errors, you can edit the text in the Problem box or select a suggested rewrite and then use one of the buttons at the right to correct the problem. The buttons are the same as for spelling errors, except that a couple of button names change:

- Click Ignore Rule to mark this text as corrected without changing it. If you ignore a rule, the rule is ignored throughout the document, so you may cause Word to miss other mistakes.

- Click Next Sentence to skip over this problem and move on; Word will flag this sentence again during the next check.

Using Spelling and Grammar Options

You can control the behavior of the spelling and grammar checkers by setting options. To display the Spelling & Grammar options, choose Options from the Tools menu and click the Spelling & Grammar tab, or click the Options button in the Spelling And Grammar dialog box. You'll see the options as shown in Figure 10-5.

If your document contains no spelling or grammar errors, the only way to access the spelling and grammar options is via the Options command on the Tools menu.

FIGURE 10-5.

There are a number of options you can use to adjust Word's spelling or grammar rules.

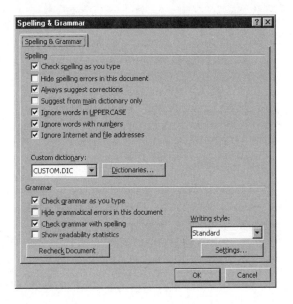

The options are divided into Spelling and Grammar areas. Except for the Recheck Document button, all of the options affect the behavior of the spelling and grammar checkers in every document, not just the one with which you're currently working. The global spelling and grammar options are described in Table 10-2 at the top of the next page.

TABLE 10-2. **Spelling and Grammar Options**

Option Name	Description
Check Spelling As You Type	Turn on automatic spelling checker.
Hide Spelling Errors In This Document	Hide wavy red underlines.
Always Suggest Corrections	Word suggests proper spellings.
Suggest From Main Dictionary Only	When selected, Word won't use custom dictionary for suggestions.
Ignore Words In UPPERCASE	Word ignores acronyms or other words with all uppercase letters.
Ignore Words With Numbers	Word ignores words with numbers in them, such as F15A.
Ignore Internet And File Addresses	Word ignores Web and e-mail addresses and file pathnames.
Custom Dictionary	Select the custom dictionary to which words are added during a check.
Dictionaries	View or change installed custom dictionaries.
Check Grammar As You Type	Turn on automatic grammar checking.
Hide Grammatical Errors In This Document	Hide wavy green underlines in document.
Check Grammar With Spelling	Clear to check spelling only.
Show Readability Statistics	Display readability statistics at the end of a grammar check.
Check Document/ Recheck Document	Check the document using the current options.
Writing Style	Select a writing style for Word to use as a guide when evaluating grammar.
Settings	Select grammar rules and style options to modify a particular writing style. *See "Changing Writing Style Settings" on page 198.*

When you click the Recheck Document button, Word rechecks the entire document again using the new options you have set and clears the lists of words or grammar problems you chose to ignore during the previous check.

> NOTE

If you open the Spelling & Grammar Options dialog box with the Options command from the Tools menu and you haven't yet checked the document spelling, the Recheck Document button is named Check Document.

About Readability and Style

When you ask Word to show the readability statistics at the end of a grammar check, you'll see a window like the one in Figure 10-6.

FIGURE 10-6.

Word can display readability information at the end of a spelling and grammar check.

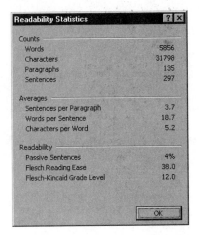

Readability Statistics	
Counts	
Words	5856
Characters	31798
Paragraphs	135
Sentences	297
Averages	
Sentences per Paragraph	3.7
Words per Sentence	18.7
Characters per Word	5.2
Readability	
Passive Sentences	4%
Flesch Reading Ease	38.0
Flesch-Kincaid Grade Level	12.0

OK

This window shows statistics not only about the document length but also about standard readability measures such as average sentence length, reading grade level, and percentage of passive sentences. This option is not available if you're not checking grammar in your document.

The Writing Style list shows the current writing style that Word is using as a guide for spotting stylistic problems. Each writing style is a collection of specific grammatical rules, or settings, that Word applies during checks. You can choose a Casual, Formal, Technical, or Standard style here, or create a Custom style of your own.

II

Writing and Editing Tools

Changing Writing Style Settings

Choosing a writing style for use in grammar checks is a crapshoot unless you know exactly which settings Word uses during checks. To see and change these settings, follow these steps:

1 Open the Spelling And Grammar dialog box.

2 Click the Options button.

3 Click the Settings button. You'll see the Grammar Settings dialog box, as in Figure 10-7.

FIGURE 10-7.

Use the Grammar Settings dialog box to change the rules Word applies during grammar checks.

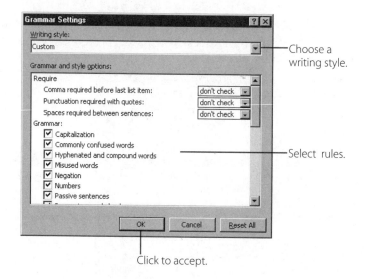

Choose a writing style.

Select rules.

Click to accept.

4 Choose a writing style to change to a specific group of preset grammar and style options or to choose a new group for the Custom style.

 TIP

Try choosing the different writing styles to see which options are set for each of them.

5 Scroll down the Grammar And Style Options list and use the menus or check boxes to set the options you want for the current writing style.

6 Click OK to save the new options you have chosen or click the Reset All button to reset all the writing styles to their default sets of options.

Working with Dictionaries

In addition to its main dictionary, Word automatically creates one custom dictionary called Custom.dic so you can store new words that aren't included in the main dictionary. You can use spelling options to add or change custom dictionaries at will, and you can edit the contents of custom dictionaries.

> NOTE

You can't remove Word's main dictionary, but you can switch to a main dictionary in another language. See "Changing a Dictionary's Language" on page 201.

The Custom Dictionary list in the Spelling Options dialog box shows all of the custom dictionaries you currently have defined for use in Word. The dictionary name that is showing in the box is the one to which new words will be added. To work with custom dictionaries, click the Dictionaries button to the right of the Custom Dictionary list. You'll see the Custom Dictionaries dialog box, as in Figure 10-8.

FIGURE 10-8.

Use the Custom Dictionaries dialog box to add, remove, or edit the contents of custom dictionaries.

The Custom Dictionaries list shows the custom dictionaries available in Word. Using the Custom Dictionaries dialog box, you can select which dictionaries are used in spelling checks, make new custom dictionaries from scratch, add dictionaries you installed or created in other ways, edit existing dictionary files, and remove dictionaries from the list. You can also set the language used for each custom dictionary.

Activating a Custom Dictionary

To activate a dictionary, select the check box next to its name in the Custom Dictionaries list.

II

Writing and Editing Tools

Adding a Custom Dictionary

If you have installed a new custom dictionary and it isn't on the Custom Dictionaries list, you can add it:

1 Click Add on the Custom Dictionaries dialog box.

2 Navigate to and select the dictionary file on your disk.

Word assumes that all custom dictionaries are stored in the folder C:\Windows\Application Data\Microsoft\Proof. Copy your dictionary file to that folder first and make sure it has the file extension .dic before adding it.

3 Click OK.

For more information about obtaining custom dictionaries from Microsoft and other vendors, choose Office On The Web from the Help menu to navigate to the Microsoft Office Web site.

Creating a New Dictionary from Scratch

If you want to create a new dictionary from scratch, there are three steps in the process:

1 Click the New button to create the new custom dictionary file and add it to the Custom Dictionaries list.

2 Name and save the file.

3 Select the dictionary in the Custom Dictionaries list and click Edit to add words to it.

Editing a Custom Dictionary

You can add, delete, or edit words in a custom dictionary at any time:

1 Select the dictionary's name on the Custom Dictionaries list and click Edit. Word opens the dictionary in a standard document window with each word listed on a separate line.

2 Press Enter at the end of any line.

3 Enter the first new word and press Enter. Word won't properly recognize a word if it isn't on its own line in a dictionary document.

TIP

Use the Paste or Insert commands to insert whole collections of words into a custom dictionary at the same time. Word doesn't care if you sort the words or not, but sorting them can make it easier for you to see at a glance if a certain word is already in the dictionary. *For sorting instructions, see "Sorting Text" on page 185.*

4 Add or edit other words if you like.

5 Press Ctrl+S to save the document when you're done.

WARNING

Don't change the name or location of an edited dictionary file when you save it. If you do, Word will continue using the older version of the file that was at the original location.

Changing a Dictionary's Language

U.S. English versions of Office 2000 include language-specific spelling dictionaries for English, Spanish, and French. When you open a document or enter text, Word detects which of these languages a word is from. However, you must set the language used for each custom dictionary so that Word will use the correct spelling rules for each. For example, if you choose the English (UK) dictionary, Word will flag "organize" as an error and will suggest "organise" as the correct spelling.

ON THE WEB

There are many custom dictionaries you can buy and install in Word for foreign languages, medical or legal terms, or other specialized word collections. For more information, choose Office On The Web from the Help menu.

There are two ways to select a different language. You can set the main language used to check the spelling in a document or a particular selection of text, or you can set the language for a specific custom dictionary.

To make Word aware of another language dictionary for use in all spelling and grammar checks, follow these steps:

1 Choose Language from the Tools menu, and then select Set Language. You'll see the Language dialog box, as shown in the figure on the following page.

2 Select a language from the list. The spelling and grammar tools will automatically support the language you select, unless you select the Do Not Check Spelling Or Grammar check box.

II

Writing and Editing Tools

3 To set the current language used in Word, click the Default button.

4 Click Yes.

To set the language for a specific custom dictionary, follow these steps:

1 Open the Custom Dictionaries dialog box.

2 Select the dictionary in the Custom Dictionaries list.

3 Select a language from the Language menu.

4 Click OK.

? SEE ALSO

For more information about storing custom dictionaries, search for *dictionary* in the Help System index and choose the topic, "Create and use custom dictionaries."

How and Where Dictionary Files are Stored

All of Word's spelling dictionaries are stored in the Proof folder. The Full Path information in the Custom Dictionaries dialog box shows the full location, which is C:\Windows\Application Data\Microsoft\Proof.

When you create a new dictionary or select a dictionary to add to Word's stable of resources, Word automatically selects this location and the .dic (Dictionary Files) file type. Do not change file types or the location, or the custom dictionary will not be available to Word.

When you create a new dictionary file in the Proof folder and click the Save button, the dictionary name is automatically added to the Custom Dictionaries list in the Custom Dictionary dialog box. If you create a dictionary file in another folder and then move it into the Proof folder, however, you'll have to add it from the Custom Dictionaries dialog box to see it on the list there.

Removing a Custom Dictionary

To remove a custom dictionary so it will no longer be used in Word, select the dictionary name in the Custom Dictionaries dialog box and click Remove. The dictionary file will be deleted from the list, but the file itself will remain in the Proof folder on your disk in case you want to add it again later.

Editing in Other Languages

With Microsoft Word 2000, it's easy to use other languages for editing your text. You can choose any of 63 languages, from Korean or Japanese to Swahili or Arabic.

To edit in a particular language, you must must enable the language for use in Word. Once you enable a language, Word adds special commands to the Format menu for editing that language with its special characters and punctuation marks. In addition, Word automatically detects many languages and sets the spelling and grammar checkers to recognize them so you don't get a lot of false red and green underlines in your document. You can enable several languages at once, and you can also choose to display all of Word's commands, dialog box options, and Help in any enabled language.

Enabling a Language

You can enable many foreign languages by using a simple dialog box, but some languages require special characters that are not in Word's built-in set or they require graphical editing or right-to-left text.

- To use Asian languages in Word, you'll need to install a Global Input Method Editor (IME) using the Microsoft Multilanguage Pack for Office 2000.

For more information about Global Input Method Editors and the ultilanguage Pack for Office 2000, look up *multilingual features* in the Help System index and select the topic called "About multilingual features in Office."

II

Writing and Editing Tools

- To input characters for Arabic, Farsi, Greek, Hebrew, Turkish, and for certain Baltic and Central European languages, as well as languages using the Cyrillic alphabet, you'll need a language-specific version of Microsoft Windows.

To enable any other language, follow these steps:

? SEE ALSO

For information about setting the language for a particular custom dictionary, see "Changing a Dictionary's Language" on page 201.

1 Choose Programs from the Start menu. From there, choose Office Tools, and then Microsoft Office Language Settings. You'll see a dialog box like this:

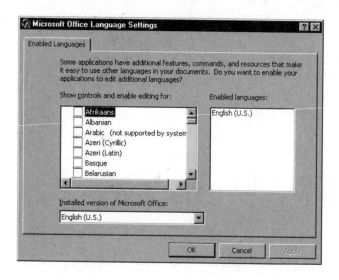

2 Select a check box for each language you want to enable.

3 Click Apply to enable the language without quitting Word or click OK to enable the language and restart Word. (Word won't know about the new language until you restart.)

Using AutoCorrect

AutoCorrect is a huge time-saver when you work with documents. It fixes common typos and punctuation errors automatically, and you can expand the list of typos it will correct. In Word 2000, AutoCorrect is even more intelligent, because rather than working solely from a list of corrections you supply, it automatically uses suggestions from the spelling checker to correct what you type.

AutoCorrect options are turned on when you begin using Word. See for yourself: begin a new sentence with a lowercase character and watch as Word capitalizes it.

Changing the AutoCorrect Rules

There are dozens and dozens of AutoCorrect rules. Some of them make it easy to enter special characters (when you enter *(r),* for example, Word converts it to ®), and others fix common typos, punctuation, or grammar problems. You can add or change these rules using the AutoCorrect dialog box, and you can also set a handful of options to adjust the way Word applies a few key rules.

Adding a Rule

If you frequently make a specific typo that AutoCorrect doesn't know about, you can add it as a new AutoCorrect rule. But AutoCorrect can also save you time by adding new rules that replace typing shortcuts. For example, if your company is named "Consolidated Dumpster Diving, Inc.," you could add the shortcut *cdd* and have Word replace it with the full company name whenever you type *cdd.*

To add a rule, follow these steps:

1 Choose AutoCorrect from the Tools menu. You'll see the AutoCorrect dialog box as shown in Figure 10-9.

FIGURE 10-9.

Scroll down the list and you'll see dozens of typos that are automatically fixed, as well as shortcuts for trademark symbols, smiley faces, arrows, and other special characters.

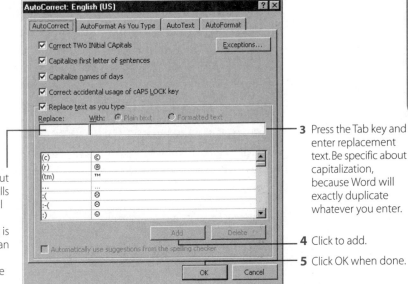

2 Enter a new shortcut or typo. The list scrolls to that alphabetical section so you can see if your shortcut is already listed. You can enter shortcuts in capital or lowercase letters.

3 Press the Tab key and enter replacement text. Be specific about capitalization, because Word will exactly duplicate whatever you enter.

4 Click to add.

5 Click OK when done.

II

Writing and Editing Tools

 **TIP**

If you select text in your document before choosing AutoCorrect from the Tools menu, the selected text will be automatically entered in the With box.

You can add as many shortcuts as you like, but be careful! Don't use letter combinations that are likely to occur in (or actually are) normal words. For example, if you replace "bin" with "binary file transfer," you'll end up with sentences like "He threw it in the trash binary file transfer."

Editing or Deleting Rules

? SEE ALSO

For information about the AutoText tab in the AutoCorrect dialog box, see "Using AutoText" on page 218. The Auto Format As You Type and AutoFormat options are covered in Chapter 18, "Formatting Automatically."

As your needs change, you may need to edit AutoCorrect rules. You might notice new typos you frequently make that aren't corrected, or perhaps you created a shortcut rule to enter a project name and the project is now complete and you no longer need the shortcut.

To edit or delete an AutoCorrect rule, follow these steps:

1 Choose AutoCorrect from the Tools menu.

2 Select the rule in the list.

3 Type new text in the With box to edit the rule and then click Replace, or click the Delete button to remove the rule.

4 Click OK.

Setting AutoCorrect Options

The options at the top of the AutoCorrect tab allow you to adjust Word's behavior. The top four options tell Word to check for specific types of capitalization errors, and the fifth option turns AutoCorrect on and off. At the bottom of the tab, you can select an option to have Word automatically use suggestions from the spelling checker.

Adding or Deleting Rule Exceptions

The Exceptions button allows you to specify exceptions to certain rules. When you click this button, you see the AutoCorrect Exceptions dialog box, like this:

1 Click a tab to choose the type of problem. Each of the three tabs is for entering or deleting a different type of exception.

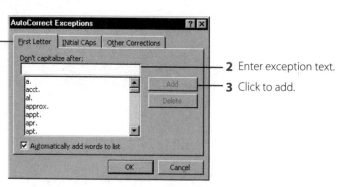

2 Enter exception text.

3 Click to add.

To add an exception, follow these steps:

1 Click the Exceptions button to display the AutoCorrect Exceptions dialog box.

2 Click a tab to select the type of exception you want to enter.

3 Enter text in the Don't Correct or Don't Capitalize After box.

> The First Letter tab already contains exceptions. Check it out for examples of rules you might enter.

4 Click Add.

5 Click OK to return to the AutoCorrect dialog box.

To delete a rule exception, display the AutoCorrect Exceptions dialog box, click the appropriate tab, select the rule, and click Delete.

What If You Want To Be Wrong on Purpose?

Word always fixes problems listed in the AutoCorrect dialog box, but this can be a problem when you want to be wrong on purpose—you make a deliberate typo and Word keeps fixing it like a patient school teacher. But since Word corrects text *as you type*, you can turn off the replace feature temporarily to make your deliberate error, and turn it back on when you're done.

1 Choose AutoCorrect from the Tools menu.

2 Click the AutoCorrect tab.

3 Click the Replace Text As You Type check box to remove the check mark.

4 Click the OK button to close the AutoCorrect dialog box.

5 Type the erroneous text.

6 Open the AutoCorrect dialog box and click the Replace Text As You Type feature to turn it back on.

7 Click OK to close the AutoCorrect dialog box.

If you make the same deliberate typo frequently and you want Word to ignore it, however, create an exception for it *(as explained above)*.

II

Writing and Editing Tools

Using the Thesaurus

Word's built-in Thesaurus helps you quickly find the right synonym for any word as you polish your prose. You can look up alternatives for words you use, have Word insert synonyms in place of selected words in your document, and even find alternatives to common figures of speech.

Finding Synonyms

To use the Thesaurus, you must select a word or phrase to look up first. To look up a synonym, follow this process:

1 Select the word or phrase for which you want to look up synonyms.

2 Choose Language from the Tools menu, and then choose Thesaurus, or press Shift+F7. You'll see the Thesaurus dialog box as shown in Figure 10-10.

FIGURE 10-10.

Use Word's Thesaurus to locate and substitute synonyms or antonyms.

3 Select a meaning for the looked-up word. Select an alternate word or phrase to see a different group of synonyms.

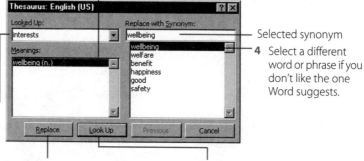

Word selected in document

Selected synonym

4 Select a different word or phrase if you don't like the one Word suggests.

5 Click to replace a selection in your document with the synonym.

Click to see additional synonyms for the selected synonym.

The Looked Up box shows the word or phrase you selected in your document. The Meanings list shows different meanings for the word or phrase—Word guesses the meaning from the context in which it was used.

The synonym list at the right shows all the synonyms found for the selected meaning. The Replace With Synonym box at the top shows the synonym that will replace your selection.

When Word Can't Find a Synonym

If you select a word for which the Thesaurus contains no synonyms, the Looked Up box is named Not Found, and a list of words or phrases appears below it that are, in Word's opinion, close to the one you selected. The Thesaurus dialog box will look like this:

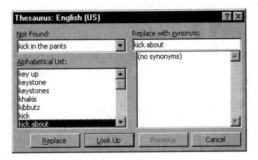

Select an alternative word or phrase from the word list and click Replace to substitute the new word or phrase in your document.

Finding Antonyms

Most thesauruses list antonyms as well as synonyms, and Word's is no exception. When you select a word or phrase that has antonyms, you'll see antonyms listed at the bottom of the list of synonyms. To use an antonym, select it and click Replace.

Looking up Other Meanings and Synonyms

People commonly use a thesaurus to cross-reference by looking up one word meaning, finding the list of synonyms, and then looking up a meaning for one of the synonyms. You can do the same thing in Word's Thesaurus dialog box with the Look Up button.

1   Select a word in the synonym list.

2   Click Look Up. Word displays synonyms for the word you selected.

By selecting alternate synonyms and looking up synonyms for them, you can quickly locate every possible variant for the word or phrase you originally selected.

Backing up Through the Thesaurus

If you're hot on the trail of the perfect synonym and you find yourself using the Look Up button to prowl among several synonyms, you may stray into lists of definitions that are nowhere near what you want. Fortunately, you can go back to words you looked up previously and display their synonyms again. Word keeps track of each word you have looked up during a given session with the Thesaurus. There are two ways to display a previous word and its synonyms:

- Choose a word from the Looked Up list box in the Thesaurus dialog box.

- Click the Previous button to go to the last word you looked up.

Hyphenating Text

Hyphens break up words into their component syllables so you can use the last bit of space at the end of one line for part of a word and then put the rest of it at the beginning of the next line. You can also use hyphens in compound words or proper names, such as Wilkes-Barre. You can insert hyphens with the keyboard as you work or use Word's automatic hyphenation feature to ensure proper word breaks and improve the look of your document.

A properly hyphenated document has a less ragged right margin, because every long word at the end of a line is hyphenated rather than being moved to the line below in its entirety. Hyphenation creates a smoother right margin for your text—Figure 10-11 shows the difference.

FIGURE 10-11.

In these two identical paragraphs, the left-hand one is hyphenated.

Yes, Type Too can handle page layout projects as small and simple as a business card or as large as a book containing hundreds of pages. Sizes can vary from business cards, through letter, legal, tabloid and custom sizes (for special projects such as boxes, catalogs, and promotional pieces. These pieces can be almost any size, cost being the only consideration).

Yes, Type Too can handle page layout projects as small and simple as a business card or as large as a book containing hundreds of pages. Sizes can vary from business cards, through letter, legal, tabloid and custom sizes (for special projects such as boxes, catalogs, and promotional pieces. These pieces can be almost any size, cost being the only consideration).

Word doesn't normally hyphenate words when they're too long to fit at the end of lines. Instead, Word moves the whole word down to the next line. However, you can use special hyphens or Word's automatic hyphenation features to adjust the appearance of your document.

Hyphens for All Reasons

There are three different types of hyphens in Word: manual, optional, and nonbreaking. Each type of hyphen behaves differently.

- **Manual hyphens** These are inserted with the hyphen key on the keyboard, and they always stay where you put them. For example, suppose you reach the end of a line and insert a hyphen to place "alter-" at the end of the line and "cation" on the next line. If later reformatting changes the word's location so it fits on one line, it will read "alter-cation." Manual hyphens are best used for compound last names or phrases, such as "Biggleswade-Smythe" or "self-conscious," that should always be hyphenated regardless of their position on a line.

- **Optional hyphens**   These are used to break up syllables when a word is too long to fit at the end of a line, but they disappear if later reformatting makes it possible for the whole word to fit on one line. With an optional hyphen, for example, what was "alter-cation" becomes "altercation" when the whole word fits on the line. To insert an optional hyphen, press Ctrl+hyphen (-). These hyphens are also inserted when you use Word's Hyphenation command.

- **Nonbreaking hyphens**   These split up compound names or parts of words, but unlike manual hyphens, they ensure that the hyphenated word or phrase is never broken up between two lines. With a nonbreaking hyphen, for example, "Puddleston-On-Thames" always appears on one line, even if it forces Word to leave an extra-large blank space at the end of the previous line. To insert a nonbreaking hyphen, press Ctrl+Shift+Hyphen (_).

 TIP

> To see optional hyphens and other special characters in your document, click the Show/Hide button (¶) on the Standard toolbar.

Using Automatic Hyphenation

If you're a big fan of hyphenation, you can set Word to hyphenate selected text or your entire document. When automatic hyphenation is on, Word looks for spaces at the ends of lines and tries to fill them by hyphenating the first word on the line below, as shown in Figure 10-11.

When you use automatic hyphenation, you can set the amount of blank space that will be left at the end of each line before Word tries to hyphenate a word. You can also set the maximum number of consecutive lines that can end with hyphenated words. (Documents become more difficult to read when there are too many hyphens.)

Activating Automatic Hyphenation

To turn on automatic hyphenation, follow these steps:

1 Select the paragraph(s) to be hyphenated in your document.

2 Choose Language from the Tools menu, and then choose Hyphenation. You'll see the Hyphenation dialog box as shown in Figure 10-12 on the next page.

II

Writing and Editing Tools

FIGURE 10-12.

Use the Hyphenation dialog box to adjust Word's automatic hyphenation options.

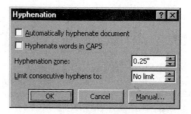

3   Select the Automatically Hyphenate Document check box.

4   Select any other options you want.

5   Click OK. Word will automatically hyphenate words to fill line endings throughout your text selection or your document.

Setting Hyphenation Options

The options in the Hyphenation dialog box let you control how Word determines when to hyphenate.

- **Automatically Hyphenate Document**   Tells Word to hyphenate the entire document, even if you have text selected in your document.

- **Hyphenate Words In CAPS**   Tells Word to hyphenate acronyms and other all-caps words that it would normally ignore.

- **Hyphenation Zone**   This is the amount of space left at the end of a line that activates automatic hyphenation. Click the arrow buttons or enter a value. Setting a smaller value will make the document's right text margin more even, but it will do so at the expense of more hyphens.

- **Limit Consecutive Hyphens To**   Tells Word not to hyphenate a line if a certain number of consecutive previous lines already contain hyphens. Setting a limit here helps you avoid over-hyphenation.

Checking Hyphenation Before Word Applies It

Setting Word loose to hyphenate your entire document could result in a lot more hyphens than you really want. You can control hyphens somewhat with the Hyphenation Zone and Limit Consecutive Hyphens options, but you may want to evaluate each proposed hyphen before Word inserts it.

To check each automatic hyphen before it is applied, click the Manual button in the Hyphenation dialog box. Word will insert the first automatic hyphen, show you how the word will be hyphenated, and ask your permission, as shown at the top of the next page.

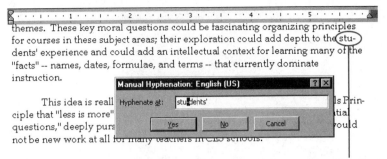

themes. These key moral questions could be fascinating organizing principles for courses in these subject areas; their exploration could add depth to the students' experience and could add an intellectual context for learning many of the "facts" -- names, dates, formulae, and terms -- that currently dominate instruction.

This idea is reall[...] [...]ls Prin-
ciple that "less is more" [...] [...]tial
questions," deeply purs[...] [...]ould
not be new work at all [...]

Hyphen being considered by Word

Click Yes to insert the automatic hyphen, or click No to skip this hyphen and jump to the next possibility. Click Cancel to stop automatic hyphenation.

Turning Hyphenation Off

If you have used Word to hyphenate your document and you decide you don't like it, you can easily remove all the automatic hyphens:

1 Choose Language from the Tools menu, and then choose Hyphenation to display the Hyphenation dialog box.

2 Clear the Automatically Hyphenate Document check box.

3 Click OK. The automatic hyphens will disappear.

⭐ **TIP**

To cancel automatic hyphenation immediately after you apply it, press Ctrl+Z or choose Undo Hyphenation from the Edit menu.

Counting Words in a Document

When you're writing to fill a specific amount of space or you're simply curious about the size of your document, you can use the Word Count command. Choose Word Count from the Tools menu. Word will count all the words in your document and you'll see the Word Count dialog box, as shown in the figure at the top of the next page.

The Word Count dialog box shows the number of words, characters, lines, paragraphs, and other elements in your document. Normally, Word includes all the text in your document as well as headers and footers when it counts. Click the Include Footnotes and Endnotes check box to include the text from footnotes or endnotes in the count as well.

II

Writing and Editing Tools

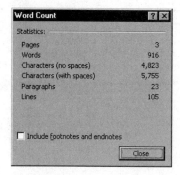

Word will not count words inside graphics, but it will count words used in captions for graphics. For more information about adding captions to graphics, *see "Inserting Captions" on page 539.*

Viewing Word Counts in the Properties Dialog Box

Another way to view the number of words in your document is to check the Statistics tab in the Properties dialog box. Choose Properties from the File menu, and then click the Statistics tab. You'll see the same word count statistics plus the number of bytes required to store the text in your document. *For more information about the Properties dialog box, see "Viewing Properties" on page 156.*

Summarizing Documents

If you're preparing a report or a long article, you may want to include an overview or executive summary at the beginning. Word can scan your document and create a summary automatically. When it creates a summary, Word tries to capture all of the key points and then group them together in a paragraph. You can adjust the size of the summary paragraph and choose four different options about the way the summary is used in your document.

To create an automatic summary, follow these steps:

1 Choose AutoSummarize from the Tools menu. (If this feature is not currently installed, you'll be given a chance to install it.) Word summarizes your document and then displays the AutoSummarize dialog box, as in Figure 10-13.

FIGURE 10-13.

You can automatically create summaries of your document's contents with the AutoSummarize dialog box.

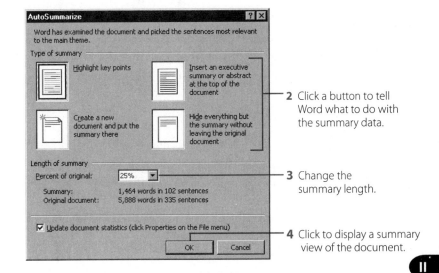

2 Click a button to tell Word what to do with the summary data.

3 Change the summary length.

4 Click to display a summary view of the document.

5 Click Close to close the summary view.

AutoSummarize doesn't always catch every key point in a document. Check the summary points against your document to make sure the summary doesn't omit something important.

Using Summary Options

The four large buttons at the top of the AutoSummarize dialog box tell Word what to do with the summary it has prepared. You can perform the following actions:

- Highlight the summary information in your document so you can easily see what Word has or hasn't included in the summary.

- Create a new document and copy the summary into it.

SEE ALSO

For more information about document sections, see Chapter 16, "Formatting Pages and Sections."

- Insert a new executive summary or abstract section at the beginning of your document and copy all the summary information into it.

- Temporarily hide everything in your document except the summary information.

- See statistics about how much of your document was included in the summary by looking in the Length of Summary section.

II

Writing and Editing Tools

- Set a limit for the length of the summary by choosing an option from the Percent of Original list, or by selecting the current value and typing a new one.

In addition, you can select the Update Document Statistics check box to have Word update the statistics shown on the Statistics tab of the Properties dialog box, if summarizing your document changes them. For example, if you use the option to copy the summary information to an executive summary section in your document, you'll increase the document's word, line, character and paragraph count.

Using the AutoSummarize Toolbar

When you summarize a document and then choose the option to highlight the summary information in your document or to display only the summary information, Word displays the AutoSummarize toolbar, like this:

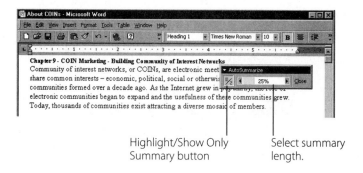

Highlight/Show Only Summary button

Select summary length.

Clicking the Highlight/Show Only Summary button on the left toggles the view between the view you chose (highlighted or summary-only) and the normal document view.

The percent slider controls the percentage of the document included in the summary, just like the Percent Of Original list in the Auto-Summarize dialog box. You can click the arrows, click in the slider box, or drag the slider bar to reset the percentage.

CHAPTER 11

Inserting Special Text, Notes, and Bookmarks

Although you'll compose most of your documents by entering text with the keyboard, you can also get help from Microsoft Word. With a few well-chosen mouse clicks, you can add special kinds of text, text symbols, bookmarks, notes, and even the contents of other files to any document.

Using AutoText

AutoText helps you work more quickly by entering specific types of text. For example, you can insert the current date or time, a page number, or various salutation or closing lines for letters. In some cases Word will offer to complete an AutoText entry when you type the first few letters of it, but you can also insert AutoText entries by selecting them from a menu or dialog box.

Inserting AutoText

You can insert AutoText from a menu, a toolbar, or a dialog box. The simplest method is to use the AutoText menu.

1 Move the insertion point to the location where you want the new text to appear.

2 Choose AutoText from the Insert menu. You'll see the AutoText submenu, like this:

The AutoText entries are grouped by type.

3 Choose a type of text to display its submenu and then select the specific text you want entered. Word inserts the text.

Using the AutoText Toolbar

If you use AutoText a lot, you can access it more easily with the AutoText toolbar. To use the AutoText toolbar:

1 Right-click in an existing toolbar and choose AutoText from the toolbar list. You'll see the AutoText toolbar, as shown in the figure at the top of the next page.

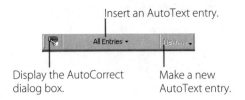

Insert an AutoText entry.

Display the AutoCorrect dialog box.

Make a new AutoText entry.

2 Click the All Entries button and you'll see the same list of text categories that you see when you point to the AutoText submenu on the Insert menu.

3 Choose a specific text entry from one of the AutoText categories.

If you want to use the toolbar to create a new AutoText entry, select the text in your document and then click the New command on the AutoText toolbar. You'll open the AutoText tab in the AutoCorrect dialog box so you can create a new text entry.

Using the AutoCorrect Dialog Box

To add or change AutoText entries, use the AutoText tab in the AutoCorrect dialog box. You can also insert AutoText from this tab.

Adding or Deleting AutoText Entries

As with AutoCorrect, AutoText can be a real time-saver by helping you enter frequently used long words or phrases. But unlike AutoCorrect, which completes your text shortcut every time, AutoText stores the entry and gives you the option to complete it. You can add an AutoText entry to a specific document template or to every document template you have open at the time.

To create an AutoText entry, follow these steps:

1 Choose AutoText from the Insert menu, and then choose AutoText again, or click the keyboard button on the AutoText toolbar. The AutoCorrect dialog box appears with the AutoText tab selected, as shown in Figure 11-1 on the next page. The tab lists any custom AutoText entries you have already defined.

2 Type a new entry in the Enter AutoText Entries Here box. Be sure to use the exact capitalization, spelling, punctuation, or spacing you want for the entry, because Word will faithfully reproduce it.

3 Use the Look In menu to choose a particular template or all active templates as the location where the AutoText will be stored.

FIGURE 11-1.

Use the AutoText tab in the AutoCorrect dialog box to add or delete AutoText entries.

Enter AutoText.

Existing Auto-Text entries.

Choose template(s) where entry will be stored.

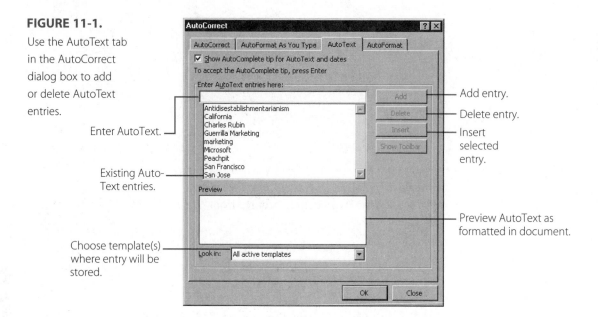

Add entry.

Delete entry.

Insert selected entry.

Preview AutoText as formatted in document.

4 Click Add or press Enter. Your new entry will appear in the list.

To delete an AutoText entry, select it in the list and click Delete.

Previewing and Inserting AutoText Entries

When the AutoCorrect dialog box is open, you can select any AutoText entry you have defined and see how it will look in your document by checking the Preview area.

To insert an entry, select it in the AutoText list and click Insert.

Inserting AutoText as You Type

If you have set the option to show AutoComplete Tips for AutoText entries, Word will offer to complete a phrase when you begin typing it. For example, if you type "Dear S" in your document, Word offers to complete the phrase with an AutoComplete tip from its standard collection, as in Figure 11-2.

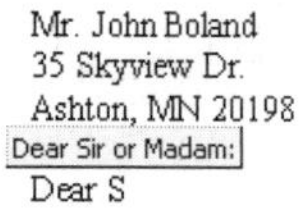

FIGURE 11-2.

Dear Sir or Madam AutoComplete tip.

Mr. John Boland
35 Skyview Dr.
Ashton, MN 20198
Dear Sir or Madam:
Dear S

To have Word complete the phrase, press the Enter key. If you don't want the phrase completed as Word suggests, just keep typing.

Word won't offer to complete AutoText entries that include both text and a date, such as the "Author, Page, and Date" entry.

To turn off the AutoComplete tips, clear the Show AutoComplete Tip For Auto-Text And Dates check box on the AutoText tab in the AutoCorrect dialog box.

Inserting Symbols and Special Characters

There are many symbols and special characters (such as accents for foreign languages) available in many fonts, but they're not shown on your keyboard. To see what characters and symbols are available and to insert them into your documents, you'll use the Symbol command from the Insert menu. You'll also find that some of the frequently used special characters have their own keyboard shortcuts, and you can define shortcuts for others if you like.

Bulleted and numbered lists contain other types of special characters, but they relate more to formatting than to text entry. *See "Creating Bulleted and Numbered Lists," on page 273.* Another type of special character you can insert is a hyperlink, which you can use to navigate quickly to another document or a Web site. *See "Using Hyperlinks" on page 772.*

Inserting a Special Character

Each font has its own special characters. If you don't find a character you want in one font, check others. To add a special character to your document:

1 Move the insertion point to the place where you want the character or symbol to appear.

2 Choose Symbol from the Insert menu. You'll see special characters as shown in Figure 11-3 on the next page.

Many fonts have unique symbols in them, and some (such as Zapf Dingbats) are nothing but graphical symbols. *See "Using Symbol Fonts" on page 224 .*

FIGURE 11-3.

Use the Symbol dialog box to insert special characters such as bullets, other graphical symbols, or accented characters for foreign languages.

All the letters, numbers, and symbols you can display with the current font are shown in the grid. The Font menu shows that Word is displaying symbols for the Symbol font.

3 Choose a font.   **4** Click a symbol.

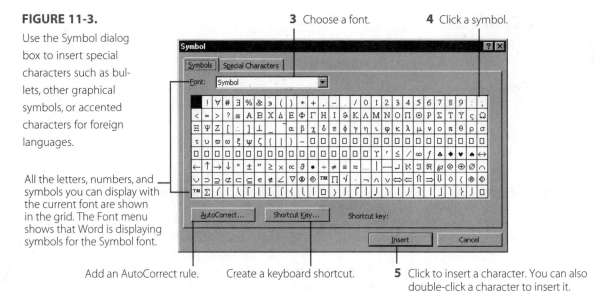

Add an AutoCorrect rule.   Create a keyboard shortcut.   **5** Click to insert a character. You can also double-click a character to insert it.

6 Click Cancel to put the dialog box away.

Adding Shortcuts for Special Characters

If you use certain symbols or special characters frequently, it can be a bit tedious to display the Symbol dialog box and select them each time. Fortunately, you can create a keyboard shortcut for any symbol or character, and you can even set up an AutoCorrect rule to replace a shortcut you type with the correct symbol. Some symbols and characters already have keyboard shortcuts or AutoCorrect rules set up.

Adding a Keyboard Shortcut

 **SEE ALSO**

For more information about defining shortcuts, see "Changing Keyboard Shortcuts" on page 172.

To add a keyboard shortcut for a symbol, follow these steps:

1 Choose Symbol from the Insert menu.

2 Select the character symbol for which you want to add a shortcut. If there is already an existing shortcut, Word displays it in the lower-right corner of the dialog box. However, you can create new shortcut keys in addition to existing ones.

3 Click the Shortcut Key button. You'll see the Customize Keyboard dialog box as shown in Figure 8-8 on page 173.

4 Press Alt+Ctrl plus the key you want to use for the shortcut. Check the Current Keys box to make sure this combination isn't already assigned.

5 Click Assign to assign the shortcut.

6 Click Close to return to the Symbol dialog box.

Adding an AutoCorrect Rule

As discussed on page 204 in Chapter 10, AutoCorrect is Word's built-in typo corrector. It can also be used to insert special characters when you type standard text.

 TIP

> To see which symbols or characters currently have AutoCorrect rules, choose AutoCorrect from the Tools menu and scroll through the list of rules in the AutoCorrect dialog box.

SEE ALSO

For more information about AutoCorrect, see "Using Auto-Correct" on page 204.

Here's how to add an AutoCorrect rule:

1 Choose Symbol from the Insert menu.

2 Select the character symbol for which you want to add an AutoCorrect rule.

3 Click the AutoCorrect button. You'll see the AutoCorrect dialog box, as shown in Figure 10-9 on page 205, except that the With box will already contain the symbol character you selected.

4 Enter the characters you want to trigger the shortcut in the Replace box.

5 Click Add.

6 Click OK to return to the Symbol dialog box.

Inserting Accented Characters

SEE ALSO

For more information about inserting international characters, look up "international characters" in the Help System index.

When your text requires the use of words from languages other than English, you'll need to use special accents on certain characters, such as the tilde in Spanish words like *piñon*. Most fonts include these accented characters, and it's easy to add them once you know the ropes.

To add a special accent to a character:

1 Press the Ctrl key along with the key that tells Word which type of accent to apply.

2 Release the two keys and then press the letter you want accented. For example, to add a tilde to an *n*, you would press Ctrl+~ and then type the *n*.

II

Writing and Editing Tools

The fonts you use in Word can produce umlauts, grave accents, circumflexes, tildes, and acute accents. Table 11-1 shows some examples plus the keyboard commands for entering these symbols.

TABLE 11-1. **Character Accent Marks and Their Keyboard Shortcuts**

Accent Name	Example	Keys to Press
Acute accent	Glacé	Ctrl+' (apostrophe), letter
Grave accent	Allègre	Ctrl+`, letter
Circumflex	Pêche	Ctrl+^, letter
Tilde	Piñata	Ctrl+~, letter
Umlaut	Mönch	Ctrl+:, letter

Using Symbol Fonts

The collection of fonts available to Word includes several fonts that are nothing but graphical symbols. You can use the Symbol command from the Insert menu and then choose a symbol font from the Font list to select these fonts, see the symbols they offer, and insert them into your documents. Once you insert the symbols, you can resize them to make them larger for such things as fliers, posters, and report title pages or to dress up other documents. Table 11-2 shows some examples.

TABLE 11-2. **Some Symbol Fonts and the Symbols They Include**

Font	Examples
Almanac MT	
Bon Appetit MT	
Directions MT	
Holidays MT	
Keystrokes MT	
Signs MT	
Sports Two MT	
Transport MT	
Vacation MT	
Webdings	
Wingdings	

> ### Dressing Up Documents with Symbol Fonts
>
> You can have lots of fun in your documents by inserting special symbols for added visual appeal. Although each character is inserted as an in-line graphic (on the same line as your other text), you can use Word's Drop Cap feature to resize a symbol and make it a graphical element, like this:
>
> ## Local Company in the News
>
> **Y** our Type, a graphics and typesetting firm in Bent Branch, was recently recognized for excellence in graphic arts design by the South Dakota Graphics Alliance. The alliance bestowed its coveted Golden Pica Stick award to Your Type for work the company did on a recent brochure and Web site project for Marshland Farms.
>
> You can also use symbols in context to save typing or to better express yourself visually. For example, add a smiley face symbol to show cheerfulness or a storm cloud to show that you're not in such a great mood after all.
>
> Spend some time cruising the various fonts and symbols in the Symbol dialog box, and you'll see lots of graphics that will make your documents more appealing.

? SEE ALSO

For instructions on using drop caps, see "Creating a Drop Cap" on page 271.

NOTE

Your system may not contain the same fonts as shown in Table 11-2.

Using Bookmarks

If you've ever done a research project, you probably used paper bookmarks and a highlighter to mark and identify specific parts of the text. You'll use bookmarks in Word for the same purpose, and more.

A bookmark is an invisible electronic marker in a document. You can set a bookmark at the insertion point's position, or you can add a bookmark to a whole selection of text. Each bookmark you create in a document has a unique name.

Once you've created a bookmark, you can use Word's Go To command to jump immediately to the bookmarked spot. If you bookmark a selection of text, Word jumps to and selects the text when you navigate to that bookmark. Bookmarking a selection of text is also useful when you insert text from that document into another document, because you can tell Word what to insert by specifying the bookmark name.

II

Writing and Editing Tools

Adding and Removing Bookmarks

You can add a bookmark to any location or selection of text in your document. To do so, follow these steps:

1   Move the insertion point to the bookmark location, or select the text you want to bookmark.

2   Choose Bookmark from the Insert menu. You'll see the Bookmark dialog box, as in Figure 11-4.

FIGURE 11-4.

Add named bookmarks to your document to identify text for faster navigation and to make it easy to insert the text into other documents.

3   Type a one-word name for the bookmark. You can't use more than one word for a bookmark name.

4   Click Add.

Deleting a Bookmark

When a bookmark has outlived its usefulness, it's easy to delete it.

1   Choose Bookmark from the Insert menu to open the Bookmark dialog box.

2   Select the name of the bookmark you want to remove.

3   Click Delete.

Displaying Hidden Bookmarks

When you add special document features such as cross-references or index entries, Word inserts hidden bookmarks so it can remember their locations. These bookmarks aren't normally displayed in the Bookmarks dialog box, but you can view them by clicking the Hidden Bookmarks check box.

Sorting the Bookmark List

You can sort the list in the Bookmark dialog box by name or by location in your document. If you sort by location, it's easier to tell where you'll be taken in the document when you double-click it. If you prefer, you can list bookmarks alphabetically. Just click one of the Sort By options below the list in the Bookmark dialog box.

Navigating to a Bookmark

Once you have created a bookmark or two, you can navigate to it with the Bookmark dialog box or with the Go To command. If you happen to have the Bookmark dialog box open already, just double-click the bookmark name or select it and click the Go To button.

If the Bookmark dialog box is not open, use the Go To command, as follows:

SEE ALSO

See Figure 4-4 on page 59 for an example of this dialog box.

1   Press Ctrl+G or choose Go To from the Edit menu to display the Go To tab in the Find dialog box.

2   Click Bookmark in the Go To What list.

3   Choose the bookmark name from the Enter Bookmark Name list.

4   Click Go To. Word scrolls through the document and moves the insertion point to that bookmark's position or selects the book-marked text.

Inserting Files

One of the great things about storing data on a computer is that you can locate and reuse the data when you need it. Recycling data is especially useful when you're creating a new document and you know that some of the data you want in it already exists in another file.

You can always move text or other data from one file to another by opening them both and cutting and pasting between them, but it can be faster to insert a whole file's contents into a document. For example, suppose you're preparing a sales proposal and you want to include a list of prices or product specifications that is stored in a Prices or Specifications file. With Word's Insert File command, it's easy to add the contents of the file to your document. When you use the Insert File command, a file's contents are inserted at the insertion point's location in your document.

Inserting a Whole File

To insert all of another file's contents into your document:

1 Move the insertion point to the place in your document where you want the other file's data to appear.

2 Choose File from the Insert menu. You'll see the Insert File dialog box as shown in Figure 11-5.

FIGURE 11-5.
Add the contents of one file to a document on your screen with the Insert File dialog box.

Select file to insert.

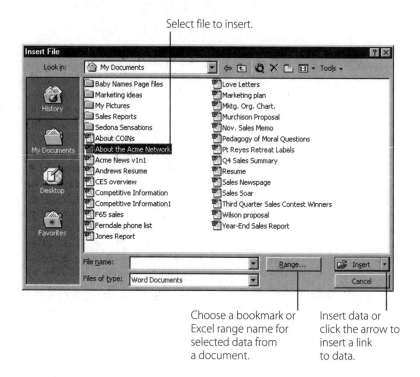

Choose a bookmark or Excel range name for selected data from a document.

Insert data or click the arrow to insert a link to data.

? **SEE ALSO**

For more about creating and using bookmarks, see page 226. For more about using Excel data in a document, see Chapter 21, "Working with Objects," and Chapter 22, "Creating Graphs, Worksheets, and Equations."

3 Locate the file you want to insert and then either double-click it or select it and click the Insert button. The file is inserted into your document.

Inserting Part of a File

If you have made judicious use of bookmarks to identify portions of text in your files, you can use them to insert only a portion of a file. You can also insert a range of cells from a Microsoft Excel worksheet if the range has a name.

To insert part of a file, follow these steps:

1 Move the insertion point to the place where you want the text or data to appear.

2 Choose File from the Insert menu.

3 Locate and select the file where the data or text is located.

4 Click in the Range box and enter the name of the bookmark whose text you want to include.

5 Click the Insert button. The data from the Excel worksheet range or Word bookmark is inserted into your document.

 TIP

To conserve file space when inserting large amounts of data from other files, insert a link to the file rather than the file itself. To do this, click the arrow button next to the Insert button on the Insert File dialog box and choose Insert As Link from the menu. *See Chapter 21, "Working with Objects," for more about linking.*

How Does Word Treat Inserted Text?

The Insert File dialog box works like the Open dialog box, but it doesn't support as many different file formats as Word does when opening files. Word will try its best to properly format any text or data you insert into a file, but Word's success has a lot to do with the type of file you try to insert.

SEE ALSO

For more information about styles, see "How Styles Work" on page 296. For more information about opening files in other formats, see Chapter 38, "Importing, Exporting, and Converting Documents."

■ If you insert a Word (.doc) file into your document and the file's text is formatted differently than the text in your document, Word will insert the text with its formatting intact. However, Word will not import any styles attached to the text you insert.

■ If you insert a file for which Word has no format converter, Word will either try to open the file anyway (with widely varying results) or it will show a message saying the file couldn't be opened.

To save yourself from lots of reformatting or other file insertion problems, stick with other Microsoft Office documents when inserting files.

II

Writing and Editing Tools

Inserting Dates or Times

You can have Word automatically insert a formatted date or time anywhere in your document. If you use dates and times frequently, this can save you a lot of keystrokes. You can insert dates or times in two ways:

■ As a static date or time entered as text. This option is best when you must refer to a specific day or time and will not need to change it later.

? SEE ALSO

Fields give you incredible powers for inserting automatically updated data into your document. For more about using fields, see Chapter 27, "Using Fields."

■ As a date or time field that will be updated to the current date or time each time you work with the document. This option is useful when you want the document to have the most recent date when you display, print, or e-mail it.

To insert a date or time, follow these steps:

1 Move the insertion point to the place in your document where you want the date to appear.

2 Choose Date And Time from the Insert menu. You'll see the Date And Time dialog box, as in Figure 11-6.

FIGURE 11-6.

Use the Date And Time dialog box to select the format dates or times and insert them in your document.

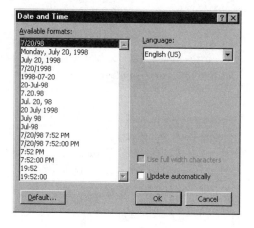

3 Select the Update Automatically check box if you want the date or time inserted as a data field that will be updated automatically.

? SEE ALSO

For more about enabling other languages in Word, see "Editing in Other Languages" on page 203.

4 Choose an alternate language if you have enabled other languages in Word. For example, dates are formatted differently in European languages.

5 Scroll through the list of formatted dates and times to find the one you want, and then either double-click it or select it and click OK. Word inserts the date or time.

NOTE

> Dates and times are common in document headers and footers. You'll notice that some of the AutoText options include standard header information such as the author, page number, and date. *See Chapter 16, "Formatting Pages and Sections," for more about headers.*

Inserting Footnotes and Endnotes

 SEE ALSO

For more information about document sections, see "Using Sections" on page 317.

Footnotes and endnotes are a staple of scholarly articles, research papers, and technical documents. Footnotes appear at the bottom of a page or at the end of a portion of text; endnotes appear at the end of a document or at the end of a document section. With Word, you can insert footnotes or endnotes, and you can set options to control where they appear and how they're identified in your document.

Inserting Notes

Use the Footnote command on the Insert menu to add a footnote or endnote to your document and to add a number, symbol, or another mark for it in the document's text. To insert a footnote or endnote:

1 Move the insertion point to the place where you want the note mark to appear.

2 Choose Footnote from the Insert menu. Word displays the Footnote And Endnote dialog box, as in Figure 11-7.

FIGURE 11-7.

When you insert a footnote or endnote, you can specify the type of note, its numbering, and other options.

SEE ALSO

For more information about setting note options, see "Setting Note Options" on page 233.

3 Click the Footnote or Endnote button to choose which type of note you want. You can use options to add footnotes either at the end of the page or at the end of a certain section of text. You can add endnotes to either the end of the document or the end of a document section.

Writing and Editing Tools

II

4 Click the AutoNumber or Custom Mark button to tell Word to insert either a note number or a custom note mark. If you choose the Custom Mark option, you can enter a custom note mark in the box at the right or click the Symbol button to display the Symbol dialog box and select one there.

5 Click OK to add the note. Word adds a number or symbol for the note in your text, and adds a footnote to the document. Figure 11-8 shows a new footnote added at the end of a page.

FIGURE 11-8.

Footnote text appears at the bottom of the document page in Print Layout view. When you insert an endnote in Print Layout view, the note text appears at the end of the document.

Footnote marker

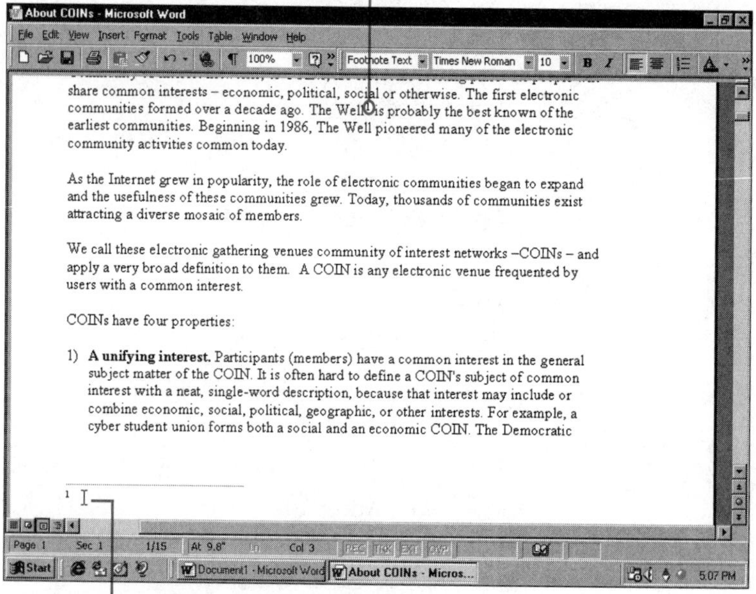

Type text of note in note area.

6 Type the text of the note.

7 Click in the document to resume editing it.

> When you work in Normal, Outline, or Web Layout view, notes appear in a separate pane at the bottom of the document window. Click the note pane's close button to close the pane or click inside the document pane to leave the note pane open and resume editing your document text.

Deleting Notes

To delete a note, select its number or symbol in your document and then press the Delete or Backspace key. Word automatically deletes the note from the note area of the document, renumbers any numbered notes, and reformats other notes there to close up the empty space.

> You must delete the note number or symbol in your text to have Word renumber and eliminate notes properly. If you try deleting the note in the note area, the note number or symbol will remain in your document.

Setting Note Options

When you insert a note, you can set specific options about its placement and the number format or symbol used to represent it. You can also change the look of the separator that divides the notes area from the rest of the text on a page.

To set note numbering or placement options:

1 Choose Footnote from the Insert menu.

2 Click the Options button on the Footnote And Endnote dialog box.

3 Click the All Footnotes or All Endnotes tab to display options for the type of note you're working with. For example, the All Footnotes tab is shown in Figure 11-9.

FIGURE 11-9.

You can modify note positions, formats, or numbers in the Note Options dialog box.

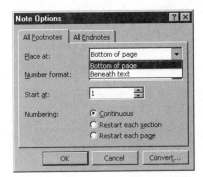

4 Choose the note position from the Place At menu. You can place notes either at the bottom of the page or after the last line of text on each page.

5 Choose a numbering scheme from the Number format menu. There are lots of number and symbol formats to choose from.

6 Enter the number you want to be used for the first automatically numbered note in the document in the Start At box, or click the arrow buttons to set it.

7 Select the numbering method. You can have notes numbered continuously through the whole document, or you can restart note numbering at the beginning of each document section or page.

8 Click OK to return to the Footnotes and Endnotes dialog box.

The options for endnotes are the same, except you can choose to place the notes either at the end of the document or at the end of the section in which they appear, and you can't restart numbering at the end of each page. (With notes at the end of the document, restarting numbering after each page wouldn't make any sense.)

Reformatting Notes

Word uses the same font you're using in your document for displaying notes, but it uses a slightly smaller font size. However, in the note area of a page you can use any of the character or paragraph formatting options that you use in your documents. You can change the line indents or alignment, reset the font, size, or style, and even insert graphics or other characters into notes.

WARNING

> Don't insert index or table of contents entries inside notes. Word won't see them there, and they won't be included when you produce the index or table. *See Chapter 25, "Creating Tables of Contents, Indexes, and Cross-References," for more about indexes and tables.*

If you don't like the plain black line that Word normally uses as a note separator, you can reformat it, too:

1 Switch to Normal view and choose Footnotes from the View menu to open the note pane.

2 Choose Footnote Separator from the Footnotes menu at the top of the note pane. You'll see the separator in an editable text line, like this:

3 Select the separator and type a new one. You can use any keyboard character, and the line can be as long as your current document margins allow. You can even use special borders with the Borders And Shading command on the Format menu or insert other graphics. *For more information about borders, see "Adding Borders and Shading" on page 288.*

TIP

> You can also use the menu in the note pane to insert note continuation separators (longer separator lines indicating that a note's text continues on the next page) or continuation notices (text in a different size that you can enter to explain that a note continues onto another page). *See "footnote options" in the Help System index for more information.*

4 Choose All Footnotes to switch back to a view of the notes themselves.

To revert back to the standard notes separator, choose Footnote Separator in the note pane's list and then click the Reset button.

II

Writing and Editing Tools

CHAPTER 12

Working with Outlines

Outlines are a great way to organize the contents of a document (or your thoughts about those contents) before you actually begin writing. Many professional writers begin all of their projects with an outline to make sure that every document flows in a logical way from one thought or subject to the next. Microsoft Word's Outline view allows you to work with any document as an outline so you can quickly see or change the way the document is organized. In this chapter, you'll learn how to make Outline view work for you.

Viewing Documents as Outlines

You can display any Microsoft Word document as an outline by choosing Outline from the View menu, by pressing Ctrl+Alt+O, or by clicking the Outline view button in the lower-left corner of the document window. You'll see the document as an outline, as shown in Figure 12-1.

FIGURE 12-1.

In Outline view, your document is organized in an outline with different organizational levels.

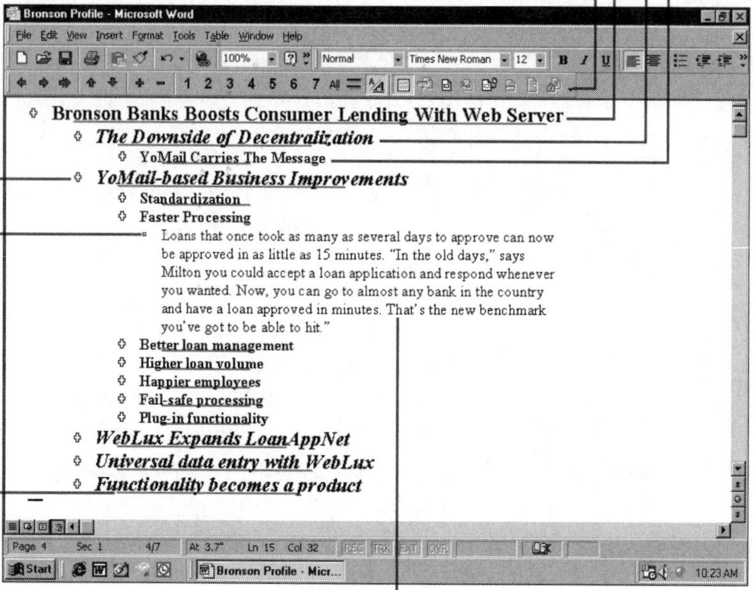

Click to expand or collapse; drag to reorganize.

Heading 1   Heading 2

Outlining toolbar   Heading 3

Topic marker

Shaded line indicates body text underneath.

Body text

(?) SEE ALSO

For more information on formatting selected paragraphs in your documents as an outline, see "Using Outline Number Formats" on page 278.

Each paragraph in the document is treated as a separate topic in Outline view, including body text paragraphs as well as headings and subheadings. Each topic is shown with a marker:

- A plus sign indicates that the topic has subtopics under it.

- A minus sign means the topic has no subtopics.

- A box indicates that the topic is body text.

You can use the toolbar to change a topic's level within the outline, to move topics up or down to reorganize the information, and to focus on certain topics by hiding others.

NOTE

If you simply want to see the general organization of your document or navigate from one heading to another, you can display your document's contents as an outline by using the Document Map, as explained on page 113 in Chapter 5.

The Outlining Toolbar

Whenever you switch to Outline view, you see the Outlining toolbar at the top of the document window, as shown in Figure 12-2.

FIGURE 12-2.

The Outlining toolbar.

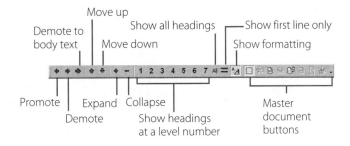

SEE ALSO

The right end of the Outlining toolbar contains buttons for use with master documents. For more information about using master documents, see Chapter 24, "Using Master Documents."

You can use this toolbar to control how text is displayed in the outline and to promote, demote, or rearrange topics, as explained later in this chapter.

How Word Creates Outline View

What you see in Outline view depends on how you have formatted the headings in your document. Word recognizes only its own built-in Heading styles (Heading 1, Heading 2, and so on) when assigning different outline levels. Word uses Heading style numbers to set the organizational level for each heading, indenting each lower-level heading 0.5 inch to the right of the level above it, as in Figure 12-1.

To make the most of Outline view, format all of your document's headings and subheadings by applying one of the Heading styles on the Style menu. Each heading has its own format characteristics. In Figure 12-1, for example, Heading 1 is 16-point Times New Roman bold, Heading 2 is 14-point Times New Roman bold italic, and Heading 3 is 12-point Times New Roman bold.

Heading styles make it easy to see each heading's importance relative to the other headings and text. If you don't use Word's Heading styles, Word will treat everything in your document as text, and all of it will appear at the same outline level, as in Figure 12-3 on the next page.

II

Writing and Editing Tools

FIGURE 12-3.

If you don't use Word's built-in Heading styles for the headings in your document, everything will be shown at one level in Outline view.

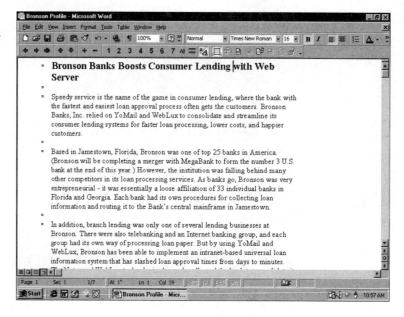

Turning a Document into an Outline

If you want to work with an existing document in Outline view, you'll need to apply Heading styles to all of its headings and subheadings. To apply them:

1 Select the first top-level heading in your document.

2 Choose the Heading 1 style from the Style menu on the Formatting toolbar.

3 Double-click the Format Painter button on the Standard toolbar. Double-clicking the button locks it so you can paste a copied format to several places by simply clicking them one after the other. *See "Copying Paragraph Formats" on page 98 for more on this tool.*

> Instead of clicking the Format Painter button to copy and paste formats, you can press Ctrl+Shift+C to copy a format and Ctrl+Shift+V to paste it.

4 Click each of the other top-level headings in your document.

5 Click the Format Painter tool to turn it off.

Repeat this process for the other heading levels in your document.

Changing the Format of Heading Styles

SEE ALSO

For more information about the Style dialog box, see Chapter 15, "Using Styles and Themes." To learn how to change an outline's numbering style, see "Creating Bulleted and Numbered Lists" on page 273.

Unless you've modified the default Heading styles in your document, they're formatted with the paragraph and character formats that were preset when you installed Word. However, you're not stuck with those formats. You can modify the Heading styles to display text in a different size, indentation level, style, font, or with other attributes by making changes to the style in the Style dialog box.

Hiding Outline Formatting

The large bold type of outline levels makes it hard to look at them for a long time. If you spend lots of time in Outline view, you can display the outline without any special heading formatting at all. Just click the Show Formatting button on the Outline toolbar. This button is a toggle; click it again to reveal heading formatting.

Starting an Outline from Scratch

When you're beginning a document, you can use Outline view to organize your thoughts. To do this:

1 Open a new Word document.

2 Choose Outline from the View Menu.

3 Enter the text for the first topic. This first topic will be formatted with the Heading 1 style.

4 Press Enter and type the second topic or subtopic. This topic will also be given the Heading 1 style, but you can change its position by applying a different Heading style to it or by promoting or demoting the outline level.

5 Continue adding and rearranging headings and text.

SEE ALSO

For information about zooming documents, see "Zooming In or Out of Documents" on page 119.

Outline view normally presents paragraphs of text in smaller type. If you find this text hard to edit, you can zoom in or out of the screen to make everything bigger or switch to Normal or Print Layout view when you want to focus on text in paragraphs rather than on headings.

II

Writing and Editing Tools

Split the Screen to See Your Document in Different Views

Outline view is best for showing your document's organization and allowing you to change it easily, while Web Layout and Print Layout views are best for showing how a document's contents will look on a page. Fortunately, you can split the document window to use Outline view and another view at the same time.

1 Drag the split box from above the vertical scroll bar down into your document or choose Split from the Window menu to divide the screen window.

2 Click in one window pane.

3 Choose Outline from the View menu. The pane changes to Outline view.

4 Click in the other window pane and, if necessary, switch to Normal, Web Layout, or Print Layout view. The document now looks like this:

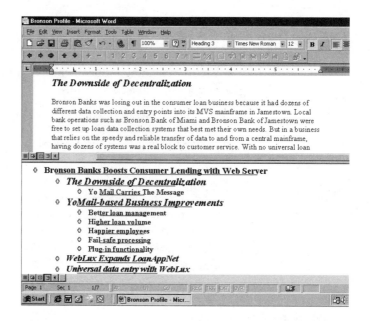

5 Drag the window pane to adjust pane sizes, if necessary.

With a split window showing both Outline view and another view, you can simultaneously reorganize your document and see how it affects the text layout.

Reorganizing Outlines

You can reorganize an outline (and thereby reorganize your document) quickly and easily in Outline view.

- Promote or demote a heading or body text paragraph, raising it or lowering it one level in the outline.

- Rearrange one or more topics or paragraphs by moving them up or down in the outline while keeping them at the same level.

Whenever you move a topic, all the subtopics underneath it move as well.

Dragging Topics

If you're reorganizing an outline extensively, the simplest way to do it is to drag topic markers with the mouse. You can drag topics or body text paragraphs up or down to rearrange the flow of information in your document or drag topics to the left or right to promote or demote them.

When you drag a topic up or down in the outline, you'll see a line that shows where the topic will be inserted when you release the mouse button, like this:

Body text paragraphs are topics, too, so you can rearrange them by dragging their topic markers.

When you drag a topic left or right to promote or demote it, you'll see a ghost topic marker at the new level to which you drag, like this:

You can promote or demote any topic, including body text paragraphs.

Writing and Editing Tools

Moving Topics with the Outlining Toolbar

You can also move outline topics with buttons on the Outlining toolbar, as shown in Figure 12-2 on page 239. First, select the topic you want to move by clicking it, and then click the Promote, Demote, Demote To Body Text, Move Up, or Move Down buttons on the Outlining toolbar.

Moving Topics with the Keyboard

If you're entering outline topics as you go, you can promote or demote them with keyboard shortcuts as well. When the insertion point is in a topic, you can demote it by pressing the Tab key or promote it by pressing Shift+Tab.

Sorting Outline Topics

In some cases you'll want the topics or subtopics in a document to be arranged in alphabetical order. You can't sort the headings in another view, because Word will try to sort every paragraph, whether it's a heading or not. But in Outline view you can sort on one heading level at a time.

Word sorts on the highest level headings in the outline portion you select, and any subheadings under the sorted ones move with them. So, for example, if you select a portion of the outline containing only level 3 and 4 headings, Word will sort the level 3 headings, and the level 4 headings under them will go along for the ride.

1   Select the portion of the outline containing the group of topics or subtopics you want to alphabetize.

2   Choose Sort from the Table menu. You'll see the Sort Text dialog box as shown in Figure 12-4.

FIGURE 12-4.

Use the Sort command on the Table menu to quickly sort a group of outline topics.

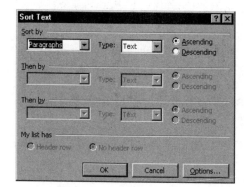

3 Click the Ascending or Descending button to choose the sort order.

4 Click OK to sort the topics.

 TIP

> To sort a group of subtopics under a particular topic, select only those sub-topics and then sort them.

Hiding or Showing Parts of Outlines

When you view an outline, you may want to focus on the topic headings at a certain level only. For example, there might be dozens and dozens of third-level or fourth-level topics, but you may want to view only the level 1 and 2 topics for awhile so you can see more of them on the screen at once. Word makes it easy to zero in on a certain topic level by allowing you to collapse individual topics or limit the outline view to a certain topic level.

Expanding and Collapsing Topics

When a topic has subtopics underneath it, the topic marker is a plus sign, as in Figure 12-1 on page 238. Many of these topics are collapsed to show only the topic label without the subtopics or text under it.

To hide subtopics underneath a topic (or collapse the topic), double-click the topic marker or select the topic and then click the Collapse button on the Outlining toolbar.

? SEE ALSO

For more information about using tables, see Chapter 17, "Working with Tables."

Rearrange Tables in Outline View

Outline view makes it easy to rearrange rows contained in tables. When you display a table in Outline view, Word converts each row to a topic, like this:

Topic marker

◇ *Third Quarter Sales Contest Winners*

Division	Sales Rep	Sales Total
Explosives	Buck Brawley	$194,577
Shrimp	Ginny Calandini	$424,603
Salmon	Horst Heitzinger	$897,335
Auto	June Thomas	$124,417
Home & Garden	Lamont Russell	$756,310

To rearrange any row, just drag its topic marker up or down or select a row and click the Move Up or Move Down button on the Outline toolbar.

Writing and Editing Tools

II

To reveal subtopics underneath a topic (or expand the topic), double-click the topic marker or select the topic and then click the Expand button on the Outlining toolbar.

Limiting the Topic Level

You can also limit the number of topic levels you can see in an outline so all topics below a certain level are hidden. To hide outline levels, click one of the level number buttons on the Outlining toolbar. This is useful when you have dozens of relatively minor topics in an outline and you want to focus on viewing or organizing the main points.

For example, to hide everything below level 2 in the outline in Figure 12-1, you would click the 2 button on the Outlining toolbar. The outline would then look like this:

- *Bronson Banks Boosts Consumer Lending With Web Server*
    - *The Downside of Decentralization*
    - *YoMail-based Business Improvements*
    - *WebLux Expands LoanAppNet*
    - *Universal data entry with WebLux*
    - *Functionality becomes a product*

Notice that the Show Level 2 button is highlighted on the Outlining toolbar. You can gradually expand the entire outline this way, by successively clicking the 3, 4, and higher level buttons on the toolbar. To display all topic levels, click the All button.

Hiding Topic Text

Finally, you can also limit each topic so that only its first line of text is displayed. This is handy when topics contain whole paragraphs of text. To display only the first line of text in each topic, click the Show First Line Only button on the Outlining toolbar. Levels with body text below them will look like this (compare this with the same headings as shown in Figure 12-1 on page 238):

- *YoMail-based Business Improvements*
    - **Better loan management**
        - By routing all loan data through the Notes databases, Bronson ...
    - **Higher loan volume**
        - By cutting the data entry time for applications from 8 minutes to ...
    - **Happier employees**
        - Loan processing employees were very happy with the new ...
    - **Fail-safe processing**
        - Loans that once took as many as several days to approve can ...
    - **Plug-in functionality**
        - The streamlined loan information system cut millions of dollars ...

Hiding Topic Formatting

When you view an outline, Word normally displays the formatting you set for text and headings as it appears in other document views, as shown in Figure 12-1. To hide the formatting, click the Show Formatting tool on the Outlining toolbar. The outline will look like this:

```
⊕  Bronson Banks Boosts Consumer Lending with Web Server
        ⊕  The Downside of Decentralization
                ⊕  Yo Mail Carries The Message
        ⊕  YoMail-based Business Improvements
                ⊕  Better loan management
                        ▫  By routing all loan data through the Notes databases, Bronson ...
                ⊕  Higher loan volume
                        ▫  By cutting the data entry time for applications from 8 minutes to ...
                ⊕  Happier employees
                        ▫  Loan processing employees were very happy with the new ...
                ⊕  Fail-safe processing
                        ▫  Loans that once took as many as several days to approve can ...
                ⊕  Plug-in functionality
                        ▫  The streamlined loan information system cut millions of dollars ...
        ⊕  WebLux Expands LoanAppNet
        ⊕  Universal data entry with WebLux
        ⊕  Functionality becomes a product
```

Special Uses for Heading Styles

Outline view is a great tool to use when you want to plan a document's organization from scratch or change its organization later. But Word also makes special use of Heading styles you use in outlines in other situations:

■ **The Document Map** When you display the Document Map (by choosing Document Map from the View menu), Word shows only headings that have been formatted with Heading styles.

■ **Master documents and subdocuments** When you create a master document, Word automatically switches to Outline view. In order to be included, each subdocument you add must have its first line formatted with the Heading 1 style.

■ **Web page navigation frames** When you add a Table of Contents frame to a Web page, Word automatically copies all of the document's Heading style headings into the frame as hyperlinks.

■ **Tables of contents** When you create a table of contents, Word uses Heading styles to determine how to indent entries in the Table of Contents it creates.

Using Templates and Wizards

Y ou don't always have to do all of the editing and formatting work from scratch when you create a new document with Microsoft Word. Templates and wizards help you do more and get better results more quickly by creating new documents that already contain special text, formatting, custom toolbars, macros, or other elements. In this chapter you'll learn more about using Word's templates and wizards.

Using Templates

Word comes with dozens of predefined templates for different kinds of documents. When you choose New from the File menu to make a new document, the New dialog box shows the predefined templates in eight different categories. Figure 13-1 shows the Letters & Faxes category.

FIGURE 13-1.

Click the tabs in the New dialog box to see and use templates for many different kinds of documents.

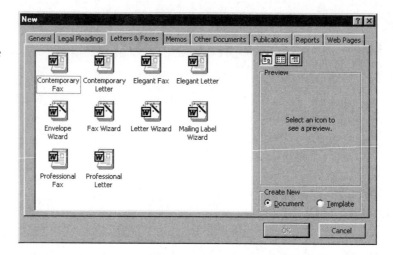

Most of the other predefined templates contain formatted text as well, such as headings and graphics for faxes, memos, letters, and other types of documents. However, even templates that create a blank document—such as the Blank Document and Web Page templates on the General tab in the New dialog box—contain custom format styles or other information. You may like and use Word's predefined templates, but if you're like most Word users, you'll want to modify these templates or create new templates of your own.

 NOTE

> The Blank Document icon you see on the General tab of the New dialog box is actually named Normal.dot. This is the name that appears on template menus and in the folder C:\Windows\Application Data\Microsoft\Templates.

For more information about using templates for formatting, see Chapter 18, "Formatting Automatically."

Exploring the Templates

You'll naturally want to see what each template looks like before deciding whether it can help you make the document you want. You can preview most of Word's document templates in the New dialog box:

1 Choose New from the File menu.

2 Select a template. You'll see a preview at the right side of the dialog box.

If a document template was not installed when you installed Word, you'll see a note in the Preview area asking if you want to install it. Insert the Microsoft Office CD-ROM and click OK to install it. If you installed Office from a network and you have permission to install other Office features, just click OK.

To better see the details of a particular template, open it as a document.

 ## Previewing Templates in the Style Gallery

The Preview box in the New dialog box is pretty small, and it can be tedious to open each document template to see how it really looks. You can get a somewhat larger view of a template in the Style Gallery dialog box. To open the Style Gallery:

1 Choose Theme from the Format menu.

2 Click the Style Gallery button at the bottom of the Theme dialog box. You'll see the Style Gallery dialog box, as shown in Figure 13-2 on the next page.

3 In the list of templates at the left, select the template you want to view. If the template is installed, you'll see a preview of the current document formatted with that template in the Preview area at the right, as in Figure 13-2. If the template is not installed, you'll see a message saying so at the top of the Preview box, and you can click the OK button to install it.

4 If you would prefer to preview the template with a generic document sample or to see how each of the template's styles will look, click the Example or Style Samples button below the list of templates.

 TIP

If a template doesn't have an example, click the Style button to view its styles, or open a document and then return to the Style Gallery dialog box to preview that document as formatted with a particular template.

FIGURE 13-2.

Use the Style
Gallery to see a larger
preview of each
template, or to see
how its styles will look
when applied to your
document.

Choose a template.

Select a view.

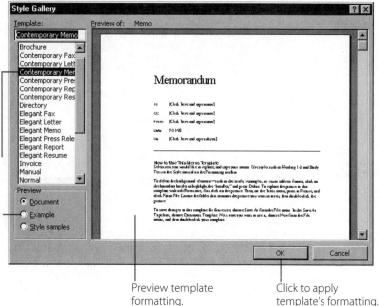

Preview template
formatting.

Click to apply
template's formatting.

Where and How
Templates Are Stored

? SEE ALSO

For more information
about the Document
Template file type, see
"How Word Handles
Documents" on
page 134.

You can turn any document into a template by saving it in the Document Template (.dot) format. Technically, you can store a template anywhere, but Word uses two specific folders as storage locations for the predesigned templates that appear on the tabs in the New dialog box.

■ The 1033 folder, stored at C:\Program Files\Microsoft Office\ Templates\1033, is where Office stores its predesigned templates.

■ The Templates folder, stored at C:\Windows\Application Data\ Microsoft\Templates, is where you'll find the Normal.dot template, and is the default location Word uses to store your custom templates.

Storing New Templates

When you save new templates that you create, you can store them anywhere you like, but you will probably want to save them so they appear in the New dialog box.

To save a template so it appears on the General tab in the New dialog box, save it inside the Templates folder (C:\Windows\Application Data\ Microsoft\Templates). The template will automatically appear on the General tab in the New dialog box.

To save a template so it appears on one of the other existing tabs in the New dialog box, follow these steps:

1   Create the template and save it anywhere on your disk.

2   Choose New from the File menu to open the New dialog box.

3   Click the tab where you want to store the new template.

4   Click the Show Desktop button in the Windows taskbar to return to your desktop, and then open the folder that contains the new template you want to store.

5   Resize the folder so it occupies a small area of the screen, and drag it to one of the corners of the desktop.

6   Click the Word button in the Windows taskbar to reactivate Word. The New dialog box should still be open with the tab you selected still open inside it.

7   In the Windows taskbar, click the button for the folder you just resized. The folder will appear, and the New dialog box will still be on the screen.

8   Select your new custom template, drag it onto the tab in Word's New dialog box, and then release the mouse button. Windows will create a shortcut for your new template on the tab in the New dialog box.

Making New Tabs in the New Dialog Box

If you want to reorganize your custom templates, you can add new tabs to the New dialog box. To add a new tab to the New dialog box, follow these steps:

1   Open the Templates folder (C:\Windows\Application Data\ Microsoft\Templates) on your hard disk.

2   Choose Folder from the New submenu on the File menu to create a new folder inside the Templates folder.

3   Rename the folder as you'd like it to appear in the New dialog box.

4 Save at least one template inside the folder you just created. The folder will now appear as a new tab in the New dialog box, and the template you saved inside it will appear on that tab. You can save other templates to the folder and so add them to the tab if you like.

> If you are saving a template and you want to place it on a new tab in the New dialog box at the same time, choose the Save command so Word navigates automatically to the Templates folder, and then click the New Folder button at the top of the Save As dialog box to make a new folder inside the Templates folder. After you name it, the new folder will then be selected as the save destination, and you can simply click Save to store the template inside it. The new folder will then appear as a tab in the New dialog box.

To remove a custom tab from the New dialog box, delete its folder.

Creating a New Document from a Template

To create a new document from any template:

1 Choose New from the File menu. Word displays the New dialog box and shows templates in the General category, as in Figure 13-1 on page 250.

2 Click a tab to display templates from another category, if you like.

3 Double-click the template you want. You'll open a new document based on that template.

> Some tabs in the New dialog box also show Wizards. *See "Using Wizards" on page 260 for more information about wizards.*

Opening a Template File

Rather than creating a new document from a template, you can instead open a template *as* a template so you can modify it. There are two ways to do this:

- Choose Open from the File menu, choose Document Templates as the file type, and then navigate to and open the template file.

- Choose New from the File menu, select a template, click the Template button in the lower-right corner of the New dialog box, and click OK.

When you open a template as a template, you must save it as a template. When you choose the Save command, you'll see the Save As dialog box with the file type locked as Document Template, like this:

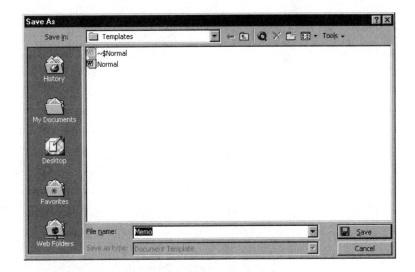

Modifying Templates

A template gives you a head start when you make a new document, but it's only a start. Once you open a new document, you'll want to change it by adding text, adjusting formatting, or making other modifications.

Most of the predefined templates in Word include headings and formatting for a particular type of document, along with instructional text. For example, suppose you open the Contemporary Memo template on the Memos tab. The new document looks like the one in Figure 13-3 on the next page.

When you use a template that includes heading text and formatting and you want to save it as a Word document, scroll through the entire document to make sure all of the instructional text and unwanted formatting is gone before you save or print it. Also, choose Header And Footer from the View menu to see and modify any standard header or footer text included in that template. *See "Using Headers and Footers" on page 320 for more information about headers and footers.*

II

Writing and Editing Tools

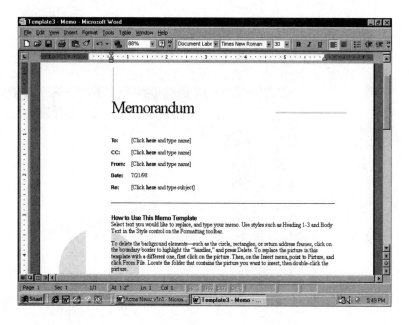

This template contains formatting and subheads for a memo, so all you have to do is to select the sample or instructional text in the appropriate areas and then replace it with the information you want this particular memo to contain. You can also change the formatting of headings or other items.

To save the modified template as a new Word document, follow these steps:

1 Press Ctrl+S or choose Save As from the File menu to display the Save As dialog box.

2 Name the document.

3 Choose Word Document as the file type.

4 Click Save.

Saving a Modified Template

When you're finished modifying a document based on a template and you want to save the changes as a template file, you have two choices:

- Replace the original template by saving it with the same name and the Document Template file type.

- Create a new template by giving the file a new name and choosing the Document Template file type.

Whenever you choose the Document Template file type in the Save As dialog box, Word automatically navigates to the Templates folder so you can save the template in the proper location.

 TIP

You can use templates to standardize company publications, and you can copy format styles or custom menus, toolbars, or keyboard shortcuts from one template to another. *See "Transferring Styles among Templates," on page 310.*

Template Ideas

You can make and use templates for all sorts of purposes. Here are some ideas to get you thinking.

- Create a company document template like the Blank Document template on the General tab and store custom format styles, keyboard shortcuts, or macros in it to enforce a standard company document style. Place it in the Templates folder on your network server or distribute the template file to others in your company with instructions about where to place it in the Templates folders on their hard disks.

- Make a custom letter or fax template for a person or company to whom you frequently send letters or faxes. You'll save typing because the person or company name and contact information will appear in every new document.

- Create different templates that store only custom format styles, keyboard shortcuts, menus or toolbars for various projects. By customizing menus, toolbars, and commands, you can create the optimum Word environment for each type of project.

- Use templates to standardize formatting of complex documents such as newsletters or books.

When you find yourself typing the same information or making the same format modifications repeatedly in your documents, create a template to expedite your work in future documents.

II

Writing and Editing Tools

Activating Additional Templates

Although you create a document from a single template, you can activate additional templates for that document once the document is open. Individual templates are a very handy place to store custom toolbar or menu settings, macros, or styles, and you may want to activate a second or third template for a document in order to gain access to the additional custom settings, macros, or styles stored there.

There are two ways to use other templates in a document:

- Attach a different template, which adds another template's information to the current document.

- Load a template, which makes the template's features available to the document during the current editing session without actually adding it to the document.

WARNING

> When you attach a template, you replace any custom styles, macros, menus, toolbars, or shortcuts that were in the original document template. If you don't want to replace the current template's features, load a template instead of attaching it.

Attaching a Template

Attach a template to a document when you want to use a particular template's styles, macros, AutoText entries, or other items and you don't care about replacing the features of the existing template. This is typically the situation when you begin a document using the Normal template, as it doesn't have any custom settings stored in it. To attach a template, follow these steps:

1 Open the document with which you want to work.

2 Choose Templates And Add-Ins from the Tools menu. Word will open the Templates And Add-Ins dialog box as shown in Figure 13-4 on the next page.

3 Click the Attach button. You'll see the Attach Template dialog box where you can select the template you want to attach.

4 Select the template you want to attach and click the Open button. Word attaches the template to the document, returns you to the Templates And Add-Ins dialog box, and replaces the old document template's name with the one you just selected.

FIGURE 13-4.

Use the Templates And Add-Ins command on the Tools menu to attach a different template to the active document.

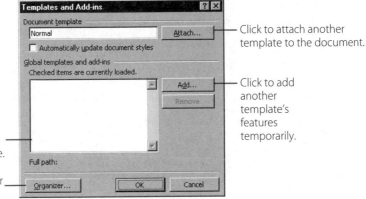

Click to attach another template to the document.

Click to add another template's features temporarily.

Added template names appear here.

Click to view styles or other information in a template.

5 Select the Automatically Update Document Styles check box if you want the new template's styles to replace those in the active document each time the document is opened.

6 Click OK to apply the new template and close the dialog box.

TIP

To see which styles, macros, AutoText entries, or custom toolbars are in the new template you're about to attach, click the Organizer button and look in the left-hand list. *For more information about the Organizer, see "Transferring Styles Among Templates" on page 310, or "Copying Macros From One Template To Another" on page 659.*

Loading a Template

When you load a template, you temporarily make its features available to the current document. You can add many different templates to a list in the Templates And Add-Ins dialog box and then select only the one(s) you want for each document-editing session:

1 Open the document with which you want to work.

2 Choose Templates And Add-Ins from the Tools menu. Word opens the Templates And Add-Ins dialog box as shown in Figure 13-4.

3 Click the Add button. You'll see the Add Template dialog box where you can select a template to add to the list at the left.

4 Locate the template you want to add, and then click the OK button. Word returns you to the Templates And Add-Ins dialog box, and the added template now appears in the list, as shown in the figure on the following page.

II

Writing and Editing Tools

Because you just added the template, its check box is already selected, so the template's features are available to the current document.

5 Click the OK button to close the dialog box.

When you want to load other templates and make their features available to the current document, repeat the procedure above. You can disable a template's features in the current document by clearing the check box next to it in the Templates And Add-Ins dialog box.

> When you load a template, its features are only loaded for the current document session.

Using Wizards

Wizards use templates to create new documents, but they make your job even easier by designing and formatting complete documents for you. Wizards are great when you know you want a certain type of document but need a lot of help in designing it.

When you use a wizard, you use a series of dialog boxes to choose options, and thereby supply information that Word needs to create the document. The Assistant may even get involved at the beginning. After you supply the information, Word creates the document for you. You'll find wizards for many kinds of documents on the tabs in the New dialog box.

Activating a Wizard

To activate a wizard, open it as you would a template in the New dialog box:

1   Choose New from the File menu.

2   Click a tab in the New dialog box to show the wizard you want.

3   Double-click the wizard. If you open the Memo Wizard on the Memos tab in the Open dialog box, for example, you'll see the wizard shown in Figure 13-5.

FIGURE 13-5.
Document wizards create new documents to your specifications by asking you questions.

4   Click the Next button. You'll see the first group of questions, like this:

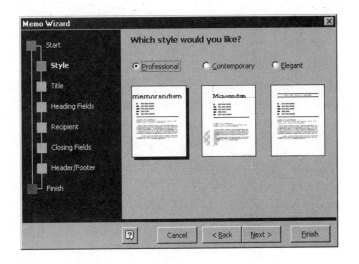

5 Choose a memo format and click the Next button.

6 Choose options and enter information in the following dialog boxes as you work through the wizard, clicking the Next button when you're finished choosing options or entering information.

7 Click the Finish button after you complete the final group of options. The wizard creates the document, as shown in Figure 13-6:

FIGURE 13-6.

When you use a Wizard, Word frequently displays the Assistant with the new document to give you some advice about what to do next.

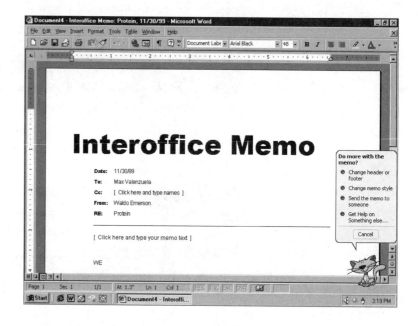

> **NOTE**
>
> Figure 13-6 shows another of Word's Office Assistant Characters. This one is called Links.

You must still enter the text in the body of your letter, but virtually everything else has been done for you. If you're using the Assistant, it offers help about changing the document in various ways.

Exploring Wizards

Investigate the other wizards on your own to see how they work. Try opening different wizards and navigating through their dialog boxes. You can always close the wizard dialog box by clicking the Cancel button. If the wizard has already created a new document, simply close the document without saving it.

Getting More Templates and Wizards

Microsoft periodically comes up with new templates and wizards and makes them available on its Office On The Web Internet site. In addition, you may not have installed all the available wizards and templates when you installed Word on your system.

ON THE WEB

To get more templates from Microsoft, you can follow the steps below:

1 Choose Office On The Web from the Help menu. Word will open your Web browser and navigate to the Microsoft Office Web site.

2 Look for the page that offers templates and other add-ins.

3 Locate the template you want and download it.

NOTE

You must have Internet access to access Microsoft's Web site and download files from it. *For more information about navigating to a Web address or getting files from the Web, see Chapter 31, "Using Word to Access the Internet."*

Writing and Editing Tools

PART III

Formatting Tools

CHAPTER 14

Formatting Special Characters and Paragraphs

When you want to add special touches such as symbols, numbered lists, or line numbers to your documents, Microsoft Word makes it easy with a suite of tools. In this chapter you'll learn more about using fonts and how to format characters and paragraphs in special situations.

Using Fonts

When you format characters with Word, you can choose from dozens of fonts to create different moods for your documents. Some fonts, such as Times New Roman or Arial, are very businesslike, while others, such as Ransom, Braggadocio, or Playbill, are more whimsical. Word makes use of all the fonts available in Microsoft Windows.

Fonts have been around for centuries, and there are thousands of them available for use in Windows. In addition to the font collection that comes with Windows, Word adds a few new fonts of its own when you install it. If you don't like your selection of fonts, you can add new ones (*see "Adding and Removing Fonts" later in this chapter*).

 ## Viewing Installed Fonts

When you're using Word, the easiest way to see which fonts are available is to examine the Font menu in the Formatting toolbar. It lists every available font, as shown in Figure 14-1.

FIGURE 14-1.

Word 2000's new Font menu shows fonts as they will appear in a document and identifies each font as a TrueType or printer font.

You can also view fonts by choosing Font from the Format menu, selecting a font from the list, and checking the Preview box at the bottom of the Font dialog box.

TrueType Fonts vs. Printer Fonts

Most of the fonts you'll use in Word are TrueType fonts, which means that the format options you see on your screen will be accurately sized, styled, and spaced when text is printed. If you use a printer font, however, what you see on your screen is an approximation; the spacing of characters may be slightly different on your printer. Each font's type is shown as an icon next to it in the Font menu or in text below the Preview area in the Font dialog box.

NOTE

If you have Adobe Type Manager installed on your computer and you're using Type1 printer fonts, those fonts will be represented accurately on your screen.

Font Families

 SEE ALSO

For more information about applying bold, italic, and other character styles, see "Formatting Characters" on page 77.

As explained in Chapter 4, "Editing Text," you can use any of Word's character formatting options to make text bold, underlined, or italic, or to apply other styles. However, most of the fonts you use belong to families. When you choose the Arial font and make text italic, for example, Word actually uses the Arial Italic font stored in Windows' Fonts folder. In addition, you can select more highly styled members of some font families right from Word's Font menu. For example, in addition to the standard Arial font, you'll see Arial Black, Arial Rounded, and Arial Narrow.

 TIP

For most normal word processing tasks, you'll be fine using a single font and then modifying its look with Word's character styles. If you're producing documents for publication on high-quality printers, however, you'll get sharper results by using font family members for extra bold, condensed, or other effects.

Monospace vs. Proportionally Spaced Fonts

The font selection includes both monospace and proportionally spaced fonts. In a monospace font like Courier, each character in the font occupies the same amount of horizontal space on the line. In a proportionally spaced font like Arial, Bookman, or Times New Roman, "I" characters take up less horizontal space than "M" characters. Figure 14-2 shows the difference.

FIGURE 14-2.

Proportionally spaced and monospace fonts.

Bookman Old Style is a proportionally spaced font –
characters like t, l, or i take up less space than
characters like m, o, or p.

Courier New is a monospaced font – each
character occupies the same amount of
space on a line.

Normally, your documents will look best when you use proportionally spaced fonts, and most of the fonts in Windows are proportionally spaced. But if you're printing text onto a preprinted form, it's better to use a monospace font. Preprinted forms were designed for typewriters,

III

Formatting Tools

and most typewriters produce monospace characters, so you'll have a better chance of matching your printed text to the spaces on a pre-printed form if you use a monospace font.

Adding and Removing Fonts

Each font available in Word is a file stored inside the Fonts folder, which is inside the Windows folder on your hard disk, as in Figure 14-3.

FIGURE 14-3.

Every font available in Word is stored in the C:\Windows\Fonts folder on your hard disk.

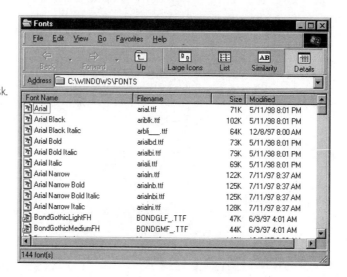

You can buy new fonts from many different sources, and there are also lots of fonts available for free or nearly free from user groups or the Internet. Microsoft also offers free fonts on its Web site.

NOTE

Your Fonts folder may contain different fonts than the ones shown in Figure 14-3.

ON THE WEB

Go to *http://www.microsoft.com/typography* for more information about new fonts and utilities available from Microsoft.

To install a new font, close Word and every other application and then copy the font file(s) into the Fonts folder. Word scans the Fonts folder every time you start it up, so any changes in the Fonts folder will register when you restart Word.

To remove a font, just drag it outside the Fonts folder or delete it. Be careful when removing fonts, though. Most fonts are there for a reason—either because they're used for dialog boxes and other text in Windows, Microsoft Office, Microsoft Internet Explorer, or other programs or because they're used in some of the styles and themes in Word.

TIP

By dragging a font outside of the Fonts folder you make it unavailable without deleting it. You may want to create one or more folders to store extra fonts on your disk so you can add or remove them easily by dragging them to or from the Fonts folder.

If you have removed a font that is used in a style or theme, you'll see a message when you try to use that style or theme and you'll be able to substitute another font. However, if you remove a font required by Word itself, you may not be able to read text in dialog boxes or menus.

WARNING

The fonts required to run Word, Windows, and Internet Explorer are Arial, Courier, Marlett, Times New Roman, Tahoma, Verdana, and Wingdings. To be on the safe side, don't remove any of these fonts or font family members.

Creating a Drop Cap

A drop cap (short for "dropped capital letter") is a popular design element used to begin text in a newsletter, magazine article, book chapter, or other publication. Each chapter in this book begins with a drop cap. It's easy to create drop caps with Word:

1 Make sure you're in Print Layout view. Word can display a drop cap in Normal view, but you must be in Print Layout view to see the drop cap in position.

2 Click anywhere in the paragraph where you want to create the drop cap. (Word makes the first character in the selected paragraph into a drop cap.)

3 Choose Drop Cap from the Format menu. Word displays the Drop Cap dialog box, as shown in Figure 14-4 on the next page.

III

Formatting Tools

FIGURE 14-4.

The Drop Cap dialog box makes it easy to create a drop cap and control its position.

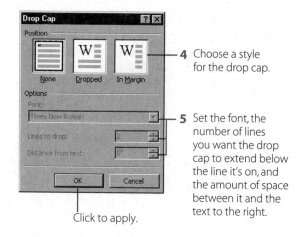

4 Choose a style for the drop cap.

5 Set the font, the number of lines you want the drop cap to extend below the line it's on, and the amount of space between it and the text to the right.

Click to apply.

6 Click OK. You'll see the drop cap like this:

In the beginning, George wanted a Pekinese or Pomeranian, but he ended up settling for a Mastiff.

SEE ALSO

For more information about creating and using frames, see "Converting a Text Box to a Frame" on page 441, or "Choosing a Text Entry Method" on page 527.

When Word creates a drop cap, it cuts the selected character from your line of text, creates a text frame, and inserts an enlarged version of the character inside the frame.

Moving and Resizing a Drop Cap

If Word has made your drop cap character too large or the spacing between it and other characters is wrong, you have several ways to change things:

- Drag one of the frame's selection handles to resize the drop cap character and its frame at the same time.

- Drag the frame's border to move it closer to or farther from other text.

- Select the character inside the frame and choose another font size for it.

- Select the frame or character, choose Drop Cap from the Format menu again, and then change the Lines To Drop or Distance From Text settings.

Viewing Character and Paragraph Formats

You can often tell in a general way how text is formatted by checking the status of the Formatting toolbar or the Ruler when the text in question is selected, but there's another way to view this information and see more details.

1   Scroll through your document until the text you want to know about is visible.

2   Choose What's This? from the Help menu. The pointer changes to a question mark.

3   Click the character or paragraph whose format options you want to view. Word displays a screen balloon with the formatting information, as seen in Figure 14-5.

FIGURE 14-5.

When you click the What's This? pointer on text in your document, you see details about the formatting options set for it.

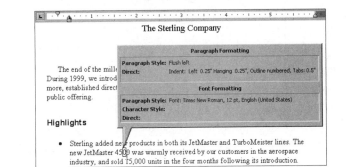

4   Press Esc to put the balloon away.

Creating Bulleted and Numbered Lists

Bulleted and numbered lists make your documents more readable by setting off key points or numbered steps. (Bullets are nonnumerical symbols that introduce the items in a list):

Acme sales increases during the last quarter were primarily due to outstanding performance by three divisions:

- Auto Products
- Salmon
- Shrimp

Steps to Success

1. Do your best.
2. Ask for help when you need it.
3. Don't take anything too seriously.

You can insert bullets or numbers anywhere in your document without resorting to special formatting, but when you want to create a whole

III

Formatting Tools

SEE ALSO

For more information
about using individual
bullet symbols any-
where in your text, see
"Inserting Symbols
and Special Charac-
ters" on page 221.

list of bulleted or numbered items, it's much easier to use Word's auto-matic bullet formatting option. You can choose a variety of bullet and number formats or create custom formats of your own. When you use a numbered list format, Word numbers items consecutively and adjusts the numbering when you rearrange or delete list items.

There are three ways to create bulleted or numbered lists:

- Create them as you type by taking advantage of Word's AutoFormat feature.

- Click the Bullets or Numbering button on the Formatting toolbar.

- Choose Bullets And Numbering from the Format menu to apply or change a bullet or number format.

 SEE ALSO

For more information
about creating para-
graph styles, see
"Defining Styles" on
page 303.

Bullets, Numbers, and Styles

While bullets or numbers are paragraph formatting options, they can be treated as enhancements to a paragraph style, rather than as a part of the style. If you apply bullets to an existing paragraph, it won't change the style defined for that paragraph.

If you use bullets and numbers a lot, however, you can create paragraph styles that include bullet or numbered list formatting so the bullets or numbers will always be applied when you choose that style.

Creating Bulleted or Numbered Lists as You Type

 SEE ALSO

For more information
about AutoFormat, see
"Using AutoFormat" on
page 380.

The simplest way to create a bulleted or numbered list is to begin one as you type. Word has predefined AutoFormat rules that recognize certain characters at the beginning of a paragraph as a signal to begin a bulleted or numbered list. To start a bulleted or numbered list as you type, follow these steps:

1 Move the insertion point to the beginning of the first line in the list.

2 Type * (Shift+8) to begin a bulleted list or a number followed by a period (such as "1.") to begin a numbered list.

3 Press the spacebar and then type the text of the first list item.

4 Press Enter to end the paragraph. Word recognizes the leading characters, turns the paragraph into a bulleted or numbered item, and begins another bulleted item in the paragraph below. The second line in a numbered list would look like this:

1. Stick porcupine quills in the microwave and heat on Medium for three minutes.
2. |

For information about discontinuing a bulleted or numbered list, see "Ending a List" on page 278.

5 Enter the text for the next list item and press Enter.

You can create as many bulleted or numbered items as you like, one after the other, by simply pressing Enter at the end of each item.

> If you don't want Word to begin a bulleted or numbered list when you type an asterisk or a number at the beginning of a line, you can change its AutoFormat rules. *See "Setting AutoFormat As You Type Options" on page 380.*

Using the Bullets and Numbering Buttons

Another way to add a bullet or number to a paragraph is to click either the Bullets or Numbering button on the Formatting toolbar. Just click in a paragraph and then choose either the Bullets or Numbering button.

When a bulleted or numbered paragraph is selected, either the Bullets or Numbering button is highlighted in the Formatting toolbar. To remove bullet or number formatting from a paragraph, click the highlighted Bullets or Numbering button.

Using the Bullets And Numbering Dialog Box

When you use AutoFormat or the Bullets or Numbering buttons, Word adds a particular style of bullet or number to a paragraph. With the Bullets And Numbering dialog box, you can choose from other predefined bullet or number formats or you can create new ones of your own. You can also use the Bullets And Numbering dialog box to change the format of existing bullets or numbers or to add a bullet or number to a paragraph that doesn't have one.

III

Formatting Tools

Creating Bulleted or Numbered Lists

To apply a bullet or number format, follow these steps:

1   Move the insertion point to the paragraph you want bulleted.

2   Choose Bullets And Numbering from the Format menu. You'll see the Bullets And Numbering dialog box as in Figure 14-6.

FIGURE 14-6.

With the Bullets and Numbering dialog box, you can add, remove, or customize bullet and numbered list paragraph formats.

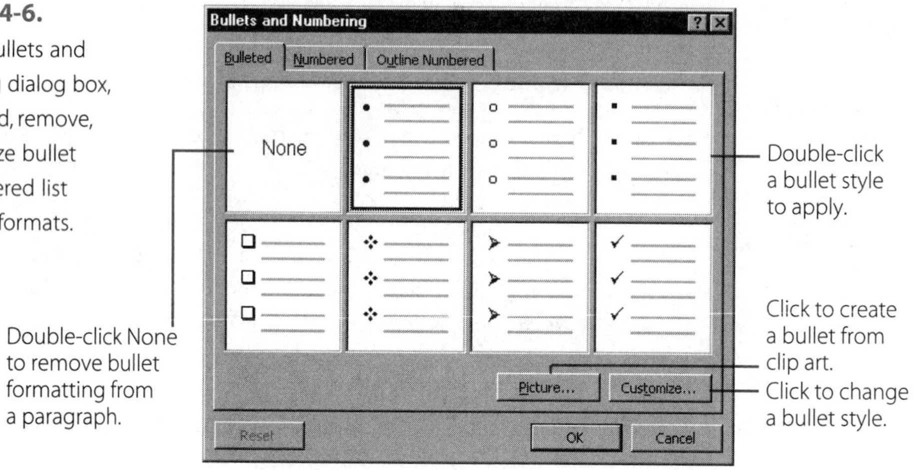

Double-click None to remove bullet formatting from a paragraph.

Double-click a bullet style to apply.

Click to create a bullet from clip art.

Click to change a bullet style.

3   Click the Bulleted or Numbered tab to display the correct set of options.

4   Double-click the format option you want and Word will add it.

You can also use the Bullets And Numbering dialog box to remove bullet or number formatting by double-clicking the None option.

Continuing Numbers in a Second List

If you enter one numbered list in a document and then begin a second list later in the same document, Word assumes the second list is a new one and restarts the item numbering accordingly. But sometimes you'll want the numbering to continue from the previous list. You can continue line numbering from one list to the next by using the Format Painter or the Bullets and Numbering dialog box.

To use the Format Painter, follow these steps:

1   Click any item in the first list and click the Format Painter button on the Standard toolbar.

2 Click inside the first item of the second list (if you have just one item), or select all of the items in the second list. Word will automatically continue numbering.

To use the Bullets And Numbering dialog box, follow these steps:

1 Place the insertion point in the first item of the second numbered list.

2 Choose Bullets And Numbering from the Format menu.

3 Click Continue Previous List at the bottom of the Numbered tab.

4 Click OK.

If the situation is reversed and you have two separate lists in your document that are consecutively numbered, the Bullets And Numbering dialog box comes to the rescue again. To restart the numbering in a second list in your document, follow these steps:

1 Click the first item in the second list.

2 Choose Bullets And Numbering from the Format menu.

3 Click Restart Numbering.

4 Click OK.

How Word Handles Automatic Numbering

Once Word has applied number formatting to a list, it automatically keeps track of the beginning and ending number in the list and changes them accordingly as you delete or rearrange text.

When you begin a numbered list, Word assigns the number 1 to the first item on the list, number 2 to the second item, and so on, unless you have set a different starting number.

When you delete an item from a numbered list, Word reformats the list and renumbers the remaining items. For example, if you delete paragraph number 3 from a list of four items, paragraph number 4 is automatically renumbered as 3. When you move paragraphs within a list, Word auto-matically renumbers them so the numbers always remain consecutive.

If you create a second numbered list farther down in the document, its number also begins with 1, but you can tell Word to continue the numbering from the previous list if you like. *See "Continuing Numbers in a Second List" on page 276 for more information.*

III

Formatting Tools

Using Outline Number Formats

The Numbered tab in the Bullets And Numbering dialog box works best for lists of items that are all indented at the same level. But you can also use the Outline Numbered tab to apply outline number formats in which items can be shown at several levels, as in Figure 14-7.

 NOTE

> You can't apply Outline Number formats in Outline view. To reformat text in Outline view, see "Changing the Format of Heading Styles" on page 241.

FIGURE 14-7.

You can format part of a document as an outline with the Outline Numbered tab in the Bullets and Numbering dialog box.

About the Acme Network

1) Overview

a) The Main Office

    i)   The network layout

    ii) Web servers and what's on them

    iii) The E-mail directory

    iv) Using a browser

b) The Shrimp division

    i)   Satellite uplink from Baja

    ii) Ship-to-shore connections

You can apply an outline number format in the same way you add a numbered list format:

1 Select the paragraphs that you want formatted.

2 Choose Bullets And Numbering from the Format menu.

3 Click the Outline Numbered tab.

4 Double-click an outline number style.

5 Press the Tab key to indent each paragraph in the outline to the appropriate level. As you indent, Word applies the correct outline number. You can also set indent and format options for outline numbers.

Ending a List

When you press the Enter key to end the last item in a bulleted or numbered list, Word automatically creates another bulleted or numbered line. To remove the bullet or number and return to your previous paragraph formatting, click the Bullets or Numbering tool or choose the current paragraph style again from the Style menu in the Formatting toolbar.

> You can remove a bullet or number by pressing either the Backspace or Enter key twice, but this also removes the paragraph indent.

Customizing Bullets

Word offers seven bullet characters in the Bullets And Numbering dialog box, but that's only the beginning. You can customize any bullet format, changing the symbol character used or even use clip art or pictures for your bullets. You can also change the style of bullet that is automatically applied when you create bullets as you type or use the Bullets button.

To customize a bullet format, you use the Customize button in the Bullets And Numbering dialog box, like this:

1 Choose Bullets And Numbering from the Format menu.

2 Click the Bulleted tab if it isn't showing.

3 Click the bullet format you want to customize, and then click the Customize button. You'll see the Customize Bulleted List dialog box as shown in Figure 14-8 on the next page.

Automating Bullet and Number Formats

If you frequently use many different bullet and number formats, having to select options in the Bullets And Numbering dialog box each time can be a little tedious. However, there are two ways to store various bullet or number formats to make them easier to apply.

- Create styles that contain various bullet or number formats so you can choose them from the Style menu in the Formatting toolbar. *For more information, see "Defining Styles" on page 303.*

- Define macros that apply different bullet or number formats so you can apply a format with a couple of keystrokes. *For more information on using macros, see Chapter 28, "Using Macros."*

You can also change the default bullet or number format that Word uses when you use the Bullets or Numbering buttons. *For more information, see "Customizing Bullets" above.*

III

Formatting Tools

FIGURE 14-8.

You can customize bullets with other symbol characters or even clip art.

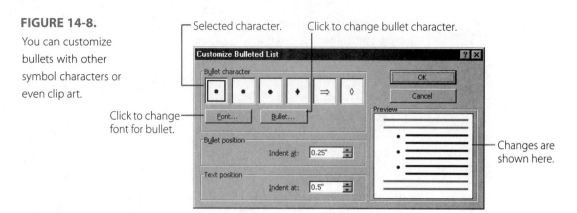

Using this dialog box, you can apply one of six alternate bullets, customize or replace any of the alternate bullets, or change the indents of bullets or text.

4 Choose the options you want. The Preview box shows the changes as you try them out.

5 Click OK to apply the changes. You'll be returned to the Bullets And Numbering dialog box, and the alternate bullet format you initially selected shows the effects of your customization.

Replacing a Standard Bullet with an Alternate Bullet

Once you have the Customize Bulleted List dialog box open, it's easy to replace the bullet you selected in the Bullets And Numbering dialog box with a different bullet character. Just double-click one of the alternate bullet formats shown. Word applies that bullet format to the current paragraph, and the format appears thereafter as an option in the Bullets And Numbering dialog box.

Changing a Bullet's Font or Style

In addition to switching among the alternate bullet characters, you can also customize them by changing the font, style, size, or color of an alternate bullet character:

1 Open the Customize Bulleted List dialog box.

2 Select the alternate bullet you want to reformat.

3 Click the Font button. The Font dialog box appears.

4 Choose the options you want.

Selecting a different font for a bullet may change the symbol used for the bullet as well.

SEE ALSO

For more information about the Font dialog box, see "Using the Font Dialog box" on page 83.

5 Click OK. The alternate character in the Customize Bulleted List dialog box reflects the changes you made.

Replacing the Bullet Character

To replace one of the alternate bullet characters with a different character, follow these steps:

1 Open the Customize Bulleted List dialog box.

2 Select the alternate character you want to replace.

SEE ALSO

For more information about using symbols, see "Inserting Symbols and Special Characters" on page 221.

3 Click the Bullet button. The Symbol dialog box appears, and you can then choose a different symbol font or a different character from any font.

4 Find the alternate symbol you want and double-click it. Word replaces the alternate symbol in the Customize Bulleted List dialog box.

5 Click OK. Word applies the new bullet to the selected paragraph in your document and adds it to the Bullets And Numbering dialog box.

To change the indent of a bullet or the text that follows it, open the Customize Bulleted List dialog box, select the bullet you want to customize, enter new values in the Bullet Position or Text Position boxes or use the arrow buttons, and click OK.

Using a Picture Bullet

If you're working on Web pages or want to add some color to your printed presentations, you can use clip art rather than symbols as bullet characters:

1 Select the paragraph where you want to add the bullet.

2 Choose Bullets And Numbering from the Format menu.

3 Select the bullet you want to replace.

4 Click the Picture button. You'll see the Picture Bullet dialog box, as shown in Figure 14-9 on the next page.

III

Formatting Tools

FIGURE 14-9.

Use the Picture Bullet dialog box to use a piece of clip art as a bullet symbol.

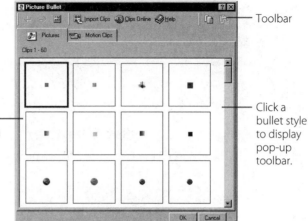

Toolbar

Click a bullet style to display pop-up toolbar.

Word offers dozens of clip art bullets you can use to add color to Web pages, e-mail, or color presentations.

? SEE ALSO

For more information about managing clip art and the clip art gallery, see "Using the Clip Gallery" on page 451.

The Picture Bullet dialog box is actually a version of Word's clip art gallery. It offers more than 60 pieces of clip art you can use. You can even import more clip art objects if you don't like the ones you see.

5   Click a bullet style. You'll see a control palette like this:

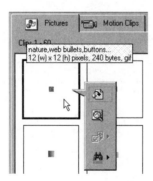

6   Click Insert Clip on the control palette. Word inserts the clip as a bullet and closes the dialog box.

 TIP

You can also use the Picture Bullet pop-up toolbar to preview a clip, save it as a favorite in the clip art gallery, or locate other clips that look like it. You can right-click a clip art object so see a shortcut menu containing other options. Click the Help button at the top of the Picture Bullet dialog box for more information.

Customizing Number Formats

You can use any character or text for automatic numbers by choosing one of the number formats on the Numbered or Outline Numbered tabs in the Bullets And Numbering dialog box. You can also customize those formats if you like.

Selecting a Different Number Format

To select a different number format, follow these steps:

1 Move the insertion point to the paragraph you want numbered.

2 Choose Bullets And Numbering from the Format menu.

3 Click the Numbered or Outline Numbered tab.

4 Double-click an alternate format to apply it to your document and add it to the Bullets And Numbering dialog box.

Customizing a Numbered Format

If the selection of Numbered format options isn't enough for you, you can customize any of them. To do this, follow these steps:

1 Choose Bullets And Numbering from the Format menu.

2 Click the number format you want to customize, and then click the Customize button. You'll see the Customize Numbered List dialog box as shown in Figure 14-10.

FIGURE 14-10.

Create your own list number formats with the options in the Customize Numbered List dialog box.

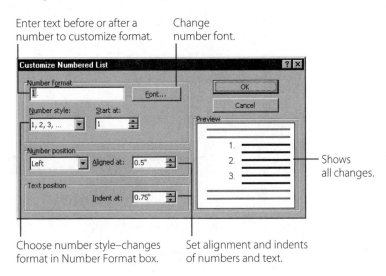

Enter text before or after a number to customize format.

Change number font.

Shows all changes.

Choose number style–changes format in Number Format box.

Set alignment and indents of numbers and text.

III

Formatting Tools

3 Choose the options you want and click OK. The number format you selected in the Bullets And Numbering dialog box will show the new format the next time you open this dialog box.

The customization options in the Customize Numbered List dialog box work as follows:

- Type an alternate number format in the Number Format box.

- Click the Font button to display the Font dialog box and change the font or character format used for the numbers.

- Choose a style from the Number Style list.

- Enter the starting number in the Start At box to change the starting number Word uses when beginning a numbered list.

Save Typing with Custom Number Formats

When you're preparing a list of items and you want to use a name and a number for each of them, you can create a custom number format to enter the text as well as the number. For example, suppose you wanted to number the list in a meeting as Item #1., Item #2., and so on. It's easy to do this:

1 Open the Numbered tab in the Bullets and Numbering dialog box, select a format, and click the Customize button (see Figure 14-10 on the previous page for an example). Notice that the number in the Number Format box has gray shading. That's because this number is automatically determined by the selection you make from the Number Style menu below. However, you can add text before or after this number if you like.

2 Click to the left of the shaded number in the Number Format box and type *Item #*.

3 Select other options if you like and then click OK. The list now looks like this:

Morale & Democracy meeting agenda 11/2/99

Item # 1.   Introductions

Item # 2.   Election of chairperson

Item # 3.   Election of recording secretary

Text that you add in front of an item number is aligned to the left of the number itself, so you may have to change the indent settings of the list to make it line up with text above or below it.

- Choose Left, Right, or Centered from the Number Position menu to change the number's alignment in a paragraph, or enter a specific ruler position at which to align the numbers in the Aligned At box.

- Enter a different value in the Indent At box to change the ruler position at which text following the numbers is aligned.

The Preview box shows the effect of your changes.

Changing Outline Number Formats

Outline number formats typically change to distinguish one outline level from another. For example, main headings may have roman numerals, while subheadings may have arabic numbers or alphabetical letters. You can change these formats if you like.

To customize an outline number format, select a format on the Outline Numbered tab and click the Customize button. You'll see the Customize Outline Numbered List dialog box. By clicking the More button in the upper-right corner, you can reveal all of the options available for formatting various outline levels, as shown in Figure 14-11.

FIGURE 14-11.
You can set the outline heading level as well as other options when you customize an Outline Numbered format.

Include a previous level number in the current level's number.

3 Set number and text indents.

1 Select the outline level number.

2 Choose a number format, style, and starting number.

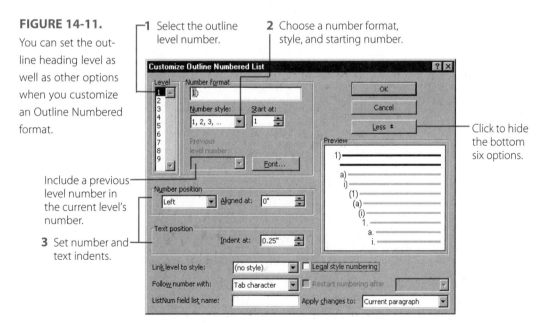

Click to hide the bottom six options.

III

Formatting Tools

Many of the format options are the same as in the Customize Numbered List dialog box shown in Figure 14-10, but there are some new ones when you work with outline numbers:

- Select a number in the Level list to choose the outline level format you want to customize.

- Choose a number or letter style from the Number Style list. You can also select bullet styles from the bottom of this list, if you prefer.

- Choose a number in the Previous Level Number list to include that number in the current level number. For example, if the current level number is 1 and the previous number format was A, this level will be numbered A1.

- Choose a style from the Link Level To Style list to format the outline level with a predefined style.

- Choose the character that follows a number at this level. (Usually numbers are separated from the text that follows them by a space or a tab.)

- Enter the name of a ListNum field in the ListNum Field List Name box if you want to generate outline numbers in special formats from a data field. Data fields can supply information to documents automatically.

- Select the Legal Style Numbering check box to set legal style numbering for the outline level. Choosing this option overrides any option you've chosen from the Number Style menu.

- Set a level at which to restart numbering with the Restart Numbering After check box and list if you want the outline numbers to automatically reset to 1 at some point.

- Use the Apply Changes To list to choose the portion of your document to which the outline number changes will apply.

? SEE ALSO

For more information about using fields, see Chapter 27, "Using Fields." For more information about the ListNum field, look up "ListNum Field" in the Help system index.

Adding Line Numbers

If you work with legal documents or have other reasons to number lines of text, you can add line numbers to all or part of your document. Line numbers appear at the left edge of your document and are only visible in Print Layout or Print Preview.

To add line numbers, follow these steps:

1   Place the insertion point on the line where you want line numbering to begin.

2   Choose Page Setup from the File menu and click the Layout tab in the Page Setup dialog box.

3   Click Line Numbers. You'll see the Line Numbers dialog box, as shown in Figure 14-12.

4   Click the Add Line Numbering check box and choose the options you want.

5   Click OK.

6   Click OK in the Page Setup dialog box to close it.

FIGURE 14-12.
Add line numbers to your document with this dialog box, accessed from the Layout tab in the Page Setup dialog box.

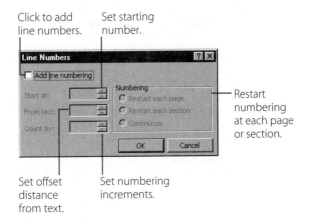

Click to add line numbers.

Set starting number.

Restart numbering at each page or section.

Set offset distance from text.

Set numbering increments.

Using Line Number Options

You can set the following options to control how and where line numbers appear:

SEE ALSO

For more information about using document sections, see "Using Sections" on page 317.

- Enter the starting line number in the Start At box.

- Enter the distance between the line numbers and the text in the From Text box.

- Enter the counting increment in the Count By box. Normally, you'll want lines numbered 1, 2, 3, and so on, so this value is set to 1.

- Click a Numbering option to tell Word how to number lines from one page or document section to the next.

III

Formatting Tools

Adding Borders and Shading

Another way to dress up your documents is with borders and shading. With borders you can place lines above, below, to the left or right of paragraphs or pages, or you can enclose paragraphs or pages in boxes. Shading applies a background pattern or color behind a paragraph. You can use borders or shading alone, or combine them to create even more interesting graphic effects. Figure 14-13 shows some examples.

TIP

You can make borders or shading part of a paragraph style definition so they're applied automatically.

FIGURE 14-13.

You can use many different options to add borders or shading to titles, headings, or ordinary paragraphs.

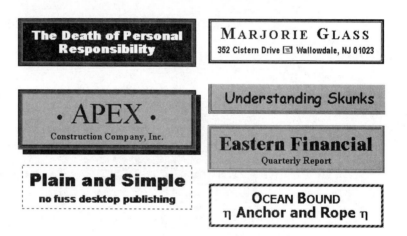

Borders and shading are great for emphasizing different parts of a document such as:

- Document titles, headings, and subheadings
- The heading row in a table
- Page headers or footers
- The name and address in a resume
- Business cards, labels, or name tags

You'll think of many other uses for borders and shading as you work.

Using Paragraph or Page Borders

You can add a box-like border around a paragraph or page or create a custom border that adds a line to only one, two, or three sides.

⭐ **TIP**

Use a bottom border to create an underline that extends from one page margin to another.

Adding a Border

When you add a border, you can select a full border or add a partial border to one or more sides of a paragraph. To add a border, follow these steps:

1 Place the insertion point in the paragraph where you want to apply a border.

2 Choose Borders And Shading from the Format menu to display the Borders And Shading dialog box.

3 Click the Borders tab or the Page Border tab, if necessary, as shown in Figure 14-14.

FIGURE 14-14.

Add predesigned or custom borders to your text with these options in the Borders and Shading dialog box.

Select a full border style. Choose a border line style, color, and width. Shows border preview.

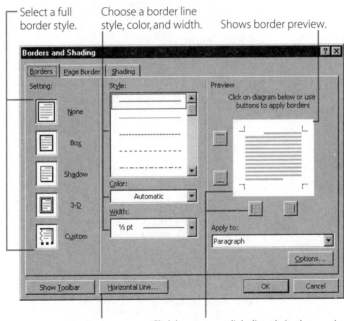

Add graphical lines to Word documents or Web pages.

Click buttons or click directly in the preview document's margins to set partial borders.

4 Click an option in the Setting area at the left to choose a border style. The Box, Shadow, and 3-D borders are full borders in different styles. Click one and in the Preview area, you'll see how the border will look. To create a partial border, click the buttons in the Preview area or click directly in one or more of the preview document's margins.

5 Choose a line style, color, and width for the border's lines with the Style, Color, and Width options. If you are creating a partial border, set these options before adding the border lines.

6 Choose a portion of your document to which the border is applied with the Apply To menu.

7 Click the Options button to change the spacing between the border lines and your text.

8 Click OK to apply the border.

> **NOTE**
>
> When the insertion point is at the end of a paragraph with borders or shading and you press Enter, the border or shading is extended into the following paragraph. To avoid this, select existing paragraphs individually and apply borders to them.

Adjusting a Border's Width and Weight

If you add a full border using the default settings in the Borders And Shading dialog box, the border outlines the selected paragraph from one paragraph indent setting to the other, like this:

About the Acme Network

This may be fine for some documents, but in others you'll want to adjust the width or height of the border line.

- To make a border narrower, drag the left or right indent markers in the Ruler toward the center of the document.

- To make a border wider, drag the left or right indent markers in the Ruler (or the left or right border line itself) toward the document margin.

- To make a border taller or shorter, drag its top or bottom line up or down.

- To reposition a single border line on one side of a paragraph, drag it.

Adding Colored Horizontal Lines

If you're doing Web page design or you just want to spice up your documents with stylized color lines, it's easy to do with the Borders And Shading dialog box.

1 Move the insertion point to where you want the line to appear.

2 Choose Borders And Shading from the Format menu and click either the Borders or Page Border tab.

? SEE ALSO

For information about moving, resizing, and managing graphics in a document, see Chapter 19, "Drawing and Manipulating Graphics."

3 Click the Horizontal Line button. You'll see the Horizontal Line dialog box, which is very similar to the Picture Bullet dialog box shown in Figure 14-9 on page 282.

4 Click one of the clip art options shown and then click the Insert Clip button on the control palette. The line is inserted as a graphic in your document.

For more information about using the Horizontal Line dialog box, click the Help button on the toolbar at the top of the dialog box.

> NOTE

A horizontal line is a graphical object and therefore cannot be used to customize a border format.

Using Border Art for Pages

When you use the Page Border tab, you have the option to apply a clip art border to your document's pages. When you click the Art menu on the Page Borders tab, you'll see a list of border art choices, like this:

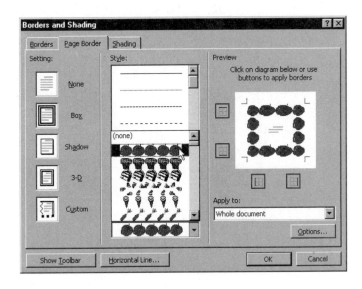

III

Formatting Tools

Select a border from the menu on the previous page and click OK. The border will be added to the document's pages. Figure 14-15 shows an example.

Click the Options button on the Page Border tab for extra options for the placement and alignment of page borders.

FIGURE 14-15.

You can create page borders out of clip art with the Page Border tab in the Borders And Shading dialog box.

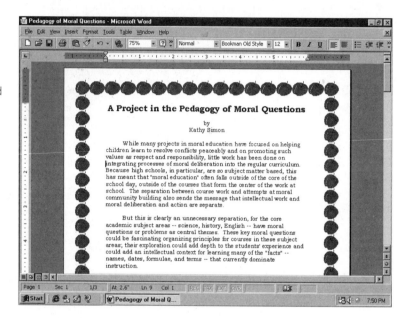

Removing Borders, Border Art, and Horizontal Lines

To remove a border, move the insertion point to the paragraph, page, or section with borders; choose Borders And Shading from the Format menu; and double-click the None option in the Setting area.

To remove a graphical horizontal line, select the line in your document and press Delete or Backspace.

Using Paragraph Shading

If you would prefer to set a paragraph off in another way, you can add a color or shaded background to it. You can also fill in a border with a colored or shaded background.

1 Place the insertion point in the paragraph you want to shade.

2 Choose Borders And Shading from the Format menu and click the Shading tab. You'll see the Shading options, as shown in Figure 14-16.

FIGURE 14-16.

Add shading to paragraphs with these options in the Borders And Shading dialog box.

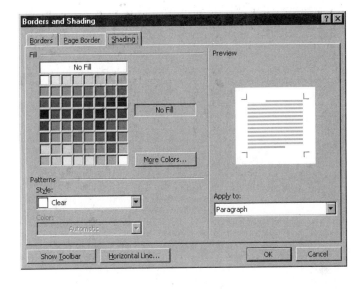

? SEE ALSO

For more information about using the Colors dialog box, see "Choosing Other Color Options" on page 429.

3 Choose a preset option in the Fill palette, or click More Colors to see the Colors dialog box, where you can choose from more than 120 colors or shades of gray, like this:

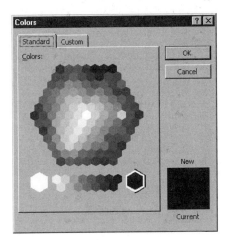

If you still don't see the color you want, click the Custom tab in the Colors dialog box to see a more sophisticated color selector where you can choose any of the colors available on your system's screen.

III

Formatting Tools

4 Choose a shading level from the Style menu.

5 Click OK.

Borders and shading are a great way to add punch to your documents, but they're only the beginning. See Part IV, "Graphics, Page Design, and Publishing Tools," to learn more about Word's other graphics and page design features. If you're designing Web pages, check out Chapter 32, "Creating Web Pages," and Chapter 33, "Using Advanced Web Features."

Displaying the Borders and Shading Toolbar

Most of Word's controls for tables, borders, and shading are available on one toolbar. To display the toolbar, right-click a toolbar in your document and choose Tables And Borders from the shortcut menu, or click the Show Toolbar button in the Borders And Shading dialog box. A floating version of the toolbar is shown in Figure 14-17.

FIGURE 14-17.

Display the Tables And Borders toolbar for easier access to the controls you need.

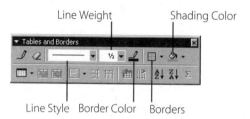

Most of the buttons and menus on this toolbar are for working with tables, but you can still set the line style or width, the border color, the border type, or the fill color with the buttons and menus here.

Using Styles and Themes

The character and paragraph formatting options in Microsoft Word allow you to create wide variations in the look of your documents, but there are so many formatting choices that it can become time-consuming to choose them one at a time for each formatting task. *Styles* are collections of formatting commands. You define a style by naming it and choosing the format options you want it to contain, and then you can apply those formatting options all at once by simply choosing the style name. *Themes* are collections of coordinated styles that give an overall look to World Wide Web pages and other HTML documents. In this chapter you'll learn how to use styles and themes to make every document look great.

About Styles and Themes

Styles have been a fixture of Word for years, while themes are a new-comer in Word 2000. Both features make it easy to apply just the right format to anything from a single character to a whole document. Many Word users never use styles or themes at all, preferring to apply formatting options one at a time with keyboard shortcuts, the Formatting toolbar, or the Format menu. But styles and themes can make formatting much faster and easier, and they can also help you maintain a consistent look in your documents.

How Styles Work

Styles can control the formatting in characters, text selections, paragraphs, table rows, or outline levels. There are two different kinds of styles:

- **A character style** contains character format options such as the font, font size, font style, position, and spacing.

- **A paragraph style** contains paragraph format options such as line spacing, indents, alignment and tabs. Paragraph styles can also contain character styles or character format options. Most styles are paragraph styles.

Every document template has a predefined collection of styles—a *style sheet*—attached to it, but you can add or change styles at any time, and you can copy styles from one template to another. You can also store styles directly in individual documents.

In Figure 15-1, the Style Gallery shows the many different styles that are defined for Word's Professional Fax template. To view the Style Gallery, choose Theme from the Format menu and then click the Style Gallery button in the Theme dialog box.

? SEE ALSO

For more information about displaying styles in the Style Gallery, see "Previewing in the Style Gallery" on page 300.

Automatic Styles and Shortcuts

At times, Word automatically applies certain styles when you enter specific types of text in documents. For example, if you enter text in a document header or footer, Word switches to a Header or Footer style. The same is true when you insert a comment or note in a document. Other styles are selected when you insert captions, index entries, and page numbers.

If you begin entering text and you find that the text style has mysteriously changed, it's probably because Word has changed it.

FIGURE 15-1.

Each template includes many different styles. Click the Style Samples button in the Style Gallery to see a template's styles and their names.

1 Select a template.   Template style names and samples are shown here.

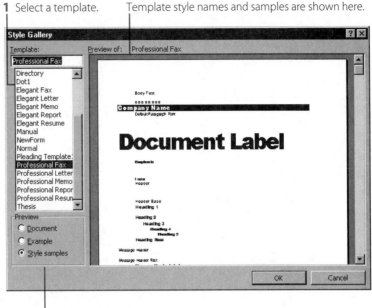

2 Click Style samples.

 TIP

Word comes with dozens of document templates, and each template has dozens of predefined styles. Before creating new styles from scratch, take a look at the styles in the different templates—you'll find a galaxy of styles that have already been created for you.

You can apply or define a style with the Style list on the Formatting toolbar, or with the Style command on the Format menu. You can always tell which style is in effect by checking the Style list on the Formatting toolbar.

 How Themes Work

Themes extend the idea of styles to the document level for Web pages. Just as a style defines the appearance of a text selection or paragraph, a theme defines the appearance of a Web page by specifying a collection of styles as well as graphics, a color background, and perhaps other elements. Figure 15-2 on the next page shows a preview of a theme in the Theme dialog box.

III

Formatting Tools

FIGURE 15-2.

Use the Theme dialog box to apply or preview themes for your HTML documents.

Select a theme.　　Theme styles, colors, and background are shown here.

NOTE

Not all of Word's themes are installed during a typical Word installation. If you select a theme to preview that is not installed, Word will offer to install it for you.

But there are some significant differences between themes and styles.

- Themes are intended for use with Web pages, for HTML documents you send via e-mail, or for documents meant only for viewing on the screen.

- You can't print the color background or background image from a theme from inside Word. (However, you can open the page in a Web browser and print it from there.)

- Themes are a built-in formatting feature of Word, so they're available in every document—they're not stored in specific document templates.

- You can't create new themes as you can with styles.

- The options for modifying themes are much more limited than for styles.

Previewing Styles

You can see the effect of any style by applying it to text in your document, but you can also examine styles in advance with either the Style dialog box or the Style Gallery dialog box.

Previewing in the Style Dialog Box

When you preview styles in the Style dialog box, you can view all the styles in the document template or just those that are currently in use. To view styles in the Style dialog box, follow these steps:

1 Choose Style from the Format menu to display the Style dialog box, as shown in Figure 15-3.

FIGURE 15-3.

You can use the Style dialog box to preview or apply existing styles as well as to create, modify, or delete styles.

Select a style.

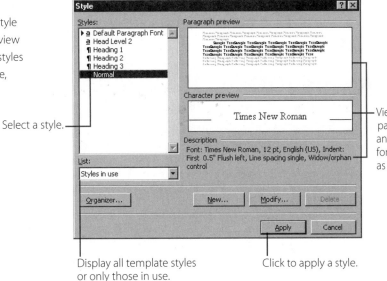

View a style's paragraph and character formatting as well as a description of it.

Display all template styles or only those in use.

Click to apply a style.

The style in use in the selected text in your document is shown in both Paragraph and Character previews, and there's a description as well.

2 Choose a style group from the List drop-down list. You can limit the Styles display to only the styles in use, only the styles that you have defined yourself, or all the styles in the template.

3 Select a style in the Styles list. You'll see previews and a description of that style on the right.

Previewing in the Style Gallery

The Style dialog box lists all the styles in the current template, but you can also open the Style Gallery from the Theme dialog box to select any other template and view the styles it contains. To view all of the styles in any document template, follow these steps:

1 Choose Theme from the Format menu to display the Theme dialog box.

2 Click the Style Gallery button. The Style Gallery appears.

3 Select a template name in the Template list.

4 Click a button below the Template list to see how the styles look in the current document, in a sample document (if one is available), or with each style name, as shown in Figure 15-1 on page 297.

If you like the Style Gallery and use it frequently, you can add a command to your Format menu so you can display it more easily. Choose Customize from the Tools menu, click the Commands tab, select the Style Gallery command near the end of the list in the Format category, and drag the command to the Format menu. *For more information, see "Adding, Deleting, and Rearranging Commands" on page 166.*

Printing a List of Styles

You may find it handy to have a printed list of all the styles and descriptions for the templates you use. To print a list of styles, follow these steps:

1 Open a document using the template whose styles you want to print.

2 Choose Print from the File menu or press Ctrl+P to display the Print dialog box.

3 Choose Styles from the Print What list.

4 Click OK to print the list of styles. Styles are printed in alphabetical order, and there's a description following each style name.

Using the Style Sheet from a Different Template

The styles available on the Style list and in the Styles dialog box are the ones stored in the current document's template. If you like a group of styles from a different template, however, you can take the style sheet from that template and use it in your document instead. To choose a style sheet from a different template, use the Style Gallery:

1 Choose Theme from the Format menu.

2 Click the Style Gallery button.

3 Select a template whose styles you want to use. If necessary, click the Style Samples option below the template list to see a list of styles in each template.

4 Click OK. These styles will replace the styles in the active document.

Applying Styles

You can apply a style to a selection of text or to one or more paragraphs, and you can use the Style list, the Style dialog box, or a keyboard shortcut to do it.

Using the Style List

The Formatting toolbar includes a Style list that displays the current style, as shown in Figure 15-4:

FIGURE 15-4.
Click the arrow button to choose a style for the selected text or paragraph.

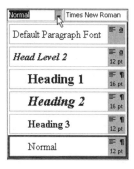

To apply a style with this list, follow these steps:

1 Select the text (for a character style only) or click in the paragraph to which you want to apply the style. To format more than one paragraph, select text in every paragraph.

2 Click the arrow button next to the Style list to display the list. Notice that Word displays each style's name in that style's character format, as shown in Figure 15-4 on the previous page.

3 Click a style on the list to apply it.

If the Style list isn't showing on the Formatting toolbar, click the More Buttons arrow at the toolbar's right edge to display it.

If you know the name of the style you want to apply, you can type it right into the Style box to apply it:

1 Select the text you want to format.

2 Click the name shown on the Style list.

3 Type the name of the style you want to use and press Enter.

Word is picky about capitalization in style names. If there are two styles named "Body" and "body," for example, be sure to enter the precise name of the style you want.

Using the Style Dialog Box

The Style list is by far the easiest way to apply a style, but you can also use the Style dialog box:

1 Select the text you want to format.

2 Choose Style from the Format menu to display the Style dialog box, as shown in Figure 15-3 on page 299.

3 Select the style name in the Styles list.

4 Click the Apply button.

Using Keyboard Shortcuts

(?) SEE ALSO

For more information about defining short-cut keys for styles, see "Defining a Style with the Style Dialog Box" on page 305.

As explained in Chapter 7, "Managing Files," you can apply a keyboard shortcut to any command in Word, and selecting a particular style is no exception. Some of Word's predefined styles already have keyboard shortcuts (as shown in Table 15-1), and you can define new shortcuts whenever you like.

To apply a style with a keyboard shortcut, select the text you want to format and then press the shortcut keys.

TABLE 15-1.   Keyboard Shortcuts for Applying Styles

To Apply This Style...	Use This Shortcut...
Normal	Ctrl+Shift+N
Heading 1, Heading 2, or Heading 3	Alt+Ctrl+1, Alt+Ctrl+2, or Alt+Ctrl+3
A style shown on the Style list	Ctrl+Shift+S, and then type the style name or press the Up or Down arrow key to select a style.

Defining Styles

Every paragraph you create in Word has a style, whether you apply one to it or not. Even when you create a new document with the Blank Document template, Word uses a default text style called Normal. A new style usually begins when you apply new formatting options to an existing word, phrase, or paragraph. When you do this, you are modifying the text's original, or *base* style.

For example, suppose you type a heading line in your document and it appears in the Normal style (12-point Times New Roman, flush left alignment, single spacing). You might modify the base style in this paragraph by selecting the heading line and choosing a larger font size or the boldface or underline format. If you decide you'll use this heading style frequently, you can define a new style that includes your modifications, but the style will be based on the Normal style.

There are two ways to define a style:

- Define a style by example by naming the style and using the format settings of the currently selected text or paragraph as the style's description.

III

Formatting Tools

■ Define a style manually by selecting a base style and then choosing font, paragraph, and other format options from menus.

To define a style, you can use either the Style list in the Formatting toolbar or the Style dialog box.

Defining a Style by Example with the Style List

You often create new styles as you work by applying new format options to existing text. The Style list is the fastest way to create a style from modified text as you work:

1 Format text as you want it to be in the new style.

2 Select the formatted text in your document.

3 Select the current style name in the Style list.

4 Type a new name for the style and press Enter. The new style name is added to the Style list, and the new style will have the base style and format settings of the selected text.

Base Styles: Good News and Bad News

Because you can base any new style on an existing style, you can save a lot of work when defining new styles. For example, suppose you have a style called Body. The Body style's description includes a font and font size, paragraph indent settings, single spaced lines, widow and orphan settings, and spacing before and after each paragraph. Now you want to create a new style called Body Double for the same paragraph, except with double spacing.

You *could* create the style from scratch, choosing all the same indent, font, and other settings all over again, but using a base style makes it much easier. Just choose Body as the new style's base style and then add double line spacing to it.

If you explore the style descriptions in Word's templates, you'll see that many of the styles are based on the Normal style.

The disadvantage to using base styles is that any change to the base style affects all of the styles based on it. If you changed the Body style's font to Arial, for example, the Body Double style's font would also change.

It's usually a time-saver to use a base style. When you want to create a style that will not be affected by changes in any other style, however, choose No Style from the Based On menu in the New Style dialog box.

Defining a Style with the Style Dialog Box

When you define a style with the Style dialog box, you can define by example or from scratch, and you have more options about how the style is applied.

1 If you want to define by example, select text or a paragraph in your document.

2 Choose Style from the Format menu to display the Style dialog box.

3 Click the New button. You'll see the New Style dialog box as shown in Figure 15-5.

FIGURE 15-5.

With the New Style dialog box, you can choose the base style and following style, along with a variety of format and style management options.

Enter a style name. Choose a base style.

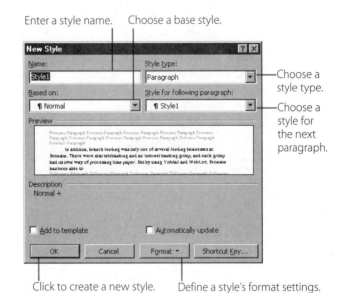

Choose a style type.

Choose a style for the next paragraph.

Click to create a new style. Define a style's format settings.

4 Click the Name box and type the new style name.

5 Choose Paragraph or Character from the Style Type menu.

6 Choose a base style from the Based On list, or choose No Style to start with a clean slate. (Word suggests the base style of the text that's currently selected in your document, but you can base your new style on any existing style.)

7 Choose a style for the paragraph that will follow paragraphs containing this style, if you like.

For more information about the formatting options you can add to style descriptions, see "Formatting with Word" on page 76, "Creating Bulleted and Numbered Lists" on page 273, or "Adding Borders and Shading" on page 288.

8 Click the Format button to display formatting commands, like this:

Choose one of the commands to open a dialog box where you can select formats to include in the style definition. You can set formats with the Font, Paragraph, Tabs, Borders And Shading, Language, Frame, and Bullets And Numbering dialog boxes.

9 Click the Shortcut Key button to define a keyboard shortcut for the style, if you like.

 TIP

You can add a keyboard shortcut to any style at any time with the Customize dialog box. *For more information, see "Changing Keyboard Shortcuts" on page 172.*

10 Select the Add to Template check box to add the new style to the document's template so that all new documents based on this template will also contain the new style. (If you don't, the style will be stored only with the current document.)

11 Select the Automatically Update check box if you want Word to automatically update the definition for this style when you set new formatting options in your document.

WARNING

The Automatically Update option can be dangerous. With this option set, you can make a minor change to one specific area of text, and as a result, change all other text formatted with the same style.

12 Click OK to save the new style and return to the Style dialog box.

13 Click Apply to apply the new style to the selected text in your document.

Save Work with Following Paragraph Styles

When you define a style, Word suggests that the following paragraph will have the same style. This is Word's normal way of formatting—it assumes you want the same style for each new paragraph you create below an existing one unless you tell it otherwise. But in some cases it's useful to set a different style for a following paragraph.

For example, suppose you have a Body Text style for the text in a report, and you're modifying the Heading 2 style for report headings. You can save yourself a lot of work by defining the Heading 2 style with Body Text as the style for the following paragraph. This way, you can type a heading in the Heading 2 style, press Enter, and then start typing in the Body Text style. Because you chose Body Text as the Heading 2 style's following paragraph, Word will automatically switch to the Body Text style so you don't have to choose it yourself.

Modifying Styles

It's easy to modify existing styles, and you will probably want to modify some of Word's predefined styles to choose alternate fonts or other characteristics you prefer. You can modify styles with the Style dialog box or the Style list.

Modifying a Style with the Style List

To modify a style with the Style list, follow these steps:

1 Select text that is formatted with the style you want to change.

2 Make formatting changes to the text.

3 Choose the same style name from the Style list. For example, if you want to modify the Body Text style, make some formatting changes to text formatted with that style and then choose Body Text again from the Style list. When you reapply the same style to text whose format doesn't match the style's existing definition, you have the option either to modify the style definition or toss out the changes and change the text back to the style's format. Word displays the Modify Style alert as shown in Figure 15-6 on the next page.

III

Formatting Tools

FIGURE 15-6.

If you reformat text and then re-apply its style, Word asks whether you want to change the style or the text.

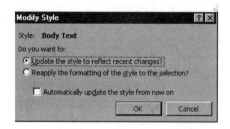

4   Click OK to modify the style.

Reapplying a Style to Delete Formatting Changes

Sometimes you'll make inadvertent formatting changes to some text. For example, one common problem is accidentally hitting the Backspace key when the insertion point is at the beginning of a body text paragraph and thereby deleting the leading indent from it.

Be Careful with the Modify Style Alert!

When you change the formatting in a paragraph and then choose the original paragraph's style from the Style menu, Word displays the Modify Style alert as shown in Figure 15-6. Consider the choices carefully before clicking OK: the choice you make can have far-reaching consequences, and the one you're most likely to make is not the default option.

When you choose the default option, Update The Style To Reflect Recent Changes, you redefine the style in the current paragraph and everywhere else it is used in the document. Be very sure you want to do this before choosing this option.

When you choose Reapply The Formatting Of The Style To The Selection, Word returns the text to the style's original formatting. This is a more common option, because there are many times when you accidentally alter a paragraph style and want to return it to the style's definition.

The Automatically Update The Style From Now On check box tells Word to modify the style definition whenever you make formatting choices. This is generally a bad idea because it means the style will change whenever you make a minor format modification for a particular situation.

Avoid a formatting fiasco by considering your choices carefully.

You can always cancel an unwanted formatting change by immediately choosing Undo from the Edit menu or pressing Ctrl+Z, but if you don't discover the mistake right away, you can undo it with the Style list.

1 Select the text with the modified formatting.

2 Choose the same style again from the Style list. You'll see the Modify Style alert shown in Figure 15-6.

3 Click the Reapply The Formatting Of The Style To The Selection button.

4 Click OK. Word will reapply the original style, and the text will be reformatted according to the original style description.

Modifying a Style with the Style Dialog Box

To modify a style, you use basically the same procedure that is used when you create a new style:

1 Choose Style from the Format menu.

2 Click the Modify button. You'll see the Modify Style dialog box, which is identical to the New Style dialog box in Figure 15-5 on page 305, except for its name.

3 Select the name of the style you want to modify from the Name menu. (If you selected text formatted with the style in your document, the style name appears here automatically.)

TIP

> You can rename a style by modifying it: just select the style in the Style dialog box, click Modify, type a new name for the style, and click OK.

4 Choose other options in the Modify Style dialog box, as you would for a new style.

5 Click OK to save the modified style and return to the Style dialog box.

6 Click Apply to apply the modified style to the selected text or click the Cancel button to put the Style dialog box away.

WARNING

> If you modify the Normal style or another style used as the base for other styles, you will also modify every style based on it. See "Base Styles: Good News and Bad News" on page 304.

III

Formatting Tools

Deleting Styles

You can delete any custom style you created in Word, as well as some of the predefined styles that are stored in your templates. Word won't allow you to delete the Normal style because many of its other predefined styles are based on it. To delete a style, follow these steps:

1 Choose Style from the Format menu.

2 Select the style name in the Styles list.

3 Click Delete. A warning message (or the Office Assistant) will ask you to confirm that you want to delete the style.

4 Click the Yes button in the warning message to delete the style.

When you delete a style, any text formatted with that style in your document returns to the format of its base style. For example, if you delete a style called Big Type that's a larger and bold version of the Normal style, any text formatted with the Big Type style in your document will be reformatted with the Normal style.

 NOTE

> If you try to delete a style that has been used in your document and for which there is no base style, Word will tell you the style is in use and you won't be allowed to delete it. To delete such a style, you must first apply a different style to any text where it has been used.

Transferring Styles among Templates

If you have spent some time defining custom styles, you may want to use them in other types of documents. For example, you might define the perfect style for the return address block in a letter template and want to use the same style on a report title page. Word makes it easy to transfer styles among templates.

Opening the Organizer

The Organizer dialog box is the place where you transfer styles from one template or document to another template or document. To view the Organizer, follow these steps:

1 Choose Style from the Format menu to display the Style dialog box.

2 Click the Organizer button. You'll see the Organizer dialog box as shown in Figure 15-7.

FIGURE 15-7.

Use the Style Organizer to transfer styles from one document or template to another.

5 Select a style. Depending upon which style you chose first, the Copy button will point to the opposite pane.

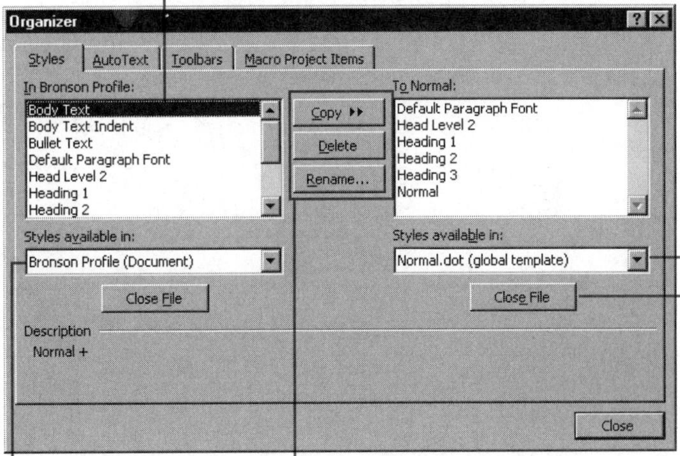

4 Select a document or template, or click Close File and open another file.

3 Select the document or its template.

6 Click a button to copy, delete, or rename the selected style.

 TIP

As shown in Figure 15-7, there are other tabs in the Organizer dialog box. You can use these tabs to transfer AutoText entries, custom toolbars, or macros between one template or document and another. Just click the tab you want and then use the same techniques covered on pages 310–312 in this chapter.

Selecting Documents and Templates

The Organizer shows styles from two different places. Normally, the list on the left shows the styles in the current document, while the list on the right shows styles from the current document template. Figure 15-7 shows the current document's styles on the left and the styles from the document's template (Normal.dot) on the right.

 TIP

You can copy styles from one document template to another in either direction: the arrows on the Copy button change direction depending on which list is selected.

However, you can (and probably will) want to select other documents and templates between which to transfer files.

III

Formatting Tools

To select a different document and view its styles, follow these steps:

1 Click the Close File button below the Normal.dot template. The list of styles above it clears, and the button name changes to Open File.

2 Click the Open File button. You'll see the Open dialog box. Word automatically navigates to the Templates folder.

3 Select a different template in the Templates folder.

4 Click the Open button. The Organizer now shows that template's styles in the list at the right.

> Word automatically switches to the Document Template file type in the Open dialog box when you open files with the organizer. To open a document instead of a file, change the file type to Word Documents so you can see documents and then navigate to a different folder on your disk.

5 Choose an option from the Styles Available In list below each document's contents in the Organizer to see styles from either a particular document or its template.

Copying, Deleting, and Renaming Styles

Between the two lists in the Organizer, you'll find buttons to copy, delete, or rename a selected style. To copy a style from one document or template to another, follow these steps: .

1 Open the Organizer and make sure the correct document or template styles are showing in both lists.

2 Select the style you want to transfer in either list.

3 Click Copy to copy the style to the other open document or template.

4 Click the Close button when you're finished.

To delete a style, select it in either list and click the Delete button.

To rename a style, select it in either list and click the Rename button. You'll see a dialog box where you can enter the new style name. Click OK when you're done.

Using Themes

 SEE ALSO

Web pages are more than just fancy formatting. See Chapter 32, "Creating Web Pages," and Chapter 33, "Using Advanced Web Features," for instructions about creating Web pages in Word.

A theme is an express ticket to fancy and evocative Web page designs. In many cases, you can simply choose a theme and begin entering the text for the page title and headings.

Selecting a Theme

To use a theme in a document, select it from the Theme dialog box:

1 Choose Theme from the Format menu to display the Theme dialog box.

2 Select a theme name in the Choose A Theme list to display a sample of it in the preview box as shown in Figure 15-2 on page 298.

 NOTE

> If the theme you select isn't installed, you'll see a notice in the preview box. Click the Install button to install it. If you installed Microsoft Office from a CD, you'll need to insert the Office CD into your CD-ROM drive.

The example shows each of the styles in the theme as they will appear in an HTML document, along with the background color or image. Notice that the Horizontal Line style is a graphic, and that the theme includes different styles for regular hyperlinks and hyperlinks that have been *followed*, or clicked to jump to another destination. You can select any theme this way to preview it.

 TIP

> To see the Active Graphics in a document, view the document in a Web browser.

3 Click OK to apply the theme to your document. Word automatically switches to Web Layout view to show how the document will look.

 NOTE

> You can view theme backgrounds only in Web Layout view, although the Normal and Print Layout views will show the theme's fonts and bulleted list styles.

III

Formatting Tools

Setting Theme Options

The Theme dialog box includes four options to change the way themes appear in your documents. Here's how they work:

- The Set Default button makes the selected theme the default formatting option for the current document template so that every new document you create with this template will already have the selected theme applied to it. This is handy when you're creating a series of Web pages and you want them all to have the same look.

- The Vivid Colors option tells Word to use brighter colors that stand out more effectively on a Web page. This option usually isn't necessary for internal Web documents.

- The Active Graphics button tells Word to use animation with some graphics. You must view the document in a Web browser to see animation.

- The Background Image option turns the background image on or off. When the background image is off, Word replaces it with a coordinated background color.

(?) SEE ALSO

For more information about using Word's e-mail features, see Chapter 36, "Sending Documents Electronically."

Setting a Default Theme for E-mail Messages

You can also use Themes to automatically format e-mail messages you send with Word. Follow these steps to choose a theme for your Word-generated e-mail:

1 Choose Options from the Tools menu to display the Options dialog box.

2 Click the General tab.

3 Click the E-mail Options button.

4 Click the Personal Stationery tab.

5 Click the Theme button to display the Theme Or Stationery dialog box.

6 Select a theme from the list and click OK.

CHAPTER 16

Formatting Pages and Sections

When you prepare simple documents, you can get along nicely using the basic page formatting and page setup options discussed in Chapter 5, "Using Basic Formatting Tools," and Chapter 6, "Viewing, Previewing, and Printing Documents." But Microsoft Word 2000 has much more powerful formatting features—features that rival some page layout programs—and you'll begin learning about them in this chapter. You'll find that Word makes it easy to add headers and footers, to number pages, to create multicolumn layouts, to vary page-level formatting options within a page, and to create layouts for bound documents.

For more information about mixing text and graphics on pages, see Chapter 23, "Designing Pages."

In this chapter, we'll cover more of Word's page formatting options. These options apply mostly to text formatting for typical printed documents, but you'll also use some of them when creating publications and World Wide Web pages.

Word comes with nearly a dozen wizards that make it easy to create certain types of documents such as mailing labels, envelopes, Web pages, calendars, and resumes. *See "Exploring Wizards" on page 262 for more information.*

Parts of a Page

So far we have been focusing on the main text areas of documents, but a page can have many different components and layouts. Figure 16-1 shows three different page layouts.

SEE ALSO

For more information about footnote or endnote formatting options, see "Setting Note Options" on page 233. For more about setting basic page format options, see "Formatting Pages" on page 100.

In this chapter you'll learn how to control more advanced page elements and formats, including:

- Sections, which allow you to apply different page formats to portions of a document

- The vertical alignment of text on the page

- The placement of header and footer text

- Page numbering

- The number of columns

- Formats for bound documents

FIGURE 16-1.

With page formatting options, you can control the placement of text in several different areas on each page.

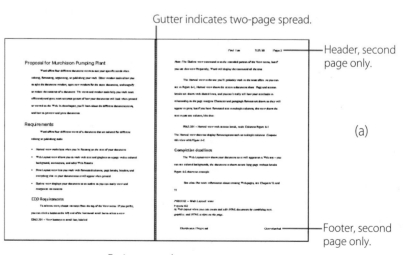

Gutter indicates two-page spread.

Header, second page only.

(a)

Footer, second page only.

Facing pages layout

FIGURE 16-1. *continued*

One-column layout

(b)

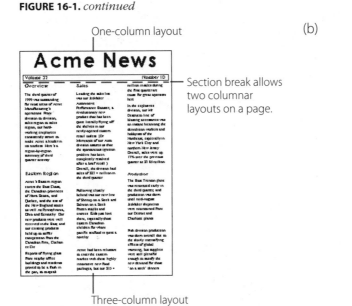

Section break allows two columnar layouts on a page.

Three-column layout

(c)

Half-page layout

Using Sections

Document sections allow you to set different page-level formatting options (headers and footers, column settings, page margins, and so on) in different parts of your document. A section is a continuous portion of your document, either a single page, part of a page, or a series of pages. You can begin and end sections anywhere, and you can add or remove them at will.

NOTE

> When you work in Print Layout view, you can't normally see section breaks, but you can display them by clicking the Show/Hide ¶ button on the Standard toolbar.

Adding a Section Break

When you need to use different page format settings in part of your document, insert a section break. It's easy to do:

1 Move the insertion point to the first line of the new section.

2 Choose Break from the Insert menu. You'll see the Break dialog box, like this:

3 Double-click one of the options in the Section Break Types area or click a button and then click OK.

Each section break type has its uses.

- **Next Page** inserts a page break along with a section break, so the new section starts at the top of a new page. Word leaves the remainder of the current page blank, although you can scroll back up to it and add text if you like. This is useful when you're beginning a new subject in a document or when you want to change page format settings from one page to the next.

- **Continuous** inserts a section break without a page break. The new section begins immediately above the insertion point's position in the middle of a page. This is helpful when you want to switch from a single column to a multicolumn layout on the same page.

- **Even Page** inserts a page and section break on the first even-numbered page following the one where the insertion point is located. If you choose this option when the insertion point is already on an even-numbered page, Word skips over the next page (the odd-numbered page), leaving it blank, and then starts the new section on the even-numbered page that follows.

■ **Odd Page**   inserts a page and section break on the first odd-numbered page following the one where the insertion point is located. If you choose this option when the insertion point is already on an odd-numbered page, Word skips over the next page (the even-numbered page), leaving it blank, and then starts the new section on the odd-numbered page that follows.

Working in a Section

As you work in your document, Word indicates the current section in the status bar, like this:

The page number indicators always show the document page, not the section page.

To make changes to the page formatting options in a section, make sure to click or select text in the section first in order to move the insertion point there and to double-check your location in the status bar. With headers and footers especially, it can be hard to keep track of which section you're in.

Changing a Section Break

After you have added a certain kind of section break, you may later find that you need to change it. You can always delete the section break and add a different one, but there's an easier way:

1   Move the insertion point into the section you want to change.

2   Choose Page Setup from the File menu or double-click in a gray area of the Ruler. You'll see the Page Setup dialog box.

3   Click the Layout tab.

4   Choose a different page break option from the Section Start menu.

5   Click OK.

III

Formatting Tools

Deleting a Section Break

To delete a section break, just select it and press the Delete key. A section break looks like this:

——————————————————————————————Section Break (Continuous)——————————————————————————

NOTE

After you delete a section break, the section above the break line is reformatted to the page format settings that were set for the section below the break.

Using Headers and Footers

The most common "extras" used in page formats are headers and footers. Headers and footers are areas in the top and bottom page margins. Any text or graphics in them are printed on every page of the document. Headers and footers are usually used to contain such text as the document name, subject, author name, page number, or date.

NOTE

For the sake of simplicity, I'll refer to headers and footers generically as "headers" from here on, unless I specifically refer to working in a footer.

When you use headers in a document, you can vary text from one page to the next, display different header text on the first document page, and even vary the position of header text from page to page. The two-page layout in Figure 16-1 on page 316 shows a header.

Adding Header Text

Header and footer areas always exist in a document's top and bottom margins, but you must add text to those areas to display header information. To add text to a header, follow these steps:

SEE ALSO

For more information about the Header And Footer toolbar, see "Adding Page Numbers and Other Special Text" on page 322.

1 Choose Header And Footer from the View menu. Word will switch to Print Layout view if you're not already in it, scroll through the document to the nearest page header area, move the insertion point into the header area, and display the Header and Footer toolbar, as shown in Figure 16-2 on the next page.

TIP

You can add header text in Web Layout view, but it won't appear on the Web page when viewed in a browser. Still, you may want to use headers on Web pages for reference when you print them.

FIGURE 16-2.

When you view the header and footer, Word switches to Print Layout view and moves the insertion point into the nearest page header area.

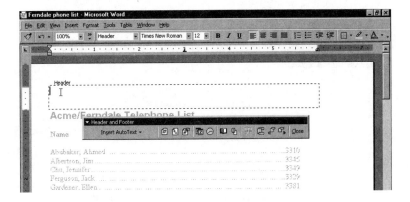

2 Type the text you want to appear in the header.

3 Use the tools either on the Formatting toolbar or on the Format menu to format the text as you want it.

4 Double-click in the document's body text or click the Close button on the Header And Footer toolbar to return to editing the document itself.

Viewing and Activating a Header

When you create a header, Word activates the header area of the document so you can enter or format text there. If you added the header from Normal, Outline, or Web Layout view, you will be returned to those views and the header text will vanish. To view the header text from these views, you must re-activate the header by choosing Headers And Footers from the View menu. If you are working in Print Layout view, you can activate a header by double-clicking inside it.

Editing and Formatting Inside a Header

Once a document header is active, you work with text in it just as you would in the body of your document. You can:

■ Type or paste text into it.

■ Add AutoText entries for dates, page numbers, and other data.

- Select a different font, font size, or other character format options.

- Set paragraph format options such as alignment, line spacing, indents, and borders.

Headers can have as many lines as you'd like—Word automatically increases the size of the page's top and bottom margin to make room for them.

> You can add graphics, borders, or shading to headers, too. Choose the Object command from the Insert menu to add a graphic to a header, or choose the Borders And Shading command from the Format menu to add a border or fill color or pattern.

Adding Page Numbers and Other Special Text

Headers frequently contain dates or page numbers, so Word makes it easy to add these and other special types of text with buttons and the Insert AutoText menu on the Header and Footer toolbar. The toolbar controls are labeled in Figure 16-3.

FIGURE 16-3.

Use the Header And Footer toolbar to quickly add text or data to a header, or to switch from one header to another.

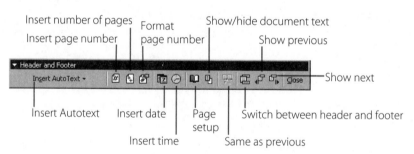

When you insert text with the Header And Footer toolbar, you actually insert a field that supplies a number or text from information stored about the document. Field information is updated each time you work with or print the document, so it always shows the correct number of document pages, page number, time, date, and other data.

- Click Insert Page Number to insert a field that displays the correct page number on each document page.

- Click Insert Number of Pages to insert the number of pages in the document.

- Click Insert Date to insert the current date.

- Click Insert Time to insert the current time.

- Choose a command from the Insert AutoText menu to insert combinations of data fields and text.

Try each option out to see how it looks. Figure 16-4 shows a header that contains field data as well as text entered manually.

FIGURE 16-4.

You can combine text and field data in a header and format it with Word's form atting tools.

Text left aligned with different character format

Text and field aligned to right tab

Date supplied by field with Insert Date button

Header

Channel Market Survey   by Paul Tse – Draft of 7/24/98
                                                                              Page 1

Text

Page number supplied by field with Insert Page Number button

TIP

Word identifies a data field by putting a shaded highlight behind it when you click it. For example, a date field supplies the date in Figure 16-4. To select a date field, you must click it twice. A selected date field has a black highlight just like any other selected text in Word. You can insert text on either side of a data field or align it with tabs or alignment settings, just as you can any other text.

Formatting Page Numbers, Dates, and Times

You can change the character format of a number, date, or time by selecting its field in a header and then choosing Word's standard character format options as you would with any other text. However, you may want to change the way these data are presented as well. For example, Word's default date format is "11/12/99," but you may prefer to have it formatted as "Friday, November 12, 1999." To change these formats, you change the display format of the field that supplies the information.

Formatting a Page Number

Page numbers are the most common data in headers, so Word puts a format control button right on the Header And Footer toolbar. To change a page number format:

1 Click the Format Page Number button on the Header And Footer toolbar. You'll see the Page Number Format dialog box like the one in Figure 16-5 on the next page.

FIGURE 16-5.

Choose the format and style of page numbers in headers with the Page Number Format dialog box.

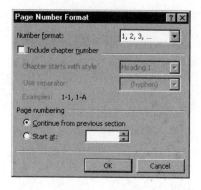

2 Choose a format from the Number Format list.

3 Select other options and click OK.

The other options in the Page Number Format dialog box work as follows:

- The Include Chapter Number check box tells Word to include the chapter number with the page number. This helps when you have several documents that are part of one large document. For example, if a document in a book is titled Chapter 2 or Section 2 or Part 2, the pages will be numbered 2-1, 2-2, 2-3, and so on.

> **NOTE**

In order to use the Include Chapter Number option, you must include the chapter number in the document's title; format the title with one of Word's Heading styles; and use that style only for the title text—and nowhere else in the document. For example, you would add a heading such as "Chapter 2 – Riding the Rockies" at the top of the document and then use the Heading 1 style to format it, making sure not to use the Heading 1 style anywhere else in the document.

- The Chapter Starts With Style list allows you to select the Heading style used to format the chapter title in your document, so Word knows where to find the chapter number.

- The Use Separator list allows you to choose the character separating the page number from the chapter number for formats such as 1-1, 1:1, 1.1, and so on.

- Page Numbering options allow you to restart page numbers in headers in the current section, to make them continuous throughout the document, or to set a starting page number for the document or a section of it.

> If you want several documents numbered continuously, you can accomplish this by setting a different starting number for each document after the first one. However, you can also use a master page to accomplish continuous numbering automatically. *See Chapter 24, "Using Master Documents," for more about master pages.*

Formatting a Date or Time Field

Unfortunately, there is no direct way to reformat dates or times inserted in headers with the Header And Footer toolbar buttons or the AutoText menu. Word uses the MM/DD/YY format for dates and HH:MM for times. If you want to use different formats for this information, delete the standard field and then insert the field again using the Insert menu:

1 Double-click the date or time field in the header and press Delete.

2 Choose Field from the Insert menu. You'll see the Field dialog box like this:

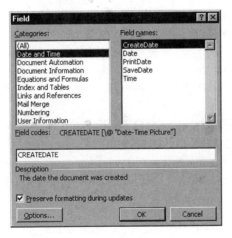

3 Select the Date And Time category and then click either the Date or Time field name in the Field Names list.

? SEE ALSO

For more information about inserting fields, see Chapter 27, "Using Fields."

4 Click Options. You'll see the Field Options dialog box, like this:

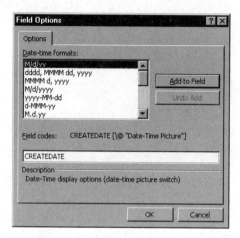

5 Select the format you want and click Add To Field.

6 Click OK to confirm your choice, and then click OK again to insert the field.

Switching Between the Header and the Footer

Word always puts the insertion point in a header when you activate headers and footers, but it's easy to jump to the footer area and back. Just click the Switch Between Header And Footer button on the toolbar or scroll to the bottom of the page and double-click inside the footer area. To move back to the header, click the Switch Between Header And Footer button again or scroll up to it and double-click in it.

Changing the Header's Position

Word normally arranges header and footer text 0.5 inch from the top and bottom of the page. However, you can change the distance if you like. To do so, follow these steps:

1 Choose Page Setup from the File menu or double-click in a gray area of the Ruler.

2 Click the Margins tab.

3 Enter a different value in the Header or Footer box in the From Edge area.

4 Click OK.

Closing the Header

When you're finished working on text in the header, click the Close button on the Header And Footer toolbar. Word puts the toolbar away and returns the insertion point to its previous position in your document.

If you're working in Print Layout view, double-click in the body of your document to close the header.

Managing Multiple Headers

You can use more than one header in a document by selecting a different first page header or by adding sections to the document. For example, you might want the first page header to include the author's name or the document's file name, while other headers contain text identifying the material covered in each document section. When you use more than one header in a document, the header area indicates this. Figure 16-6 shows three different headers from the same document.

FIGURE 16-6.

When you insert different headers in a document, Word indicates the header's location in the header view.

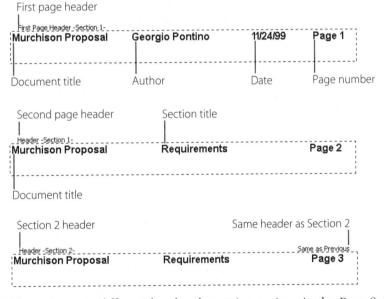

First page header

First Page Header -Section 1-

| Murchison Proposal | Georgio Pontino | 11/24/99 | Page 1 |

Document title   Author   Date   Page number

Second page header   Section title

Header -Section 1-

| Murchison Proposal | | Requirements | | Page 2 |

Document title

Section 2 header   Same header as Section 2

Header -Section 2-   Same as Previous

| Murchison Proposal | | Requirements | | Page 3 |

? SEE ALSO

For more information about creating sections, see "Adding a Section Break" on page 318.

You can create different headers by setting options in the Page Setup dialog box or by adding sections to your document. Once you have more than one header in your document, you can use buttons on the Header And Footer toolbar to copy the text from the previous section's header or to jump quickly between one section header and another.

III

Formatting Tools

Creating a First Page Header

If you want to use different text (or no text) in the header of the first page in a document, you must create a special first page header. To create a first page header, do the following:

1 Choose Page Setup from the File menu or click the Page Setup button on the Header And Footer toolbar.

2 Click the Layout tab.

3 Select the Different First Page check box in the Headers And Footers area.

4 Click OK.

The header area in the first page indicates that it's a first page header and you can enter the text you want, as in Figure 16-6 on the previous page. Word assumes you want a different header on the second page of the document, so you need to type different information in the header area there.

Creating a Header in a New Section

If your document contains two or more sections, each section can have its own header. In Figure 16-6, for example, the document has three headers: a first page header, a Section 1 header, and a Section 2 header. You'll also notice that the Section 2 header in Figure 16-6 has the same text as the Section 1 header, and that its outline box includes the designation "Same As Previous."

When you create a new section in your document, Word assumes you want the header text to be the same as in the previous section, as indicated in the header area's outline. The Header And Footer toolbar also indicates this because the Same As Previous button is highlighted. You can have Word use the information from the previous section's header in the new section header or you can use different text in the new section.

To create different text in a new section's header, follow these steps:

1 Move the insertion point into the section you want to change.

2 Choose Header And Footer from the View menu or double-click the header in Print Layout view.

3 Click the Same As Previous button on the toolbar to remove its highlight. The Same As Previous designation disappears from the header area, and you can now enter new text there.

To change a different section header to the same header that's in the previous section, view the header, click in the header you want to change, and click the Same As Previous button on the toolbar. The old text will be replaced with the text from the previous section's header.

Creating Odd and Even Headers

If you're creating a bound document, you may want to use different headers on even and odd pages in the layout, like the headers in this book. To set up odd and even headers, follow the steps below:

1   Move the insertion point to the section where you want odd and even headers to begin.

2   Choose Page Setup from the File menu or click the Page Setup button on the Headers And Footers toolbar.

3   Click the Layout tab in the Page Setup dialog box.

4   Select the Different Odd And Even check box in the Headers And Footers area.

5   Click OK. You're returned to your document, where headers and footers will now be identified as Odd Page Headers and Even Page Headers, in addition to their section designations, like this:

    ```
    Even Page Header -Section 3-
    Understanding Rodents & Marsupials              Roberta Green
    ```

You can now click inside each header area and enter different text in it.

TIP

> You can apply odd and even headers to your entire document or to a particular section by changing the Apply To setting on the Layout tab in the Page Setup dialog box.

Jumping from One Header to Another

When you work with several different headers in a document, it can be tedious to scroll down several pages to move from one header to the next. Fortunately, the Headers And Footers toolbar makes it easy. Just click the Show Next or Show Previous buttons to jump from one header to the next.

III

Formatting Tools

Troubleshooting Headers

Headers and footers are one of the most troublesome aspects of page formatting. No matter how much you concentrate when creating them, you're still liable to end up with a problem when you print your document. Perhaps a different first page header hasn't been created, or it hasn't been left blank, or different section headers aren't changing the way you want them to. The fastest and easiest way to spot header and footer problems before you print is to preview your pages with Print Preview.

First, check for missing headers or footers (or ones that aren't supposed to be there) by displaying several document pages at once:

1 Choose Print Preview from the File menu.

2 Choose a layout that shows the most pages possible with the Multiple Pages button on the Print Preview toolbar. Your document's pages are displayed as shown in Figure 16-7.

FIGURE 16-7.

Preview documents in multiple page layouts to spot problems with headers, footers, and page and section breaks.

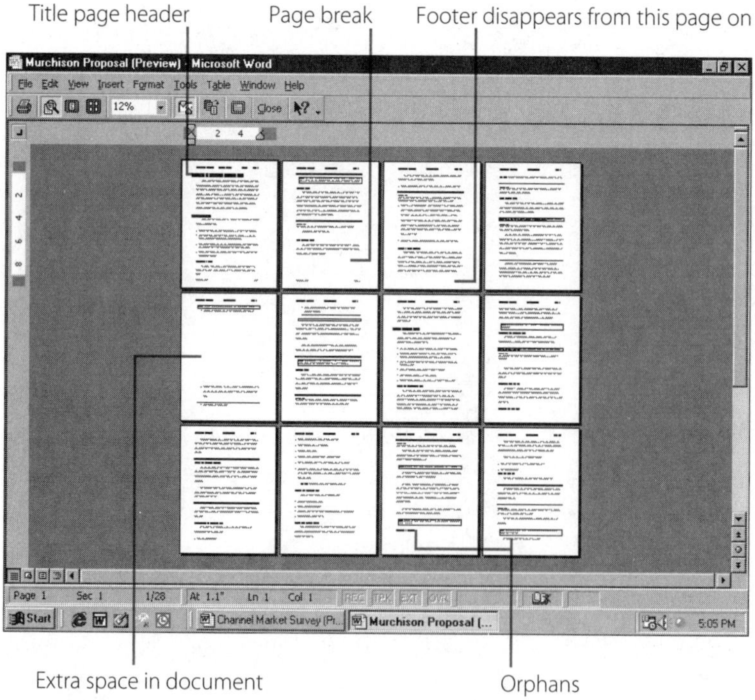

Title page header   Page break   Footer disappears from this page on

Extra space in document   Orphans

You can't read the text in this view, but the presence or absence of text in the header and footer areas at the top and bottom of each page tell you whether they exist. In Figure 16-7, for example, you can see that the footer appears in only part of the document. You can also spot extra or misplaced page breaks or section breaks by looking for blank or partially blank pages.

Next, check the text in each header to make sure it's what you want. To examine the text of a particular header or footer, double-click it to magnify the page. Make notes about the pages and headers or footers that need attention. Click once again in the document to return to the multi-page view in Print Preview.

If the header text isn't right, click the Close button on the Print Preview toolbar to return to the document view, activate the header, and edit the text there. Before editing the text in a header area, check the area's outline for the First Page Header, Same As Previous, Odd Page Header, or Even Page Header designation. Your problem may be that the header has one of these designations when it shouldn't or that it should have one of these designations when it doesn't.

If the header or footer text takes up too much room or isn't aligned properly with the rest of your document, select the text and use Word's character or paragraph formatting controls to fix it.

 TIP

> If a lone page number is aligned way out in the right or left margin, it was probably added with the Page Number command on the Insert menu. *See "Numbering Pages" below.*

Numbering Pages

When you simply want to number the pages in a document without adding a bunch of other information to a header, you can do so without even viewing your document's headers and footers. As with the automatic page numbers you add to headers, page numbers are presented in a field that Word inserts into your document.

TIP

> If you want to use any other text with a page number, such as "Page 1," it's better to use the Insert Page Number button on the Header And Footer toolbar, because it's easier to control the position of the page number field in the header.

III

Formatting Tools

Adding Page Numbers

To add page numbers to your document, follow these steps:

1 Choose Page Numbers from the Insert menu. You'll see the Page
Numbers dialog box, as shown in Figure 16-8.

FIGURE 16-8.

Set the position of a
page number with the
Page Number com-
mand on the
Insert menu.

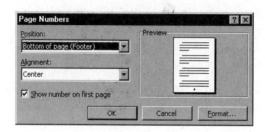

2 Choose a position from the Position menu. You can put a number in the header or the footer. The Preview area shows where
the number will appear.

3 Choose an alignment setting from the Alignment menu. There are
standard left, right, and center settings as well as inside and outside settings for two-page layouts.

4 If you don't want a number on the first page of the document,
clear the Show Number On First Page check box.

5 Click the Format button to set the page number format. You'll
see the Page Number Format dialog box shown in Figure 16-5
on page 324.

6 Choose the format options you want.

7 Click OK to close the Page Number Format dialog box, and click
OK again to close the Page Numbers dialog box.

Deleting Page Numbers

To delete page numbers after you have added them, follow
these steps:

1 Choose Headers And Footers from the View menu.

2 Double-click the page number to select it.

3 Press the Delete or Backspace key.

Arranging Text in Columns

Most documents use a single-column layout, but you can easily create multicolumn layouts for your pages. You can apply a multicolumn layout to your entire document or to a section and you can adjust the width or spacing between columns. In a multicolumn layout, text flows down the left-hand column first, and then down the next column to the right, and so on. Figure 16-9 shows an example.

FIGURE 16-9.

In multicolumn layouts, text flows from one column to the next.

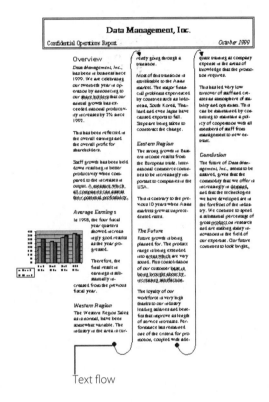

Text flow

As you edit text on the page, text moves in every column. However, you can insert column breaks to make sure that certain headings or other text appear at the top of a particular column.

 NOTE

When you apply a multicolumn layout, Word automatically switches to Print Layout view, if you're not already in it, so you can see how the columns will look. If you view a multicolumn layout in Normal view, you'll see only one column on the screen, but it will be the same width as one of the columns in Print Layout view. You can't use multicolumn layouts in Web Layout view.

III

Formatting Tools

Applying a Multicolumn Layout

There are two ways to apply a multicolumn layout. You can create equally spaced columns of the same width quickly with the Columns button on the Standard toolbar, or you can use the Columns command on the Format menu for more flexible column arrangements.

Using the Columns Button

To create a multicolumn layout with the Columns button, follow these steps:

1 Move the insertion point to the place where you want the column layout to begin, if necessary. (Just below a section break, for example.)

2 Click the Columns button on the Standard toolbar. (You may need to select it on the More Buttons palette.) You'll see a palette like this:

3 Drag across the number of columns you want and then click. If you weren't in Print Layout view to begin with, Word switches to it and displays the column layout.

Columns or Text Boxes?

Multicolumn layouts are a fast and easy way to create columns of text on a page, but they have their drawbacks. Text must always flow from the bottom of one column to the top of the next column on the right, for example, and it's very difficult to use large graphics in multicolumn page layouts.

If you're designing a flyer, newsletter, or another document and you want complete freedom in placing text and graphics on the page, use text boxes instead. With text boxes you can control how text flows around graphics, you can create boxes of any size and put them anywhere on a page, and you can link boxes so text flows from one box to another.

For more information about text boxes and other page design tools, see Part IV, "Graphics, Page Design, and Publishing Tools."

Drag to the right in the Columns palette to add even more columns to your layout. Word can add as many columns as the current page orientation and paper size options allow, but it can't create columns less than half an inch wide. To make more columns than the palette shows, try switching the page orientation to Landscape on the Paper Size tab of the Page Setup dialog box.

Using the Columns Dialog Box

To display width and spacing options as you create a multicolumn layout, follow these steps:

1 Move the insertion point to the place where you want the multi-column layout to start, if necessary.

2 Choose Columns from the Format menu. You'll see the Columns dialog box as in Figure 16-10.

FIGURE 16-10.

Use the Columns command on the Format menu to set varied column widths and layouts.

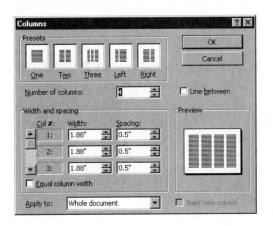

SEE ALSO

For more information about the options in the Columns Dialog box, see "Adjusting Columns with the Columns Dialog Box" on page 336.

3 Click one of the column layouts in the Presets area, or select the number of columns with the Number Of Columns box.

4 Choose the portion of your document where the layout will be applied from the Apply To menu.

5 Click OK. Word displays the column setup in Print Layout view.

III

Formatting Tools

Adjusting Column Widths and Spacing

When you have set up a column layout, the Ruler shows each column's width and the space between them, as in Figure 16-11. You can adjust the column widths and the spacing between them by dragging margin markers in the Ruler or by changing values in the Columns dialog box.

FIGURE 16-11.

The Ruler shows the width of each column and the spacing between columns. Drag the margin markers to change column widths or spacing.

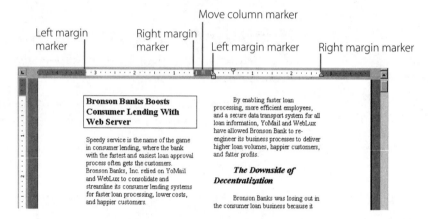

Move column marker

Left margin marker   Right margin marker   Left margin marker   Right margin marker

Adjusting Columns with the Ruler

If you already have text on your page and you want to adjust column widths or spacing, drag the margin markers in the Ruler. As you drag the Ruler's markers, you can see how the changes affect the layout of your text.

Adjusting Columns with the Columns Dialog Box

If you're setting up columns to precise specifications, you're better off using the Columns dialog box, as follows.

1   Choose Columns from the Format menu to display the Columns dialog box, as shown in Figure 16-10 on the previous page.

2   Change the Width or Spacing values for any column you want, or select the Equal Column Width check box to reset the columns to equal widths and spacing.

3   Click OK to apply the changes.

Using Column Breaks

Column breaks are like page breaks, except that they work within columns. You can use a column break to ensure that a particular line of text appears at the top of a column, or you can use a column break to switch from one column layout to another.

Inserting a Column Break

When you want a particular line of text to appear at the top of a column, there are two ways to make it happen. You can press Enter repeatedly to insert paragraph markers ahead of the line of text until it lines up at the top of the column, or you can insert a column break. It's much better to use a column break, because only this ensures that your text stays at the top of a column. (If you position text with extra paragraph markers, the text you place at the top of a column may move during subsequent editing.)

To insert a column break, follow these steps:

1   Move the insertion point to the beginning of the text that will appear at the top of the next column.

2   Press Ctrl+Shift+Enter or choose Break from the Insert menu and then double-click the Column Break option in the Break dialog box. Word moves the text to the top of the next column, as shown in Figure 16-12. Compare the layout in Figure 16-12 with the one in Figure 16-9.

FIGURE 16-12.

Insert a column break to move a heading or other text to the top of the next column.

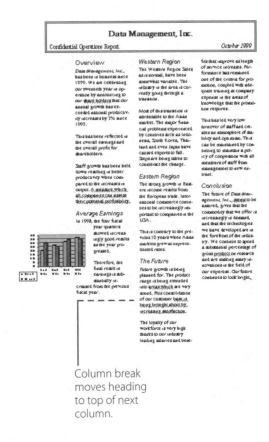

Column break moves heading to top of next column.

Changing Column Layouts with a Column Break

Any time you switch from one column layout to another within a document, you must use a section break. Word makes it easy to switch column layouts by allowing you to insert a column break and a section break at the same time:

1 Move the insertion point to the beginning of the text you want to appear at the top of the first column in the new layout.

2 Choose Columns from the Format menu.

3 Select a new column layout as described in "Using the Columns Dialog Box" on page 335.

4 Choose This Point Forward from the Apply To menu at the bottom of the dialog box and select the Start New Column check box.

5 Click OK. Word inserts a continuous section break and a column break.

TIP

When you insert a column and section break at the same time, Word always inserts a continuous section break, so the new column layout will start on the next line of the same page. To make the new column layout start on a new page, move the insertion point into the new layout, choose Page Setup from the File menu, click the Layout tab, and change the Section Start option to New Page.

Adding a Line Between Columns

In some documents, you may want a vertical line separating your columns, like this:

Bronson Banks Boosts Consumer Lending With Web Server

Speedy service is the name of the game in consumer lending, where the bank with the fastest and easiest loan approval process often gets the customers. Bronson Banks, Inc. relied on YoMail and WebLux to consolidate and streamline its consumer lending systems for faster loan processing, lower costs, and happier customers.

Based in Jamestown, Florida, Bronson was one of top 25 banks in America. (Bronson will be completing a merger with HugeBank to form the number 3 U.S. bank at the end of this year.) However, the institution was falling behind many other competitors in its loan processing services. As banks go, Bronson was very entrepreneurial - it was essentially a loose affiliation of 33 individual banks in Florida and Georgia. Each bank had its own procedures for collecting loan information and routing it to the Bank's central mainframe in Jamestown.

By enabling faster loan processing, more efficient employees, and a secure data transport system for all loan information, YoMail and WebLux have allowed Bronson Bank to re-engineer its business processes to deliver higher loan volumes, happier customers, and fatter profits.

The Downside of Decentralization

Bronson Banks was losing out in the consumer loan business because it had dozens of different data collection and entry points into its MVS mainframe in Jamestown. Local bank operations such as Bronson Bank of Miami and Bronson Bank of Jamestown were free to set up loan data collection systems that best met their own needs. But in a business that relies on the speedy and reliable transfer of data to and from a central mainframe, having dozens of systems was a real block to customer service. With no universal loan processing system, there was no way to evaluate and manage loan-processing workflow, and some consumer loans took days to process.

To add lines between the columns in your layout, follow these steps:

1 Move the insertion point to the part of your document that contains the layout.

2 Choose Columns from the Format menu.

3 Select the Line Between check box and click OK.

Creating Bound Document Layouts

If you're preparing a document that will be bound, Word has special page formatting options to take care of the gutter, or extra binding space, that you'll need in the page margin. Word can also alternate, or mirror, the page margins in facing-pages layouts so the wider margin is always on the outside of the document. Figure 16-13 shows two pages of a facing-pages layout in Print Preview.

FIGURE 16-13.

Word has special options that take care of mirrored margins for facing-pages layouts.

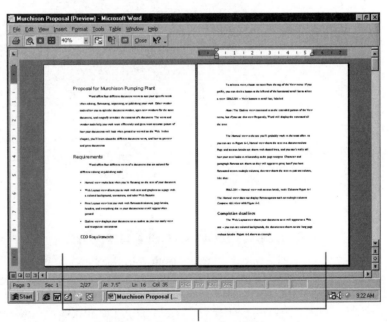

Outside margins are wider than inside margins.

Adding a Gutter

A gutter is an extra space placed in the margin of a document to allow for binding. You can add a gutter to single-page or facing-pages layouts.

To add a gutter, follow these steps:

1 Choose Page Setup from the File menu or double-click in the gray area of the Ruler to display the Page Setup dialog box.

2 Click the Margins tab.

3 Enter a value in the Gutter box. Word indicates the gutter with a wavy vertical line in the Preview area, like this:

Preview shows 0.5-inch gutter in gray.

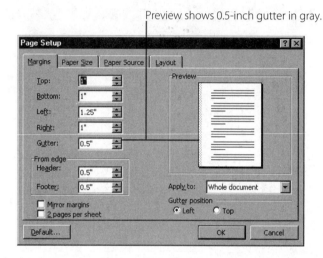

4 Select the Left or Top gutter position. Word assumes that you will bind your documents on the left side of the page, but you can set a top gutter for top bindings.

5 Click OK.

Using Mirrored Margins

The Mirror Margins option in the Page Setup dialog box is the key to facing-pages layouts in Word. When you select this option, Word mirrors the left and right page margins so that if your left page margin is usually wider, the wide margin is always on the outside of the page as in Figure 16-13. Turning on the Mirror Margins option also tells Word to place the binding gutter between the two pages. To set the Mirror Margins option, do the following:

1 Choose Page Setup from the File menu and click the Margins tab.

2 Select the Mirror Margins check box. The Preview area in the Page Setup dialog box switches to a two-page layout, as in the figure at the top of the next page.

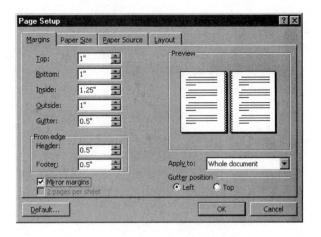

Also, notice that the Left and Right margin boxes are renamed Inside and Outside, respectively.

3   Click OK.

Setting the Vertical Text Alignment

Word leaves no stone unturned when it comes to formatting options, and there's one more that we haven't discussed: vertical alignment. In most pages, text is vertically aligned to the top margin, but you can change the alignment to suit special needs. If you want to center one paragraph on the page (the title on a title page, for example), you can set Word's vertical text alignment to place the text evenly between the top and bottom page margins.

As with other page formatting options, you can set vertical text alignment options for your whole document or for a section. To set the vertical text alignment, follow these steps:

1   Move the insertion point into the section you want to align, if necessary.

2   Double-click in a gray area of the Ruler or choose Page Setup from the File menu.

3   Click the Layout tab in the Page Setup dialog box.

4   Choose an option from the Vertical Alignment menu.

5   Click OK.

III

Formatting Tools

Setting a Default Page Layout

Normally, the Page Setup options that you set apply to the current document only. However, you can make them the default options for all new documents created with the current document template. For example, you might have a report template in which you always use a two-column layout with different odd and even headers and footers and a page border. To set default page setup options, follow these steps:

1 Choose Page Setup from the File menu or double-click in a gray area of the Ruler.

2 Set the options you want in the Page Setup dialog box.

3 Click the Default button at the bottom of the dialog box. Word will ask if you want to change the default Page Setup options for the current document template.

4 Click Yes.

Working with Tables

When you work with lists, summaries, and other data, a table is often the easiest and most efficient way to present information. Microsoft Word 2000 offers significant improvements in table making—you have far more control over table formatting, and there are handy new tools to help you create great-looking tables quickly. In this chapter you'll learn about Word's table features.

Introducing Tables

A *table* is a collection of cells arranged in rows and columns, as shown in Figure 17-1. Word uses special formatting markers to identify a table and its parts in your document. Each cell can contain text, numbers, or graphics.

> To display a table's formatting markers, click the Show/Hide ¶ button on the Standard toolbar.

Tables get special treatment in a document. You can create or resize them like a graphic, but they can contain text that can be formatted with Word's standard paragraph and character formatting tools. Essentially, a table is a container.

FIGURE 17-1.

Tables organize data in rows and columns, and they have special formatting markers in Word.

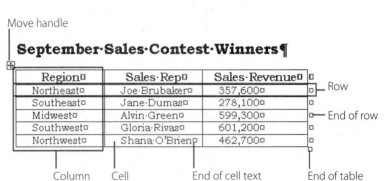

Tables Aren't Just for Data

Most of us tend to think of a table as the word processing equivalent of a spreadsheet like the example in Figure 17-1, with column labels at the top, rows of data under them, and a grid that shows the structure. But you can use tables to create all kinds of documents, from resumes to newsletters to forms.

Rather than arranging a table's cells in a regular grid as in Figure 17-1, you can make any cell, row, or column as big or as small as you like. For example, two cells can be merged into one, or you can divide one cell into many other cells. In fact, a cell can even contain another table. Figure 17-2 on the next page shows part of a resume layout that was made from a table.

FIGURE 17-2.

Tables can make it easier to format any type of document that has a columnar layout.

MORGAN·LINTON¶

OBJECTIVE¤	
¤	A·software·engineering·management·position·usingmy·demonstrated·abilities·in·application·and·utility·software·development,·personnel·management,·and·administration.¤

EXPERIENCE¤	
¤	1990–1994 → **Arbor·Software** → Southridge,·NC¶ **Engineering·Lead,·FastPlex·6**¶ ■→ Managed·team·of·20·programmers¶ ■→ Was·lead·engineering·contact·with·marketing·and·upper·management¶ ■→ Devised·innovative·new·features¤
¤	1989–1990 → **Software·Eruption** → Southridge,·NC¶ **Software·Engineer,·WordOPolis**¶ ■→ Contributed·key·ideas·for·new·features..¶ ■→ Implemented·more·than·1,500·features·under·tight·schedule¶ ■→ Named·Code·Janitor·of·the·Year.¤

Creating a Table

There are several different ways to create a table in Word. You can use the Insert Table button on the Standard toolbar, use the Insert Table command from the Table menu, or draw a table's outline and add rows or columns to it.

The Tables And Borders Toolbar

The Tables And Borders toolbar is very handy when you work with tables. To display this toolbar, right-click in any toolbar and choose Tables And Borders from the toolbar menu, or click the Tables And Borders button on the Standard toolbar. Prepare yourself for the formatting instructions in the sections that follow by noting the button and menu names on the Tables And Borders toolbar:

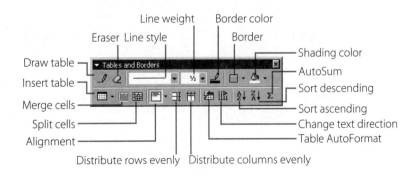

Preparing to Create a Table

When you create a table, it appears at the insertion point in your document. But before you create a table, you should have a pretty good idea of its overall size and the number of rows and columns it will contain. You can always add rows and columns later, but it's much easier to work with the table if you have some basic parameters in mind from the beginning. Ask yourself these questions:

- Can the table be any width up to the document margins, or does it need to be a specific width?

- How many columns or rows will the table contain?

- Will the table contain so many rows that it may span two pages, and can you avoid this by starting the table at the top of a page?

- Will the table contain so many columns that you'll have to change the page orientation or widen the page margins? Can you avoid this by reducing the size of text in the table?

Once you have a general idea of the table's size, you can adjust your document accordingly. For example, you might want to switch the page orientation from Portrait to Landscape to accommodate a wide table.

Here's a table setup checklist:

1 Estimate the table's size and the number of columns and rows.

2 Change the Page Setup options to accommodate the table if necessary.

3 Move the insertion point to the place where you want the table to appear. The beginning of a blank line is the best place, and it's easier to add text above the table if you don't insert the table on the first line of a document.

4 Add a break, if necessary, to place the table at the top of a new page, section, or column. *For more information about adding breaks, see "Using Sections" on page 317 or "Arranging Text in Columns" on page 333.*

5 Insert the table.

Using the Insert Table Dialog Box

When you create a table with the Insert Table dialog box, you select a particular number of rows and columns for your table and you can make formatting adjustments in advance. To create a table with the Insert Table dialog box:

1 Move the insertion point to the place where you want to begin the table.

NOTE

> If you insert a table with a line of text selected, that text will be added to the first row of the table. If you insert a table when the insertion point is in the middle of a line of text, the line will be split and the table will be inserted between the two halves.

2 Point to Insert on the Table menu and then choose Table, or display the Tables And Borders toolbar and click the Insert Table button there. You'll see the Insert Table dialog box, like this:

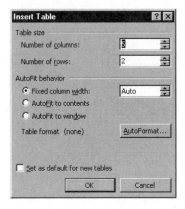

3 Enter the number of rows and columns in the Table Size area.

SEE ALSO

For more information about AutoFit options, see "Using AutoFit and Distribute Options" on page 369. For more information about AutoFormat, see "Using Table Auto-Format" on page 357.

4 Choose a different AutoFit option, if necessary (the default choice is the most common one).

5 Click the AutoFormat button to choose a table format, if necessary.

6 Click OK. Word creates the table.

III

Formatting Tools

Drawing a Table

The Insert Table button and command let you specify a table's contents and format, but they don't show you how much space the table will occupy in your document. If the exact size matters, however, you can draw a table's outer border in your document instead and then add row and column dividing lines to it as you see fit.

To draw a table, do the following:

1 Switch to Print Layout view if necessary.

2 Choose Draw Table from the Table menu or display the Tables And Borders toolbar and click the Draw Table button there. The mouse pointer becomes a pencil.

3 Point to the place where you want the upper-left corner of the table to appear—preferably the beginning of a blank line.

4 Click the mouse button and drag down and to the right until the table's outline is the size you want.

5 Release the mouse button. Word displays the table outline, like this:

The Top Five best-selling books for August were as follows:

6 Add row or column dividing lines by drawing them from one edge of the outline to the opposite edge, like this:

Word always draws straight lines when you fill in a table.

7 Click the Draw Table tool in the Tables And Borders toolbar to turn it off when you're finished so you can begin entering text.

You don't have to draw the entire line when you add a row or column divider to a table. Just drag the line a couple of inches and Word will complete it. Also, don't worry about clicking exactly on an existing line before drawing a line that will intersect with it—Word extends a partially drawn line from the nearest perpendicular line to the next one.

Customize Table Layouts with Partial Lines

When you draw lines to create a table, you're not limited to lines that span the entire table. By drawing partial lines, you can break out of the table's rigid grid structure when you have special needs. Here's an example:

	Sales (x1000)	Income (x1000)	Percent Changes	
			Last Qtr.	Last Year
Milldale	$46.9	$4.85	+11	+29
Ferndale	$33.8	$2.79	+2	+5
Cohonia	$63.2	$8.74	+30	+45

There are two ways to create partial row or column lines like the one below *Percent Changes* here.

1 Draw all of the horizontal or vertical lines first and then create a partial line by dragging only to a particular row or column line, rather than to the table's outside border.

2 Draw a line all the way across the table and then erase portions of it with the Eraser button on the Tables And Borders toolbar. Just click the Eraser tool (the pointer becomes an eraser) and then click the bottom corner of the eraser on a line segment to erase it. When you erase a line segment, the rows or columns that were divided by that segment are merged into one.

You can also use commands on the Table menu to split or merge cells or to create whole tables inside cells. *For more information, see "Rearranging Rows, Columns, or Cells" on page 361.*

III

Formatting Tools

Working with Text in a Table

Once your table has been created, you'll want to enter text into it. You enter text one cell at a time, and you can use most of the standard editing commands in Word. Because a table is a special area in a document, however, there are some different methods of navigating, selecting, and pasting information into tables.

Navigating in a Table

In a table, you enter text one cell at a time, so you'll want to move the insertion point to the correct cell before you insert text. There are three ways to move the insertion point from cell to cell:

- Click inside a cell. Word moves the insertion point to the beginning of a cell, or to the place in the cell's text where you clicked.

- Press the arrow keys on the keyboard. When a cell is empty, the arrow keys move the insertion point up, down, left, or right one cell. When the cell contains text, pressing the arrow keys moves the insertion point left or right one character or up or down one line inside the cell, unless the insertion point is at a cell border. For example, if the insertion point is at a cell's right border and you press the right arrow key, the insertion point will move to the next cell on the right.

- Press the Tab key to move forward or Shift+Tab to move backward. However, if you press Tab when the insertion point is in the bottom right cell of the table, Word adds a new row.

Entering and Editing Text in a Cell

To add text to a cell, either start typing, paste it in from the Clipboard, or insert it using one of the other methods covered in Chapter 4, "Editing Text," and Chapter 11, "Inserting Special Text, Notes, and Bookmarks." The text wraps around inside the borders of the cell just as it would between the margins of your document. When Word needs to wrap a cell's text to a new line, it makes the entire row taller to accommodate it, like this:

Name	Rank	Serial Number

In addition to multiple lines, you can have more than one paragraph in a cell—just press Enter to start a new one.

Selecting in a Table

You can select text in any cell by clicking and dragging, just as you would in other areas of the document. You can also move text from cell to cell by dragging it. Table 17-1 shows how to select parts of a table.

TABLE 17-1.   Table Selection Commands

To Select This...	Do This...
The entire table, including all text	Choose the Select submenu on the Table menu and then choose Table.
All the text in a cell	Click in the left cell margin (between the text and the cell's left border).
A cell (to apply cell shading, for example)	Click anywhere in the cell.
A group of adjacent cells	Click and drag.
A row	Click the left document margin next to the row or click in the row and choose the Select submenu on the Table menu and then choose Row.
A group of rows	Click and drag in the left document margin.
A column	Press Alt and click in the column, or click in the column and choose the Select submenu on the Table menu and then choose Column.
A group of columns	Hold down Alt and drag across columns, or point to the top table border and drag across columns.

Cutting, Copying, Moving, and Pasting Text

You can cut or copy text in a table as you would anywhere else in a document, but when you move or paste text, Word behaves a little differently in tables than it does in standard document layouts.

To move text from one cell to another, cut and paste or select the text and simply drag it to another cell. The text is added to the destination cell at the pointer's position.

III

Formatting Tools

To paste text into a cell, place the insertion point where you want the text to appear and then press Ctrl+V or click the Paste button on the Standard toolbar.

You can move or paste text from more than one cell in the same way, but you must be careful. When you select text inside cells and move or paste it elsewhere in the table, Word replaces the text in the destination cells in the same pattern it had in the original cells, like this:

When you move text from multiple cells like this...

Name	Rank	Serial Number
Jones	Sergeant	66101874
Smith	Corporal	64183521
Lee	Major	77102321
Grant	Colonel	89304821

—Move

Name	Rank	Serial Number
Grant	Colonel	89304821
Smith	Corporal	64183521
Lee	Major	77102321

... it replaces existing text in the destination cells.

Before moving or pasting text from multiple cells, make sure you won't be replacing other text that happens to be in the way. To rearrange the table by moving a whole row or column (rather than the text inside them), select the row or column and then copy and paste or drag it to the new location.

If you move and replace text by mistake, click the Undo tool on the Standard toolbar or press Ctrl+Z to cancel the action.

Formatting Cells

You can format the text inside any cell by simply selecting it and applying a character or paragraph formatting option. You can also select one or more cells and set formats for the text inside them. Figure 17-3 on the next page shows many different format options at work.

You can't use page format options such as margins or columns in tables, although you can insert a break to divide a table between one page and the next.

FIGURE 17-3.

You can use most of Word's character and paragraph formatting options on text inside cells, and Word also offers some table-specific commands for arranging text.

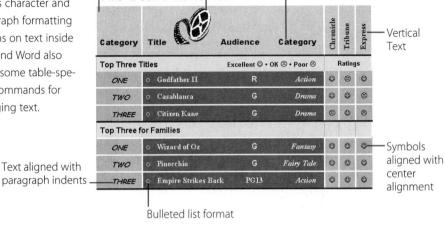

Shaded row   Clip art graphic   Text aligned with tab stops

Vertical Text

Symbols aligned with center alignment

Text aligned with paragraph indents

Bulleted list format

As you can see in Figure 17-3, you can use tab stops, indents, shading, borders, and other paragraph formats inside cells. In fact, you can set different formats for different characters or paragraphs inside a given cell.

> To create numbered rows in a table, select only the first column and then click the Numbering button on the Formatting toolbar, or choose the Bullets And Numbering command from the Format menu and then set the options you want. Word will number each row consecutively. *For more information see "Creating Bulleted and Numbered Lists" on page 273.*

Some of the format options work differently in tables than they do in normal text, so we'll look at those in detail.

> If you use special formats frequently in tables, create special character or paragraph styles for them so you can apply them easily in your next table. *See Chapter 15, "Using Styles and Themes," for more information. For more information about character and paragraph formatting, see Chapter 5, "Using Basic Formatting Tools."*

Using Tab Stops

You can set tab stops in a table by dragging in the ruler or using the Tabs dialog box on the Format menu. However, to move from one stop to the next, you must press Ctrl+Tab to move right or trl+Shift+Tab to move left. Pressing the Tab key alone moves from one cell to the next.

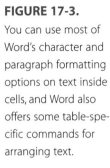

III

Formatting Tools

Aligning Text Inside Cells

You can use Word's standard paragraph alignment tools to align text horizontally in cells. However, Word also has table format options you can use to align text vertically and horizontally at the same time.

To align text in a cell, do the following:

1 Select the cell or cells.

2 Click the arrow next to the Align button on the Tables And Borders toolbar to display a palette of alignment selections, like this:

3 Select an alignment option from the palette. Word aligns the text in the selected cells.

The current alignment setting appears on the Align button itself. To apply that setting to a cell or cells, just click the button.

Use the Click and Type feature to quickly move the insertion point and change the horizontal text alignment inside a cell. *For more information about Click and Type, see "Click and Type in Web or Print Layout Views" on page 109.*

Changing the Text Direction

You can also change the direction of text in a cell with a button on the Tables And Borders toolbar. The cells containing newspaper names in Figure 17-3 on the previous page offer an example. With Word you can rotate text inside cells in 90-degree increments.

To rotate text in a cell, row, or column, first do the following:

1 Click in the cell or select the row or column.

2 Click the Change Text Direction button on the Tables And Borders toolbar. The icon on the button shows the direction text will be in after you click it.

Right-click anywhere in a table to display a shortcut menu with frequently used table commands such as Insert Table, Delete Cells, Split Cells, Borders And Shading, Cell Alignment, and AutoFit.

Adding Borders or Shading

The Tables And Borders toolbar contains its own Borders And Shading tools, or you can use the Borders And Shading command on the Format menu. You can add a border or shading to a selection of text inside a cell, to a whole cell, to a group of cells, or to the entire table.

To add a border or shading with the Tables And Borders toolbar, follow these steps:

1 Select the text or cells you want to shade or border.

2 Click the arrow next to the Borders or Shading tool in the toolbar. You'll see a palette of border or shading options.

3 Select the option you want.

Borders and shading apply to text paragraphs, so you need only click in the paragraph you want shaded or bordered to select it.

The Borders palette shows how each option will add a border to the selected cell or cells, and the selection on the Borders button shows which border is currently selected. You can add a full border or a line on any side, and you can also insert a horizontal line below the insertion point in the cell. A ScreenTip explains each option.

New tables have full borders by default, so they already have lines delineating the outside and the cell borders. If you add another border on top of the default border, you probably won't see it. To try out border options, remove the existing borders by selecting the whole table (choose Table from the Select submenu on the Table menu) and then choosing the No Border option from the Borders palette. You can then try the other options in different cells to see how they look.

III

Formatting Tools

Using the Borders And Shading Dialog Box

To add a border with the Borders And Shading dialog box, take the following steps:

1 Select a cell, text inside a cell, or a group of cells.

2 Choose Borders And Shading from the Format menu. Word opens the Borders And Shading dialog box, as shown in Figure 17-4.

FIGURE 17-4.

The Borders And Shading dialog box has special options when you work with a table.

4 Choose a border setting.

5 Choose border line style, color, and width.

6 Click lines or buttons to create a partial border, if you like.

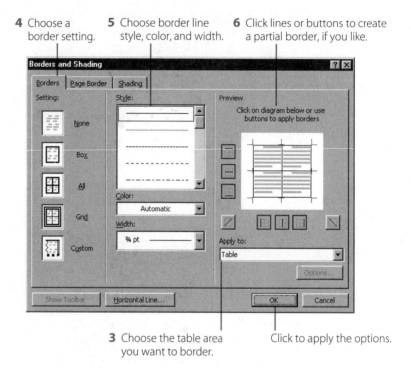

3 Choose the table area you want to border.

Click to apply the options.

? SEE ALSO

For more information about using the Borders And Shading dialog box, see "Adding Borders and Shading" on page 288.

You can apply shading options the same way by selecting them on the Shading tab. Page Border options affect the page on which the table appears, not the table itself.

The Borders And Shading dialog box has some special options that apply only to tables:

■ When you have one or more cells selected, the All and Grid border settings shown on the Borders tab in Figure 17-4 apply full borders of different types to the selected cells. Click the Help button at the top of the dialog box and then click one of these options to see a description of it.

- When you have text selected inside a cell, the Borders And Shading dialog box shows the same border styles as it does for normal text.

- On the Shading tab in the Borders And Shading dialog box, the Preview area shows a grid of cells so you can see more clearly how shading will appear in the selected text or cells.

- Whenever you work with a table, the Apply To menu in the lower-right corner of the Borders or Shading tabs allows you to apply the border or shading to the current text paragraph, to the selected cell or cells, or to the entire table.

Formatting Tables as a Whole

The best way to obtain a unified look for a table is to apply formatting to whole rows, columns, or the table itself. You can apply any of the character and paragraph formatting options mentioned previously, but there are others that affect the whole table at once.

Hiding or Showing Gridlines

Full cell and table borders are turned on by default when you create a table. However, even if you remove the borders with the Borders And Shading command, you'll still see gridlines that delineate cell and table borders so you can see the table's size and distinguish one cell from another. These gridlines don't show when you print a table, but you may also want to hide them on the screen when you're using a table to help in formatting a page layout, time line, resume, or form. Figure 17-2 on page 345 shows a table's gridlines.

If you have turned off all of a table's default borders and want to hide its gridlines as well, choose Hide Gridlines from the Table menu. (Hiding gridlines has no effect when you have the default table borders showing.)

Using Table AutoFormat

It's easy to dress up a table by selecting cells and using border and shading options on them, but Word has more than three dozen predesigned formats for tables in print and on Web pages, and you can apply them automatically with the AutoFormat feature. You can select an AutoFormat look when you first create a table with the Insert Table dialog box, or you can add a format later.

To apply a table AutoFormat to an existing table, start with the following steps:

1 Click anywhere in the table.

2 Choose Table AutoFormat from the Table menu. You'll see the Table AutoFormat dialog box as in Figure 17-5.

FIGURE 17-5.

Use the Table Auto-Format command to quickly create a coordinated look for an entire table.

3 Choose a format to see a sample in the preview area.

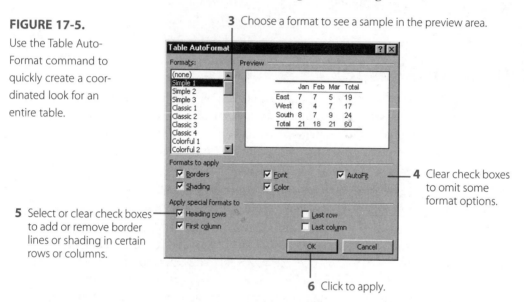

4 Clear check boxes to omit some format options.

5 Select or clear check boxes to add or remove border lines or shading in certain rows or columns.

6 Click to apply.

To apply an AutoFormat when you create a table with the Insert Table command, click the AutoFormat button on the Insert Table dialog box and then follow steps 3 through 6 above.

Breaking a Table Between Columns or Pages

When a table spans more than one column or page, Word automatically breaks it just as it would any other text. However, you can also insert manual table breaks, and you can have Word duplicate the table's original column headings at the top of each new column or page when it breaks a table.

Inserting Breaks or Splitting a Table

As with any other text, you can insert a page break manually into a table in order to move part of it to the next printed page. You can also split a table when you want to divide it into two tables or when you want to insert text before a table that is at the beginning of a document.

To insert a page break in a table, click in the row that will be the top row on the new page and press Ctrl+Enter or choose Break from the Insert menu and double-click the Page Break option.

⚠ WARNING

> Don't insert a column break in a table. Word will split the table instead.

To split a table into two tables, click in the row that will be the top row of the second table and choose Split Table from the Table menu.

★ TIP

> If you inserted a table at the beginning of a document and you now want to add some text above it, you can use the Split Table command as well: click the top row of the table and choose Split Table from the Table menu. The table will move down one line in your document and you can then enter text.

Repeating Table Headings on a New Page

When a table will span more than one page—or more than one column in a multicolumn page layout—you can have Word automatically repeat the original column headings. To do this, select the heading row or rows and choose Heading Rows Repeat from the Table menu. Word will then duplicate the headings in the next part of the table, like this:

Name	Phone		Name	Phone

⊗ NOTE

> Heading rows will not repeat when you insert a manual page break or split a table.

III

Formatting Tools

Setting Table Properties

A table is usually just one element in a document. In Word 2000, you can use the new Table Properties command to adjust the position and behavior of a table with respect to the other text around it. To set table properties, follow these steps:

SEE ALSO

For more information about the other tabs in the Table Properties dialog box, see "Rearranging Rows, Columns, or Cells" on page 361.

1 Click in the table.

2 Choose Table Properties from the Table menu. You'll see the Table Properties dialog box with the Table tab selected, as shown in Figure 17-6.

3 Choose the options you want in the Table Properties dialog box.

4 Click OK.

FIGURE 17-6.

Set a table's position and behavior in a document with the Table Properties dialog box.

Set an overall table width.

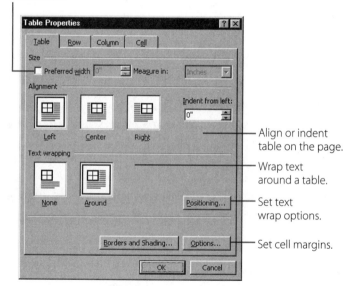

Align or indent table on the page.

Wrap text around a table.

Set text wrap options.

Set cell margins.

 **TIP**

To reposition the entire table in your document, drag the Move handle up, down, left, or right.

Here's how the options work:

■ Select the Preferred Width check box and then enter a value if you want the table to be a specific width. Choose a unit of measurement, if necessary.

- Click an Alignment button to set the table's alignment within the page margins. Enter a left indent value if you have chosen left text alignment.

- Click the Around button in the Text Wrapping area to wrap text around a table. (Normally, wrapping is set to None, so the table appears either above or below other text.) To customize the text wrapping, click the Positioning button to set options for the table's vertical and horizontal position and distance from surrounding text.

- Click the Borders And Shading button to add borders or shading to the entire table.

- Click the Options button to set default top, bottom, left, and right cell margins; spacing between cells; or automatic cell resizing to fit the content you enter.

Rearranging Rows, Columns, or Cells

Tables often begin their lives as an evenly spaced grid of rows and columns, but they don't have to stay that way. One of the features that makes tables such a flexible formatting tool is the ability to add, move, delete, or resize rows, columns, or even individual cells.

Changing Row and Column Widths

One of the simplest ways to conserve space in tables is to change the widths of columns or the heights of rows. By redistributing the space allotted for rows and columns, you can create a smaller and more efficient table. For example, suppose you create a table and enter some text, and your table looks like this:

Date	Description	Amount
7/29/99	Took 4 clients from EG blasting to lunch at the Dusty Rose.	$102.96

All three columns are the same width, even though the middle column contains far more text. By narrowing the left column and right columns, you can widen the middle column and accommodate more text

III

Formatting Tools

on one line. In doing so, you will also make the row shorter, thereby shortening the whole table, like this:

Date	Description	Amount
7/29/99	Took 4 clients from EG blasting to lunch at the Dusty Rose.	$102.96

A row will become taller automatically when the text you enter reaches a cell border and must be wrapped to a new line below. However, there are two ways to change column widths and row heights manually: by dragging a border or by using the Table Properties dialog box.

Dragging a Border

The easiest way to resize a column or row is to drag one of its borders:

1 Point to a row or column border. The pointer changes to a double arrow.

2 Drag the border to the left or right (for a column) or up or down (for a row).

You can change the borders between specific groups of adjacent cells by selecting those cells and dragging the border between them.

Using the Table Properties Dialog Box

To set a column or row to a specific width with a numerical value, use the Table Properties dialog box. For example, to change a column width, follow these steps:

1 Click in the column you want to change.

2 Choose Table Properties from the Table menu and then click the Column tab in the Table Properties dialog box. As you can see in Figure 17-7 on the next page, the number of the column you selected is shown at the top of the Column tab, because you work on one column at a time in this dialog box.

3 Change the unit of measurement if you like, and enter a different column width in the Specify Width box.

FIGURE 17-7.

Use the Table Properties dialog box to set rows or columns to specific sizes.

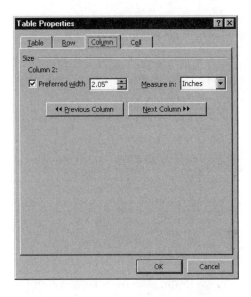

4 Click the Previous Column or Next Column button to view and change the widths of other columns.

5 Click OK.

The Row tab in the Table Properties dialog box works the same way. However, there are two additional options:

- **Allow Row To Break Across Pages** tells Word to break a particularly tall row between two pages, rather than moving the entire row to the following page.

- **Repeat As Header Row At The Top Of Each Page** is only available when you're working in the first row of a table. It works the same as the Heading Rows Repeat command on the Table menu, as explained on page 359, except it applies only to the top row in the table. If you want more than one row to repeat at the top of each page, use the Heading Rows Repeat command instead.

Adding a Row or Column

Another situation you will commonly encounter is running out of rows or columns in a table. To make a new row at the bottom of a table, move the insertion point to the end of the text in the last cell in the lower-right corner of the table and press Tab. Word will create a new row and move the insertion point into the left-hand cell in that row.

III

Formatting Tools

However, Word also gives you the flexibility to add rows or columns anywhere in a table. Here's how to add a row or column:

1 Place the insertion point in the column or row next to the place where you want new rows or columns added.

2 Choose Insert from the Table menu. You'll see the Insert submenu like this:

3 Choose an option to insert a column above or below the insertion point or to insert a row to the left or right of the insertion point. Word inserts the new row or column.

> To insert more than one row or column at a time, select the number of rows or columns you want to add before using the Insert submenu.

Deleting a Row or Column

There are two ways to delete a row or column:

- Select the row or column and choose Rows or Columns from the Delete submenu on the Table menu.

- Click in any cell, choose Cells from the Delete submenu on the Table menu and then double-click the Delete Entire Row or Delete Entire Column button.

> The Table menu doesn't offer any way to move a row from one place in the table to another, but there are two ways to accomplish this. Either insert a new row where you want one and then select and drag the text from the current row into the new row, or switch to Outline view and drag the row up or down there. *See "Rearrange Tables in Outline View" on page 245.*

Inserting or Deleting a Cell

You can also use the Table menu to insert or delete individual cells or groups of cells. When you insert a cell, other cells to the right of it or below it move over or down to accommodate it. You can also choose to insert a whole new row or column when you insert a cell. To insert a cell, follow these steps:

1 Click in the cell where you want a new cell to be added (the one you click in will move over or down when you add the new cell).

2 Choose the Insert submenu on the Table menu and then choose Cells. You'll see a dialog box like the one in Figure 17-8.

FIGURE 17-8.

Use the Insert Cells dialog box to specify how a cell is added to a table.

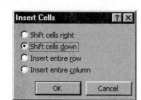

3 Double-click the option you want.

You can delete a cell in pretty much the same way. When you delete a cell or cells, the cells, rows, or columns around it will shift to take up the empty space. To delete cells, follow these steps:

1 Select the cell or cells you want to delete.

2 Choose Cells from the Delete submenu on the Table menu. You'll see the Delete Cells dialog box, which is similar to the Insert Cells dialog box shown in Figure 17-8.

3 Double-click the option you want.

Splitting or Merging Cells

When you need to create more or fewer cells without increasing or decreasing the overall size of the table, you can split one cell into multiple cells or merge two or more cells into one.

Splitting Cells

There are two ways to split cells. You can do it with a command or by using the Draw Table button on the Tables And Borders toolbar.

To split cells with a command, select the cell or cells and choose Split Cells from the Table menu. You'll see the Split Cells dialog box as in Figure 17-9.

FIGURE 17-9.

You can split a cell or cells into any number of cells.

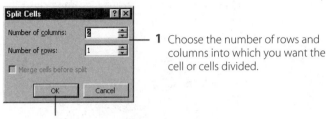

1 Choose the number of rows and columns into which you want the cell or cells divided.

2 Click OK. Word splits the cell into the number of rows or columns you specified.

To split a cell with the Draw Table button, just click the Draw Table button and then draw a line across the cell to split it. You can draw several lines to create multiple cells where the single cell used to be.

 TIP

> In Word 2000, you can nest a table inside another table. *See "Inserting a Table into a Cell" below.*

Merging Cells

To merge split cells back together, select all of the cells you want to merge and then choose Merge Cells from the Table menu. The cells will become one cell again.

If you prefer, you can merge cells by deleting lines between cells with the Eraser:

1 Click the Eraser button on the Tables And Borders toolbar. The pointer turns into an eraser when you move it into the document.

2 Click the Eraser pointer's bottom corner on the line dividing two cells—it can be either a row or column divider. Word deletes the dividing line and merges the two cells into one.

Inserting a Table into a Cell

You can use the Split Cells command on the Table menu to split a cell into a specific number of rows and columns, but you can also insert a table into a cell. These so-called nested tables are just the ticket for complex arrangements of text or data, and they're also the fastest way to add a group of preformatted cells to a part of your table. Figure 17-10 shows an example in which the cells in the right-hand column contain nested tables.

FIGURE 17-10.
Use a nested table to divide a cell into a regular grid of cells.

Night Shift Schedule – Week of November 15

Sunday through Wednesday	Location	Employee
	Counter A	Kramer
	Counter B	Ruiz
	Stock Room	Cabot
Friday and Saturday	Location	Employee
	Counter A	Luong
	Counter B	MacKenzie
	Stock Room	Espinosa

To insert a table into a cell, just select a cell and then create a table with the Insert Table command or toolbar button, as explained on page 347.

 TIP

When you insert a table into a cell, the table's borders are limited by the cell margins. To fill the cell completely with the inserted table as in Figure 17-10, reset the cell margins to 0 with the Table Properties dialog box.

 Changing Cell Margins and Other Options

Cells have text margins just like documents do. When you create a table, Word sets default cell margins, but you can reset the margins to make text, tables, or graphics fill a cell more completely. While you're at it, you can also set options to adjust the vertical text alignment in a cell or change how text wraps inside it. To set individual cell options, use the Table Properties dialog box:

1 Select the cell you want to change.

2 Choose Table Properties from the Table menu.

3 Click the Cell tab to see the options shown in Figure 17-11 on the next page.

4 Choose the options you want and click OK to apply them.

III

Formatting Tools

FIGURE 17-11.

Set a cell's alignment, size, or margins with the Cell tab in the Table Properties dialog box.

Setting a Cell's Alignment and Size

The Align button on the Tables And Borders toolbar allows you to change the vertical and horizontal alignment of text at the same time, but if you only want to adjust a cell's vertical text alignment, you can do it on the Cell tab of the Table Properties dialog box. Just click one of the vertical alignment buttons. You can also set a preferred size for a cell. These options, however, are only a suggestion to Word; Word won't resize a cell if it means resizing a whole column that is set to a different width.

> You can resize a single cell if the cell is empty. Drag across the cell until the selection highlight fills the cell, and then drag one of the cell's borders.

Setting Cell Margins

To set cell margins and other options, click the Options button on the Cell tab in the Table Properties dialog box. You'll see the Cell Options dialog box:

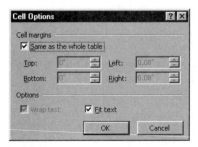

Use the options here to set the cell margins for the selected cell or for the whole table. For more information about the other options in this dialog box, click the Help button in the dialog box and then click an option.

 # Using AutoFit and Distribute Options

If you're frustrated with trying to resize individual cells, rows, or columns to accommodate the table in your document, Word 2000 can help. The new AutoFit feature offers one-click table resizing. AutoFit can resize rows and columns to fit either the page layout or the amount of text you have in the table. And if you have resized individual cells, rows, or columns and now want to return to an evenly spaced layout, Word can help there, too.

You'll find the AutoFit options on the AutoFit submenu on the Table menu. Choose AutoFit from the Table menu, and you'll see the commands like this:

Using AutoFit Options

To use the AutoFit commands, select the entire table, open the AutoFit submenu on the Table menu, and then follow these steps:

- Choose AutoFit To Contents to resize a table so the columns fit their contents.

- Choose AutoFit To Window to resize columns to fill the available text space in your document.

- Choose Fixed Column Width to set a table so it can't be widened beyond the width of the current text column. (This option is primarily for multicolumn layouts like newsletters.)

Using Distribute Options

To clean up a table by evening up the row and column widths, select the whole table and then choose Distribute Columns Evenly or Distribute Rows Evenly from the AutoFit submenu. As with the AutoFit options, you must select the entire table before applying these commands.

Sorting Text in Tables

Another way to arrange rows in a table is to sort them. You can sort text in either ascending or descending order with buttons on the Tables And Borders toolbar, or you can use the Sort command from the Table menu to specify other options.

> When you sort with the buttons on the Tables And Borders toolbar, Word sorts every row in the table except for the heading rows—*if* you have identified heading rows with the Repeat Heading Rows command. To sort selected rows only, use the Sort command on the Table menu.

Sorting with a Click

To sort a table quickly, follow these two steps:

1 Click in the column on which you want Word to sort.

2 Click the Sort Ascending or Sort Descending button on the Tables And Borders toolbar.

Using the Sort Dialog Box

The Sort dialog box offers more sorting options. To sort with this command, follow these steps:

1 Click in any cell.

2 Choose Sort from the Table menu. You'll see the Sort dialog box as in Figure 17-12.

FIGURE 17-12.

Set multicolumn sort options with the Sort dialog box.

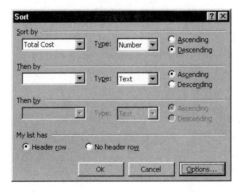

3 Click an option at the bottom to specify whether your table has a header row at the top. (If the Heading Rows Repeat command is already checked on the Table menu, these options are dimmed because Word already knows there's a header row in your table.)

4 Using the Sort By menu, select the column header name or the column number containing the text or data you want sorted.

5 Click the Ascending or Descending button to set the sort order for this column.

6 If your table contains several identical entries in the first column that will cause rows to be sorted together, use the Then By menus to choose additional columns in which to sort. However, Word always sorts whole rows whether it sorts in one column or more, so these additional sort criteria are only honored if the text or data in the primary sort column is identical.

SEE ALSO

For more information about setting a default language, see "Changing a Dictionary's Language" on page 201.

7 Click OK to sort the rows.

Word is set to sort in the default language you're using, and it normally ignores case when sorting text. To change the language used for sorting or make Word's sorting case-sensitive, click the Options button on the Sort dialog box and then set those options.

Using Formulas in Tables

Some tables you create will have numbers in them, and you can insert formulas into tables to calculate those numbers. The options are far more limited than in Microsoft Excel, but they're fine for quick calculations.

Unlike Excel, Word doesn't assign specific reference numbers to the cells in a table. As a result, table formulas must refer to cells either in terms of their direction (LEFT, RIGHT, ABOVE, or BELOW) or by a bookmark name, as explained later in this section.

NOTE

References in formulas are typically expressed in all capital letters.

For example, suppose you want Word to calculate averages in the bottom row of a table as shown in Figure 17-13 at the top of the next page.

III

Formatting Tools

FIGURE 17-13.

Use the Formula command to calculate numbers and display the results in tables.

Floor Lamp Inventory

Location	Tiffany	Bridge	Baroque	Southwest	Totals
Larkin	14	6	2	15	37
Union	11	9	7	9	36
Grand	4	12	20	2	38
First St.	8	10	5	8	31
Shenandoah	9	13	15	4	41
Curtis	7	9	6	0	22
Average	8.83	9.83	9.17		205

The table in Figure 17-13 already contains the other formulas so you can see how the averages will look, but let's assume we want to add the formula from scratch to the empty cell at the bottom of the Southwest column. Here's what to do:

1 Click in the empty cell at the bottom of the Southwest column.

2 Choose Formula from the Table menu. You'll see the Formula dialog box as shown in Figure 17-14.

FIGURE 17-14.

Use the Formula dialog box to enter formulas and calculate numbers inside tables.

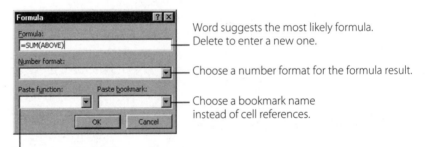

Word suggests the most likely formula. Delete to enter a new one.

Choose a number format for the formula result.

Choose a bookmark name instead of cell references.

Choose a function name to add it to the Formula box.

Word suggests a likely formula based on the location of the cell you have selected.

3 Select and delete everything except the equal sign in the current formula.

4 Choose Average from the Paste Function menu. Word inserts the function in the Formula box. The insertion point is blinking between the two parentheses following the function name.

⑦ SEE ALSO

You can use fields to calculate text and insert other types of information in Word documents. For more information, see Chapter 27, "Using Fields."

5 Type *above*.

6 Choose a number format from the Number Format menu, if you like.

7 Click OK. Word inserts a field containing the formula into the cell, and the field displays the average.

Creating Formulas

Using the Formula command on the Table menu, you can create formulas that calculate values in tables in different ways. A formula calculates by applying mathematical *functions* or *operators* to *values* in your table. A formula always begins with an equal sign (=), and the values you calculate are always listed inside parentheses. Figure 17-14 shows a very simple formula that applies the function SUM to the cells (ABOVE), or =SUM(ABOVE). Table 17-2 shows some other formulas that might be used in this table.

TIP

> You don't need to enter a formula to sum cells in the row or column directly next to the formula's cell. Just click in the cell where you want the total to appear and click the AutoSum button on the Tables And Borders toolbar.

TABLE 17-2. Formulas That Can Be Used in Tables

Formula	Result
=MIN(ABOVE)	Calculates the smallest value in the numbers above the formula's cell
=(B2+B3)	Adds the values in cells B2 and B3
=AVERAGE(PRICE)	Calculates the average of the values in the cell range with the bookmark name PRICE
=SUM(B2:B6)	Adds the values in cells B2 through B6

Using Functions

SEE ALSO

For more information about what each function does, look up *field code formula* in the Help system index.

The easiest way to use a function in a formula is to choose it from the Paste Function menu in the Formula dialog box. If you're an Excel user, you may know a number of function names by heart, but you can only use a handful of functions in Word tables, and they're all listed on the Function menu.

Using Operators

You can use any of the common mathematical operators in a table, and you can use more than one operator in compound formulas like this: =(B2-B3)+(B5*B4). To see a list of the operators you can work with in tables, look up *operator* in the Help system index and then choose the *mathematical and relational operators* topic.

III

Formatting Tools

Using References, Range Names, and Bookmarks

To specify the values you want calculated, you must tell Word the location of the cell(s) containing the values. You can do this with cell references, range names, or bookmarks.

Cells in tables are often referred to in formulas by their row and column position: rows are numbered from the top and columns get alphabetical letters from left to right. The right-hand cell in the second row of Figure 17-13 on page 372 is cell F2, for example.

⚠ WARNING

> Cell references in table formulas are always absolute (fixed) references. If you later insert a row or column that changes a referenced cell's position, the formula will be incorrect.

When you use cell references, you can specify individual cells or a range of cells. To indicate a range of cells, use a colon between two references. For example, the expression =SUM(B2:B4) would take the sum of the contents of cells B2, B3, and B4 in a table. A range must always contain a contiguous block of cells, but it can include more than one row. In Figure 17-13, the range B2:F3 includes all the values in rows 2 and 3 of the table.

❓ SEE ALSO

For more information on inserting bookmarks, see "Using Bookmarks" on page 225.

Calculating Data from Other Tables

If your document contains more than one table, you can insert a formula in one table that calculates values from a different table. To do this, follow these steps:

1 Select the table in which the values to be calculated are stored and give it a bookmark name. Make sure to select the entire table before inserting the bookmark.

2 Click the cell in which you want to enter the formula and choose Formula from the Table menu.

3 Create the formula, referring to cells in the other table with the bookmark name, followed by cell references. If the table bookmark is "Table2" and you wanted to sum cells from columns B and C, for example, the reference would be something like this: =AVERAGE(Table2 B2:C5).

To specify an entire row or column, use a range with the same row or column name on both sides, such as B:B or 2:2.

When you want to sum all of the cells above, below, left, or right of the formula's position, you can use range names instead of cell references. Tables support the ranges ABOVE, BELOW, LEFT, and RIGHT.

When you use a range name, Word includes all the values in that direction until it encounters the first blank cell or non-numeric value (such as text). Make sure there are no blank cells or non-numeric values in the middle of the range you specify, or else Word will calculate only part of the range.

To reference a range within the same table, use a bookmark. First, you must create the bookmark by selecting the group of cells within the range and then adding a bookmark to them with the Bookmark command on the Insert menu. Once you have done this, the bookmark name identifying that range will appear on the Paste Bookmark menu in the Formula dialog box. You can then select that bookmark name as a reference when you create a formula.

Converting Text to a Table or a Table to Text

Sometimes you change your mind after creating a table and you would like to turn it back into normal text. Or you may want to take the data in a table and put it into a format that can be used by database programs. In yet another situation, you may want to convert comma-delimited or tab-delimited text into a table. It's easy to make these conversions.

Converting Text to a Table

When you convert text to a table, Word takes a selection of text and creates a new table from it. To make this work, you must tell Word how to break up the text between cells and rows in the table and you must also set the number of columns in the table. Here's the procedure:

1 Select the text you want to convert.

2 Choose the Convert submenu on the Table menu and then choose Text to Table. You'll see the Convert Text To Table dialog box, as shown at the top of the next page.

III

Formatting Tools

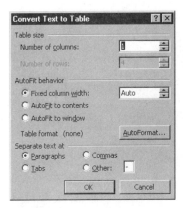

3 Enter the number of columns.

4 Select an AutoFit option to control the column and the table widths.

5 Choose a text separation option to tell Word how to break up the text from one cell to the next. If you like, enter a special character in the Other box.

6 Click OK. Word creates the table.

Converting a Table to Text

To turn a table back into standard text, you need only tell Word how to separate the text from each cell:

1 Click in the table you want to convert.

2 Point to Convert on the Table menu and then choose Table To Text. You'll see a dialog box like this:

3 Choose Paragraph Marks, Tabs, Commas, or Other as the separation option.

4 If the table contains nested tables (tables inside cells), select or clear the Convert Nested Tables option.

5 Click OK. The table disappears and the text in it is arranged in your document.

Preparing Text for Conversion

When you convert text to a table, Word creates a new cell at every occurrence of the text separation character you choose, and it makes a new row at every paragraph marker. For example, if you choose the Commas separation option, Word divides the text "Ralph Sandoval, Esquire" into two cells, because the comma is a signal to start a new cell. If your text selection has extra paragraph markers in it, Word creates a blank row for each extra mark (although it's easy enough to delete those blank rows from the table).

To avoid problems like this, check your text carefully before converting it to a table. Click the Show/Hide ¶ button on the Standard toolbar to reveal hidden tabs and paragraph marks, and then scan the selected text for potential problems. If your text contains extra commas or tabs that you want to keep, consider using a different separation character, such as an asterisk. Just insert the asterisk at each place where you want the text broken and then use the asterisk as the Other character in the Separate Text At area of the Convert Text To Table dialog box.

III

Formatting Tools

Formatting Automatically

I n Chapter 13, "Using Templates and Wizards," you saw how templates and wizards an put you on the fast track to great-looking documents with predesigned formats, but Microsoft Word 2000 has a few other tricks up its sleeve that make document formatting a breeze. AutoFormat can apply specific paragraph and character formats as you type, or it can be used to apply formatting to your finished text. And if you're preparing a letter, envelope, or label, Word has special helpers and wizards for these common documents.

Using AutoFormat

AutoFormat creates bulleted lists, numbered lists, headings, and other document formats automatically. There are two AutoFormat features in Microsoft Word:

- AutoFormat applies formatting to a document after you have created it.

- AutoFormat As You Type formats a document as you enter text.

Each AutoFormat feature has its own group of options. You can turn AutoFormat off or change the way it works.

AutoFormatting as You Type

AutoFormat As You Type is turned on by default in new Word documents, so you have probably noticed it at work already. If not, type *1/2* in a document and press the spacebar. Word changes it to the fraction character ½. Other tricks that AutoFormat performs include changing straight quotes ("") into curly ones (""), replacing ordinal numbers (1st) with superscripts (1st), and turning World Wide Web or e-mail addresses into hyperlinks.

Setting AutoFormat As You Type Options

The AutoFormat As You Type options are on a tab in the AutoCorrect dialog box. Here's how to set them:

1 Choose AutoCorrect from the Tools menu and click the AutoFormat As You Type tab. You'll see the AutoFormat As You Type options as shown in Figure 18-1 on the next page.

2 Select or clear the check boxes to change the options you want. To turn off AutoFormat completely, clear all of the check boxes.

3 Click OK to apply the changes.

The options in the Replace As You Type area in Figure 18-1 are self-explanatory.

For more about AutoFormatting an existing document, see "Using AutoFormat on a Finished Document" on page 382.

FIGURE 18-1.

You can change the AutoFormat As You Type settings in the AutoCorrect dialog box.

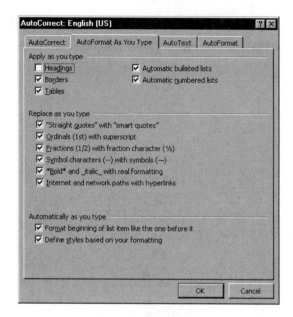

Here's a rundown on the options in the Apply As You Type area in Figure 18-1.

- **Headings** Word automatically applies Heading styles when you create single paragraphs of boldfaced text and press Enter twice.

- **Borders** Word adds a border to a new paragraph whenever you type three consecutive hyphen (-), underscore (_), or equal sign (=) characters. Typing hyphens adds a thin border; typing underscore characters adds a thick border, and typing equal signs adds a double-line border.

- **Tables** When you type a series of plus signs separated by hyphens (such as +-+-+-+) and press Enter, Word creates a table. The number of columns in the table depends on the number of plus signs you type.

- **Automatic Bulleted Lists** When you begin a line with an asterisk (*), greater-than symbol (>), or a hyphen (-) followed by a space, (or a lowercase "o" followed by two spaces), and then end the paragraph by pressing Enter, Word applies a bulleted list format.

III

Formatting Tools

⭐ **TIP**

To end a numbered or bulleted list, press Enter twice or press Backspace to delete a number or bullet.

Using AutoFormat on a Finished Document

When you tell Word to AutoFormat an existing document, it can apply standard paragraph, heading, and other styles to a document automatically. When you use AutoFormat this way, Word might remove extra paragraph markers that you have used to separate paragraphs in a document, replacing them with spacing after each paragraph instead. For example, suppose you have written a letter like this:

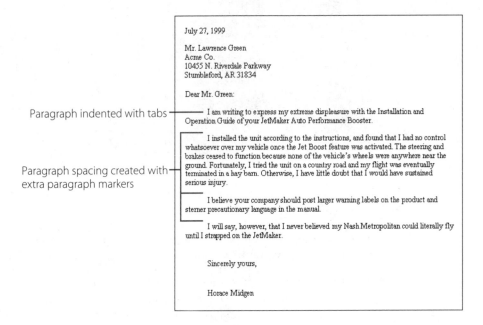

With AutoFormat, you can clean up this letter and standardize its format. To do this, follow these steps:

1 Choose AutoFormat from the Format menu. Word displays the AutoFormat dialog box, like this:

For more about the
AutoFormat options,
see "Setting
AutoFormat Options"
on page 384.

2 Choose the Letter document type from the list at the bottom.

3 Click the Options button to set AutoFormat options, if necessary.

4 Double-click the AutoFormat Now option or click OK. Word reformats the document as shown in Figure 18-2.

FIGURE 18-2.

When you AutoFormat
a document, Word
applies special para-
graph and Heading
style formats, deletes
extra carriage returns,
and does other chores.

Indents removed,
extra paragraph markers
replaced with "space after"
paragraph format

July 27, 1999

Mr. Lawrence Green
Acme Co.
10455 N. Riverdale Parkway
Stumbleford, AR 31834

Dear Mr. Green:

I am writing to express my extreme displeasure with the Installation and Operation Guide of your JetMaker Auto Performance Booster.

I installed the unit according to the instructions, and found that I had no control whatsoever over my vehicle once the Jet Boost feature was activated. The steering and brakes ceased to function because none of the vehicle's wheels were anywhere near the ground. Fortunately, I tried the unit on a country road and my flight was eventually terminated in a hay barn. Otherwise, I have little doubt that I would have sustained serious injury.

I believe your company should post larger warning labels on the product and sterner precautionary language in the manual.

I will say, however, that I never believed my Nash Metropolitan could literally fly until I strapped on the JetMaker.

Sincerely yours,

Signature
block moved

Horace Midgen

Reviewing AutoFormat Changes

AutoFormat does a pretty good job, but you may not like some of the formats it applies. Fortunately, you can review each change and then accept or reject it, rather than having Word apply them wholesale. To review AutoFormat changes, follow these steps:

1 Choose AutoFormat from the Format menu.

2 Double-click AutoFormat And Review Each Change. You'll see a dialog box like this:

3 Click Review Changes. You'll see the Review AutoFormat Changes dialog box.

4 Click the lower Find button to search for and select the first change. As you select each change, Word displays the document's non-printing characters, marks the changes, and displays them in the Review AutoFormat Changes dialog box, as shown in Figure 18-3.

FIGURE 18-3.

When you review AutoFormat changes, Word describes each change.

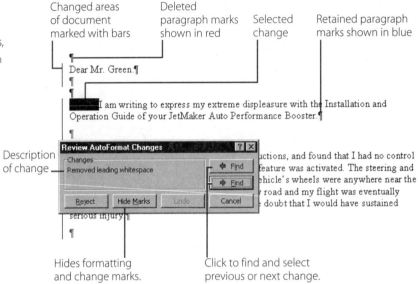

Changed areas of document marked with bars

Deleted paragraph marks shown in red

Selected change

Retained paragraph marks shown in blue

Description of change

Hides formatting and change marks.

Click to find and select previous or next change.

5 Click the Reject button to cancel the change or click the lower Find button to look at the next one.

6 When you have examined every formatting change in the document, click Cancel to put away the dialog box, and then click the Accept All or Reject All button to accept or reject the changes you didn't reject individually.

Setting AutoFormat Options

You can customize the formatting changes that AutoFormat makes in much the same way that you can change the AutoFormat As You Type options. Here's the procedure:

1 Choose AutoCorrect from the Tools menu and click the AutoFormat tab in the AutoCorrect dialog box. You'll see the options shown in Figure 18-4 on the next page.

2 Select or clear any of the check boxes to change the options.

3 Click OK to save the changes.

FIGURE 18-4.

Use the AutoFormat tab in the AutoCorrect dialog box to change the way Word formats a finished document.

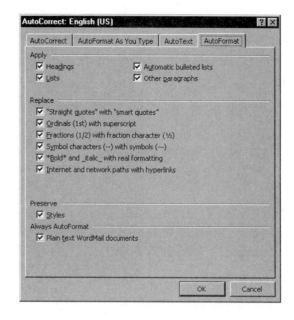

⑦ SEE ALSO

For more information about other options on the AutoFormat tab, see "Setting AutoFormat As You Type Options" on page 380.

Many of the options on the AutoFormat tab are the same as the ones on the AutoFormat As You Type tab, but some are unique to this tab. Here's what the unique options do:

■ **Apply Lists** Word applies bulleted and numbered list styles to paragraphs that begin with numbers, asterisks, lower case "o" characters, or other characters as described under "Creating Bulleted or Numbered Lists as You Type" on page 274.

■ **Other Paragraphs** Word applies the Normal style to unstyled paragraphs and uses other special paragraph styles for headers and some other types of text.

■ **Styles** When selected, AutoFormat will not override existing styles in your document. For example, if you begin your document with text paragraphs formatted with a custom My Text style, Word will not change the style to Normal.

■ **Plain Text WordMail Documents** Word applies AutoFormat to e-mail documents that are in the plain text format when you open them with Word as your e-mail editor.

III

Formatting Tools

Creating Envelopes and Labels

When it comes to getting documents to print correctly, few are more troublesome than envelopes and labels. But Word has Mailing Label and Envelope wizards help ensure they'll print right the first time. In fact, you can go beyond setting up the document layout. Using just one dialog box, you can do everything from entering addressee and return address information to adding barcodes for automated mailing.

Word's Envelopes And Labels dialog box includes correct page layout settings for dozens and dozens of standard envelope and label formats. You can use these formats as is or customize them.

 TIP

Check out the different label format options in particular. You'll find formats for business cards, name tags, post cards, ID cards, diskette labels, cassette labels, and many other documents. With some creative text formatting and perhaps a graphic, you can create custom cards or labels with a professionally printed look.

Creating an Envelope

You can create an envelope as a brand new document or add it to an existing letter so you can print them both at the same time.

SEE ALSO

For more information about creating envelopes for a list of recipients, see Chapter 26, "Using Mail Merge."

- To create an envelope by itself, open the Envelope Wizard on the Letters & Faxes tab in the New dialog box or open a new, blank document and then choose Envelopes And Labels from the Tools menu. If you open the Envelope Wizard and the Assistant asks you what sort of envelope you want, click Create One Envelope.

- To add an envelope to an existing letter or other document, open that document and then choose Envelopes And Labels from the Tools menu.

Either of these roads leads to the Envelopes And Labels dialog box, where you select or enter delivery and return addresses, choose an envelope layout, and customize the format if necessary.

To make an envelope, follow these steps:

1 Open the Envelopes And Labels dialog box as described above. It looks like the one shown in Figure 18-5 on the next page.

2 Type the delivery address in the Delivery Address box or click the Address Book icon and select the person whose address you want to use.

FIGURE 18-5.

Creating an envelope is a point and click affair with the Envelopes And Labels dialog box.

Type address or select from address book.

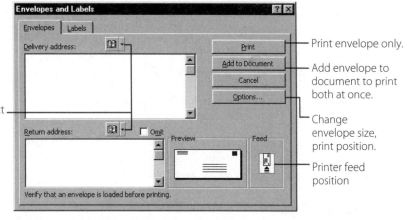

Print envelope only.

Add envelope to document to print both at once.

Change envelope size, print position.

Printer feed position

3 Type the return address in the Return Address box or click the Address Book icon and select the person whose return address you want to use.

 NOTE

If you entered your own return address on the User Information tab in the Options dialog box (choose Options from the Tools menu), it will appear in the Return Address box. Select Omit to remove it from the envelope.

4 Click the Options button and select the envelope type from the Envelope Size menu, and set other options there if you like. *See "Changing Layout Options" on page 388.*

Using Address Books

In order to access an address book from within the Envelopes And Labels dialog box, you must have the address book set up in Microsoft Outlook or in Microsoft Exchange. If you don't have an address book set up, you'll see an error message when you click one of the Address Book buttons on the Envelopes And Labels dialog box.

If you're using Word on a network, ask your network administrator for help in accessing the Microsoft Exchange address book or creating a personal address book on the Microsoft Exchange server.

If you're using Word on a stand-alone PC, choose Microsoft Outlook from the Programs submenu on your Start menu, and follow the instructions to set up the program. Once Outlook opens, choose Address Book from the Tools menu, click the New icon, and select New Contact or New Group to begin adding contacts. If you have an Outlook address book stored elsewhere, you can import it into Word. See the Help file in Outlook for instructions.

III

Formatting Tools

5 Click the Add To Document button to group the envelope with the current document so you can print them both at the same time. Click Print to print the envelope separately.

> The Add To Document button name changes to Change Document when the current document already has an envelope attached to it.

Word will prompt you to insert the envelope in your printer's manual feed tray when necessary. The Feed area in the Envelopes And Labels dialog box shows you how to feed it.

> The Feed area in the Envelopes And Labels dialog box shows Word's best guess about how to insert the envelope in your printer's manual feed tray (based on the printer you have selected). However, you should experiment with blank paper first to see just where the addresses actually print. If the Feed diagram is wrong, you can change it by resetting the envelope's printing options (*see page 389*).

Changing Layout Options

To find out which envelope format is selected or to specify a different one, click the Options button on the Envelopes And Labels dialog box. You'll see the Envelope Options dialog box with the Envelope Options tab selected, as shown in Figure 18-6.

FIGURE 18-6.

Choose a different envelope layout or other format options by clicking the Options button on the Envelopes And Labels dialog box.

Set address font and distance from edges.

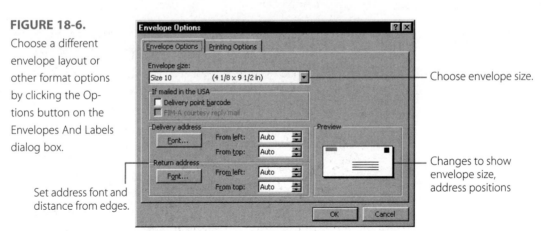

Choose envelope size.

Changes to show envelope size, address positions

Here's how to use these options.

- **Envelope Size list** Choose an envelope from this list. The default size is Size 10, which is the standard U.S. business envelope size. If you're not sure what envelope number you're using, measure it and match the dimensions next to each envelope number. The Preview area shows different envelopes as you choose them.

- **Delivery Point Barcode** This adds a delivery bar code above the envelope's delivery address so it can be handled by automated scanners at the post office. Word calculates the correct bar code based on the postal code in the address, so use nine-digit postal codes for greater sorting accuracy. If you're using a daisy-wheel printer, this option won't work.

- **FIM-A Courtesy Reply Mail** This marks the front of the envelope for special presort handling. This option doesn't work with a daisy-wheel printer.

- **Delivery Address and Return Address** Use the From Left and From Top boxes to adjust the position of each address on the envelope. The Preview area shows your changes. Click the Font button to choose a different font for each address, if you like.

Setting Printing Options

If your printer isn't printing the addresses in the proper location or is missing your envelope entirely, you can change the printer feeding options.

1 Choose Envelopes And Labels from the Tools menu.

2 Click the Options button on the Envelopes And Labels dialog box.

3 Click the Printing Options tab. You'll see the printing options as shown in Figure 18-7 on the next page.

4 Select a feed method and other options, and then click OK to return to the Envelopes And Labels dialog box.

III

Formatting Tools

FIGURE 18-7.

If an envelope isn't printing properly, change the print setup with the Printing Options tab in the Envelope Options dialog box.

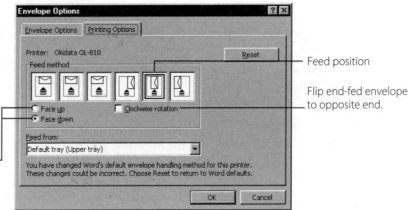

Feed position

Flip end-fed envelope to opposite end.

Set to match printer output.

Here's what the options do:

- **Feed Method** The selected icon shows the feed location that Word thinks will work best with the printer you have selected. If the addresses don't print in the right place, click another icon here. Select the Clockwise Rotation check box to change the feed location of end-fed envelopes from one side of the input tray to the other: the end-feed icons change to show the rotation.

- **Face Up or Face Down** Click a button to match the way pages come out of your printer.

- **Feed From** If your printer has an envelope feed tray, you can select it here.

- **Reset** Click this button to reset the printing options to Word's defaults for the printer you have selected.

Creating a Label

Labels are special because you usually print on label stock that contains many individual labels on each printed sheet. Word simplifies the formatting process by allowing you to select an address and choose from dozens of standard label page formats used by Avery and other manufacturers. You can print a page filled with copies of the same label or print just one label at a specific location on a sheet of labels.

You use the Labels tab in the Envelopes And Labels dialog box shown in Figure 18-8 to make labels. There are two ways to open the dialog box:

● **SEE ALSO**

For more information about creating envelopes for a list of recipients, see Chapter 26.

- Choose New from the File menu, click the Letters & Faxes tab, and double-click the Mailing Label Wizard. If you're using the Assistant, it will ask you what sort of label you want to create; click Create One Label Or A Page Of The Same Label. Word will open the dialog box with the Labels tab selected.

- Open a document and choose Envelopes And Labels from the Tools menu and click the Labels tab.

The Labels tab is shown in Figure 18-8.

FIGURE 18-8.

Enter an address and set other format options with the Labels tab in the Envelopes And Labels dialog box.

Type address or click Address Book button to insert one.

Include return address from document.

Create layout in existing document.

Create layout in new document.

Click to choose label format or add a new format.

Add a bar code.

Shows current format—double-click to change.

Print full sheet of same label or just one label.

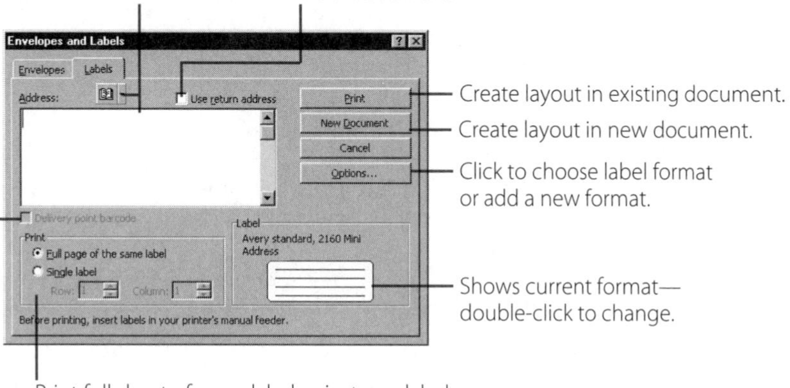

To create a label, take these steps:

1 Open the Envelopes And Labels dialog box and click the Labels tab if necessary.

2 Type either the delivery address or a return address in the Address blank, or click the Address Book icon and select the person whose address you want to use.

 TIP

If you entered your own return address on the User Information tab in the Options dialog box (choose Options from the Tools menu), click the Use Return Address check box and it will appear in the Address box. To use a return address from the document you have open, select the address in the document and insert a bookmark named EnvelopeReturn.

III

Formatting Tools

3 Select the Delivery Point Barcode check box to add a barcode to the address, if you like.

If you're using a particularly small label size, the Delivery Point Barcode check box is shaded because there isn't room to print one on the label. To use this option, select a larger label in the Label Options dialog box and then return to this tab and select the barcode check box.

4 Click a button in the Print area to print either a whole sheet of identical labels or to print just one label. If you choose to print one label, insert the row and column number of the label to be printed on the label sheet that you will use in your printer.

⭐ **TIP**

It's better to print a sheet of identical labels and use them as needed than to print single labels over and over from the same label sheet. Reusing the same label sheet can jam your printer.

5 Click the Options button and choose a different label format or change the formatting of the current label (*see "Setting Label Options" on page 394*), and then click OK.

6 Click Print to print the label, or click New Document to create a new document that shows each label's contents in a single-column table layout, as shown in Figure 18-9.

FIGURE 18-9.

To view and make changes to a label format before printing, click the New Document button in the Envelopes And Labels dialog box so Word will display the labels in a document.

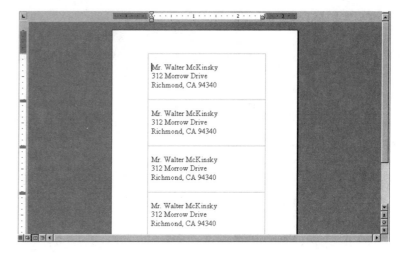

Customizing Formats in Envelopes and Labels

The Envelopes And Labels dialog box is great for creating addresses easily, but it doesn't offer all of the formatting flexibility you get in Word. You can't see an actual preview of how the label(s) or envelope will look when printed, and you can't select and format individual lines of an address. But there is a way to create envelopes or a page of the same labels easily and preview them or change their formats in any way you want.

When you use the New Document or Add To Document buttons instead and you're printing an envelope or a full page of the same labels, you can see what you'll be printing. Figure 18-9 on the previous page shows the sort of new label document you'll see when you click the New Document button when creating a label. You can select and reformat any area of text in any label, perhaps using a larger font for the name, adding a border around or shading behind the whole address, or even adding a graphic (*see "Using Graphics in Envelopes and Labels" on page 395*).

When you click the Add To Document button to create an envelope, Word inserts the envelope address (or addresses) above a new page section break in the current document. Here's an example with the page zoomed to 70% of normal size so you can see the edges of the envelope:

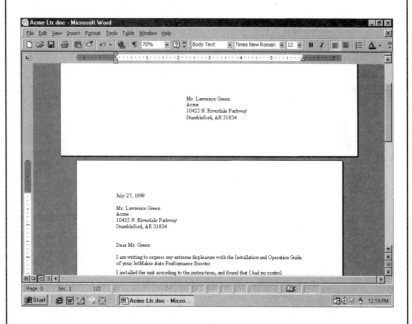

As in a new label document, you can select the text here and reformat it any way you like, and you can view the envelope section in Print Preview to see exactly how it will look when printed.

Setting Label Options

To change the type of label you print on or the specifics of its format, use the Label Options dialog box shown in Figure 18-10. To set options, follow these steps:

1 Choose Envelopes And Labels from the Tools menu.

2 Click the Labels tab.

3 Click the Options button to display the Label Options dialog box.

FIGURE 18-10.

Choose a label type and set label printing options by clicking the Options button on the Labels tab in the Envelopes And Labels dialog box.

Choose printer type—dot matrix printers can use different label sheets.

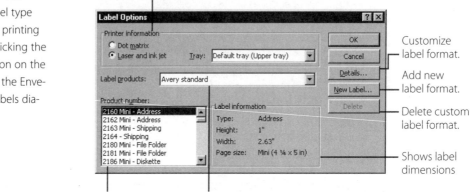

Customize label format.

Add new label format.

Delete custom label format.

Shows label dimensions

Select label format.   Choose label manufacturer.

4 Select a different printer type or input option in the Printer Information area. Dot matrix printers can often use pin-feed labels (continuous labels with feed holes at the edges) instead of single sheets.

5 Select a label products manufacturer from the Label Products list.

6 Select a label number in the Product Number list. The Label Information area shows the dimensions and the type of the label (a shipping or diskette label, for example).

7 Choose other options if you like. The other buttons on the Label Options dialog box work as follows:

• **Details** Click this button to display in all their glory the formatting details of the label you have chosen, as in the figure shown at the top of the next page.

You can use this Label Information dialog box to adjust the position of text on the label by changing the Top Margin and Side Margin settings. You'll probably want to leave the other settings alone.

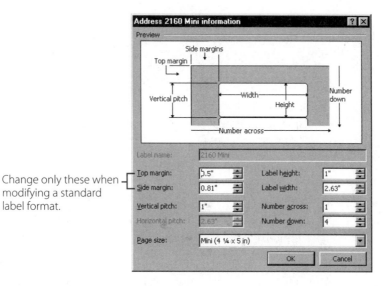

Change only these when modifying a standard label format.

- **New Label** Click this button to see a dialog box like the Label Information dialog box above, and then change any of the options you want to create a new label format and name it. Once you create a new format, its name will appear at the top of the Product Number list on the Labels tab.

8 Click OK to return to the Envelopes And Labels dialog box.

To delete a custom label, select it in the Label Products list and click the Delete button.

Using Graphics in Envelopes and Labels

When you display an envelope as part of a document or view a sheet of identical labels in a new document of their own, you are free to insert clip art, WordArt, or other graphics to dress them up.

> **NOTE**
>
> You must be able to display a label in Print Layout view in order to add a graphic to it, so you can't add a graphic to a single label with this method. To add a graphic to a single label, add the label text and graphic to an otherwise blank Word document and use the Page Setup options to format it for printing on label-sized paper. *See "Using the Page Setup Dialog Box" on page 100 for more information.*

III

Formatting Tools

You'll learn much more about managing graphics in Part IV, "Graphics, Page Design, and Publishing Tools," but here's the basic procedure for adding a graphic to an envelope or label:

1   Set up the envelope or label address.

2   Click the Add To Document or New Document button. Word displays the envelope or label page in Print Layout view.

3   Choose Picture from the Insert menu and select one of the options to paste or create a graphic.

4   Resize the inserted graphic and move it into position.

5   If you're adding graphics to a whole sheet of labels, copy the graphic from the first label and paste it into each of the other labels on the page.

? SEE ALSO

For more information about inserting, moving, and resizing graphics, see Chapter 19, "Drawing and Manipulating Graphics."

? SEE ALSO

For information about splitting a cell, see "Splitting Cells" on page 365.

You may have to reformat the text in the envelope or label to make it line up with the graphic better. If you're working in a label layout, it's easier to split the cell containing the address into two columns and then insert the graphic into the new empty cell you create.

Save Custom Return Addresses

When you spend a lot of time creating a nice-looking return address block and graphic for an envelope or a label, it would be a shame to use it to mail just one letter.

To save a whole envelope layout, first delete the text in the letter (below the section break) so you can prepare a new letter each time, and then save the document as a template. *See "Saving with a Different Name, File Type, or Location" on page 139.*

When you next make a new document from the template, the envelope will already be attached to the document and you can simply edit the address information in it.

To save a formatted return address, the address on a label, or a graphic you have sized to fit next to a return or delivery address, select it and then create a new AutoText entry with it. *See "Using AutoText" on page 218 for details.*

Using the Letter Wizard

If you write a lot of letters, the Letter Wizard can make things go much more quickly by automatically formatting your letters and entering much of the information in them for you, including the date, greeting and closing lines, your return address, and the recipient's address. The Letter Wizard can use one of four different letter templates, and you can modify any of these templates to add your own letterhead design if you like.

You can use the Letter Wizard to make a new letter from scratch or to format an existing letter that you have open:

① SEE ALSO

For more information about sending form letters to a list of re-cipients, see Chapter 26, "Using Mail Merge."

- To start a new letter from scratch, choose New from the File menu, click the Letters & Faxes tab, and double-click the Letter Wizard. Word displays a basic letter template and unless you have it turned off, the Assistant offers to help. Click Send One Letter in the Assistant's balloon. You'll see the Letter Wizard dialog box shown in Figure 18-11.

- If you have already written all or part of a letter or you have a blank document on your screen and you want help from the Letter Wizard, choose Letter Wizard from the Tools menu. You'll see the Letter Wizard dialog box as shown in Figure 18-11.

FIGURE 18-11.

Use the Letter Wizard dialog box to tell Word how you want your letter to look, to whom the letter is addressed, and which greeting and closing lines you want.

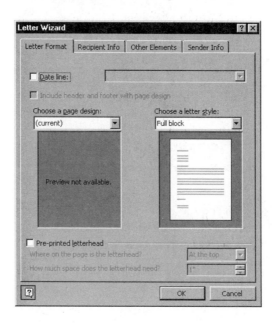

III

Formatting Tools

Using the Letter Wizard Dialog Box

You can use the Letter Wizard dialog box to format a document before you create it, or you can use it to format an existing document. Even if you have already used the Letter Wizard to create a formatted letter, you can open the Letter Wizard dialog box at any time from the Tools menu and make different choices to modify the letter's format or contents.

The Letter Wizard dialog box is organized in four tabs. Figure 18-11 shows the dialog box as opened from the Tools menu, but if you opened the Wizard with the Open dialog box, the Next, Back, and Finish buttons are at the bottom instead of OK. Click Next or Back to move from one tab to the next (rather than clicking the tabs directly, which also works). Click Finish to create the letter when you're done.

Here's a rundown on the main options on each tab. For more information about other options not mentioned here, right-click any option and select the What's This? command from the pop-up menu.

The Letter Format Tab

The Letter Format tab shown in Figure 18-11 is the place where you select the letter's overall look.

- Select the Date Line check box and then choose a date format from the list to add the current date to the letter.

- Choose the letter template you want from the Choose A Page Design list.

- Choose a letter format from the Choose A Letter Style list.

- Clear the Include Header And Footer With Page Design check box if you're writing a one-page letter.

The Recipient Info Tab

SEE ALSO

For more information about the Address Book, see the sidebar "Using Address Books" on page 387.

On the Recipient Info tab you can enter the recipient's name and address and specify a greeting line.

- Type the recipient's name and address in the Recipient's Name and Delivery Address boxes, or click the Address Book icon to select a name and address from your Address Book file.

- Click a Salutation button to select the format for the letter's greeting, and choose specific greeting text from the list if you like, or enter the greeting you want to use.

The Other Elements Tab

In many cases you can skip right over the Other Elements tab. Each of these options adds an extra line to the letter.

■ Select a check box in the Include area and then choose the text you want to use from the list to its right. If you don't like any of the choices, select the text in the box and type what you want.

■ Click the Address Book button at the bottom to select recipients of courtesy copies of the letter, or click inside the CC: box and type the names, one to a line. Each name you enter or select will appear below the signature line in the letter.

The Sender Info Tab

Use the Sender Info tab to fill out the sender's name and address and to choose options for the signature area of the letter.

■ If you filled out the User Info tab in the Options dialog box (by choosing Options from the Tools menu), your name and address appear in the Sender's Name and Return Address boxes. If they don't, you can select them from the Address Book or enter them manually.

> If you are reformatting a letter that shows a different sender's name in the signature line, Word displays it in the Sender's Name box.

■ Select options in the Closing area to add a sign-off line and to add your job title, company name, a typist's initials, or the number of enclosures below the signature. You can select and edit any of the options on these lists.

Completing the Letter

When you have selected all of the options you want in the Letter Wizard dialog box, click the OK or Finish button. Word creates the letter. Figure 18-12 on the next page shows an example.

The instructions in the letter tell you where to enter the body text and, if necessary, add your company name or other information to the header box. You can also modify the letter by selecting and reformatting any of its contents.

III

Formatting Tools

FIGURE 18-12.

When the Wizard is finished, you can enter the letter's body text or reformat it any way you like.

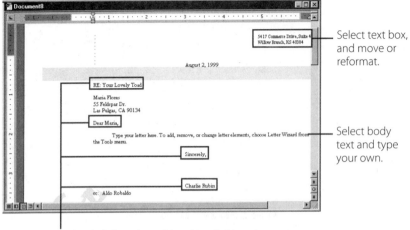

Select text box, and move or reformat.

Select body text and type your own.

Right-click the selected AutoText field to change.

The salutation, closing, reference, and many other automatically entered lines are AutoText fields (they have gray shading when you select them). To change the contents of any field, select it and then right-click it. You'll see a shortcut menu where you can select an alternate word or phrase or customize the existing one by creating a new AutoText entry.

Changing the Letter Wizard's Templates

The Letter Wizard is great by itself if you always print your letters on letterhead paper. But if you normally print your own letterhead as part of each document, it's tedious to have to add your name, address, and other contact information in the header or footer in each new letter you write.

Fortunately, there's a way around this problem. If you're careful, you can replace the Contemporary Letter, Elegant Letter, or Professional Letter templates that are used by the Letter Wizard with new ones. The replacement templates can include your name, address, a logo graphic, or any other information you always use in your letter's header or footer. You must be careful, though, because each of the Wizard's built-in templates contains specific styles and AutoText entries, and if these are not present in the templates you replace them with, the Wizard won't work.

The simplest way to substitute your own template in the Wizard is to replace one of the Wizard's own templates—create a copy of an original template and modify it without deleting any of the styles or AutoText entries. This is the best way to keep the Wizard happy, and it still gives you lots of flexibility to create custom headers and footers.

To replace a template, follow these steps:

1 Choose New from the File menu and click the Letters & Faxes tab.

2 Select the Contemporary Letter, Elegant Letter, or Professional Letter template.

3 Click Template in the Create New area in the lower-right corner of the dialog box.

4 Click OK to open the template file.

Change the text or graphics at the top or bottom of the page. You can even modify the template's styles and AutoText entries, as long as you don't delete any of them.

WARNING

Don't add a header or footer to a letter template unless you delete the existing text boxes or graphics first. Otherwise, the new header and footer will obscure other text at the top and bottom of the template.

5 Choose Save As from the File menu and save the template with the same name as the original in the folder C:\Program Files\ Microsoft Office\Templates\1033.

You should see the original template in this folder when you navigate to it in the Save As dialog box. If not, click Cancel and then choose Open from the File menu and use the Find option on the Tools menu inside the Open dialog box to locate the template you want to replace.

 TIP

You can perform the same template replacement magic to customize most other Wizards such as the Fax Wizard or Memo Wizard. There's no harm in experimenting with copies of the original templates, as long as you get them right before you replace them. However, don't replace the templates for the Mailing Label Wizard or Envelope Wizard.

III

Formatting Tools

Using AutoText Entries to Speed Formatting

If you're not comfortable with replacing a whole letter template, the next best thing is to create the header, footer, or other frequently used information you want, select it, and make an AutoText entry out of it. This way, you can simply insert the AutoText entry into each new letter.

Here's how to make sure Word creates header and footer areas in a new letter but doesn't put any text into them:

1 Open the Letter Wizard dialog box.

2 Select one of the wizard's letter templates (such as Contemporary Letter or Professional Letter) from the Choose A Page Design list on the Letter Format tab.

3 Select the Include Header And Footer In Page Design check box on the Letter Format tab.

4 Select the Omit box on the Sender Info tab.

PART IV

Graphics, Page Design, and Publishing Tools

CHAPTER 19

Drawing and Manipulating Graphics

Despite its text-oriented name, Microsoft Word includes a full set of graphics tools. You can import various types of graphics from other programs into your documents or create them from scratch, and you can place them anywhere on a page. Word also comes with a collection of clip art and some other graphics helpers that make it easy to create eye-popping graphical text and shapes. In this chapter, you'll learn the fundamentals of creating, placing, and manipulating graphics in Word.

Graphics coexist in documents with text, but you use special tools and commands to work with them. In this chapter we'll concentrate on the fundamentals of drawing lines or shapes with the Drawing toolbar and with AutoShapes and on how to select, position, manage, and format any type of graphic in a document. *For more information about inserting and manipulating clip art, WordArt, text boxes, pictures, and other graphics, see Chapter 20, "Using Special Graphics."*

About Graphics, Objects, and Pictures

There are several kinds of graphics in Word and several ways to create them, as you can see in Table 19-1. However, all graphics fall into two basic categories: objects and pictures. Objects are treated a little differently from pictures in Word, but there are some traits that all graphics have in common.

TABLE 19-1. You Can Use Many Different Types of Graphics in Word Documents

Graphic	Type	How to Create It	Samples
Lines or shapes	Object	Draw with the Drawing toolbar	
AutoShapes	Object	Create with the AutoShapes tool, then resize	
Text boxes	Object	Select Text Box from the Insert menu or draw with the Drawing toolbar or AutoShapes tool	Shipping and Receiving / If only there were a way . . .
Clip art	Object or Picture	Add from the Clip Gallery	
WordArt	Object	Insert or create with the Drawing toolbar	Wild and Crazy!
Other graphics, photos and the like	Picture	Insert from a file, scanner, or digital camera	

> **NOTE**
>
> Graphic objects are not the same as objects inserted as ActiveX components or with Object Linking and Embedding (OLE). *For more information about using these types of objects in Word, see Chapter 21, "Working with Objects."*

Every graphic in Word, whether it's an object or a picture, can exist on its own invisible layer, so you can move one graphic on top of another or in front of or behind text. Any graphic can also be *inline,* which means it is treated as a text character and can be moved only with Word's text formatting tools. You can also format graphics so that text wraps around them, and you can cut, copy, and delete graphics with the same editing tools you use for text. Finally, you can resize any graphic, either by dragging a selection handle or by specifying exact dimensions or scaling percentages.

Objects (sometimes called vector graphics) are made up of specific lines and shapes. There are several different kinds of objects in Word, as shown in Table 19-1. Objects float over text and they can usually be rotated or flipped on a page. Also, you can add shadows or 3-D effects to them or change their fill or line formats. Frequently, objects are composed of several component objects grouped together, and you can ungroup them in order to select and change the color or position of an individual component.

Pictures, or bitmaps, are collections of individual screen pixels. Pictures are created with paint programs like Microsoft Paint, or they are digitized images such as photos from a digital camera or scanned art. When you insert a picture, it is inserted as an inline graphic. A picture can't be flipped, rotated, or ungrouped, and you can't change its fill color, but you can use image control options to adjust the contrast or brightness of a picture or to change it from color to grayscale.

Creating Objects with the Drawing Toolbar

The Drawing toolbar shown in Figure 19-1 on the next page is probably the most important graphics tool in Word. With this one toolbar, you can create simple line, oval, or rectangle objects; insert AutoShapes, clip art, or text boxes; manage graphics in layers; align graphics; and select other key formatting options.

FIGURE 19-1.

Use the Drawing toolbar to create lines or shapes, manipulate them, and insert text boxes, AutoShapes, WordArt, or clip art.

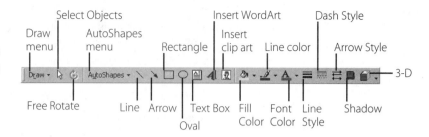

To begin drawing, start with a new blank document so you'll have plenty of room to play with. To add a graphic, follow these steps:

1 Open a new document.

2 Click the Drawing tool in the Standard toolbar or right-click in any toolbar on your screen and choose Drawing from the toolbar shortcut menu. Word displays the Drawing toolbar at the bottom of your document window.

3 Click a line or shape button on the Drawing toolbar. Word switches to Print Layout view if you're not already in it, and the pointer becomes a crosshair.

4 Point to a spot in your document where you want the line or shape to begin. When you draw a shape, you always draw from one of its corners.

? SEE ALSO

For information about changing the line color, fill color, line style, and other format options for the objects you draw, see "Changing Fill and Line Options" on page 428.

Constraining Graphics as You Draw

By holding down the Shift key as you draw a graphic, you constrain it to a specific shape or angle, as follows:

■ Straight lines are constrained to specific angles in 15-degree increments. Hold down the Shift key to draw a perfectly vertical or horizontal line, for example.

■ Rectangles are constrained to squares.

■ Ovals are constrained to perfect circles.

■ AutoShapes are constrained to the original shapes shown on the AutoShapes palettes or submenus.

It's a lot easier to create regular shapes quickly when you constrain a line or shape as you draw.

5 Click and drag to the opposite corner of the graphic's finished size. As you drag, you'll see an outline of the shape or line.

6 Release the mouse button when the graphic is the size you want. Word creates the graphic, selects it in the document, and deselects the button on the toolbar. Figure 19-2 shows four different graphics drawn with the Drawing toolbar.

 TIP

Double-click a line or shape button to lock it. You can then draw several objects with it without having to reselect the button each time. Click the same button to unlock it when you're done.

FIGURE 19-2.

When a graphic is selected, it has selection handles around it. Drag a handle to resize the graphic.

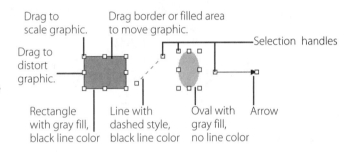

Word puts handles around a selected graphic. As you'll see in "Moving and Resizing Graphic Objects" on page 414, you can drag them to resize a graphic in various ways.

Drawing AutoShapes

The lines, boxes, and ovals on the Drawing toolbar are fine as far as they go, but Word has a whole gallery of far more interesting shapes to choose from. To see these shapes and add one to a document, follow these steps:

1 From the Insert menu, choose the Picture submenu and then AutoShapes to open the AutoShapes toolbar, or click the AutoShapes menu on the Drawing toolbar to see a list of shape categories.

2 Click a category button on the AutoShapes toolbar to display a palette of specific shapes or choose a category in the AutoShapes menu to display a submenu of shapes. Both the toolbar and a submenu are shown in Figure 19-3.

FIGURE 19-3.

To insert an Auto-Shape, either use the AutoShapes toolbar or select the AutoShapes menu on the Drawing toolbar.

AutoShapes toolbar   AutoShapes menu and submenu

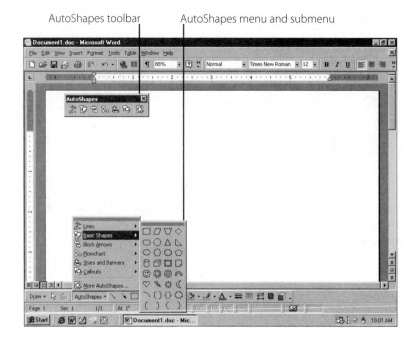

3 Select the shape you want. The crosshair pointer appears on the screen.

4 Click and drag until the shape's outline is roughly the size you want, then release the mouse button. Word creates the AutoShape and selects it in the document, like this:

Drag a colored selection handle to change object's shape.

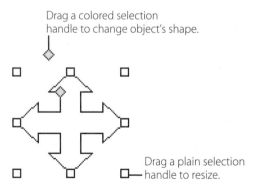

Drag a plain selection handle to resize.

Notice the two colored selection handles inside this shape. Word adds an extra handle or two to many AutoShapes so you can customize the shape as well as resize it. *For instructions, see "Changing AutoShapes" on page 417.*

TIP

> Don't overlook the Lines category of AutoShapes. You can create smooth (Bezier) curves, draw freehand, create shapes by connecting any number of lines, and create double-ended arrows with ease.

Using AutoShape Callouts

SEE ALSO

For more information about creating and formatting callouts, see "Using Text Boxes" on page 436.

When you add an AutoShape from the Callouts palette or submenu, you're actually adding a text box with a fancy border. Once you draw a callout shape, the insertion point blinks inside the text box so you can enter text.

The Callouts palette looks like this:

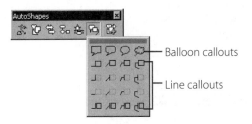

The shapes in the top row are balloon callouts that are normally used as containers for text or speech. When you select one of these, you drag in your document to create the balloon shape just as you do with other AutoShapes.

All of the other callouts are called line callouts, because they include a text box as well as a line connecting a specific place (called the *origin*) in your document with the text box. To create an AutoShape with a line, you draw the line from the origin to the margin area where you want the text box to appear, as shown on the next page.

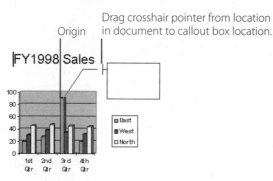

Once you place the callout you can enter and format text in it to finish it off. Figure 19-4 shows a finished callout.

FIGURE 19-4.

Use line callout AutoShapes to add notes or labels refer- ring to specific text or graphics in your document.

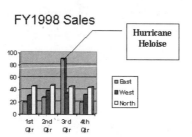

Adding Text to AutoShapes

You can add text inside any AutoShape, whether it's a callout or not. Just select the shape and click the Text Box button on the Drawing toolbar. A text box will be overlaid on the AutoShape, and the cursor will be blinking inside the AutoShape itself. You can then type the text you want. Figure 19-8 on page 422 shows a couple of examples.

Using the AutoShapes Gallery

There are dozens of arrows, boxes, and other shapes on the AutoShapes palette or menu, but that's only the beginning. When you click the More AutoShapes button on the AutoShapes palette or choose the More Auto-Shapes command from the AutoShapes menu on the Draw- ing toolbar, you'll see a whole gallery of shapes as shown in Figure 19-5 on the next page.

Scroll the window to view categories of shapes, and click a category button to see a selection of AutoShapes in that category. The More AutoShapes window stays open so you can add several shapes from it without having to reopen it each time.

FIGURE 19-5.

You can display a whole gallery of additional AutoShapes if you don't like the ones on the AutoShapes palette or menu.

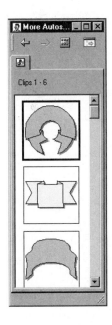

IV

Graphics and Publishing Tools

? SEE ALSO

The More AutoShapes window works the same way as the clip art window. For more information on using the gallery window, see "Using Clip Art" on page 449.

To add an AutoShape from this window, follow these steps:

1 Click a category button to view shapes inside it, and then click the shape you want. A control palette appears, like this:

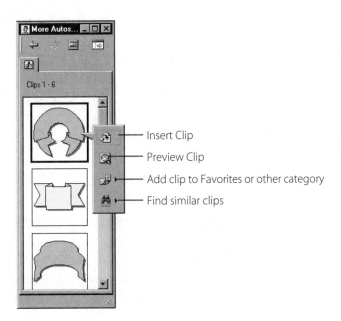

Insert Clip
Preview Clip
Add clip to Favorites or other category
Find similar clips

2 Click the Insert Clip button on the control palette, or right-click the shape and choose Insert from the shortcut menu.

Manipulating Graphics

Once a graphic is in your document, you can move it, resize it, rotate it, change the way it behaves around text, and do other things to make it look exactly the way you want.

> The techniques explained here work with all graphics in a Word document, not just shapes and AutoShapes. However, other types of graphics have additional manipulation tools. *See Chapter 20, "Using Special Graphics," for more information.*

Selecting Graphics

As with anything else in a Word document, you must select a graphic before you can move it, resize it, or do anything else with it. Shapes, AutoShapes, clip art, text boxes, WordArt, pictures, and other types of graphics are automatically selected in your document when you create them. You can tell a graphic is selected because it has selection handles around it, as shown in Figure 19-2 on page 409.

There's a difference between the default white fill color and no fill color. See "Changing the Fill Color" on page 428 for more information.

- To select a graphic, click anywhere on it. (You may have to click directly on a shape's border to select it.)

- To select several shapes at once, hold down Shift and click each of them, or click the Select Objects tool in the Drawing toolbar and then drag a selection rectangle around them.

- To delete a shape from a group of selected shapes, hold down Shift and click it.

> Right-click any selected graphic to display a shortcut menu of frequently used commands.

Moving and Resizing Graphic Objects

Once a graphic object is selected, you can drag it anywhere in the document. In fact, you can drag it completely off the edge of the document if you like. You can also drag to resize graphics. Word ignores a document's text margins when you drag graphic objects.

> Pictures are inserted as inline graphics, and you must use text formatting options to move them. For example, you can center them with an alignment tool or drag to move them to a different location within text.

- To move a graphic, drag the graphic itself or its border line, not one of its selection handles. *(See Figure 19-2 on page 409.)*

- To nudge a graphic in small increments, select it and press one of the arrow keys on your keyboard.

> Zoom your document to make fine adjustments in a graphic's size or position. (*See "Zooming In or Out of Documents" on page 119.*)

> The alignment grid is on by default and objects snap to its intersection points when you drag them. If a graphic won't stay exactly where you drag it, hold down the Alt key as you drag to temporarily turn off the Grid. *For more information, see "Aligning with the Grid" on page 419.*

Resizing a Graphic with the Mouse

You can resize any graphic by dragging one of its selection handles. When you resize a shape, however, the handle you drag (and the way you drag it) can either *scale* the graphic (making it larger or smaller while retaining its original proportions); or *distort* it (making it taller, shorter, narrower, or wider).

- To resize a line, drag a handle at one of its ends.

- To scale a shape, drag a handle at one of its corners in or out at a 45-degree angle.

- To distort a graphic, drag one of the handles up, down, left or right.

> Smaller graphics don't have side handles because there isn't room for them. To display them, zoom your document to twice its normal magnification. *See "Zooming In or Out of Documents" on page 119.*

Resizing a Graphic Precisely

To be very specific about the size or scale of a graphic, you can enter values to size or scale it.

1 Double-click the graphic or single-click and choose AutoShape from the Format menu (or whatever command is at the bottom of the extended Format menu) to display the Format dialog box.

> The name of the Format menu command and the Format dialog box will include AutoShape, Picture, Object, WordArt, or Text Box, depending on the type of object selected. For our purposes, we'll just call it the Format dialog box.

2 Click the Size tab to display these options, as shown in Figure 19-6.

FIGURE 19-6.

Set the size, scale, or rotation of an object with precise values in the Format dialog box.

3 Select options and enter values to change the graphic's size, shape, or rotation position, as follows:

- To scale a graphic and maintain its proportions, select the Lock Aspect Ratio check box in the Scale area, and then change either of the Height or Width values.

- To distort a graphic, clear the Lock Aspect Ratio check box and then change either the Height or Width values.

- To rotate the graphic, change the Rotation value. You can't rotate pictures or text boxes.

4 Click OK to apply any changes you have made.

If you don't like the effect of your changes, return to the Format dialog box and change the options again.

Changing AutoShapes

When you work with a simple shape or an AutoShape, you can replace it with another AutoShape. You can also distort AutoShapes by dragging special selection handles on them.

To replace a graphic with a different AutoShape, select the graphic and choose a different AutoShape as explained on page 412. For example, you might replace a plain rectangle with a trapezoid, rhombus, or bordered box from the Basic Shapes submenu on the AutoShapes menu.

Some AutoShapes can also be distorted. If the AutoShape has one or more colored selection handles that appear when you select them, drag a handle to change the graphic's shape. Try dragging these yourself to see how you can customize an AutoShape.

Cutting, Deleting, Copying, and Pasting Graphics

You can cut, copy, and paste graphics in a document just as you would text. This is the best way to move a graphic across several

---

Insert Graphics Easily with AutoText

If you spend a lot of time creating the perfect graphic with the Drawing toolbar or any other graphics tool, you can save it for posterity and use it later by making an AutoText entry from it. To do this, follow these steps:

1 Create the graphic.

2 Select the graphic.

3 Choose AutoCorrect from the Tools menu.

4 Click the AutoText tab in the AutoCorrect dialog box.

5 Type a descriptive name for the graphic.

6 Click Add.

Once you have stored the graphic as an AutoText entry, you can use it over and over on labels, business cards, letterheads, reports, or any other type of document. Just insert it by choosing AutoText from the AutoText submenu on the Insert menu and double-clicking the graphic's name in the list of entries.

pages in your document or from another document, and it's the simplest way to copy a graphic from one document to another.

- To delete a graphic, select it and press the Backspace or Delete key.

- To cut a graphic, select it and press Ctrl+X.

- To copy a graphic to the Clipboard, select it and press Ctrl+C.

- To duplicate a line, rectangle, or oval created with the Drawing toolbar, double-click the graphic's button on the toolbar to lock it, select the graphic, and then hold down Shift and click it.

- To paste a graphic, activate a different document or scroll to the new page where you want the graphic to appear, and then press Ctrl+V or choose Paste Special from the Edit menu.

② SEE ALSO

For more information about graphic file formats supported in Word, see "File Formats Supported in Word" on page 462.

Changing Formats with Paste Special

The objects you draw in Word are stored as MS Office Drawing Objects, but you can convert them to JPEG, GIF, PNG, Windows Metafile, or other formats with the Paste Special command.

1 Copy or cut the graphic to the Clipboard.

2 Choose Paste Special from the Edit menu. The Paste Special dialog box appears and the current format is selected, like this:

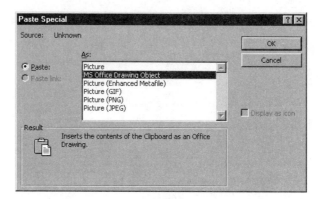

3 Select an alternate picture format. The Result box at the bottom explains the pros and cons of each format.

4 Click OK.

TIP

To move several graphics from one document to another and place them at different locations, copy them separately. They'll each be placed on the Clipboard toolbar, and they'll stay there when you switch to a different document. You can then paste any of the graphics from the Clipboard wherever you want. *For more information, see "Using Word's New Clipboard" on page 65.*

Aligning Graphics

Graphic objects float over text, so you can't use any of the text alignment tools in the Formatting toolbar to align them. Instead, you can choose commands from the Draw menu on the Drawing toolbar or use the Format dialog box to change the alignment of graphics on your page.

Aligning with the Grid

When you work with graphics, there's an invisible grid that controls the distance by which graphics are nudged (*see page 415*), and you can also use it to align graphics precisely. The grid is active by default, so when you drag graphics they "snap to" grid points. The grid makes it easy to line up graphics with one another, and in Word 2000 you can display the grid like this:

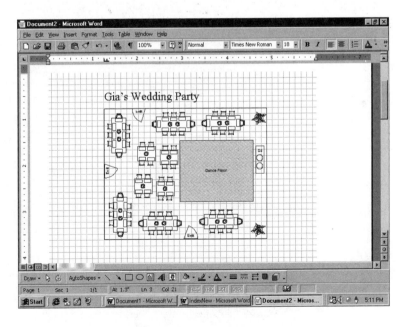

On the other hand, the grid limits your flexibility in placing graphics because every graphic must line up at a grid point. Fortunately, you can turn the grid off for more flexibility. You can also change the spacing between grid points and set other options to control it.

To set grid options, follow these steps:

1 Choose Grid from the Draw menu on the Drawing toolbar. You'll see the Drawing Grid dialog box as shown in Figure 19-7 on the next page.

2 Set the options you want for the grid. The settings work as described in Table 19-2.

3 Click OK when you're done.

TABLE 19-2. Options in the Drawing Grid Dialog Box

Setting	Description
Snap To	Snap objects either to grid points, edges of other objects, to both, or to neither. When Snap Objects To Other Objects is selected by itself, objects snap only to other objects, and can be positioned freely otherwise. Clearing both options turns the grid off.
Grid Settings	Change values to alter the spacing between Vertical and Horizontal grid lines.
Grid Origin	Enter values to set position of grid's upper-left corner, or select Use Margins to limit the grid to the area inside the page's text margins.
Display Gridlines On Screen	Select to display the grid. You can display only Vertical grid lines or both vertical and horizontal. Enter values to display all lines or every second, third, and so on.
Default button	Makes current grid settings the defaults in the current document template.

Set the Grid options before you begin drawing and positioning graphics in a document. If you change the Snap To, Grid Origins, or Grid Settings with graphics in your document, the graphics may move.

IV

Graphics and Publishing Tools

FIGURE 19-7.

You can set options for your grid with the Drawing Grid dialog box.

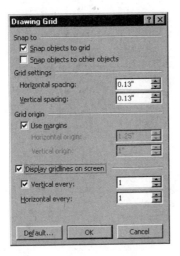

Aligning with the Draw Menu

The Grid is great for lining graphics up with each other as you drag them, but Word also has other commands you can use to automatically align graphics.

To align graphics, follow these steps:

1 Click the Select Objects button on the Drawing toolbar and then drag a selection rectangle (or hold down the Shift key while clicking) to select two or more graphics you want to align.

2 Choose Align or Distribute from the Draw menu on the Drawing toolbar. You'll see the Align or Distribute menu, like this:

The icon next to each command shows how graphics will be aligned or distributed.

3 Select the Relative To Page option at the bottom if you want to align objects relative to the page edges as well as to each other. (If you do, the menu will close and you'll have to open it again as in Step 2.)

4 Choose an alignment or distribution command. Word rearranges the objects. Figure 19-8 shows some different alignment examples.

FIGURE 19-8.

Use the Align and Distribute commands on the Draw menu to position graphics automatically.

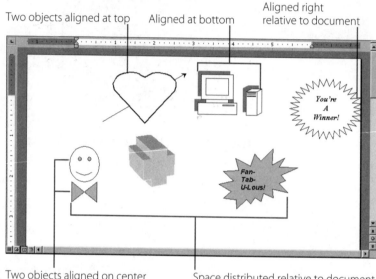

Two objects aligned at top   Aligned at bottom   Aligned right relative to document

Two objects aligned on center   Space distributed relative to document

Aligning with the Format Dialog Box

② SEE ALSO

For more information about advanced alignment, position, and text wrapping options for graphics, see "Placing Objects on a Page" on page 533.

The foregoing options align graphics with one another or to the edges of the page, but you can also align graphics relative to the left and right page margins. To do this, follow these steps:

1 Select one or more graphics in your document.

2 Double-click the selection or choose the bottom command on the extended Format menu to display the Format dialog box.

3 Click the Layout tab to display the options shown in Figure 19-12 on page 426.

4 Double-click one of the Horizontal alignment buttons to realign the graphics. For more advanced alignment options, you can click the Advanced button. *For more information, see "Setting Advanced Position Options" on page 533.*

5 Click OK.

Flipping and Rotating Graphics

For complete freedom in positioning graphics, Word allows you to rotate graphics to any angle or flip them vertically or horizontally. Figure 19-9 shows the same graphic flipped and rotated in various ways.

FIGURE 19-9.

You can flip or rotate graphics in any direction with the Rotate or Flip commands on the Draw menu.

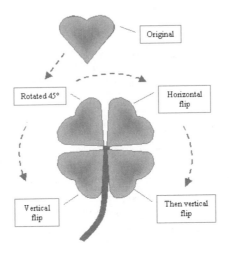

Original

Rotated 45°

Horizontal flip

Vertical flip

Then vertical flip

> **NOTE**
>
> You can't flip or rotate a text box.

You can flip or rotate a graphic in specific ways with simple commands accessed from the Draw menu on the Drawing toolbar. To use these commands, follow these steps:

1   Select one or more graphics to flip or rotate.

2   Open the Draw menu on the Drawing toolbar, and then open the Flip or Rotate submenu.

3   Choose Flip Vertical or Flip Horizontal to flip the object, or choose Rotate Left or Rotate Right to rotate the object in 90-degree increments.

Free Rotating a Graphic

You can also rotate a graphic to any position using a separate button on the Drawing toolbar. Here's how to free rotate a graphic:

1   Select the graphic.

2 Click the Free Rotate button on the Drawing toolbar. The graphic's selection handles become round and change color, and the pointer changes, too, like this:

Free Rotate pointer

3 Drag one of the selection handles.

4 Click outside of the object to cancel free rotate mode.

Managing Graphics in Layers

We have seen how you can move or rearrange graphics in two dimensions. Layers, however, allow you to move graphics in the third dimension: depth. Each time you create a graphic or insert one into your document, you can place it in its own separate, transparent layer on top of the text, so your document can become a stack of layers.

By changing the order of the layers in the stack, you specify which graphic goes in front of or behind others. This is an invaluable feature when you're creating complex graphics that are composed of several individual graphics, and you can also use it to change the relative positions of graphics and text.

> When you insert a graphic using the From File command, you can insert it into the text layer of a document if you like. A graphic inserted in the text layer is placed at the insertion point's position and becomes an inline graphic that is treated like any other text character. *For more information, see* *"Placing Objects on a Page" on page 533.*

Changing the Layer Order

To rearrange the graphic layers, follow these steps:

1 Select the graphic whose layer you want to change.

2 Click the Draw menu on the Drawing toolbar.

3 Choose an option from the Order submenu.

Here's how the Order submenu commands work:

- **Bring To Front** Moves the selected graphic to the top layer.

- **Send To Back** Moves the selected graphic to the bottom layer.

- **Bring Forward** Moves the selected graphic forward one layer.

- **Send Backward** Moves the selected graphic back one layer.

- **Bring In Front Of Text** Moves the selected graphic in front of the text layer.

- **Send Behind Text** Moves the selected graphic behind the text layer.

Figure 19-10 shows how you can create different graphic effects by rearranging layers.

FIGURE 19-10.

By changing the layer order, you can create many different graphic effects.

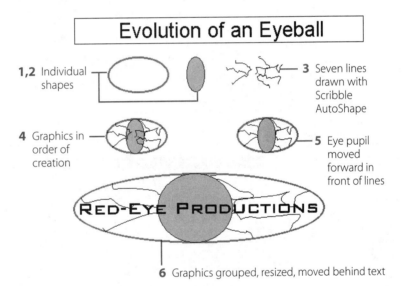

Evolution of an Eyeball

1,2 Individual shapes

3 Seven lines drawn with Scribble AutoShape

4 Graphics in order of creation

5 Eye pupil moved forward in front of lines

RED-EYE PRODUCTIONS

6 Graphics grouped, resized, moved behind text

TIP

Changing the order of the layers also helps when you're trying to select one of several tightly spaced graphics and you keep selecting the wrong one. Just select the wrong graphic and temporarily move it to the bottom of the stack.

SEE ALSO

For more information about text wrapping options, see Chapter 20, "Using Special Graphics."

Moving Graphics into the Text Layer

When you draw a graphic object, it is always created in a layer of its own on top of the text in a document, but you can move the graphic behind the text or into the text layer itself. Figure 19-10 shows a graphic placed behind text. When you move a graphic into the text layer, you can choose how the text will wrap around it. Figure 19-11 shows three different text wrapping options.

FIGURE 19-11.

By moving a graphic into the text layer, you can have text wrap around it.

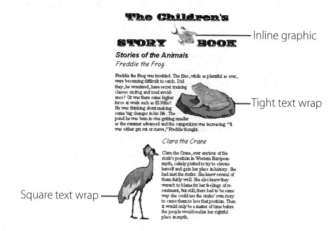

To move a graphic behind text or into the text layer, follow these steps:

1 Double-click the graphic to display the Format dialog box.

2 Click the Layout tab to display its options, as shown in Figure 19-12. Each option's graphic shows how text wraps.

FIGURE 19-12.

You can wrap text around graphics in many different ways by selecting options in the Format dialog box.

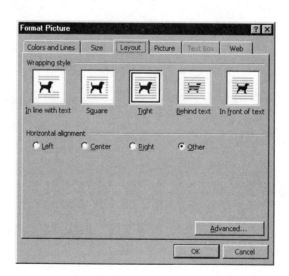

3 Double-click a Wrapping Style or Alignment option to apply it, or click the Advanced button to set additional text wrapping and graphic position options.

TIP

Word 97 users will notice that the Position and Wrapping tab options in Word 97's Format dialog box are missing in Word 2000. To see and choose these options in Word 2000, click the Layout tab and then click the Advanced button to open the Advanced Layout dialog box. *For more information about advanced text wrapping options, see "Setting Advanced Wrapping Options" on page 536.*

Grouping and Ungrouping

Many sophisticated graphics are made up of several component lines, shapes, pictures, and other items. When you create a complex graphic out of several components, you work hard to get all the pieces positioned properly, as shown in Figure 19-10 on page 425. By grouping all of the graphics that make up a complex graphic, you make it much easier to select and move the entire complex graphic as one item without fear of dislodging any of its parts.

Word allows you to group any number of graphics together as one item. You can always ungroup them later if you need to change any of the component graphics. Figure 19-13 shows the difference between a complex graphic made up of separate graphic pieces and the same graphic after the pieces have been grouped together.

FIGURE 19-13.

By grouping several graphics, you can make it easy to select and move them all at once.

Ungrouped graphics have individual selection handles.

Group has one set of selection handles.

To group several graphics, select them all and choose Group from the Draw menu on the Drawing toolbar.

 TIP

To select several adjacent graphics quickly, click the Select Objects button on the Drawing toolbar and drag a selection rectangle around all the graphics. Word selects everything inside the rectangle.

To ungroup graphics, select the grouped graphic and choose Ungroup from the Draw menu.

You can move, resize, or otherwise manipulate one or more of the component graphics in a group and then group them all again easily. Ungroup the graphic, make the modifications you want, and then choose the Regroup command to group all of the same objects again.

Changing Fill and Line Options

When you draw shapes, they are normally created with a thin black line around them and their fill color is white. But by using buttons and palettes on the Drawing menu, you can change the fill color and the weight, color, and style of the lines. These options do not affect imported pictures, but you can set special picture format options. *See Chapter 20, "Using Special Graphics," for more information.*

> The fill and line format options work with clip art and text boxes as well as with AutoShapes and with the shapes you draw with the Drawing toolbar. You can create widely varying graphic effects by filling clip art or text boxes with colors, textures, gradients, patterns, or even pictures.

Changing the Fill Color

Any shape you draw can be filled with colors, patterns, texture, or pictures. To select a different color, follow these steps:

1 Select the graphic.

2 Click the arrow button next to the Fill Color button to display the 40 colors on the Fill Color palette, like this:

3 Select a color.

When you select a fill color, that color appears on the Fill Color button, and you can apply the same color to other objects by selecting them and simply clicking the Fill Color button.

Choosing Other Color Options

If one of the 40 colors shown in the Fill Color palette doesn't suit you, you can select from more than 100 other predefined colors. And if you really want something special, you can create virtually any color of your own.

To choose from a larger palette of predefined colors, follow these steps:

1 Open the Fill Color palette and choose the More Fill Colors command. You'll see the Standard tab in the Colors dialog box as shown in Figure 19-14.

FIGURE 19-14.

You can choose from a larger group of fill colors by choosing the More Fill Colors command on the Fill Color palette.

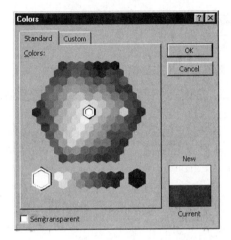

The outlined hexagon is the current selection.

2 Drag the outlined hexagon to a different color, or click an alternate color to select it.

3 Click OK. That color is applied to the selected graphic, and the alternate color is added to the bottom of the Fill Color palette so you can select it again more easily. You can add up to eight alternate colors to the Fill Color palette.

If you can't find the color you want on the Standard tab in the Colors dialog box, click the Custom tab. As you can see in Figure 19-15 on the next page, the Colors palette contains hundreds of colors, and you can drag the slider at the right to change any color's luminosity, or brightness. If you know the precise numerical values of the color you want, enter them in the boxes below the Colors palette.

FIGURE 19-15.

Create custom fill colors with the Custom tab in the Colors dialog box.

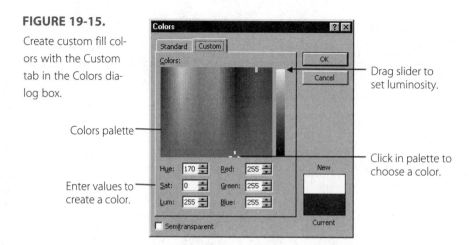

Drag slider to set luminosity.

Colors palette

Click in palette to choose a color.

Enter values to create a color.

Filling a Graphic with a Gradient, Pattern, Texture, or Photo

In addition to colors, you can fill graphic shapes with gradients, patterns, textures, or even digital photos. To see these options, open the Fill Color palette and choose the Fill Effects command. You'll see the Fill Effects dialog box, as shown in Figure 19-16.

FIGURE 19-16.

You can fill graphics with gradients, textures, patterns, or digital pictures by choosing Fill Effects on the Fill Color palette.

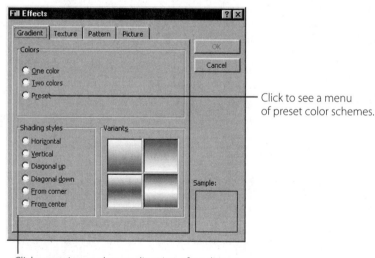

Click to see a menu of preset color schemes.

Click an option to change direction of gradient.

To apply a gradient, click the Gradient tab to see the options shown in Figure 19-16. Notice that you can select one or two colors for the gradient and choose the direction in which the gradient progresses.

TIP

Check out the Preset gradients. Microsoft has included 24 preset gradients from which to choose. To use a gradient you have created with other another program, import it with the Texture tab and apply it as a texture.

To apply a texture, click the Texture tab to display the options shown in Figure 19-17 and select the texture you want.

FIGURE 19-17.
You can add prede-signed textures or import your own tex-tures when you fill objects.

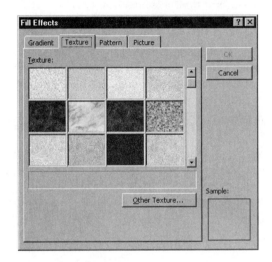

Word comes with a built-in selection of textures, but you can use any other texture you like by importing it. A texture is simply a graphic created with a paint program and saved as a file on your disk. To import a new texture, click the Other Texture button on the Texture tab and open the new texture file.

To fill a graphic with a pattern, click the Pattern tab and select the pat-tern you want. Each pattern has two colors (foreground and back-ground), and you can change these colors if you like.

SEE ALSO
For information about the graphic file for-mats supported in Word, see "Inserting Pictures" on page 461.

To fill a shape or clip art with a picture, click the Picture tab and then click the Select Picture button to open a picture file from your disk.

Changing the Line Color, Weight, or Style

Another way to vary graphic shapes is by changing the color, weight, or style of their border lines. These options work with the rectangle, oval, and line shapes on the Drawing toolbar as well as with AutoShapes, text boxes, and clip art. They do not affect pictures.

SEE ALSO

For more information about color options, see "Choosing Other Color Options" on page 429.

You use buttons, menus, and palettes on the Drawing toolbar to change the line color, weight, or style. You can adjust the color options in the same way you adjust the fill color:

■ To change the line color, select the graphic and choose a different color from the Line Color palette.

■ To change the line weight or style, select the graphic and choose a different weight or style from the Line Style or Dash Style palette on the Drawing toolbar.

■ You can also change the line ending styles for individual lines in your document by selecting them and choosing another option from the Arrow Style menu on the Drawing toolbar.

White Fill, No Fill, and Semitransparent Fill

The shapes you draw with AutoShapes or the Drawing toolbar are filled with the color white by default. Although the white color may look transparent when the shape is by itself in a document, it's not. Shapes filled with the white color will obscure shapes, lines, or text beneath them, while shapes filled with the No Fill option are transparent, so objects beneath them show through, like this:

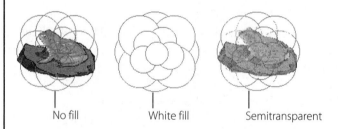

No fill   White fill   Semitransparent

You can also make colors semitransparent so objects under them will show partially through. Just choose the More Colors option on a color palette and then select the Semitransparent check box in the Colors dialog box. You can create some interesting screen effects with semitransparent colors.

Setting the No Fill option is an easy way to make a shape look as if it's behind text without having to change its layer position.

Experiment with these options to see the difference and to discover how much you can vary the look of graphics in your documents.

Setting Fill and Line Options with the Format Dialog Box

There are many options available when you reformat a graphic with the Line Color, Weight, and Style options on the Drawing toolbar, but there are even more in the Format dialog box. To use them, double-click the graphic you want to reformat and then click the Colors And Lines tab in the Format dialog box. The Colors And Lines options look like this:

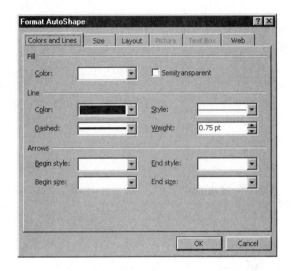

With this one tab, you can change the fill color or the line color, weight, or style. You can specify the line weight in precise values, and you can also customize arrow lines by changing the style and size of each end independently.

Adding Shadows or 3-D Effects

To make graphics stand out even more, you can apply shadow or 3-D effects to them. To do this, select a graphic and then choose an option from the Shadow or 3-D palette at the right end of the Drawing toolbar.

You can apply either a shadow or a 3-D effect, but not both. Figure 19-18 on the next page shows some examples. You can get particularly great results by applying shadow or 3-D effects to shapes or WordArt.

FIGURE 19-18.
Use the Shadow or 3-D palettes on the Drawing toolbar to create a wide variety of visual effects.

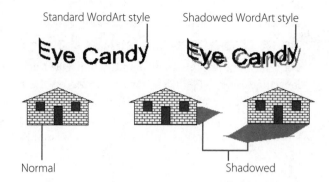

Adjusting Shadow Settings

You can add a shadow effect to a shape, line, WordArt, or clip art graphic. And if the preset shadow styles aren't enough, you can adjust them to create lots of other effects. To adjust a shadow, click the Shadow Settings button on the Shadow palette. You'll see the Shadow Settings toolbar
like this:

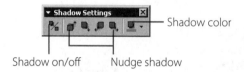

Use the buttons here to change the position of a shadow, change its color, or turn it on and off so you can easily see the difference that the change makes.

CHAPTER 20

Using Special Graphics

Microsoft Word 2000 has basic tools you can use to draw graphic objects, but a tool is only as good as its user. Since most of us aren't trained graphic artists, Word offers special types of objects that are easy to make and look great in print or on the Web. In this chapter you'll learn how to create text boxes or stylized graphical lettering and how to use clip art, digital photos, and other graphic files in your documents.

Any of these graphics can be sized, scaled, rotated, and otherwise manipulated in your document. Chapter 19, "Drawing and Manipulating Graphics," explains the basic graphics manipulations, but special graphics have some additional manipulation tools. *For more information about positioning text boxes, WordArt, or other graphics precisely in a page layout, see "Placing Objects on a Page" on page 533.*

Using Text Boxes

A text box is a graphical object that contains text. Since Word is one of the best text processing programs, you might wonder why you would need to create a graphic with text inside it. But such boxes are very useful in page design. A text box is a graphic, which means that you can fill it with a color, texture, pattern, or picture; you can change the thickness and style of the line that surrounds it; and you can set your document's main text to wrap around it in various ways. You can also link one text box to another anywhere in the document to create newspaper-style columns that jump from page to page. Figure 20-1 shows some text boxes in action.

FIGURE 20-1.

Text boxes give you total freedom in arranging your text with respect to other text and graphics on a page.

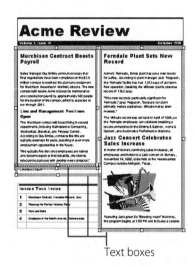

Text boxes

Creating a Text Box

There are three ways to create a text box:

- Use the Text Box command on the Insert menu.
- Click the Text Box button on the Drawing toolbar.
- Click AutoShapes on the Drawing toolbar and choose a shape from the Callouts menu.

When you use one of these three options, Word switches to Print Layout view (if you're not already in it), and the pointer becomes a crosshair. Drag the pointer to draw the text box and release the mouse button when the box is the size and shape you want. The box is selected and the insertion point is blinking inside it, as shown here:

 TIP

To create a callout, draw a line from the place in the document you want to label to the place where you want the callout's text box to appear. *For more information, see "Using AutoShape Callouts" on page 411.*

 NOTE

Text boxes are anchored to a specific place in a document. If you are displaying formatting characters in your document with the Show/Hide ¶ button, each text box or other graphic has an anchor symbol near it. *For more information about anchoring a graphic object, see "Placing Objects on a Page" on page 533.*

Entering Text into a Text Box

Since the insertion point is blinking inside a text box after you create it, you can simply begin typing to enter text. To add text to a text box later, just click inside it and begin typing. As you type, the text wraps inside the borders of the text box, but it isn't hyphenated automatically—words are broken in half when Word runs out of room on a line, like this:

If you type more text than the box can display or the words in it are broken in the wrong places, you can either resize the box by dragging one of its handles or use a smaller font size so that more characters can fit on a line.

> **NOTE**
>
> If you have linked a text box to another text box, text flows from the first box to the second when it reaches the bottom of the first box. *See "Linking Text Boxes" on page 443.*

Inside a text box, you can use any of Word's text editing features except for page or section formatting. For example, you can create multiple paragraphs, insert symbols or special characters, and insert AutoText. AutoCorrect also works, and so do the spelling checker and the thesaurus.

> **TIP**
>
> To use line numbering, footnotes, or comments in a text box, convert it to a frame. *See "Converting a Text Box to a Frame" on page 441.*

Formatting Text Inside a Text Box

You format text inside a text box just as you do any other text in a document. For example, you can change the font, size, or style, change the indents, spacing, or alignment, set tabs, use bulleted or numbered lists, align paragraphs, or add borders or shading to accent portions of the text. AutoFormat works, too. Figure 20-1 on page 436 shows some formatting examples.

> **TIP**
>
> You can also change the size of the margins that separate text from the text box border. *See "Changing the Internal Margins" on page 439.*

Changing the Text Direction

In addition to standard text formatting, you can change the direction of text in a text box so it runs vertically up or down the page. To change the text direction, select the text box, choose Text Direction from the Format menu, and choose a direction option from the Text Direction dialog box.

> **TIP**
>
> If the Text Box toolbar is open, you can also click the Change Text Direction button on it to change the direction of text. *For more information, see "Linking Text Boxes" on page 443.*

Formatting a Text Box

A text box is a graphic object, so you can move or resize it by dragging its border or one of its selection handles. When you move a callout, the line between the place in the document to which the callout refers (the *origin*) and the text box automatically adjusts to the new location.

> **NOTE**
>
> You can't rotate or flip text boxes.

SEE ALSO

For more information about resizing a text box, see "Resizing a Graphic Precisely" on page 416. For more information about positioning a text box relative to other graphics or text on a page, see Chapter 23, "Designing Pages."

And as with other graphic objects, you can also change a text box's fill or line color, line weight or style, size and location, or text wrap options as explained in Chapter 19, "Drawing and Manipulating Graphics."

In addition to the standard graphic format options, however, you can change the internal margins in a text box, set special format options for callouts, or turn a text box into a frame.

Changing the Internal Margins

Text boxes have default internal margins that separate text inside a box from the box's border. To change the internal margins, follow these steps:

1 Double-click the text box border to open the Format dialog box.

2 Click the Text Box tab to display its options, like this:

3 Change the values in the Left, Right, Top, and Bottom internal margin boxes.

4 Click OK.

? SEE ALSO

Charts created with MS Organization Chart 2.0 are embedded objects in your document. See Chapter 21, "Working with Objects," for more information about embedded objects.

What About Organizational Charts?

Organizational charts are a business staple everywhere, but arranging and formatting all of those little boxes can be a real pain. You can use text boxes and connecting lines to create such charts with the Drawing toolbar, but the Microsoft Office CD also comes with MS Organization Chart 2.0, a program that automatically arranges organization charts for you. (To create a chart with MS Organization Chart 2.0, choose Object from the Insert menu, select MS Organization Chart 2.0 from the Object Type list on the Create New tab, and click OK.)

Each approach has its pros and cons:

- Text boxes give you more formatting flexibility. You can arrange the boxes any way you want, fill boxes at different organizational levels with various colors or patterns, or use different paragraph formatting inside each box. You can also select and edit the contents of any text box without having to activate a different program. However, you'll have to do a lot of manual drawing, resizing, and alignment to set up your chart layout properly.

- MS Organization Chart 2.0 lays out boxes automatically, offers a selection of predefined chart layouts, and automatically sizes and positions text and boxes so they fit on a page. On the other hand, you must reactivate the MS Organization Chart 2.0 program to edit the text in boxes, and you can't change the color, position, or line style of the chart once you create it.

For quick organization charts, MS Organization Chart 2.0 is the way to go, but if you want to create a more visually appealing chart, you'll have more options if you do it yourself with the drawing tools in Word.

Formatting a Callout

? SEE ALSO

For more information on creating line callouts, see "Using AutoShape Callouts" on page 411.

If you used the AutoShapes command to create a text box in the shape of a line callout, you have some additional formatting options.

To change formatting options for callouts, follow these steps:

1 Double-click the border of the callout text box or select it and choose Text Box from the Format menu.

2 Click the Text Box tab in the Format dialog box if necessary, and then click the Format Callout button. You'll see the dialog box shown in Figure 20-2.

FIGURE 20-2.

Set special callout formatting in the Format Callout dialog box.

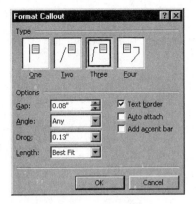

The Format Callout options work as follows:

- **Type** Sets the type of line that connects the text box to its origin in the document. You can choose a straight line, an angled line, a two-segment line, or a three-segment line.

- **Gap** Sets the distance between the callout line and the text box.

- **Angle** Changes the angle of the callout line in the document. The Any option leaves the line as you drew it.

- **Drop** Sets the distance from the top of the text box to the point where the line connects with it. You can also connect the line at the box's top, bottom, or center.

- **Length** Changes the length of the line segment (or first line segment) from the origin to the text box. The Best Fit option leaves the line as you drew it.

- **Text Border** Shows or hides the border line around the text box.

- **Auto Attach** Automatically changes the callout line position when the origin's position changes.

- **Add Accent Bar** Adds a vertical accent bar between the callout line and the text box.

Converting a Text Box to a Frame

Text boxes will meet most of your flexibility requirements when you place text on a page, but they do have limits. You can't insert footnotes or reviewer comments into a text box, nor can you insert index, cross-reference, or table of contents entries. You can't place text boxes inside other text boxes or wrap text around graphics in a text box, either. If you want to do any of these things, you'll need to convert the text box to a frame.

Here's how to convert a text box to a frame:

1 Double-click the text box's border to display the Format Text Box dialog box.

2 Click the Text Box tab, if necessary.

3 Click the Convert To Frame check box. Word will warn you that you may lose some formatting when you convert to a frame.

4 Click OK. The text box becomes a frame and moves all of its text into the frame.

> It's hard to tell the difference between a frame and a text box by looking at them, but a frame has smaller, filled selection handles. In addition, the Line and Fill options on the Drawing toolbar are not available, and the command at the bottom of the Format menu reads Format Frame.

To set a frame's formatting options, double-click its border or choose Frame from the bottom of the Format menu. You'll see the Frame dialog box as shown in Figure 20-3.

FIGURE 20-3.

When you convert a text box to a frame, you can set all of the frame's formatting options in this one dialog box.

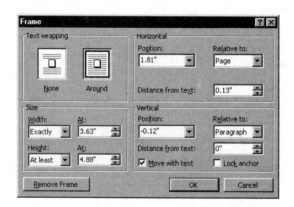

> You will also notice a Frames command on the Format menu. This command is for inserting and managing scrollable frames in Web pages. *See "Using Frames" on page 790 for more about them.*

The Text Wrapping and Size options in the Frame dialog box are like those covered in Chapter 19, "Drawing and Manipulating Graphics."

IV

Graphics and Publishing Tools

For more information about the Position options, see "Placing Objects on a Page" on page 533. For additional information on any item, click the Help button at the top of the dialog box and then click an option to see a description.

To remove a frame, double-click its border and then click the Remove Frame button in the Frame dialog box. Word deletes the frame, moves its contents into the document, and adds a border around them. You can't convert a frame back into a text box.

Linking Text Boxes

When you're creating a newspaper, newsletter, or magazine-style layout, linked text boxes give you much more freedom about how and where text appears, and you can use linked text boxes to contain different sections of the same article. Linked text boxes can be on different pages of a document if you like.

When you link text boxes, they are linked one to another in a chain. Text flows from one box to the next as Word inserts or deletes lines during editing and formatting. You can create a link to any empty text box.

Creating or Removing a Link

To link two text boxes, follow these steps:

1 Select an origin text box from which you want to create a forward link, or draw a new one. Word displays the Text Box toolbar, as shown in Figure 20-4.

FIGURE 20-4.

Use the Text Box toolbar to create or remove links between text boxes.

Previous text box   Next text box

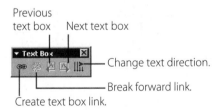

Change text direction.

Break forward link.

Create text box link.

2 Click the Create Text Box Link button on the toolbar.

3 Click inside an empty destination text box to create the link.

 NOTE

You can link only to an empty text box.

To remove the link between two text boxes, select the origin box and click the Break Forward Link button on the Text Box toolbar.

To navigate from one linked box to the next, select any linked text box and click the Next Text Box or Previous Text Box button on the Text Box toolbar.

Using WordArt

WordArt is highly stylized text that can be moved, rotated, sized, and placed on a page as a graphical object. Commercial artists frequently use type-rendering programs to create graphical text (or type effects) like the ones in WordArt for presentations, posters, document titles, advertisements, brochures, and other designs. WordArt is not as powerful as a commercial type-rendering program, but it's much easier to use and you can use it to create thousands of different type effects. Figure 20-5 shows some WordArt effects, including a sign created by overlaying a WordArt effect on a shaded background.

FIGURE 20-5.

WordArt's graphical text effects add eye appeal to posters, signs, document titles, and other projects.

⭐ **TIP**

The WordArt Gallery offers 30 different type effects, but you can customize these with the WordArt and Drawing toolbars to create thousands of different looks with format options. Options in a 3-D format are especially interesting.

Creating WordArt

When you create WordArt, you use a dialog box to select a WordArt style, enter the text of your title, and choose the type font or font size. To do this, follow these steps:

1 Choose Picture from the Insert menu and click WordArt, or click the Insert WordArt button on the Drawing toolbar. Word displays the WordArt Gallery like this:

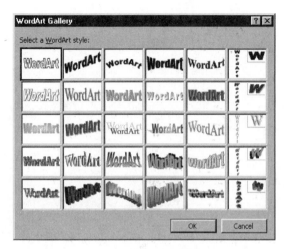

2 Double-click a WordArt style. Word opens the Edit WordArt Text dialog box, like this:

3 Type the text you want. It will replace the sample text. Text wraps inside the Edit WordArt Text dialog box, but it appears on one line in your document. Press the Enter key to break a line when you want your WordArt object to contain text on more than one line.

4 Choose a font, font size, or the Bold or Italic type styles with the menus and buttons at the top of the dialog box. The text window shows the effect of your changes. The text formats apply to all of the text—you can't format individual characters.

5 Click OK to insert the WordArt. It appears in your document and the WordArt toolbar is displayed, as shown in Figure 20-6.

FIGURE 20-6.

Use the WordArt toolbar or the Drawing toolbar to rotate, flip, or change the fill options in WordArt.

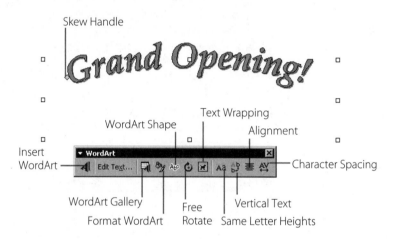

Editing WordArt Text

To edit WordArt text after it appears in a document, double-click the WordArt object or select the object and click the Edit Text button on the WordArt toolbar. Word reopens the Edit WordArt Text dialog box so you can change the text or its font or style settings.

Formatting WordArt

SEE ALSO

For more information about moving, re-sizing, flipping, or rotating graphics or adjusting their layer position, see "Manipulating Graphics" on page 414 and "Managing Graphics in Layers" on page 424.

WordArt is treated as an object in a document, so you can resize it, flip it, rotate it, change its fill or line format, add shadow effects, and set other format options, just as you can with most other graphic objects. You can also adjust the layer position of WordArt to place it in front of or behind other graphics or to put it into the text layer of a document.

There are additional formatting options you can use with WordArt to give you even more flexibility in your designs.

TIP

Some WordArt titles appear cramped when you create them, but you can increase their legibility by resizing them.

Changing the WordArt Shape

When you first create WordArt, you select the basic WordArt style, but after it's in your document you can change its shape. You can select a completely different shape if you like, or you can drag a special selection handle to change the amount of curve or slant in the current shape.

Here's how to choose a totally different shape:

1 Select the WordArt object.

2 Click the WordArt Shape button on the WordArt toolbar to display the shape palette, which looks like this:

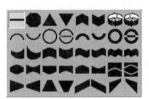

3 Select a different shape.

To alter the current shape, select the WordArt object and drag the yellow selection handle. The type of adjustment Word makes as you drag this handle depends on the WordArt style you originally used.

Changing the Text Arrangement

The four buttons on the right end of the WordArt toolbar allow you to change the appearance of text, as follows:

- **WordArt Same Letter Heights** Makes all the letters in your text the same height.

- **WordArt Vertical Text** Positions the text vertically rather than horizontally, or vice versa. Notice that the vertical letters remain upright but they're arranged one below the other. When you rotate the text, on the other hand, the letters are rotated.

- **WordArt Alignment** Sets the alignment of text within the WordArt object according to the option you select from the menu. This feature is most useful when the WordArt text is on two or more lines.

SEE ALSO

For more information about character spacing and kerning, see "Character Spacing Options" on page 84.

■ **WordArt Character Spacing** Applies spacing options between letters, from Very Loose to Very Tight. You can't specify the number of points by which to separate letters as you can with the Character Spacing tab in the Font dialog box, but you can adjust spacing by a percentage of the original. You can also turn on kerning for pairs of characters that would benefit from it, such as the "Ve" and "Yo" in "Very" or "Your."

Figure 20-7 shows some examples formatted with various text arrangement options.

FIGURE 20-7.

Use text arrangement options on the Word-Art toolbar to vary the spacing, height, direction, and alignment of text.

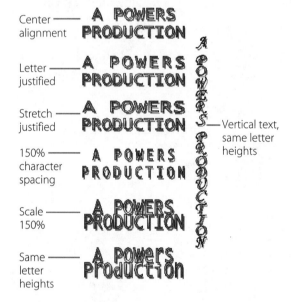

Changing the Fill and Line Options

You can change the fill color, line color, and line weight in WordArt, like the example shown here:

When you change the fill color, you change the surface of the WordArt text. You can't change the color of the sides of 3-D text or the color of any shadow or background text that's part of the WordArt style.

 **TIP**

> Try filling WordArt with textures, patterns, and pictures, or using the Shadow or 3-D options on the Drawing toolbar to create even more incredible type effects.

When you change the line color or style, you change the color of the line that borders the surface of WordArt text.

Using Clip Art

Word comes with a large collection of ready-made graphics, or clip art, that you can insert in your documents, and the revamped Clip Gallery in Word 2000 makes it easier to locate, manage, and insert specific graphics. Figure 20-8 shows how clip art can enhance a document.

FIGURE 20-8.

Clip art helps break up text in a layout, adds eye appeal, and helps create a mood.

Some clip art graphics are objects and some are pictures, but you use the Clip Gallery to insert them all. Clip art objects are formatted like other graphics in Word, as explained in Chapter 19, "Drawing and Manipulating Graphics." Clip art pictures are formatted like pictures. *For more information about formatting clip art pictures, see "Formatting Pictures" on page 463.*

Inserting Clip Art

To insert a clip art graphic, follow these steps:

1 On the Insert menu, point to Picture and click Clip Art, or click the Insert Clip Art button on the Drawing toolbar. Word opens the Clip Gallery, as shown in Figure 20-9.

FIGURE 20-9.

The new Clip Gallery in Word 2000 stays open after you insert a graphic, sound, or video clip, and you can search for clip art items by keyword.

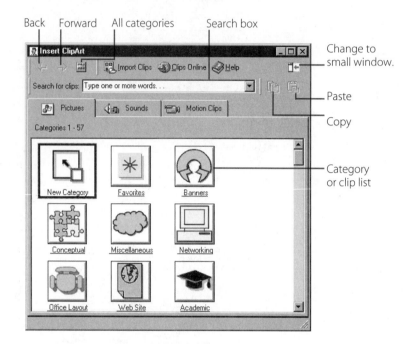

2 Click a category name to see clips in that category.

3 Select a clip. Word shows a control palette, like this:

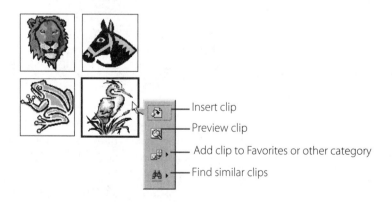

4 Click the Insert Clip button or drag the clip into the document window.

TIP

> Point to any clip for a couple of seconds to see a ScreenTip showing the clip's size in pixels and the keywords associated with it.

Using the Clip Gallery

The Clip Gallery in Word 2000 is much improved over the one in previous versions of Word. You can now drag clips directly from the gallery into your document, and you can search for more clips that are similar to the one you have already selected. There's also an improved Preview function so you can see more accurately how a clip will look in your document.

Managing the Gallery Window

SEE ALSO

Motion clips and sounds are primarily for Web pages. For more information about adding them to Web pages, see "Adding Sounds and Movies" on page 797.

The Clip Gallery is in its own window, as shown in Figure 20-9. Clip Art (Pictures), Sounds, and Motion Clips are on individual tabs in the Gallery window, and the clips are organized in dozens of categories in a scrolling list. You can move, resize, minimize, maximize, or close the gallery window just as you can a document window, but there are also two distinct versions of the window.

To switch to the small or large version of the gallery window, click the Change To Small Window/Change To Full Window button in the top-right corner. The small window doesn't show all of the gallery control buttons. It looks like this:

Navigating in the Gallery

The Clip Gallery can contain hundreds of clips. Word offers several different ways to find exactly the one you want:

- Click the Pictures, Sounds, or Motion Clips tab to see categories of clips. Scroll through the list to see more categories.

- Click a category name to view specific clips and scroll through the list to see more clips.

- Click the Forward button (or press Alt+→) or Back button (or press Alt+←) to go to the previous or next category.

- Click the All Categories button (or press Alt+Home) to return to the main Categories list for the current tab.

Searching the Gallery

Another way to locate clips is by searching for them. You can search by a descriptive keyword or have Word find more clips like the one you have selected.

To search by keyword, follow these steps:

1   Click a tab to indicate the type of clip you want to find.

2   Select the text inside the search box at the top of the Gallery window.

3   Type a descriptive keyword, such as "office," and press the Enter key. If you are searching for clip art on the Pictures tab, Word finds all the clips that are identified with that keyword and displays them like the figure on the following page.

   Notice that when you search the Clip Gallery, Word collects clips from all categories (including AutoShapes) and displays them on the tab for your convenience.

There are dozens of new clip categories in Word 2000, including several with Web graphics such as bullets, divider lines, backgrounds, and banners. Be sure to take a look at them when you're creating Web pages.

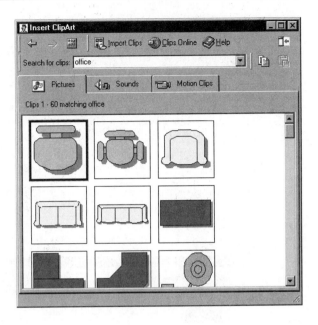

If you find one clip and want Word to locate more like it, you can use a button on the control palette:

1 Select the clip to display the control palette.

2 Click the Find Similar Clips button. Word presents buttons and keywords you can use to search for similar clips, like this:

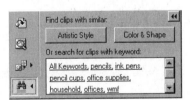

3 Click a button to see additional clips with a similar style, color, or shape, or click a keyword to see all clips associated with that keyword.

Previewing a Clip

To see a larger version of a clip, select it and click the Preview Clip button on the control palette. The clip appears in a larger preview window. Click the Close button at the upper-right corner of the preview window to put it away.

Changing Clip Properties

Each clip is stored in the Clip Gallery in certain categories and with certain keywords, and each clip has properties that you can edit. For example, you might add more keywords so that a particular clip is included in a search you frequently conduct, or you might include the clip in more categories so it shows up more often when you browse the gallery window.

To see and change a clip's properties, follow these steps:

1 Right-click a clip to display a shortcut menu, and choose the Clip Properties command. You'll see the Clip Properties dialog box, as seen in Figure 20-10.

FIGURE 20-10.

You can assign a clip to more categories or keywords with the Clip Properties dialog box.

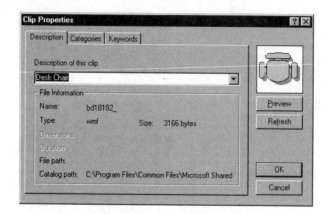

2 Click the Categories tab. You'll see options like this:

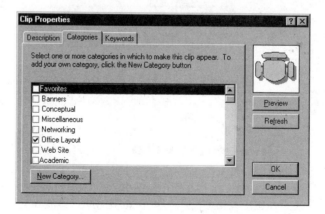

3 Select the check boxes next to the names of categories in which you want the clip to be included or clear check boxes to exclude the clip from categories. To create a new category, click the New Category button and enter a name for it.

 TIP

You can also make a new category by clicking the New Category button in the list of categories in the main gallery window. Add a clip to one category at a time by clicking the clip to display the control palette, clicking the Add Clip To Favorites Or Other Category button, and then choosing a category from a menu.

4 Click the Keywords tab. You'll see a list of keywords associated with the clip, like this:

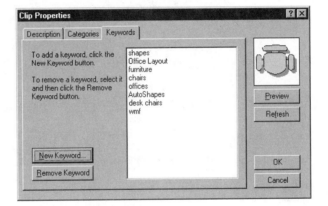

5 Review, add, or delete keywords.

6 Click OK to save the changes.

Importing and Arranging Clips

There are hundreds of clips in the Clip Gallery, but you can add others by importing them from files on a disk or from the Web. You can also copy and paste clips into documents or other categories in the Clip Gallery window.

Importing a Clip from Your Disk

Here's how to import a clip from a file on your disk:

1 Click the Import Clips button at the top of the full window version of the Clip Gallery window. You'll see a dialog box like this:

Select location.

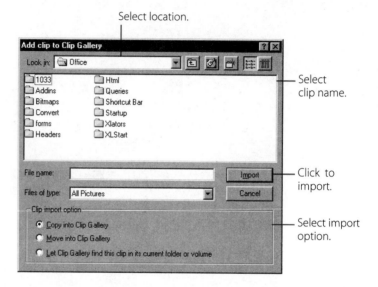

Select
clip name.

Click to
import.

Select import
option.

? **SEE ALSO**

For more information
about linking, see "Importing a Clip from
Your Disk" above or
see Chapter 21, "Working with Objects."

How and Where the Gallery Stores Clips

The Clip Gallery stores all of its clips in the C:\Program Files\Common Files\Microsoft Shared\Clipart folder on your hard disk. The clips are arranged in folders within the Clipart folder by type, not by category. When you import a clip from a file on your disk, Word automatically places it in the appropriate folder, but you do have a choice about whether the file is copied into the Clipart folder, moved there, or installed there as a link to its original location.

Each option has its advantages:

■ Copy a graphic to the Clipart folder when you want to access it from the gallery window and yet leave it stored in its original location (perhaps for easier access from other programs).

■ Move a graphic to the Clipart folder when you will primarily use it from the Clip Gallery.

■ Install a link to the graphic when you don't want to increase the size of the Clipart folder. This is useful if you're short of disk space or if you frequently access graphics from a collection on a CD-ROM or a network server.

2 Use the navigation buttons and Files Of Type menu to locate the clip you want.

3 Select the clip.

4 Choose an import option.

- Copy the clip to the Clipart folder on your disk (Copy Into Clip Gallery)

- Move the file into the Clipart folder (Move Into Clip Gallery)

- Insert a link to it in the Clipart folder (Let Clip Gallery Find This Clip In Its Current Folder Or Volume).

5 Click Import. You'll see the Clip Properties dialog box as shown in Figure 20-10 on page 454.

6 Add keywords on the Description or Keywords tabs, and choose or create new categories on the Categories tab, as explained on page 454-455.

7 Click OK. The clip is added to the categories you selected with the keywords you supplied.

Importing a Clip from the Web

Microsoft has more clips available on its Web site, and if you have an Internet connection, you can import them directly from there into the Gallery. To import clips from the Web, follow these steps:

1 Click the Clips Online button at the top of the Gallery window. You'll see a message like this:

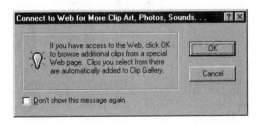

2 Click OK. Word takes you to the Microsoft Clip Gallery Live Web site. You'll be asked to accept a software license agreement, and once you click the Accept button, you'll see the main Clip Gallery Live page as in Figure 20-11 on the next page.

FIGURE 20-11.

You can review more clip art graphics online and download the ones you want for use in the Clip Gallery.

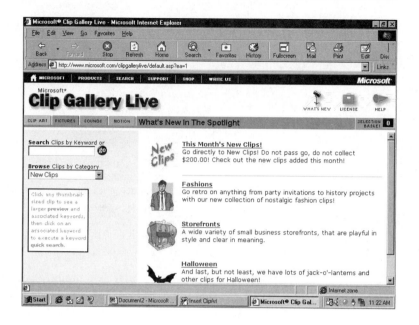

3 Click a hyperlink to see clips in a particular category, like this:

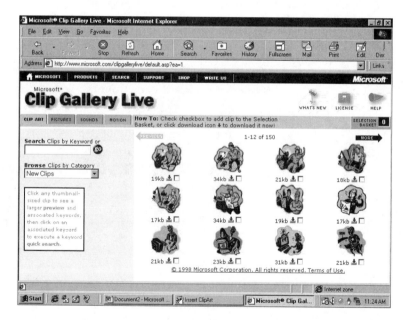

4 Click the arrow button below a clip to download a clip. To download more than one clip at a time, click the check box below each clip to add it to the Selection Basket, and then click the

Selection Basket button at the top of the Web page and follow the instructions to download all the clips in the basket.

5 Open the Downloaded Clips category in the Clip Gallery window to see or use the clips you downloaded.

> If you follow the procedure above, all downloaded clips appear in the Downloaded Clips category in the Clip Gallery window. However, you can always change any clip's properties to add it to other categories.

Copying, Pasting, and Deleting Clips

If you want, you can move clips by using Copy and Paste commands. You can also delete them.

■ To delete a clip, right-click it and choose Delete from the shortcut menu. You'll be asked to confirm the deletion by clicking OK.

WARNING

> Deleting a clip eliminates it from the Clip Gallery entirely and removes it from all gallery categories. Use the Recover command on the shortcut menu if you change your mind (*see page 460*). To remove a clip from one or more categories without removing it from the Clip Gallery, use the Clip Properties dialog box.

■ To copy a clip, select it and click the Copy button at the top of the gallery window, or right-click the clip and choose Copy from the shortcut menu.

■ To paste a clip into another category, open that category and then click the Paste button at the top of the gallery window, or right-click in the list of clips and choose Paste from the shortcut menu.

■ To insert the clip in your document, right-click the clip and choose Insert from the shortcut menu. If you copied the clip, you can also use the Paste Special command on Word's Edit menu to paste it in with a different format.

> When you copy a clip, it is placed on the Clipboard so that you can paste it into more than one place. *For more information, see "Using Word's New Clipboard" on page 65.*

Deleting or Renaming a Clip Category

There are dozens of categories in the Clip Gallery, and there could well be some you believe you'll never use. You can delete individual clips or entire categories if you want to avoid cluttering the gallery window with clips or categories you don't want. You can also rename categories.

To delete a category, follow these steps:

1 Display the list of categories in the Clip Gallery window.

2 Right-click the category you want to remove and choose the Delete Category command from the shortcut menu. You'll be asked to confirm the deletion.

3 Click the OK button to delete the category.

WARNING

If you delete a category that you created yourself, the category will be deleted for good—it can't be recovered. However, the clips in that category will remain on your disk and can be accessed using other gallery features.

To rename a category, right-click the category button on the gallery window, choose the Rename Category command, and then type a new name for the category.

Recovering Deleted Clips and Categories

To recover a deleted clip or category or to restore a clip's original properties if you have changed them, right-click in the category or clip list, choose Recover from the shortcut menu, and click the Restore button in the dialog box that follows. You'll see the Recovery dialog box like this:

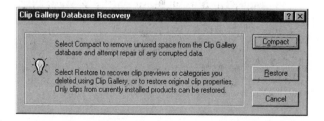

Click a button here to recover deleted categories or clips or to reset a clip's properties to their original state. You can only recover categories and clips that were initially installed with Word, not categories or clips you added yourself.

Conserving Clip Gallery Space

The Clip Gallery takes up a lot of space on your disk, but you can compact it to eliminate unused space from it if you're using a laptop or another computer where conserving disk space is important. To do this, right-click anywhere in the category or clip list, choose Recover from the shortcut menu, and then click the Compact button.

Inserting Pictures

Although Word's built-in graphics tools give you lots of design options, you can also insert pictures into your documents. For example, you might want to use a digital photo of your company's new office for a Web page or add the company logo to a newsletter. As far as Word is concerned, a "picture" is a digital photograph or a bitmap graphic. Some graphics in the Clip Gallery are pictures, and you can also insert pictures from your disk, a network server, a digital camera, or a scanner.

To insert a picture from a file on your disk, choose Picture from the Insert menu, and then choose From File. You'll see the Insert Picture dialog box. Use the Insert Picture dialog box to locate the picture you want, and then double-click the picture file or select it and click the Insert button to insert the picture into your document.

To insert a picture from a scanner or digital camera, follow these steps:

1 Plug the scanner or camera into your computer and turn it on. Place the picture you want to scan in the scanner, if necessary.

2 On the Insert menu, point to Picture and choose From Scanner Or Camera. Word opens the Insert Picture From Scanner Or Camera dialog box, like this:

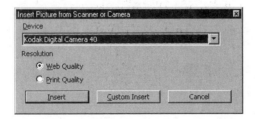

3 Choose the scanner or camera name and model from the Device menu. (This menu should list every scanner or camera for which you have installed a driver.)

4 Choose a resolution option.

5 Click the Insert button to insert a single image from a scanner or camera. Word connects to the scanner or camera and presents a dialog box where you can set the scanning options or choose the picture you want from the camera's memory.

6 Set the options you want in the camera or scanner dialog box, and then click the appropriate button to operate the scanner or to get the picture you want from the camera. Word inserts the picture in your document.

TIP

To choose a picture from among several stored on a digital camera, click the Custom Insert button to launch the image management software from the camera and then use that software to select a picture to insert.

NOTE

Each digital camera and scanner has its own image management and driver software, which must be installed on your computer before Word can get pictures from it. When you tell Word to insert a picture from a scanner or camera, you'll see a dialog box with scanner or camera options. This dialog box is supplied by the camera or scanner driver and varies from one model to the next.

File Formats Supported in Word

Word makes it easy to insert pictures or other graphic files from many programs. You can insert pictures in the following graphic file formats:

- AutoCAD Format 2-D (.dxf)
- Compressed Windows Enhanced Metafile (.emz)
- Compressed Windows Metafile (.wmz)
- Computer Graphics Metafile (.cgm)
- Corel Draw (.cdr)
- Encapsulated Postscript (.eps)
- Graphics Interchange Format (.gif, .gfa)
- Joint Photographic Experts Group format (.jpg, .jpeg, .jff, .jpe)

- Kodak Photo CD (.pcd)

- Macintosh PICT (.pct)

- Micrografx Designer/Draw (.drw)

- PC Paintbrush (.pcx)

- Portable Network Graphics (.png)

- Targa (.tga)

- Tagged Image File Format (.tif)

- Windows Bitmap (.bmp)

- Windows Enhanced Metafile (.emf)

- Windows Metafile (.wmf)

- WordPerfect Graphics (.wpg)

Support for so many different file formats means you can use a graphic from just about any source. Even if a program's native file format isn't on the list above, nearly every graphics program can save its pictures in one of these formats.

 TIP

The file format converters listed above are all available from the Microsoft Office program CD, but they probably weren't all installed on your computer. To install more graphics converters, use the Add or Remove Features button in the Microsoft Office Installation Wizard. *For more information, see "Customizing an Office Installation" on page 802 in the Appendix.*

Formatting Pictures

 SEE ALSO

For information about moving and manipulating graphics, see Chapter 19, "Drawing and Manipulating Graphics."

When you select a picture in a document, Word opens the Picture toolbar as shown in Figure 20-12 on the next page. You can use this toolbar to change the contrast, brightness, line style, fill color, or other format options for clip art. Click a button to change a specific setting like the brightness or contrast, or click the Format Picture button to open the Format dialog box and choose more options there. In addition to using these formatting options, you can move, resize, align, and change the layer position of pictures just as you can other graphic objects.

FIGURE 20-12.

Use the Picture toolbar to format clip art as well as pictures.

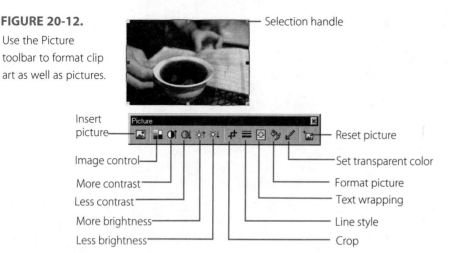

Selection handle

Insert picture

Image control

More contrast

Less contrast

More brightness

Less brightness

Reset picture

Set transparent color

Format picture

Text wrapping

Line style

Crop

NOTE

You can't rotate, flip, or free rotate pictures.

Changing Clip Art Fill and Line Formats

Most clip art graphics and pictures are inserted into documents with no fill or line color. However, you can change the fill color to create a colored backdrop for a clip art graphic, and you can change the line color or style to create a border around a piece of clip art.

To change the fill or line color or style, use buttons on the Drawing toolbar, as explained in Chapter 19. There's also a Line Style button on the Picture toolbar that works like the one on the Drawing toolbar, and you can click the Format Picture button on the Picture toolbar to set color or line options on the Colors And Lines tab in the Format Picture dialog box.

SEE ALSO

For more information about shadow or 3-D effects, see "Adding Shadows or 3-D Effects" on page 433.

Adding Shadow Effects

You can also add a shadow background behind any clip art graphic (object or picture). To do this, click the Shadow button on the Drawing toolbar and choose a shadow style from the palette. Only a few of the shadow styles are available when you work with clip art, and you can't use 3-D effects at all. In addition, you can't use shadow or 3-D effects with pictures inserted from files, scanners, or cameras.

Cropping a Picture

In addition to resizing clip art objects and pictures, you can crop them. When you crop a picture you drag a handle to resize it, but instead of resizing the object, you reduce the amount of the picture that is showing, like this:

Original picture

Resized to fit

Cropped to fit

Final image size
in document

> **NOTE**
>
> You can crop a picture only when it is an inline graphic in a document. Once you move a picture out of the text layer, you can't crop it anymore. *See "Changing A Picture's Layer Position" on the next page.*

To crop a picture, follow these steps:

1 Select the picture.

2 Click the Crop tool on the Picture toolbar. The pointer turns into a crop frame icon.

3 Drag one of the corner selection handles on the picture to reduce its size and eliminate part of it.

> **TIP**
>
> If you crop too much of a picture you can restore it to its original size by clicking the Reset Picture button on the Picture toolbar.

Changing a Picture's Layer Position

You can change the layer position of clip art graphics and pictures just as you can other types of graphics. In fact, you'll find it necessary to change the layer position in order to move and resize pictures easily. When a picture is inserted in your document, it is added as an inline graphic in the text layer, like this:

Theresa's New Beverage

Theresa went out for a cup of   coffee, but Giggolo's was closed and Ishmael's was out of the question. Nobody went there anymore, which actually didn't bother her, but it was clear across town on a cold, windy night.

You can tell that the object is an inline graphic because it is treated as a text character. Text does not wrap around the picture, so it can only be moved by inserting or deleting text in front of it or by using the controls in the Formatting toolbar. In addition, the picture selection handles are inside the picture instead of outside it, and the height of the picture affects the line spacing between the line it's in and the line above (the title in the example above).

SEE ALSO

For more information about text wrapping options, see "Moving Graphics into the Text Layer" on page 425.

To convert a picture into a floating graphic, click the Text Wrap tool in the Picture toolbar and choose any of the wrapping options from the menu. Once a picture or clip art object is a floating graphic, you can change its layer position as you would with other types of graphics by clicking the Draw menu on the Drawing toolbar and choosing a command from the Order submenu.

TIP

If a picture is too large when inserted into your document, double-click it to display the Format Picture dialog box, click the Size tab, and change the Height and Width values in the Scale area to 50%. At half size, the graphic should be small enough to move and reformat with ease.

Setting Image Options

When you work with a picture, you can modify its appearance with tools on the Picture toolbar. By clicking the following buttons one or more times, you can achieve these effects:

- **More Contrast or Less Contrast** Changes the contrast.

- **More Brightness or Less Brightness** Makes the picture lighter or darker.

- **Image Control** Changes the color display style. You can choose among these styles:

  - Automatic—displays the image's original colors as faithfully as possible.

  - Grayscale—converts a color image to shades of gray.

  - Black and white—changes the image to only black and white.

  - Watermark—converts the image to very pale, transparent shades.

Figure 20-13 shows examples of images that have been modified by using the Picture toolbar.

FIGURE 20-13.

By changing a picture's brightness, contrast, and image control settings, you can make significant changes in its appearance.

Original picture

Enhanced with brightness and contrast changes

I wandered lonely
as a cloud that
floats on high o'er
vales and hills

Watermark picture as a page background

Using Transparent Colors

If you have used a fill color behind a clip art picture or object, you can make it semitransparent for a softer look, like this:

Original
fill color

Semitransparent
fill color

You can also make colors in bitmapped graphics transparent so a background color or texture shows through.

To make part of a digital photo or bitmapped image semitransparent, click Set Transparent Color on the Picture toolbar and then click the area in the picture that you want to make semitransparent. For example, click the white background of a corporate logo to make the logo semitransparent on a Web page.

 NOTE

> The Set Transparent Color button is only active when you have a digital photo or bitmapped image selected.

To add a semitransparent background to a clip art picture, do the following:

1 Click the Format Picture button on the Picture toolbar.

2 Click the Colors And Lines tab.

3 Select the Semitransparent check box and then click OK.

Resetting a Picture's Format Options

You can play around with a picture's size, cropping, and image control options, but you may end up with results you don't like. You can use the Undo button on the Standard toolbar to cancel the last formatting change, but you can also reset a picture back to the original size, location, and image settings it had when you first inserted it in your document. Once you select the picture, there are two ways to do this:

■ Click the Reset Picture button on the Picture toolbar.

■ Click the Format Picture button on the Picture toolbar, click the Picture tab on the Format Picture dialog box, click the Reset button, and then click OK.

Using the Format Picture Dialog Box

To access the Format Picture dialog box and set a picture's line, fill colors, layout options, size, cropping, and image control options all at once, double-click the picture or select it and click the Format Picture button on the Picture toolbar. The options on the Colors And Lines, Size, and Layout tabs have been covered in Chapter 19, but you can also use the Format Picture dialog box to set a picture's image control options. Here's how to do this:

1 Double-click a picture to display the Format Picture dialog box.

2 Select the Picture tab if necessary. You'll see its options, like this:

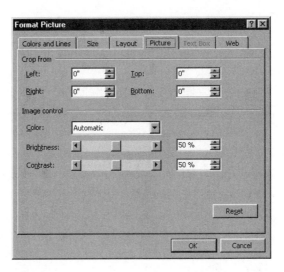

3 Rather than using the Crop button on the Picture toolbar, you can set a specific crop area with the Crop From options here. It's handy to use specific dimensions when you're trying to reduce a picture to an exact size.

4 To change the brightness, contrast, or image control options, change the settings in the lower half of the Picture tab.

5 Click the Reset button to return all of the settings in this dialog box to their defaults if you want to start again from scratch.

6 Click the OK button to make the changes.

If you don't like the effect of the changes you make, return to this tab and click the Reset button.

Ungroup Clip Art Objects to Customize Them

Many clip art objects are actually collections of component objects arranged together in the proper layers. When you work with a clip art object that isn't an inline graphic, you can ungroup it to change the shape or color of different components. For example, suppose you want to use a redder red as the color of the schoolhouse building below:

To change the building color, follow these steps:

1 Select the object, click the Text Wrapping button on the Picture toolbar, and choose a different wrapping style to change it from an inline to a floating graphic.

2 Choose Ungroup from the Draw menu in the Drawing toolbar. Lots of selection handles appear and it's hard to see which ones belong to the building.

3 Zoom the document to 200 percent of its original size or more. The graphic becomes larger, and its handles grow farther apart.

4 Shift-click to select only the building and the bell tower.

5 Change the fill color to a brighter red using the Fill button on the Drawing toolbar.

Sometimes a graphic has been grouped in layers. This means that if you ungroup it once, portions of it still contain smaller groups of objects. If this is the case, just select a smaller group and ungroup it again.

By ungrouping graphics, you can customize them for many different uses.

Exploring the Microsoft Photo Editor

In addition to using Word's built-in tools to edit pictures, your Office CD includes Microsoft Photo Editor, an image editing program you can use to add special effects to pictures or to control their formats much more precisely. For example, you can blur or smudge areas of photos or apply charcoal or watercolor effects to them. Naturally, you're free to use any photo editing or graphics program to create artwork for Word documents, but the Microsoft Photo Editor comes free with Office.

The Microsoft Photo Editor is not installed with a typical Office installation. To install it, you must do so separately using the Office Installation Wizard. *See "Customizing an Office Installation" on page 882 in the Appendix for more information.*

Once you have installed the Microsoft Photo Editor, here's how to open the program and learn more about it:

1   Click the Start menu in the Windows taskbar and then choose Programs from the menu.

2   Choose Office Tools from the Programs submenu, and then choose Microsoft Photo Editor from the Office Tools submenu. Microsoft Photo Editor will start up.

3   Choose Photo Editor Help Topics from the Help menu to get started.

CHAPTER 21

Working with Objects

You can use Microsoft Word to add all kinds of specially formatted text and graphics to your documents, but the possibilities don't stop there. You can also insert data objects from many other programs. Examples of objects you can insert into Word documents include organization charts from MS Organization Chart, graphics from programs like CorelDraw or Microsoft Paint, data charts from Microsoft Chart or Microsoft Excel, Excel worksheets, or Microsoft PowerPoint slides. In fact, you can access data from any program that supports Object Linking and Embedding (OLE) or Dynamic Data Exchange (DDE), as many programs do.

When you insert an object, you can edit the data using the original program from inside Word or you can have the object's data automatically updated whenever it changes in the source file so your document is always current. In this chapter you'll learn how to use objects in Word documents.

? **SEE ALSO**

Word also allows you to use ActiveX objects to make Web pages interactive. For more information about ActiveX, see Chapters 32, "Creating Web Pages," and 33, "Using Word's Advanced Web Features."

Objects in Word documents are made possible with an underlying technology called Object Linking and Embedding (OLE). OLE maintains connections with other programs' files automatically, so that all you have to do is insert objects into a document to include data created with those programs. Naturally, you can use any sort of data in a Word document by simply pasting it from another program, but when you copy and paste data it is static. To change static data, you must replace it with a new copy from the original program. In contrast, objects in Word documents are "live." Live data can be stored right inside your Word document, or it can be linked to the original file so that it changes whenever the file changes.

For example, suppose you're working on a corporate marketing presentation and you want to include a slide from the PowerPoint presentation in an advance report for your boss. If you insert the slide as a linked object, the object in your document will always show the latest changes from the original PowerPoint file, right up to the time you print or e-mail the report document. Figure 21-1 shows a linked PowerPoint object.

FIGURE 21-1.

A linked object looks like any other graphical object in a document, but the data in it is updated to reflect changes in the source file.

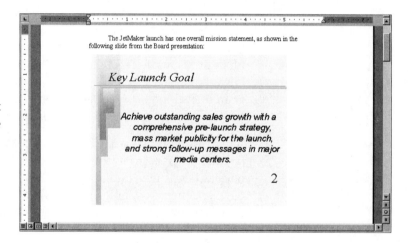

? **SEE ALSO**

For more detailed information about embedding worksheets or charts from Excel or graphs from Microsoft Chart, see Chapter 22, "Creating Graphs, Worksheets, and Equations."

You can also embed objects from other programs. (Worksheets and charts are the most commonly embedded objects.) Instead of creating a link to a source file, an embedded object contains the object's data itself. Read on to learn more about the difference between linked and embedded objects.

Linking vs. Embedding

OLE makes it possible to insert data into a Word document in two different ways: as a linked object or an embedded object.

- **A linked object** represents the current state of data in the source file. The linked object knows the location of the source file and maintains a connection with it. When the source file changes, so does the representation shown in the document.

- **An embedded object** is data from another program (or from Word, for that matter) stored inside your Word document. You must open the object's program from inside Word to edit the object.

You can add linked or embedded objects with equal ease, but each has its own advantages and disadvantages.

About Linked Objects

Using linked objects is the simplest way to ensure that the latest data is always shown in your Word documents. To create a link to an object, you must either select a source file or select data inside a source file. A linked object is updated from its source file, and you can edit the link to specify when the data is updated. You can also lock or break the link to prevent further changes in your document.

Word maintains links to files anywhere on your disk or network, and it even keeps track of links when source files are moved from one place to another. You can add as many links to a document as you like, and you can create multiple objects with links to the same source file.

You edit a link's data by editing the source file. When you double-click a linked object, Word opens the source file and its program. If the object is linked to a Microsoft Excel or PowerPoint file, Word's menus are replaced with Excel's or PowerPoint's menus when you edit the object. Otherwise, the program and source file open in a separate window.

Links are also a more efficient way to present data from other programs in your document. Since each link is only a pointer to the source file plus a representation of the data, it doesn't take up as much storage space as an embedded object. Also, since you can create several links to the same source file, you can store and maintain the actual data in just one place and have it updated in many places.

The Downside of Linking

On the other hand, links can be tricky when you share your files with other people. You can't update or edit a linked object unless you have access to the source file and the program used to create it. So, for example, if you send a Word document containing a PowerPoint slide to someone else, they must also have access to the source file and to PowerPoint in order to maintain updates to the linked source file. If you're on a company network, you can store source files on a server to which your document's recipients have access, but even then the recipients must also have the source file's program installed as well.

 NOTE

> When you share linked Excel or PowerPoint files with another Microsoft Office 2000 user who doesn't have Excel or PowerPoint installed, the Install On Demand feature of Office 2000 will install them on the recipient's computer. *For more information about "Install on Demand," see the Appendix.*

If you link to a file on a network server, another possible problem is that it will be changed or deleted by someone else. For example, suppose you insert an Excel chart object from the marketing department into your corporate report. Just before you print the report for distribution, however, someone in marketing accidentally deletes a key data point from the original Excel worksheet, the chart is updated, and it's now wrong. You probably won't notice the change until you hear nasty things from the report's readers. To avoid problems like this, use the manual linking option when you insert a linked object, and then check the source files before you tell Word to update the linked data.

Performance is also a potential issue when you use links. If your document contains lots of linked objects, it will take much longer than normal to open, and you may have to wait during updating.

About Embedded Objects

An embedded object is data from another program that is stored in a Word document. You can create a new embedded object from scratch using another program, or you can embed an existing file. Either way, the object's data is stored in the document. If you embed an object from an existing file, there's no link to the original file.

IV

Graphics and Publishing Tools

You can edit an embedded file from inside Word. When you do, Word starts up the original program and copies the object's data into its window so you can change it.

There are two major advantages to embedding:

- The object's data is stored in your Word document and it doesn't change unless you edit it directly. As a result, you can share the document with others without having to provide another source file. However, others must still have the program used to create the file in order to edit the object.

 TIP

If you know a document's recipients don't have the program they need to edit an object, you can convert the object's data to another format. *For more information, see "Converting an Embedded Object" on page 488.*

- You can create a new object from scratch, rather than having to create a file in advance, so you can add a drawing, Excel Worksheet, PowerPoint slide, or data chart on the fly.

There are two major disadvantages to embedding:

- Each embedded object stores actual data rather than a pointer to a source file, so the larger the object (or the more linked objects you have), the larger your document file. Documents with several embedded objects will be quite large, especially if the objects are bitmapped graphics or photos.

- When you need to change one or more embedded objects, you must edit them individually from inside Word.

Distinguishing Embedded and Linked Objects

Because the procedures for adding embedded and linked objects are very similar and you can double-click either type of object to edit it, it can be hard to tell which objects are linked and which are embedded. Table 21-1 on the next page lists some of the differences.

TABLE 21-1. Linked vs. Embedded Objects in Word Documents

Linked Object	Embedded Object
Double-clicking to edit always opens a separate program window.	Double-clicking an Excel or PowerPoint object replaces Word's menus with Excel's or PowerPoint's.
Object data is copied into the original program's window for editing.	Object data is edited in place in the Word document.
Edit and shortcut menus have Linked Object command.	Edit and shortcut menus have Object command.

Inserting Linked Objects

In Word, there are two ways to insert linked objects. You can use the Object command on the Insert menu or you can copy and paste using the Paste Special command on the Edit menu. It's easier to use the Paste Special command, so we'll cover that first.

Linking with Paste Special

To add a linked object with the Paste Special command, you must have both your document and the other program and its file open on your computer. The major advantage to taking this route, besides ease of use, is that you can select part of the data in a source file rather than having to link to the entire file. To insert a linked object, follow these steps:

1   Select the object's data in the source file and choose the Copy command (which is usually on the Edit menu).

2   Activate the Word document and move the insertion point to the place where you want the object inserted.

3   Choose Paste Special from the Edit menu. You'll see the Paste Special dialog box as shown in Figure 21-2 on the next page.

4   Choose the object's data format from the As list (this is the format the object will have in your document). The Result area below the As list explains how each type of object will behave in the document.

5   Click the Paste Link button to paste the object as a link. (If you choose the Paste button, the object is embedded in your document.)

6   Click OK. The object is pasted into your document as in Figure 21-1 on page 474.

FIGURE 21-2.

Use the Paste Special dialog box to paste copied data into a Word document as a linked object. You can set the object's data format here as well.

Source file type and location.

Click to insert object.

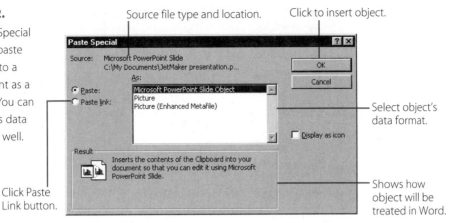

Select object's data format.

Shows how object will be treated in Word.

Click Paste Link button.

 NOTE

Microsoft Word 97 users will notice that in Word 2000, the Float Over Text check box has been deleted from the Paste Special and Object dialog boxes. *For more information about changing an inline graphic to a floating graphic, see "Changing a Picture's Layer Position" on page 466.*

Linking Word Documents

One of the object types to which you can link is a Word document. It may seem redundant to link to another Word document when you're already using a Word document, but it's useful to link to other documents when you collaborate with others or work on parts of a document separately.

For example, suppose you're preparing advertising copy for a new product. You're writing the sales copy, but your legal department is reviewing the disclaimer information for potential loopholes. By making the disclaimer a separate Word document, inserting it as a linked object into the ad copy document, and storing both documents in a mutually accessible place, your legal eagles can refine the final words while you work on the rest of the piece.

Linked Word objects are also handy when you add a frequently changing table to your documents.

Links don't have to be between documents, either. By inserting objects linked to selections of text or graphics from elsewhere in the same document, you can ensure consistency between them.

Once you see how easy it is to link objects, you'll find other ways to make them work for you.

Linking with the Object Command

When you insert a linked object by using the Object command on the Insert menu, you must link to an existing file, so the object you insert will contain all of the file's data. To insert a linked object, follow these steps:

1 Move the insertion point to the place in your document where you want the object to appear. (The file you will insert as an object does not have to be open.)

2 Choose Object from the Insert menu. You'll see the Object dialog box.

3 Click the Create From File tab to display the options as shown in Figure 21-3.

FIGURE 21-3.

To create a linked object with the Object command on the Insert menu, you must link to an entire file.

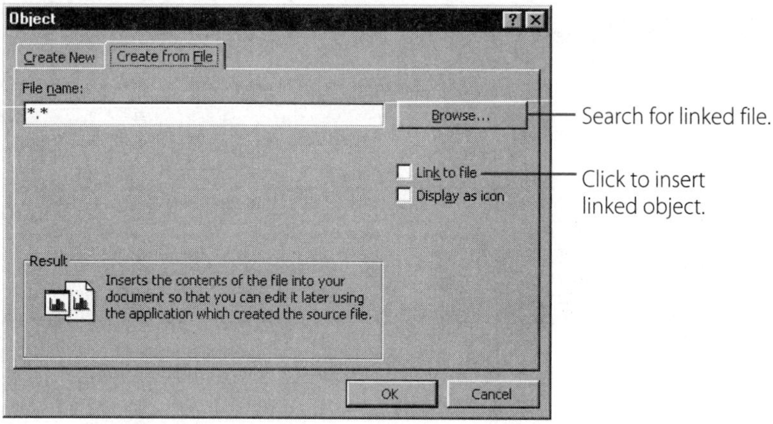

Object

Create New | Create from File

File name:

.

Browse... ——— Search for linked file.

☐ Link to file ——— Click to insert
☐ Display as icon   linked object.

Result

Inserts the contents of the file into your document so that you can edit it later using the application which created the source file.

OK   Cancel

4 Type the name of the source file in the File Name box if you know it, or click the Browse button to search your disk and then select the file and click the Insert button.

5 Select the Link To File check box. Notice that the Result area's text changes to explain the difference between a linked and embedded object.

6 Click OK. Word inserts the linked object in your document, as shown in Figure 21-1 on page 474.

> You can delete, copy, format, and manipulate linked or embedded objects using the same techniques used to format graphic objects or pictures. *For more information, see Chapter 19, "Drawing and Manipulating Graphics," and "Formatting Pictures" on page 463.*

IV

Graphics and Publishing Tools

Managing Linked Objects

Once a linked object is in your document, you can edit its data, change the way a link is updated, or change its appearance with formatting options. A linked object looks and acts like any other graphical object when you insert it. However, you can also open a linked object to edit its data or change the nature of the link itself.

Editing Data in a Linked Object

To edit the data in a linked object, you must open the linked source file and its associated program. There are several ways to do this from inside Word:

- Double-click the object—unless it's a PowerPoint presentation or a sound, animation, or video clip. (Double-clicking a PowerPoint presentation starts a slide show of the presentation to which you linked, while double-clicking a media clip plays it.)

- Select the object, choose Linked [Object Name] Object, from the Edit menu, and then choose Edit Link or Open Link. When you work with linked objects, both the Edit and Open commands do the same thing.

> **NOTE**

The [Object Name] part of the Linked Object command name on the Edit or shortcut menu refers to the name of the selected object. For example, if it's an Excel Worksheet object, the command name is Worksheet Object.

- Right-click the object to display a shortcut menu, and then choose the Edit Link or Open Link command from the Linked [Object Name] Object submenu.

After any of these actions, Word opens the source file and its associated program so you can edit the data. Depending on the link update options you have set, the data will either be updated immediately as you change the source file, or it can be changed when you update manually.

Editing a Link

When you insert a linked object, it is set by default to be updated automatically whenever the source file changes. However, you can edit a link to change the way data is updated, change the source file, or break the link completely. To edit a link, choose Links from the Edit menu. You'll see the Links dialog box as shown in Figure 21-4 on the next page.

FIGURE 21-4.

Use the Links dialog box to change the way links behave.

Shows location of linked data when linking to a selection rather than a whole file.

Update a manual link.

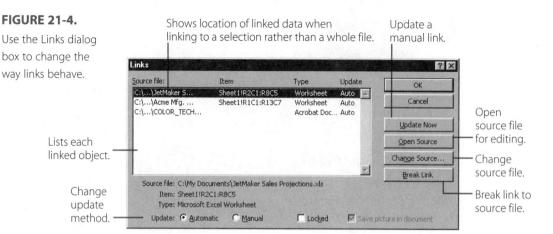

Lists each linked object.

Change update method.

Open source file for editing.

Change source file.

Break link to source file.

This dialog box lists each linked object in your document. You see the location of the source file, the specific data items linked from the object, the type of object it is, and the link update setting. You can use the Links dialog box to change any of these features except the specific data that is linked.

Changing When a Link is Updated

As mentioned previously, every linked object you insert into a document is updated automatically, but that may be a little risky when you link to a file that is accessed by others on a network. By changing a link from Automatic to Manual, you have total control over when the object's data is updated. To do this, click the Manual button on the bottom of the Links dialog box.

Double-Clicking to Edit PowerPoint Presentations or Slides

You can double-click most linked or embedded objects to edit those objects, but not always.

If you link to or embed a single PowerPoint slide in a Word document, you can double-click the slide in Word to display PowerPoint's menus to edit the slide's contents.

If you link or embed a whole PowerPoint presentation file (by using the Object command on the Insert menu to select the file name), Word displays the first slide in the presentation as the representation of that object in your document. When you double-click an embedded presentation, Word displays the slides one by one as a slide show in Full Screen mode.

To edit a linked or embedded PowerPoint presentation from within Word, right-click the object to display a shortcut menu, and then choose Edit Link from the PowerPoint Object or the Linked PowerPoint Object submenu.

When a link is set to Manual, you must update it yourself by returning to the Links dialog box, selecting the link in the list, and clicking the Update Now button.

 TIP

> You can update all manual links at once by holding down the Shift or Ctrl key, clicking them in the list in the Links dialog box, and then clicking Update Now.

If your document is set to update automatically, you can set Word to trigger an automatic update each time you print the document. This last-minute update is a good way to make sure your linked data is current. To trigger an update before printing, follow these steps:

1   Make sure the link is set for Automatic updates in the Links dialog box.

2   Choose Options from the Tools menu and click the Print tab in the Options dialog box.

3   Select the Update Links check box in the Printing Options area.

4   Click OK.

Changing a Link's Source File

A link works fine as long as the source file is edited, but sometimes a source file is actually deleted. A link is broken when the source file is deleted, but you won't immediately notice the difference in your document because the most recent representation of the data remains there as an object. If you close the document and reopen it later, Word will tell you the object can't be edited if you try to open or edit it. The Links dialog box also shows you when a link is broken because the Update column reads *N/A* (Not Available) for that particular link.

If a link is broken, you can change the link's source file:

1   Select the link in the Links dialog box and click the Change Source button. You'll see the Change Source dialog box, which looks a lot like the Open dialog box.

2   Navigate to the new source file and double-click it. The new link is established and data from the new source file replaces the data in your document.

3   Click OK to close the Links dialog box.

Locking, Unlocking, and Breaking Links

If you like automatic updating but want to disable it temporarily, you can lock a link so that updates don't occur and then unlock it when you want it to accept updates again. You can also break a link completely when you have no further use for updates from the source file.

■ To lock a link, choose Links from the Edit menu, select the link in the list, and select the Locked check box on the Links dialog box.

■ To unlock a link, select it in the Links dialog box and clear the Locked check box.

■ To break a link, choose Links from the Edit menu, select the link in the list, and click the Break Link button. You'll be asked to click Yes in a message box to confirm the break.

 WARNING

If you break a link, it can only be reconnected if you choose Undo immediately after breaking it. Otherwise, you'll have to change the link's source file or delete the object from your document and reinsert it.

Save File Space with Linked Pictures

When you insert a linked object, Word stores a representation or "picture" of the linked data in your document. You can hide this data by displaying the object as an icon if you like—*see "Hiding an Object's Data" on page 490*—but the snapshot itself is still stored in the document. Pictures of linked graphics are especially large, and if your document contains a lot of these, your document will be much larger than it needs to be.

To conserve file space, you can tell Word not to save pictures of some linked graphics in your document by following these steps:

1 Choose Links from the Edit menu.

2 Select a picture's link.

3 Clear the Save Picture In Document check box. If the Save Picture In Document check box is dimmed, it's because Word must save the link's picture and you have no choice in the matter.

4 Click OK. The picture will be replaced by the link's name in your document, and the document's file size will be reduced.

To view a linked graphic when its picture isn't stored in a document, just double-click the link name and Word will open the source file and transfer the image.

Embedding Objects

When you want to share files with others without having to provide access to the source files for linked objects, you can embed objects instead. Embedded objects store their data in a Word document.

As with linked objects, you can insert embedded objects with either the Object command on the Insert menu or the Paste Special command on the Edit menu. Unlike linked objects, however, embedded objects can be created from scratch, and you can convert an embedded object to another data format to make it easier for others to work with it.

Creating a New Embedded Object

To create a new embedded object, use the Object command on the Insert menu as follows:

1 Move the insertion point to the place in your document where you want the object to appear.

2 Choose Object from the Insert menu to display the Object dialog box as shown in Figure 21-5.

FIGURE 21-5.

When you insert an embedded object, you can create a new one from scratch.

List objects for all OLE-compliant programs on your disk.

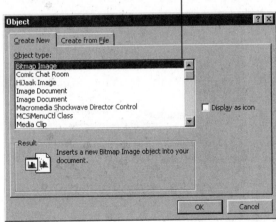

3 Select an object type in the list. The Result area at the bottom of the dialog box offers a brief description of each object type.

4 Select the Display As Icon check box if you want the object to be represented by an icon in your document instead of showing the actual data. If you choose this option, readers of the document can double-click the icon to view the data.

5 Click OK to insert the object. Word opens the program you need to create the object and activates its window. In most cases, the new object appears right inside your document and you add data to it there. For example, Figure 21-6 shows how a Word document looks when you embed a new bitmap object.

FIGURE 21-6.

When you create a new embedded object, you use a different program to create it.

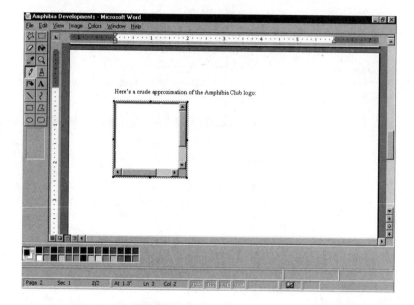

6 Create the object.

7 Click inside the Word document window or close the other program. Word places the object in your document, like this:

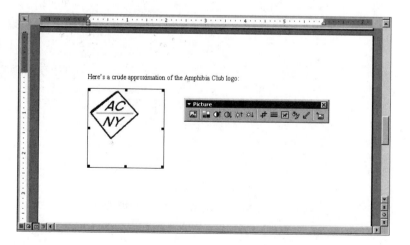

Notice that since a bitmapped object was created, Word inserts it as a picture and displays the Picture toolbar.

Inserting Existing Data as an Embedded Object

To insert existing data as an embedded object, you can use the Paste Special command on the Edit menu or the Object command on the Insert menu. The procedures are much the same as for inserting a linked object.

Use Paste Special when you want to insert a selection of data. To use the Paste Special command, follow these steps:

1   Open the file containing the data you want to embed.

2   Select data inside the file and choose Copy from the Edit menu (or the program's alternate Copy command).

3   Activate the Word document and move the insertion point to the place where you want the object to appear.

4   Choose Paste Special from the Edit menu. Word displays the Paste Special dialog box as shown in Figure 21-2 on page 479.

NOTE

> The Paste Special dialog box lists different data formats depending on the type of object you copied, so your Paste Special dialog box may not look the same as the one shown in Figure 21-2.

5   Select the [Object Name] Object option in the As list.

6   Make sure the Paste button to the left of the As list is selected, rather than the Paste As Link button.

7   Click OK. The object appears in your document.

TIP

> To display an embedded object as an icon rather than as the object's data, select the Display As Icon check box in either the Paste Special or Object dialog box. (This option is available in the Paste Special dialog box only if you have already selected [Object Name] Object in the As list.) *For more information about using icons to represent objects, see "Changing an Object's Icon" on page 491.*

To embed an existing object with the Object command on the Insert menu, follow these steps:

1   Move the insertion point to the place in your document where you want the object to appear.

2   Choose Object from the Insert menu to display the Object dialog box, and then click the Create From File tab to display the options shown in Figure 21-3.

3   Click the Browse button to locate and select a file and click the Insert button to select it and return to the Object dialog box.

4   Click OK to insert the object into your document.

Editing Embedded Objects

To edit the data in an embedded object, you must open the program originally used to create the object. Since the data itself is part of the Word document, the only way to edit an object is to open its source program from inside Word. There are several ways to do this:

- Double-click the object, unless it's a PowerPoint presentation, sound, video, or animation clip. (Double-clicking a presentation launches a full-screen slide show, and double-clicking a media clip plays it.)

- Select the object, open the Edit menu, open the [Object Name] Object submenu, and choose Edit or Open.

- Right-click the object to display a shortcut menu, and then choose Edit or Open from the [Object Name] Object submenu.

When you do any of the above, Word opens the object's file in its source program and you can make changes to the object there. When you're finished making changes, click inside the Word document or choose the source program's Exit command to return to your document.

⭐ **TIP**

If you see artifacts from the source program left on your screen after you edit an object (partial window borders or white space, for example), scroll down a screen or two in the Word document and then back up to make them go away.

Converting an Embedded Object

The main benefit of using embedded objects instead of linked ones is that they make your document more portable. Since the data is stored in the document itself, you don't have to provide any source files when you share your document with others. But if other readers want to edit the data, they'll still need the object's source program. To make your documents even more accessible to others, you can convert embedded objects to other file formats for programs your readers are more likely to own or have access to over a network. For example, you can convert a

SEE ALSO

For more information
about the Microsoft
Photo Editor, see
"Exploring the
Microsoft Photo
Editor" on page 471.

CorelDraw picture into a Windows bitmap so it can be edited with the
Paint program found in all installations of Windows. You might also convert a picture image created with an obscure photo-editing program into
Microsoft Photo Editor format, because anyone with Microsoft Office has
access to Microsoft Photo Editor. The Microsoft Photo Editor comes with
Office, but you have to install it individually. *For more information
about installing additional Office components, see the Appendix.*

It's easy to convert an embedded object from one format to another.
Here's how to do it:

1   Select the object.

2   On the Edit menu, point to [Object Name] and then click Convert.
    You can also right-click the object, point to [Object Name] and click
    Convert on the [Object Name] submenu. You'll see the Convert dia-
    log box, like this:

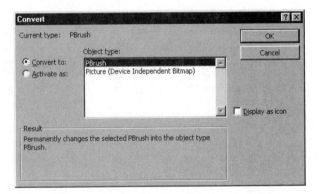

In this case, the selected object was a bitmapped drawing
from Windows Paint, so you have the option to convert it to a
device independent bitmap.

3   Select the new file type in the Object Type list.

NOTE

> The file types listed in the Object Type list will depend on which type of ob-
> ject you have selected in your document and which file converters are in-
> stalled in your copy of Word. You can't convert to another application's format
> if that application or the proper converter isn't installed. *For information
> about installing more file format converters, see the Appendix.*

4 Make sure the Convert To button is selected (it should be by default).

5 Click OK to convert it.

If you want to leave the data format as is but have the object open another compatible program when you edit it, click the Activate As button instead of the Convert To button on the Convert dialog box.

Hiding an Object's Data

Just because you insert a linked or embedded object, it doesn't necessarily follow that you must display the object's data. The data in a linked or embedded object may be quite large or it may represent supporting data that many of your readers won't necessarily want to see. In situations like this, you can display the objects as their names or as icons rather than as data.

Hiding All the Objects in a Document

To display object names instead of their data, follow these steps:

1 Choose Options from the Tools and click the View tab in the Options dialog box if necessary.

2 Select the Field Codes check box in the Show area at the top.

3 Click OK. Word displays all linked and embedded objects in your document with their geeky names, like this:

{ EMBED MS_ClipArt_Gallery.5 }{ LINK Word.Document.8 "C:\\My Documents\\oledoc.doc" "OLE_LINK3" \a \r }
{ LINK Excel.Sheet.8 "C:\\My Documents\\ACME. 98 ACTIVITY.XLS" "" \a \p }

This option affects every object in the document, however. Your readers will have to clear the Field Codes option to see the object data.

Displaying Objects as Icons

To hide the data in an object and yet still make it easy for readers to view it, display the object as an icon. When you display an object as an icon, readers can simply double-click it to view the object's data. You can do this when you create or insert objects, or you can change an object's display setting later on.

To show an object as an icon when you create it, select the Display As Icon check box in the Paste Special or Object dialog box.

To change an object's display setting at a later time, follow these steps:

1   Select the object.

2   On the Edit menu, point to [Object Name], and then click Convert to open the Convert dialog box.

3   Select the Display As Icon check box and click OK. The object is now shown as an icon, like this:

The sales summary in the worksheet below amply illustrates our need to rethink the Blasting Products division's marketing strategy and budget. Double-click on the icon to see the worksheet.

"Acme Sales.xls"

Changing an Object's Icon

By default, the icon that represents a linked object is the source program's standard program icon. This icon is shown below the Display As Icon check box when you select it. However, you can select a different icon if you want something special. To change the icon for an object that is already in your document, follow these steps:

1   Right-click the object to display a shortcut menu.

2   Open the [Object Name] Object submenu and choose the Convert command to open the Convert dialog box.

3   Click the Change Icon button. You'll see a list of alternative icons you can select in the Change Icon dialog box, like this:

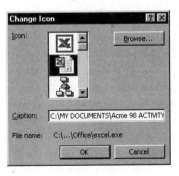

4 Scroll through the Icon list or click the Browse button to prowl your disk for other icons you may want to use.

5 Select the alternate icon and click OK to replace it.

6 Click OK to put the Convert dialog box away.

You can also select a different icon when you insert an object by selecting the Display As Icon check box in the Object or Paste Special dialog box and then clicking the Change Icon button below it.

Creating Graphs, Worksheets, and Equations

There's nothing like hard data to back up your assertions, whether you're submitting an audit report, projecting sales or expenses, or preparing other documents where you must be at your most mathematically persuasive. Microsoft Word 2000 makes it easy to create graphs, worksheets, or complex mathematical equations and to display them in your documents. In this chapter, you'll learn how to use Microsoft Graph, how to insert worksheets or charts from Microsoft Excel, and how to create equations with Microsoft Equation 3.0.

Graphs and worksheets are the most commonly used data objects in business, so we'll start with those and leave Microsoft Equation 3.0 for last. If you work in marketing, sales, accounting, or other business areas, graphs and worksheets give essential visual support to your strategies, reports, and ideas. You can create colorful and detailed graphs without knowing anything about Microsoft Excel or any other spreadsheet program.

> **NOTE**
>
> I use the words "chart" and "graph" interchangeably except when referring to the Microsoft Graph program.

Your worksheet and chartmaking options in Word are as follows:

- Use Microsoft Graph to create a chart from scratch.

- Add a new Excel worksheet to your document as an embedded object.

SEE ALSO

For more information about OLE, see Chapter 21, "Working with Objects."

- Link or embed a worksheet or chart object from Excel or another OLE-compliant spreadsheet or graphing program.

Which method you use to insert these items depends on your expertise with worksheet and charting programs and whether you have an existing worksheet from which to insert data.

If you're familiar with Microsoft Excel or another charting or worksheet program, you'll probably want to use it to create the worksheet or chart. By clicking a button, you can link or embed an existing Excel chart or worksheet in a document or you can create a new Excel worksheet in your document. With Excel or another spreadsheet program, you can make complex calculations that produce the data or chart that you then display in Word.

SEE ALSO

For more about using linked and embedded objects, see Chapter 21, "Working with Objects." For information about formatting objects, see "Formatting Pictures" on page 463 or consult Chapter 19, "Drawing and Manipulating Graphics."

If you're not familiar with Excel or another spreadsheet or graphing program, you'll want to use Microsoft Graph. Compared to Excel or some other spreadsheet programs, Graph has very few worksheet features, but it is much less complex and it offers the same abundance of chart types as Excel.

Microsoft Graph charts and Microsoft Equation 3.0 equations are always inserted into a document as embedded objects. Charts and worksheets from other programs, on the other hand, may be either linked or embedded objects. Once these objects are in your document, you can edit, move, resize, or reformat them just as you would any other linked or embedded object.

Using Microsoft Graph

Microsoft Graph 2000 is one of several bonus programs that come with Word on the Microsoft Office 2000 CD. You can use Graph to create pie charts, area charts, column or bar charts, line graphs, or scatter charts. You can embellish charts by combining two or three chart types, adding 3-D effects, or adding titles or other text. The main advantage of using Graph over Excel or another spreadsheet or charting program is that Graph is built into Word, which means you can distribute your document to other Word users without worrying about whether they have the program they need to edit it.

Microsoft Graph Basics

The general procedure for using Microsoft Graph is as follows:

1 Open a Word document and move the insertion point to the place where you want the graph to appear.

2 Choose Object from the Insert menu.

3 Scroll through the Object Type list to locate Microsoft Graph 2000 Chart and then double-click it. Word embeds a new chart object in your document. As you can see in Figure 22-1, you see not only the chart object but also the datasheet window, which stores the numbers being charted. In addition, Microsoft Graph's menus replace Word's menus at the top of the document window.

FIGURE 22-1.

Microsoft Graph is the easiest way to create charts and graphs in a document.

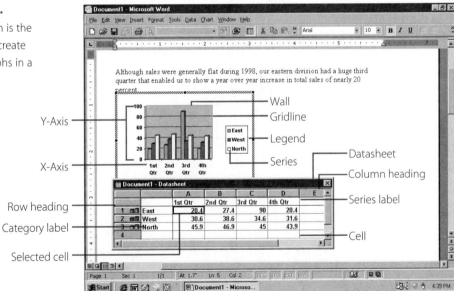

NOTE

If you don't see Microsoft Graph Chart listed in the Object dialog box, it's not installed on your computer. To install Graph, run the Setup program on the Office installation CD, click the Add/Remove Features button, and then locate Microsoft Graph and install it. *See the Appendix for more information.*

4   Enter the data you want to graph into the datasheet. New graphs have sample data in their datasheets, but you can replace the data by selecting cells and typing new values or labels. As you enter values or labels, the graph changes instantly.

TIP

You can also use values and labels from a Word table that already exists in your document. Just select the data in the table before inserting the Graph object, and the data will appear inside the datasheet window.

5   Use Microsoft Graph's menus to choose a chart type or customize the chart format.

6   When you have finished customizing the chart, click anywhere outside the chart or datasheet in the document. The datasheet window disappears and the chart becomes an embedded object, like this:

Although sales were generally flat during 1998, our eastern division had a huge third quarter that enabled us to show a year over year increase in total sales of nearly 20 percent.

TIP

Graphs are always embedded in a document as inline graphics. When you create a graph, be careful where the insertion point is, because any text to the right of the insertion point will move to make room for the new object. If you want to avoid disturbing text, you can make a graph float over it. *For more information, see "Moving a Chart" on page 504 or "Changing a Picture's Layer Position" on page 466.*

Understanding Charts and Datasheets

Before we delve into the details of creating charts, let's explore some key charting concepts. Every time you create a chart, you work with two items: a *datasheet* and a *chart*. The *datasheet* appears in a window that you can hide, move, or resize. The *chart* is an embedded graphic object that represents the numbers in the datasheet.

Elements of a Datasheet

A datasheet is a matrix of cells arranged in rows and columns, much like a spreadsheet or a Microsoft Word table. You can use up to 256 columns and 4000 rows in the datasheet, but charts get pretty cluttered if you use more than a few of either. Here's a rundown on the datasheet elements shown in Figure 22-1 on page 495.

- **Cells** Each contain one value that will be plotted in the chart. The *active cell* has a heavy border around it.

- **Rows** These are horizontal groups of cells. Rows are numbered from 1 down.

- **Columns** These are vertical groups of cells. Columns are numbered from A to Z, AA to ZZ, BA to BZ, and so on.

- **Row and column headings** Each designates the row or column numbers. These headings also show whether or not a row or column's data appears in the chart. Double-click a heading to hide its data—if the data is not shown, the bar icon disappears from a row heading or the values in a column are shaded.

- **Series labels** These identify different bars, lines, or pie slices in a chart. In a chart, one row or column is a series. Series labels must be entered in the first column in the datasheet—the column to the left of Column A.

- **Category labels** These identify the data categories from the series in the chart, often periods of time. In Figure 22-1, the category labels are the labels atop the columns containing data in the datasheet. Category labels must be entered in the first row of the datasheet, or Word won't recognize them.

Elements of a Chart

A chart interprets the data in the datasheet window and displays it graphically according to the options you set. Here's how the elements labeled in Figure 22-1 present data.

- **X- (or horizontal) axis** This usually shows the category labels.

- **Y- (or vertical) axis** This typically shows a scale of values so you can see how the lines, bars, or area points on the chart measure up.

3-D charts also have a z-axis, which lists series names. *See "Using 3-D charts" on page 503.*

- **Data series** This is plotted as a group of bars, a line, a pie slice, or an area with a distinctive color or pattern.

- **Gridlines** These can extend into the chart from either axis to help readers distinguish series or categories more easily.

- **Wall** This is the background behind the chart's data points.

- **Chart legend** This identifies each series so you can tell which is which.

Charts can also have titles or additional explanatory text. *See "Adding or Editing Chart Text" on page 508.*

Entering Values in the Datasheet

When you create a chart object, the datasheet has sample labels and values in it. You can easily add your own data by typing in cells or pasting it from another location.

Before entering data into a cell, you must select the cell. To select a cell, click it or use the arrow keys on your keyboard to move the insertion point into it. The selected cell has a heavy black border, as shown in Figure 22-1 on page 495. To select several adjacent cells, click the first one and drag across other cells or select the first one and then hold down Shift and click the last one.

TIP

> To view more of the datasheet window, make it larger by dragging one of its sides or the resize button at its lower-right corner. To select a cell that is out of view, just continue pressing an arrow key or hold the key down to scroll rapidly.

To select a row or column, click its heading area at the top or left edge of the datasheet window. You can also select several rows or columns at once by dragging across their heading areas or by selecting the first one and then holding down Shift and clicking the last one.

To enter data in the datasheet, follow these steps:

1 Select a cell.

2 Type or paste the data into the cell. The value or label you type or paste automatically replaces any existing data.

3 Press Enter to confirm the entry and move the cell selection down, or press an arrow key to confirm the entry and move the selection to the adjacent cell. You can also press the Tab key to confirm the entry and move the cell selection to the right, or press Shift+Tab to confirm the entry and move the cell selection to the left.

 TIP

> You can move data from one cell to another by dragging the selected cell border. If this doesn't work, choose Options from the Tools menu in Graph, click the Datasheet Options tab, and select the Cell Drag And Drop check box.

Formatting a Datasheet

When you first open a datasheet, the columns are set to a width of nine characters and the text and values are in 10-point Arial font. In addition, numbers are formatted exactly as you enter them, so they may or may not have dollar signs, commas, or decimal points.

To display labels and values more clearly in a datasheet, you can change the widths of columns, the type font or size, or the data format shown in cells.

Changing the Column Width

To change a single column's width, point to the column heading and drag the dividing line between it and the column to the right.

You can also size a column by the number of characters you want it to contain. To set a precise value, follow these steps:

1 Select a cell in the column you want to change. To change more than one column at a time, select cells in all of them.

2 Choose Column Width from the Format menu to display the Column Width dialog box, like this:

3 Enter the column width in characters and click OK.

The Column Width dialog box has other uses. You can reset a column to its default width by selecting the Use Standard Width check box, and you can have Graph automatically set the optimum width for one or more columns by clicking the Best Fit button.

Adding and Deleting Rows or Columns

To insert a row or column, select the row above or the column to the left of the place where you want the new one to be added and choose Cells from the Insert menu. If you select part of a row or column, Graph will ask you whether you want to add a new column to the right, a new row below, or if you want to add just one cell and move others in that row or column down or to the right.

To delete a column or row, select it and choose Delete from the Edit menu. (If you press Delete or Ctrl+X, you delete the values in the row or column but not the row or column itself.)

You can add or delete several rows or columns at once by selecting them all. To add four rows to a datasheet, for example, select four rows and then choose Cells from the Insert menu. Graph will add four new rows to the datasheet.

SEE ALSO

The Font dialog box in Graph is less extensive than the one in Word, but it works the same way. For more information about the Font dialog box, see "Using the Font Dialog Box" on page 83.

Changing the Font, Size, or Style

Since the datasheet usually isn't the star of the charting show, the cell formatting options are limited. To change the font or size of the text in the datasheet, select other options with the Font and Size boxes or character style buttons on the Formatting toolbar, or choose Font from the Format menu and select options in the Font dialog box.

Changing the Data Format

If you include data labels in your chart or choose to display the datasheet along with the chart in your Word document, you may want to change the data format. To change the data format for a cell or cells, use the Format Number dialog box by completing the following steps:

1 Select the cell(s).

2 Choose Number from the Format menu. You'll see the Format Number dialog box, as seen here:

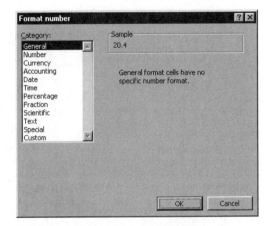

3 Choose a format category in the Category list. You'll see more options for many individual categories at the right, and the Sample area at the top shows how numbers will look in the datasheet. For example, if you choose the Date category, you can then select the specific date format you want.

4 Select format options for the category and click OK.

Choosing a Chart Type

Data in the datasheet window is automatically shown as a column chart in which bars rise up from the x-axis. However, there are dozens of different chart types and each type has variations. Some chart types are totally unsuitable for certain types of data, of course, but when you choose a chart type, Word briefly explains how that chart type presents data.

You can see what each chart type and variation looks like by viewing it in the Chart Type dialog box. To see chart types and select one, do the following:

1 Insert a new chart object or double-click an existing one to display the Graph menus at the top of your screen.

2 Choose Chart Type from the Chart menu. Graph displays the Chart Type dialog box, as shown in Figure 22-2.

FIGURE 22-2.

Microsoft Graph offers dozens of chart types and variations.

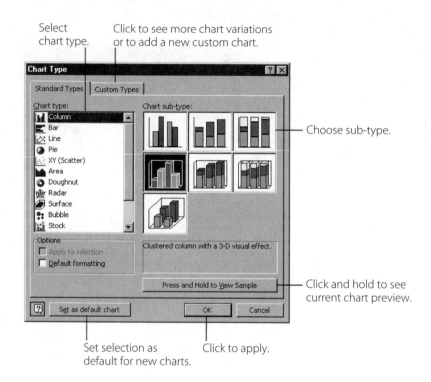

Select chart type.

Click to see more chart variations or to add a new custom chart.

Choose sub-type.

Click and hold to see current chart preview.

Set selection as default for new charts.

Click to apply.

3 Select a chart type in the Chart Type list. A group of variations (or sub-types) appears at the right, and the area below the chart variations briefly explains how the chart displays data.

Click the Custom Types tab to see even more chart types. If you select a chart type and then customize it, you can add it to the Custom Types tab by selecting the User Defined button and then clicking Add.

4 Select a different chart variation if you like.

5 Click the Press And Hold To View Sample button to see how the chart will display the current datasheet contents, if you like. The sample replaces the chart variations above.

6 Click OK to set the new chart type.

⭐ TIP

If you dislike the Column chart type shown by default when you insert a new graph, open the Chart Type dialog box, choose a chart more to your liking, click the Set As Default Chart button, and click Yes when you're asked to confirm the change.

To get assistance inside the Chart Type dialog box, click the Help button in the lower-left corner.

Using 3-D Charts

3-D charts show depth as well as height and width. You can use 3-D charts to add visual appeal, and they can demonstrate important trends more dramatically than 2-D charts, as you can see in Figure 22-3.

FIGURE 22-3.

When you use a 3-D chart effect, Word adds a third, or z-axis to the chart.

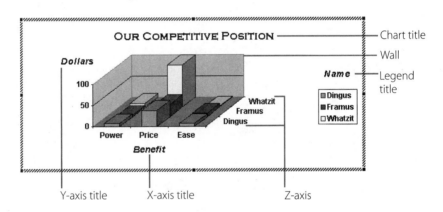

This chart, like other 3-D charts, has a third set of values and a z-axis. In this case, the Z-axis shows the product names.

To make a 3-D chart, choose one of the 3-D subtypes in the Chart Type dialog box. Some chart types don't have any 3-D variations.

⭐ TIP

Although not a 3-D chart, the bubble chart type is also designed for plotting three sets of values. Each bubble represents a data series. The first two values are plotted on the x- and y-axes, and a bubble's size relative to other bubbles indicates the third value.

Modifying a Chart

Once you have inserted a chart into your document, you can work with it in many ways. You can move or resize it, change its layer position, change specific elements of it, and add or edit text.

Reactivating Microsoft Graph

Once you insert a chart and click in the Word document anywhere outside the chart (or datasheet), Word is reactivated and the datasheet disappears, along with the Graph menus. If you want to set any chart formatting options, you'll have to reactivate Microsoft Graph. There are four ways to do this:

- Double-click the chart object inside your document.

- Right-click the chart object and choose Edit from the Chart Object menu on the shortcut menu.

- Select the object and choose Edit from the Chart Object submenu on the Edit menu.

- Select the object and choose Open from the Chart Object submenu on the Edit menu. This method opens Microsoft Graph in a separate window.

If you close the datasheet window by clicking its Close box, Microsoft Graph remains active, as you can tell by the menus at the top of your screen. To re-open the datasheet window when Graph is active, choose Datasheet from the View menu.

Resizing a Chart

Since a chart is treated as an object in a Word document, you can resize or move it just as you would any other embedded object. To resize a chart, drag one of its selection handles. You can do this whether you're working in Graph or in Word. If you're working in Word, however, you can also change the chart size more precisely by selecting the chart object, choosing Object from the Format menu, clicking the Size tab, and setting values for the chart's size or scaling percentages.

Moving a Chart

Every chart you make with Microsoft Graph is inserted as an inline graphic, so you can only move it by adding or removing text, tabs, or paragraph marks in front of it or by using Word's text alignment features.

For more flexibility in moving a chart, turn it into a floating object. To do that, follow these steps:

1 Click outside the chart to return to Word.

2 Select the chart object and choose Object from the Format menu in order to display the Format Object dialog box.

3 Click the Layout tab and choose any Wrapping Style button other than In Line With Text.

4 Click OK.

Once the graph is a floating object, you can move it anywhere.

Setting Overall Chart Display Options

You can, in one convenient place, set lots of options to determine how a chart is displayed and which elements are shown on it. Just choose Chart Options from the Chart menu. You'll see a dialog box like the one in Figure 22-4.

FIGURE 22-4.

You can set dozens of options for a chart's appearance all at once in the Chart Options dialog box.

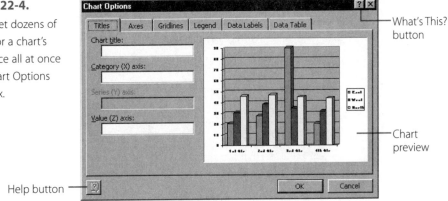

What's This? button

Chart preview

Help button

Here's a quick rundown on what you can do in this dialog box, tab by tab:

■ **Titles** Add an overall title inside the chart object or add titles for any axis.

■ **Axes** Show or hide any chart axis and choose the type of value scale on the x-axis.

■ **Gridlines** Hide or show major or minor gridlines on any axis. If you're working with a 3-D chart, you can also change the gridlines and walls to 2-D.

- **Legend** Change the position of the chart legend or hide it entirely.

- **Data Labels** Add labels to all data points showing their values.

- **Data Table** Display the datasheet in your document along with the chart and hide or show series symbols in the datasheet's value rows.

These options are generally easy to understand, and you can see how any of them affects the look of your chart by selecting it and watching the chart preview change. If you need more help, click the Help button in the lower-left corner of the Chart Options dialog box or check out Graph's Help menu.

Setting 3-D Chart Options

All 3-D charts have depth, and you can skew or rotate a chart to change the viewing angle. Often a small change in perspective makes a 3-D chart easier to grasp at a glance. To set 3-D options, do the following:

1   Make sure Microsoft Graph is active and that you're working with a 3-D chart type.

2   Choose 3-D View from the Chart menu. You'll see the 3-D View dialog box, as shown in Figure 22-5.

FIGURE 22-5.

With the 3-D View dialog box, you can change the angle or rotation of a 3-D chart to present your data more clearly.

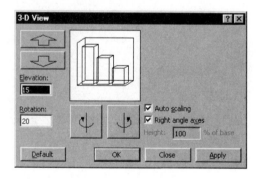

3   Select the options you want.

4   Click the Apply button to change the chart in your document without closing the dialog box. If you don't like the changes, you can reset them in the dialog box.

5   Click OK to close the dialog box when you're done.

Try these options on your own to set the optimum viewing perspective for your 3-D charts.

Formatting Chart Elements

You can be quite specific about the type of chart you create when you choose it in the Chart Type dialog box and set options in the Chart Options dialog box. But once you see the chart by itself in your document you may decide to change the look of one element or another. For example, you may want to move the legend, add a background fill color or pattern, or change the color of a line, bar, or pie slice. With a few mouse clicks, you can set formats for many individual chart components.

In general, you can change the fill color, the line width or style, or the text formats of any chart element. These elements include the chart's axes, gridlines, legend, individual data series, and the wall behind the data series, but they vary from one chart type to the next.

To see which elements you can format individually in a chart, follow these steps:

1   Reactivate Microsoft Graph if it isn't active.

2   Click in a blank area inside the chart object to select the chart area. You can tell it's selected because there's an additional set of selection handles just inside the object's border, as shown in Figure 22-6.

FIGURE 22-6.

When the chart area is selected inside a chart object, you can point to any chart element to see a ScreenTip.

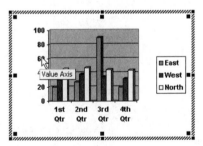

3   Move the mouse pointer slowly over the chart. As you do, you'll see ScreenTips that identify discrete elements of the chart, as shown in Figure 22-6.

To change an element's format, double-click the element, or right-click it and choose Format [Chart Element Name] from the shortcut menu. You'll see a Format dialog box with options available for it. Figure 22-7 on the next page shows format options for one of the columns (a data series) in Figure 22-6.

When you select the legend or a title you have added to a chart, you can drag it to move it. *For more information, see "Adding or Editing Chart Text" below.*

FIGURE 22-7.

You can set individual format options for chart series, axes, legends, gridlines, and other elements with Microsoft Graph.

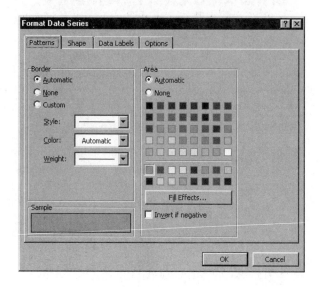

Most of the options in the format dialog boxes are self-explanatory. Notice that you can set the line weight or style of each data series as well as its color. For example, you can make the points on a line or scatter chart larger or change the symbols used for them. You can also fill bars or pie slices with textures, patterns, gradients, or even pictures. Check out all of these options to see just how much chart formatting power you have within your grasp.

If you need help understanding a formatting option, click the Help button and then click an option for more information, or choose Microsoft Graph Help from the Help menu to use the online Help system.

Adding or Editing Chart Text

Microsoft Graph automatically adds a legend, a value scale, and data category labels to new charts, but you can add other text if you like. For example, you may want to add a title inside the chart object or add a more descriptive label to the y-axis or x-axis. You might even want to call out a particular data point and offer an explanation about it.

There are three ways to add text to a chart:

- Add a chart title or axis labels with the Chart Options dialog box.

- Add floating text by typing inside the chart object.

- Add floating text by creating a callout or text box in Word.

Let's take a look at each alternative.

Adding Titles or Axis Labels

Chart titles are placed in specific places in the chart window, like the ones seen in Figure 22-3 on page 503. To add titles or axis labels, do the following:

1   Reactivate Microsoft Graph if necessary.

2   Choose Chart Options from the Chart menu and click the Titles tab. You'll see the options shown in Figure 22-4 on page 505.

3   Type the title text in the appropriate box. You'll see how the title looks in the preview chart at the right. With certain 3-D chart types, you may be able to add up to three different axis titles.

4   Click OK. The label or title appears in the chart in your document as a selected text box. You can then drag the box to move it or click inside it to edit the label text.

★ TIP

Click the text inside a text box and press Enter to create a two-line title. To change the font or style of a title or label, right-click it in the chart and choose Format Chart Title from the shortcut menu to display a dialog box with font, size, and style options.

Adding Floating Text to a Chart Object

To add formatted text to other areas of a chart object, you can create a floating text box right inside it. Just click anywhere in the chart object's frame and start typing. Graph immediately creates a floating text box:

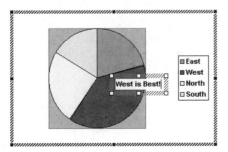

When you're finished typing, you can drag the box anywhere you want inside the chart object. Click outside the text box when you're done.

> You can display the actual data represented by each data point in the chart by choosing Chart Options from the Chart menu and then selecting options on the Data Labels tab, but these options add data labels to every data point in the chart. Use a floating text box to show the data for just one pie slice, bar, or other data point.

Adding Text Boxes, AutoShapes, or Callouts with Word

Although you can add text inside the chart object with Microsoft Graph, you can do the same thing with Word, and you'll have more formatting options. Here's an example:

This chart also includes data labels to show the values of the pie slices. To embellish a chart with special text and AutoShapes, follow these steps:

1 Click outside the chart object in the document to reactivate Word.

2 Choose Text Box from the Insert menu or AutoShapes from the Picture submenu on the Insert menu to create a new text box or AutoShape.

3 Add the text you want to the text box or AutoShape and then move it into position with respect to the chart.

Chart Tips

With so many kinds of charts and formatting options available in Microsoft Graph, it's easy to run amok and end up with a chart that doesn't make your point. Charts are nice visual additions to a document, but don't forget that the point of a chart is to show a relationship more clearly than a spreadsheet, table, or text can. Here are some tips to keep you on track.

- Choose the right chart type. If you can't clearly see the relationship you hope to show in one chart type, try another. For example, because you can display more lines than bars or columns in a chart, use line charts for plotting lots of different data series.

- Use short words or abbreviations in the x- (category) axis. Category labels tend to run together and become unreadable, especially when the chart shows data groups over more than four time periods.

- Use two charts when one isn't enough or would invite confusion. Don't combine several data sets and series in a chart to show more than two or three key relationships at the same time.

- Don't plot too many data points. Don't plot sets of values that are far apart in value, such as two groups in the five-digit range and another group in the three-digit range. If you do, the y-axis scale will have to be so broad that you won't be able to distinguish the smaller numbers.

- Avoid cluttering the chart with text. The plotted data is the point, and text distracts readers from it. If you need lots of text to explain the chart, you should probably be using a different chart type, one that shows the data more effectively. If you must add explanatory notes, use AutoShapes in Word to create callouts.

- Don't select too many data points. The more data points there are, the closer they'll be and the harder it will be to read the chart. You can always resize the chart to make it bigger, of course, but that may impair your document's layout.

- Be careful with 3-D effects. They add drama, but they can also make charts harder to read. If a 3-D chart seems confusing, try the 2-D version.

- Test print every chart. Charts that look great on your screen may be hard to read on paper, especially when printed on a black and white printer. If your printer doesn't print grayscale values well, you may need to substitute patterns for colors.

TIP

> To make eye-popping charts, add callout AutoShapes to point to a chart element with a line or combine other AutoShapes or lines with text boxes, WordArt, or even clip art or pictures. *For more information about inserting drawing objects and other graphics, see Chapter 19, "Drawing and Manipulating Graphics," and Chapter 20, "Using Special Graphics."*

Inserting Excel Worksheets and Charts

? SEE ALSO

For information about adding a linked or embedded object from an existing Excel worksheet or chart. See Chapter 21, "Working with Objects."

You can insert a worksheet or chart into a Word document from any OLE-compliant spreadsheet or charting program, but because Microsoft Excel is part of the Office productivity suite, Word allows you to embed a new Excel worksheet in your document by clicking a toolbar button.

Embedding a New Excel Worksheet

To embed a new Excel worksheet object, you can use the Object command on the Insert menu or a button on the Standard toolbar. The toolbar button is easier.

1 Move the insertion point to the place in your document where you want the worksheet to appear.

2 Click the Insert Microsoft Excel Worksheet button on the Standard toolbar. You'll see a palette like this:

3 Drag across and down the palette to choose the number of cells you want the worksheet to have and release the mouse button. A blank Excel worksheet of that size is added to your document, and Excel's menus appear at the top of the document window, as shown in Figure 22-8 on the next page.

FIGURE 22-8.

When you embed an Excel worksheet in a Word document, Excel's menus replace Word's in the menu bar.

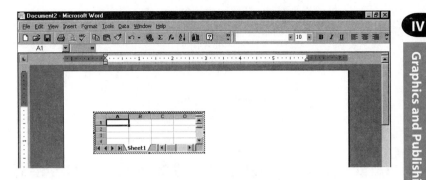

4   Enter the data you want the worksheet to contain, and then use Excel's menus to format the worksheet. For more information about using Excel, consult the Help menu in Excel's menu bar.

5   Click outside the worksheet to return to Word.

> When Word's menus are active, click the worksheet object and then use any of Word's object formatting options to make the worksheet float over text, to resize it, or to add a fill color behind it. *See Chapter 19, "Drawing and Manipulating Graphics," for more information.*

Embedding a New Excel Chart

To embed a new Excel chart in a Word document, use the Object command on the Insert menu, as described above, and choose the Microsoft Excel Chart object instead of the Microsoft Excel Worksheet object. You'll see an Excel worksheet window with the chart on a worksheet tab, like this:

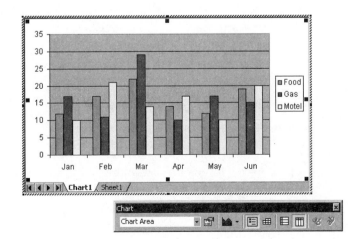

To change the labels or values in the chart, click the Sheet 1 tab at the bottom of the object to display the worksheet from which the chart was plotted. Then edit the labels and values in the worksheet. Click the Chart 1 tab to see your changes in the chart.

When you're finished modifying the Excel chart, click outside the object to return to Word.

Adding Equations to a Document

If you work in a technical field such as mathematics, engineering, or physics, you need to be able to convey your ideas with complex equations. In Microsoft Word, you can use Microsoft Equation 3.0 to create equations and place them in your documents. Microsoft Equation 3.0 lets you insert equations like this:

The fundamental basis of our discovery is simplicity itself:
$$x - \left\{ \frac{y\dfrac{4\sin x}{4}}{\sin y} \right\} + 3x2^2$$

Incredibly enough, this deceptively simple formula turns out to be the secret of the universe. This one formula guides the very fabric of life with harmonic vibrations.

These equations do not calculate a result the way the formulas in a table or worksheet do. Rather, they allow you to express mathematical concepts.

⭐ **TIP**

> Microsoft Equation 3.0 is a "light" version of MathType, the renowned equation editing program from Design Science, Inc., that has been customized for use with Office. If you use equations frequently, consider upgrading to MathType itself.

Ⓦ **ON THE WEB**

For information about upgrading Microsoft Equation 3.0 to MathType, go to *http://www.mathtype.com/msee*.

Starting the Equation Editor

The only way to start the Equation Editor is to insert an Equation Editor object into your document. To do that, follow these steps:

1 Move the insertion point to the place where you want the equation to appear.

2 Choose Object from the Insert menu and select Microsoft Equation 3.0 as the object type.

NOTE

If Microsoft Equation 3.0 isn't listed in the Object dialog box, it's not installed, and you'll need to restart the Office Installer to add it. *See the Appendix for more information.*

3 Click the OK button. The Equation Editor's menus replace Word's menus at the top of the document window and the equation object appears, as shown in Figure 22-9.

FIGURE 22-9.
Microsoft Equation Editor gives you the tools you need to insert complex mathematical expressions into a document.

Use menus to set character styles.

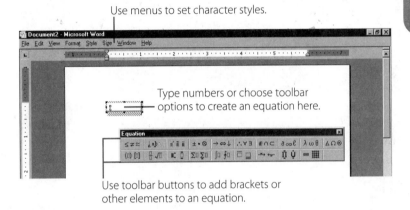

Type numbers or choose toolbar options to create an equation here.

Use toolbar buttons to add brackets or other elements to an equation.

Creating and Editing Equations

If you know enough about mathematics to create complex equations, you'll quickly figure out how to use these buttons and palettes to build the equation you want. In general, you use the Equation toolbar to add expressions to the equation, and you type numbers on your keyboard to enter them. To format the equation, use the Format, Style, and Size menus at the top of the document window.

TIP

Press F1 or choose Equation Editor Help Topics from the Help menu for more information about using the Equation Editor.

To exit the Equation Editor and return to Word, click outside the equation object. To edit the equation later, just double-click it to open the Equation Editor toolbar and menus.

CHAPTER 23

Designing Pages

Most of the chapters in this book tell you how to use individual features of Microsoft Word to create and format text, objects, graphics, and format elements such as headers and footers. This chapter, however, tells you how to pull all of these elements together into complete page designs. So far, you may have been content simply to create and format text, but as the examples in this chapter will show, you can combine text and other objects to create truly stunning page layouts in Word. When you see how easy it is to combine and position graphics, text, and other page format elements, the chances are that your documents will be in for a more visually appealing future.

While Word doesn't compete with stand-alone page layout programs such as Quark XPress, Adobe FrameMaker, or Adobe PageMaker, it does have the basic tools you need to create great looking documents in all sorts of formats. If you're a typical Word user, you'll find everything you need in Word, and you can learn how to put pages together fairly quickly. Word's page design tools are also much easier to use than those in a stand-alone layout program.

Although you'll learn about the basic components of a page layout and how to produce layouts with Word in this chapter, you'll be referred to other chapters for details about creating objects, text boxes, text, headers and footers, and other page elements. However, this chapter goes more deeply into layout-related tasks such as placing objects precisely on a page, using the drawing grid to assist placement, and wrapping text around objects.

Principles of Page Design

A page design can be anything from a single column of ordinary text to a rich arrangement of text, objects, headings, and other components. But no matter what sort of document you're creating, there are some common elements in all page designs.

Elements of a Design

A page design consists of several different elements, as you can see in Figure 23-1. You may not use all of these elements in a given design, but once you know what they are, you can keep them in mind as you create page layouts on your own. These elements are standard players in page designs.

 TIP

Word comes with dozens of predesigned templates that show you a variety of different layouts and page design elements. Choose New on the File menu and take a look at the templates on the tabs in the dialog box to see templates for reports, letters, calendars, resumes, newsletters, manuals, brochures, and other documents. *For more information about using templates, see "Using Templates" on page 250.*

FIGURE 23-1.

A page design consists of several elements arranged to present information in the clearest and most efficient way while delivering as much visual impact as possible.

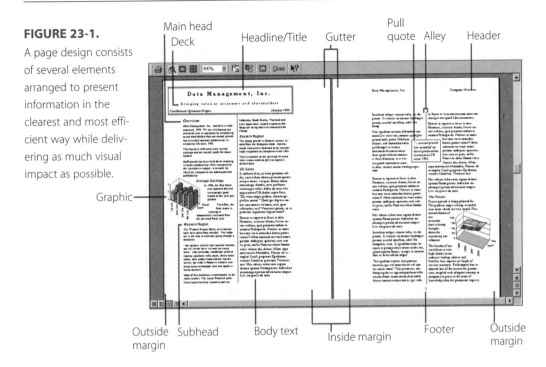

Main head
Deck
Headline/Title
Gutter
Pull quote
Alley
Header

Graphic

Outside margin
Subhead
Body text
Inside margin
Footer
Outside margin

Here's a brief rundown of the standard page elements shown in Figure 23-1 along with some tips about how to handle them in Word.

Headline/Title

The headline or title should be formatted in larger, bolder, or otherwise different type than anything else in the document. Word has a built-in Title style you can use for this. If you're producing a book or a manual, the headline is the document's title and is usually on a page by itself. In a brochure, invitation, flier, or other short document, you might use a different font or WordArt for the title.

Byline

The author's name usually goes directly beneath the heading or title. If you filled out the User Information tab in the Options dialog box, you can insert your name using the AutoText feature.

? SEE ALSO

For more information about using AutoText, see "Using AutoText" on page 218.

Deck

This is summary or teaser text that appears below the title. The deck captures the main point of the piece or highlights an interesting point that entices people to read the whole article.

Pull Quote

A pull quote is a brief phrase taken from the body of the article that appears as an object by itself. Pull quotes are used as design elements to break up a page visually, but they also serve as teasers by showcasing interesting quotations or points from the article. You typically use text boxes to create pull quotes in Word.

Main Heads and Subheads

Main heads and subheads identify sections of a document. You'll want to use Word's Heading styles for these. *See "Headings" on page 528 for more information.*

Body Text

The body text of a document is the main text in the article, report, or book. You can create body text with Word's normal text tools, or you can use text boxes or frames to create text objects that can be arranged more flexibly on a page.

> Frames for print publications are not the same as frames in Web pages. *For more information about using frames in Web page layouts, see "Using Frames" on page 790.*

Graphic

For more information about linked or embedded objects, see Chapter 21, "Working with Objects."

For our purposes in this chapter, a graphic is any object other than a text box. It might be a piece of clip art, a linked or embedded object such as a Microsoft Excel worksheet or a chart, a table, a drawing object, an AutoShape, or a WordArt object. *For more information about drawing objects and about using AutoShapes, see Chapter 19, "Drawing and Manipulating Graphics." To learn about WordArt, see Chapter 20, "Using Special Graphics."*

Caption

A caption describes a graphic, but some graphics are self-explanatory and don't need them. Captions appear in smaller type directly below the graphic that they describe, as shown in the figure on the facing page.

You can insert captions easily with the Caption command on the Insert menu. *For more information about this, see "Inserting Captions" on page 539.*

IV

Graphics and Publishing Tools

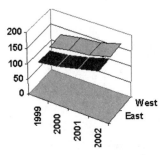

Figure 1 - Projected employee growth

Header and Footer

 SEE ALSO

For more information about creating headers, see "Using Headers and Footers" on page 320.

These display the document title, section title, page number, or other information on every page of the document. In a book-style layout where header and footer text changes, these are called *running heads* and *running feet*. Headers and footers can also include graphics.

Notes

Although not shown in Figure 23-1 earlier, footnotes or endnotes are used in books, manuals, technical papers, and other information-heavy documents. *For more information, see "Inserting Footnotes and Endnotes" on page 231.*

Callout

SEE ALSO

For more information about creating callouts, see "Using AutoShape Callouts" on page 411.

A *callout* or *label* is an explanatory note with a line pointing to something else in the document. The text and lines identifying parts of Figure 23-1 are callouts, for example. You use the AutoShapes menu on the Drawing toolbar to create callouts automatically in Word, or you can create them on your own by adding a text box and then connecting it with a line to the item being described.

Continuation

In newsletters, magazines, and other layouts in which articles continue from one page to another (and not necessarily on the next page), a continuation element either tells readers that an article continues or tells them specifically where to turn to find the next part of the article, as shown in the figure on the following page.

The loyalty of our workforce is very high thanks to our industry leading salaries and benefits that improve as length of service increases. Performance has remained one of the criteria for promotion, coupled with adequate training at company expense that the promotion requires.

Continued on page 2 —— Continuation

Sometimes a continuation is simply an arrow, which usually indicates that the article continues on the next page, but it can also be text that tells people where to turn, such as: "See *Frog Olympics* on page 4."

⭐ **TIP**

> You can add continuation text as a cross-reference, and Word will automatically keep track of the page number or other location to which it refers. *For more information, see "Creating Cross-References" on page 577.*

Sidebar

This is a short, related article that is set off in a box by itself from the body text. You can use a text box, a frame, or a small table to create a sidebar. A sidebar typically has its own title and a border or *screen* (a fill pattern or color) to set it off visually, like this:

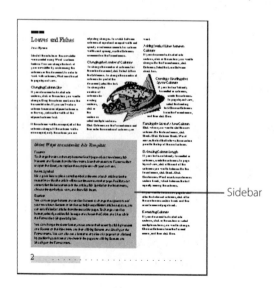

——— Sidebar

SEE ALSO

For more information about setting margins for layouts, see "Setting Margins" on page 101.

Margins

Every page in every layout has top and bottom margins. In magazine, newsletter, book, or other two-page layouts, there are also inside and outside margins that change depending on whether the page is a *verso* (left-hand) or *recto* (right-hand) page. You use the Margins tab in the Page Setup dialog box to specify margin sizes; click the Mirror Margins check box on this tab to set up a two-page layout and specify inside and outside margins.

⭐ **TIP**

> When you use floating graphics in a layout, the graphics can be placed outside the page margins. However, make sure you don't place them so close to the edge of the paper that they're cut off. Each printer has a maximum "printable area" and can only print so close to the edge of a page. Consult your printer's manual for more information.

Gutter

The gutter is extra space added to the inside margin of a two-page layout to allow space for binding the pages together. You can specify the gutter width on the Margins tab in the Page Setup dialog box.

Alley

SEE ALSO

For more information about creating columns, see "Arranging Text in Columns" on page 333.

An alley is the space between two columns in a layout. Word refers to the alley as "spacing" in the Columns dialog box. The alley can be empty or it can contain a vertical line as a divider between columns. If you created columns with the Columns command on the Format menu, you can specify the alley's width and add a vertical line at the same time. If you create columns by arranging text boxes or frames on the page, you set the alley's width by dragging the text objects.

Table of Contents and Index

Although not shown in Figure 23-1 on page 519, long documents such as books or manuals usually contain a table of contents and an index. *For more information, see Chapter 25, "Creating Tables of Contents, Indexes, and Cross References."*

Basic Design Principles

The fundamental goal of every page design is to communicate clearly and effectively. Creating such a design involves several basic principles. You must know the document's purpose, its intended audience, its intended effect, and how it will be reproduced (color or monochrome, for example). Then you create a design that delivers the document's information in the most effective and appropriate way.

Knowing Your Purpose

To determine a document's purpose, think about the goals that you hope to achieve with it. Every document conveys information, but beyond communicating clearly, you probably also want readers to have a certain feeling after reading the document, whether it's a renewed respect for your abilities, a desire to buy a product, or an understanding of a technical procedure.

Knowing Your Audience

The style of your text and of the layout itself will vary with the audience. For text, you need to consider your audience's reading level. If certain key points in the document are important, you may want to emphasize them visually. And there's a big difference between a businesslike layout for a corporate report and a party invitation. Finally, consider whether your audience has a built-in motivation to read the document or whether it must be enticed into doing so. These considerations will greatly influence your design.

Projecting an Appropriate Image

Based on your knowledge of the document's purpose and its intended audience, you can begin thinking about how the overall design will look. A straight columnar design is more businesslike, while a freer design with text boxes of varying sizes is more casual. Consider the difference between *The Wall Street Journal* and *The National Enquirer*, for example.

Using a Grid to Lay Out Each Page

? SEE ALSO

For more information about displaying and adjusting the grid, see "Aligning with the Grid" on page 419. For more information about basing a design on a grid, see "Layout Decisions" on page 525.

Most professional page designs are based on a grid, which is a system of vertical columns and horizontal lines that guides the placement of text and graphics on a page. The grid is such a standard design tool that professional page layout programs automatically allow you to choose the grid style and then display it in the background as you create pages. Word doesn't go to this length, but it has a grid and you should use it.

Matching Form to Content

In professional publishing, there is often a conflict between the art directors who create the page designs and the writers who create the text. The artist's job is to create an inviting document, and the writer's job is to convey information with the printed word. Try to balance these two needs for your purpose and audience. For example, if the text information is the star of the show, as in a critical report, fact sheet, book, or instruction manual, you'll want to make the text as easy to read as possible. This may mean sacrificing some design elements such as variable-width columns or graphics in the middle of the page. If visual entertainment is more important, as in a brochure, sales sheet, or flier, you might sacrifice the readability of some text to create a more engaging design.

 TIP

Strive for designs in which the reader's eye is led to the most important items on a page by using varied column widths, drop caps, headlines, graphics, or pull quotes.

Planning a Design

The best document designs result from careful planning. Before you start assembling text and graphics in a Word document, you should make some key decisions about how the document will look, what it will contain, and how those contents will be presented. In effect, you create a set of design rules that you then follow as you create the document. When you know and follow the rules, you'll create clear, consistent designs and you'll have fewer mishaps along the way. The more specific you can be about these rules, the better.

Layout Decisions

The first decisions to make are about the type of layout you want. Here are some questions to consider:

- Will you use a portrait or landscape layout?

- Will it be a two-page (book style) layout or a one-page layout?

- Will the document print on standard-size paper? (You might use different paper for a tri-fold brochure, a postcard, or an invitation, for example.)

Choosing a Layout Grid Style

Once you decide on the page size, layout orientation, and layout type, you can choose a layout grid style to suit your design goal. Figure 23-2 on the next page shows three different layout grid styles. It's usually better to use variations of the same grid style than to use different grids on different pages, especially in business documents.

FIGURE 23-2.

Most layouts are based on a layout grid that guides the placement of titles, text, and objects on each page.

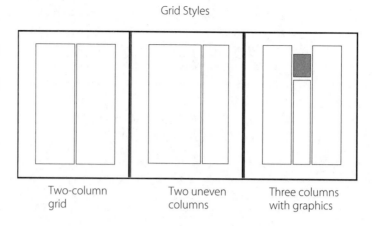

Grid Styles

Two-column grid

Two uneven columns

Three columns with graphics

> **NOTE**
>
> Don't confuse a layout grid with the built-in drawing grid whose options you can set with the Draw menu on the drawing toolbar. *For more about the drawing grid, see "Aligning with the Grid" on page 419.*

Choosing a Layout Method

The type of layout you choose will help you determine the best way to create it. There are three different ways to create a page layout in Word:

SEE ALSO

For more information about using tables, see Chapter 17, "Working with Tables."

- Use Word's standard text formatting options.

- Create a table that matches your grid design and then place text or graphics in its cells.

- Use text boxes, frames, and other objects only.

TIP

> The tabs in the New dialog box contain documents that show each of Word's layout-creation options. Click the Publications tab and open the Brochure template to see how Word's standard formatting tools were used to create a layout. To see text boxes at work, open the Newsletter Wizard and follow its instructions. To see an example of how a table was used to create a layout, click the Other Documents tab and open the Contemporary Resume template.

Each approach has its pros and cons, but since Microsoft Word is a word-processing program rather than a page layout program, your decision will likely be based on the method you typically use to insert text into the document.

IV

Choosing a Text Entry Method

There are four ways to position text in a document: standard text entry, a table, text boxes, and frames. Each method has advantages, however, and whenever you combine text and graphics on a page, you'll want to consider them. Here are the advantages and disadvantages of using each method of text entry:

> You don't have to use just one text entry method. Many designs include standard document text as well as text boxes, for example.

- **Standard text** The only kind of text you can wrap around graphic objects. Standard text and heading styles are also required if you want Word's help in creating cross-references, a table of contents, or an index. However, you can't drag standard text and place it anywhere in a page—you must use columns, margins and indent settings to change its position.

- **Tables** You can replace the format of an entire page, or you can use them within text when you want more placement flexibility in the midst of standard text. For example, a table in text allows you to switch quickly from a single-column to a two-column layout and back again without inserting section breaks; it also allows you to change the direction of text if you like.

- **Text boxes** These give you complete placement flexibility. You can even change the direction of text inside them. However, Word can't include the contents of a text box in a table of contents or an index, and you can't wrap text around a graphic inside a text box.

For more information about creating a frame, see "Converting a Text Box to a Frame" on page 441.

- **Frames** These are a holdover from older versions of Word that didn't offer text boxes. However, you may still need them in Word 2000. You can wrap text around graphics inside a frame if you like, and a frame can include reviewer comments, footnotes, endnotes, or certain fields such as automatic numbers or dates. To make a frame, create a text box and then convert it to a frame.

> Don't confuse text frames, which are converted text boxes, with Web page frames inserted with the Frames command on the Format menu. *See "Using Frames" on page 790 for more information about Web page frames.*

Text Boxes vs. Frames

Text boxes will suit your needs in most layouts. They're easier to create and you have more formatting flexibility with them. But in some cases you'll need to use a frame. The table below compares the features available in text boxes and frames.

Feature	Text Box	Frame
Link boxes so text flows from one to the other.	Yes	No
Rotate or flip.	No	No
Select more than one object.	Yes	No
Group several text objects.	Yes	No
Change object alignment or distribution with the Draw menu on the Drawing toolbar.	Yes	No
Change the text direction.	Yes	No
Use the Drawing toolbar's format options to add a fill color or pattern, shading, or a 3-D effect, for example.	Yes	No
Wrap text around a graphic.	No	Yes
Add reviewer comments to text.	No	Yes
Include footnotes or endnotes.	No	Yes
Include the contents in a table of contents, index, or use autonumber fields.	No	Yes

Text Formatting Decisions

In addition to the text entry method, you'll want to decide in advance, as much as possible, how text will be formatted throughout the document. Here are some issues to consider.

Headings

You know your document will have a title, but what other headings will it have? Before you place any text in the document, come up with a standard system of heading styles (Word helpfully provides one for you) and use them consistently. Think about the document's contents

IV

and consider which sections deserve Level 1, Level 2, or Level 3 heads based on Word's Heading 1, 2, and 3 styles. If the document will contain sidebars or tables that have titles, will those titles be one of the regular heading levels or different ones?

Styles

For information about copying styles, see "Transferring Styles Among Templates" on page 310.

Decide which fonts, font sizes, character styles, and paragraph formats you'll need in your document, and make sure there's a style for each format you'll use. Often, you can use the Organizer to copy styles you have already defined in other documents, or you may have a document template ready to go that contains your favorite styles.

Document Sections or Subdocuments

For more information about using master documents, see Chapter 24,"Using Master Documents."

If your document will contain mostly standard Word text, will it contain different sections? If so, you should plan in advance where the section breaks will occur. If you're creating a long document, you should use a master document and decide which subdocuments it will contain.

Numbering

If you create a document containing multiple sections that begin new pages, decide how the document's pages will be numbered. Will you number consecutively from the first page or will numbering restart with each new section?

If you're creating a long document, will it have a table of contents, title page, or index, and will it end with an appendix, glossary, index, or endnotes? If so, do you want to number these special pages—often called *front matter* and *back matter*—separately? In books, for example, front matter is usually numbered separately in Roman numerals.

Headers and Footers

For more information about creating a table of contents, table of figures, or index, see Chapter 25,"Creating Tables of Contents, Indexes, and Cross-References."

Do you want to use the same headers and footers throughout the document, or do you want running heads that change from one section or chapter to the next? You may want to suppress the header and footer on the first page of a document, for example. In a two-page layout, you may want to have separate left-page and right-page headers or footers.

Front Matter and Back Matter

If the document will contain a table of contents, a table of figures, or an index, decide which information you want these elements to contain and whether you want Word's help in creating them.

Graphics Decisions

You should also make some basic decisions about graphics in your design before you begin creating it.

Black and White, Grayscale, or Color

Your choice of graphics will depend considerably on whether the document will be printed in black and white, grayscale, or color. This will affect your choice of fill colors, line colors, text colors, and the kinds of photos, clip art, or other objects you use. For example, some of the art in Word's Clip Gallery is in color, and it doesn't look as good in grayscale or black and white.

 TIP

Test print every color or grayscale graphic to see how it will look on paper and adjust it if necessary using the Picture toolbar, the Format Object or Format Picture dialog box, an image editing program, or the program originally used to create it.

Types of Graphics

It helps to know in advance whether you'll be using photos, clip art, drawing objects, WordArt, AutoShape callouts, or linked or embedded objects in your document. You can then plan the size and placement of these objects based not only on the document's overall look, but also on the amount of space needed to show the graphic clearly.

Placement

You can place graphics or other objects behind or in front of text, inline with standard text, or you can wrap text around them. The choice you make will affect your placement flexibility as well as the arrangement of text on a page.

Captions and Numbering

Will your graphics have captions, and will the captions include numbers? In this book, for example, many of the graphics have numbers as well as captions. If you decide to use captions or numbers, plan a numbering system and create a style for the caption text in advance.

 TIP

Word has a built-in Caption style that it applies when you use the Caption command on the Insert menu. Modify this style to suit your page design. *For more information, see "Modifying Styles" on page 307.*

Creating a Page Design, Step by Step

Other chapters in this book cover the specifics of creating the text, text boxes, and graphics that you place on a page. In addition to those steps, the process of creating a design involves a lot of trial and error. But there are some basic rules you can follow to minimize problems as you go along:

1   Decide on the layout orientation, paper size, and layout grid style for your design.

2   For areas that require distinct formatting, sketch each page on paper to make basic visual decisions about where text and graphics will go. You'll want to refer to the sketches as you work.

3   Create a new document. You may be able to use a predesigned Word template that matches the type of document you're creating or a custom template of your own that contains the styles you'll need.

4   Use the Page Setup command to set appropriate options for the paper size, page orientation, and margins.

? SEE ALSO

For information about using the Organizer, see "Transferring Styles among Templates" on page 310.

5   Using the Organizer, copy styles from other documents that you want to use in your new design. If you're planning to include a table of contents or an index, make sure to use Word's Heading styles for the document's headings.

6   Display the Drawing toolbar in Print Layout view.

7   Use the Grid command on the Draw menu to display the built-in grid, turn on the Snap To Grid feature, and display the document's text boundaries as reference points, if necessary. You may want to change the distance between grid points, too.

8   Add the document text, including body text, headings, notes, headers, footers, linked or embedded objects, and fields according to the basic layout grid you chose in Step 1. *See Chapter 21, "Working with Objects," for more about adding linked or embedded objects, and see Chapter 26, "Using Mail Merge," and Chapter 27, "Using Fields," for more about using fields.*

9   Place the graphics and set text wrap options for them according to the basic layout grid you chose in Step 1.

10 Add the index, table of contents, or other reference items.

11 Carefully check the alignment of everything using test printouts.

12 Update any linked objects or fields in the document.

13 Print the document.

Now let's look a little more closely at the process.

Working with Text

Text is the basic information the document will convey, so you should add it first. The type of text you add to each part of your layout will depend on the sort of layout you're creating, but here are some suggestions.

1 Insert or create the standard text in the document first. Insert any page and section breaks you'll need (subdocuments, for example), and create multicolumn layouts if you're using the Columns command on the Format menu to create columns. Use the spelling and grammar checker and scan the text yourself to make sure it's the way you want it. (If you need to make significant deletions or additions later, these changes might affect the positions of other objects in the layout.)

 TIP

Use the Columns command on the Format menu to create a multicolumn layout with equal length columns of text in it. Use text boxes rather than the Columns command when you want to vary the length, width, or position of individual columns.

2 Add text boxes next. Create the text boxes and add the text inside them. Text boxes automatically float over text when you insert them, so you can move them into their approximate locations by dragging them. If necessary, convert text boxes to frames.

Adding Graphics and Other Objects

Chapters 19, 20, and 21 explain the details of inserting objects on a page, but here are some general steps to follow:

1 Place the objects on one page at a time.

2 When an object is inserted as a picture and you want to move it independently of the document's text, select it, right-click the object and choose Format Object or Format Picture from the shortcut menu to display the Format dialog box. Then, click the Layout tab, choose one of the text wrap options there other than "In Line With Text," and click OK. The object will then float on the page and you'll be able to wrap text around it.

3 Drag all objects into their approximate positions on the page and set the appropriate text wrap options to see how things look in general.

Placing Objects on a Page

Even though each floating graphic is created in its own layer, it is anchored to a particular place on a page—inline with or on top of normal document text, for example.

If the object is an inline object (like a picture), it moves with your text—if you insert more text above the object, it moves down the page to maintain its anchored position. You can also drag the object and move it to a different location with the text by dragging, just as you would with text. Normally, you use an inline object because you want to anchor it to a specific place in your text so that if the text moves, the object will too.

If the object floats, you can simply drag it anywhere you like. In addition, you can set position options that lock it to a specific place relative to the page margins or to specific text elements.

 TIP

You can set precise position options for a picture by converting it from an inline graphic to a floating graphic. *See step 2 under "Adding Graphics and Other Objects" on page 532.*

Setting Advanced Position Options

You can do pretty well by dragging floating objects and aligning them to points on the drawing grid (if the grid is on) or using the Horizontal Alignment options on the Layout tab in the Format Object dialog box. Sometimes, however, you want to anchor an object to a specific margin, column, line, or character of text. To do this, follow these steps:

1 Right-click the object and choose Format Object from the Format dialog box. (The dialog box name will be Format Text Box, Format, AutoShape, Format Picture, or Format Object, depending on the type of object you clicked.)

2 Click the Layout tab and click the Advanced button.

3 Click the Text Wrapping tab if necessary, select any wrapping style except "In Line With Text," and then click the Picture Position tab to display the options shown in Figure 23-3.

FIGURE 23-3.

You can set the alignment or absolute position of a text box.

Align to text.
Align to margin.
Specify position.
Align one side of object to text.

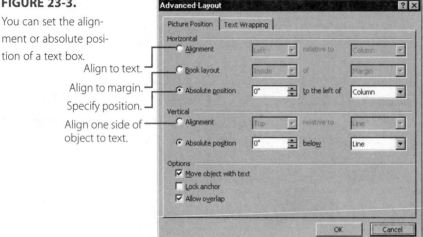

To align the object vertically or horizontally, click Alignment, choose an alignment option, and then choose a page landmark from the Relative To menu. You can align a text box relative to the page edge (Page), page margin (Margin), or the nearest column or character.

If you're working in a two-page layout, click the Book Layout option and then choose options to align the text box relative to the inside or outside page edge or margin.

To set an absolute vertical or horizontal position, click the Absolute Position option, enter a value, and choose a page landmark from the To The Left Of list.

To position graphics by points, picas, centimeters, or millimeters instead of inches, choose Options from the Tools menu, click the General tab, and change the Measurement Units selection. You can also position Web page elements by pixels by selecting an option on the General tab.

Here's what the options on the Advanced Layout tab do:

■ **Move Object With Text** The object moves when you change the vertical position of the text to which it is anchored so it's always the same distance from the text.

- **Lock Anchor** This fixes the object at its position on the page so it no longer moves with adjacent text when the text moves, although you can still move the object by dragging it.

- **Allow Overlap** When this is cleared, the object cannot overlap other objects. Normally, objects without a set wrapping style can overlap each other.

Wrapping Text around Objects

You can select any floating object, anchored or not, and change the way text wraps around it. You'll find basic text wrapping options in the Format Object dialog box. However, there are more advanced wrap options on the Picture toolbar and on the Text Wrapping tab in the Advanced Layout dialog box.

Editing Wrap Points

When you format a picture with the Picture toolbar, you can edit the wrapping area around the picture by dragging individual wrap points. To do this, follow these steps:

1 Select the picture.

2 Click the Text Wrapping button on the Picture toolbar and choose Edit Wrap Points. The picture is outlined with a border filled with handles, like this:

Drag any wrap point to change wrap area.

Local Company in the News

Yes, **Type Too** was recently featured in a survey of the best graphics arts firms in the East Bay. Our fearless leader, Mel, took a reporter and photographer from the East Bay Blade on a tour of our palatial facility and served a nice catered lunch afterwards.

3 Drag one or more of the handles on the border to change the shape of the wrapping boundary around the object.

4 Choose Edit Wrap Points from the Text Wrapping menu when you're done to hide the handles again.

Setting Wrapping Options

The Format Picture dialog box has two levels of wrapping options you can use. There are basic options on the Layout tab, and you can set more options with the Advanced Format dialog box.

Here's how to set a wrapping option:

1 Right-click the picture and choose Format Picture from the shortcut menu to display the Format Picture dialog box.

2 Click the Layout tab to display its options, as seen in Figure 23-4.

FIGURE 23-4.

Set basic text wrapping and layout alignment options with the Layout tab in the Format Picture dialog box.

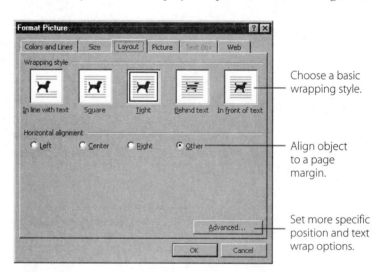

Choose a basic wrapping style.

Align object to a page margin.

Set more specific position and text wrap options.

3 Click a basic option and then click OK to see how it looks in your document.

Setting Advanced Wrapping Options

To set other text wrapping options, follow these steps:

1 Display the Layout tab in the Format Picture dialog box.

2 Click the Advanced button.

3 Click the Text Wrapping tab. You'll see the Advanced Layout dialog box as in Figure 23-5.

FIGURE 23-5.
For more specific layout options, use the Advanced Layout dialog box.

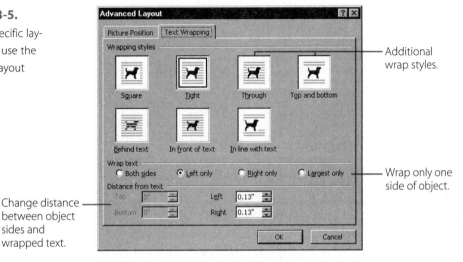

Additional wrap styles.

Wrap only one side of object.

Change distance between object sides and wrapped text.

Notice that in addition to the choices on the Layout tab, you can set text to wrap through a graphic or to wrap above and below it. You can also specify which side of an object the text wraps around when you choose certain wrapping styles, or you can set specific distances between the text and the object being wrapped.

NOTE

When text wraps through a graphic, it wraps tightly to the outer edges of the object (like tight wrapping), but text also fills any blank or "open" areas inside the graphic. Look closely at the icons representing the Tight and Through options in the Advanced Layout dialog box to see the difference, or click the Help button at the top of the dialog box and then click the Through option for more information.

4 Choose a Wrapping Style option.

5 Choose a Wrap Text option.

6 Set specific values for the distance from the sides of the object. The values that are available depend on the wrapping style you chose.

7 Click OK to return to the Layout tab, and click OK again to apply the change.

Creating a Watermark

Another way to position a picture is to turn it into a *watermark*, which places it behind text and displays it in a lighter shade so that text or other objects show over it easily. You can also turn text into a watermark. Figure 23-6 shows a watermark.

FIGURE 23-6.

You can turn any picture or text into a watermark for your page.

To create a picture watermark, select the picture, click the Image Control button on the Picture Toolbar, and then choose Watermark from the Image Control menu.

To create a text watermark, follow these steps:

1 Click the Text Box button on the Drawing toolbar or choose Text Box from the Insert menu to create a text box and enter its text.

2 Adjust the text size and style for a watermark. You may want larger or bold text so it can be clearly read even though it's a watermark.

3 Position the text box where you want it on the page.

4 Select the text and choose the 25% Gray text color with the Font Color palette on the Formatting toolbar.

5 Double-click the text box border to display the Format Text Box dialog box.

6 Click the Layout tab, set the Behind Text wrapping style, and click OK.

Inserting Captions

If you like to label the diagrams, pictures, tables, or other graphic elements you add to your documents, you can have Word help you insert captions. Word's caption feature can insert a caption with or without a number in it. You can add any text you want to a caption, and you can have Word automatically add captions whenever you insert various types of objects with the Object command on the Insert menu.

Inserting a Caption

Here's how to insert a caption directly above or below an object:

1 Select the object.

2 Choose Caption from the Insert menu. Word displays the Caption dialog box, as shown in Figure 23-7.

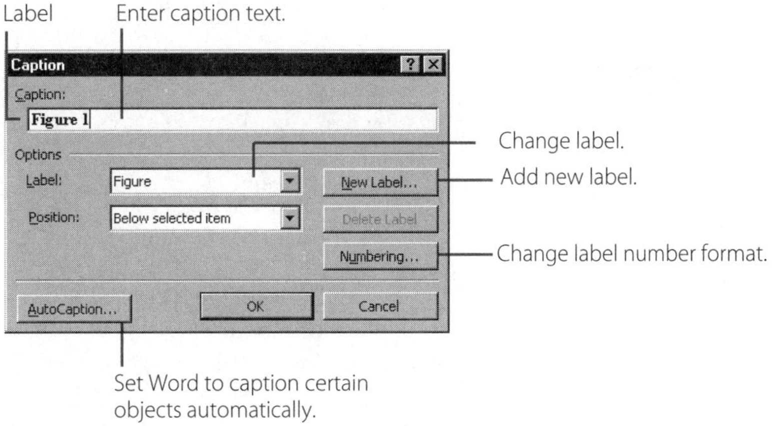

FIGURE 23-7.
Word helps you add captions to graphics when you use the Caption dialog box.

Label   Enter caption text.

Change label.
Add new label.

Change label number format.

Set Word to caption certain objects automatically.

3 Type the caption's text in the Caption box. You can completely replace the suggested figure label and number if you like.

4 Select a different predefined label by choosing an option from the Label list (you can choose Equation, Table, or Figure here) or by clicking the New Label button and creating a new one.

5 Select a different number format by clicking the Numbering button and choosing an alternate format there.

6 Choose an option from the Position menu to determine the caption's placement.

7 Click OK. If you selected an inline graphic, Word adds the caption on the line below or above the graphic. If you selected a floating graphic, Word inserts a text box containing the caption, like this:

Figure 1 - Male African Lion

8 Move or resize the text or text box to your liking, or select the text inside it and apply different style or other character formatting options.

> Word uses a built-in style called Caption to format the caption text. Modify this style if you want a different look for the text. (*See "Modifying Styles" on page 307.*) If you want to give a floating object a caption without using a text box, just type a caption below the graphic in your document.

Using AutoCaption

AutoCaption automatically adds a caption to each object you add to a document. You can set AutoCaption to kick in when you add specific types of objects, and as with adding one caption, you can choose the label and number format you want. To use AutoCaption, follow these steps:

1 Choose Caption from the Insert menu to display the Caption dialog box.

2 Click the AutoCaption button. Word opens the AutoCaption dialog box, as shown in Figure 23-8 on the next page.

SEE ALSO

For more information on OLE-compliant objects, see Chapter 21, "Working with Objects."

3 Select the check box for the type of object you want to create an autocaption for. The list shows every OLE-compliant object on your computer. Notice when you scroll through the list that it includes tables and documents from Word itself.

4 Choose label, position, and numbering options as explained above.

FIGURE 23-8.

With AutoCaption, you can set Word to add captions automatically to specific types of objects when you insert them.

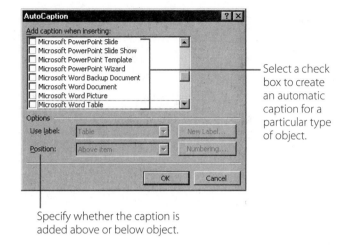

Select a check box to create an automatic caption for a particular type of object.

Specify whether the caption is added above or below object.

5   Repeat the process to select and specify options for other types of objects if you like.

6   Click OK. Word will create captions for the types of objects you selected as you add them to the document from then on. (However, Word will not caption objects that are already in the document.)

Finishing Up

After you have placed text and objects where you want them, it's time to look at the document as a whole and add some final touches. Here's a checklist:

- Check headers and footers and make sure they change from section to section as necessary.

- Add any graphic accents such as AutoShape bursts, continuation marks, or extra lines that divide columns or separate articles.

- Check the alignment of text and graphics on each page.

- Closely examine every text box or frame to make sure no text is cut off.

- Create the document index or table of contents and make sure they have titles and proper formatting.

SEE ALSO

For more information about linked files, see "Managing Linked Objects" on page 481.

- Make sure any linked files are available and that all links are updated.

- Test print any pages containing fill colors, text colors, or shading if you're not sure how they will look on your printer, and change them if necessary.

- Use the spelling checker for a final check (text boxes and frames are checked automatically, but not WordArt).

- If you're sending the document elsewhere to be viewed or printed and you have used custom fonts in it, be sure to include the font files as well as any linked object files along with the document.

Using Master Documents

I f you work with especially long documents or you manage collaborative efforts where several people contribute sections to one document, master documents can make your life a lot easier. A master document contains other Microsoft Word documents as discrete objects (or subdocuments), so you can apply formatting, check spelling, create indexes, add continuous page numbers, print, or perform other tasks with a whole group of related documents at once while maintaining them as separate documents for editing. In this chapter, you'll learn how to make the most of master documents.

Essentially, a master document allows you to view, reorganize, and otherwise work with a group of documents all at once. If you're writing a book, for example, you might create individual chapter documents and then assemble all of them into a master document in order to apply consistent formatting or page numbering, to run the spelling checker on all the files at once or to print them all in sequence as one book. If several people are working on a big corporate report, using a master document allows each person to work on the file they need while you format it as part of the master document.

Why Use a Master Document?

There are, of course, several other ways to insert the *contents* of other Word documents into a single document. You can copy and paste, use the File command on the Insert menu, or insert a linked or embedded Word document object inside your current document. But each of these other methods has disadvantages when you want to work with chapters or sections independently while retaining the ability to format all of those chapters or sections as one document.

For example, inserting a file or cutting and pasting from other documents puts the contents of those documents into the destination document. If you insert or paste lots of other files, your document becomes much larger. What's more, you can't edit the source files independently and have the changes reflected in the main document. You can remedy this problem by inserting another Word file into your document as a linked object, but if you do, you'll have to format the linked object as a separate document.

In a master document, you can display other files' contents as *subdocuments*. Subdocuments retain their identity as individual files, but they're also part of the master document. You can edit a subdocument directly inside the master document or you can open it separately and edit it, but either way, any changes you make to subdocuments are reflected in the master document.

There are lots of advantages to using master documents:

- Simplify collaborative projects by allowing different people to work on various subdocuments and yet format or print them all as one document.

- Use Outline view to reorganize subdocuments.

- Apply continuous page numbering to all of the subdocuments in the master document.

- Set one group of consistent styles or other formatting for the master document and all subdocuments.

- Check the spelling of the master document and all subdocuments with one command.

- Create a book-length index or table of contents that includes all of the headings in all of the subdocuments as well as any in the master document.

- Print the master document as one finished document with all of the subdocuments in order.

Elements of a Master Document

A master document can contain text, graphics, and other objects just like any other Word document, but its real power is in subdocuments, which are other files contained within the master document. A master document is any document that contains subdocuments. Figure 24-1 shows some subdocuments in a master document, as you would see them in Outline view.

FIGURE 24-1.

A master document allows you to combine the contents of many other documents into one document.

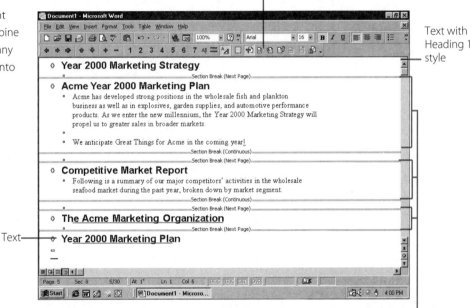

Master document buttons in Outlining toolbar

Text with Heading 1 style

Text

Subdocuments

At first glance, this looks like normal Outline view, but notice that each subdocument is separated by section breaks. You can insert a subdocument from an existing file or you can create a new one from scratch. You can also lock subdocuments so they can't be edited, and subdocuments stored on network servers are automatically locked when someone else is editing them.

Creating a Master Document

It's easy to create a master document. All you have to do is switch to Outline view in any document and start adding subdocuments to it. You can start a new master document with a blank document or with an existing document that already has other contents. Here's how to create a master document from a new, blank document:

1 Choose New from the File menu to create a new, blank document.

2 Switch to Outline view. Word displays the Outlining toolbar, which includes several buttons for master documents, as shown in Figure 24-2.

FIGURE 24-2.

The right end of the Outlining toolbar contains these master document buttons.

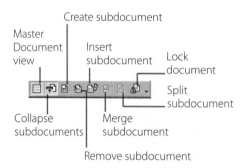

Create subdocument

Master Document view

Insert subdocument

Lock document

Split subdocument

Collapse subdocuments

Merge subdocument

Remove subdocument

 NOTE

In Word 2000, the master document buttons have been added to the Outlining toolbar. There's no longer a separate Master Document toolbar or a Master Document command on the View menu as in Word 97.

3 Enter a title or introductory text into the document, and then move the insertion point to the place where you want a subdocument to appear. As subdocuments are inserted after a section break, be sure to place the insertion point at the beginning of a blank line.

TIP

Make sure there's at least one blank line between the insertion point and the top of the document or between the insertion point and any subdocument above it when you create or insert a new subdocument. The extra space will make it a lot easier to rearrange subdocuments later.

4 Click the Create Subdocument button to make a new subdocument, or click the Insert Subdocument button to insert one from an existing file.

Adding Subdocuments

SEE ALSO

For more information about the Heading 1 style, see "Headings" on page 528.

Subdocuments are added directly below the insertion point in a master document. You can create a new subdocument in the master document and then enter text in it, or you can insert a subdocument from an existing file. However, subdocuments should all begin with a heading formatted in Word's Heading 1 style.

Creating a New Subdocument

To create a new subdocument, follow these steps:

1 Move the insertion point to an empty line below which you want the subdocument to appear.

2 Apply the Heading 1 style to the line, if necessary.

3 Click the Create Subdocument button on the Outlining toolbar. Word creates the new subdocument like this:

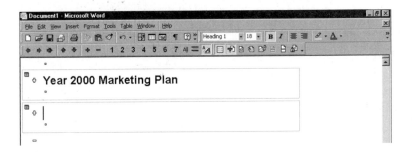

You can then enter the title and text for the new subdocument. You can create other headings inside the subdocument, insert objects, or do anything else that you would do in Outline view. And by switching to Print Layout or Web Layout view, you can see how the subdocument will look as part of the master document.

When you're finished inserting text or objects into the subdocument, save the master document. Word automatically saves the subdocument as a separate file in the same folder. The Heading 1 heading at the top of the subdocument is used as the new file's name.

Inserting an Existing File as a Subdocument

If some parts of your master document already exist as separate files, you can insert them as subdocuments. To do this, follow these steps:

1 Open the master document if necessary.

2 Move the insertion point to the line below which you want the new subdocument to appear.

3 Click the Insert Subdocument button on the Outlining toolbar. You'll see the Insert Document dialog box, which looks just like the Open dialog box from the File menu.

4 Locate the subdocument file in the Open dialog box, select it, and click the Open button. The subdocument is added to the master document.

If you insert a subdocument that contains different styles than the master document, you'll be asked to indicate what to do about the difference. *For information about this, see "Formatting Subdocuments" on page 553.*

Working with Subdocuments

Figure 24-1 on page 545 shows a master document in Outline view as it looks when you create it, which is fine for organizing several subdocuments and perhaps arranging some text or headings above or below them. But you can also use any of Word's other document views to see how the whole master document will look when printed or viewed on the Web. You can also switch to Master Document view to check the status of each subdocument.

Using Master Document View

For more information about making subdocuments available for editing, see "Locking and Unlocking Subdocuments" on page 550.

Outline view is fine for reorganizing a group of subdocuments, but when you're in Outline view, it's not easy to see which headings are subdocuments and which of these subdocuments are available for editing.

Master Document view is a variation of Outline view that uses border lines and document icons to indicate subdocuments. It also shows you when a subdocument is locked.

Master Document view is on by default when you select Outline view. To turn it on or off at other times, click the Master Document View button on the Outlining toolbar. Figure 24-3 on the next page shows how a document looks in this view.

Subdocuments are shown in all their glory in this view, and you can click inside any subdocument to edit it (as long as the subdocument isn't locked—*see page 550*).

To select a whole subdocument, click its document icon.

FIGURE 24-3.

Use Master Document view to see which subdocuments are locked and which are available for editing.

Document icon identifies each subdocument.

Lock icon means subdocument can't be changed.

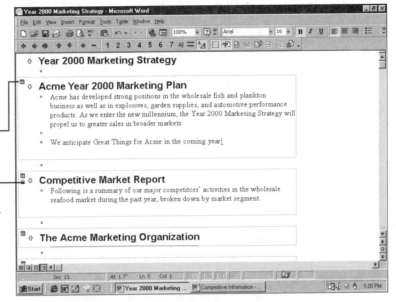

For more information about working with outline headings, see Chapter 12, "Working with Outlines."

Since this is Outline view, you can double-click any heading to view subtopics beneath it, you can use the heading level buttons on the Outlining toolbar to hide or display headings up to a certain level, and you can drag subdocuments to rearrange them.

Collapsing Subdocuments

If your document contains a lot of subdocuments, you may want to view as many of them on the screen as possible. You can collapse subdocuments to fit more of them on the screen at once. Figure 24-3 shows how Master Document view looks with several very short subdocuments open. Notice that each subdocument has a box border around it. When a subdocument is long and the entire document is showing, it will still have a box border around it to help you remember that it's a subdocument.

You can collapse subdocuments in either Master Document or Outline view.

To collapse all of the subdocuments in a master document, click the Collapse Subdocuments button on the Outlining toolbar. The subdocuments are then shown as hyperlinks that include each subdocument file's name and location, like this:

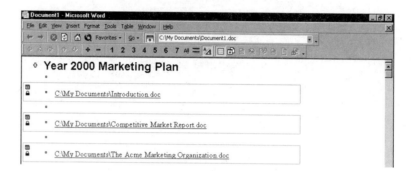

By reducing each subdocument to a hyperlink, the Collapse Subdocuments button automatically reduces each subdocument to its minimum size in the master document.

Deleting a Subdocument

If you change your mind about including a subdocument in your master document, you can delete it or merge it into the master document as ordinary text.

To delete a subdocument, make sure you're in Master Document view (the Master Document View button in the Outlining toolbar should be highlighted, and you should see a document icon at the top of each subdocument), click the document icon, and press the Delete key.

To merge a subdocument's contents into the master document as regular text, expand the subdocument, select its document icon, and then click the Remove Subdocument button on the Outlining toolbar.

Locking and Unlocking Subdocuments

Notice the lock icon below the Competitive Market Report subdocument's icon in Figure 24-3. This indicates that the subdocument is locked and can't be edited from the master document. Only Master Document view shows you if a subdocument is locked. You can also use Master Document view to lock documents. There are three ways in which a document becomes locked:

- The subdocument's file is open in a separate window on your computer.

- The subdocument is stored on a network server and is open on someone else's computer.

- You have locked the subdocument to prevent further changes to it.

SEE ALSO

For more information about using files on a network server, see Chapter 34, "Sharing Documents on a Network."

To lock a subdocument without opening its file, select or click inside the subdocument and then click the Lock Document button on the Outlining toolbar.

The Lock Document button is a toggle, so if you use it to lock a document, you can click it again to unlock the document.

Opening and Editing Subdocuments

Master Document view is fine for revealing locked subdocuments and showing the contents of smaller subdocuments (a page or two, perhaps), but it's not very effective when those subdocuments are large. Because you're working in a master document, you can't scroll inside subdocuments with the scroll bars—you must use the arrow keys on your keyboard to move down within a subdocument.

If you're planning to do a lot of editing or formatting work in a subdocument, you should open the subdocument itself. There are three ways to do this:

- Open the subdocument's file from its original location.

- Double-click the subdocument's icon in Master Document view.

- Collapse the subdocuments and then click a subdocument's hyperlink.

Splitting and Merging Subdocuments

When two subdocuments are fairly small, you may want to combine them into one subdocument so you'll have one less subdocument file to keep track of. Conversely, you may want to split a subdocument into two so that different people can work on parts of it separately. It's easy to split and merge subdocuments.

Splitting a Subdocument

When you split a subdocument, you create a new subdocument file. You can split a subdocument anywhere you like, as long as the line you choose to become the first line in the new subdocument is formatted with the Heading 1 style.

To split a subdocument, follow these steps:

1 Expand all subdocuments so you can see their text (if you see only hyperlinks in your document, click the Expand Subdocuments button on the Outlining toolbar).

2 Expand all of the subdocument's headings to reveal all of its text if you can't find the specific place where you want the split to occur.

3 Move the insertion point to the beginning of the line that will begin the new subdocument. If this line isn't formatted with the Heading 1 style, apply this style with the Style menu in the Formatting toolbar.

4 Click the Split Subdocument button on the Outlining toolbar. Word creates a new subdocument using the first line in the new subdocument as its file name.

Merging Subdocuments

When you merge two subdocuments, you add the contents of one subdocument to another subdocument. To do this, follow these steps:

1 Switch to Outline view and Master Document view and then arrange the two subdocuments so the subdocument you want to end up with is directly above the one to be merged into it. Delete any blank lines or outline markers between them if necessary.

2 Select both subdocuments by clicking the first subdocument's document icon and then Shift-clicking the second subdocument's document icon.

3 Click the Merge Subdocuments button on the Outlining toolbar. Word adds the contents of the lower subdocument to the upper subdocument.

Formatting Subdocuments

You can use any of Word's normal formatting options in a subdocument. Since a subdocument may very well have its own document template and styles, however, you may have to make some formatting decisions when you insert a subdocument. In addition, each subdocument is surrounded by section breaks, and you may want to change or delete them.

Working with Styles

When you insert a subdocument that contains different styles or is based on a different template than the master document, the subdocument takes on the master document's characteristics when it is inserted. However, if Word finds the same style name in both the new subdocument and the master document, it alerts you like this:

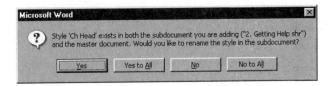

You then have the option to either rename the incoming styles from the subdocument (Word usually adds "1" after the original style name) so you can keep them or to have Word simply use the master document's styles instead.

If an incoming subdocument contains styles that are not in the master document template, Word simply adds them to your master document's template.

Because one of the main advantages to using a master document is being able to apply the master document's styles uniformly to all subdocuments, Word automatically checks for duplicate style names as it inserts a subdocument from an existing file.

Working with Section Breaks

Word inserts each subdocument with section breaks before and after it. These section breaks are shown when Master Document view is turned off, as in Figure 24-1 on page 545. You can change the section breaks or remove them if you like:

■ To remove a section break, select the section break marker and press the Delete key.

■ To change a section break, set different options on the Page Layout tab in the Page Setup dialog box. *For more information, see "Changing a Section Break" on page 319.*

Managing Master Document Projects

Master document projects will go much more smoothly if you follow these five suggestions:

1 Before you begin, create a separate folder to store your master document and its subdocuments and then move any existing subdocument files into it. This will help you avoid subdocument file name conflicts.

2 If possible, use the same document template for the master document and all subdocuments. If this isn't possible, compare the style sheets of your master document and a potential subdocument before inserting the subdocument and delete any styles in the subdocument that don't exist in the master document.

3 Plan a consistent strategy for headers and footers that will work for all subdocuments and any master document pages before you begin, and then make sure to apply it consistently in each master document section. For example, if you're creating a two-page layout, make sure *all* your subdocuments are set up for the two-page layout, with separate left and right headers.

4 Format any subdocuments in advance using Word's Heading styles for headings.

5 Don't rename or move any subdocument files. If you do, Word will have problems finding them.

You won't always be able to adhere to these suggestions, but you'll have less reformatting work to do if you try. *For more information about managing collaborative projects, see Chapter 37, "Managing Collaborative Projects."*

Saving Master Documents

You can open, edit, and save subdocument files individually, of course, but whenever you edit a subdocument file inside the master document and then save the master document, Word automatically saves changes to any affected subdocument files. To save a master document, just press Ctrl+S, or click the Save button on the Standard toolbar, or choose Save from the File menu as you would for any other document.

If your master file contains newly created subdocuments, Word saves the subdocument files with the names you used for their Level 1 headings in the master document. Newly created subdocument files are saved in the same folder as the master document.

 NOTE

> If the location where you save a master document already contains files with the same names as new subdocuments, the subdocument file names will be modified with a numeric extension. For example, if you save a master document to a folder that contains an unrelated file named "Marketing Report" and the master document contains a subdocument called "Marketing Report," the subdocument's file name will automatically be changed to "Marketing Report1."

Printing a Master Document

Printing a single large document from a group of subdocuments is another great benefit of master documents. You can print all of the docu-ment's contents by printing from Web Layout, Print Layout, or Normal view, or you can print a detailed outline of it by printing from Outline view.

To see what will print from each view, switch to that view and choose Print Preview from the File menu. To preview a Web page in your browser, choose Web Page Preview from the File menu.

To print from any view, press Ctrl+P or choose Print from the File menu.

Creating Tables of Contents, Indexes, and Cross-References

When you create long documents, you'll often want to include navigation aids for the reader such as a table of contents, a table of figures, an index, or cross-references. Microsoft Word can create these aids quickly and easily. Word can scan your document and automatically create a table of contents or table of figures, and you can insert special marks to identify cross-references, index entries, or other items for other automatically generated tables. In this chapter you'll learn how to create reference tables, indexes, and cross-references.

Word has built-in facilities that make it fairly simple to create several different navigation aids in documents:

- **A Table of Contents** (or TOC) that lists all of your document's chapter or section headings, subheadings, and other contents if you like.

- **A Table of Figures** (TOF) that lists all of the figures in a document.

- **A Table of Authorities** (TOA) that lists cases cited in legal documents, book titles, authors cited in research papers, or other references.

- **An Index** that lists alphabetically entries you identify, with their page numbers.

- **Cross-references** that direct readers to other parts of the document for more information about a topic.

You can add tables and other document references to any kind of Word document for print or for the World Wide Web using the techniques covered in this chapter. However, you can also add a table of contents frame to a Web page using a different procedure. *For more information see "Creating a Table of Contents Frame" on page 796.*

Creating a Table of Contents

For more information about using Word's Heading styles for a document, see "Headings" on page 528.

Word can quickly generate a table of contents from any document that uses Word's Heading styles. Word gathers up the text from every heading formatted with a Heading style and arranges the headings in order in the TOC. The Heading style level determines the indent level in the TOC. For example, Heading 2 styles are indented to the right of Heading 1 styles. In addition, you can instruct Word to include text formatted with any other style when it builds a TOC.

When you create a TOC, Word creates a new section at the insertion point and puts the TOC into it. The TOC is actually a large data field, but you can select, edit, or reformat individual table entries or move the table.

Here's how to create an automatic TOC based on Heading styles in a document:

1 Format all of the document's headings with Word's Heading styles.

2 Proofread your document and use Word's proofing tools to check spelling, grammar, and readability so that the text is exactly the way you want it.

3 Place the insertion point where you want the TOC to appear.

4 Choose Index And Tables from the Insert menu to open the Index And Tables dialog box.

5 Click the Table Of Contents tab to display the options shown in Figure 25-1.

FIGURE 25-1.

Use the Index And Tables dialog box to create tables of contents, indexes, and other navigation aids.

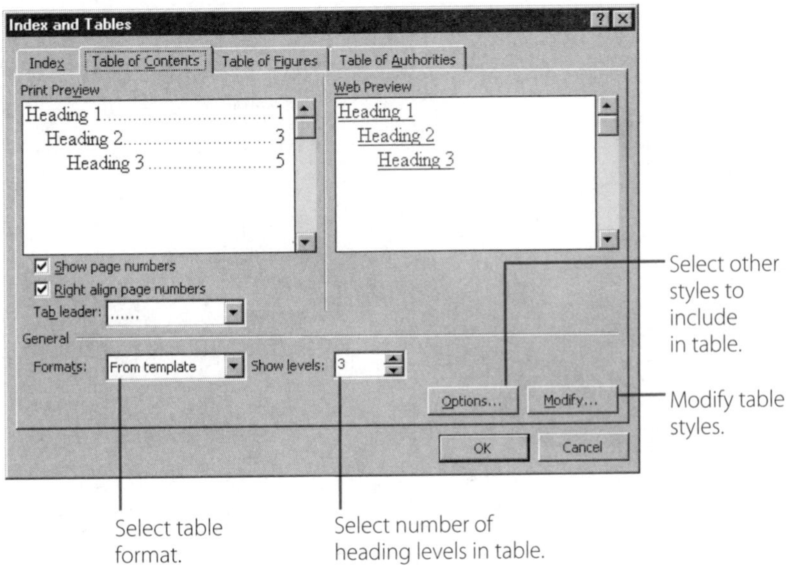

Select other styles to include in table.

Modify table styles.

Select table format.

Select number of heading levels in table.

6 Choose any of the TOC formats from the Formats list at the bottom and check out its preview above.

In Word 2000, you'll find separate previews for Web pages and for printed documents. On Web pages, table entries are inserted as hyperlinks.

7 Enter a different number in the Show Levels box to change the number of Heading style levels that will be included in the table, if you like.

8 Change the tab leader or page number display options if you like.

9 Click OK. Word adds the table to your document. Figure 25-2 shows a table in the Distinctive format.

FIGURE 25-2.

A table of contents appears in your document as one object, but you can select and edit any of its text if you like.

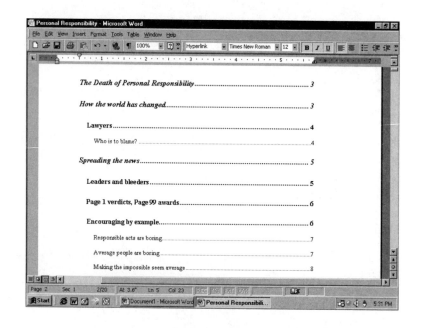

 **TIP**

Use Word's regular text entry and formatting tools to insert a title for the Table of Contents.

Although a table of contents is a large field, you can select and edit portions of it. In addition, each entry that Word creates is also a hyperlink—clicking it navigates you to the heading or other text area it names.

 TIP

When Word creates a TOC, it assigns TOC level styles to each line, rather than keeping the Heading styles you originally used in your document. The TOC styles include the indentation, text size, and other formatting options you see. You can modify individual TOC styles to change the look of a TOC. *For more information, see "Modifying Table Styles" on page 562.*

Adding Custom TOC Entries

You can add other entries to a table of contents to be more specific. When you add entries, you specify which text you want added and then recreate the table. You can specify new TOC entries in two ways:

- Use a Table Entry field to mark the text you want to include. *See "Defining a Marker Field" on page 635.*

- Add more styles to the list of styles from which Word gathers TOC entries.

Expanding a TOC by Including More Styles

To expand your TOC by including more styles, follow these steps:

1   Format the head or text you want to add to the table with a style that is not currently used in the TOC.

2   Choose Index And Tables from the Insert menu and click the Table Of Contents tab, if necessary.

3   Click the Options button. You'll see the Table Of Contents Options dialog box like this:

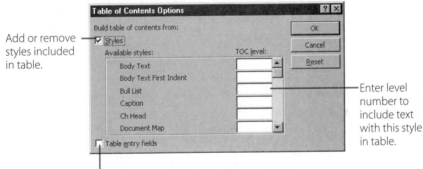

Add or remove styles included in table.

Enter level number to include text with this style in table.

Include text marked with table entry fields.

4   Scroll through the list of styles until you find the one(s) you want to add to the TOC.

5   Assign a TOC level number to each style you want to use. A checkmark appears next to the style name to show that it will be included in the TOC.

6   If you have inserted Table Entry fields into your document, select the Table Entry Fields check box to include them in the revised table as well.

7   Click OK to return to the Table Of Contents tab and set other formatting options for the new levels or items you have added.

8   Click OK, and then click Yes when Word asks if you want to replace the selected TOC.

Reformatting a TOC

Once a TOC is inserted in your document, you can change or add new text to it, reformat specific lines or words, or make general changes to its appearance by modifying its styles.

■   To change specific text, select it and then edit or reformat it. When selecting text, make sure to drag across it immediately after clicking inside the TOC, or else Word will assume you want to jump to that part of your document.

■   To create a new listing in the TOC, move the insertion point to the end of a line and press Enter, just as you would in any text paragraph. Enter the text, press Tab to create the tab leader, and then enter the page number.

WARNING

Any individual formatting changes you make to a TOC will disappear if you re-create it. To make a permanent formatting change to a TOC, modify a style used in the TOC.

NOTE

When you add a new line to a TOC by typing it in, Word does not add a hyperlink to the line. To add a hyperlink, select the text and use the Hyperlink command on the Insert menu. *For more information about this, see "Using Hyperlinks" on page 772.*

Modifying Table Styles

To make wholesale changes to every TOC listing that is formatted with a particular style and to ensure that the changes will remain even if you recreate the TOC, change the style itself. You can always do this using the Style command on the Format menu, but if you have selected the From Template format for the table and the Table Of Contents tab in the Index And Tables dialog box is already showing, there's an easier way:

1   Click the Modify button. Word displays a TOC-only version of the Style dialog box, as shown in Figure 25-3 on the next page.

FIGURE 25-3.

You can change the appearance of a table by modifying the styles Word uses to format it.

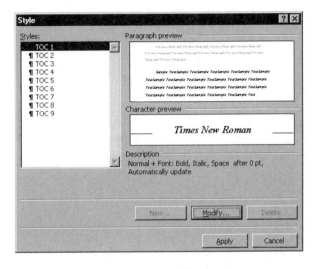

② SEE ALSO

For more information about modifying a style, see "Modifying a Style with the Style Dialog Box" on page 309.

2 Select the TOC style you wish to modify from the Styles list and click the Modify button. You'll see the Modify Style dialog box, where you can change any aspect of the style.

3 Change the style and click OK to return to the Style dialog box, and then click Apply to apply the new style to the selected text.

4 Click OK, and then click OK again when Word asks if you want to replace the selected TOC.

Changing the TOC Levels

Another way to change the look of a TOC is to change the level of one or more entries or to change the number of levels shown.

To change the level of one entry, select it and choose another TOC style from the Style menu in the Formatting toolbar.

To change the number of levels shown in a table, follow these steps:

1 Choose Index And Tables from the Insert menu.

2 Click the Table Of Contents tab, if necessary.

3 Choose a new value in the Show Levels box.

4 Click OK, and then click Yes when Word asks if you want to replace the selected table of contents.

Updating a Table

It's best to create the TOC at the end of the document creation process so it captures all the latest headings, table entry fields, and other elements you want to include. If you end up changing your document after you create a TOC, you can update the TOC at any time.

1 Right-click in the TOC and choose Update Field from the shortcut menu. Word asks if you want to update the whole table or just the page numbers shown for its listings, like this:

FIGURE 25-4.

You can choose what information to update in a TOC.

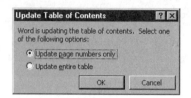

2 Click OK to update page numbers only, or select Update Entire Table and click OK. Word will perform the update.

Creating a Table of Figures

If your document is heavily illustrated and the figures have captions, Word can create a table of figures (TOF) from them. When it creates a TOF, Word collects the text from all of the captions in the document that were created with the Caption command on the Insert menu, or from any other text that is formatted with the Caption style.

> You can also create a TOF by inserting table entry fields into your document. *See Chapter 27, "Using Fields," for more information.*

The process is similar to the one used to create a table of contents.

1 Add a caption to every figure you want included in the table by using the Caption command on the Insert menu, or select existing figure captions and apply the Caption style to them.

2 Move the insertion point to the place where you want the TOF to appear.

3 Choose Index And Tables from the Insert menu to display the Index And Tables dialog box.

4   Click the Table Of Figures tab to display the options shown in Figure 25-5.

FIGURE 25-5.

Use the Table Of Figures tab in the Index and Tables dialog box to set content and format options for a table of figures.

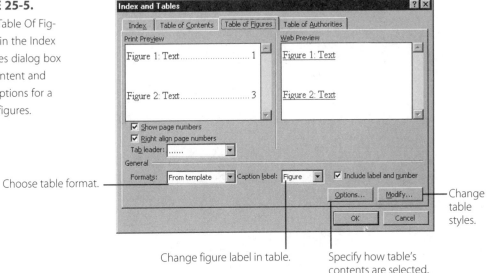

Choose table format.

Change figure label in table.

Specify how table's contents are selected.

Change table styles.

5   Select a table format from the Formats list at the bottom to see how various formats will look in the Preview boxes above.

6   Set other options to change the label used for figures, to hide page numbers or change their alignment, or to hide the figure label and figure number and display only the text in each caption.

Using More than One Table of Contents

If a long document contains lots of subheadings, a single TOC listing all of them can span several pages. If you don't want to intimidate your readers with such a detailed table at the beginning of the document, you can insert a basic TOC showing main sections or chapters at the beginning of the document and then add a secondary TOC at the beginning of each chapter or section.

To insert a secondary TOC to your document, move the insertion point to the place where you want it to appear and follow steps 1–9 on pages 559–560. When you click the OK button to insert the TOC, however, Word asks if you want to replace the existing TOC.

Click No to insert the new TOC instead of updating the main table for the document.

7 Click OK. Word creates the table of figures, as shown in Figure 25-6.

FIGURE 25-6.

A table of figures lists every captioned figure or graphic in your document.

Modifying and Updating a Table of Figures

 SEE ALSO

For information on modifying a table style, see "Modifying Table Styles" on page 562.

As with a TOC, you can modify a TOF's contents by selecting and changing text in it manually, or you can use a dialog box to set certain options. Here's how to change a TOF using the Table of Figures Options dialog box:

1 Choose Index And Tables from the Insert menu and click the Table Of Figures tab, if necessary.

2 Click the Options button. Word displays the Table Of Figures Options dialog box, like this:

Select one or both options to specify how table contents are selected.

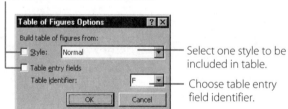

Select one style to be included in table.

Choose table entry field identifier.

3 Select either the Style or Table Entry Fields check box. If you select the Style check box, choose the style that identifies text you want included in the TOF. If you choose the Table Entry Fields option, you must choose the letter that identifies the TOF. Typically, this letter is F for a Table of Figures entry field, but you can change it to collect text from other table entry fields instead if you like.

4 Click OK to return to the Index And Tables dialog box and click OK to recreate the TOF. Word will ask if you want to replace the TOF. Click Yes to replace the old TOF or No to add a new TOF.

> **NOTE**

You can choose only one style for inclusion in a table of figures. If you pick a different style and recreate the TOF, it will contain only the figure captions formatted with that style. Any previously listed captions formatted with a different style will be deleted from the TOF.

★ **TIP**

A table of figures uses only one indent level and one style, so it's easy to reformat the TOF's text by modifying the style. If you are using a format style from the current document template, you can modify it by clicking the Modify button in the Index And Tables dialog box. If you choose one of Word's built-in table formats, you can select that format's style in the Style dialog box and modify it there.

? **SEE ALSO**

For more about updating a TOF, see "Updating a Table" on page 564.

To update an existing table of figures to reflect changes in your document, right-click in the TOF and choose Update Field from the shortcut menu.

Creating a Table of Authorities

A table of authorities (TOA) is used mostly for legal documents where cases, rules, statutes, constitutional language, treaties, or other documents are cited. The TOA shows each such reference and its document location.

To create a TOA, your document must contain reference names or citations that are specially marked as such. You must add these marks before creating the TOA. Once you insert all of the marks, Word arranges all the marked text in a list that's similar to a table of contents.

It's standard practice to refer to a citation completely the first time you use it in a document, and then refer to it elsewhere by a shorter name. For example, the first reference to a legal case might be *Hatfield v. McCoy, 66 Can 2d 216 (1993)*, while the short version would simply be *Hatfield v. McCoy*. When you mark all of the citations in your document, you can tell Word to search for and mark both the long and short forms of the citation, and you can edit the citation names that appear in the TOA if you like.

Marking Citations

There are two ways to mark citations in a document. You can use the Mark Citation dialog box or you can insert a table entry field.

Using the Mark Citation Dialog Box

To mark a citation with the Mark Citation dialog box, follow these steps:

1 Select the first occurrence of a citation in your document (the long version) and press Alt+Shift+I to display the Mark Citation dialog box, as shown in Figure 25-7. (To display the dialog box using menus, choose Index And Tables from the Insert menu, click the Table Of Authorities tab on the Index And Tables dialog box, and click the Mark Citation button.)

FIGURE 25-7.

Use the Mark Citation dialog box to mark reference citations for inclusion in a Table of Authorities.

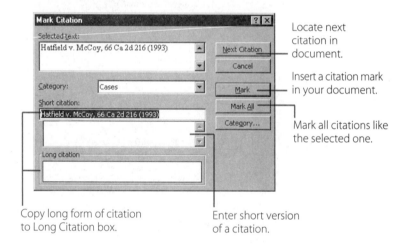

Locate next citation in document.

Insert a citation mark in your document.

Mark all citations like the selected one.

Copy long form of citation to Long Citation box.

Enter short version of a citation.

2 The text you selected appears in the Selected Text box and in the Short Citation box. The Selected Text box shows the way the text will appear in the table of authorities when it is created.

3 Edit the text in the Selected Text box to change the way it will appear in the table, if you like.

4 Edit the text in the Short Citation box to match the shorter version of the citation in your document. For example, if the short version in Figure 25-7 is "Hatfield v. McCoy," delete the case and court number and date from the end of the text.

5 Choose an authority category from the Category list. (When you create the table of authorities, the category name appears in **bold** in the table of authorities, above the list of references selected for that category.)

TIP

You can choose from predefined category names or add new ones of your own. Click the Category button to open the Edit Category dialog box, select an existing category from the list, type a replacement name, click Replace, and then click OK.

6 Click Mark. Word inserts a Table Entry field next to the citation in your document, like this:

The·case·was·very·similar·to·Hatfield·v.·McCoy,·66·Ca·2d·216·(1993){·TA·\l·"Hatfield·v.·McCoy,·66·Ca·2d·216·(1993)"·\s·"Hatfield·v.·McCoy"·\c·1·},·and·should·have·had·a·similar·verdict,·however·the·judge·relied·on·tainted·courtroom·testimony·to·rule·in·favor·of·the·defendant.¶

NOTE

Word automatically displays the document's nonprinting characters in your document so you can see the table entry field code. This field code is invisible when you don't display nonprinting characters in your document, and Word won't print the field code unless you choose a special printing option. *For more information about printing field codes in a document, see "Using Advanced Printing Options" on page 127. See Chapter 27, "Using Fields," for more about fields.*

TIP

To hide table entry fields and other nonprinting characters, click the Show/Hide ¶ button on the Standard toolbar.

7 The Mark Citation dialog box remains open so you can select and mark lots of different citations. Click in your document to select other citations, and then click in the dialog box to reactivate it. You can drag the dialog box around your screen to reveal text if necessary.

8 When you're finished with the Mark Citation dialog box, click Close to put it away.

Marking Several Citations Automatically

Once you enter a short citation name, you can use the Mark Citation dialog box to have Word automatically locate and mark all citations with that name. You can also have Word locate each successive citation in your document so you can mark them one by one.

To mark all citations in a document that are like the one you have selected, press Alt+Shift+I, select the short citation text in the Short Citation list, and click the Mark All button.

To locate the next citation you may want to mark, click the Next Citation button.

> Word locates citations by searching for a text string that contains *v.* or *ibid.* or which is preceded by legalese such as *in re* or *sess.*

Selecting a Format and Creating the Table

After marking all of the citations in the document, the next step is to choose formatting options and create the table. You use the same basic procedure you use for TOC or TOF entries:

1 Place the insertion point where you want the table to appear and choose Index And Tables from the Insert menu.

2 Click the Table Of Authorities tab if necessary. You'll see the options shown in Figure 25-8 on the facing page.

> For more information about the check box options on the Table Of Authorities tab, click the Help button at the top of the dialog box and then click one of the options to see a description.

SEE ALSO
For more information about modifying styles, see "Modifying Styles" on page 307.

3 Choose a format style from the Formats list and check the Print Preview box to see how it looks. If you select the From Template format, Word formats the table using the current template's Table of Authorities styles. Click the Modify button to modify these template styles if you like.

4 Choose the category of citation you want to include in the table, or leave the option set to All.

FIGURE 25-8.

Use the Table of Authorities tab to set table options or create a table of authorities.

Select citation category to show in table or leave option set to All.

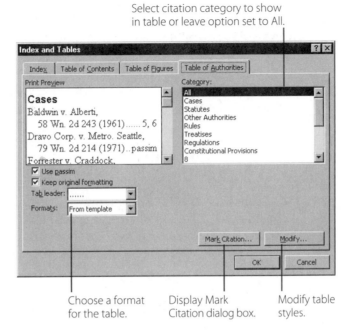

Choose a format for the table.

Display Mark Citation dialog box.

Modify table styles.

5 Click OK to create the table. The TOA appears in your document like this:

Cases¶
Hatfield·v.·McCoy,·66·Ca.·2d·216·(1993) ....→..............................1¶
Montague·v.·Capulet,·83·Mi.·2d·338·(1594) ....→..............................1¶
Trump·v.·Trump,·22·Ny.·2d·486·(1988) ....→..............................1¶
¶

Notice that this particular table includes citations in the Cases category, and that the category name is used as a heading for the table. As with a TOC or TOF, the table is one large field.

Modifying or Updating the Table

❓ SEE ALSO

For more information on modifying a TOA, see "Reformatting a TOC" on page 562.

You can select and edit or reformat individual lines in a table of authorities just as you can in a TOC or TOF. And as with other tables, you can also reopen the Index And Tables dialog box and choose a new format or other options for the TOA.

The procedure for updating a TOA is also the same as with other automatically generated tables. Since the TOA is a field, you can click anywhere in the table and then press F9 to update it or right-click in the table and choose Update Field from the shortcut menu.

> When you modify a TOA by making changes in the Index And Tables dialog box and clicking OK to apply the changes, you're asked if you want to replace the selected table category. If your table contains more than one category (Cases, Statutes, and Constitutional Provisions, for example), Word only modifies one of them at a time. To modify a particular category in a table, click in the category before you open the Index And Tables dialog box.

Creating an Index

Word can automatically create an index in your document by collecting entries you have identified with special index field markers, or it can gather up all occurrences of words or phrases based on a list you create separately. Like other tables, an index is created as one large field.

Making an Index from Marked Text

To create an index from marked text, you must mark each word or phrase you want listed in the index. If you're creating a long document, it's best to do this as you go through the document during final proofreading. To insert an index marker, follow these steps:

1 Select the text you want to mark.

2 Press Alt+Shift+X to open the Mark Index Entry dialog box, as shown in Figure 25-9, on the next page. (To display this dialog box the hard way, choose Index And Tables from the Insert menu, click the Index tab, and click the Mark Entry button.)

3 Click the Mark button to mark this one entry, or click Mark All to mark every occurrence of this entry throughout the document. The dialog box stays open after you mark an entry so you can select other text in your document and mark it as well.

4 Click outside the dialog box and select another index entry, and then click the Mark Index Entry dialog box to reactivate the dialog box so you can mark the selection. Repeat this step until all index entries are marked.

5 Click Close on the dialog box to put it away when you're finished.

FIGURE 25-9.

When you mark an index entry, you can edit the text of the entry, add text for a subentry, or specify how the entry's location is shown in the index.

Selected text in document— Edit if necessary.

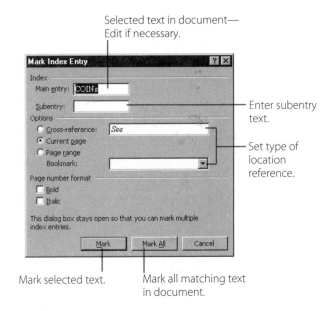

Enter subentry text.

Set type of location reference.

Mark selected text.

Mark all matching text in document.

WARNING

Be careful when using the Mark All button to mark index entries. Unless the selected text is a proper name or technical term, the chances are that Word will mark entries that don't really belong in the index.

Setting Index Entry Options

When you mark an index entry with the Mark Index Entry dialog box, you have several options about how the entry will be formatted in the index.

Editing Main Entry Text

The text you selected in your document is shown in the Main Entry box when you first open the Mark Index Entry dialog box. You can select and edit this text if you like. You may very well want to create several different index entries for the same marked text. Indexes commonly include multiple references to the same text in a document, because people use different words to refer to the same concepts. For example, text that refers to "profitability" might also appear in the index as "cash flow" or "financial performance." To create alternate index entries for the same text, just edit the Main Entry text and click Mark after each alternate listing.

Creating Subentries

Subentries are index entries that are indented under a more general main entry. For example, a report on commodity futures might have main entries for each commodity (corn, wheat, soybeans, and so on) with separate subentries under each for specific investments in each.

> To see an example of a subentry, open the Index And Tables dialog box, click the Index tab, and scroll the Print Preview box.

Here's how to create a subentry:

1 Select the Main Entry text in your document.

2 Press Alt+Shift+X. The Mark Index Entry dialog box appears and the Main Entry text is in the Main Entry box.

3 Enter the subentry text in the Subentry box.

4 Click Mark.

Setting Entry Options

The Options area of the Mark Index Entry dialog box lets you decide how an index entry's location will be listed.

- **Cross-reference** Adds a cross-reference entry to the index listing rather than a page number. The cross-reference usually points to another Index entry. When you select this option, the word "See" is already entered in the Cross-Reference box, and you can type a cross-reference name in it to refer readers to another index entry. For example, a cross-reference entry for the index entry "Net Revenues" might read, "*See Cash Flow.*"

- **Current page** This is the default option—it tells Word to simply show the current page on which the index entry appears. If you use the Mark All button to mark all occurrences of an entry, Word lists every page number where the entry appears.

For more information about inserting a bookmark, see "Using Bookmarks" on page 225.

- **Page Range Bookmark** Allows you to specify a range of pages rather than a single page number for an index entry. For example, "Frog Habits, 32–34." To use this option, you must first select the range of pages in the document and insert a bookmark for it. The bookmark name will then appear on the Page Range Bookmark menu, where you can select it.

IV

Graphics and Publishing Tools

- **Page Number Format options** Allows you to format individual index entries in bold or italic type as you create them. Of course, you can always select individual entries in the index itself and reformat them later if you like.

Creating the Index

Once you have marked all of the entries you want to appear in the index, creating it is easy. The process is very similar to the ones you use to create a table of contents or other tables in your document.

1 Move the insertion point to the place where you want the index to appear, usually at the end of your document.

2 Choose Index And Tables from the Insert menu and click the Index tab if necessary. Word displays the Index options, as shown in Figure 25-10.

FIGURE 25-10.

When you create an index, you can choose different predefined formats from a list and set other formatting options.

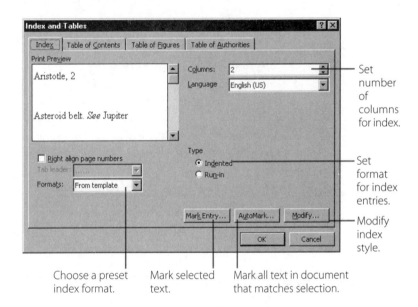

Set number of columns for index.

Set format for index entries.

Modify index style.

Choose a preset index format.

Mark selected text.

Mark all text in document that matches selection.

3 Select an index format from the Formats list. You can see how each format looks in the Print Preview box above.

⭐ **TIP**

Scroll down in the Print Preview box to see how various types of entries are formatted with each of the different options.

4 Choose the number of columns for the index.

If you have marked dozens of index entries, the index can span many pages. If your index contains mostly short entries, you can save paper by arranging the index in three columns, rather than two.

5 Select other options if you like, and click OK. Word adds the index to your document as one large field.

Reformatting an Index

For more information on modifying styles, see "Modifying a Style with the Style Dialog Box" on page 309.

Once you have an index in your document, you can select any text in it and reformat it manually, or you can reformat text at certain levels by modifying the index styles. There are two ways to modify an index style:

■ Open the Index tab in the Index And Tables dialog box, click the Modify button, and modify the style.

■ Choose Style from the Format menu and modify the style.

Updating an Index

If you mark additional index entries or modify the document's text so that the locations of index entries change, you'll need to update the index. You can update the index whenever you want. Just click in the index and press F9 or right-click in the index and choose Update Field from the shortcut menu.

Creating an Index from a List

Rather than marking index entries throughout your document, you can prepare a list of words or phrases and then have Word find them in your document, mark them, and put them in an index automatically.

WARNING

Creating or modifying an index from a word list is dangerous because Word automatically finds and marks every occurrence of the words or phrases you list, and you may not want all of them marked. For example, you might add "Airports" to the index of a travel guide only to find out after creating the index that many casual references to airports were included when they shouldn't have been. It's best to use a list to supplement an existing index created from entries you have marked by hand and to list only words or phrases that are unique enough to appear only on those pages that you want listed in the index.

The following steps show how to supplement an existing index or create a new index from a list:

1   Create a new document.

? SEE ALSO

For more information about tables, see Chapter 17,"Working with Tables."

2   Insert a two-column table by choosing the Table command from the Insert submenu on the Table menu.

3   Type in the left-hand column of the table the word or phrase that you want Word to locate in your document. Type the word *exactly* as it appears in your document, being sure to use correct capitalization. For example, Word won't locate "manufacturing statistics" if you enter "Manufacturing statistics" in the column.

4   Type in the table's right-hand column the index entry as you want it to appear in the index.

5   Repeat steps 3 and 4 for each index entry.

6   Save the document.

7   Return to the document where you want to create or supplement the index.

8   Choose Index And Tables from the Insert menu and click the Index tab if necessary.

9   Click the AutoMark button. Word displays the Open dialog box.

10   Double-click the file containing the two-column table. Word locates and marks all of the matching words or phrases in your document.

11   Choose Index And Tables from the Insert menu again and click OK to create the index. If you're updating an existing index, click Yes when Word asks if you want to replace the existing one.

Creating Cross-References

Cross-references are bits of text that refer readers to other places in a document. Often displayed in italics or parentheses, cross-references point to a particular document location, such as a chapter or page number.

You can always create cross-references manually by simply typing the appropriate text in your document, of course, but when you insert a cross-reference with Word, it automatically creates the reference text and includes the page, chapter, or other location reference. In addition, Word will automatically change location references if you later modify your document, and cross-references can be inserted as hyperlinks that readers can click to jump to the cross-referenced location in the document.

> **NOTE**
>
> Word can create cross-references only to other locations in the same document or master document. To create cross-references to other documents, use hyperlinks. *For more information about using hyperlinks, see "Using Hyperlinks" on page 772.*

To insert a cross-reference, follow these steps:

1 Move the insertion point to the place where you want the cross-reference to appear and type the beginning of the cross-referenced text, such as "See" or "See page" followed by a space.

2 Choose Cross-Reference from the Insert menu to display the Cross-reference dialog box as shown in Figure 25-11.

FIGURE 25-11.

Specify which text you want the cross-reference to contain.

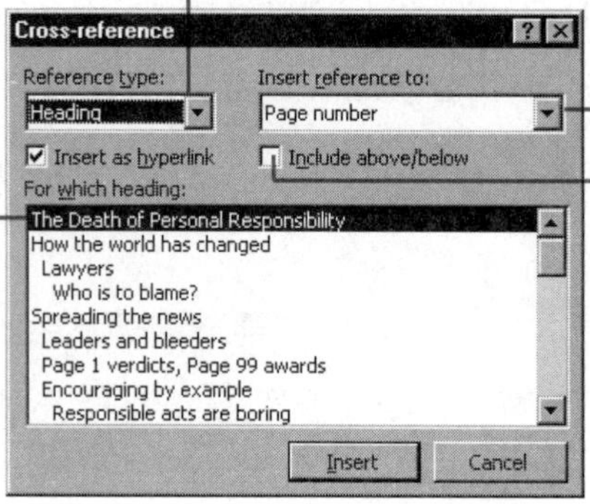

Select type of text for entry.

Choose specific heading, figure, or other item, depending on Reference Type above.

Choose type of location reference.

Add "above" or "below" to cross-reference text.

3 Using the Reference Type list, select the type of item to which you want a cross-reference. For example, if you select Heading, you'll see a list of the document's headings in the For Which Heading list below, as shown in Figure 25-11.

4 Select the specific document heading, bookmark, or other element from the list. This indicates the location in the document to which you want the cross-reference to refer.

5 Using the Insert Reference To list, select the reference information you want shown. You can show a reference to heading text, a page number, or an item number in a list, for example.

6 Select or clear the check box to insert the reference as a hyperlink or to add the word "above" or "below" to the reference text, depending on the relative location of the item to which you are referring. (This check box is not available for all reference types.)

> **TIP**
>
> Select the Insert As Hyperlink check box when you insert cross-references, if it isn't already selected. This way, you or others reading the document on a computer can click the cross-reference to jump immediately to the referenced location.

7 Click Insert to insert the reference. Word inserts the text of the reference you selected and the Cross-reference dialog box stays open so you can insert others. Click the Close button to close this dialog box.

> **TIP**
>
> When Word inserts a cross-reference, it is actually inserting a field. To show the field name rather than the cross-reference text, choose Options from the Tools menu, click the View tab, and select the Field Codes check box.

PART V

Data Handling and Automation Tools

Using Mail Merge

When you want to mail the same item to many people, mail merge is the answer. Microsoft Word can automatically combine a document's text with names, addresses, and other information to create personalized form letters, mailing labels, and other products. Mail merging is a powerful data management feature, but Word makes it easy with the Mail Merge Helper.

The most common items made by mail merge are form letters, envelopes, and mailing labels. However, since you can insert fields into any Word document and format the document any way you like, you can also use the Mail Merge Helper to create catalogs, purchase orders, telephone lists, schedules, and many other documents.

The Mail Merge Helper in Word 2000 is mostly unchanged from the one in Word 97. If you use database queries to select records for a data source, however, you can now use Microsoft Query to do it. *See "Querying a Data File" on page 597.*

About Merge Documents

You need two things to create a mail merge document:

- A *main document* that contains the text you want to distribute along with *fields* that tell Word which data to insert where. A main document is a standard Word document, but you must identify it as a main document using the Mail Merge Helper dialog box.

- A *data source* that contains the names, addresses, and other information to be inserted into the main document. You can create a new data source using the Mail Merge Helper, or you can use data from an existing file.

When you perform a merge, these two items are combined to produce merge documents, one for each address or other record in the data source. In Figure 26-1, the document at the top of the screen is a form letter inviting customers to a new product demonstration, and the document at the bottom of the screen is the data source.

FIGURE 26-1.

Mail merge combines names, addresses, and other information from a data source file (bottom) with a main document (top). Fields in the main document indicate which data goes where.

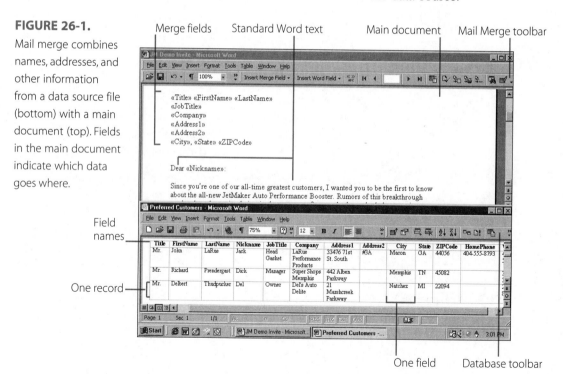

You use the Mail Merge Helper dialog box shown in Figure 26-2 to create main documents, select data sources, and set merge options.

FIGURE 26-2.

The Mail Merge Helper makes mail merging simple.

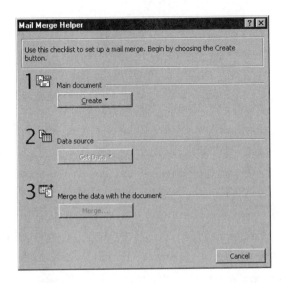

You can use Microsoft Excel or Microsoft Access files, Microsoft Outlook address books, and many other types of files as data sources. However, any data source you use must be divided into *records* and *fields*. In Figure 26-1, each row in the data source table is one record, and each column represents a field, or category of information. The top row in the data source is the *header*, which shows the name of each field.

When you create merge documents, Word makes one copy for each record in the file. You can create merge documents on a printer, as separate e-mail messages, or as individual sections of one new Word document. If you don't want to create a merge document for every single record in the data source, you can sort or filter records in a data source before merging.

Understanding the Mail Merge Helper

The Mail Merge Helper separates the mail merge process into three areas, but it's actually a little more complex than that. We'll look at every step in detail, but for now here are the basic steps to creating a merge document:

1   Choose Mail Merge from the Tools menu. Word opens the Mail Merge Helper, as shown in Figure 26-2.

Don't confuse the Mail Merge command on the Tools menu with the Merge Documents command on the Tools menu. The Merge Documents command is for consolidating reviewer comments from several copies in a document into one. *See Chapter 35, "Tracking Changes in a Document," for more information.*

2 Click the Create button to create a main document. You can choose the type of document you want to create, or you can use the document that's currently active. The choice you make affects the way Word creates merge documents.

Keep an eye on the messages at the top of the Mail Merge Helper dialog box. They tell you which stages of the merge process have been completed or which step you need to handle next. Also, text below the Main Document, Data Source, and Merge buttons tells you which main document or data sources are currently selected and which options are set for them.

3 Click the Get Data button to select a data source. You can create a new data source from scratch at this point or you can open an existing one.

4 Add merge fields to the main document, and then add or edit other text or graphics in it and make final formatting adjustments.

5 Select and sort the records in the data source to specify which records are used to create merge documents.

6 Check the merged documents for errors. You can have Word check for data errors or create merge documents on the screen so you can scan them visually.

7 Merge the data source with the main document to create merge documents.

Now let's look at the process in more detail.

Creating a Main Document

A main document looks and acts the same as any other Word document, except that Word knows it's a target for merged data. There are two ways to create a main document:

■ Create a document in advance (a form letter, for example) and then turn it into a main document with the Mail Merge Helper.

- Use the Mail Merge Helper to create a new blank document as the main document and then enter the text.

Here are the basic steps to creating a main document:

1   Open the document containing the form letter or other text if you created it in advance.

2   Choose Mail Merge from the Tools menu.

3   Click the Create button in the Mail Merge Helper and choose the type of document you want to create. Word asks if you want to use the active document or make a new one, like this:

4   Click a button to make your choice. Word creates a main document or converts the active document into a main document and returns you to the Mail Merge Helper.

Choosing a Main Document Type

The type of main document you choose determines how Word merges information as well as how you arrange fields in the document. Keep the following distinctions in mind when creating a main document, and be sure to choose the right type of document for the job.

? SEE ALSO

For more information about formatting and adding fields to mailing labels, envelopes, or catalogs, see "Adding Fields to a Main Document" on page 599.

- **Form Letters** You want to create a merged letter, invitation, invoice, or any other type of document for which you want to print one document for each record in the data source.

- **Mailing Labels** You want to create labels or other documents that include blocks of data repeated on a page, such as name tags. When you choose this option, you use the Label Options and Create Label dialog boxes to format and add fields to the document.

- **Envelopes** You want to create one envelope for each record in the data source. When you choose this option, you can use the Envelope Options and Create Envelope dialog boxes to set up the envelope format and add fields to it.

■ **Catalog** You want to create a list or directory of phone numbers, customers, employees, team members, or other data. You use a standard Word document to arrange the fields in a catalog layout. Word prints as many records from the data source as will fit on each page.

Adding Text to a Main Document

? SEE ALSO

For more information, see "Adding Merge Fields to a Main Document" on page 599.

If you're creating a merge document that includes text or graphics as well as fields, you'll want to enter and format everything before adding fields from the data source. When the Mail Merge Helper dialog box is open, you must put it away before you can edit the document. To do this, either click the Edit button and select the document's name on the pop-up menu or click the Close button on the Mail Merge Helper dialog box.

Switching Main Documents

Once you have created a main document, you can use the Mail Merge Helper to change the main document type, create a new main document, or convert a main document back into a standard Word document. You can make such changes whenever you like.

Changing the Document Type

To switch document types, follow these steps:

1 Choose Mail Merge from the Tools menu to open the Mail Merge Helper.

2 Click Create in the Main Document area and choose another document type from the pop-up menu. Word will ask whether you want to change the document type or create a new main document.

3 Click Change Document Type.

Restoring a Main Document to a Word Document

Since a main document has an association with a data source, you may want to eliminate that association, especially if you want to allow others to use the main document in other merging projects with other data sources. To convert a main document back into a normal Word document, follow these steps:

1 Activate the main document and choose Mail Merge from the Tools menu.

2 Click the Create button in the Main Document area, choose Restore To Normal Word Document, and then click Yes when Word asks you to confirm this choice.

Selecting a Data Source

Before you can add merge fields to a main document, you must select the data source so Word knows where to get the information that will be merged. To select a data source, click the Get Data button on the Mail Merge Helper dialog box, and then choose an option from the menu.

You can create a new data source from scratch; you can use an address book from Outlook or another program; or you can open a data file from Excel, Access, or other database, spreadsheet, or word processing programs. Each process is a little different, so we'll go into details in the sections that follow.

Constructing a Useful Data Source

No matter which program you use to create a data source for a merge project, it's important to capture all of the information you might need in the merge document and to do so in a way that gives you maximum flexibility in using the information.

This means making sure there are enough separate fields in the data source to capture your data so you can use it the way you want. In addition to the fields offered in the Create Data Source dialog box, for example, you might add fields for a fax number or e-mail address. In a merge project using invoices, you might include an Amount Due field so you can put the invoice total right into the merge document.

The same is true when it comes to separating data among different fields. For example, you might be tempted to include only one Name field to store each person's first and last name because it makes data entry a little easier. But when you add fields to a main document later, you'll be forced to use both names in every situation—you'll end up saying "Dear John Smith" instead of "Dear John." You might also want to use separate Area Code and Number fields instead of one Phone field so you can sort or select records by area code or local prefix.

Creating a New Data Source

If you don't have an existing file that you can use as the data source, you'll have to create one. With the Mail Merge Helper, you can create a new Word document as a data source. The process is much like setting up a database file: you select the fields you want the file to contain as you create the source file, and then you enter the information. Here's how to begin:

1 Choose Mail Merge from the Tools menu to open the Mail Merge Helper if necessary.

2 Click the Get Data button and choose Create Data Source from the pop-up menu. Word opens the Create Data Source dialog box, as seen in Figure 26-3.

If the Get Data button appears dimmed in the Mail Merge Helper, you need to first create a main document as explained on page 586.

FIGURE 26-3.

When you create a new data source, you can choose the fields (or data categories) it will contain.

Type new field name and click button to add to data source.

Remove selected field from data source.

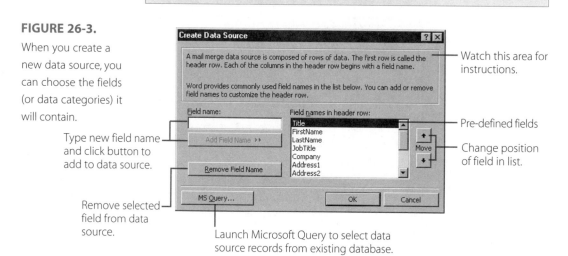

Watch this area for instructions.

Pre-defined fields

Change position of field in list.

Launch Microsoft Query to select data source records from existing database.

Setting Up the Data Source Fields

The Create Data Source dialog box lists the names of fields that are commonly used in mail merge projects. All of these fields will be included in the new data source unless you remove some of them or create new fields. Word adds fields to the new data source table from left to right according to their place on the list, but you can move fields up and down in the list if you like.

■ To remove a field name from the data source list, select it and click Remove Field Name.

- To add a new field name to the data source list, type the name in the Field Name box and click Add Field Name.

- To reorder a field, select its name and click one of the Move arrow buttons to the right of the list.

You can't use field names that contain spaces.

Creating a Data Source Document

Once you have made your field selections, you're ready to create the data source document. Here's what to do:

1 Click OK in the Create Data Source dialog box. Word opens the Save dialog box so you can name the new file and save it.

2 Type a file name and click Save. Word then asks whether you want to add new records to the data source or add merge fields to the main document, like this:

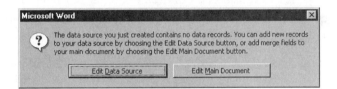

3 Click Edit Data Source. Word opens the Data Form shown in Figure 26-4.

FIGURE 26-4.

When you first create a data source, Word presents a handy form you can use to enter data.

Enter each field's data for one record.

Scroll to view other fields.

Click to close.

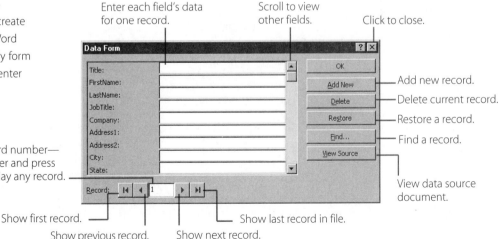

Add new record.

Delete current record.

Restore a record.

Find a record.

View data source document.

Current record number— type a number and press Enter to display any record.

Show first record.

Show previous record.

Show next record.

Show last record in file.

V

Data Automation Tools

Entering Data

? SEE ALSO

Data sources you create with the Mail Merge Helper arrange data in tables. For more information about entering and editing data in tables, see Chapter 17, "Working with Tables."

You can open a data source document itself to enter or change data, but it's easier to use the Data Form shown in Figure 26-4.

To enter data with the Data Form:

1 Click in the first field and enter the data for that field for the first record you want to store.

2 Press Tab to move the insertion point down one field, and enter the second field's data.

3 Continue entering data until the whole form is filled out and then press Enter or click Add New. Word stores the data for that record and displays a new, blank one.

4 Repeat the above steps for each record you want to store and click OK to close the Data Form dialog box when you're finished.

Editing Data

? SEE ALSO

For more information about the Mail Merge toolbar, see "Using the Mail Merge Toolbar" on page 600. For more information about finding records with the Data Form dialog box, see "Finding Records" on page 616.

You can open the Data Form at any time to view or edit the data in your data source, to see how many records are in the source, or to locate a particular record.

1 Click the Edit Data Source button on the Mail Merge toolbar or open the Mail Merge Helper, click the Edit button in the Data Source area, and then choose the data source name from the pop-up menu. Word opens the Data Form dialog box.

2 Use the arrow buttons at the bottom or use the Find button to locate a particular record.

 TIP

> If you know the number of the record you want to view, select the current record number, type the number of the record you want, and press Enter to display it.

3 Select and edit the data in any field.

4 Click OK to save the change, or click Restore to discard changes and revert to the record's original state.

Viewing a Data Source Document

In addition to using the Data Form dialog box, you can view or edit data directly in the data source document. Editing directly in the data source document can be easier because you can use Word's Find and Replace commands to locate or change data throughout the document. You can see several records on the screen at once, you can delete rows to delete records, or you can use the Paste command to append records copied from another file.

To open the data source document:

1   Choose Mail Merge from the Tools menu.

2   Click the Get Data button to create a new data source or open an existing one, if necessary.

3   Click the Edit button and choose the data source name from the pop-up menu to display the Data Form.

4   Click the View Source button in the Data Form dialog box. Word will open the data source document like the one shown at the bottom of Figure 26-1 on page 584.

Whenever you view a data source document, Word displays the Database Toolbar. *For more information about the Database toolbar, see "Using the Database Toolbar" on page 614.*

Using Existing Data

If you have existing data in a file, you can use that file as a data source. The file might be a *data source document* you created with Word for a previous merge project, or it might be a *data file* from another program. You can use all of the data from such a file, or you can query it to use only a subset of its records. The specific procedure depends on whether the file is a data source document or a data file from another program. And if you work with a data source document, you can add records to it as well.

You can also select which records to merge from a file before creating final merge documents. *For more information, see "Filtering Records" on page 616 or "Creating Merge Documents" on page 620.*

Opening an Existing Data Source Document

You can open an existing data source when you begin a merge project, or to change from one data source document to another during a merge project. To open an existing data source document, do the following:

1   Open the Mail Merge Helper dialog box, click the Get Data button, and choose Open Data Source from the pop-up menu. Word presents the Open Data Source dialog box as shown in Figure 26-5.

2   Select the data source document and click the Open button. (If you had a data source document open before you opened this one, you'll be asked if you want to save the data source being replaced; click Yes to save it if you like.)

Editing Records in a Data Source Document

When you open a data source, you generally know which data you want to use in a merge project, but sometimes you change your mind. For example, you may have two closely related data source files and decide that the one you're using is lacking an important field or important records. There are two ways to remedy this situation: either open a different data source to replace the current one (as described above), or edit the existing data source.

Before you can edit the data in a data source or copy records into it from another data source, the current data source document must be open on your screen. *For instructions on viewing a data source, see "Viewing a Data Source Document" on page 592.*

Editing or Deleting Data in a Data Source Document

? SEE ALSO

For more information about working with tables, see Chapter 17, "Working with Tables."

Since a data source document is a standard Word table, as shown at the bottom of Figure 26-1, you can edit the data in it by selecting individual cells and changing their contents, adding rows or columns to create new fields or records, or deleting data. For example, you can:

■ Add a new record by pressing Tab when the insertion point is at the end of text in the last cell in the table, and then enter data into the new record.

■ Add a new field by inserting a column with the Columns command on the Table menu's Insert menu.

■ Delete data using the Delete submenu on the Table menu.

Copying New Records to a Data Source Document

To add a group of records from another data source document to the current data source document, you can open both documents and copy between them. However, you'll want to make sure that the same number of fields are in each document, and that both files contain the same types of data in their fields.

1   Open each data source document using the Open command on the File menu.

2   Activate the document from which you want to copy records, and select the rows containing the records you want to copy.

3   Press Ctrl+C or choose Copy from the Edit menu.

4   Activate the original document, and click immediately below the data source table.

5   Press Ctrl+V to paste in the data from the other table. Word creates a new row (or rows) and pastes the data into them.

Using Data from Other Programs

You can also use a data file from another program as the data source for your merge project. Here's what to do:

1   Open the Mail Merge Helper dialog box, click the Get Data button, and choose Open Data Source from the pop-up menu. Word displays the Open Data Source dialog box, as shown in Figure 26-5.

FIGURE 26-5.

When you open a data source file, you can limit the view to a certain type of data file or query a data file to select records from it and copy them into a new data source.

Change file type to view external data files.

Select to link external data rather than embed it.

Launch MS Query to select records from external file.

V

Data Automation Tools

2 Choose the type of file you want to open from the Files Of Type menu at the bottom. The default choice here is All Word Documents, and you won't be able to see other types of files unless you change the file type.

3 Select the file and click the Open button.

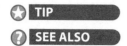

SEE ALSO

For more information about linked and embedded files, see Chapter 21,"Working with Objects."

External data source files are usually embedded in the main document. If the data file you want to use is large or is used for other purposes and you would prefer not to embed it, select the Select Method check box. The file will then be linked to the main document rather than embedded in it.

Opening Access or Excel Files

Because Access and Excel are parts of Microsoft Office, you get extra help in selecting data from those types of files when you open them as data sources.

When you open an Excel file, Word asks if you want to open the entire spreadsheet or a named range of cells, like this:

When you open an Access database, you can select a particular table and query:

Select a table on the Tables tab, and then click the Queries tab to select or modify a record selection query. When you make your selection and click OK, only those records will be used as the data source.

> You can also export an Access table as Word data and then open it as a Word document.

Querying a Data File

If you select a data file that contains thousands of records, you will probably want to merge only certain ones. If the data file supports Dynamic Document Exchange (DDE) and has an Open Database Connectivity (ODBC) driver installed, you can query it and then place only the records matching the query in a new data source file. To find out whether your company's database file supports DDE and has an ODBC driver, contact your network administrator.

SEE ALSO

For more information about files you can query, see "Using External Data" on page 599.

To query a data file, follow these steps:

1 Open the Mail Merge Helper dialog box, select or create a main document (if you haven't done so already), click the Get Data button, and choose Open Data Source from the pop-up menu.

2 Select the file you want to query.

3 Click the Microsoft Query button at the bottom of the Open Data Source dialog box. Word launches the Microsoft Query program and the Assistant offers to help you with it, as in Figure 26-6. (The Assistant character shown in this figure is called F1.)

FIGURE 26-6.

Use Microsoft Query to select records from data files created by other programs.

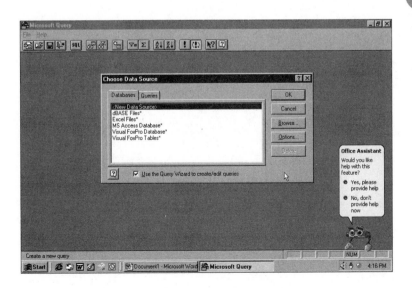

V

Data Automation Tools

SEE ALSO

For more information about using Microsoft Query, choose Microsoft Query Help from the Help menu or use the Assistant.

You use Microsoft Query to select records. Once you have completed the query, Word copies the records you selected into a new data source document and selects it as the data source for your main document.

Importing Data from an Address Book

If the names, addresses, or other information you want to merge are already stored in your e-mail address book from Microsoft Exchange Server, Outlook, or another program, you can use the address book as a data source. Word can use any address book created with Exchange, Outlook, Schedule+ 7.0, or any other MAPI-compatible contact management program.

 NOTE

> MAPI (Mail Application Programming Interface) is a standard data exchange method supported by many e-mail and scheduling programs.

Before you can use an address book as your data source, you must install the e-mail program, configure it as the default e-mail program on your computer, and restart the computer. Once you have done this, here's how to use data from an address book:

 TIP

> You will be asked if you want to make your e-mail program the default program when you first install it. See your program's Help file for more information.

1   Open the Mail Merge Helper dialog box, click Get Data, and choose Use Address Book from the pop-up menu. You see the Use Address Book dialog box like this:

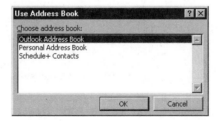

2   Select the mail program whose address book you want to use and click OK. Word displays a message that there are no merge fields in the main document.

? SEE ALSO

To learn more about specifying an alternate database header, see "Using a Different Header Source" on page 619. For more information about Word's file converters, see Chapter 38, "Importing, Exporting, and Converting Documents," or consult the Appendix.

Using External Data

Here's a list of external file types you can use as data sources in a merge project:

- Microsoft Access databases or database tables.

- Microsoft Excel worksheets or cell ranges.

- A personal address book from Microsoft Outlook, Microsoft Exchange Server, Schedule+ 7.0, or any other MAPI-compliant messaging server.

- Database files for which you have installed an Open Database Connectivity (ODBC) driver. Drivers for several database file types are included on the Microsoft Office installation CD.

- Any other file for which Word has a converter, such as ASCII text; older versions of Word for Windows, for MS-DOS, and for the Macintosh; WordPerfect; and Lotus 1-2-3.

Keep in mind that in any file you use as the data source, the first row of worksheet cells or the first record in a database file must contain the field names unless you create a separate header source file. *For more information about using a different header source, see "Using a Different Header Source" on page 619.*

V

Data Automation Tools

3 Click the Edit Main Document button to return to your main document so you can begin inserting merge fields from the new data source.

Adding Merge Fields to a Main Document

With the source data stored, selected, and properly identified, you're ready to add merge fields to the main document. In fact, each time you select a data source for a new main document, Word prompts you to begin inserting merge fields in it. The method you use to add merge fields depends on the type of main document you initially chose, so we'll look at each document type in detail. But first, let's take a quick tour of the Mail Merge toolbar, since you'll need it to add fields.

Using the Mail Merge Toolbar

When you edit a main document, Word displays the Mail Merge toolbar:

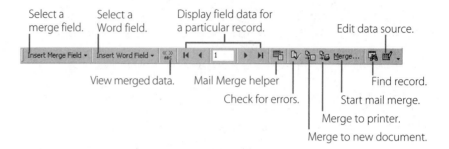

Select a merge field. Select a Word field. Display field data for a particular record. Edit data source.

View merged data. Mail Merge helper Find record.

Check for errors. Start mail merge.

Merge to printer.

Merge to new document.

At the click of a button, you can view data from the data source rather than field names in the main document. You can use the arrow buttons to select any record from the data source and view its data. You can also perform a merge, locate a particular record, view the data source, or open the Mail Merge Helper by clicking various buttons, as we'll see.

Setting up Form Letters

If you're working in a form letter, you can insert fields into the document anywhere you like. Just move the insertion point to the place where you want the field's data to appear and then select the field with the Insert Merge Field menu on the Mail Merge toolbar.

For example, suppose you want to insert a field called Nickname as part of the salutation line of the form letter shown in Figure 26-1 on page 584. The following steps show you how:

> **! WARNING**
>
> The instructions below assume that you have already made the form letter document a main document and have inserted its text, and that you have selected a data source for it. You can't insert merge fields without opening a main document and selecting a data source for it.

? SEE ALSO

For more information about the Letter Wizard, see "Using the Letter Wizard" on page 397.

1 Move the insertion point to the end of "Dear" in the salutation line and press the spacebar. (If you created a letter with the Letter Wizard, the "Dear Sir or Madam" text is a field, and you must delete it and type "Dear" as plain text.)

2 Click the Insert Merge Field button on the Mail Merge toolbar to display a menu of fields like this:

This menu shows all of the fields in the current data source. You may see different fields than the ones shown above.

3 Choose Nickname from the menu. Word inserts the Nickname field into your document.

4 Type a colon (:) after the field marker, because you want the salutation line to end with a colon. This line now looks like the one in the main document in Figure 26-1.

5 Add any other fields to your document (such as the recipient's address in the letter's address block) to finish the project.

After you create merge documents, one letter might look like this:

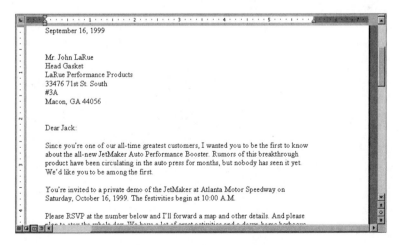

If you don't see the field you want on the Merge Field menu, you either have the wrong data source open or you have added or changed a field name in the data or header source and Word hasn't caught up to the change yet. To update the Merge Field menu with the current information from the data or header source, save and close both the main document and the data or header source and then open them again. *For more information about header sources, see "Using a Different Header Source" on page 619.*

When you edit a form letter, you can treat the field markers the same as you would any other text. You can insert field markers anywhere you want, add punctuation or other text around them, and format them with the same techniques you use with standard Word text.

Don't bother formatting data in the data source—it will take on the format of the text around it in the merge document anyway. To format data prior to merging, select the appropriate field marker in the main document and format it.

Setting Up Mailing Labels

SEE ALSO

For more information about using the Label Options dialog box to select a label format, see "Creating a Label" on page 390.

When you set up a Mailing Labels document, you use Word's built-in label formatting tools. You'll set up the label format after you choose a data source. Here are the steps:

1 Open the Mail Merge Helper, click the Create button in the Main Document area, and choose Mailing Labels from the pop-up menu.

2 Choose a data source.

3 Choose a label product and product number and click OK. Word opens the Create Labels dialog box as in Figure 26-7.

FIGURE 26-7.
The Create Labels dialog box allows you to insert and arrange fields and text on a label.

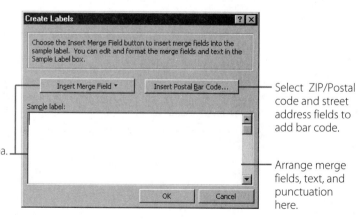

Add a merge field to sample label area.

Select ZIP/Postal code and street address fields to add bar code.

Arrange merge fields, text, and punctuation here.

4 Click the Insert Merge Field button and choose the first field you want to insert on the label. Word adds the field to the upper-left corner of the Sample Label area.

5 Insert additional fields the same way. You can use the Enter key, press the spacebar, or add punctuation or other text to the label as well.

6 To add a barcode to the label for faster mailing, click the Insert Postal Bar Code button and then indicate which field names contain the Postal code and street address information on the label.

> **NOTE**
>
> If any of the Postal codes in your data source have been changed recently, you may get a message saying the code isn't valid when you try to add a barcode.

7 Click OK. Word creates the label layout in the main document with the fields in the right places, like this:

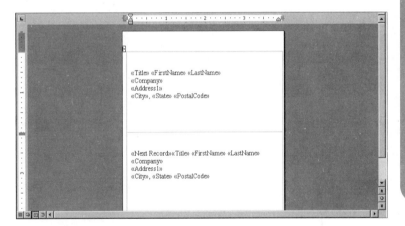

> **TIP**
>
> Once you set up a Mailing Labels document, the Edit button in the Main Document area of the Mail Merge Helper changes to Setup. Click this button to adjust the label layout at any time.

Setting Up Envelopes

When you set up an envelope, it's a lot like setting up a label. You select fields in a special dialog box rather than in the main document itself. To set up an envelope layout and add fields to it, follow these steps:

1 Choose Envelope as the main document type in the Mail Merge Helper dialog box.

2 Choose a data source.

SEE ALSO

For more information about using the Envelope Options dialog box to select a label format, see "Creating an Envelope" on page 386.

3 Choose an envelope size and set the mailing address format, if necessary. Don't worry about adding a return address here now—you can add it to the main document in a moment.

4 Click OK. Word displays the Envelope Address dialog box, like this:

5 Enter text in the Sample Envelope Address box or use the Insert Merge Field button to add fields.

6 Click OK to return to the Mail Merge Helper dialog box, and then click Close. Word displays the envelope layout in the document window.

7 Add a return address to the envelope if necessary.

8 The finished layout looks like this:

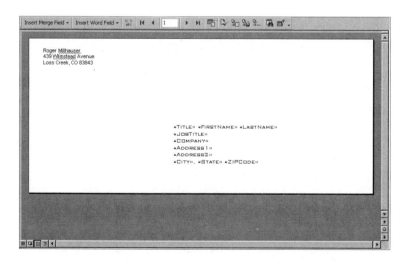

Setting Up a Catalog

A Catalog document works much like a Mailing Label document in that Word prints more than one record on each page. Unlike a Mailing Label or Envelope document, however, Word doesn't offer a handy tool that makes it easy to set up the catalog's format or add merge fields to it. However, it's fairly easy to create a catalog if you remember three things:

- When you select the Catalog main document type, Word will add multiple records to the page—as many as there are room for.

- Since records are repeated to fill each catalog page, you need only insert field names once. To create a parts catalog, for example, you would need to insert the PartNum, Description, and Price fields only once in the entire document, and this data would be repeated down the page for as many records as data will fit.

- Everything you type in the main document is repeated for each record during a merge. Don't enter the catalog title or the column headings for a list in the main document unless you want that text repeated for each record.

If you keep these points in mind, it's easy to produce catalogs, lists, agendas, schedules, and other documents with mail merge. Follow these steps to see how:

1 Create a new Catalog main document.

2 Create or open a data source.

3 Click the Edit Main Document button in the message you get after creating or selecting the data source.

4 Press Enter a few times to create some blank lines at the top of the main document. (You'll need the space for a title or other information after creating the merge document.)

5 Set up tab stops or create a one-row table to divide the catalog into columns as shown in figure 26-8 on the next page. (If you use a table, each row and cell in the catalog will have borders.)

6 Click in the left-hand column or cell, and then click the Merge Field button on the Mail Merge toolbar to insert the field you want in that column.

7 Move the insertion point to the next column or table cell and insert the field or fields that belong there.

V

Data Automation Tools

8   Continue adding fields to the table until you have added all of the ones you want.

9   If necessary, insert explanatory text or change the formats of the fields. Remember, though, that any explanatory text will be repeated in each record in the data source. Still, you might enter text such as *Size* before the Size field's data.

10 Merge the document to a Word document (*see "Creating Merge Documents" on page 620*).

11 Once the merge is complete, add the column labels or document title to the first document page, and if necessary, copy the column labels to the first pages of other documents. You can insert column labels as text in a line above the data in a merged document. Or, if you used a table to lay out the merge fields initially, you can insert a new row at the top of the table and add the column labels there.

? SEE ALSO

For more about inserting rows in tables, see "Adding a Row or Column" on page 363.

★ TIP

> Use a running document header or footer for the title, and you won't have to copy and paste the same title text onto each merged document page.

Figure 26-8 shows a finished customer list created with tab stops between columns. The title text is in a document header, and the column labels are text that was added after the merge.

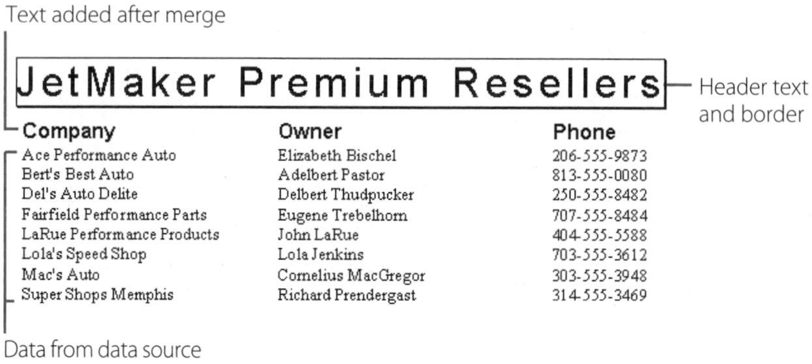

FIGURE 26-8.

Use Catalog main documents to create lists or directories of customers, parts, team members, meeting agendas, class schedules, and many other types of documents.

Text added after merge

JetMaker Premium Resellers ── Header text and border

Company	Owner	Phone
Ace Performance Auto	Elizabeth Bischel	206-555-9873
Bert's Best Auto	Adelbert Pastor	813-555-0080
Del's Auto Delite	Delbert Thudpucker	250-555-8482
Fairfield Performance Parts	Eugene Trebelhorn	707-555-8484
LaRue Performance Products	John LaRue	404-555-5588
Lola's Speed Shop	Lola Jenkins	703-555-3612
Mac's Auto	Cornelius MacGregor	303-555-3948
Super Shops Memphis	Richard Prendergast	314-555-3469

Data from data source

Viewing Merge Data in a Document

When you're checking the formatting of any document, you can view actual data from merge fields rather than just the merge field names. This is an essential ability when you're working within tight field length restrictions, such as in a label, catalog, or form letter layout.

For example, if one person's first and last names are long, the data may not fit in a small label, and it's better to know this before you print the labels.

To view merge data in a main document, activate the main document and click the View Merged Data button on the Mail Merge toolbar. You can then use the record selection buttons on the Mail Merge toolbar to scroll through the data source and view data from different records, or use the Find Records button to locate a specific record based on the data in a certain field.

Inserting Word Fields

In addition to merge fields, which identify the fields to be merged from the data source, you can also insert Word fields, which allow you to further customize documents during the merge process. For example, you can insert a Word field that asks for additional information at some point or that inserts one of several different data strings based on the contents of a field in the data source.

⚠ **WARNING**

Word fields are not for the faint of heart. You can create fabulous merge documents without Word fields, and when you do use Word fields you will probably have to do quite a bit of troubleshooting to get things running smoothly.

To insert a Word field:

1 In the main document, move the insertion point to the location where you want the field to appear.

2 Click the Insert Word Field button on the Mail Merge toolbar and then choose a field name from the menu. When you insert most Word fields, you must use a dialog box to select options for it before the field appears in the main document.

You can use as many Word fields as you want in a main document, and you can use more than one of any type of Word field. Here's a rundown on the Word field types.

Ask and Fill-In Fields

Ask and Fill-In fields allow you to create dialog boxes that pop up and ask for additional information during the merge process. This is a good way to add data to a merge document that you can't obtain from the data source. For example, you might want to enter a personal message for each customer in a form letter invitation or add a personal note to a standard holiday letter. Such messages probably won't be stored in the data source, but you could create an Ask or Fill-In field to request the information for each merge document.

Here's the difference between Ask and Fill-In fields:

- Ask fields rely on bookmarks as data locations when merging. Since you can add the same bookmark to as many places in a document as you like, you can insert the same data in every bookmark location.

- Fill-In fields use field markers to insert data, so one Fill-In field inserts data in only one place in a merge document.

Adding an Ask Field

For more information about bookmarks, see "Using Bookmarks" on page 225.

When you add an Ask field, you define the contents of the dialog box that Word presents when it asks for information during the merge and you link those contents to a bookmark name.

Here's how to add an Ask field:

1 Move the insertion point where you want the data to appear.

2 Choose Ask from the Insert Word Field menu in the Mail Merge toolbar. Word displays a dialog box as in Figure 26-9.

FIGURE 26-9.

To add data with an Ask field, you must identify the text that will be inserted.

Enter bookmark name or choose one from list.

Ask user for data only when first merge document is created.

Enter instructions for user to complete dialog box.

Enter text suggested as data entry.

3 In the Prompt box, enter the text of the message you want the dialog box to contain. To prompt for a special customer message, for example, the message might be, "Enter special customer message."

4 In the Default Bookmark Text box, enter the text for Word to suggest as the entry—a proposed special message for the customer, for example.

5   Select an existing bookmark name from the Bookmark list or type a new bookmark name to attach to this data. If you choose an existing bookmark name, Word will insert the Ask field's data into that bookmark's location. If you don't have a predefined bookmark in the main document, you can add one to the current location by typing a new bookmark name.

6   Select the Ask Once check box to have Word ask for more data only when it merges the first record from the data source. If you select this check box, Word asks you for data only once and then enters the same text in every merge document. When the check box is clear, Word asks for data with each new merge document.

7   Click OK to store the field definition. Word displays the dialog box that will appear during the merge, as shown in Figure 26-10.

FIGURE 26-10.

After you define an Ask or Fill-in field, Word displays the dialog box that will appear during merging.

8   Click OK to put the sample dialog box away.

Adding a Fill-In Field

When you add a Fill-In field, Word inserts data in just one place in the merge document. Here's what to do:

1   Move the insertion point to the place where you want the data to appear.

2   Click the Insert Word Field button in the Mail Merge toolbar, and choose Fill-In from the pop-up menu. Word opens the Insert Word Field: Fill-In dialog box, like this:

V

Data Automation Tools

3 In the Prompt box, enter the text for the prompt message that will appear during merging.

4 In the Default Fill-In Text box, enter the suggested fill-in text that will appear during merging.

5 Click OK to create the field. Word displays the dialog box you have defined so you can make sure it looks the way you want.

6 Click OK in the sample dialog box to return to the main document.

> You can also select the Ask Once check box to have Word ask for input only for the first merge document. *See step 6 under "Adding an Ask Field" on page 608 for more information.*

Responding to an Ask or Fill-In Field

When you merge a main document containing an Ask or Fill-In field, Word displays the dialog box you defined. You'll see the dialog box once for every record in the data source unless you selected the Ask Once check box when you defined the Ask field. Either accept the suggested response or type a new one, and then click OK to insert the data into the merge document.

If...Then...Else Fields

With an If...Then...Else field, you can have Word insert one of two different text strings based on its evaluation of the contents of another field in the data source. This is a very powerful capability, because you can use it to completely change the contents of a form letter based on data in one of the data source fields.

Here's an example. Suppose you want to send out holiday letters and vary the tone of the letters according to whether the recipient is a customer, colleague, acquaintance, or relative. You could insert an If...Then...Else field that evaluates a ContactType field in the data source and then inserts one of two different versions of a paragraph—or even the entire text of the letter—based on whether or not the ContactType field contains "Customer."

To insert an If...Then...Else field, follow these steps:

1 Move the insertion point to the location where you want the field's result to appear.

2 Choose If…Then…Else from the Insert Word Field menu in the Mail Merge toolbar. Word displays the Insert Word Field: If dialog box shown in Figure 26-11.

FIGURE 26-11.

You can have Word insert one of two different text strings in each merge document based on the contents of a field in the data source.

Select field name. Choose a comparison operator. Enter comparison text.

Enter text to be inserted if comparison matches.

Enter text to be inserted if comparison doesn't match.

3 Choose a field name from the Field name list. This is the field whose contents you want Word to evaluate when determining which data to insert.

4 Choose an operator from the Comparison menu.

5 Enter the comparison text in the Compare To box.

6 In the Insert This Text box, enter the text you want inserted if the condition is true.

7 In the Otherwise Insert This Text box, enter the text you want inserted if the condition is not true. In our holiday letter example, the dialog box might now look like this:

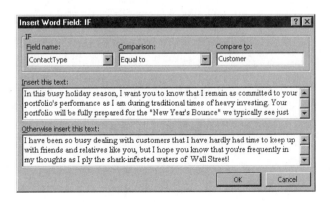

8 Click OK to insert the field.

Merge Record # Fields and Merge Sequence # Fields

You use Merge Record # fields and Merge Sequence # fields to insert data source record or document numbers into your merge documents. There's no dialog box to fill out when you insert either of these fields.

- The Merge Record # field inserts the number of the current record being merged from the data source.

- The Merge Sequence # field inserts the number of each particular merge document. For example, if the third form letter in a merge is being produced, Word adds the number 3 to it.

If you are merging every record from the data source, record and sequence numbers are identical, but they may differ if you have used a filter to select a subset of records. For example, if you have selected a group of records by Postal code from a data source, the first merge document may contain data from record number 3 in the data source. In this case, the sequence number is 1, but the record number is 3. *For more information about selecting records, see "Filtering Records" on page 616.*

Next Record and Next Record If Fields

These fields are a quick way to insert data from more than one record into a single merge document without having to create a label or catalog layout. Add the Next Record field when you want Word to insert data from the following record in the data source to the same merge document. Use the Next Record If field if you want Word to decide whether or not to insert the next record's data based on the contents of another field in the data source.

You can insert the Next Record or Next Record If fields to add two, three, or as many records as will fit in one merge document. If you need to insert multiple records into one merge document, however, it's probably easier to select only the records you want in the data source and then create a Catalog or Mailing Label layout.

When you add a Next Record If field, you define its evaluation rule much as you do with an If...Then...Else field. *See page 610 for more information.*

Set Bookmark Fields

Use a Set Bookmark field when you want to insert the data associated with a bookmark into every merge document. Unlike the Ask field, a Set Bookmark field inserts the data associated with a particular bookmark into every merge document, so the data never changes from one document to the next. If a product name changes, for example, you can enter the new product name as a Set Bookmark field.

When you add a Set Bookmark field, Word displays a dialog box like the one in Figure 26-12.

FIGURE 26-12.

When you use a Set Bookmark field, you can have Word insert the same bookmarked text into every merge document.

Enter value to be entered in merge documents.

Enter bookmark name or select one from list.

If you have already defined a bookmark in the main document for the text you want to insert, you can select the bookmark's name in the Bookmark list and click OK to insert it. Otherwise, enter the bookmark text in the Value box, type a new bookmark name in the Bookmark box, and click OK.

Skip Record If... Fields

Use the Skip Record If field when you want Word to omit certain records from the merging process based on an evaluation of a field in the data source. For example, if you're sending out dunning notices to a customer list, you might use a Skip Record If field to keep Word from creating merge documents for customers whose accounts are current.

When you add a Skip Record If field, Word displays a dialog box like this:

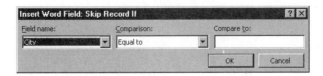

Data Automation Tools

V

For example, suppose you're sending out dunning letters and you want to create letters only for customers who owe you more than $10. Your data source includes a field called *AmtDue* that shows what each customer owes. Here's how to define the field in the Skip Record If dialog box:

1 Choose the *AmtDue* field from the Field Name menu.

2 Choose *Greater Than* from the Comparison menu.

3 Enter *10* in the Compare To box.

4 Click OK to define the field.

Managing Data Sources

Once you have created or chosen a data source, you can easily locate specific records, filter the data to select a subset of records to merge, or sort the data so that merge documents are created in a certain order.

> Most of this section describes working with data sources that can be viewed in Word document windows. *See "Managing External Data Sources" on page 620 for information about working with data not stored in a Word document.*

Using the Database Toolbar

When you view a data source inside a Word document window, Word displays the Database toolbar like this:

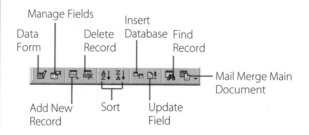

With one mouse click, you can zoom through various data management tasks without having to return to the Mail Merge Helper dialog box.

Adding or Changing Fields

If you want to add, remove, or change the names of fields in the data source, there are two ways to do it. You can make these changes directly in the data source table if you like by altering header text or by adding or removing columns, but it's usually easier to use the Manage Fields dialog box. Here's how to use the Manage Fields dialog box:

1 Display the data source window. *See "Viewing a Data Source Document" on page 592 for more information.*

2 Click the Manage Fields button on the Database toolbar to open the Manage Fields dialog box. This dialog box looks similar to the one in Figure 26-3 on page 590. It lists all of the fields in the data source, and you can delete fields, enter field names, add new fields, and even rename fields if you like.

Changing Field or Header Data

You can also change the contents of a field or field header in the data source, and if the main document is open at the same time, the change should be reflected there. However, you may sometimes need to refresh the connection between the data source data and the merge fields in the main document. There are two ways to update a data source and main document after you have changed any of the data:

■ Save the data source and the main document, close both windows, and open them again.

■ Click the Update Field button on the Database toolbar when you're viewing the data source.

Changing a Field Name

When you change a field name in the data source document and return to the main document, the name of the merge field does not automatically change in the main document. Instead, Word will alert you that a field in the main document is not found in the data source with a message like this:

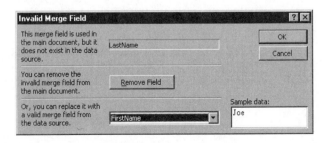

To handle this situation, either select the renamed field's name from the list, or click the Remove Field button to remove the invalid merge field from the document. (You can always insert the updated field again by using the Insert Merge Field menu in the main document.)

Finding Records

Here's how to find a particular record in the data source:

1   Click the Find Record button on either the Database or Mail Merge toolbar to display the Find In Field dialog box, like this:

2   Click in the Find What box and type the data you want to search for.

3   Choose the name of the field that contains the search data.

4   Click Find First. Word locates and highlights the first record in your file that contains matching information in that field. To locate the next matching record, click Find Next.

5   Click the Close button when you're finished searching.

Filtering Records

If you don't want to merge all of the records in the data source, the simplest way to limit the selection is to create a filter with the Mail Merge Helper. To do this, follow these steps:

1   Display the Mail Merge Helper and click the Query Options button to open the Query Options dialog box.

2   Click the Field list's arrow to display a list of fields as shown in Figure 26-13 on the next page.

Each row on the Filter Records tab represents one selection rule. You can create up to six selection rules to be very specific about the records you want.

3   Choose the name of the most important field you want used as the selection criterion.

FIGURE 26-13.

Click the Query Options button in the Mail Merge Helper dialog box to select or sort records in the data source file.

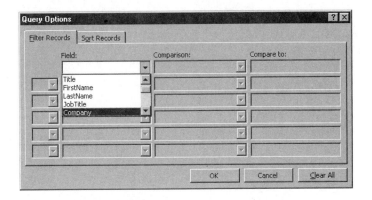

4   Click the Comparison list's arrow button and select a comparison operator from the menu.

5   Click the Compare To box and type in the comparative information.

6   To create a filter with more than one criterion, choose And or Or from the operator menu in the second row, and fill out the rest of the row and any additional rows if you like. Here's a filter containing three criteria:

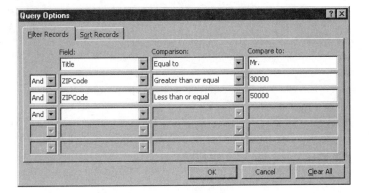

In this case, the filter will select all records for males living in Postal/ZIP Codes between 30000 and 50000.

 TIP

Use the AND operator at the beginning of a filter row to combine criteria such as the ZIPCode range above, and use the OR operator to have Word match one criteria row or another, for example, *State Equal to CA OR State Equal to NY.*

7   Click OK when you're finished. Word selects only the records that match your search filter and returns to the Mail Merge Helper.

V

Data Automation Tools

Sorting Records

It's often useful to sort the records in the data source before a merge. For example, you might sort addresses by Postal code, companies by name, or items in a schedule by time or date so they print out in order. In the catalog in Figure 26-8 on page 606, the records were sorted by company name before merging.

You can sort records from the Mail Merge Helper at any time or use the Database toolbar when you view a data source. To use the Mail Merge Helper, follow these steps:

1 Open the Mail Merge Helper, click the Query Options button, and click the Sort Records tab. Word displays options like this:

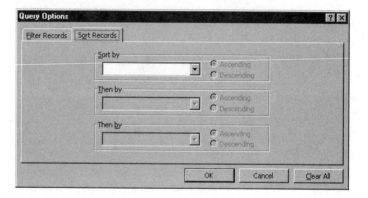

2 Choose the most important field by which you want to sort from the Sort By menu.

3 Click the Ascending or Descending option to the right to set the search order.

4 Select up to two other fields and their sort order options.

5 Click OK. Word sorts the records and returns to the Mail Merge Helper dialog box.

To sort with the Database toolbar, follow these steps:

1 Display the data source document.

2 Select the entire column that represents the field by which you want to sort.

3 Click the Sort Ascending or Sort Descending button on the Database toolbar.

TIP

If you're filtering records from a data source and sorting them for the same project, it's best to filter first and sort afterwards.

Using a Different Header Source

When you create a new data source from scratch, you have the opportunity to select or create the fields that will be contained in the first row, or header. However, if you use an existing data file, you may find the field names indecipherable because a database programmer created them. If so, you can create a different header source that contains the field names you want, and you can use it with another data source file at the same time. Just as with a data source, you can create a header source by selecting one from an existing file or by creating it from scratch.

NOTE

When you create an alternate header source, it must include a name for every field in the data source. Otherwise, Word won't allow you to merge the file. Also, the field names must be in the correct order so they accurately identify the data in each field. For example, you wouldn't want to use a header that labels the City field as "State," or else the city data won't end up in the right place when you create merge documents.

To create an alternate header source, follow these steps:

1 Display the main document and open the Mail Merge Helper dialog box.

2 Click the Get Data button in the Data Source area and choose Header Options from the pop-up menu. You'll be asked if you want to create a new header source from scratch or open an existing one, like this:

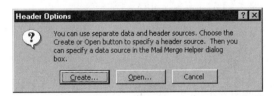

3 If you want to use a header from an existing file, click the Open button and select the file you want. To create a new header source file, click the Create button. You'll see a dialog box like

the one in Figure 26-3 where you can select, remove, or create new field names to be included in the header. *For more information on this process, see "Setting Up the Data Source Fields" on page 590.*

WARNING

> Make absolutely sure that you select the same number of fields for the header source as there are in the data source. It doesn't matter how many merge fields you currently have in the main document, but the header source and data source must have the same number of fields. If the number of fields in the header source doesn't match the number of fields in the data source, Word will alert you when you save the header source document.

4   When you're finished selecting the field names, the new header source file is complete. Click OK to display the Save As dialog box.

5   Name the new header source file and click Save. Word returns you to the Mail Merge Helper dialog box, where the new header source is listed below the Data Source area's buttons.

Managing External Data Sources

The data management options discussed earlier in this section apply only to data sources that are Word documents. When you open an entire Access database, Excel worksheet, or a file from another program as the data source for your merge project, Word does not create a Word document as the data source. Since the data remains in its native format, you must use the original program's features to select and sort records prior to the merge. For example, when you use the Mail Merge Helper to edit an Excel worksheet, Word opens Excel so you can make any edits or changes to the original worksheet file.

Creating Merge Documents

When your main document is formatted to your liking, when your data source is selected, filtered, and sorted the way you want, and when the right fields are in the right places in the main document, the only thing left to do is perform the merge. Any mistakes you have made along the way will now be magnified several, dozens, hundreds, or even thousands of times as your printer or e-mail program spews forth personalized documents for each record in the data source.

Fortunately, the Merge dialog box that you'll use has some features you can employ to spot problems and deal with them before they occur. Figure 26-14 on the next page shows the Merge dialog box.

FIGURE 26-14.

When you're ready to create merge documents, the Merge dialog box has the options you'll need to make things go smoothly.

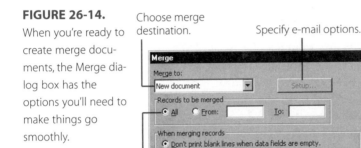

Choose merge destination.

Specify e-mail options.

Click to merge.

Check for data errors.

Filter or sort records in data source.

Choose a range of records to merge.

Checking for Data Errors

To make a last crucial check before merging, you can have Word simulate the merge and check for errors or create one merged Word document and then scan it visually for problems. It's best to use both approaches. It all starts with the Merge dialog box.

1   Open the Mail Merge Helper dialog box and click the Merge button to display the Merge dialog box as in Figure 26-14.

2   Click the Check Errors button. Word asks you how you would like it to report errors, like this:

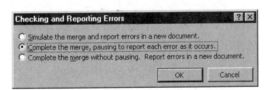

3   Click an option and then click OK to return to the Merge dialog box.

4   Click Merge. Word performs the merge or simulated merge and reports the errors either in a new document or in a message box during the merge. Typically, errors result from fields in the main document that don't exist in the data source, something that can easily occur if you switch data sources for your main document after inserting fields.

V

Data Automation Tools

While Word can check for missing data fields or other such problems, it won't report formatting problems such as merged data not fitting properly in the merge document. For example, maybe you have added the City, State, and Postal Code fields to one line on a label. This is fine for most labels, but when a label comes along for the addressee in Whatzamattawidyou, New Jersey, 01832-9238, there isn't enough room on that line for all of the data in those fields. As a result, some data is simply chopped off.

To be sure that there are no problems with merge documents, you'll have to scan the documents yourself before printing or e-mailing them. Fortunately, you can choose options to create one big Word document in which each separate merge document is separated by a section break, and report any data errors in a separate document at the same time. To do this, follow these steps:

1. Open the Mail Merge Helper dialog box and click the Merge button.

2. Select New Document from the Merge To menu, if necessary. (It should be selected by default.)

3. Click the Check Errors button to display the Checking And Reporting Errors dialog box, as shown on the previous page.

4. Select either the top or bottom option in this dialog box and then click OK. (Despite the wording, there is no functional difference between these two options.)

5. Click Merge to create the new document. If there are data errors, you'll either see messages about problems with individual records, or you'll see the Invalid Merge Field dialog box, and you can handle the problems there. *See "Changing a Field Name" on page 615 for more information.*

6. Once you deal with the data errors, choose the new document's name from the View menu to display it, and then scroll through each merge document to scan it visually for errors such as typos, merge fields in the wrong places, data that doesn't fit in the space allowed, or punctuation problems.

   If you find any errors, you can edit them or discard the new document and fix the problems with the main document and data source options.

Selecting Final Merge Options

The Merge dialog box also has other options you'll want to set properly before performing the final merge.

Choosing the Merge Document Target

To tell Word what sort of merge document you want, choose the type of merge document from the Merge To menu.

- If you choose to merge to a new document, Word puts all of the merge documents in one big Word document and separates them with new page section breaks.

SEE ALSO

For more about printing options, see "Setting Printing Options" on page 126.

- If you choose to merge to a printer, you'll see the Print dialog box when you actually perform the merge so you can choose printing options.

- If you choose to merge to an e-mail document, the Setup button to the right becomes active because Word needs to know where to send each electronic merge document. Here's how to satisfy its curiosity:

   1 Click the Setup button to display the Merge To Setup dialog box, like this:

   2 Select the data field that contains the e-mail or fax address in the data source, and enter the subject line for the merged e-mail documents. You can also choose whether to send the merge documents as attachments or as ordinary text within the e-mail message itself.

   3 Click OK to return to the Merge dialog box.

Printing or Suppressing Blank Lines

The final decision is whether or not to print blank lines in merge documents when a field for a particular record contains no data. Missing data is one of the most common mail merge problems, especially if you choose an existing file as your data source.

V

Data Automation Tools

Most of the time you'll want Word to act as if the field isn't there in that particular merge document, closing up any text on either side of it. That's why Don't Print Blank Lines When Data Fields Are Empty is the default option in the Merge dialog box. For example, if the Street2 or Address2 field is missing from the address block in a particular form letter, you'll probably want the empty line deleted from rest of the address block so there isn't a gap. This particular letter will be one line shorter than the others as a result, but it won't matter.

But in some cases, you'll want to have Word leave a blank space where the data should have gone. For example, if the Title field is missing from a single-column name tag layout, you may want Word to leave a blank space for the missing data. This way, you can fill it in by hand. Also, if you don't leave a blank line where missing data should go on a single-column label layout, that particular label or name tag will be one line shorter than the others below it. All the data below that particular label will move up one line, so that the top lines of records below that label may overlap the dividing line between the actual labels.

Merging, at Last

To create the merge documents with the settings you have chosen, click the Merge button. If you're merging to a printer you'll be able to select printing options. If you're merging to e-mail documents, you may be asked to choose options for your e-mail program. But if you've prepared the project carefully, it should otherwise go off without a hitch. If it doesn't, use the Help window to search for mail merge topics. You'll find lots of troubleshooting tips there.

CHAPTER 27

Using Fields

Fields are devices that allow you to insert information into a document automatically. Whether you know it or not, you have already used fields if you have created headers or footers, made calculations in tables, or created mail merge documents. But fields can make it easy to customize your documents or save repetitive typing in many other ways. There are many fields available in Microsoft Word, and in this chapter, you'll learn how to use them.

A field is essentially a set of instructions. This set of instructions is inserted into your document as a *field code*, but your document usually displays the result of the instructions rather than the instructions themselves. Figure 27-1 shows the difference.

FIGURE 27-1.

When you insert a field, you tell Word to produce information in a certain way.

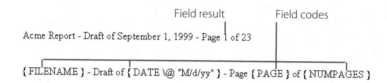

There are dozens of different fields and dozens more options, or *switches*, that you can set for them to perform a wide variety of tasks. For example, a field can:

- Tell Word to insert the current page, section, or line number.

- Display a picture or text from another file.

- Calculate mathematical formulas and display the results.

- Ask the document viewer to enter information.

- Mark text for insertion into an automatic table of contents or index.

You use the Field command on the Insert menu to select a field by name. You add other instructions if necessary, and then Word inserts a field code in the document at the insertion point. You can insert as many fields as you like into a document.

When you use the Field command on the Insert menu, you'll see fields in several different categories, but essentially there are three types of fields:

- **Result fields** calculate or retrieve information. These include the Formula field, Date and Time fields, Hyperlink fields, AutoText fields, and fields that retrieve document information such as the title or author name. When you insert a result field, Word displays the result immediately.

- **Action fields** require further action from the document's viewer to produce a result. For example, the Ask or Fill-In fields ask the viewer to enter text, and the MacroButton field runs a macro when double-clicked. *See Chapter 28, "Using Macros," for more information.*

- **Marker fields** simply identify text for inclusion in an index, a table of contents, a table of figures, a footnote section, or another reference item in the document.

Many result fields need to be updated periodically. For example, if the InsertText field tells Word to insert text from another file and that file is changed occasionally, you must update the field to display the file's most recent contents. After insertion, fields are updated each time you open the document, or you can tell Word to update them at other times.

It helps to know which type of field you're using because it lets you understand in advance just how the result will look and behave in the document. As you'll see, Word helps explain the purpose and result of each field when you insert it.

Field Definitions and Field Codes

A field tells Word to perform a certain action at a certain place in a document, but in most cases Word needs to know more than that. After selecting a field name, you must complete the field code by entering additional instructions. For example, a Formula field must include numbers or an expression to calculate, and an IncludeText field must know which text to include. And since a field code is text, it must be enclosed in special markers so Word recognizes it as a field code. Here are all of the elements in a field definition:

- **Field characters** The curly brackets that begin and end a field code.

NOTE

> Field characters look like the curly brackets you can type from the keyboard, but they're not the same.

- **Field name** The name itself.

- **Field instructions** Examples are the text, a number or expression, or the name of a bookmark you want to insert.

- **Switch** Optional instructions about how to present the data.

Figure 27-2 shows a field definition that includes all of these elements. This particular field inserts the contents of a bookmark named Sales and capitalizes the first letter of that entry.

FIGURE 27-2.

Every field definition contains field characters and a field name.

Data Automation Tools

V

Inserting Fields

You can insert a field anywhere in a document's body text, header, or footer. You can even include some fields in text boxes if you like. There are several different ways to insert fields into a document, some of which you have probably used already:

? SEE ALSO

For more information about using fields in a header, see "Adding Page Numbers and Other Special Text" on page 322.

- Use buttons or choose the AutoText menu on the Header And Footer toolbar to insert result fields that show the current date, page number, time, number of pages, document author, or other information.

? SEE ALSO

For more information about the Formula command, see "Using Formulas in Tables" on page 371.

- Choose the AutoText command on the Insert menu to insert document information such as the author name, title, subject, or number of lines.

- Choose the Formula command on the Table menu to insert a formula into a table or anywhere else in your document.

- Choose the Field command on the Insert menu.

? SEE ALSO

For more information about inserting fields with the Mail Merge toolbar, see "Adding Merge Fields to a Main Document" on page 599 or "Inserting Word Fields" on page 607.

- Enter field codes with the keyboard.

- Use the Mail Merge toolbar to insert Merge fields and Word fields during a mail merge project.

In the remainder of this chapter you'll learn how to define and work with fields using the Field command on the Insert menu or your keyboard.

Using the Field Command on the Insert Menu

The Field command on the Insert menu is the simplest way to explore the whole range of fields that Word has to offer, because you use a dialog box where you can see a description of each field and field option. To add a field with this command, follow these steps:

1 Move the insertion point to where you want the result of the field to appear. If you're inserting a marker field, place the insertion point next to the text you want to mark.

2 Choose Field from the Insert menu to open the Field dialog box as shown in Figure 27-3 on the next page.

FIGURE 27-3.

The Field dialog box is the easiest way to insert fields, and you can also use it to get a brief description of each field.

Select category.　　Select field.

Enter text in Field Code box.

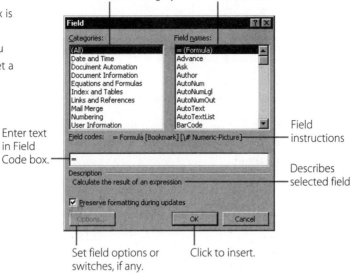

Field instructions

Describes selected field

Set field options or switches, if any.

Click to insert.

3 Select a field category in the Categories list.

4 Select a field name in the Field Names list. The Field Codes area below shows the instructions that are needed for that field, and the Field Code box is where you enter the actual field code. For example, if you select the IncludeText field in the Links and References category, the Field Codes area looks like this:

Required instruction

Field name　　Optional instructions

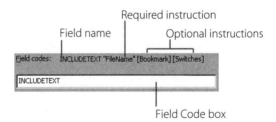

Field Code box

The field instructions for this field must include the field name (which is automatically inserted in the Field Code box) and the name of the file (in quotation marks) whose text you want to insert. The bracketed instructions are optional: you can specify a bookmark in the file you have named in order to select specific text from it, or you can include one or more switches to change the way Word displays the result.

TIP

> When instructions in the Field Codes area include optional items in brackets such as [Bookmark] and [Switches], you can choose those options by clicking the Options button at the bottom of the dialog box.

5 If necessary, enter instructions in the Field Code box. Some fields such as Date and AutoNum don't require any instructions.

SEE ALSO

For more information about using switches, see "Using Field Switches" on page 636.

6 Click the Options button and set switches or other options for the field if you like. Not all fields have optional instructions, but many do.

7 Click OK to insert the field.

If you make an error when defining the field, Word displays an error message in your document. For example, if you choose an AutoText field to add your name to a return address block and then fail to specify the AutoText entry you want inserted, Word displays a message like this:

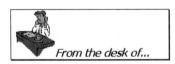

From the desk of...

Error! No AutoText entry specified.
3348 Vista Drive
San Rolondo, NM 88340

Getting More Help with Fields

There are far too many field switches and other variables to go into detail about here, but you can easily get more information about any field, instruction, or switch with the online help system in Word.

To get an overview of fields or see all of the Help topics that cover them, type *fields* in the Office Assistant's balloon and click the About Fields option or open the Help window and type *fields* in the Answer Wizard box.

To see more information about a particular field, follow these steps:

1 Choose Field from the Insert menu to open the Field dialog box.

2 Select a category and a field name.

3 Click the Help button at the top of the dialog box and then click on the selected field name. The Help window opens and you see a description of that particular field, its instructions, and its switch options.

Inserting a Field with the Keyboard

If you know the precise field name, instructions, switch characters, and other options you want, you can type all of this information directly from the keyboard without going through the Field dialog box. Here's how to do this:

1 Move the insertion point to where you want the field result to appear.

2 Press Ctrl+F9. Word inserts a pair of field character brackets into your document and places the insertion point between them, like this:

{|}

3 Type the field name and press the spacebar.

4 Type the field instruction, if any, and press the spacebar.

5 Type the field switches and other options, if any.

6 Click outside of the field code to complete the definition.

When you insert a field with the keyboard, Word displays the field code rather than the result in your document. To display the result instead, click anywhere in the field and press Shift+F9.

Let's look at some examples to get a better idea of how the process works.

? **SEE ALSO**

For more information about switching from field codes to field results in a document or setting other display options for fields, see "Viewing Fields" on page 638.

Defining a Result Field

When you insert a result field, Word displays text, a number, date, time, or a picture. With some result fields, Word can determine the result from the state of the document or from your computer (the current date, time, or page number, for example), so you don't need to enter an instruction. In most cases, however, you must tell Word exactly how or where to get the result you want or how to format it.

Suppose, for example, that you're adding an executive summary to the beginning of a document. To save time, you want to have Word insert the introductory paragraph from each main document section into the executive summary. You could simply copy and paste, of course, but if

V

Data Automation Tools

the sections are likely to change it's better to use Ref fields and a few bookmarks instead. With Ref fields, you can ensure that the executive summary will always contain the current version of each paragraph each time you open the document. Here's how to use Ref fields in this situation:

? SEE ALSO

For more information about bookmarks, see "Using Bookmarks" on page 225.

1 Select each paragraph you want to be included in the executive summary and insert a unique bookmark for each one.

2 Place the insertion point at the beginning of the executive summary text.

3 Choose Field from the Insert menu to open the Field dialog box.

4 Select the Links And References category.

5 Select the Ref field name in the Field Names list. The field name is added to the Field Codes box and the instructions for the field appear above it, like this:

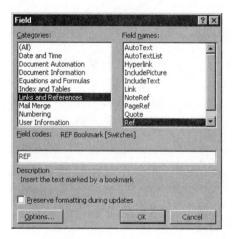

The Field Codes area shows that the next part of the field code is the bookmark name.

6 Click the Options button to open the Field Options dialog box and click the Bookmarks tab to show its options, as shown on the facing page.

7 Double-click the name of the bookmark whose paragraph you want to appear first in the executive summary, or select the bookmark name and click Add To Field.

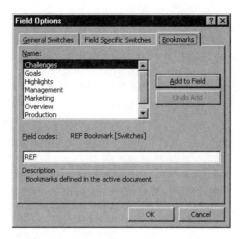

8   Click OK to return to the Field dialog box. The Field Codes box now includes the bookmark name.

9   Click OK to insert the field.

10 Repeat steps 2-10 to add a Ref field for the lead paragraph in each section you want to include in the executive summary.

Defining an Action Field

An action field requires further action on the part of the document's user before it can display a result. There are four action fields in Word: Ask, Fill-In, GoToButton, and MacroButton.

SEE ALSO

For more information about the Ask and Fill-In fields and the difference between them, see "Ask and Fill-In Fields" on page 607.

- **Ask and Fill-In fields** allow you to display a dialog box that asks the user to enter text. In both cases, the dialog box appears immediately after you insert the field or whenever the field is updated. The dialog box contains a prompt that tells the user what to do and a space for the user's input. Once the user fills out the dialog box, the text is then attached to a bookmark or displayed in the document.

- **A GoToButton field** navigates to another part of the document when the user double-clicks the text associated with it. You create a GoToButton field by entering the text that you want to appear in your document and then defining a bookmark or other location in your document to which double-clicking the text will lead.

 **TIP**

> To see the various types of Go To locations you might want to use with the GoToButton field, choose Go To from the Edit menu and examine the Go To What list in the Find and Replace dialog box.

■ **A MacroButton field** runs a macro when the text associated with it is double-clicked in the document. To define a MacroButton field, you enter the text you want to appear in your document and then enter the name of the macro you want Word to run when the text is double-clicked.

For example, suppose you have created an invoice form for use by your employees and you want to add a MacroButton field to it so they can simply double-click the field to print the invoice. The field will appear as a text prompt that reads, "DOUBLE-CLICK HERE TO PRINT." When double-clicked, the field will execute a macro named PrintInvoice that sets special page setup and printing options and then prints the document. To create a field like this, follow these steps:

1 Move the insertion point to where you want the clickable text to appear.

2 Choose Field from the Insert menu to open the Field dialog box.

3 Select the Document Automation category.

4 Select the MacroButton field name.

5 Click the Options button to open the Field Options dialog box. It lists all of the macros currently stored in the document template, like this:

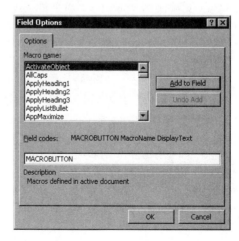

6 Select the PrintInvoice macro from the list and click Add To Field.

> NOTE

The PrintInvoice macro was created especially for this example. It will not appear in your Field Options dialog box unless you have created a macro with the same name.

7 Click OK to return to the Field dialog box.

8 Click in the Field Codes box to the right of the macro name and type *DOUBLE-CLICK HERE TO PRINT.* The Field Codes box now looks like this:

Field codes: MACROBUTTON MacroName DisplayText

MACROBUTTON PrintInvoice DOUBLE-CLICK HERE TO PRINT

V

9 Click OK. Word adds the field to the document, like this:

DOUBLE-CLICK HERE TO PRINT

Defining a Marker Field

For more information about creating indexes, tables of contents, and cross-references, see Chapter 25, "Creating Tables of Contents, Indexes, and Cross-References."

You use marker fields to identify index and table of contents entries or other references in your document. You can insert marker fields either by using the Index And Tables dialog box or by inserting them directly from the keyboard. The keyboard approach is handy when you want to add a new entry to an existing table or index.

For example, suppose you have already created a table of contents using the Index And Tables command and you now want to add a new listing in the table. Here's what to do:

For more information about how Heading styles are used in tables of contents, see "Creating a Table of Contents" on page 558.

1 Select the heading you want to mark and press Ctrl+C to copy it.

2 Click on either side of the heading to move the insertion point there.

3 Choose Field from the Insert menu to open the Field dialog box.

4 Select the Index And Tables category, and then select the TC name to add it to the Field Codes box.

Data Automation Tools

> Don't insert the TOC field name by mistake. If you do, Word creates a table of contents at the insertion point. To make sure you're adding the right field for the job, before adding the field be sure to read the description of the field you select at the bottom of the Field dialog box.

5 Click in the Field Codes box and type an open quotation mark (").

6 Press Ctrl+V to paste in the heading text you copied in Step 1.

7 Type a close quotation mark (").

8 Click OK. Word adds a marker field to your document. *For information on how to view the field you've just inserted, see "Viewing Fields" later in this chapter.*

9 Right-click in the Table of Contents in your document and choose Update Field from the shortcut menu.

10 Click the option to update the entire table. The heading you marked will now appear in the table.

Using Field Switches

Another way to change the way Word displays a result is to use *switches*. If a field has switches, the [Switches] option appears in the Field Codes area of the Fields dialog box. There are dozens of different switches, but the selection you have available will depend on which field you're defining.

Every switch name begins with the backslash character (\) followed by a symbol, letter, or keyword that denotes the type of switch. Switch symbols describe four basic types of field options:

- Format (*), for setting capitalization and other text format options.

- Numeric (\#), for setting number formats.

- Date-Time (\@), for setting date or time formats.

- Lock Result (\!), for preventing fields contained in a reference used in Bookmark, IncludeText, or Ref field from being updated. For example, if an IncludeText field refers to a document called "Sales Report," which itself contains Date and Time fields, using the Lock Result switch prevents the date and time information from being updated unless the fields are updated in the Sales Report file.

Some other switches are identified simply by a backslash and a letter. To use a switch, you usually include it in the field instructions when you define the field. Here's the basic process:

TIP

You can edit a field code to add a switch after the field is in your document. *See "Editing a Field" on page 640 for more information.*

1 Choose the Field command from the Insert menu.

2 Select a field that has switches.

SEE ALSO

For more information about using switches, type *switches* in the Office Assistant's balloon or in the Answer Wizard box in the Help window.

3 Click the Options button. Word displays a selection of switches, like this:

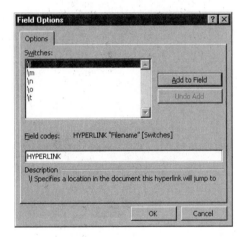

4 Select a switch. Word explains what the switch does in the Description area at the bottom of the dialog box.

NOTE

With some fields, the Field Options dialog box offers groups of switches on more than one tab.

5 Click Add To Field and then click OK to return to the Field dialog box.

6 Click OK to close the Field dialog box and insert the field.

Data Automation Tools

V

Why Mess with Switches?

Because Word selects default switches for you, you can create any field without selecting any. But switches can save you a lot of manual labor when it comes to formatting or otherwise altering the results of fields. Here are some examples:

- Use a date-time format switch to change the format of a date or time in a document header. The Insert Date button on the Header and Footer toolbar inserts dates as *mm/dd/yy*, but you can insert the field with the keyboard and add the date-time format switch \@ "MMMM d, yyyy" to have Word spell out the name of the month and use four digits for the year.

- Use a case conversion switch like * FirstCap to capitalize the first letter of every word in a result of a field when you use a field to generate a proper name.

- Use a format-conversion switch to format a number as currency, a Roman numeral, or a word. To display a document's page number as a Roman numeral, for example, you might use the Page field with the numeric-conversion switch \# Roman to insert the current page number at a specific place in your document. (Changing this one field's format does not change the default page number format set for the document, however.)

If you're willing to spend a little effort learning about switches through the Field Options dialog box or Word's help system, you'll discover many more uses for them and for the fields they modify.

Viewing Fields

You can display either field results or field codes in a document. You may want to display field codes if a field's format isn't quite right and you want to change the switch, but in most cases, you'll want to display field results. You can change what you see at any time, and you can make fields stand out a little more by shading them.

To change the view of one field, click anywhere in the field and press Shift+F9.

To change the view of every field in the document at once, use the Options dialog box, like this:

1 Choose Options from the Tools menu to open the Options dialog box.

2 Click the View tab.

3 Select or clear the Field Codes check box. When the check box is clear, field results are shown.

4 Click OK.

Adding Field Shading

When you display field results, it's hard to tell which text in your document is a field and which is just plain old text. You can make it easier to distinguish fields by shading them like this:

Motorcycling in the Rockies, by ░░░░░░   Page ░ of ░

Chapter 3

More than a dozen incredibly beautiful mountain passes cross the Continental Divide between Pagosa Springs in the south and Steamboat Springs. Elevations range from 7,000 feet up to more than 14,000 feet on Trail Ridge Road in Rocky Mountain National Park.

When you add shading, it appears only on the screen, not when the document is printed or viewed on the World Wide Web. You can set fields so they're shaded all the time, shaded only when you select them, or never shaded at all.

Here's how to set field shading:

1 Choose Options from the Tools menu and click the View tab.

2 Choose an option from the Field Shading menu and then click OK.

Editing and Formatting Fields

Once you have inserted a field, you can treat it as you would any other text in your document. You can select it, move it, cut it, paste it, or format it, and you can also edit the field code or field result.

Selecting a Field

A field may look like ordinary text, but Word knows the difference and shows it when you select a field. You can select the text inside a field to edit or format specific characters, or you can select the entire field when you want to cut or copy it or drag it to a new location.

- To select text inside a field, double-click anywhere inside the field or drag the I-beam pointer across some of the text inside the field.

- To select an entire field, drag the I-beam pointer across it.

> Selecting text inside a Table of Contents or Table of Figures is particularly tricky because each listed item is a hyperlink that takes you to the item's location in the document when you click it. To select the table or text inside it, be sure to hold down the mouse button and drag to select the text you want.

Whenever you select a field or any text inside it, Word adds a normal text selection highlight to the selected area. If you have field shading on, the selection highlight appears on top of the shading like this:

Selected text in field

9/8/98 9:07 AM

Field shading

SEE ALSO

For more information about displaying field codes or field results, see page 638.

Editing a Field

If your needs change, you may want to edit a field's codes to change its result. You may also want to edit a result directly. To edit text in a field, make sure Word is displaying the right view (the field codes or the field result), then select the text inside the field and change it.

TIP

> If you need to view and edit a number of fields at different places in your document, there's an easy way to jump from one field to the next: press F11 to jump to the next field in the document or press Shift+F11 to jump to the previous field. You can also use the window browse buttons or the Find or Go To commands to jump to a specific field. See *"Navigating in a Document"* on page 56.

Formatting Fields

You can format some aspects of the field by using switches, but you'll want to use Word's text formatting tools to change the overall look of the field codes or results in your document. For example, you should use a switch to change a field's number, date, time format, or capitalization, but you'll need to select the field in the document and choose format options to change its font, size, or style.

Printing Field Codes

Whenever you print a document containing fields, Word normally prints the field results rather than the field codes. However, you may want to print a copy of the document that shows the field codes so you'll have them for reference. To print a document with its field codes, follow these steps:

1   Press Ctrl+P or choose Print from the File menu to display the Print dialog box.

2   Click the Options button to display the print options.

3   Select the Field Codes check box in the Include With Document area and click OK.

4   Click OK in the main Print dialog box to print the document.

> **NOTE**

Once you choose the Field Codes option for printing a document, it remains in effect until you cancel it. Don't forget to return to the Print dialog box and clear the Field Codes check box before printing the document for its readers.

Updating and Locking Fields

Result fields produce text in a document by "reading" the current state of the information to which they refer (such as the text of a bookmark, the date or time on your computer's clock and calendar, or the contents of a file) and then displaying it. Fields are always updated when you open a document, but otherwise Word doesn't know the current state of the data to which a field refers. However, Word makes it easy to update one or all of the fields in a document any time you want, and you can also have all fields updated automatically when you print a document.

If a field in your document contains a result that you don't want to change anymore, you can lock the field to prevent further updates. Later you can unlock it to allow more updates. You can also convert a field to text when you want to permanently discontinue updates.

Updating a Field

To update a field manually, click it and press F9, or right-click it and choose Update Field from the shortcut menu.

To update all of the fields in a document, press Ctrl+A to select the entire document and then press F9.

To have Word automatically update all of a document's fields before printing, follow these steps:

1 Press Ctrl+P to display the Print dialog box.

2 Click the Options button.

3 Select the Update Fields check box in the Printing Options area and then click OK to return to the Print dialog box.

4 Click OK to update all of the fields and print the document.

Locking a Field

When you want to prevent updates to a field temporarily, you can lock it. This action is temporary because you can just as easily unlock the field later. If you need to print form letters over a span of several days, for example, you might lock a Date field to print the same date on every letter no matter when it is printed.

■ To lock a field, select the field and press Ctrl+3 or Ctrl+F11.

■ To unlock a field, select it and press Ctrl+Shift+F11.

★ TIP

To determine whether a field is locked, right-click it and examine the shortcut menu. If the Update Field command appears dimmed, the field is locked.

Converting a Field to Text

If you have no further use for a field, you can convert it to the text of its result by unlinking it. For example, if a form letter's date is supplied by a date field, you can select the date field and unlink it so that the field will no longer change to reflect the current date every time you open up the form letter. To unlink a field, select the field and press Ctrl+6 or Ctrl+Shift+F9.

   TIP

> You can't turn text back into a field, but you can undo the conversion immediately after you perform it by pressing Ctrl+Z or by choosing Undo Unlink Fields from the Edit menu. You may also be able to undo the conversion later by choosing Undo Unlink Fields from the Undo menu on the Standard toolbar.

Using Keyboard Shortcuts with Fields

You can use a keyboard shortcut to insert three of the most common fields or to perform other field operations. You'll want to select the field or put the insertion point where you want the field to appear before using these shortcut keys.

Table 27-1 shows a list of shortcuts you can use:

TABLE 27-1.   Shortcut Keys for Working with Fields

Shortcut Keys	Description
Alt+Shift+D	Insert DATE field
Alt+Shift+P	Insert PAGE field
Alt+Shift+T	Insert TIME field
Ctrl+F9	Insert field characters
F9	Update selected field(s)
Shift+F9	Toggle display of field codes/field results
F11	Go to next field
Shift+F11	Go to previous field
Ctrl+F11	Lock selected field(s)
Ctrl+Shift+F11	Unlock selected field(s)

V

Data Automation Tools

Using Macros

Microsoft Word 2000 has a lot of features that automate aspects of the document creation process, but none of them compares with macros. A *macro* is a set of instructions that Word executes at your command. The instructions can include virtually any task that Word can perform, from entering text to formatting and printing, checking the spelling, creating a table or index, and creating and printing form letters. You can even use macros to export Word documents to Microsoft Excel or Microsoft Access. Macros can automate simple tasks such as selecting a group of Page Setup settings, or they can automate complex sequences of operations that might take you minutes or even hours to do yourself. In this chapter and the next, you'll learn how to use macros to make your life much easier.

Macros save you time and effort by executing groups of commands without your intervention and much faster than you could on your own. You can assign a keyboard shortcut or a toolbar button to any macro, so you can run it with a couple of keystrokes or a mouse click. While you might have to locate and choose dozens of individual commands and dialog box options to carry out a series of tasks, a macro tells Word to execute all of the tasks instantly when you press just a couple of keys or click a button.

The more you use a certain complex procedure that can be handled with a macro, the more time you save. For example, if you often choose several custom page formatting options before printing a certain type of document, you can create a macro to handle them and then save time whenever you print that sort of document. Macros can also help eliminate errors in documents that are prepared by others because they faithfully carry out the same instructions time after time.

You can activate, or run a macro whenever you like. You can also create macros that run automatically when a document is opened or closed, or when you start or exit Word.

How Macros Work

Macros are actually programs written in Microsoft Visual Basic for Applications (VBA). VBA is a version of Microsoft Visual Basic that includes dozens of special control features specifically for Word. You can use these special controls to create complete custom applications that use Word's basic code but that look completely different on the screen. For example, you could write a Visual Basic program that turns Word into a tightly focused form letter generator where the user completes a series of custom dialog boxes or uses custom menus to create a form letter.

> **NOTE**
>
> VBA also has program-specific controls when you use it in Excel, Access, or other Microsoft Office programs. In Excel, for example, you can use VBA to create a full-featured accounting application.

By default, macros are stored in the Normal template that Word uses for blank documents, but they can just as easily be stored in a particular document or a custom template. Each macro has a unique name, and you can store as many of them as you like in any document or template. You can also copy macro collections from one document or template to another.

SEE ALSO

For more information about creating or editing macros with the Visual Basic Editor, see Chapter 29, "Working with Microsoft Visual Basic."

There are two ways to create macros: you can have Word record the commands or dialog box options you choose, or you can use the Visual Basic Editor to write macros from scratch or edit any macro that is already stored. You'll probably get started with macros by recording your actions, but you may want to use the Visual Basic Editor to modify macros or to create macros that are too sophisticated to be recorded.

Macros can also be nested inside other macros. This feature allows you to create macros for specific operations and then pick and choose among them to create a new, more complex macro that does many different things at once. For example, you could create individual macros that change line spacing, indentation, or capitalization, and create others that print a document with various page setup and printing options. You could then create one macro that runs some of these other macros in order to format and print a document automatically.

TIP

Most of the individual commands you can choose in Word are already stored as Word Command macros. By nesting Word Command macros inside another macro you can easily combine a series of events. *For more information, see "Nesting Macros inside Other Macros" on page 658.*

What Can Macros Do for You?

You could spend your entire career working in Word without ever using a macro, but it's really very easy to create simple macros that can save you time and energy when you have to do the same things over and over again. Here are some examples of how macros can help you.

Text Entry

Macros can enter text, insert text from bookmarks or other files, select spelling and grammar options, run checks, summarize documents, add information to a document's properties, and perform other editing chores.

If you use Word to distribute forms or questionnaires, for example, you can create a macro that runs each time the document is opened and presents a dialog box that provides instructions or asks the user for certain information.

If you routinely prepare contracts or similar documents, you can use macros to insert boilerplate paragraphs in certain places or to choose which paragraph is inserted based on the contents of other paragraphs.

Formatting

Formatting documents often requires many steps, but you can combine them all into one macro to complete tasks more quickly and with fewer mistakes.

For example, if you frequently copy text from e-mail messages or other files into Word documents, you may often need to manually remove extra return characters at the ends of lines manually. You can use the Find command to locate extra return characters and remove them one by one, but a macro can repeat (or *loop*) the find-and-delete operation from the beginning of the document to the end, thereby eliminating all of the extra return characters in one fell swoop. The macro can even help distinguish when return characters shouldn't be removed.

If you often use text boxes, logos, or other objects of a particular size and frequently place them in similar locations in various documents, you can create a macro that automatically creates, positions, and sets format options for such objects.

And Much More...

Macros can handle any other Word operation or group of operations that would normally require you to choose commands or specify dialog box options. For example, you might use macros to set the Insert Table options and then create a table, to set up an index or table of contents in a certain way, or to add an AutoShape or WordArt graphic. Macros can start up other programs, open or save documents, transfer information from one Microsoft Office document to another, and handle nearly any other task you need to perform.

The Dark Side of Macros

Macros can speed up your work incredibly, but they execute a series of commands regardless of whether they're appropriate for the context in which you run them. You have a choice about whether to run a macro (unless it's an automatic macro), but once the macro is running, you're powerless until it's finished. If you run a macro in the wrong situation, you'll probably spend some quality time with the Undo menu reversing the damage.

With a little planning and care, however, you can set up macros to do what you want, when you want, and without unpleasant side effects.

When Should You Use a Macro?

Macros can do anything, but that doesn't mean they should do everything. When you want Word's help in automating various tasks, there are other ways to automate the process without using a macro. You can do the following:

- Create document templates to store specific formatting, toolbars, menus, macro collections, or style choices so you don't have to reset them each time you open a new document.

- Use styles to apply groups of character and paragraph format options.

- Set AutoFormat options to apply formatting.

- Set AutoCorrect or AutoText options to insert text as you type.

- Use fields to insert text, dates, times, or numbers, to make logical evaluations and produce a result, or to request more information from a user.

- Use hyperlinks to navigate instantly to other files, Web sites, or bookmarked text.

- Choose Options from the Tools menu and then use the Options dialog box to update hypertext links or fields when a document is printed or to create a backup copy of each document.

Determining Likely Macro Candidates

With so many other automation options in Word, it can be difficult to decide when it's appropriate to use a macro. Here is an important question to help you determine whether to macro or not to macro.

Can the Macro Do the Job at All?

Macros are extremely capable, but they're not omnipotent. Macros can't read your mind, and they can't capture mouse movements. For example, when you select an option in a dialog box, a macro doesn't care which method you choose to complete a command—it only cares about the command itself. It makes no difference whether you used Ctrl+P or chose Print from the File menu to open the Print the dialog box, because the macro simply records a command to print the document using any settings that were in effect when you recorded the macro.

Recording Macros

To record a macro, you name the new macro, turn on the macro recorder, complete the commands you want to store in the macro, and then turn the recorder off. Word saves the new macro when you save your document. You can record only new macros; to edit an existing macro you must use the Visual Basic Editor. But before you start recording a new macro, you'll want to make sure that Word and your document are in optimum condition.

Preparing To Record a Macro

Once you begin recording a macro, it's Show Time: you're on the air and everything you do (mistakes included) will be recorded. To make the recording process as smooth and organized as possible, follow this prerecording routine:

1 Open the document in which you'll use the macro. To store the macro in a particular document or template, make sure to open that document or template.

2 Think of a short name for the macro. If you'll want to assign a keyboard shortcut or button to the macro, you should also have a button name or keystroke combination in mind.

> **NOTE**
>
> Macro names can't contain spaces, so it might help to capitalize each of the words in a macro, as in "SetUpEnvelope."

3 Determine whether the macro involves selected text or a specific location in a document. If it involves working either one, insert a bookmark to identify the selection of text or the location.

4 If the macro will rely on selecting a certain style, Web page theme, fill option, external file, or other named item, make sure the item is available before you begin.

5 Run through the actions you plan to record to make sure you aren't planning to do something that can't be recorded. If necessary, write down every single keystroke or mouse movement in order and then review it. You may find a more efficient way to do it, or you may realize that you need to find a keyboard alternative for the part of the process you had planned to handle with the mouse.

Once you're confident that you can record the macro without any backtracking or unrecordable actions, you're ready to begin.

Recording a Macro

 SEE ALSO

For more information about using Auto-Format with tables, see "Using Table Auto-Format" on page 357.

To see how the recording process works, let's try recording a sample macro. Let's assume you frequently use three-column, four-row tables formatted with the Classic 4 AutoFormat. You want to record a macro named Tab3x4 that will automatically insert such a table whenever you press a keyboard shortcut.

You will always run this macro after moving the insertion point to the place where you want the table to appear, so it's immaterial where the insertion point is (or for that matter, what the document looks like) when you create it. However, you'll want to make sure to open the document or template in which you want to store the macro.

Turning On the Recorder

 SEE ALSO

For more information about templates, see "Copying Macros from One Template to Another" on page 659.

1 Open the template or document in which you want to store the macro.

2 Choose Record New Macro from the Macro submenu on the Tools menu. Word opens the Record Macro dialog box shown in Figure 28-1.

FIGURE 28-1.

Use the Record Macro dialog box to name a new macro and start recording it.

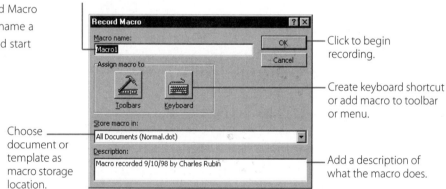

Enter macro name.

Click to begin recording.

Create keyboard shortcut or add macro to toolbar or menu.

Choose document or template as macro storage location.

Add a description of what the macro does.

3 Type *Tab3x4* in the Macro Name box.

4 Choose the location where you want to store the macro from the Store Macro In menu. The Record Macro dialog box suggests the normal.dot template, but any other template you currently have open is also on this list, as is the particular document you have open.

5 Type a description for the macro in the Description box.

Data Automation Tools

It's extremely useful to add a description of every macro you create. You'll often have several macros with very similar names, and the descriptions will help you sort out the differences or jog your memory about older macros you seldom use.

SEE ALSO
For more information about assigning commands or buttons to macros, see "Creating Macro Commands, Buttons, and Keyboard Shortcuts" on page 654.

6   Click the Toolbars or Keyboard button to assign a button or keyboard shortcut to the macro.

7   When you close the Customize or Customize Keyboard dialog box, Word turns on the macro recorder and displays the Stop Recording toolbar, like this:

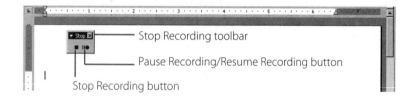

The recorder is now on, waiting for you to start recording commands. To pause the recorder temporarily, click the Pause Recording button on the toolbar, and click it again to turn the recorder back on. To cancel recording, click the Stop Recording button or choose Stop Recording from the Macro submenu on the Tools menu.

Recording the Macro Steps

When you record the steps of a macro, take your time. Word records commands but not the time delays between them, so take the time to make sure you're choosing the right command. To continue our example of creating a table, follow these steps:

1   Choose Table from the Insert submenu on the Table menu to display the Insert Table dialog box.

2   Enter 3 in the Number Of Columns box.

3   Enter 4 in the Number Of Rows box.

4   Click the AutoFormat button to display the Table AutoFormat dialog box.

5   Select the Classic 4 format in the Format list.

6 Click OK to return to the Insert Table dialog box.

7 Click OK to insert the table.

Word always executes the commands you choose when you record a macro, so in addition to saving the steps, you also produce the results of those commands in your document.

Working Around Macro Limitations

Although Word can't record mouse movements, such as scrolling or resizing the document window or selecting and resizing text, there are frequently ways to work around these limitations by using the keyboard or a dialog box. Here are some examples:

- Rather than scrolling to a particular part of a document, use the Go To command.

- Rather than selecting text with the mouse, create a bookmark for the text and then use the Go To command to select it.

- Rather than clicking or dragging markers in the ruler to set indents and tab stops, use the Paragraph and Tabs dialog boxes.

- Rather than dragging to resize the document window, use commands on the window or application control menus and press the arrow keys on the keyboard.

- Rather than selecting a shape in the Drawing toolbar and dragging to create it, store the shape in a file first and then create a macro that uses the Picture command on the Insert menu to place it in your document. Since the inserted object remains selected, you can also record settings in the Format Picture dialog box to size and position the object precisely or to set its text wrapping options.

- Rather than dragging to create a text box, use the Text Box command on the Insert menu.

You'll probably find a way to work around most mouse-driven activities in Word, and if one doesn't exist, you may be able to create it by defining a new keyboard shortcut or toolbar button.

V

Data Automation Tools

Creating Macro Commands, Buttons, and Keyboard Shortcuts

During the naming process you go through just before you record a macro, you have the opportunity to assign the macro to a toolbar button or menu command, or to give it a keyboard shortcut.

Adding a Macro to a Menu or Toolbar

② SEE ALSO

For more information about customizing toolbars, menus, and keyboard shortcuts, see Chapter 8, "Customizing Toolbars, Menus, and Commands."

To add a new macro to a menu or toolbar, follow these steps:

1 Open the Record Macro dialog box, enter a name and description for the macro, and choose a template in which to store it, as explained in steps 1–4 on page 651.

2 Click the Toolbars button. You'll see the Customize dialog box like this:

The Commands list shows the name of the new macro you are about to record.

3 Choose a storage location for the command or button from the Save In menu.

4 Drag the command to a menu or toolbar to create a button or menu command for it. The command or button name will be the same as the name shown in the Commands list.

5 Click the Close button to close the Customize dialog box.

Assigning a Keyboard Shortcut to a Macro

Here's how to assign a keyboard shortcut to a macro:

1 Open the Record Macro dialog box, enter a name and description for the macro, and choose a template in which to store it, as explained in steps 1–3 on page 651.

SEE ALSO

For more information about editing buttons or copying button icons, see "Changing Buttons and Commands" on page 167.

Customizing a Macro Toolbar Button

When you add a new macro to a toolbar, the button shows the name of the macro and the template where it's stored, like this:

New button for Tab3x4 macro
on Formatting toolbar

However, you can customize a macro's button by adding an icon to it. The best way to do this is to use a predesigned icon. Word comes with several predesigned button icons, or you can make a new icon using a drawing or paint program and then copy it onto the macro's button. To customize a macro button:

1 Add the new macro to a toolbar as described in this chapter.

2 If you created a new button icon yourself, open the file containing the icon, select the icon, and copy it to the Clipboard.

3 Choose the Customize command from the Tools menu.

4 Open the toolbar that contains the macro button, if necessary, and then right-click the button on the toolbar to display a shortcut menu.

5 Choose Paste Button Image from the menu to paste the image from the Clipboard (if you copied one there), or choose Change Button Image to open a palette of icons that come with Word, and then select an icon from that palette.

6 Click the Close button to close the Customize dialog box.

V

Data Automation Tools

2 Click the Keyboard button. Word opens the Customize Keyboard dialog box like this:

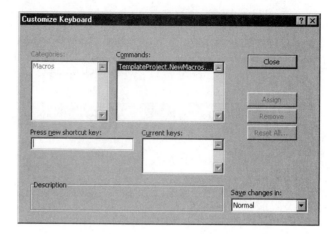

As with a button, the name of the macro you are about to record is shown in the Commands list.

3 Select the template or document where you want to save the custom command or button from the Save Changes In menu.

4 Press the shortcut keys you want to use to run the macro. Make sure to use Alt or Ctrl or both as part of the key combination. The area below the Press New Shortcut Key box tells you if the macro is already assigned to another command or if it is unassigned and therefore available, like this:

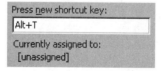

 **TIP**

Nearly every built-in keyboard shortcut in Word uses the Ctrl key, so many key combinations that include this key are already assigned. You'll have an easier time finding previously unassigned key combinations if you use the Alt key in macro key combinations.

5 Click the Assign button.

6 Click the Close button to close the Customize Keyboard dialog box.

If you forget to define a button or keyboard shortcut for a macro, there are two ways to solve the problem. You can record the same macro again and define the button or shortcut when you name it, but if the macro is complex, this may be a lot of work. Another solution is to create a new macro that includes a button or command assignment and then use it to record the act of selecting and running the previous macro with the Macros dialog box.

Running Macros

If you have the same instincts as most Word users, your first thought upon completing a macro is to try it out and see if it works. You can run a macro with the Macros dialog box or by choosing the button, command, or keyboard shortcut that you assigned to it.

Running a Macro with the Macros Dialog Box

To run a macro with the Macros dialog box, follow these steps:

1 Press Alt+F8 or choose Macros from the Macro submenu on the Tools menu. Word opens the Macros dialog box as in Figure 28-2.

FIGURE 28-2.

Use the Macros dialog box to select and run a macro.

Select a macro.

Choose macro collection to display its macros in the list above.

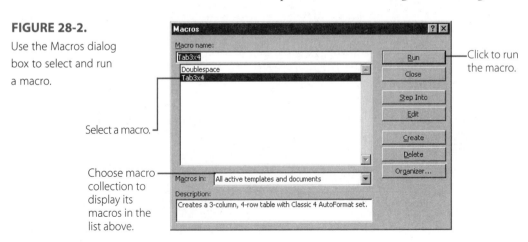

Click to run the macro.

2 Using the Macros In menu, select the template or document that contains the macro you want. (You may have alternate collections of macros stored in the current document, the current document template, or the Normal template.)

3 Double-click the name of the macro you want to run, or select it and click the Run button. The macro runs and the Macros dialog box vanishes.

Managing Macros

When you create macros, they are stored in the document or template as a Visual Basic project called NewMacros. If your macros prove useful in one template, however, you may want to copy them all to another template or document where they can also be of help. In addition, you'll want to periodically examine your macro collection and eliminate outdated macros or perhaps rename them. You can perform all of these tasks with the Macros dialog box, as shown in Figure 28-2.

Nesting Macros inside Other Macros

While you're recording a macro, you can run other macros to execute them automatically from within the main macro. To do this, you simply choose Macros from the Macro submenu on the Tools menu while the macro recorder is on, select a macro, and click the Run button. You can do this a number of times to include or nest several macros inside the one you're recording so that they will all run automatically, one after the other.

The list of macros you see in the Macro dialog box depends on which template or macro collection is selected on the Macros In menu. In addition to the current document and template and the Normal template, the Macros In menu also includes a location called Word Commands. The Word Commands location includes dozens of predefined macros that execute individual Word commands. If you know the name of a Word Command macro you want to use while recording, you can select it in the Macros dialog box and click the Run command to include it.

By running other macros while recording a macro, you can create very powerful macros that perform many sophisticated operations all at once.

Deleting or Renaming a Macro

To delete a macro, open the Macros dialog box, select the macro name, and click the Delete button.

To rename a macro, you'll need to edit it with the Visual Basic Editor and then save it with a different name. *See Chapter 29, "Working with Microsoft Visual Basic," for details.*

Copying Macros from One Template to Another

If you have already read up on styles in Chapter 15, "Using Styles and Themes," you're familiar with the Organizer. When you copy macros, you use the Organizer to copy macro projects from one template to another.

About Macro Projects

In the Organizer, a macro "project" is a collection of custom macros you have recorded and stored in a particular document or document template. Technically, macros you create are stored in the current document template as a Visual Basic program module called NewMacros.

Macro projects are only one type of project you can create with Visual Basic. *For more information about Visual Basic projects,* see *"Using Procedures, Modules, and Projects" on page 678.*

When you create a macro, you can store it in the NewMacros module for the current template, in a new module for the current document or template, or in a module called All Active Templates And Documents, which is available to any document you have open.

To copy macros from one template or document to another, you use the Organizer to select and copy the entire macro module that contains them. To select and copy just one of a template's macros, you must first use Visual Basic to copy that macro into a new module, and then use the Organizer to copy the new module.

If you will use only a few of the macros in a particular macro module that you copy, just open the Macros dialog box in the document to which you copied the project and then delete any macros you don't want.

V

Data Automation Tools

Using the Organizer to Copy Macros

Once you understand the concept of macro projects, it's easy to use the Organizer to move a project from one document or template to another. Here's an example.

Let's assume you want to copy the NewMacros macro collection from the normal.dot document template to the current document, which is a new document called Document4 and is based on a different template. Here's what to do:

1   Choose Macros from the Macro submenu on the Tools menu to display the Macros dialog box.

2   Click the Organizer button. Word opens the Organizer, as shown in Figure 28-3.

FIGURE 28-3.

Use the Organizer to copy macro projects between documents or templates.

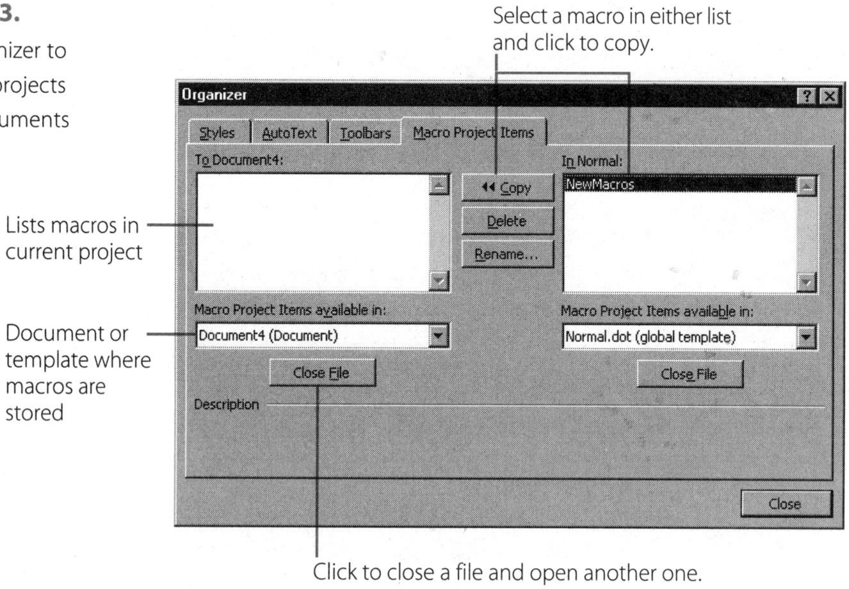

Select a macro in either list and click to copy.

Lists macros in current project

Document or template where macros are stored

Click to close a file and open another one.

The Organizer allows you to copy macro projects from one document or template to another, and you can also use it to open or close specific documents. In Figure 28-3, the left side of the Organizer shows the contents of Document4 and the right side shows the contents of the normal.dot template. Notice, too, that the macro project stored in the normal.dot template is called NewMacros.

WARNING

You can't copy a macro project to another document or template that already contains a macro project of the same name. Since the default name for the macro project is NewMacros in every template, you'll need to rename this project before copying it to another document that already contains a NewMacros project. *For more information, see "Renaming Macro Projects" below.*

TIP

You can also use the Organizer to copy styles, AutoText entries, or custom toolbar, command, or keyboard shortcuts from document to document or template to template. Just click the tab for the type of information you want to copy and proceed as above.

3 Using the Macro Project Items Available In list on the right-hand side of the dialog box, choose the normal.dot template. The macro projects stored in that document or template will be listed above. In our example, there's only one macro project (called NewMacros) stored in the normal.dot template, as shown in Figure 28-3.

4 Select the NewMacros project in the list above. (It is already selected in Figure 28-3.)

NOTE

The left-hand list in the dialog box in Figure 28-3 doesn't show the name of a macro collection because it lists macros stored in the active document, and the macros are stored in that document's template, not the document itself.

5 On the left side of the dialog box, use the Macro Project Items Available In list to select the template or document to which you will copy the macro project. We want to copy the macro project to the Document4 document, so we would select that document as in Figure 28-3.

6 Click the Copy button. Word copies the NewMacros project to Document4.

7 Click the Close button in the lower-right corner to close the Organizer dialog box.

V

Data Automation Tools

Renaming Macro Projects

As mentioned previously, Word's default name for macro projects is NewMacros, and every document template has a NewMacros project. You can't copy an identically named collection to a template or document, so if you record new macros in a NewMacro collection and then want to copy them to another document, you must rename the project before you copy it. You may also want to rename a macro project to store a collection of macros for a particular purpose. For example, you might have separate macro projects for formatting, editing, or printing documents.

Here's how to rename a macro project:

1 Choose Macros from the Macro submenu on the Tools menu, and click the Organizer button.

2 Select the macro project name.

3 Click the Rename button. Word displays the Rename dialog box.

4 Enter a new name for the project and click OK. Word returns you to the Organizer dialog box.

Deleting a Macro Collection

You can also delete macro collections using the Organizer. To do this, select the collection name in the Organizer and click the Delete button.

Opening and Closing Templates and Documents

When you first open the Organizer dialog box, Word presents the contents of the current document on the left side and the contents of the normal.dot template on the right side. To copy macro projects from other documents or templates that are not currently open in the Organizer, follow these steps:

1 Click the Close File button underneath either macro project list. The button name changes to Open File.

2 Click the Open File button to display Word's Open dialog box.

3 Select a document or template in the Open dialog box and click the Open button. Word returns you to the Organizer dialog box, where you may now copy macro projects to or from the newly opened document or template.

Editing a Macro with the Macro Recorder

For information about using Visual Basic, see Chapter 29, "Working with Microsoft Visual Basic."

The best way to edit a macro is to press Alt+F11 to open the Visual Basic Editor. You'll see the macro's code, and you are then free to modify the macro instructions to your heart's delight. Of course, you need to know something about Visual Basic to edit macros this way. Without the Visual Basic Editor, however, the only way to edit a recorded macro is to record a new one with the same name. Here's how to do this:

1 Choose Record New Macro from the Macro submenu on the Tools menu.

2 In the Macro Name box, enter exactly the same name as the macro you want to replace.

3 Click OK. Word will ask if you want to replace the existing macro.

4 Click Yes and then record the replacement macro.

Preventing Macro Viruses

Since it is arguably the most popular productivity program ever created for personal computers, Word has often been the target of malicious viruses. Viruses sometimes display screen messages that you can't get rid of, or they do even worse things like erase files on your hard drive.

Viruses spread through files, and Word viruses in particular attach themselves to Word documents as AutoOpen macros that run automatically when the document is opened. You may contract a Word macro virus by opening files that you downloaded from the Internet or from disks you got from other people. Typically, you need only open a virus-infected document once, and then the virus goes about its evil business.

Preventing Viruses in Word Documents

Since the only way to activate a virus is by opening a file or running a macro that contains one, there are two ways to protect yourself from macro viruses in Word:

■ Install a virus detection and removal program such as McAfee VirusScan or Norton AntiVirus so that every file on your disk is scanned each time you start up your computer and any viruses are automatically removed. This is the best defense against viruses of all kinds.

To download an evaluation copy of VirusScan, navigate to *http://www.nai.com/ download/default.asp*.

V

Data Automation Tools

For more information about preventing macros from running, see "Setting the Macro Security Level" on the next page.

■ Prevent Word from loading macro collections in the documents you open, so that any macro viruses in them never get a chance to run.

In the previous version of Word, the program automatically scanned every document as it was opened and reported the presence of any suspicious macros. You could then disable all of the document's macros, enable all macros, or cancel to avoid opening the document at all. Word 2000 offers stronger and more flexible macro security options.

Using Digital Signatures

For more information about digital signatures, see "Adding a Digital Signature" on page 701.

Word 2000 includes a third defense against macros: digital signatures and the Security dialog box. Digital signatures are unique, unbreakable codes that identify individual computer users. You can use either an *authenticated* digital signature that is issued and guaranteed by a third party supplier, or you can create an *unauthenticated* digital signature for your own use.

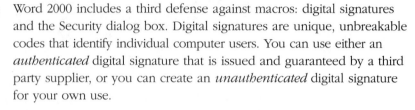

For information about obtaining an authenticated digital signature or to obtain one, go to the Verisign, Inc., site at *http://www.verisign.com* or visit Microsoft's Security Advisor at *http://www.microsoft.com/security*.

Once you have a digital signature, you can use the Visual Basic Editor to "sign" any macro with it. The signature then becomes a trusted means of identifying yourself as the macro's author.

> **NOTE**
>
> Digital signatures work only when you have Microsoft Internet Explorer version 4.0 or later installed. If a user opens a document containing digitally signed macros on a computer that doesn't have Internet Explorer 4.0 or later installed, Word displays the old macro virus dialog box that simply offers a choice between enabling or disabling all macros.

Word 2000 allows you to set three levels of security based on the presence or absence of digital signatures. The settings are:

■ **High** Word allows only digitally signed macros to run. You can add a digital signature to macros you create with the Visual Basic Editor. All other macros are disabled.

■ **Medium** Word identifies the presence of macros in any document and lets you choose whether or not to disable them.

■ **Low** Word allows all macros to run. This option is recommended only if you have a virus scanning and prevention program installed on your computer.

Setting the Macro Security Level

To set the level of macro security, follow these steps:

1   Choose Security from the Macro submenu on the Tools menu. Word opens the Security dialog box, as shown here:

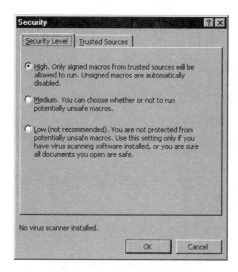

The Security dialog box indicates whether you have a virus detection program installed on your computer, so you can decide if you want to set the Low security level.

2   Click the Security Level tab if necessary.

3   Select the High, Medium, or Low security option.

4   Click OK.

NOTE

> Word detects only the presence of virus scanning programs that have been specially programmed to identify themselves to Word. If you're running a virus scanner and the Security dialog box says, "No virus scanner installed," you'll need to install a newer version of the scanner program.

Viewing and Removing Trusted Sources

When you set the High security level in the Security dialog box, Word relies on a Trusted Sources list to determine whether macros will be allowed to run. Macros that include digital signatures are considered to be from trusted sources, but each time you open a document containing signed macros from a trusted source that is not on Word's list, you can choose whether or not to enable those macros. (After all, a hacker can add a digital signature to a macro as easily as a legitimate programmer, and digital signatures can expire.) If you enable the macros, the trusted source's name is automatically added to the Trusted Sources list.

To view the Trusted Sources list, choose Security from the Macro submenu on the Tools menu and click the Trusted Sources tab. You'll see a list that shows all of the macro sources that are currently trusted by Word, as shown here:

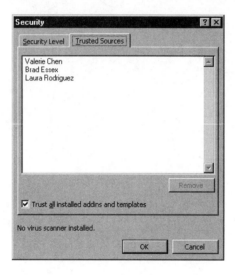

To remove a trusted source, select it and click the Remove button. You can use the check box on the Trusted Sources tab to set security for add-ins and templates you may later install using the Microsoft Office Setup program or the Templates and Add-Ins command on the Tools menu. If you clear the check box, Word allows you to install these components only from trusted sources.

> If you're using Word on a company network, your network administrator may have locked the Trusted Sources list so you can't change any of the list items or options on it.

Now that you've learned the basics of recording and managing macros, turn to Chapter 29, "Working with Microsoft Visual Basic," for information about how to edit macros or create much more sophisticated ones with Visual Basic.

CHAPTER 29

Working with Microsoft Visual Basic

This chapter deals with the programming language called Visual Basic. It is one of Microsoft's programming languages for developing Microsoft Windows applications, and Microsoft Word 2000 includes a version of Visual Basic called Visual Basic for Applications (VBA).

SEE ALSO

For more information about ActiveX controls, see "Using ActiveX Controls" on page 722.

Although the idea of using a programming language may seem daunting, it's worthwhile to learn something about VBA, as you will see. By opening the Visual Basic Editor in Word, you can use VBA to write or edit macros, to define ActiveX controls, and to create whole custom applications for Word. In this chapter, you'll learn how VBA works and how to use it to write and edit macros or to define ActiveX controls.

WARNING

> Visual Basic programming is complicated. In this chapter, I have attempted to bring it into focus within the context of editing and enhancing a Word macro, but if you're serious about learning Visual Basic, you'll need more help than the overview offered here.

Visual Basic offers a complete set of programming tools that are powerful enough for professional programmers but simple enough for ordinary Word users. It is, however, a general programming language intended for people who want to create custom programs from scratch. VBA, on the other hand, is a custom version of Visual Basic that you can access only from within Word or another Microsoft Office program. In Word, VBA includes a suite of Word-specific features that you can use to control Word in specific ways.

NOTE

> VBA is also included with other Microsoft programs such as Microsoft Excel and Microsoft PowerPoint. The program-specific features available in VBA will depend on the program from which it's opened.

This chapter introduces the essential concepts—and a few of the major tools—of Visual Basic for Applications. You can work through the three exercises in this chapter to get a good basic understanding of how VBA works and how you can use it to work more effectively in Word.

For more information on Visual Basic, get a book like the Microsoft Visual Basic 6.0 Programmer's Guide *or* Microsoft Word 97 Visual Basic Step by Step *from Microsoft Press.*

 NOTE

> Visual Basic has its own online Help system that will prove to be an essential reference as you write programs. If Visual Basic Help is not installed on your computer, you can add it with the Microsoft Office Installation CD. *See the Appendix for more information.*

Why Visual Basic?

Visual Basic is a relatively simple programming language, but it's a programming language all the same, and you may be wondering why you should get involved with it all. There are several reasons.

 NOTE

> For the sake of simplicity, I will refer to VBA and Visual Basic both as "Visual Basic" from here on.

As Chapter 28, "Using Macros," explains, you don't need to know anything about Visual Basic in order to record a macro or set a keyboard shortcut for it, but Visual Basic is the language in which every Word macro is stored. The macro you record becomes a *procedure* in a Visual Basic program module, or *macro project*. And since macros are stored as Visual Basic program modules, you can open the Visual Basic Editor to view or change their code.

? SEE ALSO

For more information about screen forms and the Control Toolbox toolbar, see Chapter 30, "Creating Forms."

Visual Basic is also the language you use to define any ActiveX controls you have added with the Control Toolbox toolbar. As you'll see in Chapter 30, you can use Word to create data entry forms that users fill out on the screen. When you create data entry forms, you can use the Control Toolbox toolbar to add specific controls such as drop-down lists, scrolling text boxes, or check boxes. However, once you have added a control to a form, you must use Visual Basic to define how the control looks and behaves. For example, you might use the Control Toolbox toolbar to add a drop-down list to a screen form, but you would need to use Visual Basic to describe the options that appear on that list, and what happens when the user selects each of them.

Although it's not necessary to know about Visual Basic when you use Word, you will need to know about it to edit macros, to create advanced macros, and to define ActiveX controls for use in forms or on Web pages.

About Visual Basic

To develop a new application in Visual Basic, you might begin by selecting the *objects* that will eventually make up the "look and feel" of your new program—objects such as the screen window that presents it, along with its scroll bars, buttons, menus, and so on. Visual Basic offers many kinds of objects you can select, and VBA includes many more objects that are specific to Word or other Microsoft Office programs. Each object you use in a program has a unique name.

V

Data Automation Tools

> Every Word macro is a Visual Basic program, but not every Visual Basic program is a macro. Macros are programs that you run from within Word, for example, while you could write a Visual Basic program that looks and acts like an entirely different program than Word. For the most part, however, the words "macro," "application," and "program" are used interchangeably in this chapter to describe the Visual Basic programs you develop in Word.

For example, to create a custom dialog box for a new application in Word, you would create a *form object*. A form object in Visual Basic is used to present a set of options on the screen. You would then put other objects inside it—such as command buttons, drop-down lists, text boxes, and labels for all of them. If the dialog box allows the user to select from a list of predefined Word documents, each of the documents that can be opened is identified in the program as a Word-specific object.

Properties, Events, and Methods

Every object that you create in Visual Basic is defined by *properties*, *events*, and *methods*. For example, the form object for a custom dialog box has a specific height and width, which are two of the form object's properties.

Properties

Each object has its own properties, and the Properties window lists all of them, as shown in Figure 29-1 on the next page. You can scroll through the list and change the settings of various properties to modify the way an object appears or behaves.

For example, in Figure 29-1 you see a command button labeled "Create Heading." The text, or caption, that is displayed on the face of that button is determined by the Caption property. In the same way, the Font property defines the font used for the caption and the Height property controls the height of the button.

Other properties control the behavior of an object. For example, the Default property determines whether a command button will be the default control in a dialog box. If you set the Default property to True, the user can select the command button simply by pressing the Enter key.

FIGURE 29-1.

The Properties Window lists the properties for a selected object.

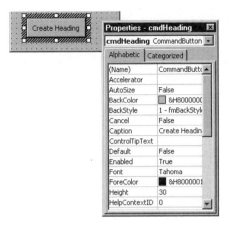

Events

In Visual Basic, you design a program to respond to specific *events* that occur while that program is running. Many events are initiated when the user clicks a command button or drags the slider in a scroll bar, but others are generated by the application itself. For example, a program might scan a document for extra paragraph markers and delete them upon finding them. When an event occurs, the program can be defined in such a way that it will carry out an appropriate action in response. To define what this response will be, you write an *event procedure*. For example, an event procedure named CommandButton1_Click might define the action that will result when the user clicks the command button named CommandButton1.

Methods

A *method* is a predefined Visual Basic procedure that performs a specific action on an object. Methods simplify the task of designing a program—rather than writing a complex procedure yourself to manipulate an object, you can often call on a method to do the job for you.

For example, suppose you want to have a simple way of making sure that the user enters a response into a particular text box at a certain point in your program's performance. To do so, you could use the TextBox.SetFocus method. The TextBox.SetFocus method causes a flashing cursor to appear inside the text box, indicating that an entry is required there.

How Macros are Stored in Visual Basic

? SEE ALSO

For more information on viewing macro projects with the Organizer, see "Copying Macros from One Template to Another" on page 659.

Applications in Visual Basic are organized as *projects*. Each project may include a variety of components, such as *forms* or *modules*. A form would contain the objects needed to display a screen form such as a dialog box. A module contains the program code that handles a specific procedure or aspect of the overall program. For example, one module might contain the program instructions that govern how text appears in a document window in the program. When you record macros in a blank document that is created from the normal.dot document template, the name of the project is Normal—which is the Visual Basic equivalent of the normal.dot template—and the code module that contains the macros is called NewMacros. When you view a document's macros in the Organizer dialog box in Word, NewMacros is listed as a macro project.

Steps to Creating a New Program

When you create a new program in Visual Basic, it can involve a lot of jumping back and forth between adding objects, selecting methods, and creating events or specifying properties. To create a program, you use the Visual Basic Editor shown in Figure 29-5 on page 676. You can follow some specific examples later in this chapter to get a feeling for the process yourself, but overall, there are three major steps in the process:

1 Select and arrange the objects that will make up the visual part of your application—the data window, dialog boxes, menus, and so on. You use Visual Basic forms to present dialog boxes for your program. For example, create a form and arrange a selection of controls—command buttons, text boxes, options, check boxes, scroll bars, and so on—inside that form.

   Whenever you create a new form in the Visual Basic Editor, you'll also see the Toolbox palette, which contains buttons representing the various classes of controls you can place in a form. Figure 29-2 shows the Toolbox palette. You can see the name of any control by pointing to the control on the palette.

FIGURE 29-2.

The Toolbox palette shows the controls available to you in Visual Basic.

2 Set the properties for the objects in your program. The properties available to change will depend on the object you have selected to work with.

> When you create an electronic form in a Word document, you can also use the Control Toolbox to add programmable ActiveX objects to the form. If you do, you'll use the same Visual Basic techniques described here to program them. However, the forms you create to produce custom dialog boxes with the Visual Basic Editor are not the same as data collection forms you create directly in Word documents or Web pages using the Forms, Control Toolbox, or Web Toolbox toolbars in Word. *See Chapter 30, "Creating Forms," and Chapter 33, "Using Word's Advanced Web Features," for more information about creating screen- or Web-based data collection forms.*

3 Write the procedures that will be performed while the program or the macro is running. The statements in a procedure are known as the program's *code*. Much of the code you write will be organized as event procedures, that is, they will be performed in response to the user's actions. When you write these procedures, you can use specific methods to manipulate your program's objects. For example, the PargraphFormat method manipulates the Selection object in a program, telling Word to set a particular paragraph format option for the selection text or at the location of the insertion point. Writing code is the most demanding part of programming, but you can make this step much easier by first selecting the right objects for your program and by judiciously setting their properties.

Creating a Macro

To see how you might use Visual Basic to edit and enhance a macro initially recorded in Word, let's go through a simple example. Think of the example that follows as the Letterhead macro. Its initial purpose will be simply to store the specific lines of text that you place at the top of letters that you write in Word and then, when you want to, place that text at the top of new documents. You can store a complete letterhead as a template, of course, but this macro will give you a lot more flexibility. After you create the macro, it will display a Letterhead dialog box like the one shown in Figure 29-3 on the next page. Using the dialog box, you can select the specific information you want to include in a particular heading. When you click the Create Heading button in the dialog box, the macro inserts only the information you've selected.

V

Data Automation Tools

FIGURE 29-3.

The Letterhead macro will produce this dialog box.

 NOTE

This letterhead macro may seem like a complicated way to do something you might handle more easily as a template or as an AutoText entry, but it's only the starting point. Macros frequently begin as fairly simple procedures that are later enhanced in ways that are not possible with any other feature in Word.

Recording the Initial Macro

To see how recording a macro actually creates Visual Basic instructions, we'll begin this macro with the following basic steps:

1 Open the Tools menu, choose Macro, and then choose the Record New Macro command. The Record Macro dialog box appears.

2 Enter *Letterhead* as the name for the new macro. Also enter a brief description of the project, like this:

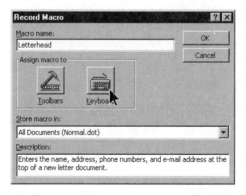

3 Click the Keyboard button. In the resulting Customize Keyboard dialog box, press Alt+L as the keyboard shortcut for performing this macro. (You could use another key combination, of course, but let's stick with this one for now.)

4 Click the Assign button to confirm the keyboard shortcut, and then click the Close button to put the dialog box away and begin recording the macro.

You can tell when macro recording is on because the Stop Recording toolbar appears on the screen and the pointer becomes a tape cassette as shown in Figure 29-4.

5 Press Ctrl+E to center the text you're about to enter, and choose the Arial font and 16-point font size from the Formatting toolbar.

6 Type your name and press Enter twice.

7 Choose the 12-point font size, and type the remaining lines of the heading: your address, phone and fax numbers, and e-mail address. Figure 29-4 shows the completed Letterhead text. To match the example, press Enter twice after typing the second line of the postal address, after typing the second phone number line, and after typing the e-mail address.

FIGURE 29-4.

The text you type is recorded in a macro so that Word can enter it automatically in the future.

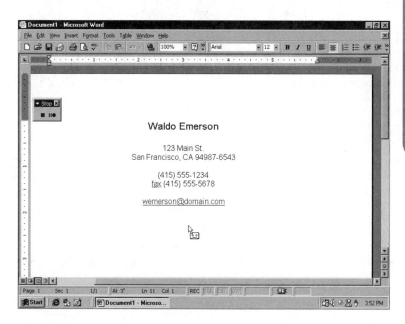

8 Click the Stop Recording button on the Stop Recording toolbar to turn off macro recording.

Data Automation Tools

Viewing the Macro's Instructions

To see how the tasks you just recorded look in Visual Basic, open the macro for editing in the Visual Basic Editor. Here are the steps:

1 Open the Tools menu, choose Macro, and then choose the Macros command to display the Macros dialog box.

2 Select the Letterhead macro name and click the Edit button. Word displays the macro's code in the Visual Basic Editor as shown in Figure 29-5.

FIGURE 29-5.

When you edit a macro, its code appears in the Visual Basic Editor's Code window.

Code window

Project Explorer

Properties list

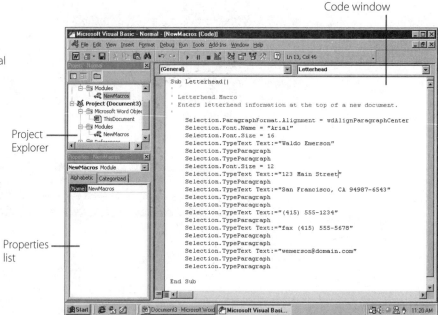

The Code window at the right shows the macro's code, and the Project window (also called the Project Explorer) at the left shows other modules in the project. Notice that the title bar on the Visual Basic Editor's window shows the project's name as Normal. Each group of macros you store in a particular document or template is a separate Visual Basic project; this project is called Normal because it's stored in the normal.dot template.

How Visual Basic Controls Word

The macro's name appears at the top of the Code window in the Visual Basic Editor. It is followed by the description that you entered in the Record Macro dialog box. The actual lines of code that tell Word how to behave appear next.

As you look through the macro's code, you can understand what each statement does because you just recorded the actions they describe. In this macro, each statement begins with the word Selection. This refers to the current selection (in this case the insertion point's location) in the Word document window. Each of the statements in this macro therefore performs an action at the insertion point's location.

Using Property Settings and Methods

This macro contains both property settings and methods. The macro assigns new settings to a variety of properties that are associated with the Selection object, and uses methods to specify in general the type of action being taken with the Selection object. You're not required to specify a method for each object, but often you'll use methods just the same. For example, in the statement

```
Selection.ParagraphFormat.Alignment =
    wdAlignParagraphCenter
```

Selection is the object, ParagraphFormat is the method, Alignment is the property, and wdAlignParagraphCenter is the property setting.

The macro includes other methods that control the Selection object. In the code above, for example, the ParagraphFormat method changes the format of the paragraph where the insertion point is located. Also, the TypeParagraph method inserts a new paragraph at the insertion point, which is the equivalent of having the macro press the Enter key.

Notice the general syntax for referring to the properties and methods of an object in Visual Basic. The name of the object is followed by the name of the relevant method and property, and the names are separated by periods:

```
Object.Method.Property
```

When you specify a property, the property setting follows the property name after an equal (=) sign:

```
Object.Method.Property = Setting
```

V

Data Automation Tools

The first three actions you took after turning on the macro recorder were to select center paragraph alignment, choose the Arial font, and choose the 16-point font size. These property settings appear in the Code window as

```
Selection.ParagraphFormat.Alignment =
    wdAlignParagraphCenter
Selection.Font.Name = "Arial"
Selection.Font.Size = 16
```

For some Visual Basic objects, a property-related statement is equivalent to changing a setting in Visual Basic's Properties box. For example, you might use a property statement to change the color of a button in a custom dialog box after the user clicks it. For other objects, such as the Selection objects in our example, a property change in macro code is equivalent to selecting a specific command in Word itself.

This macro also contains several statements that apply a method called TypeText to a Selection object. The first TypeText statement is

```
Selection.TypeText Text:="Waldo Emerson"
```

The TypeText method inserts a text entry (or *string* in programmerese) at the insertion point. The macro includes six statements containing this method for inserting the name, street address, city, state, postal code, phone number, fax number, and e-mail address of the letterhead. Each TypeText statement is followed by one or more statements containing the TypeParagraph method, because each line of text appears in its own paragraph.

The general syntax of the TypeText method is as follows:

```
Selection.TypeText Text:="Text"
```

Notice that the text entry itself is enclosed within quotation marks.

Now that we've examined the specific lines of code that make up the Letterhead macro, let's take a brief look at the format of this macro and how it fits into the organizational scheme of Visual Basic projects.

Using Procedures, Modules, and Projects

When you record a macro in Word, the resulting Visual Basic code is structured as a procedure—that is, a named sequence of statements enclosed within Sub and End Sub lines. (The keyword Sub refers to the term *subroutine,* a somewhat outdated synonym for *procedure.*) In Figure 29-5 on page 676, you can see that the first line of the Letterhead procedure is a Sub statement:

```
Sub Letterhead()
```

This statement marks the beginning of the procedure and defines the procedure's name. The last line in the procedure is (you'll have to scroll down in the code window to see it)

    End Sub

The statements between Sub and End Sub represent the actions that will occur whenever you run the macro.

At the top of the Letterhead procedure, just below the Sub line, you can see *comment* lines containing the macro name and description. A comment in Visual Basic code is any line of text that begins with a single quotation mark ('). When you run the macro, these comments have no effect on its performance, but their presence in the code is an important way of providing essential information about what the macro does and how it works. You can place comment lines anywhere inside the code of a macro. It's a good idea to write comments of your own whenever you revise or expand a macro from its original recorded content.

You can examine the components of the Normal project inside Visual Basic's Project Explorer. As you can see in Figure 29-6, the Project window organizes the components of the Normal project into folders named Forms, Modules, and Microsoft Word Objects.

Press Ctrl+R or choose Project Explorer from the View menu if this window isn't showing in the Visual Basic Editor.

FIGURE 29-6.

The Project window shows the module components of a Visual Basic project. Macros are stored in the NewMacros module.

If the Modules folder is closed, click the plus sign (+) just to its left to open it and view its contents. You'll see that it contains a module named NewMacros. This is the default location of all recorded macro procedures that you store in a template. (If your Project window doesn't include a Forms folder, choose User Form from the Insert menu and one will be created.)

Finding a Macro in the Code Window

The Code window lists every macro that you've added to a document or template. If you have added a lot of macros, you may have to scroll through the window quite a ways to find the one you want. But if you're not in the middle of editing another macro in the Code window, you can locate a particular macro easily through the Macros dialog box. To locate it, do the following:

1 Click the Minimize button on Visual Basic Editor's title bar or click the Word document button in the Windows taskbar to return to your Word document.

2 Point to Macro on the Tools menu, and choose Macros. You'll see the Macros dialog box, which contains a list of the macros stored in the current document or document template.

3 Select the macro you want to edit and click the Edit button. Word opens the Visual Basic Editor and moves the insertion point to the beginning of that macro's code in the Code window.

If you switch to the Visual Basic Editor and you don't see the Code window, you can select your macro projects and display them in the Code window at the same time. To view the Code window, do the following:

1 Open the Project Explorer, and then open the Modules folder in the Normal project.

2 Double click the NewMacros entry in the list. Visual Basic opens the code window.

As an alternative, choose Code from the View menu in the Visual Basic Editor. You can resize the Code window just as you would any other window.

Enhancing a Macro with Functions and Decisions

So far, we have used the Visual Basic Code window only to examine the lines of the Letterhead macro and to figure out how the procedure is organized. But one of the primary reasons to use Visual Basic in Word is to revise macros—to change the way they work or to incorporate them into a larger programming project.

For example, suppose we want to add a simple dialog box to the basic Letterhead macro that appears when the Letterhead macro runs. The dialog box will offer a choice between inserting a partial heading that includes only the name and address and inserting a complete heading that also includes phone numbers and an e-mail address. We can easily add the necessary dialog box with another Visual Basic tool called a *function*. We can then have the macro interpret the choice the user made in the dialog box with a *decision statement*.

About Functions

A function is a procedure that performs a defined task within a program and then provides the program with a relevant item of information. In our Letterhead macro, we'll add a function called MsgBox. It will ask the user to make a choice and then it will relay that choice back to the program within a *decision statement* that tells Word how to interpret the user's choice.

To use a function, you write a statement that invokes, or *calls,* the function by name. When the function's task is complete, the function returns a value to the program—that is, it provides an item of data: a number, a text string, or some other type of value.

Using Automatic Macros

There are five automatic macros that run on their own whenever a document is opened or closed or whenever you perform other Word operations. You can make a macro run automatically by giving it a special automatic macro (or automacro) name when you create it. Each automacro name causes the macro to run at a different time. Here's a brief description:

- **AutoNew** runs automatically when you create a new document based on a template containing the macro.

- **AutoOpen** runs automatically when the document containing it is opened.

- **AutoClose** runs automatically when the document containing it is closed.

- **AutoExec** runs automatically when you start Word.

- **AutoExit** runs automatically when you exit Word.

You can also use these macro names within more complex Visual Basic procedures. *For more information about using these special macros in Visual Basic, look up "Auto Macros" in the Visual Basic Help file.*

In Visual Basic you can learn to write functions of your own or you can make use of its large library of built-in functions. MsgBox is one of Visual Basic's most useful built-in functions. Before we get into actually editing our macro, let's take a closer look at how the MsgBox function and decision statements are used in Visual Basic.

About the MsgBox Function

The MsgBox function is a convenient tool for eliciting a simple response from the user while a macro is running. Here's how the function works:

1   The MsgBox function displays a message box on the desktop. The box typically contains a line or so of text, and it may also contain one or more command buttons. For example, the message box might contain a Yes button and a No button: the text in the box will ask a question, and the user can click Yes or No to answer it. This is how we'll use the MsgBox function when we enhance the Letterhead macro.

2   After the user clicks a button on the message box, the function returns a numeric value describing which button was clicked (0 = No and 1 = Yes, for example). The box then disappears from the desktop, and the action of the MsgBox function is complete.

3   The statement that made the call to the MsgBox function receives the numeric value from the function. Now the program knows which button the user clicked inside the message box.

The message box that we'll add to the Letterhead macro contains a simple question with Yes and No buttons. If you click Yes, this information will be included; if you click No, the heading will contain only the name and address. A sample of this message box is shown in Figure 29-7.

FIGURE 29-7.

The MsgBox function displays a prompt on the screen.

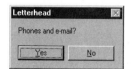

Of course, to carry out this new option, it's up to you to make sure that your Letterhead macro uses the MsgBox function correctly. Let's add the function to the Letterhead macro to see how the process works.

Writing a Function Statement

In Visual Basic, a function call consists of the function's name followed by a specific list of *arguments* enclosed in parentheses. The function call looks like this:

```
FunctionName(argument1, argument2, argument3, …)
```

To control the way the function works, you specify the arguments. But different functions require different arguments, and you'll need to know the argument format for each function you use.

Learning More about Functions

Visual Basic has lots of functions, and you will have to gain some experience before you can remember the arguments and usage for the functions you'll use frequently. To look up a function, type the name of the function in the Code window and press F1. The Visual Basic Editor opens the Help window and provides the information you need. For example, the help page for the MsgBox function looks like this:

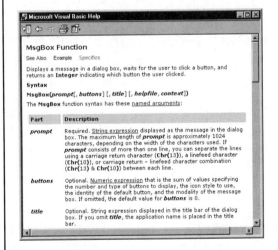

When a function has optional arguments—that is, arguments that you can omit if you don't need them in your particular application—they are shown in square brackets like the buttons, title, and help file options above.

For our MsgBox function, we'll use the following argument format:

```
MsgBox(prompt, buttons, title)
```

In this syntax, *prompt* is the text string that will be displayed inside the message box; *buttons* is a code that indicates which set of buttons you want to include inside the message box; and *title* is the text string that will appear on the title bar of the message box. We want the message box to ask whether the user wants to include phones and e-mail information and to offer Yes and No buttons. We'll use "Letterhead" as the title for the message box. As a result, the MsgBox function call in our macro should read:

```
MsgBox("Phones and e-mail?", vbYesNo, "Letterhead")
```

The first and third arguments, *prompt* and *title*, are text values that you supply, enclosed in quotation marks. Each argument is separated from the next by a comma; note that the comma appears *outside* of the quotation marks between the first and second argument. Conveniently, you can write the second argument simply as vbYesNo. This is a Visual Basic *constant*—in this case, a constant that represents the correct numeric code for Yes and No buttons.

Writing a Decision Statement

Although we have now worked out the syntax for the MsgBox function statement, there's another issue to deal with before the message box will work properly. A function call in Visual Basic may not stand alone as a statement by itself—something has to be done with the value it returns. Since a function returns a value to the procedure that calls it in the first place, the function call must be part of a larger statement, one that makes some specific use of the return value.

In the Letterhead macro, the purpose of the MsgBox function is to find out whether the phone numbers and e-mail address should be included in the heading. This involves a decision: if the user clicks the Yes button, the program should include the additional information; if the user clicks No, the heading should end after the address.

Visual Basic's If statement allows your program to choose a course of action depending upon the outcome of a particular condition. You can use the If statement in several versatile formats, as outlined in the Visual Basic Help window shown in Figure 29-8 on the next page.

FIGURE 29-8.

Visual Basic's If statement can be used in several different formats, depending on the needs of a particular application.

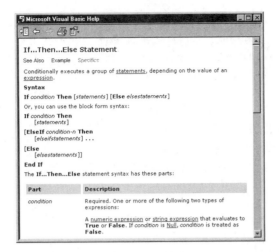

If you don't want the program to do anything in the event of an Else situation, you simply leave that part of the statement blank. We want the macro to do nothing if the condition is not met, so the statement in our Letterhead macro is formatted like this:

```
If condition Then
    Statement
    Statement
    ...
End If
```

This is known as a decision *structure*, because the If and End If statements serve as markers for the beginning and end of a block of code. You can insert any number of statements between If and End If.

The *condition* in the If statement is an expression that Visual Basic can evaluate as either True or False:

- If the condition is True, all the statements between If and End If are performed. The program then continues to perform any statements that appear after End If.

- If the condition is False, the program skips all the statements between If and End If without performing any of them. The program then goes on to execute any statements after End If.

In the Letterhead macro, the condition to be determined is whether or not the user has clicked the Yes button in the message box. If the return value from the MsgBox function indicates that the user has clicked Yes, the macro should perform all the statements that provide the phone numbers and the e-mail address. But if the MsgBox function indicates that the user has clicked No, all of these statements should be skipped. Here's how to express this decision:

```
If MsgBox("Phones and e-mail?", vbYesNo,
    "Letterhead") = vbYes Then
  ...
End If
```

In other words, if the call to MsgBox returns a value of vbYes—another Visual Basic constant, this time representing the code for a click of the Yes button—the statements between If and End If should be performed; otherwise they'll be skipped.

About Control Structures

The If statement falls into a category of programming features known as *control structures*. The default flow of control for a procedure in Visual Basic is simply from one statement to the next, starting at the beginning of the procedure and continuing to the end. A control structure, however, creates a departure from this line-by-line flow. In the Letterhead macro, for example, a False If decision causes the macro to skip an entire block of code.

A *loop* is another kind of control structure. A loop structure contains instructions for a specified block of code to repeat itself for a particular number of *iterations*. The number of repetitions in a loop can be specified by a number or by a condition that indicates when the looping should stop. For example, when you click the Replace All button on the Find And Replace dialog box to replace one word with another throughout a document in Word, a loop condition tells Word to repeatedly find and replace the word until all of its occurrences have been changed. When all of the occurrences have been changed, this condition causes Word to display a message box reporting the number of changes made.

The Visual Basic keywords for loop structures are For and Do. To learn more about looping, press F1 in the Visual Basic Editor and search for "loops" in the Help file.

Editing the Macro Code

You can edit macro statements right inside the Code window by using the basic text-handling features available in any word processor. You can easily select, insert, and delete lines of code, perform cut-and-paste and copy-and-paste operations, and edit the content of individual lines.

To see how easy it is to edit a macro, let's add the MsgBox function and its supporting decision statement to the Letterhead macro:

1 Press Alt+F11 to open the Visual Basic Editor if it's not showing on your screen.

2 If necessary, use the Project Explorer window to locate the NewMacros module in the Normal project, and then double-click the module name to open the Code window.

3 Find the Selection.TypeText statement that produces the second line of the address, the one containing the city, state, and postal code. Just beneath this line are two Selection.TypeParagraph statements. Move the insertion point to the end of the second of these TypeParagraph statements and press the Enter key twice. This makes room for the new If statement that we're about to add.

4 Insert a two-space indent in front of each of the final eight Selection statements. This indent is simply a visual indication that these statements are part of a decision block.

5 Move the insertion point back up to the blank line just before the first indented statement. This area of the Code window should now look like this:

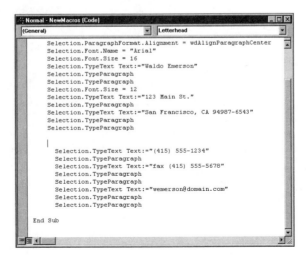

6 Type *If MsgBox (*. As soon as you type the opening parenthesis
for the MsgBox function, Visual Basic's automatic Quick Info feature pops up to show the entire syntax of the MsgBox function,
as shown here:

```
If MsgBox(
    S MsgBox(Prompt, [Buttons As VbMsgBoxStyle = vbOKOnly], [Title], [HelpFile], [Context])
    S As VbMsgBoxResult
    Selection.TypeText Text:="fax (415) 555-5678"
    Selection.TypeParagraph
    Selection.TypeParagraph
    Selection.TypeText Text:="wemerson@domain.com"
    Selection.TypeParagraph
    Selection.TypeParagraph
```

   QuickInfo is an instant reference to syntax for any built-in
function that you begin entering in the Code window. The Visual
Basic Editor watches as you type in the Code window and offers
other help as you go.

7 Continue typing to enter the Prompt argument so the statement
reads:

```
If MsgBox("Phones and e-mail?",
```

8 After you type the comma to separate the Prompt argument
from the next argument, Visual Basic knows you'll need a Buttons argument next, and it displays a list of constants you can
choose for the Buttons argument, as seen here:

9 Scroll to the bottom of the list and click vbYesNo, and then type
a comma to indicate that you're ready to enter the next argument. Visual Basic automatically enters vbYesNo as the second
argument.

10 Type the Title argument *"Letterhead"* within quotation marks, and
then type the closing parenthesis and an equal sign so the statement reads:

```
If MsgBox("Phones and e-mail?", vbYesNo,
    "Letterhead") =
```

11 The Quick Info feature offers a menu of Visual Basic constants representing possible return values from the MsgBox function:

```
If MsgBox("Phones and e-mail?",vbYesNo,"Letterhead")=
    Selection.TypeText Text:="(415) 555-1234"
    Selection.TypeParagraph
    Selection.TypeText Text:="fax (415) 555-5678"
    Selection.TypeParagraph
    Selection.TypeParagraph
    Selection.TypeText Text:="wemerson@domain.com"
    Selection.TypeParagraph
    Selection.TypeParagraph
```

```
vbAbort
vbCancel
vbIgnore
vbNo
vbOK
vbRetry
vbYes
```

12 Choose the last entry on the menu, vbYes, and then press the spacebar once.

13 Type the final keyword of this line, *Then*, and press Enter to complete the entry. It should now read like this:

```
If MsgBox("Phones and e-mail?", vbYesNo,
    "Letterhead")= vbYes Then
```

14 Move the insertion point down near the end of the procedure, just above the End Sub line. Press Enter to make room for a new line of code and enter it as "End If." The decision statement within the Letterhead procedure now looks like the example shown here.

```
If MsgBox ("Phones and e-mail?", vbYesNo,
    "Letterhead") = vbYes Then
  Selection.TypeText Text:="(415) 555-1234"
  Selection.TypeParagraph
  Selection.TypeText Text:="fax (415) 555-5678"
  Selection.TypeParagraph
  Selection.TypeParagraph
  Selection.TypeTextText:=wemerson@domain.com
  Selection.TypeParagraph
  Selection.TypeParagraph
 End If
End Sub
```

In the revised code, the statements located between If and End If are neatly indented. That's because you inserted two spaces in front of each one back in Step 4. Visual Basic doesn't require this indentation; it's just a way to make the code a little more readable. Similarly, the space between the comma and the vbYesNo constant in the statement is optional.

You've now completed this revision of the Letterhead macro. The next step is to switch back to Word and try running the macro.

V

Data Automation Tools

Testing the Macro

To return to Word from the Visual Basic Editor, choose Close and Return to Microsoft Word from the File menu or press Alt+Q. When you exit the Visual Basic Editor, any changes you've made to a macro are saved in the Normal template.

> To save macro changes as you work in the Visual Basic Editor, choose Save Normal from the File menu.

Once you're back in Word, you'll see the original document in which you recorded the first macro steps, but you'll want to try the macro out in a new document. Here's how to test the macro:

1. Open a new document based on the Normal template.

2. Press Alt+L to run the Letterhead macro. The macro enters your name and address at the top of the document and then displays the Letterhead message box as shown in Figure 29-9.

FIGURE 29-9.

The macro code's MsgBox function produces a decision box when the macro runs in Word.

3. Click Yes to complete the heading with phone numbers and an e-mail address, or click No to display only the name and address on the current document. The message box disappears as soon as you click a button.

Debugging a Macro

If the macro doesn't work because you mistyped something, you'll know it right away. Word will open the Visual Basic Editor and highlight the problematic statement in the macro inside the Code window. You can then use options on the Debug menu to figure out what's wrong.

TIP

If you select a macro in the Macros dialog box and click the Step Into button, Word also opens the Visual Basic Editor and highlights that macro's name in the Code window. Then, by choosing Step Into from the Debug menu in the Visual Basic Editor, you can have Word move from command to command to see how each command affects your document.

Debugging is a science unto itself, but you can learn about it by looking up "debugging" in the Visual Basic Help window.

Creating a Custom Dialog Box

As you may recall, Figure 29-3 on page 674 shows a custom dialog box that gives you even greater flexibility in producing a letterhead for a particular document. To create a custom dialog box like the one in Figure 29-3, you use a Visual Basic *form.* Specifically, this form offers the options of including or omitting any of the four elements of the heading: the name, the address, the phone numbers, and the e-mail address.

About Visual Basic Forms

In Visual Basic, you can always add new forms to the Forms folder in the Normal project. Like the macros you store in the Normal template, forms in this location are available globally—that is, they are available wherever you wish to use them in Word. Sometimes you may want to develop general-purpose forms that will be useful in any number of macros you create. In other cases, such as our present situation, you'll create a form for a single, specific macro.

Adding a Form

To begin creating the custom dialog box, you must create a form that will contain the command button and check boxes for the dialog box. To create a form, do the following:

1 Press Alt+F11 to switch to the Visual Basic Editor if you're in Word.

2 If you don't immediately see the Project Explorer window, press Ctrl+R to open it.

3 Select Normal in the list of projects in the Project Explorer.

4 Choose UserForm from the Insert menu. Visual Basic adds a form to the Normal project and displays the new, empty form on the screen inside the Project window. (When you create a form, the Project window replaces the Code window in the Visual Basic Editor.)

When you examine the Project Explorer, you may find that your Normal project already has a Forms folder containing a form called UserForm1 to develop the Letterhead dialog box.

If this is the first form you've created, its initial name is UserForm1, as shown in Figure 29-10.

5 Click the form. You'll also see the Toolbox palette, which contains controls you can select and add to the new form.

6 Double-click the (Name) property in the Properties window, enter "frmLetterhead" as the new name of the form, and press the Enter key. This new name now appears inside the Project window. As you'll discover shortly, the purpose of the Name property is to give the form a unique identifier that will be used in creating code.

7 Select the Caption property and enter *"Letterhead"* as the new setting. This caption now appears in the title bar of the form.

Now you're ready to place controls on the Letterhead form.

FIGURE 29-10.

A new form is stored in the Forms folder for the template in the Project Explorer window.

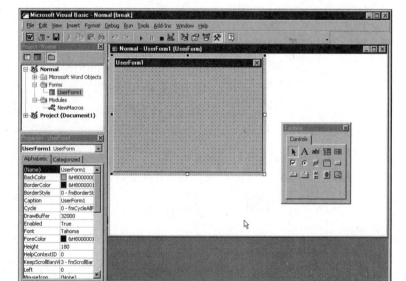

Arranging Objects on Visual Basic Forms

When it comes to arranging and aligning objects on a form in the Visual Basic Editor, you have many of the same options that you have when you work with graphics in Word documents:

- You can select multiple objects by holding down Shift while you click them.

- The form has a built-in grid, and each of the dots in it is a grid point to which objects snap when you drag them.

- The Align submenu on the Format menu allows you to quickly align objects to the grid or to themselves.

- You can group or ungroup objects.

- You can automatically size objects or arrange several of them in a line along the bottom or right side of the form.

Check out the options on the Format menu in the Visual Basic Editor. You'll find a lot of commands that make form layouts a breeze. *For more information about manipulating graphic objects, see Chapter 19, "Drawing and Manipulating Graphics."*

V

Data Automation Tools

Using Controls to Design the Form

As shown in Figure 29-3 on page 674, the form will have a total of five controls: four check boxes and one command button. It takes only a few minutes to add these controls to the form by using the Toolbox palette.

1 Click inside the form to display the Toolbox palette, if necessary.

2 Click the CheckBox button on the Toolbox palette, and then click the upper-left corner of the Letterhead form to place the first check box control in the form, as shown here:

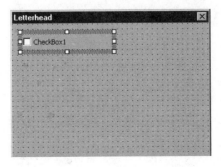

The control's default name is CheckBox1, but you'll change this later with the Properties window.

3   Repeat Step 1 three times to add CheckBox2, CheckBox3, and CheckBox4 below CheckBox1.

 SEE ALSO

For more information about arranging items on forms, see "Arranging Objects on Visual Basic Forms" on the previous page.

4   Using commands on the Align submenu, arrange the four check boxes in a column at the left side of the form.

5   Click the CommandButton control on the Toolbox palette and click below the column of check boxes in the form. A control called CommandButton1 appears beneath the check boxes, as seen here:

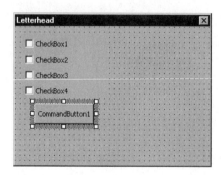

6   With CommandButton1 still selected as the active control, select the Name property in the Properties window and change it to *cmdHeading*.

7   Select the Caption property and change it to *Create Heading*. The new caption appears across the face of the command button, as seen here:

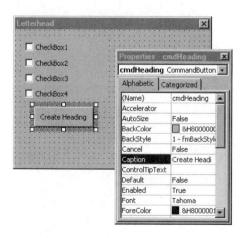

The Properties window has been moved next to the command button in this example to show it more clearly.

⭐ **TIP**

> Select a button and choose Size To Fit from the Format menu to automatically resize the button to accommodate any caption.

8 Select each of the four check box controls in turn and enter new settings for their Name and Caption properties in the Properties window, as indicated in Table 29-1.

TABLE 29-1. New Properties for the Letterhead Form

Original Check Box Name	New Name Property	New Caption Property
CheckBox1	chkName	Include name
CheckBox2	chkAddress	Include address
CheckBox3	chkPhones	Include phones
CheckBox4	chkEmail	Include e-mail address

9 Select the entire form object by clicking its title bar, and then drag one of its corner selection handles to eliminate wasted space. The resized form should be about the same size as the one in Figure 29-3 on page 674.

We have now completed the first two steps in traditional Visual Basic project development: we have designed a form by adding controls to it and arranging them, and we have changed selected properties of the controls. The third step in the process is writing code to handle specific events that occur when the form is used. In this case, however, we already have a sequence of code—the code from our edited macro—that we can move to the form module and then revise for use in this new context. Let's do just that.

Preparing Code for the Form

Under our plan for revising the macro, the Letterhead dialog box will open when the macro is run. The user decides which lines of text will be included in the letterhead by selecting one or more of the four check boxes in the dialog box. When the user clicks the Create Heading

V

Data Automation Tools

button, the macro inserts the selected lines. Here are the main issues we need to take care of when revising the code:

- The macro procedure itself will have the task of opening the Letterhead dialog box. Once the dialog box is open, its code controls the program until the action is complete.

- Because the macro must respond to the Create Heading button, we have to move the existing macro code that actually inserts text into a particular event procedure related to the Letterhead form. Specifically, the cmdHeading_Click procedure will be performed when the user clicks the Create Heading button. All the text entry is initiated by this one event procedure.

- We need to add four decision structures inside the cmd_Heading Click procedure. These will allow the procedure to determine which lines of the text to write to the document, based on the four check box settings. When a box is checked, the procedure writes the line.

Even though this design is a big departure from the actions of the original macro, the coding portion of this project is relatively simple. Using the Code window, we'll move a large block of code from the original macro procedure to the cmdHeading_Click procedure. Then we'll write a new line of code to open the dialog box in the macro procedure. Finally, we'll add a sequence of decision statements in the cmdHeading_Click procedure to handle the text entry correctly.

Here are the steps for implementing this new code design:

1 If necessary, press Ctrl+R to open the Project Explorer.

2 Open the Modules folder in the Normal project and double-click the NewMacros entry to open the corresponding Code window.

? SEE ALSO

For a refresher on how the original code looked after you recorded the macro, check Figure 29-5 on page 676.

3 In the Letterhead procedure, select and delete the If and End If statements that you wrote during the previous exercise. Also, delete any blank lines and indents that set off the decision statement so that the code looks the same as it did when you initially recorded the macro.

4 Select everything in the Code window from the beginning of the Selection.Font.Size statement down to the final Selection statement, as shown in the figure at the top of the next page.

```
Sub Letterhead()
'
' Letterhead Macro
' Enters letterhead information at the top of a new document.
'
    Selection.ParagraphFormat.Alignment = wdAlignParagraphCenter
    Selection.Font.Name = "Arial"
    Selection.Font.Size = 16
    Selection.TypeText Text:="Waldo Emerson"
    Selection.TypeParagraph
    Selection.TypeParagraph
    Selection.Font.Size = 12
    Selection.TypeText Text:="123 Main Street"
    Selection.TypeParagraph
    Selection.TypeText Text:="San Francisco, CA 94987-6543"
    Selection.TypeParagraph
    Selection.TypeParagraph
    Selection.TypeText Text:="(415) 555-1234"
    Selection.TypeParagraph
    Selection.TypeText Text:="fax (415) 555-5678"
    Selection.TypeParagraph
    Selection.TypeParagraph
    Selection.TypeText Text:="wemerson@domain.com"
    Selection.TypeParagraph
    Selection.TypeParagraph

End Sub
```

> **NOTE**

The first two Selection statements in the macro can stay where they are, because they control formatting for every line that could possibly be inserted.

5 Press Ctrl+X to remove these lines from the macro procedure and to copy them to the Clipboard.

6 Enter "frmLetterhead.Show" as seen here:

```
Sub Letterhead()
' Letterhead Macro
' Enters letterhead information at the top of a
' new document.
    Selection.ParagraphFormat.Alignment =
        wdAlignParagraphCenter
    Selection.Font.Name = "Arial"
    frmLetterhead.Show
End Sub
```

> **NOTE**

If you see a QuickInfo box after typing the period after "frmLetterhead", click the Show method name to enter it in the statement.

V

Data Automation Tools

This statement uses the Show method to load and display the Letterhead dialog box and to give it control of the program. Notice that since we cut out the decision statement's code, the entire Letterhead macro now contains only three statements: two to perform formatting tasks and the third to display the Letterhead form as a dialog box.

7 Double-click the Letterhead form in the Project Explorer window to once again display the form. Once you see the form, double-click the Create Heading command button to view its code.

> **NOTE**

In the Visual Basic Editor, double-clicking a control in a form opens the default event procedure for that control in the Code window. For a command button the default event is Click, so the Code window will display the first and last lines (Sub and End Sub) of the cmdHeading_Click procedure.

8 Click between the Private Sub and End Sub lines inside the Code window to place the insertion point inside the procedure, and then press Ctrl+V to paste the code from the Clipboard into the procedure. The result is shown below.

```
Private Sub cmdHeading_Click()
  Selection.Font.Size = 16
  Selection.TypeParagraph
  Selection.TypeParagraph
  Selection.Font.Size = 12
  Selection.TypeText Text:="123 Main Street"
  Selection.TypeParagraph
  Selection.TypeText Text:="San Francisco, CA
      94987-6543"
  Selection.TypeParagraph
  Selection.TypeParagraph
  Selection.TypeText Text:="(415) 555-1234"
  Selection.TypeParagraph
  Selection.TypeText Text:="fax (415) 555-5678"
  Selection.TypeParagraph
  Selection.TypeParagraph
  Selection.TypeTextText:="wemerson@domain.com"
  Selection.TypeParagraph
  Selection.TypeParagraph
End Sub
```

The final task in revising this macro is to organize the check box control code into a sequence of four decision structures, as shown in Figure 29-11, so the macro knows how to interpret user selections from each check box on the form.

FIGURE 29-11.

These decision structures in the macro code tell Word how to respond to check box options in the Letterhead dialog box.

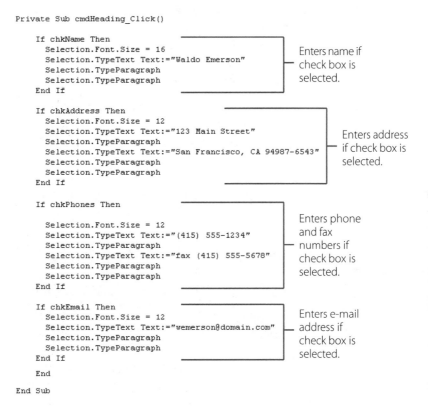

```
Private Sub cmdHeading_Click()

    If chkName Then
        Selection.Font.Size = 16
        Selection.TypeText Text:="Waldo Emerson"
        Selection.TypeParagraph
        Selection.TypeParagraph
    End If

    If chkAddress Then
        Selection.Font.Size = 12
        Selection.TypeText Text:="123 Main Street"
        Selection.TypeParagraph
        Selection.TypeText Text:="San Francisco, CA 94987-6543"
        Selection.TypeParagraph
        Selection.TypeParagraph
    End If

    If chkPhones Then

        Selection.Font.Size = 12
        Selection.TypeText Text:="(415) 555-1234"
        Selection.TypeParagraph
        Selection.TypeText Text:="fax (415) 555-5678"
        Selection.TypeParagraph
        Selection.TypeParagraph
    End If

    If chkEmail Then
        Selection.Font.Size = 12
        Selection.TypeText Text:="wemerson@domain.com"
        Selection.TypeParagraph
        Selection.TypeParagraph
    End If

    End

End Sub
```

Enters name if check box is selected.

Enters address if check box is selected.

Enters phone and fax numbers if check box is selected.

Enters e-mail address if check box is selected.

9 To create decision structures for each check box option, insert *If* and *End If* statements at each end of the code that defines the name, the address, the phone number, and the e-mail address lines, as shown in Figure 29-11.

★ TIP

When you need to repeat the same line several times in a program, it's faster and more accurate to copy and paste than it is to retype it each time.

The controlling condition in each of the If statements is simply the name of the corresponding check box. In effect, the value of a given check box is True if the user has checked the box and False if the box is unchecked.

V

Data Automation Tools

NOTE

> Indents were added for visual clarity in Figure 29-11. Your Code window will look different if you don't add these indents.

10 Add new Selection.Font.Size = 12 statements at the top of the phone and e-mail portions of this procedure. Since each of these lines can now be selected separately in the dialog box, the macro must ensure the correct font size for each line. This new code is shown in Figure 29-11.

The original macro ended with an End statement (as do all Visual Basic procedures), and so the End statement at the end of this procedure terminates the macro once it has written the desired text to the document.

Testing the New Dialog Box

To make sure the new dialog box works properly, return to Word, create a new document, and press Alt+L. The Letterhead dialog box should appear as shown in Figure 29-12.

FIGURE 29-12.

The finished dialog box appears whenever you run the Letter-head macro.

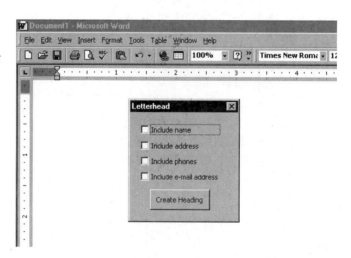

Try selecting several of the check boxes and then click the Create Heading button to see the result. The macro should enter only the parts of the heading text that you requested in the dialog box. If you see an error message at any time, use the Visual Basic Editor to debug the procedure. To test the macro fully, try selecting different sets of options in the dialog box to make sure they all work.

Adding a Digital Signature

In Word 2000, you can now verify your macros with a digital signature. As explained in "Preventing Macro Viruses" on page 663, Word 2000 can recognize macros that are "signed" with digital signatures and allow only those macros to run when a document is opened. You can add a digital signature to any Visual Basic project or macro to ensure that other users will have no trouble getting it to run on their computers.

> **NOTE**
>
> A digital signature is actually the code representation of your digital identity, but it is attached to a *digital certificate* that contains your name, the name of the agency that issued the signature, the expiration date, and other information. The terms "digital signature" and "digital certificate" are used interchangeably in Word, which is why you can choose the Digital Signature command from the Tools menu in the Visual Basic Editor to display the Select Certificate dialog box.

Getting a Digital Signature

> **SEE ALSO**
>
> For more information about digital signatures in general, see "Using Digital Signatures" on page 664.

There are three ways to get a digital signature:

- Create an *unauthenticated* digital signature for your own use or for sharing macros in a small workgroup.

- Get an *authenticated* digital signature from your company. Some organizations set up their own digital signature authorities to create digital signatures with tools such as Microsoft Certificate Server. Ask your network administrator or computer services department manager for information about this option.

- Get an authenticated digital signature from a commercial vendor like VeriSign, Inc. Your digital signature will come with instructions for installing it for use in Visual Basic.

> **NOTE**
>
> If your organization has restrictions on the use of digital signatures, you may not be allowed to create your own digital signature or sign your own macros.

Making Your Own Digital Signature

Microsoft Office includes a utility called Selfcert.exe that allows you to create your own, unauthenticated digital certificate. To create an unauthenticated digital certificate for self-signed projects, follow the steps on the next page.

V

Data Automation Tools

1 Close the Visual Basic editor and Microsoft Word.

2 Choose Run from the Windows Start menu.

3 Click the browse button and locate the Selfcert.exe program inside the C:\Program Files\Microsoft Office\Office folder.

> If you can't find the Selfcert.exe program, you need to install the Digital Signature For VBA Projects feature using Disc 1 of the Office program CD set. You'll find this feature inside the Office Tools category in the Setup program. *For more information about installing new features in Word, see "Customizing an Office Installation" on page 882.*

4 Select the program and click Open, and then click the OK button on the Run dialog box. The Selfcert program runs and displays a dialog box like the one shown below:

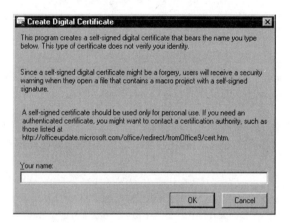

5 Type your name and any other identifying information you want in the Your Name box and then click OK. The program will create and install an unauthenticated signature that you can select with the Visual Basic Editor.

Adding a Signature to a Macro

Once you receive or create a digital signature and install it properly, it's easy to sign any macro or other Visual Basic project. To sign a macro or Visual Basic project, do the following:

1 Open the document or template that contains the macro or Visual Basic project you want to sign.

2 Open the Visual Basic Editor.

3 In the Project Explorer, select the project you want to sign.

 NOTE

> You affix a digital signature to a project rather than to an individual macro.

4 Choose Digital Signatures from the Tools menu. The Digital Signature dialog box shows which signature, if any, is currently attached to the project, and allows you to choose a signature, as seen below:

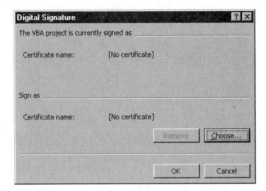

5 Click the Choose button to see a list of signatures that are currently installed. Figure 29-13 shows the Select Certificate dialog box with one certificate in it.

FIGURE 29-13.

You can install many different digital signatures in the Visual Basic Editor and then choose the one you want to sign each macro project.

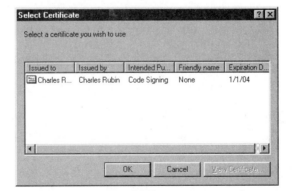

6 Select the digital signature you want to use and click OK.

7 Click OK again to close the Digital Signature dialog box.

Creating Forms

Many businesses use standard forms for the purpose of collecting data. These forms can include expense reports, employment applications, purchase order requests, and so on. But forms are valuable data-gathering tools for business and nonbusiness users alike. With Microsoft Word 2000, you can create elegant forms that efficiently gather the information you need. Not only can you can make printed forms, but you can also make electronic forms that other Word users fill out on the screen. In this chapter, you'll learn how easy it is to create forms with Word.

A *form* collects specific data by requiring the user to fill out data fields and labels, so you must create and arrange those fields and labels when you create a form. You can create three types of forms with Word:

- Printed forms that are distributed on paper and filled in by hand.

- Electronic forms that are distributed as Word documents and filled out on the screen.

- 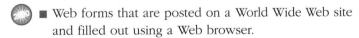 Web forms that are posted on a World Wide Web site and filled out using a Web browser.

In this chapter, we'll look at printed and electronic forms; Word has a separate group of tools used to design forms for Web pages. *For more information about Web forms, see "Making Web Forms" on page 805.*

The point of a form is to capture accurate data in a systematic way. This means creating the right fields and arranging them in such a way that it's obvious to the user just which data you want. You have the same flexibility in laying out forms as you do with other documents in Word. You can create a basic layout for the form and then add text, graphics, or fields.

? SEE ALSO

For more information about ActiveX controls, see "Using ActiveX Controls" on page 722.

When creating either a printed or electronic form, you can use the Forms toolbar to add fields to it. If the form is electronic, however, the fields you add with the Forms toolbar work like other electronic fields, such as the options in Word dialog boxes. For example, in an electronic form containing a drop-down list field, clicking that field displays a list of options that you can choose for that field. Providing a predefined list of choices for users is a great way to improve the accuracy and consistency of the data you gather, but Word offers even more. You can add macros or ActiveX controls to automate the form even further. For example, a macro might save the data from a completed form automatically when the user closes it.

Creating Printed Forms

Every well-designed form has a structure, and if it's structure you want, Word's table features are just the ticket. When you begin your form by using a table, you can use the table's cells as places to put data fields and their labels. And thanks to the flexibility you have with tables, you can hide or show cell borders, resize rows, columns, or individual cells, and split or merge cells to arrange fields and present them any way you want. Figure 30-1 shows a check request form that was laid out in a table.

FIGURE 30-1.

You can use any of Word's formatting tools to create efficient, attractive forms for work or pleasure.

Bees' Knees Knitting Company
CHECK REQUEST FORM

Date of Request:	/ /	Date Check Needed:	/ /
Person Requesting:		Department:	
Check Date:	/ /	Check Amount:	$
Check Payable To:			
Expense Type:	Travel ☐ Entertainment ☐ Supplies ☐ Services ☐ Other ☐
Reason for Expense:	
	Authorized Signature:

? SEE ALSO

For more information about working with tables, see Chapter 17, "Working with Tables." For more information about basic formatting, see Chapter 5, "Using Basic Formatting Tools."

Figure 30-1 is essentially a four-column table, but some of its rows have been resized, some of its cells have been merged and resized, and the vertical text alignment has been changed in some cells. The Expense Type check boxes were added with the Forms toolbar. Most of the techniques required to create this form have been covered elsewhere in this book, but we'll look at them here in the context of creating a form.

Creating a Form

As with any document that has a fairly complex format, it's a good idea to sketch the form on paper before you begin. If you're adapting a pre-existing paper form, use a copy of it it as a guide. Next, use Word to create a table that duplicates the layout you have sketched, and then fill it in.

Here are the basic steps you would take to create the form in Figure 30-1:

1 Create a new blank document.

2 Choose Page Setup from the File menu and reset the page margins to 0.5 inch on every side. You can change the table's overall size or its cell borders later, but it's a good idea to give yourself as much room on the page as possible.

3 Choose Options from the Tools menu, click the View tab if necessary, and select the Text Boundaries check box in the Print and Web Layout Options area so you can see the margins.

4 Right-click in any toolbar and choose Forms from the shortcut menu. You'll see the Forms toolbar like this:

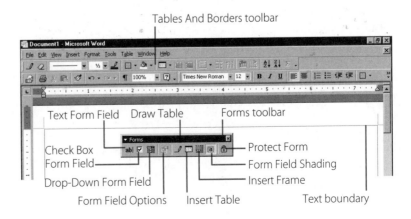

V

Data Automation Tools

In this example, the Tables And Borders toolbar is also shown at the top of the screen—Word displays this automatically when you draw a table.

5   Click the Draw Table tool and draw a rectangle of the table's outline just inside the top, left, and right text boundaries and about halfway down the page. The table is now one giant cell, so you need to draw dividing lines to break it up into rows and columns.

6   Draw a series of lines completely across or down the table to create the basic structure of four columns and nine rows shown in Figure 30-1.

TIP

You can also use the Table command from the Insert submenu on the Table menu to create a new table.

7   Click the Eraser tool in the Tables And Borders toolbar and click on cell dividing lines to merge some of the cells as shown in Figure 30-1. Click the Eraser tool when you're done to switch it off.

8   Enter the form title and the field labels into the appropriate cells. Don't worry about the font or alignment settings for this text for now.

9   In row 7, column 2, enter *Travel* as the label for the first expense type option, press the spacebar, and then click the Check Box Form Field button on the Forms toolbar to add a check box. Word adds the check box. Figure 30-2 shows an example in which the text has been reformatted as 12-point Times New Roman.

FIGURE 30-2.

Use the Forms toolbar to add a check box.

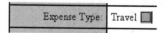

The check box is inserted as an inline graphic, so it can be moved or formatted with text formatting options. In addition, the field is shaded, but you can turn off field shading by clicking the Form Field Shading button on the Forms toolbar.

TIP

Clicking the Form Field Shading button on the Forms toolbar turns shading on or off for all fields in a form. To shade some of the fields on a form but not others, apply shading to individual cells in the table.

10   Repeat the previous step for the other expense categories in this cell.

11   Select cells, rows, or columns and set the font and size options for them using the Formatting toolbar. As you resize text, notice that the check boxes you added are resized along with the text in row 7.

12   Select text as needed and align it using the alignment button on the Tables And Borders toolbar. The button's default setting is Align Top Left, but you can click the arrow button next to it to display a palette of options. You can even center text vertically in a cell if you like.

13   Drag the remaining cell borders to adjust the sizes of the field label and field data cells. If necessary, resize the whole table to make it fit better on the page.

14   Click in the cell in the lower-left corner and use the Borders tool in the Tables And Borders toolbar to add both diagonal borders to it. This will create the "X" shown in Figure 30-1 on page 706.

15   Select each of the date fields and add the date dividing lines, either by typing slash characters with the keyboard or by drawing them with the Line tool on the Drawing toolbar.

16   Add cell shading or change the widths or styles of cell or table borders, if you like, by using either the Tables And Borders toolbar or the Borders And Shading dialog box.

⭐ **TIP**

When you apply shading with the Borders And Shading dialog box, make sure the Apply To menu has the correct setting (Table or Cell).

That's all there is to it. As you design printed forms of your own, you can experiment with these and other features. Here are some other things to try:

■   If you don't want to work with a table, try using the Insert Frame button on the Forms toolbar. Just click the Insert Frame button and then draw an outline for the frame to indicate its

V

Data Automation Tools

size. You can then add one or more fields inside the frame. By arranging two or more frames in the document, you will have more flexibility in positioning data field areas.

> Frames are always inserted as inline graphics. If you use the Insert Frame button in the middle of the table, the frame will divide the table in half. *For more information about formatting frames, see "Converting a Text Box to a Frame" on page 441.*

SEE ALSO

For more information about inserting graphics, see Chapter 19, "Drawing and Manipulating Graphics."

- Add graphics by dragging floating graphics on top of blank spaces in the form or by clicking in any cell and adding them in the text layer.

- Add extra rows or columns to a table and then hide their borders to add extra space between parts of the form.

Using Merge Fields in Printed Forms

If you use forms to report delinquent accounts or similar information to individual customers, you can use Word's Mail Merge features to produce personalized documents quickly and easily. Figure 30-3 shows a past due form with merge fields in it.

FIGURE 30-3.

You can use Mail Merge features with a form to create monthly invoices or other routine documents.

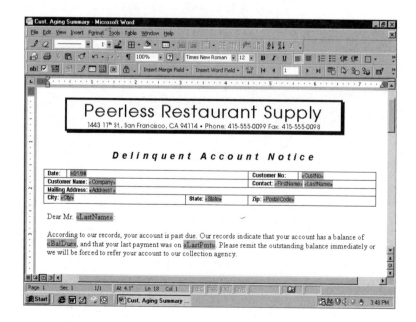

Here are the basic steps:

1 Create the form with data field labels only.

2 Choose Mail Merge from the Tools menu and use the Mail Merge Helper to convert the form to a main document.

3 Use the Mail Merge Helper to select your accounts receivable database or another data source. (You may need to select records from the database for each monthly run.)

4 Insert merge fields for the customer-specific data you want to appear on each merge document.

5 Perform the merge.

? SEE ALSO

For more information on mail merge, see Chapter 26, "Using Mail Merge."

You can use this technique to create personalized forms of all kinds, from monthly performance evaluations to student grade reports and service club assignments. Microsoft Word will take you wherever your imagination wants to go.

Creating Electronic Forms

When you create a form that will be filled out on the screen in Word, you can use automated form fields to make the form easier to complete. Such fields not only guide the user in supplying information, but also help ensure that the information is correct. You can also add macros or ActiveX controls to perform much more sophisticated data handling, and you can even add online Help to the forms you create.

Since you will use Word to create an electronic form that will also be filled out using Word, you must use two special techniques to prevent the form's users from changing it.

- Create each electronic form as a template rather than as a Word document. That way it will display empty fields each time users open it.

? SEE ALSO

For more information about protecting forms, see "Protecting a Form" on page 725.

- Protect the form to prevent users from changing its text, layout, or field properties. When a form is protected, it works as a form: its fields drop down or change states when clicked and its text boxes accept data entries. When you design a form, however, it is unprotected, which lets you insert text, add fields, and format it properly.

Planning a New Form

? SEE ALSO

For more information about the Control Toolbox toolbar, see "The Control Toolbox Toolbar" on page 723.

As with a printed form, the best way to launch a new electronic form is to have a basic design in mind before you begin laying it out in Word. It also helps if you know in general which kinds of fields and other automated features you can add to a form. For example, if you know you can present instructions in a Help window that appears when the form is opened, you won't have to leave space for those instructions on the form itself. Before you start designing, skim through this chapter and check out the tools on the Forms and Control Toolbox toolbars.

Creating a Form Template

Because you will distribute your form electronically, you want to create it as a template. That way, each new form document will contain blank data fields. To create a new template, follow these steps:

1   Choose New from the File menu to display the New dialog box.

2   Select a document template on which to base the new form (usually the Blank Document template).

 TIP

> If you're creating a form whose contents are similar to an existing one, select the existing form in the New dialog box and create a new template from it. Then you can simply modify the old form to suit your new purpose. See *"Modifying Templates" on page 255 for more information.*

3   Click the Template button on the lower-right corner of the New dialog box.

4   Click OK. Word creates a new template document.

Creating a Layout

You can create a basic layout for the new form in several ways: by using a table as described in "Creating Printed Forms" on page 706; by adding frames; or by simply entering text, adding fields, and arranging them with Word's other formatting tools. Since the form is electronic, you'll want to take advantage of the form fields on the Forms toolbar. You'll also need the Forms toolbar to protect the form whenever you want to view form fields as they will appear to the form's users. And if you're technically adventurous, you can also add macros and ActiveX controls to perform more sophisticated data handling.

Using Form Fields

The form fields that you add to a form with the Forms toolbar can be defined to present data entry options, instructions, or other information each time the end user clicks a field. You could insert the fields without defining them (as with the check box added to a printed form on page 708), but the main reason for using these fields in an electronic form is to add predefined data entry options or to help the user in other ways. These are the general steps for adding and defining any form field:

1 Place the field on the form by clicking its button on the Forms toolbar.

2 Double-click the field (or select the field and click the Form Field Options button on the Forms toolbar) to display its options dialog box.

3 Select field options in the dialog box and click OK to apply them.

Let's see how this works with each of the form fields.

Form Field Samples at Your Fingertips

To see how you might use check boxes, drop-down lists, and other fields or controls on the Forms or Control Toolbox toolbars, you need look no further than Word's own dialog boxes. Some of the more complex dialog boxes such as the Options, Style, or Page Setup dialog boxes contain examples of every type of form field you can add to a form.

Adding a Check Box Field

Check box fields are used to indicate yes/no or true/false decisions on an electronic form. To add a check box, do the following:

1 Move the insertion point to the place where you want the field to appear, usually to the left or right of the field name text.

2 Click the Check Box Form Field button on the Forms toolbar. The check box is added, as shown in Figure 30-2 on page 708.

You can reposition the box by dragging it to another location in the form's text, or copying and pasting it to other locations in your document.

To define the check box field, double-click it. Word opens the Check Box Form Field Options dialog box, as shown in Figure 30-4 on the next page.

FIGURE 30-4.

Use the Check Box Form Field Options dialog box to define the behavior of a check box field.

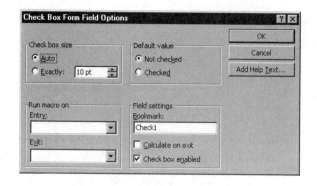

Setting Check Box Field Options

The Check Box Form Field Options dialog box lets you determine the behavior and appearance of the field. Many of these options are also available when you define other form fields. Here's what the options do:

- **Check Box Size** allows you to set a specific size for the box. With this set to Auto, which is the default, the box is resized to match the font size of the surrounding text.

- **Default Value** sets whether the box is shown as checked or cleared when the user views the form. For example, you might want an option such as "Salaried" checked by default in a new employee information form.

- **Run Macro On** allows you to select predefined macros that will run when the field is first selected (Entry) or when the user moves from the field to another part of the form (Exit). For example, you might create a macro that asks for a certain type of information when the user selects the field and then attach it as an Entry macro.

? SEE ALSO

For more information about using other fields on a form, see "Using Other Fields on Forms" on page 721.

- **The Bookmark box** under Field Settings allows you to name a bookmark for this field. Although Word automatically creates a bookmark for each field you add and suggests a name for it, you can change the name here if you like. By adding a bookmark to each form field, Word makes it easy to refer to fields by their bookmark names in formulas or in other fields.

- **Calculate On Exit** tells Word to recalculate all the fields in this document based on the new contents of this field.

- **Check Box Enabled** allows you to lock a check box to keep the user from altering it in any way. Clear this check box to prevent user changes to the check box setting. This option is available when you define other form fields, although its name changes to match that of the field you're defining.

- **The Add Help Text button** at the right side of the dialog box allows you to present instructions that pop up when the field is selected.

After you have set the options you want, click OK to define the field.

Adding a Text Form Field

A Text form field is a place where the user enters text on the form. You could always create a blank space as you would on a printed form, but when you use a Text form field, you can specify parameters, such as the maximum length of the entry or whether it must be text, a number, a date, or a time. You can even enter default text of your own when there's a standard response. Figure 30-5 shows a form that uses text fields along with one drop-down field.

FIGURE 30-5.

Text form fields can store any text or number, and they can include default text.

Unlimited length, text format

Maximum length 3 characters; default text

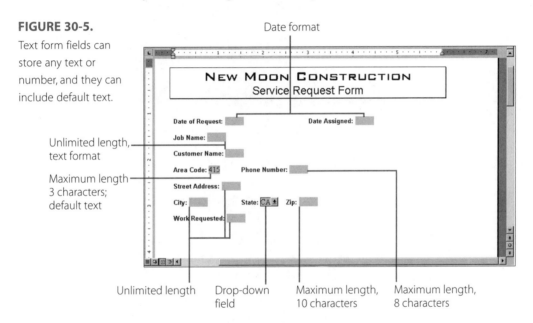

Date format

Unlimited length   Drop-down field   Maximum length, 10 characters   Maximum length, 8 characters

Here's how to add a Text form field:

1   Move the insertion point to the place where you want the field to appear, usually to the left or right of the field name text.

2   Click the Text Form Field button on the Forms toolbar. Word inserts the field and shades it, as shown in Figure 30-5. The field looks pretty small, but it expands to accommodate the default data you enter in it or to accept data from the form's user.

**TIP**

If you can't see the field, click the Form Field Shading button on the Forms toolbar.

3 Double-click the field to display the Text Form Field Options dialog box, as shown in Figure 30-6.

4 Choose the options you want and then click OK to apply them.

FIGURE 30-6.

When you add a Text form field, you can set a variety of options for it.

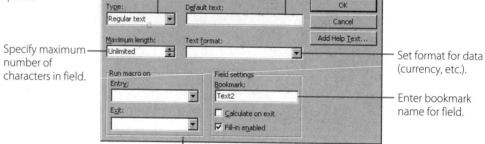

Set data type (text, number, date, etc.).

Enter default text for field.

Specify maximum number of characters in field.

Set format for data (currency, etc.).

Enter bookmark name for field.

Add a macro that runs when field is selected or when user moves from field to another part of form.

Setting Text Form Field Options

The Run Macro On and Field Settings options in the Text Form Field Options dialog box work as they do in every form field. *For more information about them, see "Setting Check Box Field Options" on page 714.* Here's what the other options do:

- **The Type menu** allows you to set the data type for the field. The choices are Regular Text, Number, Date, Current Date, Current Time, and Calculation. Choose this option first, because the choice you make here affects the options on the other menus in the top half of the dialog box.

- **The Default Text box** allows you to enter a default entry for this field, as shown with the Area Code field in Figure 30-5. If you choose the Current Date or Current Time data type on the Type menu, this option is unavailable. If you choose the Calculation option on the Type menu, you must enter a formula or expression here.

- **The Maximum Length box** lets you set a limit on the number of characters or numbers that can be entered in the field. For example, if you are inserting an Area Code field, you could avoid incorrect entries by limiting it to 3 numbers, as was done in Figure 30-5 on page 715.

- **The Format box** allows you to select format options for the data type you choose on the Type menu. If you select a number format, for example, you can choose a decimal, currency, percentage, or commas format.

Which Data Type Should You Use When?

The Type menu for a Text form field lets you force users to enter a specific type of data in the field. It also lets you make the field produce its own result. However, these restrictions may hinder text entry options in ways you don't expect. Here are some tips about using the different field data types.

- Use the Regular Text type for maximum flexibility. This way, users can enter either text or numbers or a combination of the two in the field, such as the dashes and parentheses that occur in a Postal/ZIP code or Phone Number field.

- Use the Number type when you want to prevent anyone from entering text in the field. An example would be a part number or a job number.

- Use the Date or Time data types when you want to force users to enter dates or times in a particular format. You can choose the data format from the Text Format menu.

   If you select Current Date or Current Time on the Type menu, Word inserts the current date or time in the format you choose. Users are not allowed to modify the field's contents.

- Use the Calculation field type to produce a result based on other fields in the form. For example, a calculation field called Charge might contain the formula =Hours × Rate to calculate hours worked or labor rate data entered in two other fields. In order to use a formula like this, you must use bookmark names that refer to the fields whose data you want to calculate.

V

Data Automation Tools

Adding a Drop-Down Form Field

Use a Drop-Down form field when you want to give users a list of predefined options to enter. Drop-down lists prevent a lot of typographical errors because the choices are already defined and the user can simply pick one. The first item on the list shows at all times, and the others appear when the field is clicked. Here are two Drop-Down form fields, one of which has been clicked:

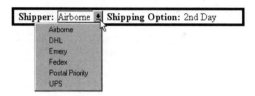

Users can simply drag down the list to select an option and then release the mouse button to enter it.

> When you add a Drop-Down form field, entries in the field are limited to items that can be chosen from the drop-down list. To create a drop-down list that will allow alternate inputs from the user, add a Combo Box object with the Control Toolbox toolbar. *For more information about the Control Toolbox toolbar, see "Using ActiveX Controls" on page 722.*

To add a Drop-Down form field, do the following:

1 Place the insertion point where you want the field to appear.

2 Click the Drop-Down Form Field button on the Forms toolbar. The field appears in the document.

3 Double-click the field to display the Drop-Down Form Field Options dialog box as in Figure 30-7.

FIGURE 30-7.

When you define a Drop-Down form field, you can define the options that appear on its list.

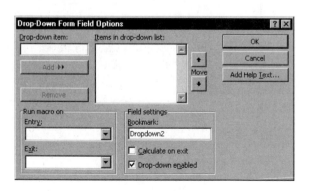

4 Add entries to the field's drop-down list, arrange them the way you want, and then click OK to define the field.

NOTE

To see a Drop-Down form field as it will appear to the user, you must protect the form by clicking the Protect Form button on the Forms toolbar.

Setting Drop-Down Form Field Options

SEE ALSO

For more information about the Run Macro On or Field Settings options, see "Setting Check Box Field Options" on page 714.

As with the other form fields, most of the options in the bottom half of this dialog box are common to every field. Here's what the field-specific options do:

■ **The Drop-Down Item box** is the place where you enter each item that you want to appear on the drop-down list. To add a list item, enter it in the Drop-Down Item box and then click the Add button below.

■ **Items In Drop-Down List** shows the items you have added so far. To remove an item from the list, select it and click the Remove button at the left. To change an item's position on the list, select it and click one of the Move arrows.

■ **The Drop-Down Enabled check box** in the Field Settings area makes the drop-down feature active or inactive. When this check box is cleared, the drop-down list won't appear and the first item on it will be the only possible entry in the field.

Inserting Help Text

No matter which kind of form field you add with the Forms toolbar, you can attach help text to it to avoid user confusion. You can have the text appear in the Status Bar when the field is selected, or you can have it pop up in a Help window when the field is selected and the user presses F1. The Help window looks like this:

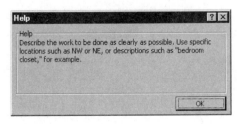

TIP

> You can also create an AutoOpen macro that displays help text in a dialog box whenever the form is opened. *For more information about AutoOpen macros, see the sidebar "Using Automatic Macros" on page 681.*

To add help text to a field, follow these steps:

1 Double-click the field to display its options dialog box.

2 Click the Add Help Text button. Word displays the Form Field Help Text dialog box, as shown in Figure 30-8.

FIGURE 30-8.

You can add help text to any form field.

3 Click either the Status Bar or Help Key tab to determine where the help will appear. The options are the same on both tabs. (You can enter help text on both tabs if you like so it will appear both in the status bar and in a pop-up Help message.)

4 To enter custom Help text, click the Type Your Own button and then enter the text you want to display in the box below.

5 If you would rather use a previously-defined AutoText entry, click the AutoText entry button and choose an option from the list at the right.

6 Click OK to add the text, and click OK again to close the Field Options dialog box.

 TIP

> To see how help text will look to the form's users, click the Protect Form button on the Forms toolbar, select the field, and press F1 if necessary.

Using Other Fields or Macros

Although you can do a lot just by using the Forms toolbar by itself, you can considerably expand the possibilities of forms by using other fields or macros in them.

- Fields can calculate information from other fields, copy information from one field to another, or ask the user for input.

- Macros allow you to combine a number of Word operations into one event and then have Word execute the event automatically, as described in Chapter 28, "Using Macros."

Using Other Fields on Forms

Fields allow you to recycle information in a form or perform other automated data entry procedures. Here are three examples:

- Use a Formula field to copy data from one field to another on the same form. For example, when the Mailing Address field on an invoice form includes a customer address, the Ship To field could contain a formula that inserts the data from the Mailing Address field's bookmark. This way, the Ship To field will contain the same data as the Mailing Address field. (When the shipping address is different from the mailing address, users could be allowed to edit the Ship To field.)

- Use a Formula field to produce a calculated result from two or more other fields on the form. For example, a PastDue field might include the formula =((Date-LastPmt)-30) to calculate the number of days a payment is past due.

- Add an Ask field to present a dialog box containing a detailed description of the data you want entered along with an entry box where the user can enter the information.

Read up on fields in Chapter 27, "Using Fields," and you'll find lots of uses for other fields as you design forms.

Adding a Macro to a Form

You can add any macro to a form just as you would add a macro to any other document. Just open the form template and either record the macro using the Record New Macro command on the Macros submenu on the Tools menu, or open the Visual Basic Editor and create the macro there. Once you have created the macro, be sure to save the form again as a template so the new macro will be stored and will be available each time users create new forms.

Macros can carry out complex data-handling procedures, such as saving a form's data to a new document, opening that new document and selecting the data, and pasting the data into a Microsoft Excel worksheet. You can also create a macro that presents a dialog box that offers options about how the form is saved or printed.

Chapter 28, "Using Macros," and Chapter 29, "Working with Microsoft Visual Basic," explain macros in detail. Be sure to read the sidebar "Using Automatic Macros" on page 681 for ideas on how to use automatic macros to add Help text to each new form, to print the form when it is closed, or to perform other processing tasks.

Using ActiveX Controls

ActiveX controls are special objects in documents. You define the objects' functions using Visual Basic. The Control Toolbox toolbar offers a selection of objects that look like standard form fields, and you can choose from more than 100 other objects if you like.

> You must have a solid understanding of Visual Basic in order to define ActiveX controls. See Chapter 29 for more information.

When you work with an ActiveX control in Word, you do so in Design Mode. Design Mode allows you to select, move, resize, or define control objects. When you want to see how an ActiveX control will look to the end user of a form, you must exit Design Mode.

> A form must be unprotected in order for you to add ActiveX controls or use Design Mode. See "Protecting a Form" on page 725 for more information.

The Control Toolbox Toolbar

All ActiveX controls are added with the Control Toolbox toolbar. To open the Control Toolbox toolbar, right-click in any toolbar and choose Control Toolbox from the shortcut menu. When docked at the top or bottom of the document window, the Control Toolbox toolbar looks like this:

Adding a Control

SEE ALSO

For more information about each of the controls on the Control Toolbox palette, search for "ActiveX Controls" in the Help system.

The controls on the toolbar are common form components. The name of each control appears for a second or two when you point to it. To add a control to a form, do the following:

1 Move the insertion point to the place where you want the field to appear.

2 Click a button on the Control Toolbox toolbar to insert the type of control you want. Word inserts the control object with selection handles around it and adds the Exit Design Mode toolbar to your screen like this:

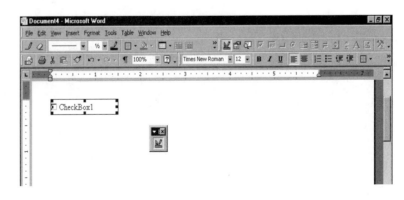

When you add an ActiveX control, Word switches to Design Mode so you can move, resize, or define the control object.

3 Insert text or spaces or use text formatting tools to move the control object, or drag one of its selection handles to resize it.

> ActiveX controls for forms are added as inline graphics. To make an ActiveX object float over text, right-click an object, choose Format Control from the shortcut menu, and then set a different text wrap option on the Layout tab. *For more information about setting an object's format, see Chapter 19.*

4 Click outside the control to deselect it.

To see how the field will actually look in the form, click the Exit Design Mode button.

Defining an ActiveX Control

For details about setting an object's properties see "Properties" on page 670.

Besides dragging and resizing it in Design Mode, there are two additional steps you must take to define an ActiveX control. You change its display properties with the Properties window, and you write a Visual Basic program that defines its behavior.

Changing an Object's Properties

To view or change an object's properties, follow these steps:

1 Select the object and click the Properties button on the Control Toolbox toolbar, or right-click the toolbar and choose Properties from the shortcut menu. You'll see the Properties window like this:

In this example, the Properties list has been widened to show its contents more clearly.

2   Select the property text for the property you want to change and then enter new text to describe it. For example, if you add an ActiveX Command Button control, you would change the button's label by selecting and editing the text for the Caption property.

3   Click the Close button to close the Properties window when you're done.

⭐ **TIP**

Changing the format of an ActiveX control is another way to adjust some of its properties. To change an object's format, right-click the object and choose Format Control from the shortcut menu.

Programming an Object

❓ **SEE ALSO**

See Chapter 29, "Working with Microsoft Visual Basic," for more information on programming with Visual Basic.

To program an object's behavior, do the following:

1   Double-click the object or select it and click the View Code button on the Control Toolbox toolbar. Word opens the Visual Basic Editor.

2   Write a Visual Basic program that tells the object how to behave.

3   Click the Close button on the upper-right corner of the Visual Basic Editor window to return to the form, or choose Close And Return To Microsoft Word from the File menu.

▷ **NOTE**

As long as the Visual Basic Editor is running, you can't move, resize, or display the shortcut menu for an object. When you want to return to Design Mode, make sure to close the Visual Basic Editor window rather than minimizing it.

V

Data Automation Tools

Protecting a Form

To see how a form will look to an end user, you must protect it. Protecting a form locks its fields and text, preventing any formatting changes and making it possible for the fields to collect data. When a form is protected, its drop-down lists, check boxes, Help windows, and other field options work as intended. In addition, only fields can be selected in the form.

You will want to protect every form you create before sending it out to users, but because anyone familiar with the Forms toolbar can unprotect a form, you should consider setting a document password that prevents anyone from changing it, no matter how much they know about Word's form features.

Using the Protect Form Button

As you go about designing a form, you'll want to protect and unprotect it often. Doing so will let you make that sure each field looks and acts the way you want. To protect a form, click the Protect Form button on the Forms toolbar. The button will be highlighted. Click the Protect Form button again to unprotect the form.

Protecting the Form with a Password

Since anyone familiar with the Forms toolbar can unprotect a form at will, you can use a password to make absolutely sure the form can't be changed by anyone but you. To set a password, follow these steps:

1 Unprotect the form.

2 Choose Protect Document from the Tools menu. Word opens the Protect Document dialog box, like this:

3 Select the Forms button if it isn't already selected.

4 Enter a password of up to 15 characters in the Password box and click OK. Word displays the Confirm Password dialog box.

5 Enter your password into the Confirm Password dialog box and click OK. Word protects the form.

WARNING

Make sure to write down your password or to choose one you're certain you'll remember. There is no way to open a password-protected document without its password.

To unprotect a document that has a password, do the following:

1 Click the Protect Document button on the Forms toolbar or choose Unprotect Document from the Tools menu. Word displays a dialog box with a space for your password.

2 Enter the password and click OK. Word unprotects the document.

Saving the Form Template

When your form is exactly the way you want it to look, save it as a template. If you created the form from a new template, the Document Template file type option will already be selected in the Save As dialog box when you save the form. Otherwise, be sure to select Document Template in the Save As Type box in the Save As dialog box before saving it. Here's a checklist of other things to do before saving the final version of the form:

- Scroll through the whole form and delete any practice data, text, or other objects that you may have entered in various fields while designing and testing the form.

- Put away the Forms, Control Toolbox, and other toolbars that the user won't need.

- Select the document view that you want to be showing when the form is opened.

- Resize the document window if you want it to open at a preset size.

Using a Form

Once your form is complete, protected, and saved as a template, you're ready to distribute it. Here are the general instructions for distributing a form template and creating individual forms from it.

Distributing the Form

? SEE ALSO

For more information about storing files on a network server, see Chapter 34, "Sharing Documents on a Network."

To make your electronic form available to others, you can pass it around on floppy disks or store it on a network server to which all of its intended users have access. When you distribute the form, you may also want to include a printed or electronic set of guidelines for using

V

Data Automation Tools

the template. For example, you may want individual forms created from the template to be named a certain way or saved to a specific place on a network server. Consider what your form's users will need to know about how and where to save each filled-in copy of a form, and then explain it when you distribute the form.

Entering Data in a Form

When the form is opened by an end user, any AutoOpen macros you added to the form will run. Once any AutoOpen macros have run, users can click in any field to enter data or select an option. They can also press the Tab key to jump from one field to the next or Shift+Tab to jump from one field to the previous one. As each field is selected, any help text you created for it either appears in the status bar or pops up when the user presses F1.

Saving Completed Forms

To save a form, just press Ctrl+S or choose Save from the File menu and then enter a name and choose a location for the file. Saving in this manner saves the entire form, including any field names, graphics, and the form's title, along with the data in each field.

If you plan to use each form's data in a database or spreadsheet, you can instruct its users to set a save option that saves only the form's data as a text file. To save only the form's data, follow these steps:

1 Choose Options from the Tools menu and click the Save tab.

2 Select the Save Data Only For Forms check box.

3 Click OK.

If you instruct users to do this the first time they use a form, the option will be set and will remain that way unless the user later deselects it.

TIP

You can ensure that the Save Data Only For Forms option is set by including an AutoClose macro in the form template which sets the Save Data Only For Forms option each time the form document is closed. *For more information about macros and Visual Basic, see Chapters 28 and 29.*

Printing a Form

For more information about printing, see "Printing Documents" on page 125.

When you print a form, you have three options available. You can print the form's text, fields, and data; print only the data; or print only the fields and text. Here's how to print what you want:

- To print the form's data along with any text or field labels, just print it as you would any other document. Press Ctrl+P, choose Print from the File menu, or click the Print button on the Standard toolbar.

- To print a blank form (fields and text without any data in them), open a new form using the form template and print it as you would any other document.

- To print only a form's data, follow these steps:

  1 Press Ctrl+P to open the Print dialog box.

  2 Click the Options button.

  3 Select the Print Data Only For Forms check box in the Options For Current Document Only area.

  4 Click OK to return to the main Print dialog box.

  5 Click OK to print just the document's data.

Add an AutoClose macro to a form to select the Print Data Only For Forms option on the user's computer when the first form is printed. For more information about using Visual Basic to create macros, see Chapter 29.

Modifying a Form

Once you put a form into circulation, you may find that some fields aren't as effective as you thought or that you need to collect information in a different way. Fortunately, you can modify a form whenever you like. To make modifications, follow these steps:

1 Choose New from the File menu, select the form template, click the Template button in the lower-right corner of the New dialog box, and then click OK.

2 Display the Forms toolbar if necessary.

3 Select individual fields and move them or change their shading, size, or other format options.

4 Double-click individual fields to change their behavior, their bookmark names, or any macros attached to them.

5 When you have made the modifications you want, save the template with the same name. Word selects Template as the file type and asks if you want to replace the existing file. Click Yes and the original template is replaced with your modified one.

? SEE ALSO

For more information about using the Go To command, see "Navigating with the Go To Command" on page 59.

Identifying and Locating Form Fields

If you haven't attached descriptive text names to each field that you inserted on a form, it can be difficult to tell which field is which. However, you can use each field's bookmark to identify it, and then use the Go To command to locate and select it in your document.

To change a field's bookmark name, make sure the form is unprotected and then double-click the field to display the field's options dialog box. Change the name in the Bookmark box and click OK.

To find and select a particular field using its bookmark name, Press Ctrl+G to display the Go To tab in the Find and Replace dialog box. Then select Bookmark from the Go To What list, choose the bookmark name from the Enter Bookmark Name drop-down list, and press Enter or click the Go To button.

PART VI

Web and Internet Tools

CHAPTER 31

Using Word to Access the Internet

By now you probably know that the Internet is the biggest thing in personal communication since the telephone. The Internet has become such an important resource that most software manufacturers now provide some sort of link to it from their products. Microsoft is no exception. In Microsoft Word 2000 and other Microsoft Office programs, you can access Internet locations, view Web pages, and open files from Internet servers as easily as you can open a file in Word. In this chapter, you'll learn the different ways to access the Internet from inside Word.

We'll begin our exploration of Word's Internet capabilities with a survey of how the Internet works.

⚠ **WARNING**

> Word's Internet access features work only if you are able to connect directly to the Internet using a Web browser and an e-mail program, not if your access is through a host computer system such as America Online or Prodigy. If you use America Online or Prodigy to access the Internet, you must use the America Online or Prodigy software to do so, and the Word features described in this chapter will not work for you.

About the Internet and Intranets

The Internet is a communications network that links computers around the world. Internet technologies—especially the World Wide Web—have become so popular that private companies have set up *intranets*, which are like the Internet, except that they operate only within a company network. Since most every computer these days has a Web *browser* (a program used to view Web pages), companies use intranets to set up private Web servers so their employees can exchange graphically rich documents. Most intranet users can also access the Internet through a link (or *gateway*) to it from their company's network.

▷ **NOTE**

> For the sake of simplicity, I'll use *Internet* to refer to both the Internet and an intranet, and use *intranets* only when I'm referring to them alone.

What You Need to Access the Internet

In order to view or download files stored on the Internet, you need the following:

▷ **NOTE**

> If you're on a company intranet, you need only a browser, newsgroup, and e-mail software because the network connection has already been set up for you.

- **A computer with a connection to the Internet** You'll need either a modem and telephone line, a cable modem setup, or a network connection, like the ones companies provide their employees.

- **An account with an Internet service provider** If you're accessing the Internet from a company network, your company has an Internet account and you probably use your network user ID and password to access it.

If you're an individual Word user, Microsoft Windows 98 comes with account setup wizards for several major Internet service providers.

- **Internet connection software** This comes with Windows and includes either the Dial-Up Networking control panel or the Network control panel. When you access an intranet, you use the same software that connects you to the whole network.

- **A Web browser for viewing Web pages** You can access Microsoft Internet Explorer, or other browsers such as Netscape Navigator, from Windows.

The sample browser screens in this book are from Internet Explorer version 5, and the instructions about using a browser from within Word assume you are using either Internet Explorer version 4 (or newer) or Netscape Navigator version 3 (or newer). Your results may vary if you use other browsers or versions older than these.

- **Additional software for reading e-mail or accessing Internet discussion groups** Web browsers these days have built-in support for e-mail and newsgroups, but if you're using an older version of Microsoft Internet Explorer or Netscape Navigator, you may need to add e-mail or newsgroup programs.

About Servers and Clients

There are two kinds of computers on the Internet: *servers,* which are repositories of files, and *clients,* which are individual computers used to access the files on the servers. When you use Word to access information on the Internet, your computer is a client.

Every computer that stores files and makes them available on the Internet is a file server, but there are several different kinds of Internet servers. The most common kinds of servers are:

- **Web servers** contain collections of Web pages

- **FTP servers** contain files that are downloaded to a user's computer

- **News servers** store messages for discussions called *newsgroups*

- **Mail servers** store e-mail messages

You can open Web pages and FTP files from right inside Word. To view messages on a news server or to transfer e-mail, you need either

VI

Web and Internet Tools

a Web browser or a special e-mail program. For example, you can use Microsoft Internet Explorer to access newsgroups, and you can use Microsoft Outlook or Outlook Express to read e-mail messages.

About URLs

Web servers and ftp servers each use a different set of communications rules (or *protocols*) to transfer files over the Internet. Each file stored on a Web or ftp server has a unique Internet address called a *Uniform Resource Locator* or *URL*. The URL includes the protocol used to access the file along with the file's name and location in a format like this:

> *http://www.domain.com/sales/index.htm*

In this URL, the "http" before the slashes indicates the Internet communications protocol—in this case, HTTP, or *Hypertext Transfer Protocol.* This identifies the resource as a Web page. The text after the slashes is the address of the actual page, which in this case is a page named "index.htm" stored on the server called "sales" at the network (or *domain*) called *www.domain.com.*

A URL for an ftp resource looks like this:

> *ftp://ftp.domain.com/graphics/logo*

In this case, the protocol is FTP, or *File Transfer Protocol,* the file being accessed is named "logo," and the file is stored in the "graphics" directory on the server *ftp.domain.com.* When you access FTP servers, you transfer files to your computer rather than opening and viewing them on the server.

In today's Web browsers, you can frequently dispense with the protocol and simply type the URL as *www.domain.com.* The browser assumes that the addresses you specify are Web addresses, so it uses the *HTTP* protocol by default unless the URL tells it otherwise.

URLs vs. Pathnames

Just as a URL is the standard way to specify the address of an Internet resource, a *pathname* is a standard way to specify the name and address of a file stored on your computer or a file on a network file server that isn't a Web server. And while a URL typically includes slashes to separate the network protocol type from the actual file address, a pathname uses backslashes. Here are two examples:

> C:\Program Files\Microsoft Office\Word
>
> \\Marketing\Plans\JetMaker Launch Plan.doc

The first pathname is the location of the Word file on a computer's hard disk. The pathname specifies first the disk name (in this case the C: drive), the directories in which the file is located (Program files\ Microsoft Office) and the file name (Word).

The second pathname is the location of a Word file on a network server. The double backslash indicates that it's a network resource, the server name is Marketing, the directory name is Plans, and the file name is "JetMaker Launch Plan.doc."

The words "URL" and "pathname" are sometimes used interchangeably, but we'll keep them separate in this chapter.

How Word Accesses the Internet

To establish a connection to the Internet, Word uses an Internet connection and your computer's Web browser and e-mail program. But Word uses these resources in different ways, depending on which type of file you open and how you open it.

There are four different ways in which you can access Internet resources from within Word:

- **Open a Web page in Word itself** You can use the Open command on the File menu to access a Web page and download a copy of the page into a new Word document window. In this case, Word opens a connection to the Internet just long enough to transfer the file into a new document window, and the connection is closed after that. The file you open is a read-only copy of the Web page—you can't enter data into it or change it in any other way. You can also follow this procedure to open any Web page that you created with Word and stored on a local disk. You can then use Word's features to edit it.

- **Use the Web toolbar** When you go to a Web page using an address on the Web toolbar, Word opens your default Web browser, which accesses and displays the file. If you have permission to enter data into or edit the contents of the page, you can do so using your Web browser.

- **Click a hyperlink** If a Word document contains a hyperlink, clicking the hyperlink launches the Web browser on your computer, and the browser then displays the link and opens the page.

SEE ALSO

For more information about the Web toolbar, see "Using the Web Toolbar" on page 739. For more information on inserting and managing hyperlinks in Word documents, see "Using Hyperlinks" on page 772.

VI

Web and Internet Tools

- **Open an FTP file** You can download and open a file from an FTP server by using the Open command on the File menu. However, you must add the FTP server as a location in the Open dialog box first. *For more information about opening an FTP file, see "Opening Files from FTP servers" on page 747.*

Opening a Web Page as a Word Document

When you use the Open command on the File menu to display a Web page, the page is opened in a new Word document window. The way in which Word behaves, however, depends on whether you open the page from a Web server or from another location:

> **NOTE**

As you'll see in Chapters 32 and 33, you can create Web pages right in Word's document window and save them in the HTML format needed to display them on a Web server. When you're working on a Web page, you will probably store it on your local hard disk or on a network file server. *For more information about HTML, see Chapter 32, "Creating Web Pages."*

- If you open the page from a Web server, the page is read-only— you can't make any changes to it.

- If you open the page from a network file server or from a local disk, you can edit the page using Word.

To open a page from a Web server, follow these steps:

1 Choose Open from the File menu.

2 In the File Name box, enter the address for the Web page you want.

3 Click the Open button. Word opens a new document window and copies the Web page into it, as shown in Figure 31-1 on the next page. During the process, you may see a progress indicator box that says Word is transferring the file.

If you click a hyperlink on this Web page, Word fetches the new page and replaces the contents of the current document window with those of the new page. However, you can go back to the previous page (or forward again to the current one) by clicking the Back or Forward buttons on the Web toolbar. *For more information about using the Web toolbar, see "Using the Web Toolbar" on page 739.*

FIGURE 31-1.

When you open a Web page using Word's Open command, the page is copied into a new Word document window as a read-only file.

Back Forward Web toolbar

Insertion point

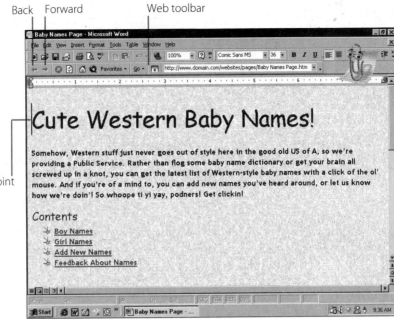

? SEE ALSO

For more information about creating and editing Web pages with Word, see Chapter 32, "Creating Web Pages," and Chapter 33, "Using Word's Advanced Web Features."

Here's how to open a Web page from a local or network disk rather than from a Web server:

1   Choose Open from the File menu.

2   Choose Web Pages from the Files of Type list at the bottom of the Open dialog box.

3   Navigate to the Web page you want to open and then double-click it. The page opens as a Word document so you can edit it.

Using the Web Toolbar

The Web toolbar brings the features of a Web browser right inside Word. In most cases, using the Web toolbar's controls or buttons launches your Web browser and retrieves the page you want to see.

To display the Web toolbar, right-click in any toolbar and choose Web from the shortcut menu. Figure 31-2 on the next page identifies the buttons on the Web toolbar along with the Insert Hyperlink button on the Standard toolbar.

As you'll see, there are several ways to explore the Web with the Web toolbar.

Don't confuse the Web toolbar with the Web Tools toolbar. The Web Tools toolbar is used for adding HTML objects to Web forms. *See "Using the Web Tools Toolbar" on page 798 for more information.*

FIGURE 31-2.

The Web toolbar has all the controls you need to find and display any Web page.

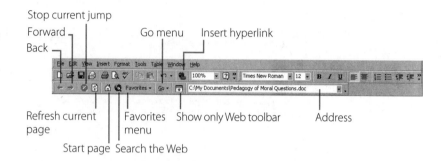

Specifying a URL

The most direct way to open a Web page is to specify its URL. On the Web toolbar, you can use either the Address box or the Go menu to do this.

The Web toolbar's controls generally work just as their counterparts in a Web browser do. For example, you can omit the HTTP protocol and the leading slash marks from a Web URL and Word will add them automatically.

Using the Address Box

To go to a new address, click the Address box, enter the URL, and then press Enter. Word opens the page in your computer's browser.

In addition, there's a drop-down list attached to the Address box that can display the URLs of the last several places you viewed, like this:

To return to a recently visited URL, click the arrow button to display the list and then choose the URL you want.

Resetting the Address List

The list of recently viewed pages in the Web toolbar is maintained by Windows, and it shows the pages you have opened during a specified number of previous days. The Address list can include files you have opened from anywhere on your network as well as Web pages. You can erase this list or reset it to cover a longer or shorter period of time.

Here's how to do this:

1 Point to Settings on the Start menu, and choose Control Panel.

2 Double-click the Internet icon. You'll see the History options on the General tab, and you can then clear the recent history list or change the number of days it covers.

If you're using Windows 95, the History options are on the Navigation tab in the Internet Properties dialog box.

Using the Go Menu

The Go menu on the Web toolbar also offers several ways to jump to a particular Web page.

1 Click Go on the Web toolbar. The Go menu opens as in Figure 31-3.

FIGURE 31-3.

The Go menu in the Web toolbar offers lots of ways to get to a Web page.

2 Choose the Open command to display the Open Internet Address dialog box, as seen here:

3 Enter a URL in the Address box or choose a recently visited URL from the drop-down list. To locate a file on your network, click the Browse button and you'll see a dialog box where you can search for and open a particular file.

4 Select the Open In New Window check box to open the page in a new document window rather than in the existing window.

5 Click OK to open the page.

Using the Favorites Menu

Since the World Wide Web is so vast, it can take quite a bit of exploring to find the exact page you want. When you find a page that you'll want to access again, you can add it to the Favorites menu in the Web toolbar.

Web Toolbar Precautions

When you use the Web toolbar to open a Web page, Word launches your computer's browser and displays the page there. The entire browser window replaces the current Word document on your screen, but the browser is actually "contained" in the original document window. (If you open a Web page from the Web toolbar without having a Word document open, Word opens a new document to contain it.)

Because the browser window is contained in the Word document, some actions you take in the browser can affect the state of the original document:

■ If the Back button is active when you first display the Web page in the browser, clicking the button will return you to the insertion point's position in the Word document you had open before you displayed the page.

■ Closing the browser window also closes the Word document you had open before you displayed the page.

To avoid this linkage between the current document window and the Web browser, use the Open command on the Go menu on the Web toolbar to open Web pages. When you use this command, the Open Internet Address dialog box offers you the option to open the page in a new document window so the browser won't replace your current document.

When you add a URL to the Favorites menu in the Web toolbar, it is also added to the Favorites menu in Internet Explorer.

Adding to the Favorites Menu

You can add any Web page or any other file to the Favorites menu. Here's how:

1 Use the Open command on Word's File menu to open the Web page or file you want to add.

2 Choose the Add to Favorites command from the Favorites menu. Word displays the Add To Favorites dialog box, like this:

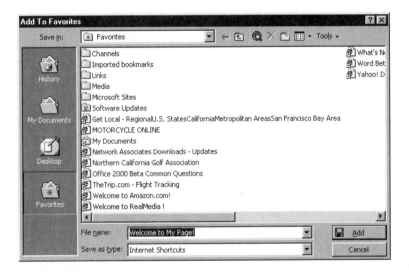

This dialog box works like the Save As dialog box that you use in Word, except that it shows the contents of the Favorites folder on your hard disk. The File Name box contains the name of the file you currently have open.

3 Click the Add button. Word places a shortcut to the file inside the Favorites folder, and the name is added to the Favorites menu.

Accessing a Favorite

To go to a page listed on the Favorites menu, just click the menu and then click the page name. The Favorites menu can list individual pages, and you can organize pages into folders if you like, as shown in Figure 31-4 on the next page.

VI

Web and Internet Tools

FIGURE 31-4.

The Favorites menu on the Web toolbar stores locations and names of Web pages or files you frequently open.

Customizing the Favorites Menu

? SEE ALSO

For more information about managing files in the Open or Save As dialog boxes, see Chapter 7, "Managing Files."

You can use the Favorites menu to store shortcuts not only to Web pages, but also to individual files or folders. You can also reorganize the Favorites menu's contents by adding new folders, deleting folders, or deleting or rearranging shortcuts. You can perform these actions by working directly on the Windows desktop or by using commands on the Favorites menu. When you choose the Add To Favorites or Open Favorites command from the Favorites menu in the Web toolbar, you'll see a standard Save As or Open dialog box. You can then use all of the same file management tools in the dialog box to add, delete, or rename files or folders.

★ TIP

Click the Favorites icon in the Places bar in the Open or Save As dialog box to jump to that folder quickly. When you add a new folder inside the Favorites folder, it appears as a folder on the Favorites menu in the Web toolbar, like the Microsoft Sites folder shown in Figure 31-4.

You can also work directly on the Windows desktop to move, rename, or delete items inside the Favorites folder, which is located inside the Windows folder on your hard disk. Any changes you make will be reflected on the Favorites menu in the Web toolbar.

Jumping Back or Forward

Clicking hyperlinks to jump to different pages is a key to getting around the Web or a network. In Figure 31-5 on the next page, for example, each underlined word or phrase is a hyperlink, and some of the graphics are, too. Each hyperlink stores a URL or pathname, and you can jump to the stored location by clicking the hyperlink. You may also want to jump back to a page you previously viewed.

FIGURE 31-5.

When you search the Web, the search engine usually returns with a list of hyperlinks to pages containing your search words or phrase.

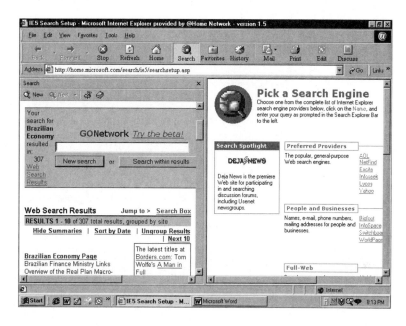

To jump back to the previous page or location you visited with the Web toolbar, click the Back button at the left end of the toolbar.

Once you have jumped back to a previous page, you can jump forward again to the next page by clicking the Forward button on the Web toolbar.

Searching for a Web Page

With more than 100 million Web pages out there, you will probably need some help finding the one you want. Within a Web search page, you can find pages by searching for certain keywords they contain. You can access a search page by clicking the Search The Web button on the Web toolbar, or by choosing the command of the same name on the toolbar's Go menu. To see an example, follow these steps:

1 Click the Search The Web button or choose the Search The Web command from the Go menu on the Web toolbar. Word opens your browser and locates either your browser's default search page or a Microsoft Web page where you can choose from a selection of search engines.

VI

Web and Internet Tools

> The default search location in Internet Explorer 5.0 is Microsoft's Pick A Search Engine page, but your default search page may be different. *See "Resetting the Search Page" below.*

2 If you're using the Pick A Search Engine page, click a link to select a search engine from the list on the page. That search engine's page appears in a new frame at the left side of your screen.

3 Enter *Brazilian economy* in the search box and click the Search or Go button. The search page scours the Web for pages containing the keywords you specified and returns a list of pages that match your search, as shown in Figure 31-5 on the previous page.

4 Click a hyperlink to take a look at a particular page. If you open a page you don't want, click the Back button on the browser's toolbar to return to the list of matching pages and try another one.

Resetting the Search Page

There are lots of search pages on the Web, but your browser always goes to the same default search page when you click its Search button or use the Search the Web features on the Web toolbar. To change the default search page, follow these steps:

1 Open an alternate search page in the Word document window using Word's Open command. (You can't use the Web toolbar to open the page because you need access to the Web toolbar, and your browser window replaces Word's toolbars.)

2 Choose the Set Search Page command from the Go menu on the Web toolbar. Word will ask if you want to save the change.

3 Click Yes.

Accessing or Changing the Start Page

The start page (or home page as it's also called) is the page your browser automatically loads when it opens. To get to this page from the Web toolbar, click the Start Page button or choose Start Page from the Go menu.

There are three ways to change the start page:

- Open the page you want to be the start page using Word's Open command, choose Set Start Page from the Go menu on the Web toolbar, and click Yes when Word asks if you want to reset the start page to the current page's URL.

TIP

> You use basically the same procedure to reset the start page as you do to reset the search page. *For more information, see "Resetting the Search Page" on the previous page.*

- Open your browser and use its options to reset the page there.

- Point to Settings on the Start menu and choose Control Panel; then click the Internet icon to display the Internet Properties dialog box. Move to the Home Page section on the General tab to reset the start page.

Refreshing the Current Page

Web pages change frequently, especially those that have "live" feeds of news, weather, sports scores, or stock prices. Since most pages don't change automatically, you must reload, or refresh them to display any new information that has been added since you last downloaded it. You can do this easily with the Web toolbar by clicking the Refresh Current Page button.

Hiding Other Toolbars

If you're opening files or Web pages directly in the Word document window and you're focused on moving from one page to the next, you may want to hide all of the other toolbars. Click the Show Only Web Toolbar button on the Web toolbar to hide all other toolbars or to reveal them if they're already hidden.

Opening Files from FTP Servers

As mentioned at the beginning of this chapter, FTP servers store files that can be downloaded directly into a Word document window. FTP servers have been around on the Internet since long before the Web, and unlike Web servers, they require you to log in for access.

Some FTP sites are for public use—these "anonymous FTP" sites grant access to any user with a default user name of "anonymous." Other FTP sites are for private use and require you to have a specific user name and password.

Once you know the address and password for an FTP site, you can use Word's Open command to view a directory of the site from inside Word and then select any file to download. Before you can view an

VI

Web and Internet Tools

FTP server's directory, however, you must add that server's location to the list of available locations in Word's Open dialog box, as explained below.

Adding an FTP Location

To add an FTP site to the list of FTP locations, follow these steps:

1 Choose Open or Save As from the File menu, and then choose the Add/Modify FTP Locations command from the Look In or Save In list at the top of the dialog box. You'll see the Add/ Modify FTP Locations dialog box, as shown in Figure 31-6.

FIGURE 31-6.

Before you can download a file from an FTP server, you must add the server to the list of locations in Word's Open dialog box.

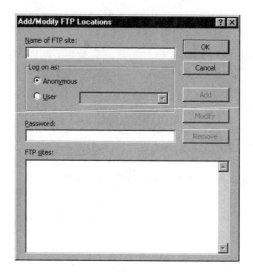

2 Type the address of the FTP site in the Name Of FTP Site box.

3 Click Anonymous if the site allows anonymous log-ins, or click User and select or enter your user name.

4 Type your password if the site requires one. (If the site allows anonymous log-ins, you may want to enter your e-mail address as a courtesy to identify yourself to the server's owner.)

5 Click the Add button and then click OK.

You can also use the Add/Modify FTP Locations command and dialog box to delete or change the login or address of an FTP location. Just select the location you want to delete or change and then click the Remove or Modify button.

Opening a File Using FTP

Once you have added an FTP server as a location in Word using the procedure just described, the server's URL appears as a location in both the Open and Save As dialog boxes. In the Open dialog box, it looks like this:

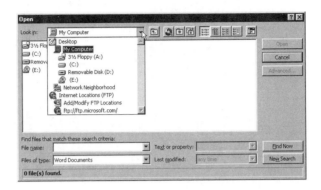

To open a file from this server, do the following:

1   Select the server name and click the Open button. Word displays the main directory of the server in the Look In list.

2   If the list shows only folders, double-click a folder to open it or select a folder and click the Open button.

3   Double-click a file name or select a file name and click the Open button. Word downloads the file and displays it in a new Word document window.

As you have seen in this chapter, Word gives you access to Internet pages and files in a number of different ways. But that's just the beginning. Word also makes it very easy to create Web pages of your own, and you can start learning how by going on to Chapter 32.

VI

Web and Internet Tools

Creating Web Pages

B y offering a simple, universal method for viewing pictures and other graphically rich documents on the Internet, the World Wide Web has smashed communications barriers. Anyone with a Web browser such as Microsoft Internet Explorer can view documents on the Web. You can also access the Web from within Microsoft Word, as explained in Chapter 31, "Using Word to Access the Internet." In Word 2000, it's easier than ever to create a Web page of your own. Word 2000 has dozens of incredible capabilities that allow you to create dazzling, sophisticated Web pages as easily as you create other documents. In this chapter you'll learn the basics.

As the Web has soared in popularity, it has become a force in commerce, education, and everyday communications around the world. You can use Web pages to publish corporate documents on an internal company network; to broadcast news of your product, service, family, or hobby on the global Internet; to sell products; and to collect information. Figure 32-1 shows a Web page for a small business.

FIGURE 32-1.

The home page for a small business Web site announces the company to the world.

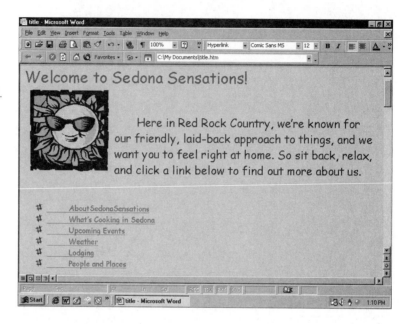

To publish information on the Web, you need two key ingredients:

- **A Web server** presents the pages on the Web. Any computer can become a Web server if it runs Web server software and has a continuous connection to the Internet or an intranet (so that the connection is available at all times). Web server software is generally inexpensive, and some programs are even free, but your computer can't be a Web server and a client at the same time.

 NOTE

Some of Word's Web publishing features (such as browsing Web folders) require that additional *server extension* software be installed on the server along with the Web server software. Microsoft has a special Office Server Extensions package that is required to use some of the Web and collaboration features of Microsoft Office applications. To determine which extensions are installed on your network's Web servers, contact your system administrator or Internet service provider.

- **Web pages** contain the information you want to present. Web pages are documents stored in *Hypertext Markup Language* format (HTML). HTML is simply text that contains special instructions, or *tags*, that tell the Web server how to format text, where to get any graphics included on the page, how to present information, and how to perform other housekeeping operations as a page is viewed.

> **NOTE**
>
> Many people refer to Web sites as "Web pages" or "home pages," but there is a difference. For our purposes, a Web page is a single HTML document; a Web site is a collection of Web pages that is accessed through a particular location on the Web; and a home page (or start page) is the default page that loads when a viewer accesses a Web site. The home page usually contains the site's title, a description, and a directory of its contents.

Publishing Documents on the Web

Publishing a document on the Web is quite a bit different from publishing it in print. There are whole books devoted to creating Web pages with HTML and the details of Web servers, Java scripting, and other topics. These subjects are beyond the scope of this book, but here are some key points to keep in mind if you're new to Web publishing.

A Web Page is Many Files

A Web page is often a collection of individual objects. It can contain body text, hypertext links to other pages, text boxes, frames, pictures, graphics, sounds, video clips, scripts, and objects such as drop-down menus or scrolling text boxes. Since the HTML format is a text-only format, any graphical objects, scripts, or other page elements must be stored in separate files and identified in the page itself with HTML codes that specify the object's name and location. Figure 32-2 on the next page shows some of the HTML text of the Web page in Figure 32-1.

You'll notice in Figure 32-2 that the HTML text is mostly *tags* or instructions that indicate formatting or the location of graphics, but it also contains the text that will be displayed on the page in a browser.

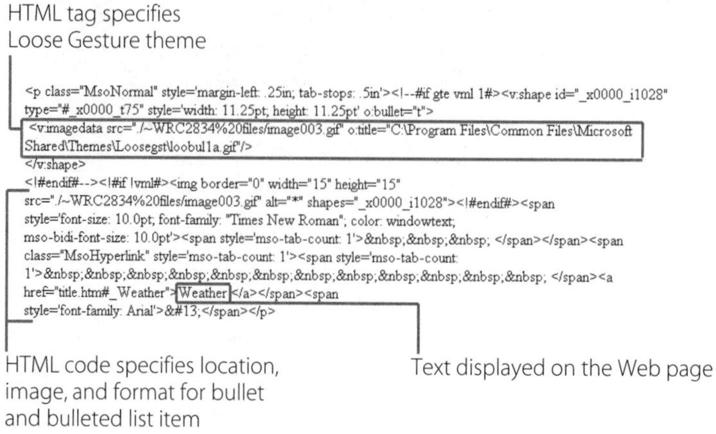

FIGURE 32-2.

Behind the graphics and format of every Web page is HTML text that describes how to present the page.

HTML tag specifies
Loose Gesture theme

```
<p class="MsoNormal" style='margin-left: .25in; tab-stops: .5in'><!--#if gte vml 1#><v:shape id="_x0000_i1028"
type="#_x0000_t75" style='width: 11.25pt; height: 11.25pt' o:bullet="t">
  <v:imagedata src="./~WRC2834%20files/image003.gif" o:title="C:\Program Files\Common Files\Microsoft
Shared\Themes\Loosegst\loobul1a.gif"/>
</v:shape>
<!#endif#--><!#if !vml#><img border="0" width="15" height="15"
src="./~WRC2834%20files/image003.gif" alt="*" shapes="_x0000_i1028"><!#endif#><span
style='font-size: 10.0pt; font-family: "Times New Roman"; color: windowtext;
mso-bidi-font-size: 10.0pt'><span style='mso-tab-count: 1'>    </span></span><span
class="MsoHyperlink" style='mso-tab-count: 1'><span style='mso-tab-count:
1'>           </span><a
href="title.htm#_Weather">Weather </a></span><span
style='font-family: Arial'>&#13;</span></p>
```

HTML code specifies location, image, and format for bullet and bulleted list item

Text displayed on the Web page

When the page is viewed in a browser, the browser loads the HTML text and converts it to formatted text and graphics. Since the HTML commands refer to specific objects at specific locations, if any of those objects are moved, renamed, or deleted, they will become unavailable, and the displayed page won't contain them.

What You See Is Relative

Your Web page will be viewed by different people whose computers have varying collections of fonts, screen sizes, and screen resolution and color settings. Your pages may also be viewed with different browser programs. While the HTML format specifies how things should look in any browser, viewers may see slightly different versions of the page because of varying screen resolution settings or fonts available on their own computers. For example, if you design a full-screen page using 1024x768 screen resolution you'll have more room to work with, but viewers using 640x480 resolution won't be able to see your entire "page" without scrolling.

Speed Matters

Since each Web page is usually created from a collection of files, every would-be viewer of the page has to wait until all of the component files are loaded before the page appears in all its glory. These days, browsers load page components incrementally, which means that you see and read the text of the page as soon as it is loaded, even though you're waiting for the other objects to load. Even large pictures can be presented in an "interlaced" mode that displays a lower-resolution or monochrome version of the picture quickly and then gradually improves in quality as the rest of the picture file is loaded.

Nevertheless, pages with lots of large component files can take a long time to load—especially if the viewer is using a dial-up Internet connection—and with so much to see and do, users often have limited patience. When you design each page, remember that the more graphics, text, scripts, or other objects a page contains, the longer it will take for a viewer to see it all.

? SEE ALSO

For more information about creating online forms that are distributed via e-mail or as Word documents, see Chapter 30, "Creating Forms."

What's Good for the Web...

Some of Word's Web document features work for any document that is viewed on the screen. Although you will likely use most of these features for Web pages, you can also add animation, drop-down lists, or other Web-like controls to any electronic Word document.

How Word 2000 Makes Web Pages Easy

Word 2000 makes it as easy to create a Web page as any other document. Word 2000's Web-page creation tools are so simple that anyone can use them, yet they're powerful enough to deliver advanced Web page features such as frames, animation, scripts, HTML objects, and ActiveX controls. Before we go into the details of creating Web pages, here's an overview of Word 2000's Web page creation features.

What You See Is What You Get

Because any Word document can become a Web page, the page you create in Word is pretty much what viewers will see on the Web. Word faithfully reproduces on the Web any feature that appears in a Word document, including tables, fields, graphics, text wrapping, backgrounds, styles, and other format enhancements.

- Web Layout view allows you to create pages without being distracted by page breaks, margins, or other print-oriented page elements, and it also shows the actual positions of graphics, buttons, and other page objects.

- Word's standard editing and formatting commands help you create Web pages, and most options will faithfully translate to the Web. (Word warns you if a page contains format options that

VI

Web and Internet Tools

won't translate to the Web.) There are also several special commands for adding Web-specific components such as frames, backgrounds, and graphical lines or bullets to your pages.

- The Web Page Preview command launches your Web browser and displays your page in it so you can double-check the format and the operation of any controls in the page.

Web Form Tools

? SEE ALSO

For more information about form tools, see "Making Web Forms" on page 805.

One of the most important features of many Web pages is that they're "live." Animated features such as scrolling text capture the viewer's attention, while other live features such as drop-down menus and scrollable text boxes make it easy to fill out forms on the Web. In Word 2000, you can use either the Web Tools toolbar or the Control Toolbox toolbar to create Web forms.

Frames

? SEE ALSO

For more information about frames, see "Using Frames" on page 790.

Frames are now a standard Web page feature typically used to provide navigation controls for the site on each of its pages. A frame usually contains navigation hyperlinks, but you can also add text, graphics, or ActiveX objects to a frame. You can scroll through frames independently of the rest of the page. Figure 32-3 shows an example.

FIGURE 32-3.
You can add frames to Web pages to provide onscreen navigation links for every page on a Web site.

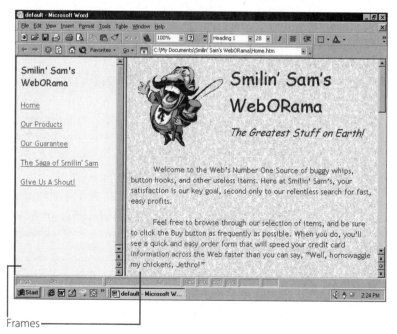

Frames

Themes

With millions and millions of Web pages in cyberspace, it can be hard to make a page stand out. Word has built-in themes that instantly apply background graphics and collections of coordinated styles to a page. Themes can save you from a lot of trial and error when creating an overall look for your page. In Figure 32-1 on page 752, the overall look was created by applying the Cactus theme.

NOTE

> Word only installs a handful of themes when you perform a typical installation, but you can easily install others as you work. If a theme is not installed, Word will give you the chance to install it from the Office program CD by clicking a button. *See the Appendix for more information on customizing Word.*

Instant Publishing

SEE ALSO

For more publishing details, see "Publishing Web Pages" on page 781.

Word 2000's new Save As Web Page command and Web Folders location allow you to save a Web page and publish it on your Web server at the same time. When you choose the Save As Web Page command instead of Save As, Word makes a copy of the document, converts it to HTML format, and then copies the page and any related files to the location you select. If you have set up one or more Web folders, saving to a Web folder also copies the pages to a Web server.

NOTE

> To fully support Web folders, a Web server must be running Microsoft's Office Server Extensions. You can still use Web folders on Web servers that don't have the Office Server Extensions, but some functions (such as browsing for a Web folder on the server) are disabled.

Round-Trip Editing

When you save a Word document as a Web page, it is converted to the HTML format, which supports only text characters. However, you can click the Edit button in Internet Explorer version 5 to open any Web page for editing in Word 2000. When you do this, you see the page in Web Layout view with all of the graphics, formatting, and other features of the original document just as they were when you created the page.

VI

Web and Internet Tools

Web File Housekeeping

Word helps ensure that each Web page you create or edit will always display the proper information. It does this by automatically updating links to any component files included in the page. For example, if you delete a graphic from a document, Word deletes the link to that graphic from the Web page and removes the graphic file itself from the page's folder of component files.

Creating a Web Page

Now that we've seen how Word 2000 makes it easy to create Web pages, let's get down to business. There are several ways to create a Web page with Word:

 TIP

> If you have the Premium edition of Microsoft Office, your package includes Microsoft FrontPage 2000, a program specifically designed for creating and managing Web sites. FrontPage 2000 has more features that make it easy to create Web pages. You may want to use FrontPage 2000 for making new Web sites from scratch, and only use Word for turning individual documents into Web pages.

- Open an existing document and save it as a Web page.

 SEE ALSO

For more information, see "Publishing Web Pages," on page 781.

- Create a new document, add text and graphics to it, and save it as a Web page.

- Open one of Word's Web page templates for a head start on page layout and formatting.

- Use the Web Page Wizard to create a new page or group of pages based on preferences you select.

 NOTE

> If you thoroughly understand HTML, you can create a Web page in Word by entering HTML code into a document and saving the document as a text file, just as you can with any text editing program. But Word's other methods make the job much easier.

For now, let's focus on starting a page from scratch, using Web page templates and the Web Page Wizard.

Designing an Effective Web Page

You can organize text, graphics, and other elements on a Web page any way you like, but there are some basic principles that are followed by all successful Web designers.

- ■ **Make it easy to navigate.** If the page is long or includes lots of links to other pages on the same site, use a frame as a navigation area and then add descriptive hyperlinks, buttons, or other clickable graphics to the frame so viewers can easily jump from place to place. *For more information, see "Using Frames" on page 790.*

- ■ **Explain what you want.** If your page requires an action or input from the viewer, make it clear what you want the viewer to do. If you want the user to fill out a form, for example, explain exactly which information you want in each box and how to submit the form. Whenever possible, use sample input, menus, or drop-down lists to prevent confusion and eliminate typos. *For more information about user input forms, see "Making Web Forms" on page 805.*

- ■ **Beware of large graphics and multimedia files.** Graphics, sounds, movies, and animation can make your page more interesting, but they usually make it larger and slower to load. Use small graphics and multimedia files so the page loads as quickly as possible.

Creating a Web Page from Scratch

You can create a new Web page with the File menu's New command just as you create any other new Word document. And since you can save any Word document as a Web page, you can use the Blank Document or any other template to begin a new page if you like. However, the General tab in the New dialog box also includes a Web Page Template, and it's best to use that. Although a new Web Page document looks the same as a new Blank Document document on your screen, it isn't:

- ■ When you create a document with the Web Page Template, Word sets the document's file type to Web Page rather than Word Document, and displays the page in Web Layout view.

? SEE ALSO

For more information about opening documents and setting file types in the Save As dialog box, see "Creating New Documents" on page 134 and "Saving Documents" on page 137.

■ Word adds the HTML Source command to the bottom of the View menu. By choosing the HTML Source command, you can see the HTML text and formatting tags rather than the formatted text that will appear in a browser, as shown in Figure 32-2 on page 754.

Using Predesigned Web Page Templates

If you've never created a Web page before, Word gives you a head start with a selection of predesigned templates. To use one, open it as you would any other Word template by doing the following:

1 Choose New from the File menu.

? SEE ALSO

For more information about using and installing templates, see Chapter 13, "Using Templates and Wizards."

2 Click the Web Pages tab in the New dialog box. You'll see icons of the templates and wizards available for you to use, like this:

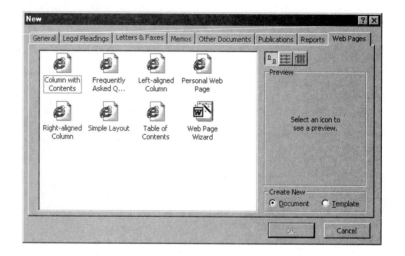

3 Double-click any page template to open it. Figure 32-4 on the next page shows the Personal Web Page template. (Notice The Genius, another of Word's Assistant characters, in the upper right corner of the screen.)

Templates contain instructional text or text placeholders to show you how the page might be laid out. To create your own page content, just select any of the existing placeholders and replace them with new text or objects.

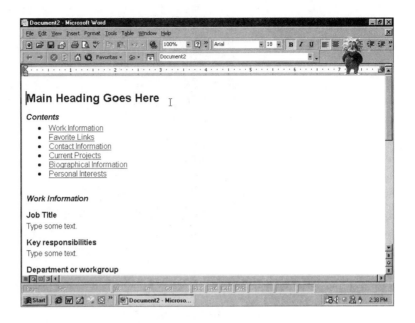

Using the Web Page Wizard

While templates create individual Web pages, the Web Page Wizard creates a whole Web site that contains multiple pages. With the Wizard, you can choose a storage location for the site, select a navigation system, add and organize the individual pages that make up the site, and add a theme for the site's overall look. Word then creates the entire site to your specifications. This is much easier than creating individual pages from scratch and then trying to link and organize them yourself.

Suppose we want to create a new Web site called Al's Grab Bag to sell a few products. Here's how to do a lot of the work quickly with the Web Page Wizard:

1 Choose New from the File menu and click the Web Pages tab in the New dialog box.

2 Double-click the Web Page Wizard icon on the Web Pages tab. The Wizard's dialog box opens and an introductory screen explains what the Wizard does.

3 Click the Next button. You'll be asked to name the Web site and choose a location for it. Type *Al's Grab Bag* as the site name and either enter a different location, click the Browse button to select a different location, or accept the location that's suggested, as shown at the top of the next page.

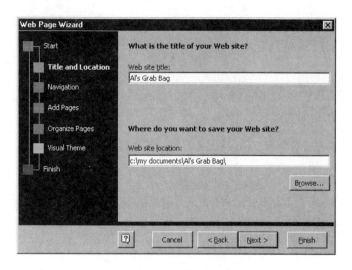

Word suggests the default document location, in this case *My Documents*.

4 Click Next. You'll be asked to choose where the site's navigation controls will appear on the page, like this:

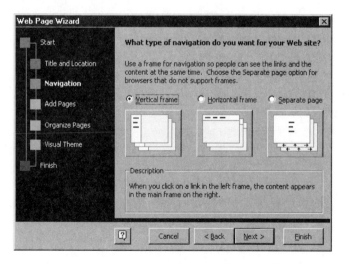

5 The Vertical Frame option is selected by default. Click Next, and you'll be asked to determine how many pages you'll need for your site, as shown at the top of the facing page.

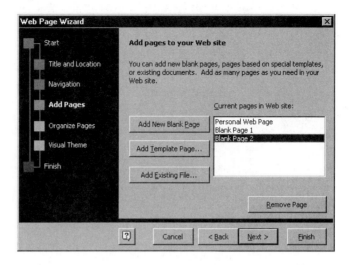

Word has already selected three pages for you to use. The Personal Web page is from one of the Web Page templates. For our site, we'll need to select the Personal Web page, click the Remove Page button to remove it, and then add four new blank pages. Don't worry about the page names yet: you'll have a chance to rename them in the next step.

6 Click the Next button after removing and adding the pages. You'll be given the chance to rearrange and rename pages, like this:

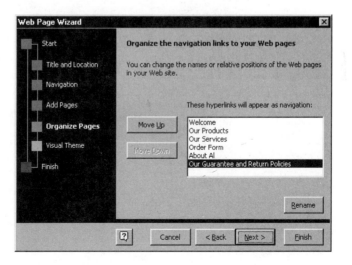

This example shows the pages we added, but renamed as they'll appear in Figure 32-5 on the facing page. To move a page up or down in the list, select it and click the Move Up or Move Down buttons. To rename any page, select it, click the Rename button, type a new name, and click OK.

★ TIP

As you create a site using the Wizard, you can click the Back button to revisit previous steps. If you get to the Organize Pages step and discover that you need another page or that you have one too many, you can return to the previous step and add or delete a page.

7 Rearrange and rename the pages the way you want and click Next. You'll be given a chance to choose a theme for the site, like this:

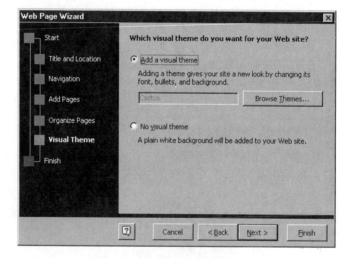

Click the Browse Themes dialog box to open the Theme dialog box and check out Word's built-in Web page themes. The one used in Figure 32-5 is Citrus Punch. *See "Using Themes" on page 313 for more information.*

8 Click Next to display the final Wizard screen, and then click Finish. Word creates the site and saves its files within one folder. Figure 32-5 on the next page shows the site immediately after it was created with the Web Page Wizard.

FIGURE 32-5.

The Web Page Wizard can create a structurally complete Web site with multiple pages, a navigation system, and a graphically consistent look.

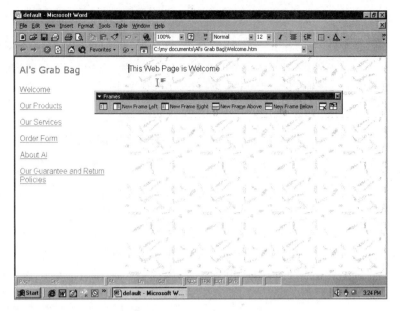

When the Wizard creates a site, it automatically creates the pages you specified for inclusion in it and saves them in the location you chose. (In Figure 32-5, the vertical frame we chose in Step 5 is on the left.) It also adds hyperlinks to the site's other pages in the order in which you arranged them with the Wizard, and includes placeholder text at the top of each page in the site. From this beginning, you can view all the other pages and add text, graphics, or other elements to them.

 NOTE

Since our new Web site contains a navigation frame, the Frames toolbar is also opened when the pages are created. *For more information about the Frames toolbar, see "Using Frames" on page 790.*

Adding Content to a Web Page

SEE ALSO

For more information about adding frames, sounds, or movie clips, see Chapter 33, "Using Word's Advanced Web Features."

To add text, graphics, or other content to a Web page, just insert individual items as you would in any Word document. You can format items as you go or, if you prefer, leave all of the formatting for later. If you're working from a template or from a page created with the Web Page Wizard, you can select the placeholder text or a graphic on the page and replace it by inserting something else.

When you work on a Web page, you can use any of Word's standard features for inserting text and graphics on a page, including the Insert menu commands, borders and shading, bulleted or numbered lists, or tables. These features are covered elsewhere in this book. In this chapter, let's look at some editing and formatting techniques that apply specifically to Web pages.

Working in Web Layout View

When you create a new Web page from a template or with the Web Page Wizard, Word automatically switches to Web Layout view. But even if you create a page from scratch, you'll want to work in Web Layout view because it more accurately represents how a page will look when viewed on the Web.

In Web Layout view, Word shows the background pattern or color you have chosen for the page. It also ignores or disables formatting options that don't apply to Web pages, such as page breaks, margin settings, headers and footers, tab stops, or multicolumn formatting.

Pixels are the standard unit of measurement for Web page objects, and you can set Word to show object sizes in pixels. If you're creating graphics or other objects on a page, you can set Word to show the size of the objects in pixels. To do this, choose Options from the Tools menu, click the General tab, select the Show Pixels For HTML Features check box, and click OK.

Creating a Page Design

For more page design tips and general information about how to create an effective design, see Chapter 23, "Designing Pages."

If you plan to combine text and graphics on a page, it's best to approach the page as you would a page layout project. For example, you will want to decide in advance whether you will enter text into the document's text layer or add it with text boxes. You will also want to sketch a design for the page before you begin adding content to it.

You must also remember that the page will be viewed on the screen. Although you will have greater flexibility with colors and graphics, you must be careful not to make the page hard to read. For example, yellow body text on a blue background may look interesting, but it's not very legible.

Use a table to create an organizing structure for elements on a page. *For more information about using tables, see Chapter 17, "Working with Tables."*

Formatting Text

Most of the text on a Web page will probably be standard Word body text. It's important to use styles to create a consistent, readable look for all of the text on the page. You can always reformat specific words or lines individually if you like, but styles will not only keep your document's appearance uniform, they'll also increase the likelihood that what you create will be what others see.

Themes are the simplest way to create a consistent format for a page. As explained in Chapter 15, "Using Styles and Themes," a theme controls the overall look of a Web page with a set of coordinated styles along with a background color or pattern and preselected graphic styles for bullets or horizontal lines.

You can select a theme for a new set of pages when you use the Web Page Wizard, and once you're working with a page, you can apply a theme at any time. To apply a theme, choose Theme from the Format menu and select a theme from the Theme dialog box.

> **NOTE**
>
> A theme is always applied to the active frame on a page. If your page has a separate navigation frame, be sure to click either in that frame or in the other part of the page so you'll apply the theme to the correct area.

SEE ALSO

For more information about applying a theme, see "Using Themes" on page 313.

When you apply a theme, Word adds several additional Heading styles to your document. Instead of using font, size, or style to distinguish the importance of text, HTML uses Heading level format tags. This way, larger type will always be larger for each viewer, regardless of the specific fonts installed on that person's system. The Heading styles that come with a theme are recognized HTML heading tags.

> **TIP**
>
> Even if you don't use a theme, there's another reason to use Word's Heading styles to format your page's title, headings, and subheadings. When you add a frame to a page, Word creates hyperlinks for all of the headings and subheadings in the page or site. *For more information, see "Creating a Table of Contents Frame" on page 796.*

Finally, use paragraph formatting options rather than spaces or tabs to align text on the screen. HTML ignores more than one space between any two words, and you can't use tabs in Web Layout view. When you use the Ruler or the Paragraph dialog box to set indents, however, Word translates the settings into HTML screen position tags.

VI

Web and Internet Tools

Adding a Scrolling Text Object

In an electronic document like a Web page, few things grab a viewer's attention more than text that scrolls across the screen. To add a scrolling text object, you'll need to insert a special HTML object using the Scrolling Text tool on the Web Tools toolbar. Here's what to do:

1 Right-click any toolbar and choose Web Tools to display the Web Tools toolbar if it isn't already open. Figure 32-6 shows this toolbar as a floating palette.

FIGURE 32-6.

To add scrolling text to a Web page, use the Scrolling Text tool in the Web Tools toolbar.

Scrolling Text tool

2 Move the insertion point to the place where you want the text to appear.

3 Click the Scrolling Text button on the Web Tools toolbar. Word displays the Scrolling Text dialog box as in Figure 32-7.

4 Delete the sample text in the Type The Scrolling Text Here box and enter the text you want. The Preview area shows how the text will move in your document.

FIGURE 32-7.

When you create a scrolling text object, you can specify its behavior and format.

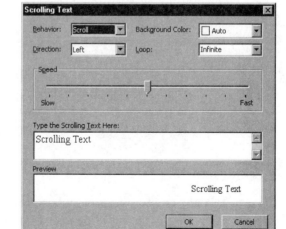

5 Select the text behavior from the Behavior menu, and then choose options on the Background Color and Direction menus. The Preview area shows how the text will look.

6 Choose an option from the Loop menu. You can have the text scroll from one to five times when the page is opened and then stop after that, or you can have it scroll continuously in an infinite loop.

7 Drag the slider to set the scrolling speed.

8 Click OK. The scrolling text object is embedded in your document, as seen in Figure 32-8.

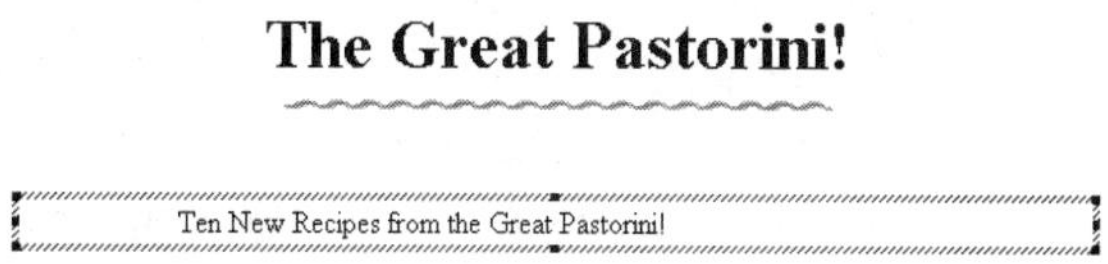

FIGURE 32-8.

Scrolling text objects can be moved or re-sized like other objects.

The Great Pastorini!

Ten New Recipes from the Great Pastorini!

? SEE ALSO

For more information about the formatting options for a scrolling object, see "Formatting Pictures" on page 463. For more information about the other tools on the Web Tools toolbar, see "Using the Web Tools Toolbar" on page 798.

Notice that the object is essentially a window inside which the text scrolls. You can move or resize the object by dragging its border or one of its handles or by choosing the Control command from the Format menu, but this doesn't change the size of the text inside it.

To reformat the text inside a scrolling object, select the object in your document and choose character formatting options by using the Font command on the Format menu or the Formatting toolbar.

To alter the text itself or reset the scrolling options, double-click inside the object to reopen the Scrolling Text dialog box and then make the changes you want.

Adding Graphics

To insert or format a graphic, use one of the techniques covered in Chapter 19 or Chapter 20, "Using Special Graphics." You can use any of Word's graphics tools when you create a Web page, whether you're drawing lines or shapes; inserting pictures, clip art, or text boxes; or adding AutoShapes or WordArt.

You'll want to keep graphics file sizes as small as possible so they load quickly into the page. There are two main ways to accomplish this:

- Resize the graphic to make it smaller. The smaller the graphic is on the page, the smaller its file will be.

VI

Web and Internet Tools

■ Use a lower-resolution version of the graphic. Low-resolution graphics files are much smaller than high-resolution graphics files. Most Web users have their screens set to a pixel resolution of either 640x480 or 800x600, so it's a needless waste of file space and loading time to use graphics that have higher resolution than that.

When a graphic is especially important on a page, you might consider adding a smaller, lower-resolution "thumbnail" version of it along with a hyperlink that users can click to see a larger or sharper version.

Adding Alternative Text to a Graphic

Many Web surfers browse pages without viewing any images on them, because the pages load more quickly that way. As a result, it's a good idea to add alternative text for the graphics on your pages so that text-only viewers will at least see a description of each graphic. Alternative text is positioned behind the graphic and is only visible when the graphic itself is not displayed. If you don't include alternative text and the graphic itself doesn't appear on the page, the viewer sees only a generic icon in place of the picture.

To add alternative text to a graphic, follow these steps:

1 Double-click the graphic to display the Format Picture dialog box.

2 Click the Web tab. You'll see a place where you can enter alternative text, like this:

3   Type the alternative text you want to appear when the picture is not loaded.

4   Click OK. The text is added to the page but you won't see it. To review the text or edit it, repeat the steps above to select the graphic and view the text on the Web tab of the Format Picture dialog box.

 TIP

Alternative text is stored in the page's HTML code, so it can be located by search engines on the Web. Web surfers often use widely varying terms when they search the Web, so by adding lots of alternative keywords behind the graphics on your pages, you'll increase the chances that your page will be listed in search results.

Adding Horizontal Lines

SEE ALSO

For information on the steps you take to add a horizontal line, see "Adding Colored Horizontal Lines" on page 291. For more information about formatting graphics, see Chapter 19, "Drawing and Manipulating Graphics," and Chapter 20, "Using Special Graphics."

Dividing lines are a staple of Web pages, and Word has a built-in capability for creating them. You can always draw a line with the Drawing toolbar and then change its fill color or pattern, but Word has a collection of predesigned lines you can choose with the Borders And Shading dialog box.

When you add a horizontal line to a Web page, it looks something like the wavy line under the page title in Figure 32-8 on page 769. When you click the line you'll see selection handles. You can select the line and drag it to another location, drag one of its selection handles to resize it, or double-click it to view and change its formatting options.

Graphic Formats on the Web

The two main graphic file formats used on the Web are GIF (Graphic Interchange Format) and JPEG (Joint Photographic Experts Group). You'll want to use these formats to ensure that graphics will be viewable in any browser.

When you include graphics in a Word document and then save the document as a Web page, the graphics are automatically stored as either GIF or JPEG, depending on their type. Word saves all line art or drawing objects as GIF files, and it saves all photographs, pictures or bitmaps in the JPEG format.

For details on how to add a picture bullet, see "Using a Picture Bullet" on page 281. For more information about how to create bulleted lists in general, see "Creating Bulleted and Numbered Lists" on page 273.

Adding Picture Bullets

You can create a bulleted list on a Web page the same as you can in any document—either by using the Bullets button on the Formatting toolbar or by choosing options in the Bullets And Numbering dialog box. Web pages, however, typically use picture bullets, and Word offers a collection of them. Themes include picture bullets, as well.

Formatting a Page Background

You can spice up any page by adding a background to it. Themes automatically add backgrounds to your pages, but you can add a background independently if you like. To do this, choose Background from the Format menu and choose one of the colors from the palette that appears. If your page contains more than one frame, the background is applied only to the frame where the insertion point is currently located.

You can also click the Fill Effects command on the Background palette to fill the background with a texture, gradient, or picture. For example, you might fill the home page from your travel services site with a photo of the beach at Acapulco. *For more information about filling backgrounds with custom colors, textures, gradients, or pictures, see "Changing the Fill and Line Options" on page 448.*

Using Hyperlinks

Along with the combination of text, graphics, and multimedia content on a viewable page, another feature that makes the Web so popular is the *hyperlink*. Rather than having to know a lengthy network address, you can navigate to a remote location by simply clicking a hyperlink. A hyperlink stores the address and is the basic method for navigation in a Web site. A hyperlink can navigate to other parts of the same Web page, to other pages within the same site, or to any other Web page on any server on the network. In addition, you can use hyperlinks as navigation aids in standard Word documents.

A hyperlink usually appears in a different color and is often underlined in a document, as seen as in Figure 32-1 on page 752. In addition, a hyperlink typically changes color after you click it the first time. This feature is handy when a document contains a lot of hyperlinks, because it tells you which ones you have already used.

Word 2000 has a much-improved system for inserting and managing hyperlinks.

Inserting a Hyperlink

You can insert a hyperlink in two ways. You can select text, a picture, or another object and turn it into a hyperlink, or you can create the text for a hyperlink and insert it at the same time. Here are the general steps for adding a hyperlink:

1   Move the insertion point to the place where you want the hyperlink to appear, or select the text or object you want to represent the hyperlink in your document.

> ### Hyperlinks Aren't Just for Web Pages
>
> Hyperlinks are prominent on Web pages, but you can use them elsewhere in Word as quick and easy navigation aids for any document that is viewed on the screen. Here are some ideas:
>
> - Add hyperlinks to Web resources so your readers can easily jump from a document to Web pages containing more information about specific topics.
>
> - Create a navigation table for a large report that you distribute via e-mail, and convert the section headings to hyperlinks so readers can simply click them to navigate.
>
> - Refer to hyperlinks in fields to navigate to text in the current document or to jump to and open a completely different file.
>
> - Specify hyperlinks in the Advanced Find dialog box when you conduct searches.
>
> As you come to know hyperlinks, you'll find them to be the most effective way to navigate in many kinds of documents.

VI

Web and Internet Tools

2 Press Ctrl+K, choose Hyperlink from the Insert menu, or click the Insert Hyperlink button on the Standard toolbar. Word opens the Insert Hyperlink dialog box, as seen in Figure 32-9.

FIGURE 32-9.

When you insert a hyperlink, you must specify the link's characteristics in the Insert Hyperlink dialog box.

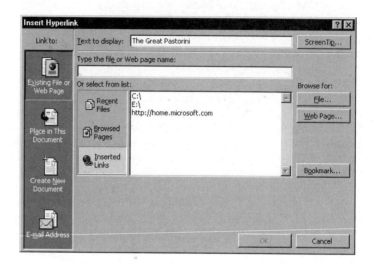

You can also right-click any word and choose Hyperlink from the shortcut menu to add a hyperlink to that word.

3 If you didn't select text beforehand, enter it in the Text To Display box. (If you selected text before inserting the hyperlink, the text you selected appears in the Text To Display box, as shown in Figure 32-9.) If you selected an object or graphic, you don't need to enter text because the object itself will become the hyperlink.

4 If you want a ScreenTip to appear when the viewer points to the hyperlink when viewing the page with Internet Explorer 4.0 or later, click the ScreenTip button and enter the text of the ScreenTip. For example, a ScreenTip for Figure 32-9 might lead to a biography of the Great Pastorini, and the tip might read, "Click here for Bio."

5 Select the general location where the hyperlink will go by using the Places bar at the left. The location contents and options in the middle of the dialog box change according to the general location you select here.

6   Select a navigation location in the list or type in the pathname to the location in the Type The File Or Web Page Name box. If you don't see the location you want and you don't remember it, click one of the buttons in the Browse area. Notice that there are specific browse buttons for locating a file, a Web page, or a bookmark in the current document.

> **NOTE**

> If you're adding a hyperlink to a Web page that contains frames, you'll see additional options at the bottom of the Insert Hyperlink dialog box that allow you to choose the frame where the hyperlink will appear. *For more about these options, click the Help button at the top of the Insert Hyperlink dialog box and then click a frame option.*

7   Click OK to insert the hyperlink.

Now let's look at the process in more detail. We'll assume you have already positioned the insertion point or selected text or an object in your document and have pressed Ctrl+K to display the Insert Hyperlink dialog box.

Linking to a Web Page or a File

Here's how to add a hyperlink to a Web page or a file:

1   Click the Existing File or Web Page icon in the Places bar at the left. You'll see options like the ones in Figure 32-9. Notice that the list of locations has its own miniature Places bar. You can click icons in this bar to see a list of files you have recently opened, Web pages you have recently browsed, or other links you have inserted.

2   Select a location from the list and click OK.

Linking to a Document Location

You can also create a hyperlink to a location in the current document:

1   Click the Place In This Document icon in the Places bar. If you're in a standard Word document at the time, the Insert Hyperlink dialog box will look something like the graphic at the top of the next page.

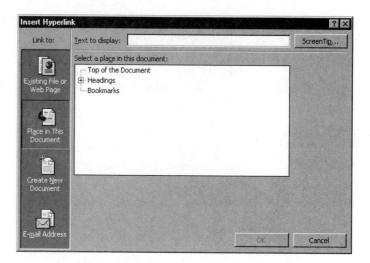

2 Click a location to select it. If there are headings and bookmarks in the document, these locations will indicate this with a plus sign, just as you see in the Headings group above. Click the plus sign to display individual document headings or bookmarks so you can select one of them.

3 Click the ScreenTip button and enter text for a ScreenTip attached to the hyperlink, if you like.

4 Click OK to create the link.

Linking to a New Document

If you haven't yet created the document to which you want the hyperlink to point, you can create it by using the Insert Hyperlink dialog box.

1 Click the Create New Document icon in the Places bar. The dialog box will then look something like the graphic at the top of the next page.

2 The current path name is shown in the Full Path area. Click the Change button to change the path name, if you like.

3 Enter the name of the new file in the Name Of New Document box.

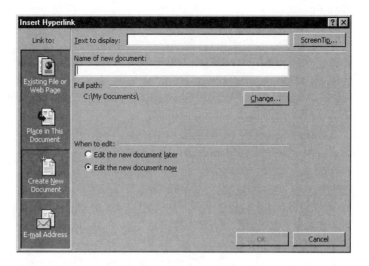

4   Click the ScreenTip button and enter text for a ScreenTip attached to the hyperlink, if you like.

5   Click one of the buttons in the When To Edit area. If you choose Edit The New Document Now, Word will open a blank document after you insert the hyperlink.

6   Click OK to insert the hyperlink.

Linking to an E-mail Message

When you link to an e-mail message, you create a "mailto" hyperlink that presents a preaddressed e-mail message when clicked. Mailto links are used when you want to make it easy for viewers to submit feedback, ask questions, or contact the owner of the page for any other reason.

When a mailto hyperlink is clicked, Word or the browser being used to view the document opens a blank e-mail form that already includes an e-mail address in the To box and a subject in the Subject box. (The e-mail form is supplied by the viewer's default e-mail program.) To complete the message, the user enters message text in the space provided and then clicks the Send button.

VI

Web and Internet Tools

To create a mailto hyperlink, follow these steps:

1 Click the E-mail Address icon in the Places bar. The Insert Hyperlink dialog box now looks something like this:

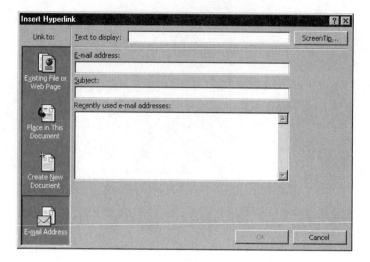

If you have created other mailto hyperlinks recently, the Recently Used E-mail Addresses list shows them. This is handy when you want to add the same mailto link to several different Web pages.

2 Select a previous e-mail address and display text from the list, or click in the E-mail Address box and enter the e-mail address to which you want these e-mail messages sent.

3 Click the ScreenTip button and add a ScreenTip to the hyperlink, if you like.

4 Enter a subject for the e-mail messages in the Subject box.

5 Click OK to create the link in your document.

Formatting a Hyperlink

Once you have inserted a hyperlink, you have a lot of options for formatting it, although it doesn't seem so at first glance. By default, all text hyperlinks you create appear underlined and in the same font as that of the surrounding paragraph, but they appear in a different color. For example, if you aren't using a theme in the document, a new hyper-link appears in blue text. Once the hyperlink has been clicked, or "followed," it appears in purple. But you're not stuck with these options.

Here's how to reformat a hyperlink:

- To modify one hyperlink, right-click it to display a shortcut menu, choose Font, select options in the Font dialog box, and then click OK.

- To modify every hyperlink in a document, choose Style from the Format menu and modify the Hyperlink or Followed Hyperlink styles (the "Followed Hyperlink" style is the way the hyperlink appears after it has been clicked).

? SEE ALSO

For more information about modifying styles, see "Modifying Styles" on page 307.

Word's Normal document template includes Hyperlink and Followed Hyperlink styles. Every hyperlink you create is automatically formatted with the Hyperlink and Followed Hyperlink styles, so you can easily reformat every hyperlink in a document by modifying one or both of these styles. By selecting and modifying these styles in the Style dialog box, you can change the text color, remove the underline, add another stylistic enhancement, or even change the font or size of hyperlinks in your documents. If you like, you can create custom hyperlink styles for different documents so that the style, size, and color of the hyperlinks will blend more harmoniously with the rest of the page.

★ TIP

To add to the consistent look of a Web page, set the hyperlink color to match that of the corporate logo, horizontal lines, or the most prominent graphics.

Selecting a Hyperlink

You can copy and paste hyperlinks just as you can any other text in your document. However, since a hyperlink jumps you to another location when you click it, you usually have to be a little careful about how you select it.

- To select an entire hyperlink, move the pointer to the space just to one side of the hyperlink, and then drag across to the space on the other side of the hyperlink.

- To select part of the text in a hyperlink, click and drag across the text, being careful not to release the mouse button until everything you want is selected.

- To select a graphic with an attached hyperlink, select it with the selection pointer on the Drawing toolbar.

VI

Web and Internet Tools

Copying and Pasting a Hyperlink

 SEE ALSO

For more information on the Paste Special command, see "Using the Paste Special Command" on page 66.

To copy and paste a hyperlink, use the same copy and paste techniques you would use to copy text: press Ctrl+C, move the insertion point to the place where you want the copy to appear, and press Ctrl+V. Word copies the hyperlink's HTML tag as well as the text.

To paste only the text of a hyperlink but not the link itself, use the Paste Special command and choose Unformatted Text to insert it as plain text.

Editing or Removing a Hyperlink

To remove a hyperlink or change the location to which it refers, use the Edit Hyperlink dialog box. This dialog box has the same options as the Insert Hyperlink dialog box featured in Figure 32-9 on page 774. To display the Edit Hyperlink dialog box, right-click the hyperlink and choose Edit Hyperlink from the Hyperlink submenu on the shortcut menu.

■ To change the hyperlink's location, edit the navigation details in the Edit Hyperlink dialog box and click OK.

Turning Off Automatic Hyperlinks

Word is set by default to recognize any URL or e-mail address you type and convert it into a hyperlink in every document. This is a good idea because even if you're preparing a document for printing, the hyperlink format lets readers identify these references as hyperlinks. Still, you may want to disable the automatic hyperlink formatting or convert a hyperlink back into ordinary text.

To disable automatic hyperlink formatting, follow these steps:

1 Choose AutoFormat from the Format menu and click the Options button to display the AutoCorrect dialog box.

2 Click the AutoFormat As You Type tab.

3 Clear the Internet And Network Paths With Hyperlinks check box in the Replace As You Type area.

4 Click OK to return to the AutoFormat dialog box, and then click OK again to return to your document.

To disable automatic hyperlink formatting when you use the AutoFormat command to format a whole document, click the AutoFormat tab in Step 2 above and then complete steps 3 and 4.

To convert one hyperlink back into ordinary text, right-click the hyperlink and choose Remove Hyperlink from the Hyperlink submenu on the shortcut menu.

- To remove a hyperlink, click the Remove Link button in the Edit Hyperlink dialog box. When you remove a link, you remove the link only, not the text or graphic to which it is attached.

You can also remove a hyperlink by right-clicking it and choosing Remove Hyperlink from the Hyperlink submenu on the shortcut menu.

Saving a Hyperlink as a Shortcut

Word can create shortcuts for your favorite hyperlinks, and it will even add them to your Favorite Places folder with the click of a mouse. To save a hyperlink as a shortcut, do the following:

1 Right-click the hyperlink and choose Add to Favorites from the Hyperlink submenu on the shortcut menu. You'll see a dialog box like the standard Save As dialog box, with the save location preset to the Favorites folder on your hard disk.

2 Change the save location if you like, and click Add to save the link. Word saves the hyperlink with a special hyperlink icon. For example, here's the icon for a hyperlink called Products:

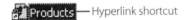—Hyperlink shortcut

Publishing Web Pages

There's a difference between saving Web pages and publishing them, even though from your perspective the two may appear much the same.

How Word Saves and Manages Web Pages

There are two ways you can save your Web page. You can use Word's Document format, or you can save it in the Web Page format, which converts it to HTML. When you save a document as a Web page, Word sets up a folder to contain any graphics, frames, or other components you have added to the page. For example, if you save a page called Welcome as a Web page, Word creates a folder called Welcome Files in the same location and stores the page's component files inside it.

When you create a whole Web site with the Web Page Wizard, Word automatically creates a master folder for the site, stores each of the site's pages in it, and creates a subfolder for each page to hold its components. You specify a location for the site folder as you work through the Wizard. If you want to edit any of the site's pages or component files later, however, you'll have to open and save them individually.

You can save Web page files anywhere you want, but if you save them to a Web folder in the Web Folders directory, they will automatically be copied to the Web server to which the Web Folder points. Essentially, saving to a Web folder simultaneously saves your pages locally and publishes them on the Web. Web folders are especially useful when you work with pages that must be edited frequently—you can simply open the page in Word, make the edits, and press Ctrl+S to save and publish the changes.

Previewing a Web Page

Before you publish a page, make sure it will look the way you want by viewing it in a browser. To do this from Word, just choose Web Page Preview from the File menu. Word launches your default browser and loads the page into it. You can then see exactly how the page will look to others on the Web who are using the same browser with a similar screen setup.

If you have both Netscape Navigator and Microsoft Internet Explorer on your computer, it's a good idea to see how your pages look in both browsers before publishing them, so you can adjust for any display variations. To view your pages in a browser that isn't your computer's default browser, open the browser itself and then use its Open command to locate and open the page you want to see.

Creating a Web Folder

Before you can save pages to the Web Folders location, you must create a folder inside that location that will contain all the pages and supporting files you wish to publish. To create a Web folder, do the following:

1 Choose Open from the File menu and click the Web Folders icon in the Places bar. Word navigates to the Web Folders location on your hard disk.

2 Click the Create New Folder button on the Open dialog box. The Add Web Folder Wizard appears, as shown on the next page.

3 Type the URL of the Web server directory where you want to publish the pages from this folder or click Browse to launch your Web browser to search for and open a Web directory using the browser's navigation controls.

 NOTE

> You can browse for a Web folder only if the Web server you plan to use has the Office Server Extensions installed. Contact the server's administrator for information.

4 Click Next. Word verifies that the location is a valid one and asks you to enter a name for the folder.

NOTE

> You cannot create a Web folder in the Web Folders location without linking that folder to a valid Web server directory.

5 Type a name for the new folder and click OK. The folder now appears inside the Web Folders location, and your pages are stored and ready to be published. When you save Web pages to this folder, they will also be transferred automatically to the Web server associated with the folder.

Saving and Publishing Web Pages

There are two steps to saving and publishing a Web page: saving the page in HTML format and saving the HTML version of the page on a Web server. If you have set up a Web folder as explained in the

VI

Web and Internet Tools

previous section, Word can handle both of these tasks with just one command. But even if you don't have a Web folder set up, the process is very simple. Here's the procedure:

> You must have permission to publish to a Web server. If you try to save to a directory on a Web server and you get a message that says your access is denied, contact your Internet service provider or your company's network administrator.

1   Open the welcome, default, or home page for your Web site, or open the individual page you want to publish.

2   Choose Save As Web Page from the File menu. Word opens the Save As dialog box and sets the Save As Type list to Web Page, as shown in Figure 32-10.

FIGURE 32-10.

When you save a Web page, you can add or change a page title in the Save As dialog box.

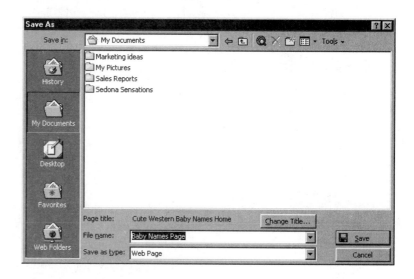

3   Enter a different file name in the File Name box if you like.

> Web servers don't recognize files as Web pages unless they have the .htm extension, but Word adds the extension automatically when you save a file as a Web page.

4   If you have already set up a Web folder to contain the page, that folder is listed as the save destination. If you haven't set up a

? SEE ALSO

For instructions about setting up a Web folder, see "Creating a Web Folder" on page 782.

Web folder, save the page and its component files to any directory, and then either use the Windows desktop or Windows Explorer to copy them to a Web server on your company intranet; or use FTP to transfer them to a directory on a Web server maintained by your Internet service provider.

5 Click the Change Title button above the File Name box and add or edit the page title, if necessary, and then click the Save button.

6 If the page contains format elements that can't be reproduced in a browser, Word will alert you with a dialog box like this:

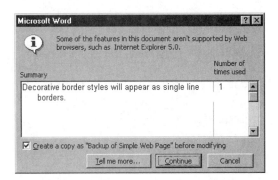

The alert box lists the page's incompatible features and the number of times they are used. If you click Continue to save the page, Word saves it in HTML format, but without the incompatible features. At the same time, Word will create a backup copy of the page in Word document format so the original features will be preserved there. If you don't want Word to save the backup copy, clear the Create A Copy As Backup check box.

 TIP

Click the Tell Me More button to get more information about how to work around incompatible features.

7 Click the Continue button to save the page.

Updating and Managing Web Pages

Keeping track of the myriad files that can be involved with a Web site is one of the major hassles of being a Webmaster, but Word handles the organization and updating chores for you. In addition to organizing files as described above, Word also manages Web page links and content automatically.

VI

Web and Internet Tools

For example, as mentioned earlier in the chapter, if you edit a Web page and delete a graphic, Word also deletes the graphic's file from that page's folder. And whenever you save a Web page, Word automatically verifies and updates all hyperlinks that are used to refer pages in the site to one another.

⭐ **TIP**

> Don't delete files inside a Web page's folder or subfolder unless you know exactly what you're doing. The files and folders are all there because they're required to present the pages you design.

Adding a Page to a Site

To add a new page to a Web site, you must create the page, save it to the same location as the other pages, and add hyperlinks to the site's default or home page (and perhaps to other places) so users can jump to the new page from anywhere else in the site. Here's the general procedure:

1 Create a new document from a Web page template, and work with it in Web Layout view. If you used a certain theme, background, or group of styles in the other pages in the site, you'll probably want to use the same format in the new page so it blends in. Check the page in your browser to make sure it looks the way you want.

2 Save the document as a Web page inside the folder that contains all of the other pages for the site. For example, if your Web site was originally saved in a folder called My Site, make sure to save the new page inside the My Site folder. When you do, Word will also create a subfolder to contain any of your page's component files, such as graphics, sounds, or movies.

3 Open the default or home page of the site, and add a new hyperlink to the navigation frame or to the contents area of the page that points to the new page. Save the page when you're done.

4 Open any other pages in the site, if necessary, and add hyperlinks to the new page from those as well. Save each page when you're done.

5 Open the default page in your browser and check the new hyperlinks to make sure each one jumps properly to the new page.

Removing a Page from a Site

There are two ways to delete a page from a Web site. You can delete the page or move it to a different location, or you can simply delete any hyperlinks that lead to it from the site's default page or other pages. If you've spent a lot of time designing a page, you'll probably want to preserve it on your disk so you'll still be able to modify it and use it again.

If you delete every hyperlink to a page, it is effectively inaccessible unless the user knows the page's specific URL. However, you may want to go farther and remove the page and its folder of component files from the Web server completely, retaining a copy of it on your local disk for possible future use.

If you remove the page and its folder from the Web server, you should also move the page and its folder outside the Web site's folder in the Web Folders location on your hard disk. This way, you won't accidentally republish the page to the Web server the next time you save pages from that Web folder.

Editing a Web Page with Internet Explorer

Since Word publishes copies of your Web files rather than the files themselves, you can always use the standard Open command on the File menu to open and edit pages that aren't stored on a Web server. When you do this, however, you must republish any changed pages in order to transfer your edits to the Web. If you're using Internet 0Explorer 4.0 or later, there's an easier way: initiate editing right from inside your browser. Here's how to do this:

1 Open Internet Explorer and navigate to the page you want to edit.

2 Click the Edit button on the Standard toolbar or choose Edit With Microsoft Office 2000 from the File menu. Word opens with the Web page in its document window.

3 Make the changes you want to make.

4 Press Ctrl+S to save the changes. Word automatically saves the page in HTML format at the same Web server location.

5 Return to your browser and click the Refresh button. The changes you made will appear in the document.

Now that you've learned the basic procedures for creating and publishing a Web page, go on to Chapter 33 for information about adding zip to your pages with special features.

CHAPTER 33

Using Word's Advanced Web Features

Although the quality of the information on your Web pages will be their biggest attraction, that doesn't mean they have to be static and boring. You can make any Web page more interesting or easier to use by adding navigation frames, sounds, animation, or movie clips. And if you want to collect information as well as present it, Microsoft Word 2000 makes it easy to create interactive forms that viewers can fill in and send to you with a click of the mouse. In this chapter you'll learn how to use these advanced features of Microsoft Word.

With Word, you can add sophisticated enhancements such as frames, sounds, and movie clips to your Web pages with ease. And if you're familiar with Visual Basic or a Web scripting language such as Java, you can do far more sophisticated tasks.

Using Frames

A frame is a separate document in the browser window, and it is stored as a separate file. When you add a frame to a Web page, the page is divided into two frames, which appear as separate panes in the document window. A frame is a good way to present navigation options that will appear on every page the viewer visits. In Figure 33-1, for example, the navigation frame on the left contains hyperlinks that viewers can click to see other parts of the document or to display other documents. When the viewer selects a hyperlink, the navigation frame remains in position while the frame on the right changes.

FIGURE 33-1.

Use a frame to present navigation links that stay on the screen no matter which page in the site is viewed.

Frame border

Frame ⎯⎯⎯⎯

You can also use a frame to display a corporate logo, a document header, a document summary, or anything else that you want the viewer to see at all times while viewing your Web site.

It's simple to add a frame to any Web page in Word. When you insert a frame, you indicate where you want it to be and Word puts it there automatically. You can choose to display a scroll bar in the frame if you like, and you can add text, hyperlinks, graphics, or form components to it as you can to any other document. As we'll see, Word makes it particularly easy to create a "table of contents" frame that acts as a navigation bar for a Web site.

How Word Handles Frames

 SEE ALSO

For more information about linking and embedding objects, see Chapter 21,"Working with Objects."

Word stores frames in special Frames pages. This means that if a Web page doesn't already contain a frame, Word will turn it into a Frames page when you add a frame to it. The new frame is a separate file, but it is embedded in the page where you insert it. The original document is then designated the Main Frame or Frame 1 and the new frame is called the Top Frame, Left Frame, Right Frame, Bottom Frame, or simply Frame 2, depending on where you insert it. To avoid confusion, we'll use *frame* to refer to only a frame that's been added.

When you add a frame to a Web page, the specific page to which you add the frame is the *initial document*. After you create a frame, you can embed it in a different initial document if you like. For example, if you initially add a frame to a page that is the home page of your Web site but you later create a new home page, you can attach the frame to the new page instead. You can also link the frame to a document rather than embed it.

 TIP

> You can add several frames to the same page, but it's not a good idea. Most viewers get confused pretty quickly when a page has more than two scrolling frames. However, you might add one frame without a scroll bar to display a group of navigation icons or a corporate logo, and then use a second, scrolling frame to show the site's contents as a list of hyperlinks in an outline format.

Creating an Empty Frame

When you create an empty frame, you must indicate whether you want the frame at the top, bottom, left side, or right side of the document window. For example, suppose your personal Web page has grown to the point where some navigation options would really help users find different areas of the page, and you want to create a new frame on the left side of the page. To do this, follow these steps:

1 Open the page in Web Layout view.

2 On the Format menu, point to Frames and choose New Frames Page. Word converts the document into a Frames page, and opens the Frames toolbar as shown in Figure 33-2 on the next page.

 TIP

> When you work with a Frames page, the Frames submenu on the Format menu contains the same commands you see in the Frames toolbar.

VI

Web and Internet Tools

FIGURE 33-2.

The Frames toolbar allows you to insert or reformat frames.

Table of contents in frame   Delete frame   Frame properties

3 Click the New Frame Left button on the Frames toolbar.

4 Word adds a new, empty frame on the left side of the document window:

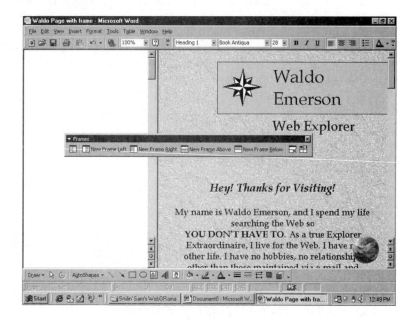

(The globe in the lower right corner of the page is another one of Word's Office Assistant characters—this one is called Mother Nature.)

 **SEE ALSO**

For more information about adding content to a frame and formatting that content, see "Adding Content to a Web Page" on page 765.

Adding Content to a Frame

You can add text, graphics, hyperlinks, or other objects and format the frame's contents using any of Word's standard editing and formatting tools. Just make sure to click inside the frame first before you begin typing, drawing, inserting, or pasting so Word knows where to put the content.

⭐ **TIP**

The spelling and grammar checkers work inside frames just as they do in other documents.

Formatting a Frame

Although a frame always runs the length or width of the document window, you can resize it, add a background color to it, or set other properties for it.

Resizing a Frame

The simplest way to resize a frame is to drag it with the mouse pointer. Just point to the border between the frame and the initial document—you'll see the double-headed Resize arrow when the pointer is on the border—and then drag the border.

You can also specify a precise width for the frame with the Frame Properties dialog box, as we'll see next.

Opening the Frame Properties Dialog Box

You can set a frame's size, border width, and other options all at once with the Frame Properties dialog box shown in Figure 33-3. To display the Frame Properties dialog box, click the Frame Properties button on the Frames toolbar or right-click in a blank portion of the frame and choose Frame Properties from the shortcut menu.

FIGURE 33-3.

You can change a frame's document link, resize it, or change its border or scroll bar options with the Frame Properties dialog box.

Enter or select the URL or path name of the Web page where the frame first appears.

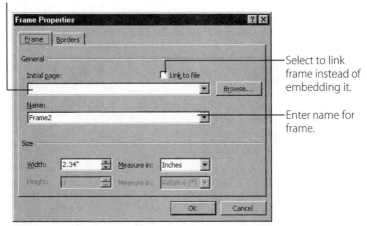

Select to link frame instead of embedding it.

Enter name for frame.

To set options here, click the tab you want, choose or specify the options you want, and then click OK to make the changes. The sections that follow show how the options work.

Changing a Frame's Properties

To change the frame's width, height, or initial page, click the Frame tab in the Frame Properties dialog box (if necessary) to display the options shown in Figure 33-3.

Depending on whether a frame is vertical or horizontal, you can change its width or height. Just choose an option from the Measure In menu and enter a new value in the Width box. When you choose the Relative option, the Width or Height box values are multiples of the frame's default width or height. You can also set the width and height in terms of inches or as a percentage of the window space.

> To change page measurements to pixels, choose Options from the Tools menu and click the Show Pixels For HTML Features check box on the General tab.

To change the initial page that displays the frame, enter the new page's path or URL in the Initial Page box or choose a name from the drop-down menu. The Link To File check box is automatically selected when you change the initial page so the frame is linked to the new initial page rather than embedded in it, but you can clear the check box to embed the frame in the new initial page.

Changing Border or Scroll Bar Options

To change the frame's border or scroll bar options, click the Borders tab to display the options shown in Figure 33-4.

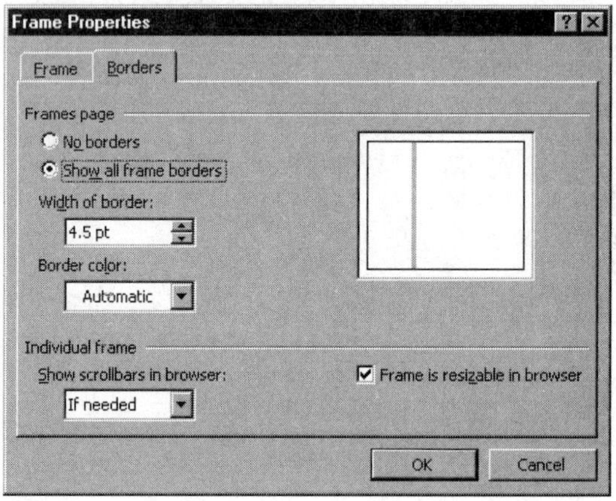

FIGURE 33-4.

By using the Borders tab in the Frame Properties dialog box, you can set a frame's border or scroll bar options.

The border is normally a thin shaded line between the frame's scroll bar and the rest of the document window, as shown in Figure 33-1 on page 790.

- To hide the frame border, click the No Borders option.

⭐ TIP

When you use a frame to display a corporate logo or a graphic in a permanent banner on the page, hide the border and scroll bar so the banner blends seamlessly with the rest of the page.

- To change the border's width, click the arrows on the Width Of Border box or enter a value in the box itself. (The border in Figure 33-1 on page 790 was widened to show it more clearly.)

- To change the border color, choose a color from the Border Color palette.

- To hide the frame's scroll bar or to set it to appear only when it's needed, choose If Needed or Never from the Show Scrollbars In Browser menu.

⚠ WARNING

There is no way to scroll a frame when its scroll bars are hidden, so make sure the frame shows all of its contents before hiding the scroll bars.

❓ SEE ALSO

For more information about the Frame Properties dialog box, click the Help button on the dialog box and then click on any option.

- To lock the frame so it can't be resized by dragging its border in a browser, clear the Frame Is Resizable In Browser check box. A viewer normally has the option to drag and resize a frame in the browser, but you can lock the frame if a resized frame will interfere with your design or the page's overall readability.

Changing the Background Color or Applying a Theme

New frames have a white background, but you can make a frame stand out on your Web page by setting it off with a different background color or by applying a theme to it.

To change the background color, click anywhere inside the frame, choose Background from the Format menu, and then select a color from the palette that appears.

VI

Web and Internet Tools

⊛ TIP

You can use a color, texture, pattern, or picture as the background of a page or a frame. *For more information about fill options, see "Changing the Fill and Line Options" on page 448.*

⑦ SEE ALSO
For more information about the Theme dialog box, see "Using Themes" on page 313.

To apply a theme to a frame, click inside the frame, choose Theme from the Format menu, and then select a theme in the Theme dialog box.

Deleting a Frame

If you decide you can live without a frame after all, it's easy to get rid of it: Click inside the frame and then click the Delete Frame button on the Frames toolbar. If the frame contains text or graphics or you have done any editing in it at all, Word will ask whether you want to save the frame's contents as a separate document before deleting it.

⊙ NOTE

You can't cut, copy, or paste frames.

Creating a Table of Contents Frame

A frame is most often used as a navigation area or table of contents. If you have formatted all of the page's headings and subheadings with Word's Heading styles, Word can automatically create a table of contents frame that contains hyperlinks to each of them.

⊙ NOTE

When you add a table of contents frame, Word only includes links formatted with its Heading styles, so you must add hyperlinks to other documents or other Web pages by inserting them manually in the frame. *For more information, see "Inserting a Hyperlink" on page 773.*

To add a table of contents frame, follow these steps:

1 Display the Web page to which you want to add the frame.

⑦ SEE ALSO
For more information on applying styles, see Chapter 15, "Using Styles and Themes."

2 Select each document heading or subheading and apply a Heading style to it.

3 Click Frames on the Format menu or click the Table Of Contents In Frame button on the Frames toolbar. Word adds the frame and places the appropriate hyperlinks inside it.

NOTE

If you're working with a new Web page and haven't saved it yet, Word will ask you to save the page before creating the frame. Word needs to learn the name and location of the frame's initial page before it knows where to save the frame.

4   Select the hyperlinks inside the frame and reformat them. You can add extra lines to create spaces between main categories, apply styles to change text indents or character formats, add bulleted or numbered list formatting, or use the Ruler to change the indent settings for any of the links. Figure 33-5 shows a table of contents frame with some additional formatting added.

FIGURE 33-5.

When you add a table of contents frame, Word automatically adds hyperlinks for each heading in your document to the new frame.

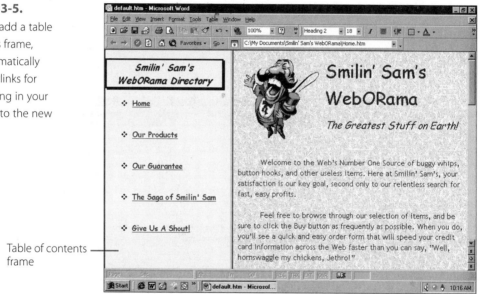

Table of contents frame

Adding Sounds and Movies

Sounds and movies can add a lot to a Web site. Movies can show events or demonstrate techniques, and sounds can add a background "sound-track" to a site, or you can use them to present audio clips or music samples. You can add sounds and movies to Web pages with a few mouse clicks using the Web Tools toolbar.

VI

Web and Internet Tools

NOTE

In order to play a sound or movie, the computer being used to view the page must have sound or movie playback software installed as an extension to its browser, along with a sound card and speakers or headphones. The newest versions of Microsoft Internet Explorer and Netscape Navigator include sound and video playback capabilities.

Using the Web Tools Toolbar

You can add sounds and movies to a Web page using the Object command on the Insert menu, but it's easier to use the Web Tools toolbar. To open the Web Tools toolbar, right-click in any toolbar and choose Web Tools from the shortcut menu. The Web Tools toolbar is shown in Figure 33-6.

FIGURE 33-6.

The Web Tools toolbar is the easiest way to add Web form objects, sounds, and movies to a page.

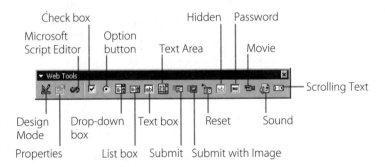

Multimedia Is Great, But...

Sounds and movies, like other elements of a Web page, are stored in individual files, and those files can be quite large. Before you run amok adding sounds and movies to your pages, consider your audience. If most of them have dial-up connections to the World Wide Web, it can often take anywhere from 30 seconds to several minutes for them to download movies. And if the viewer is using a slower (pre-Pentium) computer, the sound or movie probably won't play at its normal speed anyway.

When you are designing Web pages, it's best to give the viewer as much control over the experience as possible, and multimedia elements are definitely something you want the user to be able to control. Rather than simply embedding a sound or a movie in a page so that it plays automatically when the page is viewed, let users decide whether to play the clip. To do this, add a button or hyperlink to the sound or movie that must be clicked in order to play the clip. (See "Creating a Sound Hyperlink" on page 800).

Adding a Background Sound

When you add a background sound to a Web page, Word assumes that you want the sound to play automatically when the page is loaded into a browser, as a kind of sound track for the page. To add an automatic background sound to your Web page, follow these steps:

1 Click the Sound button on the Web Tools toolbar. Word opens the Background Sound dialog box, as seen here:

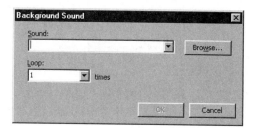

2 If you have selected other sounds previously and want to use one of those, click the Sound menu's arrow button to select one. You can also type in the path name for the sound you want to add, or click the Browse button to navigate to and select a sound.

 TIP

When you click the Browse button, Word opens the Media folder inside the Windows folder on your hard disk, where you'll see a list of sounds used by Windows for various alerts or other actions on the desktop. You can create new sound files by recording them on your PC, or by copying them from another source. There are lots of collections of sound files available from computer user groups or commercial sources. Try searching the Web for "Multimedia files" to find other sources. *For more information about recording sounds on your PC, choose Help from the Windows Start menu and search for "Sound Recorder" in the Help system index.*

 ON THE WEB

Choose Office On The Web from the Help menu to check for new sounds and video clips available from the Microsoft Office Web site.

 NOTE

You can insert sounds in WAV, MID, AU, AIF, RMI, SND, and MP2 (MPEG) format.

3 Choose an option from the Loop menu. If you choose the Infinite option to repeat the sound endlessly, the sound will continue playing as long as the page is displayed.

VI

Web and Internet Tools

4 Click OK to insert the sound. Word immediately plays the sound and inserts an icon to represent it on your page.

You can also use the Object command on the Insert menu to insert a sound of a specific type. When you choose the Object command, you'll see the Object dialog box, and you can create a new sound or select an existing one here.

For more information about inserting objects, see Chapter 21, "Working with Objects."

SEE ALSO

For more information about creating hyperlinks, see "Inserting a Hyperlink" on page 773.

Creating a Sound Hyperlink

By adding a hyperlink to a sound, you can let your viewer decide when to play it—or whether to play it at all. You can also insert several sounds that can be played individually. Here's how to insert a sound hyperlink:

1 Move the insertion point to where you want the hyperlink to appear, or select the text on your page that you want to represent the hyperlink.

2 Press Ctrl+K to display the Insert Hyperlink dialog box.

3 Click the File button in the Browse For area and then locate and select the sound file you want.

4 In the Text to Display box, enter text to represent the hyperlink on your page (unless you select text before opening the Insert Hyperlink dialog box.)

Sound Advice

Here are three things to keep in mind when you add sounds to your pages:

- Once a sound begins playing, the only way the person viewing the page on the Web can stop it is to load a different page. Don't use the Infinite option as a Loop value in the Background sound dialog box unless you're using a soothing sound.

- Don't add more than one background sound to a page unless you're trying to create harmony. All background sounds play at the same time, so if you add more than one, the viewer will hear them all at once. To give page viewers access to more than one sound (such as segments from different songs on your Favorite Music page), insert the sounds as hyperlinks.

- When you are finished adding sounds to a page, set your computer to a medium sound level, open the page in your browser, and play the sound(s). You may find that a sound is too soft or too loud. If so, you may need to rerecord it at a different level.

5 Set other options if you like and then click OK to insert the hyperlink.

Adding a Movie

When you add a movie to a Web page, you can choose whether it plays automatically or only when the user points to it. Since movie files are especially large, you can also select an alternate image to display when movie viewing is turned off or is unavailable in the viewer's browser. You can also add alternate text so that if the viewer can't see the movie or its alternate image, there will be something to read instead.

To add a movie to your Web page, follow these steps:

1 Move the insertion point to the place where you want the movie image to appear.

2 Click the Movie button on the Web Tools toolbar. Word opens the Movie Clip dialog box as in Figure 33-7 on the next page.

Movie Formats and Movie Players

There are different movie formats and different movie players. Microsoft Office programs and Microsoft Internet Explorer offer built-in support for two common digital movie formats, AVI and MPEG. Windows also comes with a built-in movie player accessory called the Windows Media Player. (To see it, choose Programs from the Start menu, open the Accessories subfolder, open the Entertainment subfolder, and choose Windows Media Player.) The Windows Media Player supports AVI and MPEG files as well, but it also gives you more control over a movie when it plays: the Media Player window shows the movie's length, and you can easily rewind a movie or play a certain segment of frames.

Other movie formats such as QuickTime and RealMedia aren't compatible with Office programs or the Windows Media Player. In order to insert and view QuickTime and RealMedia movies on your Web pages, you must install Apple's QuickTime or RealPlayer from RealNetworks, respectively.

For more information about RealPlayer or QuickTime products, visit http://www.real.com *or* http://www.apple.com, *respectively. For more information about Media Player, open the Media Player program from the Start menu and choose Help Topics from the Help menu.*

VI

Web and Internet Tools

FIGURE 33-7.

When you add a movie to a Web page, you can also specify options to control its appearance.

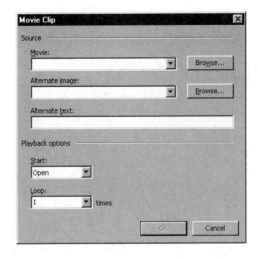

3 In the Movie box, enter the path for the movie clip you want to add or click the Browse button to navigate to and select a movie clip. If you have selected other movie clips previously and want to use one of those, you can also click the arrow button on the Movie menu to select one of them.

 ON THE WEB

To look for movies you can download from the Web and try out in your Web pages, choose Office On The Web from the Help menu or open your browser and search for "multimedia files."

4 In the Alternate Image box, enter the path for the alternate graphic file that will be displayed if the viewer's browser can't play movies or if the viewer has turned that function off. You can also click the Browse button or choose a recently used image from the Alternate Image menu.

5 In the Alternate Text box, enter the text that will appear when neither the movie nor its alternate image are showing in a browser. For example, the alternate text for a product demonstration video might read: "Video of the JetMaker in action."

6 Use the Start menu to specify when the movie will play. You can have the movie play when the page is opened (Open), when the viewer points to it (Mouse-over), or both (Both).

TIP

To include a movie that will play only when the viewer clicks it, insert a picture showing one frame of the movie and add a hyperlink to the picture that will open the movie and play it when the link is clicked.

7   Choose an option from the Loop menu. You can have the movie play from one to five times or repeat infinitely.

8   Click OK to insert the movie. If you haven't selected an alternate image, a message will warn you that some browsers don't support inline movie clips.

9   Click the Select Image button to choose an alternate image or click the Continue button to insert the movie. If you are inserting a movie compatible with Word or the Windows Media Player and you used the Open option, you'll see the first frame of the movie on your screen, like this:

My vacation video is here!

 If you're inserting a movie in QuickTime or RealMedia format but you don't have QuickTime or RealPlayer installed, you'll see a generic movie icon.

If you inserted a movie compatible with Word or the Windows Media Player using the Mouse Over or Both option, the movie will begin playing.

If you have RealPlayer or QuickTime installed, you'll see an icon from one of those programs.

Playing a Movie or Resetting Its Options

You can review a movie right on your Web page as you work, if you like. You can change its display options or choose a different movie or alternate image for the page as well.

■   If the movie is in AVI or MPEG format, right-click it and choose Play from the shortcut menu. You can stop the playback by right-clicking the movie and choosing Stop.

■   If the movie is in RealMedia or QuickTime format, you must have RealPlayer or QuickTime installed on your computer in order to view it. To view the movie, right-click it and choose Play to launch its viewer program. The RealPlayer or QuickTime viewer's window will open and you can use its controls to play the movie.

■ To reset the display options for any kind of movie, right-click it and choose Properties from the shortcut menu. You'll see the Movie Clip dialog box, where you can reset the movie's options.

Adding Animation Clips

Animated graphics, or "animated GIFs" as they're often called, are an easy way to add life and color to a Web page. Word 2000 comes with a selection of animated graphics called Motion Clips, and you'll find them in the Clip Gallery.

NOTE

> Motion clip animations appear only when you view them in a Web browser. When you view a clip in Web Layout or other Word views, you see the graphic but not the animation.

SEE ALSO

For more information on using the Clip Art Gallery, see "Using Clip Art" on page 449.

To add a motion clip, follow these steps:

1 Move the insertion point to the place on a Web page where you want the clip to appear.

2 Choose Clip Art from the Picture submenu on the Insert menu to open the Clip Gallery, or click the Insert Clip Art button on the Drawing toolbar. The Insert ClipArt window opens.

3 Click the Motion Clips tab to see categories of motion clips, like this:

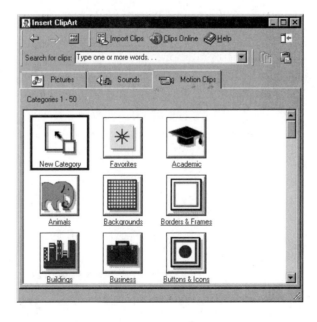

4 Click a category icon to view clips in that category.

5 Click a specific clip to display a control palette, and then click the Insert Clip icon at the top of the palette. The clip is added to the Web page.

6 Click the Close button on the Clip Gallery window.

 ON THE WEB

Click the Clips Online button at the top of the Insert ClipArt window to access a Microsoft Web page where you can view and download animation clips. Downloaded clips are placed in the Downloaded Clips category in the Insert ClipArt window.

Making Web Forms

A form is by far the most efficient way to compile information from viewers of your Web page. You can use a registration form to learn the names of the people who access your page and how to contact them; you can take a survey; and you can build order forms which viewers can use to order and pay for things.

 **TIP**

The simplest way to get feedback from viewers is to include a *mailto:* hyperlink on the page, along with some text asking viewers to send you e-mail messages. *See "Linking to an E-mail Message" on page 777.*

Using FrontPage 2000 to Create Forms

Although Word offers a complete selection of tools for adding drop-down lists and other controls to Web forms, you must understand Visual Basic or a Web scripting or programming language in order to use them. If your installation of Office includes Microsoft FrontPage 2000, it is much easier to create forms with that program. In FrontPage 2000, you'll find several page creation wizards that automatically add lists, check boxes, buttons, and other controls to a page and arrange them in several different kinds of forms. There's also more online Help available in FrontPage about how to program those components so they work properly.

If you're new to Web forms, FrontPage 2000 is the best place to start learning about them.

VI

Web and Internet Tools

With a form, you can be very specific about the kinds of information you request and how that information is compiled and transmitted back to you. You can use drop-down lists, check boxes, radio buttons, and other *form controls* to prevent data entry errors or simply to make forms easier to complete. You can also add a Submit button that automatically sends the contents of the form via e-mail to any address you choose.

To create a Web form with Word, you must use either the Web Tools toolbar (shown in Figure 33-6 on page 798) or the Control Toolbox toolbar shown in Figure 33-8 to add form controls one by one and then arrange them on a Web page.

NOTE

> In order to use controls from the Control Toolbox or Web Tools toolbars, you must know how to write programs using (respectively) Visual Basic or a scripting or programming language such as Visual J++. These subjects are beyond the scope of this book, but there's a good general overview of Visual Basic in Chapter 29, "Working with Microsoft Visual Basic."

Using the Web Tools or Control Toolbox Toolbars

As mentioned earlier, you can use either the Web Tools toolbar or the Control Toolbox toolbar to add form controls to a Web page. The Web Tools toolbar is shown in Figure 33-6 on page 798, and the Control Toolbox toolbar appears in Figure 33-8 below.

FIGURE 33-8.

The Control Toolbox toolbar allows you to add sophisticated controls to a Web page.

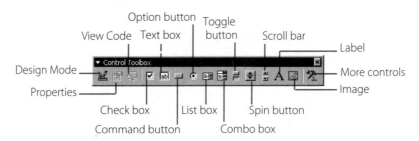

SEE ALSO

For more information about formatting controls in Design Mode, see "Formatting Controls" on page 809.

It's pretty simple to add form controls with either of the two Web-related toolbars, but once you add them, you'll need to define them with a Properties window and a programming language. To add a form control with either toolbar, follow these steps:

1 Move the insertion point to the place where you want the form control to appear on the page.

2 Click the button representing the control you want to add. Word will add the control and switch to Design Mode so you can move, resize, or define it. Figure 33-9 shows a new List Box control from the Web Tools toolbar.

FIGURE 33-9.
Boundary lines surround the new form control.

List box control

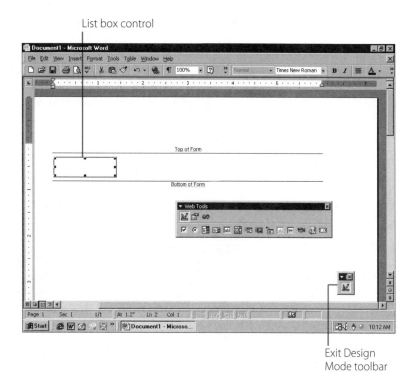

Exit Design Mode toolbar

❓ SEE ALSO

For more information about properties, see "Properties" on page 670.

3 Right-click the object and choose Properties from the shortcut menu, or select the object and click the Properties button on the Web Tools or Control Toolbox toolbar (whichever is appropriate for the object) to display the Properties window:

VI

Web and Internet Tools

> **NOTE**
>
> When you use the Web Tools toolbar and you add the first control to a page, Word also inserts form boundary lines to help you work with the form as a distinct part of the page. These lines are guides only—they don't appear when the page is viewed in a browser.

4 Name the object and adjust its other properties if you like.

5 If you added a Web Tools control, click the Microsoft Script Editor button on the Web Tools toolbar to display the Microsoft Development Environment, as shown in Figure 33-10. (The Script Editor is actually Microsoft Visual Studio 6.0.) If you added a Control Toolbox control, double-click it or click the View Code button on the Control Toolbox toolbar to open the Visual Basic Editor as shown in Figure 29-5 on page 676.

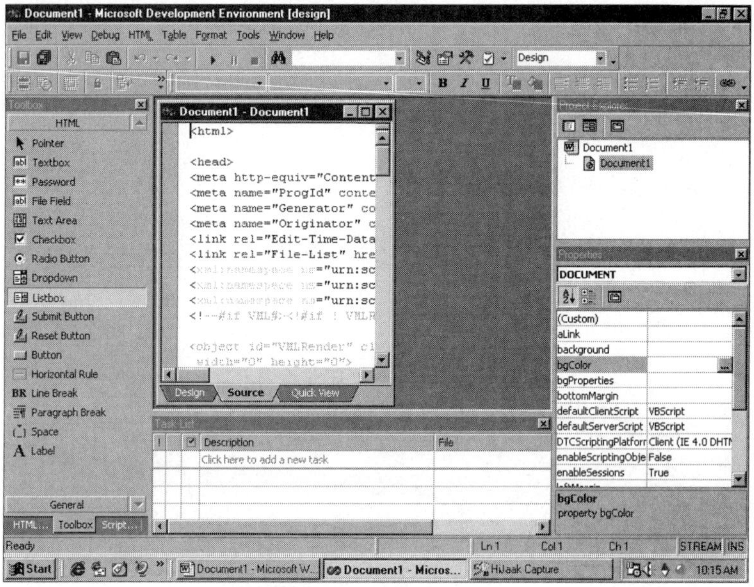

FIGURE 33-10.

The Script Editor is a complete programming environment for defining Web Tools objects.

![Screenshot of the Microsoft Development Environment showing the Script Editor with Toolbox, Document window with HTML code, Project Explorer, and Properties panes.]

6 Write a procedure for the object.

ON THE WEB

See Chapter 29, "Working with Microsoft Visual Basic," for more information about programming in Visual Basic, or for more information about the Microsoft Development Environment, look up "VisualStudio 6.0" on Microsoft's Web site at http://www.microsoft.com.

7 Click the Close button on the Microsoft Development Environment or Visual Basic window to store the script in your page and return to Word's document window.

Formatting Controls

When you add a control to a form, Word automatically switches to Design Mode. While in Design Mode, you can move, resize, and set other format options for each control. When you add a control, it is inserted into the text layer of the document as an inline graphic. To move an inline graphic, you must insert or delete text or spaces on either side of it or use the alignment controls in the Formatting toolbar or in the Paragraphs dialog box.

Creating Well-Designed Forms

In addition to defining the controls on a form, you must also arrange controls, text, and graphics so the form is as clear as possible to the user. Here are some ideas about how to create well-designed forms:

- **Don't reinvent the wheel.** The Web is practically awash in forms, and there are plenty of examples that show both good and bad designs that you can use as guides. Visit prominent Web sites and look at their forms to see how to arrange items or get ideas about how to define controls. Try various controls to see what options they offer, and notice how each form is laid out.

- **Consider the user.** Ask others to review your form in a browser before publishing it. You'll get valuable feedback from a user's perspective about how to improve your form. You might especially want to check the form's operation in older versions of browsers such as those prior to Internet Explorer 4.0 and Netscape Navigator 3.0, as not all of the controls on forms are compatible with older browsers.

- **Think globally.** Forms on the Internet are viewed by people all over the world, and your form should take this into account. If the form captures address data, for example, make sure there's a Country field. If you're selling items through the form, make sure you allow for variances in shipping costs to foreign countries, and be very specific about which credit cards you accept.

- **Offer navigation controls.** If your form is more than two screens long, consider adding hyperlinks to it so users can quickly jump from place to place.

- **Use white space.** Cramming too many controls onto a form usually makes it harder to understand and therefore more error-prone. It's nice to have a form that occupies only one screen, but don't insist on this at the expense of clarity.

VI

Web and Internet Tools

To give yourself more flexibility about the placement of a control, move it out of the text layer. To do this, follow these steps:

1 Right-click the control and choose Format Control from the shortcut menu to open the Format Object dialog box.

2 Click the Layout tab.

3 Select any other Wrapping Style option on the Layout tab and click OK. Word will convert the object to a floating graphic so you can place it anywhere on the page.

 NOTE

Some text wrapping options may not be compatible with all Web browsers. If so, you won't be able to select them when creating a Web page.

Just as you can with any other graphic, you can use any of Word's other graphics formatting options to change the appearance of a control. *For more information about formatting graphic objects, see Chapter 19, "Drawing and Manipulating Graphics."*

Viewing Finished Controls

When you add, define, or format controls on a Web page, you work in Design Mode—the control can be moved or resized like a graphic object, and you can view its code or properties. But before publishing the form, you'll want to view the form as it will look on the Web. There are two ways to do this:

■ Click the Exit Design Mode button on the Web Tools or Control Toolbox toolbar (or on the mini-toolbar elsewhere on the screen that contains only the Exit Design Mode button). Word will display the form controls as they will look in a browser.

■ Choose Web Page Preview from the File menu. Word opens your computer's Web browser and displays the page.

Editing Form Controls

When you test your form, you'll probably find some things that don't work properly, and you'll need to edit the program you wrote for one or more of its controls. To do this, right-click the control and choose View Code from the shortcut menu. Word will open the Visual Basic Editor or the Script Editor so you can edit the program or script. When you exit the Visual Basic Editor or the Script Editor, the edited script is automatically saved.

PART VII

Collaboration Tools

Sharing Documents on a Network

Many Microsoft Word users work in places where the computers are linked by a network. If you work on a network, you can use Word's file management features to save or open files on a network server, to control access to those files, and to prevent changes to those files. In this chapter, you'll learn how a network file server differs from your local disk drive, how to share documents on a network file server, and how to protect your document from other network users.

Working on a Network

Technically, a *network* is any means of communication that allows computers to exchange information. In the simplest terms, a network might be two computers that are connected by a cable so that a user at one computer can access files on the other computer's hard disk. In most companies, however, a network includes one or more *file servers,* which are computers whose sole purpose is to store files and programs for use by anyone on the network. The Internet is also a network, of course, but in this chapter we'll focus on internal company networks.

> You can also share documents directly from Word with other network users by e-mailing them, by sending them to a public folder on a Microsoft Exchange server, or by distributing them to participants in an online meeting. *See "How Word Transmits Documents" on page 846 for details.*

For some time now, the aim of software design has been to make it as easy to open and save files on a network as it is to open and save them on a local disk. To that end, Microsoft Windows treats a network file server like any other location you can access from the Windows desktop. Unlike a local disk, however, a network file server is available to dozens, hundreds, or even thousands of users, so there are additional considerations you need to keep in mind when you save or open files on a server.

> File servers can store programs as well as files. You may be running portions of Microsoft Office from your network server, or installing additional components of Office from a server as you need them.

Access Privileges, User Names, and Passwords

First of all, there must be someone who has responsibility for the network and control of its resources. Every network has one or more *network administrators,* people in charge of keeping the network running, explaining how to use its resources, and setting up *access privileges* to different network resources for each user.

Each user on a network must have a unique identity or *user name* so that access to the network can be restricted to certain people. Passwords add a second level of access control by preventing anyone else from logging on to the network by simply using a valid user name. You are asked to log on to a network with your user name and password each time you start your computer. Unique user names make it possible to assign access privileges on an individual basis, and they may also be used for e-mail addresses.

? SEE ALSO

For more information about creating and using an Office Profile, see "Running Word from Another Computer" on page 820.

Although you probably have a computer for your own use, you can log onto the network from any computer on it. For example, if you happen to be working in a different department for the day, you can log onto the network using a computer there. If you work on a network, you can store an Office Profile for Word and the other Microsoft Office programs. The Office Profile can automatically transfer your custom desktop settings and preferences to any computer you use to log on to a network.

Not only can access privileges restrict access to a select group of people, but they can also restrict the type of access each person has to a folder or server. For example, a marketing department may have its own file server, and the network administrator may have set the server's access privileges so that only members of the marketing department can see the folders stored in it. Or it may be that some of the folders are available to everyone in the marketing department, while others are restricted to use only by upper management.

As a network user, you have no control over network access privileges, although you may be able to ask your network administrator to change the access privileges for a certain folder or server. As we'll see, however, you also can control access to the individual Word documents that you store on a network server.

File Locking

Although most files stored on network servers can be opened and changed by many people, only one person at a time is allowed to change a file. File-saving privileges are doled out automatically on a first-come, first-served basis: the first person to open the file can edit it and save the changes, and anyone else who opens the file while it is in use by the first person opens a read-only version.

? SEE ALSO

For more information, see "Protecting a Network File" on page 817.

When you initially save a file to a network server, you become the file's *owner*, and you may have other file-protection options available to you at that time. When you save a file to a network server from Word, for example, you have the option to store a special read-only version of it that can't be changed by anyone but you.

Adding Word Components from a Network Server

As you use Word, you'll probably notice that the program periodically asks you to install a new component, such as a Web page theme, a wizard, or a template. If you're on a network, the chances are that your network administrator has placed the Office installation files in a directory on a network server and that your copy of Word automatically searches that directory for new components when you need to add them.

With Office 2000, network administrators can create custom installation templates that determine which of the many Office components each user is allowed to install. If you try to install a new component from your network server and you see a message that the component isn't available, contact your network administrator.

For more information about installing additional Word components, see the Appendix.

Now that we've covered the basic concepts of network file sharing, let's look at how you share network files with Word.

Working with Network Files

The process of opening or saving files at a network location is basically the same as opening or saving files on your own local disk. The only difference is that you choose a network location in the Open or Save As dialog box. When you save a file to a network server, however, you may want to use special options to save a restricted copy of the file so that others on the network can't change it.

Saving a File to a Server

To save a file, simply locate the network directory where you want to save it using the Save As dialog box. For example, let's say you want to save a document inside the Promotions folder on a file server called Marketing on your network. Here's what to do:

1   Choose the Save As command from the File menu. Word displays the Save As dialog box.

2   Click the arrow button on the Save In list and navigate to the Desktop level. Figure 34-1 shows the Save As dialog box with the desktop level shown in the Save In list.

FIGURE 34-1.

The Network Neighborhood icon on your desktop shows the file servers available on your network.

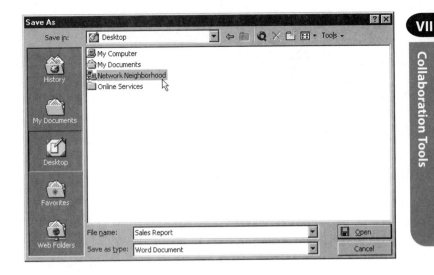

3 Double-click the Network Neighborhood icon to reveal a list of the file servers and work groups on your network.

4 Double-click the Marketing file server icon to reveal the folders and files on that server.

NOTE

> If you don't have access to a particular file or folder, Word will show a message that tells you so.

5 Open the Promotions folder.

6 Click Save to save the file there.

TIP

> To save navigation time, you can map any network server folder as a drive on your Windows desktop. When you do, Windows will assign a new drive letter to that folder, and you can then select it from the desktop itself without having to go into the Network Neighborhood. *For instructions on mapping a network drive, see "Mapping a Network Drive to Your Desktop" on page 150.*

Protecting a Network File

When you save a file to a network location, anyone else who has access to that location can open, change, and resave the file. But you may want to allow others just to read the file and not change it, or you may want to restrict access to the file with a password. There are two ways to protect a file on a server:

? SEE ALSO

For instructions on saving a file with a password, see "Securing a File with a Password" on page 140.

- Use a password so that only those who have the password can open or change the file. You can use two different passwords: one to open the file and another to change it.

- Change the file's properties, so it can be viewed but not changed.

Here's how to create a read-only file:

1   Save the file to the network server folder.

2   Open Windows Explorer or switch to the Windows desktop and open the network server's folder.

3   Right-click the file you saved and choose Properties from the shortcut menu. You'll see the Properties dialog box.

4   Click the General tab to reveal its options, as shown in Figure 34-2.

FIGURE 34-2.

The General tab in the Properties dialog box allows you to make a file read-only.

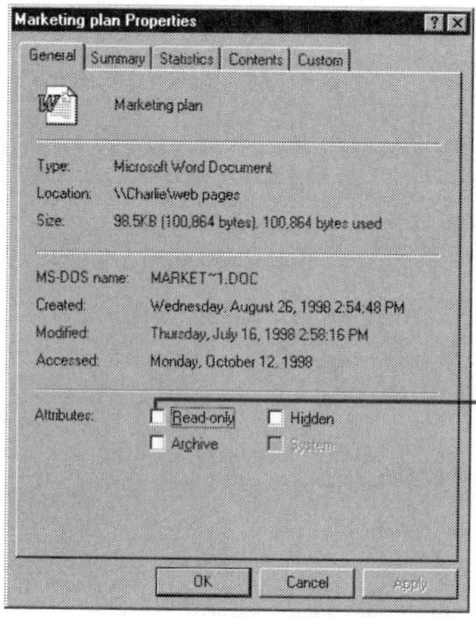

Select the Read-only check box to prevent changes to a file.

5   Select the Read-only check box at the bottom of the tab.

6   Click the Apply button to apply the change, and then click the Close button to close the dialog box. The file is now read-only, so anyone who opens it will not be able to save any changes to it.

> NOTE

When you make a file read-only using the Windows desktop, anyone can select the file and remove the read-only designation from the Properties dialog box. To truly protect a file from changes, use a password that controls a user's ability to modify it.

Opening a File from a Network Server

If you need to work on a Word file that was stored on your network by another user, you can open it with the Open dialog box. However, if the file has been protected with a password, you will have to take a couple of extra steps. Here's the procedure:

1 Choose Open from the File menu to display the Open dialog box.

2 Click the arrow button next to the Look In list and select Network Neighborhood from the list. Word shows you available servers or workgroups on your network.

Your network may be divided into sections called workgroups. If so, the Network Neighborhood location list will include icons for those workgroups, and you must open a particular workgroup icon to see the servers in that area of the network. Also, you may have to double-click the Network Neighborhood icon to see the servers or workgroups on your network.

3 Open a workgroup if necessary, and then open the server that contains the file.

4 Open a folder on the server and select the file you want to open.

5 Click the Open button.

Opening a Protected File

If you open a read-only file, you will be able to make changes to it, but when you try to save the file, you'll see a message that the file is read-only, as shown here:

If you try to open a file that is protected with a password, you'll be asked to enter the password to open it. The message looks like this:

Enter a password and click the OK button to open the file.

If the file is protected with a second password in order to restrict changes to it, you'll see a second message after entering the first password:

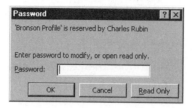

If you know the modification password, enter it and click OK. Otherwise, click Read Only to open a read-only copy of the file.

Editing a File Stored on a Server

Your ability to edit a file stored on a network server depends not only on whether you have the right password, but also on whether someone else is editing the file. When you open a file that is in use by someone else, Word presents a File In Use message like this:

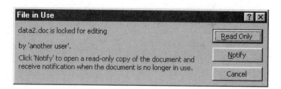

Click Read Only to open a read-only copy of the file, or click Notify to open a read-only copy of the file and have Word notify you when the other user has stopped editing the file.

Running Word from Another Computer

When you work on a network for a large company, you sometimes have to use a computer besides your own. Fortunately, you can create and save an Office Profile that saves your personal styles, macros, toolbar settings, keyboard shortcuts, and AutoText entries. When you install your Office Profile on another computer, Word and the other Microsoft Office programs on that computer adopt the same preferences and other custom settings as your own copy. The Office Profile is invaluable for transferring your custom settings to another version of Word on your laptop, home computer, or another computer on your company network.

Creating an Office Profile

To create an Office Profile, you need to get a copy of the Office Profile Wizard from your network administrator. You may be able to run the Office Profile Wizard from a network file server, or you may be able to obtain a copy of your own. Once you have access to the wizard, it's easy to create a profile:

1 Close any open applications on your computer.

2 Using the Windows desktop, locate the Office Profile Wizard on your network server or your local disk and open it. You'll see a title screen. Click Next. You'll see the Save or Restore Settings dialog box as shown in Figure 34-3. The option to save your machine's settings is selected by default.

FIGURE 34-3.

By creating an Office Profile, you can easily transfer your custom Word settings to any other computer.

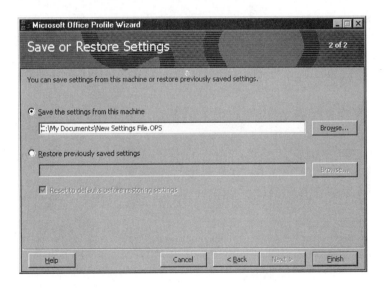

3 Click Browse to select a name and location for the profile file you're about to create if you don't like the location that is currently set.

4 Click Finish. The wizard creates the profile and saves it in the location you chose.

Using an Office Profile

To activate your profile in any of the Office programs on another computer, simply log on the network from that computer with your own user name, and Word will automatically load your profile from the network server.

> In order for an Office Profile to load automatically when you use Office on a different computer on the network, your network administrator must have set up Office correctly on the network server. If the above procedure doesn't work, contact your network administrator.

Copying Your Office Profile to a Second Computer

If you use a second computer (a laptop or home computer, for example), you can copy your Office profile to that computer and then install it so that all of the custom settings you made to Office on your computer at work will automatically be transferred to the second computer. To copy your office profile, follow these steps:

1 Locate your Office Profile and the Office Profile Wizard on your network server and copy them via floppy disk or some other means to the second computer.

> Every Office Profile has the file extension .ops, so you can use the Windows Find command to locate profiles by searching for that extension.

2 Run the Office Profile Wizard on your second computer.

3 Click Next on the title screen to display the Save or Restore Settings dialog box, as shown in Figure 34-3.

4 Select the Restore Previously Saved Settings button.

5 Click Browse, if necessary, to locate and select the Office Profile you copied from the network server.

6 Click Finish. The Profile Wizard installs that profile for use with the Office programs on the computer you're using. Word and other Office programs will now have your custom settings.

For more information about the Office Profile Wizard, contact your network administrator.

Using a network server is just one of the ways you can share documents. To learn how to share documents with e-mail or other electronic transmission methods, see Chapter 36. To learn how you can track and manage revisions during a collaborative editing project, check out the next chapter.

Tracking Changes in a Document

Because many projects are team efforts in which several people work on the same document, Microsoft Word has built-in features that allow you to keep track of how a document is changed. You can keep track of changes by author or by document version, you can insert reviewer comments into a document, and you can consolidate changes or comments into a final document. These features make it much easier to work with documents in a group and to keep track of which person made which change. In this chapter, you'll learn how to track changes, add reviewer comments, and manage document versions.

How Word Tracks Changes, Comments, and Versions

Tracking changes, inserting comments, and comparing versions are three different ways to collect and incorporate each team member's contribution during a collaborative effort. Each of these features allows you to distinguish one contributor's comments or changes from another's. You can use any or all of these features.

■ **The track changes feature** allows you to track and identify each author's changes to a document. When you turn this feature on, Word marks each author's changes with colored text. In addition, a ScreenTip accompanies each change: when you point to a marked change, the tip pops up to show the author's name and the date and time of the change. If there is more than one copy of the same document and each one contains changes, you can merge the changes into a single copy of the document.

■ **Comments** are notes that are attached to a document's text. Comments can be inserted anywhere and can be displayed either at the point of insertion or in a special Comments pane at the bottom of the document window. Comments are numbered consecutively as you or others insert them. As with changes, each comment is color-coded and identified by its author, and you can merge comments from multiple copies of a document into one copy. You don't need to have the track changes feature turned on in order to insert comments.

■ **Versions** store the changes made to a document during a particular editing session. When you turn on the versioning feature, Word can save each editing session's changes as a separate version in the same document file, complete with comments from the person who made those changes. You can't merge information from different document versions, but you can view more than one version on the screen at a time to compare them.

Word identifies the author of a change, comment, or version by reading the Name and Initials boxes on the User Information tab in the Options dialog box. If you're adding comments to or editing a document on someone else's computer—or if you're not sure about this information on your own computer—it's a good idea to check and perhaps update the user information before opening a document for comment or editing.

To check or change the user information, do the following:

1 Choose Options from the Tools menu. Word displays the Options dialog box.

2 Click the User Information tab. The User Information tab looks like this:

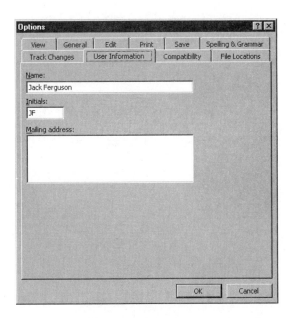

3 Click in the Name box and enter or change the name, if necessary. Word uses the name to identify the author of comments or changes.

4 Click in the Initials box and enter or change the initials, if necessary. Word uses these to identify comments in a document.

5 Click OK to save the changes and put the dialog box away.

If you enter a mailing address in the Mailing Address box on the User Information tab, Word can automatically add it to envelopes. *For more information about creating envelopes, see "Creating an Envelope" on page 386.*

Tracking Document Changes

It's really very easy to keep track of changes in a Word document. Once you turn on the track changes feature, Word automatically identifies every editing or formatting change with a special text color or symbols. Each editor's changes are shown in a different color. Once all reviewers have had a chance to look at a document, you can merge all of the changes into a final document.

Activating Change Tracking

Track Changes is normally turned off in Word documents. To turn on this feature, double-click the Track Changes button on the status bar (it's labeled TRK), or press Ctrl+Shift+E, or point to Track Changes on the Tools menu and choose Highlight Changes. The TRK button becomes active on the status bar, like this:

Track Changes button

If you choose Highlight Changes from the Track Changes submenu, you'll see the Highlight Changes dialog box shown in Figure 35-1.

FIGURE 35-1.

The Highlight Changes dialog box.

To use this dialog box, do the following:

1 Select the Track Changes While Editing check box.

2 Clear either of the two check boxes below it to hide changes in either the screen version or printed version of the document, if you like. (By default, Word shows changes and prints them as well.)

3 Click the Options button to select a different color or marker for the changes you make, if you like, and then click OK. *See "Setting Change Colors or Formats" on page 830.*

4 Click OK to close the Highlight Changes dialog box.

Making and Viewing Changes

Once change tracking is turned on, any editing changes you make from then on appear in a different color from the color of the original text. By default, text additions are underlined and text deletions are marked with a strikethrough, as shown in Figure 35-2.

FIGURE 35-2.

With change tracking on, changes in a document appear marked and in a different color.

Bar in margin also indicates changed area of document.

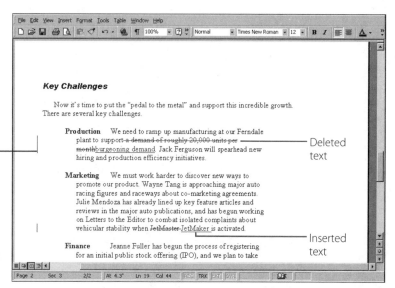

As each author makes changes, Word assigns a new color to that author's changes, cycling through a selection of more than a dozen colors or shades.

To get more details about who made a change and when they made it, point to the change. In a second or two, a ScreenTip will appear that identifies the author of the change, the date, the time, and the nature of the change, like this:

Key Challenges

Now it's time to put the "pedal to the metal" and support this incredible growth. There are several key challenges.

Production   We need to ramp up manufacturing at
plant to support a demand of roughly 20,000 units per
month burgeoning demand. Jack Ferguson will spearhead new
hiring and production efficiency initiatives.

Kiko Shimada, 10/5/98 3:00 PM:
Deleted

When you're finished editing a document, save it as you normally would. All of the marked changes are automatically saved with it.

Using the Reviewing Toolbar

Word has a special Reviewing toolbar that makes it easier to review and work with changes or comments. The Reviewing toolbar is shown in Figure 35-3.

FIGURE 35-3.

The Reviewing toolbar.

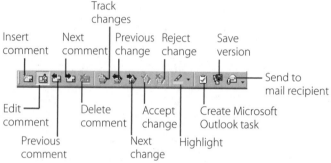

The Reviewing toolbar does not appear automatically when you track changes or insert comments, but you can display it by right-clicking in any toolbar and choosing Reviewing from the shortcut menu.

Other Buttons on the Reviewing Toolbar

The three buttons on the right of the Reviewing toolbar are used to carry out other steps in the revision process. Here's what they do:

- **Create Microsoft Outlook Task**   creates a Microsoft Outlook task for the document and includes a shortcut to the document in the task note so you can open up the document from the Outlook task list. *For more information, consult the online Help system in Microsoft Outlook.*

- **Save Version**   instructs Word to create a new version of the document each time you save it. *For more information about versions, see "Saving Document Versions" on page 837.*

- **Send To Mail Recipient**   opens an e-mail form and attaches the document to it so you can send it to someone else. *For more information about routing documents via e-mail, see "Mailing a Document" on page 849.*

Accepting and Rejecting Changes

After other reviewers return an edited document to you, you can either accept or reject each change.

- Accepting a change converts the marked change into standard document text and deletes the old version of the text.

- Rejecting a change deletes the marked change and converts the old text back into standard document text.

In either case, the special change marks are removed and this area of the document is no longer marked as having been changed.

Reviewing Individual Changes

You can use either the Reviewing toolbar or a shortcut menu to review changes individually as you read a document.

- To accept a change, click anywhere in the change and then click the Accept Change button on the Reviewing toolbar. As an alternative, right-click any part of the change and choose Accept Change from the shortcut menu.

- To reject a change, click anywhere in the change and then click the Reject Change button on the Reviewing toolbar. As an alternative, right-click any part of the change and choose Reject Change from the shortcut menu.

> **NOTE**
>
> Word will not automatically convert a change to normal text and delete the old or revised text in the same operation. You must separately select the old text and the new, changed text and then accept or reject each area.

Navigating from One Change to the Next

If a document has a lot of changes, you can jump quickly from one change to the next. There are two ways to do this:

- Click the Next Change or Previous Change button on the Reviewing toolbar.

- Choose the Accept Or Reject Changes command from the Track Changes submenu on the Tools menu and then click one of the Find buttons shown in Figure 35-4 on the next page.

VII

Collaboration Tools

Accepting or Rejecting Changes Automatically

If you're sure what you want to do with a set of changes, you can use the Accept Or Reject Changes dialog box to handle the process automatically. Here's the procedure:

1 Click the first change in the document.

2 Choose the Accept Or Reject Changes command from the Track Changes submenu. You'll see the Accept Or Reject Changes dialog box as shown in Figure 35-4.

FIGURE 35-4.

To automatically accept or reject changes, use the Accept Or Reject Changes dialog box.

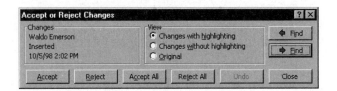

The Accept Or Reject Changes dialog box shows the author of the currently selected change, the type of change, and the date and time of the change.

3 Click one of the buttons in the View area to temporarily alter the way changes are shown in the document. For example, the Changes Without Highlighting option shows the document as if all changes have been accepted.

4 Click the Accept or Reject buttons to accept or reject the current change, or click the Accept All or Reject All buttons to accept or reject all changes in the document.

5 If you accept or reject only the current change, click one of the Find buttons to navigate to the next or previous change.

> If you accept or reject a change by mistake, click the Undo button immediately afterwards.

6 Click Close when you're finished.

Setting Change Colors or Formats

As you can see in Figure 35-2 on page 827, Word normally displays changed text in three ways: by adding a change bar to the document margin; by showing the changed text in a different color; and by adding an underline or strikethrough color to the changed text. You can set options to control how changes appear.

To choose a different format for changes, follow these steps:

1   Point to Track Changes on the Tools menu and choose Highlight Changes. You'll see the Highlight Changes dialog box as shown in Figure 35-1 on page 826.

2   Click the Options button. Word opens the Track Changes dialog box, as shown in Figure 35-5. There are four sets of options in the Track Changes dialog box: you can change the color or marker used to identify inserted text, deleted text, or changed formatting; and you can adjust the color or location of the revision bars that identify changed lines in the document's margin.

FIGURE 35-5.

Use the Track Changes dialog box to reformat changes.

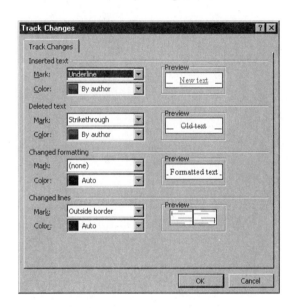

3   Choose a different mark or color in the Inserted Text, Changed Text, or Changed Formatting areas, or choose a different position or color in the Changed Lines area. As you choose different options in each area, the Preview area at the right shows how the change will look.

4   Click OK to save your changes, and then click OK again to close the Highlight Changes dialog box. The document will change accordingly.

TIP

The By Author option for Inserted or Deleted text marks each author's changes with a different color. It's best to leave this setting alone unless you have agreed in advance that each editor on a project will use a specific color.

Using the Highlighter

 SEE ALSO

For more information about selecting colors with the Highlight button's palette, see "Choosing Other Color Options" on page 429.

The Highlight button on the Reviewing toolbar works the same way as its counterpart on the Formatting toolbar. You can use this button to mark text with a colored highlight: just click the Highlight button, drag across the text to highlight it, and then click the Highlight button again to turn the highlighter off. You can set an alternate color for the highlighter by clicking the arrow button next to it and then selecting a different color from the palette that appears.

Printing Changes

When you have change tracking turned on, Word prints changes and change marks by default. However, you can use the Highlight Changes dialog box so that these changes and change marks won't be printed. To do this, follow these steps:

1 Point to Track Changes on the Tools menu and choose Highlight Changes. You'll see the dialog box shown in Figure 35-1 on page 826.

2 Clear the Highlight Changes In Printed Document check box.

3 Click OK to close the dialog box.

With this check box cleared, Word prints the latest changes to the document as normal text without showing any deleted text or change marks.

Adding Comments to a Document

When you work with others on a document, it's often important to be able to make suggestions or to add notes that explain changes that you have made. Word allows you to insert comments anywhere in a document's text. Comments are automatically identified by their author's name and initials. When you open a document that contains comments, you can view the comments as pop-up notes in the document's text or in a special pane at the bottom of the document window.

> **NOTE**
>
> You don't need to have the track changes feature on in order to insert comments.

Inserting a Comment

You can insert either text or voice comments into a document. Here's how to insert a text comment:

1   Move the insertion point to where you want the comment to appear.

2   Choose Comment from the Insert menu or click the Insert Comment button on the Reviewing toolbar. Word adds a yellow highlight to the word to the left of the insertion point, inserts a comment marker with your initials on it, opens the Comments pane, and moves the insertion point into the Comments pane so you can enter the text of the comment, as seen in Figure 35-6.

FIGURE 35-6.

When you insert a comment, Word marks the comment's location and opens the Comments pane.

Comments are formatted with a unique style.

Comment is marked as a change when change tracking is on.

Comment is highlighted and marked with author's initials.

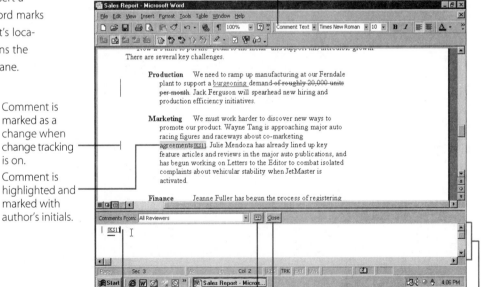

Type a comment here.   Insert sound object   Close Comments pane   Comments pane

3   Enter the text of your comment.

4   Click Close on the Comments pane if you like, or click inside the document pane to return to editing the document.

TIP

When you insert a comment, it is numbered relative to the beginning of the document and to any other comments. If you insert a comment above one or more existing comments, all comments below it are renumbered. As a result, it's not a good idea to refer to comments in a document by number, because the numbers can change as others add more comments.

To insert a voice comment, you must have a sound card and a microphone installed on your computer. If you have the audio hardware, here's how to add a voice comment:

1 Move the insertion point to the place where you want the comment to appear.

2 Choose Comment from the Insert menu or click the Insert Comment button on the Reviewing toolbar. Word inserts a new comment, opens the Comments pane if it isn't already open, and moves the insertion point to the new comment in the Comments pane.

3 Click Insert Sound Object at the top of the Comments pane. Word inserts a sound icon in the Comments pane and displays the Sound Object dialog box, as shown in Figure 35-7.

FIGURE 35-7.

You can record voice comments in the Comments pane by clicking the Sound Object button.

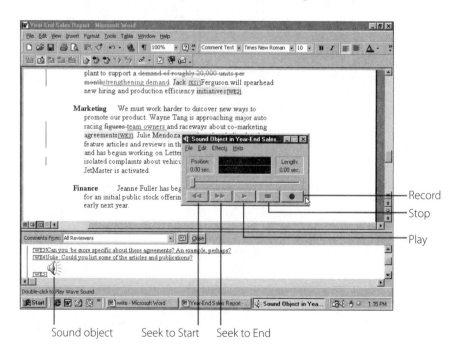

4 Click Record and begin talking into your computer's microphone.

5 Click Stop when you're finished. The sound is stored.

Reviewing Comments

When you open a document that contains comments, you'll see highlight marks in the text indicating the positions of attached comments. To view a text comment, point to the highlight for a second or two and the comment will appear as a ScreenTip, like this:

Move the pointer away from the comment to make it disappear.

To view all of the comments in a document and display the initials of each person who inserted a comment, choose Comments from the View menu. The Comments pane appears as in Figure 35-8. The Sound Object icon indicates a voice comment.

FIGURE 35-8.

The Comments pane shows each author's comments in a different color.

To listen to a sound comment, right-click its Sound Object icon and choose Play from the Wave Sound Object submenu on the shortcut menu.

To display only the comments from one particular author, choose the author's name from the Comments From list in the Comments pane.

Editing Comments

You can move, cut, copy, delete, or edit the text in any comment, and you can also edit a sound comment if you like.

■ To select a comment in the document, drag the selection pointer across it.

■ To move a comment, use the Cut and Paste commands on the
Edit menu, or drag the comment marker to a new location in the
document. When you move a comment below or above another
comment, all of the comments in the document are automatically
renumbered.

⚠ **WARNING**

Don't move comments by dragging them in the Comments pane, because it
changes the comment author's name.

■ To edit a text comment, click the comment's text in the Comments pane and then edit the text. If you have change tracking
turned on, Word marks the changes you make.

❓ **SEE ALSO**

For more information
about using the
Sound Object dialog
box, choose Help Top-
ics from the Help
menu inside the
Sound Object dialog
box.

■ To edit a sound comment, right-click the sound object's icon
in the Comments pane and choose Edit from the Wave Sound
Object submenu on the shortcut menu. Word opens the Sound
Object dialog box, and you can then record over all of the comment or drag the slider to move to a particular place in the
comment and then rerecord from there on.

■ To delete a comment, select the comment's marker in the
document and then click the Delete Comment button on the
Reviewing toolbar or press the Delete or Backspace key on your
keyboard. You can't delete a comment from inside the Comments pane.

Navigating Among Comments

You can easily jump from one comment to the next, and you can also
use the Comments pane to navigate quickly to a specific comment in
your document.

■ To jump from one comment to the next, click the Previous Comment or Next Comment button on the Reviewing toolbar.

■ To automatically scroll through the document to a comment
marker's location, click inside the Comments pane and scroll to
the comment. As the Comments pane scrolls, the document
scrolls with it.

⭐ **TIP**

You can also use the Go To command to locate comments by number or by a
particular reviewer name. *For more information about using the Go To command, see "Navigating with the Go To Command" on page 59.*

VII

Collaboration Tools

Printing Comments

Comments normally don't appear when you print the document, but you can print them on a page at the end of a document, or in a separate document if you like.

- To print only the comments from a document, choose Print from the File menu, select Comments in the Print What menu at the bottom of the Print dialog box, and click OK.

? SEE ALSO

For more information about printing, see "Printing Documents" on page 125.

- To print comments at the end of the document, choose Print from the File menu, click the Options button, and select the Comments check box in the Include With Document area. Click OK twice to close the Options dialog box and print the document.

Saving Document Versions

Suppose you want to keep track of the changes to a document by storing the different renditions as separate files. You can do this by saving document versions. A document version is stored as part of the document, and it contains information about which changes were made since the previous version, along with the name of the version's author, the date and time the version was saved, and any comments the author has saved with the version. When you open a version, however, it contains all of the text in the document as the version's author saved it. You can open an older version of a document if you like, and you can even open two or more versions at once to compare them.

Turning on Version Control

You can save a document version using either the Versions command on the File menu or the Save Version command on the Tools menu in the Save As dialog box. Either way, you turn on Word's version control feature and set the document up to store multiple versions.

When the version control feature is on, you'll see the Versions button on the status bar, like this:

Versions button

Saving with the Versions Dialog Box

When you use the Versions command on the File menu to save a version, you open the Versions dialog box, which shows any previous versions of the document and allows you to set version control options. Here's the procedure:

1 Choose Versions from the File menu. You'll see the Versions dialog box, which will look like the example in Figure 35-10 on the next page, except without the versions listed in it.

2 Click the Save Now button. You'll see the Save Version dialog box shown in Figure 35-9.

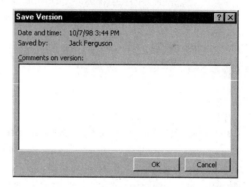

The Save Version dialog box already contains your user name information and the current date and time.

3 Enter any comments you have about the version and click OK. Version control will be turned on.

Saving with the Save Version Command

If you want to save the current version without viewing other versions in the Versions dialog box, you can use a command from the Tools menu in the Save As dialog box. Here's what to do:

1 Choose Save As from the File menu to open the Save As dialog box.

2 Choose Save Version from the Tools menu at the top of the dialog box. You'll see the Save Version dialog box shown in Figure 35-9.

3 Enter any comments you have about the version and then click OK.

Saving Versions Automatically

You can also use the Save Version dialog box to set a document so that a new version is automatically saved each time the document is closed. To do this, follow these steps:

1   Choose the Versions command from the File menu to display the Versions dialog box as shown in Figure 35-10.

FIGURE 35-10.

Use the Versions dialog box to view or delete versions.

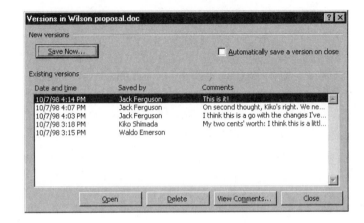

2   Select the Automatically Save Version On Close check box.

3   Save the current version by clicking the Save Now button if you like.

4   Click the Close button. From now on, a new version will be saved each time the document is closed.

Viewing Versions

To view information about various versions, you also use the Versions dialog box. Figure 35-10 shows an example of the Versions dialog box with a few versions in it.

Viewing a Version's Comments

The Comments column in the Existing Versions list shows partial comments for each version. To view the complete comment for a version, select the version and click the View Comments button to display the View Comments dialog box, as shown on the next page.

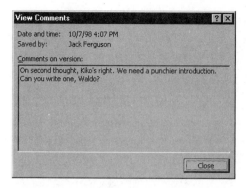

Comparing the Current Version with a Previous Version

Different versions of a document contain different text, and you'll probably want to compare two versions side by side. Here's how:

1 Open the version you want to compare with another.

2 Choose Versions from the File menu to open the Versions dialog box.

3 Select the version you want to compare with the current one.

4 Click Open. Word opens the version and arranges it on the screen below the current version, as shown here:

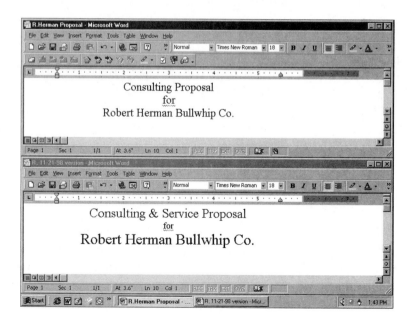

TIP

Double-click the Versions icon in the status bar to open the Versions dialog box.

 **TIP**

You must compare versions visually to see how they differ. To make comparisons easier, turn on change tracking when you first activate the versioning feature for a document. That way, each reviewer's version will show that person's changes in a different color.

VII

Collaboration Tools

Deleting a Version

You can also use the Versions dialog box to delete one or more versions of a document when you no longer need them. To do this, follow these steps:

1   Choose Versions from the file menu or double-click the Versions button on the status bar to open the Versions dialog box.

2   Select one or more versions in the Existing Versions list (hold down Shift or Ctrl and click to select more than one version).

3   Click Delete, and then click Yes to confirm the deletion.

4   Click Close to put the Versions dialog box away.

Consolidating Changes and Comments

If you have distributed several copies of the same document to other Word users, you'll want to consolidate the changes and comments into one copy for final editing. You can merge or compare only two documents at once, so if several copies of a document are out there on the editorial circuit, you'll have to consolidate them one at a time.

To simplify our discussion of merging, we'll call your original copy of the document the *master copy* and refer to others as simply copies. There are two ways to consolidate changes in Word:

- Merge the changes from another copy into the master copy of the document. When you merge two documents, you'll see both sets of changes and comments in the document, just as if both authors had edited the same copy of the document.

- Compare the master copy of the document with another copy. When you compare documents, Word inserts the other copy's changes and comments into the master copy, but it automatically marks all of them as deleted. You can then reject individual changes to make them part of the master copy.

> **NOTE** Word only merges changes that have been tracked, so you can't merge changes from documents in which the track changes feature was turned off during editing.

Word always merges changes into the active document, so you'll want to have the master copy of the document open on the screen before either merging or comparing.

Merging Documents

Here's how to merge another document's changes into the master copy of the document:

1 Open the master copy of the document.

2 Choose Merge Documents from the Tools menu. Word opens the Select File To Merge Into Current Document dialog box, which is basically the same as the Open dialog box.

3 Double-click the file you want to merge or select it and click the Open button. Word merges the file's changes and comments into the master copy and identifies them by their author.

> **NOTE** If a document was edited with change tracking turned off after initial changes were tracked, it contains untracked changes. When the master copy of the document contains untracked changes, Word will alert you and it will merge changes only up to the first unmarked change in the master document.

Comparing Documents

Comparing documents is very similar to merging them, but the results are a little different. Here's the procedure:

1 Open the master copy of the document.

2 Choose Compare Documents from the Track Changes submenu on the Tools menu. Word opens the Select File To Compare With Current Document dialog box, which is basically the same as the Open dialog box.

3 Double-click the file you want to merge, or select it and click Open. What happens next depends on whether you have enabled the track changes feature in either the master document or the copy.

- If *neither* of the two documents contains tracked changes, Word merges the file's changes and comments into the master copy and marks them all as deleted by the master document's author. You can then accept or reject the deleted changes.

- If *either* the master document or the copy contains tracked changes, you'll see a message that confirms this. Click the Yes button to merge the changes anyway, and you can then accept or reject the changes in the master document.

NOTE

If a copy of the document contains untracked changes, Word will alert you before merging them into the master document. Word can't merge untracked changes.

Word's e-mail and other collaboration features allow you to use electronic routing to help control a collaborative editing project. For more information about transmitting documents electronically with Word, read on in Chapter 36.

VII

Collaboration Tools

CHAPTER 36

Sending Documents Electronically

When you want to get a document to someone quickly and inexpensively, there's nothing like electronic transmission. Virtually everyone on a company network has access to network file servers or Web servers and has an e-mail address, and millions of others who use the Internet at home have World Wide Web access and e-mail addresses as well. Many more who don't have an e-mail address have a fax machine. Microsoft Word makes it easy to save documents on network file servers or Web servers and to send documents to e-mail or fax recipients, and you never have to leave the document window to do it. In this chapter, you'll learn how to send documents electronically.

How Word Transmits Documents

The Send To command's submenu on the File menu offers several different types of electronic document transmission, as you can see in Figure 36-1.

FIGURE 36-1.

All of Word's commands for sending documents electronically are on the Send To submenu on the File menu.

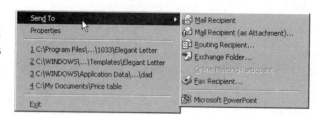

There are lots of ways to send documents, as you can see. Here's a brief rundown of the Send To submenu's commands and the reasons for using each of them.

- **Mail Recipient** When you send a document to an e-mail recipient, Word attaches an e-mail header to your document. You can select one or more recipients, add a message subject, and then send the document as a message. When the message is read on the recipient's computer, your document's contents appear inside the e-mail message window. Use this option when recipients may not have a copy of Word they can use to read an attached Word document (see the next item).

- **Mail Recipient (As Attachment)** When you send a document to an e-mail recipient as an attachment, Word opens the new e-mail message form from your computer's e-mail program and attaches the current document to the message. You can select one or more recipients, add a message subject and a message, and then send the message along with the attached document. Recipients must have Word 97 or Word 2000 to open the attachment and read it properly. Use this option when you are sending to people who you know are also using Word.

- **Routing Recipient** When you send a document to a routing recipient, Word transmits it via e-mail, but it first displays a routing slip where you can select the people to whom you want to send the message and set the order in which they receive it. The message is sent to the first recipient on the list, and that person then sends it on to the next person. Use this option when you want a document reviewed by people in a particular order (for example, by a staffer, and then a manager, and then a vice president).

> **NOTE**
>
> When you send mail with a routing slip, each recipient must have a copy of Microsoft Word 97 or later in order to use the routing slip feature. However, any recipient can receive the document copy and send it to the next recipient manually by attaching it to a standard e-mail message.

■ **Exchange Folder** When you send a document to an Exchange folder, you place it in a public folder on a Microsoft Exchange server where other users of the network have access to it. This option is only available if your network includes a server that's running Microsoft Exchange Server software. Contact your network administrator for more information.

■ **Online Meeting Participant** When you send a document to an online meeting participant, you send it to one or more of the people attending an online meeting by using Microsoft NetMeeting or other online collaboration software. The meeting must be in progress in order for you to use this option.

Integrating Your E-mail Program with Word

In order to integrate an e-mail program with Word, the program must support either the Messaging Application Programming Interface (MAPI), or the Vendor Independent Messaging Standard (VIM)—such as Eudora or Lotus Notes. Most stand-alone e-mail programs support at least one of these standards, but e-mail functions inside other applications such as America Online do not. If you installed all of the Microsoft Office 2000 programs, Word will automatically use Microsoft Outlook Express as its e-mail program. If you use a different program to send e-mail, you can select it for use with Word:

1 Choose Control Panel from the Settings submenu on the Start Menu.

2 Double-click the Internet icon in the Control Panel folder.

3 Click the Programs tab in the Internet Properties dialog box.

4 Choose the alternate program from the Mail menu. If your program doesn't appear on that menu, it is either not properly installed or it isn't MAPI-compliant or VIM-compliant.

The examples in this chapter are based on Outlook Express, so your screens and e-mail options may vary if you're using another program.

> Microsoft NetMeeting is part of Microsoft Internet Explorer. If you're using Netscape Communicator, the meeting software is called Netscape Collabra.

- **Fax Recipient** When you send a document to a fax recipient, you usually transmit it from your computer to the recipient's fax machine, network fax server, or internal fax/modem. When you choose this command, Word opens the Fax Wizard so you can select a fax program to use, choose a cover sheet template, enter or select the recipient's fax number, and perform other tasks. You can't use this option unless you have a fax program installed on your computer.

- **Microsoft PowerPoint** If you are working in Outline view, you can convert your Word outline into a PowerPoint presentation by choosing this option. PowerPoint uses the Heading styles in the outline to break up text from your document into slides: Each Heading 1 topic in the outline is used as the title for a new slide, and lower heading levels beneath each Heading 1 topic are arranged in outline format on each slide. *See Chapter 12, "Working with Outlines," for more information about outlines.*

Other Document Sharing Alternatives

The Send To command offers a number of ways to transmit a document, but there are two other ways to share documents:

- Use the Save As command on the File menu to save the document to a network file server. *For more information, see "Saving a File to a Server" on page 816.*

- Create a Web page and publish it on a Web server. *See Chapter 32, "Creating Web Pages," for more information about creating and publishing a Web page.*

For more information about the best ways to share a document with others in various situations, see "Routing vs. Broadcasting" on page 852 and check out Chapter 37, "Managing Collaborative Projects."

Mailing a Document

Mailing a document from within Word saves you time because you don't have to open your e-mail program separately and manually attach the document to a new message. Word handles these chores for you. You can send a document as an e-mail message itself, or attach it to an e-mail message, depending on which command you choose from the Send To submenu.

To send a document as an e-mail message, do the following:

1   Open the document you want to send.

2   Choose Send To on the File menu, and then choose Mail Recipient from the Send To submenu. Word adds an e-mail address header to your document as in Figure 36-2.

> The jigsaw puzzle icon in Figure 36-2 is another of Word's Office Assistant characters. This one goes by the name Office Logo.

FIGURE 36-2.

When you send a document to an e-mail recipient, Word adds an e-mail header to the document itself.

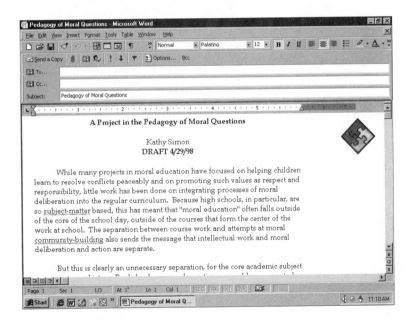

3   Enter one or more e-mail addresses in the To or Cc lines in the header. To send to a recipient whose address is stored in your e-mail program's address book, click the To or Cc icon to see the address book list and to select recipient names there.

4 Click in the Subject line and edit the subject if you don't like the one Word proposes.

5 Click the Send A Copy button in the header's toolbar. Word places the document as an outgoing message in your e-mail program's outbox and returns you to the standard document window.

To mail a document as an attachment, do the following:

1 Open the document you want to send.

2 Choose Send To on the File menu, and then choose Mail Recipient (As Attachment) from the Send To submenu. If you're using Microsoft Outlook Express as your e-mail program, you'll see a new e-mail message like the one shown in Figure 36-3. The insertion point is blinking in the To line in the message header so you can enter the address of the recipient there, and the current document is already attached to the new message.

FIGURE 36-3.

When you send an e-mail message as an attachment, you work with your e-mail program's window.

Click to send when you're done.

Enter recipient name(s).

Enter a subject and a message, if you like.

Word automatically attaches the document.

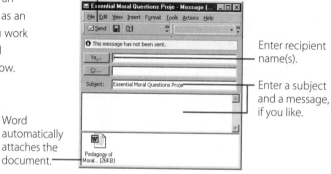

3 Enter one or more e-mail addresses in the To or Cc lines in the header, or click the Address Book icon in the Outlook toolbar to view names in your e-mail address book and to select recipients there.

4 Click in the Subject line and edit the Subject box if you like.

5 Click in the message area and type a message to accompany your document. You can also use formatting options in your e-mail program to select stationery for the message, add an e-mail signature, or format the text to dress it up.

6 Click the Send button to send the message. The message window closes and you are returned to your document.

NOTE

If you're using Microsoft Outlook or Outlook Express, you can also encrypt mail messages and attach digital signatures to them. *For more information about these features, consult the Help menu in Outlook or Outlook Express.*

Mailing with a Routing Slip

If you have worked in an office for very long, you have probably seen documents with small paper routing slips attached to them. The routing slip contains the names of several people, and the document bounces from one inbox to another until it is returned to the person who started it. There's usually an initial blank or check box next to each name so each person can indicate that they have seen the document. Word lets your computer's e-mail program accomplish the same thing electronically.

When you route a document to a group of recipients, you can select the order in which the document passes from person to person, and you can protect the document to limit what others can do to it.

To route a document, do the following:

1   Open the document.

2   On the File menu, point to Send To and choose Routing Recipient. Word displays the Routing Slip dialog box, as shown in Figure 36-4.

FIGURE 36-4.

When you route a document, you specify recipient names and choose other options in the Routing Slip dialog box.

Lists recipients in order

Click to select recipients from your e-mail address book.

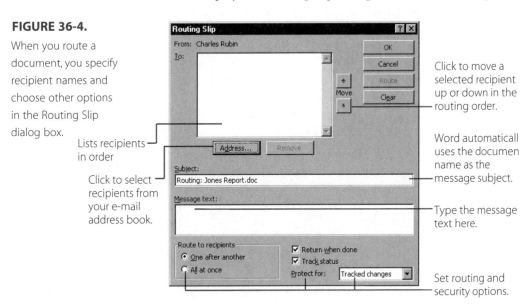

Click to move a selected recipient up or down in the routing order.

Word automaticall uses the documen name as the message subject.

Type the message text here.

Set routing and security options.

3 Click the Address button to open your e-mail program's address book, and then use it to add one or more recipient addresses to the message header.

4 Click OK to add the names to the routing slip and close the Address Book dialog box. The recipients are listed on the slip, like this:

To rearrange the list order, select a name and click the up or down arrow button to the right of the list.

5 Edit the Subject box if you like.

6 Click in the Message Text box and enter a message to accompany the document.

Routing vs. Broadcasting

Because you can use the Mail Recipient or Mail Recipient (As Attachment) commands to send a document to several people, it's not always clear why you might want to use the Routing Recipient command instead.

When you use the *Mail Recipient* or *Mail Recipient (As Attachment)* option, you send a copy of the document to each person at the same time. Each person can edit the document (unless you send a read-only version), and each person will return a unique copy of the document to you. You will then have to consolidate the changes from all of these copies into one final document.

When you use the *Routing Recipient* option, Word attaches a routing slip to the document, so that you can route the document from one person to the next rather than sending it to all of them at once. The slip indicates where the document should go next after the current person sees it. The advantage to this option is that you can protect the document in specific ways to limit what can be done to it. Also, there's only one copy of the document in circulation, so it's easier to consolidate changes from multiple reviewers.

TIP

When a recipient receives a routed message, Word automatically includes a generic message that explains how to send the document on to the next recipient, so you don't have to add these instructions to the message text.

7 Choose routing and protection options below the Message Text box. The protection options are explained below.

8 Click Route to close the Routing Slip dialog box and send the document to the first recipient. To add the routing slip to the document without immediately sending it, click the Add Slip button instead.

 TIP

If you add addresses to the routing slip and want to continue editing the document before sending it, click the Add Slip button instead of the Route button in the Routing Slip dialog box. To route the message later, open the Routing Slip dialog box and click the Route button.

The first recipient will get an e-mail message with the subject line that you chose in the Routing Slip dialog box. The recipient then uses his or her e-mail program to open the message. The message contains the attached document, and it explains how to open the document in Word to edit it and send it on again. Depending on the options you set when you routed it, each recipient may or may not be able to edit the document.

When a recipient is finished with the document, he or she chooses the Next Recipient command from the Send To submenu to route it to the next person. If you added your own name at the end of the recipient list or you selected the Return When Done check box in the Routing Slip dialog box, the last recipient returns the document to you by choosing the Next Recipient command.

WARNING

A routing slip helps automate the process of moving a document from one person to another, but if one of the recipients isn't there to receive the mail, the entire process comes to a stop until that person returns. To reduce the chances of this happening, make your reviewer deadlines clear in the e-mail message that goes with the routing slip, use the Track Status option in the Routing Slip dialog box as explained on the next page, and follow up immediately when the document stops moving from one person to another.

Setting Routing Options

The options at the bottom of the Routing Slip dialog box allow you to set the way a document is routed and what each person can do with it. Here's how to use these options:

- **Route To Recipients area** Select one of these options to determine whether to route the document to one person after the other (the default) or to send it to all of them at once. Choosing the All At Once option here sends a copy of the document to each recipient rather than forwarding a single copy from one person to the next. If you send a document to all recipients at once, each recipient returns the document to you when he or she is finished with it.

- **Return When Done check box** This is selected by default, and tells Word to route the document back to you. When the last reviewer on the slip chooses the Next Recipient from the Send To submenu, the document is returned to you.

- **Track Status command** This instructs your e-mail program to send you a message each time a recipient forwards the document to the next recipient, so you'll know just where the document is at all times. This option may not work with all e-mail programs.

- **Protect For menu** This allows you to limit changes to a document. You can prevent recipients from editing any previously tracked changes in the document, from adding any comments to the document, or (if you're routing a form) from making any changes other than filling in the form's data fields. If you prefer, you can choose None from this menu to allow all changes.

Faxing a Document

When e-mail fails, try faxing. Many small businesses and others who have come late to e-mail have fax machines, and you can use the Send To submenu to send a fax just as easily as an e-mail message.

 NOTE

You must have fax software installed on your computer to send a fax from Word. When you first use the Fax Recipient command, Word will offer to install the Fax Wizard so you can set up your fax software for use with Word. *For more information about faxing, see "Fax" in Word's Help system index.*

There are two ways to send a fax:

- Include a fax number in the recipient list of a routing slip or in the To or Cc box in an e-mail message header.

In order to send an e-mail message to a fax address, you must set up your e-mail program to tell it which fax software to use. If you use a fax address in a routing slip, the recipient won't be able to use Word's routing features to send it along to the next recipient.

- Choose the Fax Recipient command from the Send To submenu.

When you use the Fax Recipient command, Word opens the Fax Wizard. Now you can select the fax program you want to use, you can specify a cover sheet template, and you can set other options. Here's the procedure:

1 Open the document you want to fax.

2 Choose Fax Recipient from the Send To submenu on the File menu. Word opens a new document window along with the Fax Wizard. The Fax Wizard dialog box is shown in Figure 36-5.

FIGURE 36-5.

Use the Fax Wizard to create a new fax document and attach it to the document you want to send.

3 Work through the steps as the wizard presents them. You'll be asked which document you want to fax and whether you want to add a cover sheet, which fax software you have installed, who the fax is going to, and which style of cover sheet you want to use. You'll then have a chance to add sender information such as your phone number or address.

4 Click Finish on the final page to close the wizard and display the fax cover sheet on your screen as shown in Figure 36-6.

Add any additional information to the cover sheet if you like, and then click the Send Fax button in the Fax Wizard toolbar to send the fax.

FIGURE 36-6.

When you fax a document, you can choose a cover sheet template and then Word will fill the template out based on information you provide.

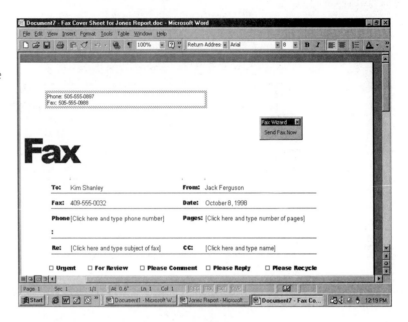

Now that you've read up on all of the features in Word that make collaboration easier, turn to Chapter 37 for advice on how to select the right collaboration tools for any job.

Managing Collaborative Projects

Microsoft Word 2000 has a number of features that make collaborative projects much simpler, and you'll find instructions about how to use them elsewhere in this book. But *managing* a collaborative project often involves combining two or more of Word's collaboration features. In this chapter, we'll review the purpose of each collaboration feature and look at a couple of strategies for combining them to streamline project management.

There are many ways to collaborate on documents with Word. As the manager of a collaborative project (or the person responsible for the final document), you should think of Word's collaboration features as a set of tools that can be tailored to suit any project. Before we look at some strategies for managing a collaborative project, let's examine the issues involved in collaboration and see how you can address them with Word.

How Word Aids Collaboration

There are three basic issues to resolve when you're managing a collaborative document project: access, tracking changes, and consistency.

- Access is important because everyone involved in the project must be able to see or edit the document. You may also need to implement some sort of security to prevent unauthorized people from viewing or changing the document.

- Tracking changes is important because you usually want to know which team member has made which contribution.

- Consistency in formatting, style, word usage, and spelling is important because the finished document must usually appear as if one person wrote it, and because company documents often have a standard format or style.

Word's collaboration features give you several ways to address these issues.

Access and Security

Everyone on a team must have access to the document being created, but you may not want people outside the team to have access. Depending on the type of project and your company's equipment, you can use e-mail, a network file server, a Web server, floppy disks, or even an online meeting to distribute a document. When you distribute the document, you'll also want to preserve the original document so you can compare it with the changed versions. Here are the ways you can electronically share and secure documents with Word:

SEE ALSO

For more information about the Exchange Folder command, see "How Word Transmits Documents" on page 846.

- **Save to a network server with the Save As command** If the document is open to anyone, save it in an unrestricted folder on a network server. If you want to secure it, save it to a folder to which only the team members have access, or create a password for the document itself. If your network has a Microsoft

Exchange server, you can also save the document to a public folder on that server using the Exchange Folder command on the Send To submenu on the File menu.

SEE ALSO

For more information about sending Word documents via e-mail, see "Mailing a Document" on page 849.

- **E-mail a document** To send a document to a selected group, send it as an e-mail message or attached to an e-mail message. Since you can address an e-mail message to more than one person, you can send the document to several people at once this way, and because you are using e-mail instead of saving to a server, only the people to whom you send the document will have access to it.

TIP

If you use Microsoft Outlook 98 or later, you can encrypt e-mail messages to prevent outsiders from viewing them. For more information, open Outlook, choose the Microsoft Outlook Help command from the Help menu, and search for "encrypt Web discussions."

SEE ALSO

For more information about using routing slips, see "Mailing with a Routing Slip" on page 851. For more information about creating and publishing a Web page, see Chapter 32, "Creating Web Pages," and Chapter 33, "Using Word's Advanced Web Features."

- **Attach an e-mail routing slip to a document** If you want a single copy of a document routed to several people one after the other, or if you want to limit the changes others can make to a document in specific ways, use an e-mail routing slip.

- **Publish a Web page** You can share a document by publishing it as a Web page on an intranet or Internet Web server. The main advantage of this method is that anyone with a Web browser can view or edit the document. You can restrict access to a Web page by requiring a password.

- **Comment on a Web page** If a Web server on your network includes the Microsoft Office Web Server Extensions and your network administrator has set up a Web discussion server, you can allow others to add comments to any Web page. To connect to a discussion server, choose Web Discussions from the Online Collaboration submenu on the Tools menu.

NOTE

In order to use Web discussions in Word, your network administrator must install the Office Server Extensions on a network server. *For more information, contact your network administrator. For more information about Web discussions, search for "Web discussions" in the Help system.*

SEE ALSO

For more information about NetMeeting, contact your network administrator.

■ **Save the file to one or more floppy disks** Not everyone has access to or is comfortable with using a network server or e-mail, but most people know how to insert a floppy disk and open a file from it. When all else fails, use this "sneakernet" approach to hand carry floppies to team members or distribute them through inter-office or postal mail.

■ **Share the document in an online meeting** Microsoft Internet Explorer includes Microsoft NetMeeting, which allows you to meet with one or more people at the same time over a network. NetMeeting connects you to other users simultaneously and allows you to collaborate on a document, exchange typed or spoken remarks, transmit documents to all discussion participants, and even see a live video of participants.

 TIP

If you're using Netscape Communicator, you can set Word up so you will access Netscape's Collabra meeting software when you choose the meeting options. *For more information, contact your network administrator.*

Tracking Changes

 SEE ALSO

For more information about tracking document changes, consolidating changes, adding comments, and creating multiple document versions, see Chapter 35, "Tracking Changes in a Document."

When several people work on a document, you need a way to identify each person's contributions and to keep track of the latest version of the document. A document may take days or weeks to create, so you'll want to be able to distinguish the latest contributions from earlier ones. You can use Word to track changes in several ways:

■ **Track and merge changes** Whether you route a single copy of a document from one team member to the next or you distribute individual copies, change tracking lets you identify each person's changes and merge them into one document.

■ **Collect comments** In addition to changes, anyone on a team can insert comments into a document. The comments might be editing suggestions, questions about the text, or notes about why a change was made. Each comment, like each change, is stamped with its author's name and the date and time it was made, and you can merge comments from several copies of a document into one.

■ **Use versions** When you save one copy of a document on a network server, you can use Word's versioning feature to identify each saved copy as a unique version of the document. Each version is stamped with the date and time it was saved as well as with the author's name. You'll find the Versions command on the File menu.

Maintaining Consistency

A document may have several contributors, but in most cases, you'll want the final text to read as if one person created it. This means enforcing consistent formatting and stylistic conventions throughout the document. Word offers several ways to standardize the look and writing style in a document.

? SEE ALSO

For more information about using templates, see Chapter 13, "Using Templates and Wizards."

- **Use a template** By creating the original document in a custom template, you can distribute copies of the document that already contain certain styles, keyboard shortcuts, AutoText entries, or macros. If you're managing a project that will include several documents from different authors, you can standardize the format options in all of them by distributing the same template to everyone involved. For example, you might distribute a template called Report Section so that when users contribute different documents to different sections of a report, all the documents will look the same.

★ TIP

Even if you distribute a template that contains the styles you want to be used in a collaborative document project, it's a good idea to attach a style guide and a few sample pages to show which styles should be used where.

? SEE ALSO

For more information about using master documents, see Chapter 24, "Using Master Documents."

- **Use a master document** Another way to standardize the look of documents created by different authors is to create a master document to contain them. For example, if you're preparing an annual report in which each section has a different author, you can create a master document for the entire report, set the formatting options you want, and then add each section as a subdocument to the master document. Subdocuments automatically take on the styles and format characteristics set in the master document, and you can print the master document as one document with consecutive page numbering and standard page format options.

? SEE ALSO

For more information about using macros, see Chapter 28, "Using Macros," and Chapter 29, "Working with Microsoft Visual Basic."

- **Use macros** By including macros in the documents or document templates you distribute, you can automate complex procedures so that each member of the group performs them in the same way. For example, you might create an automatic macro that saves a revised copy of a document to a certain network server with the author's initials attached to the file name.

Collaboration Strategies

Before you begin a collaborative project, first consider the issues of access, change tracking, and consistency. Then plan a strategy for applying Word's features to handle those issues. As a rule, you want to keep things simple: automated routing and access control are great when you really need them, but they're often in the way when you don't. Here are some guidelines:

- **Make access easy** Don't protect a document with a password or save it in a restricted network folder unless it's really necessary. Invariably, people lose or forget passwords or someone not part of the original team needs access, and when that happens you'll have to spend time dealing with the problem. Full access presents no such problems.

- **Allow changes, but track them** Word's change tracking features are very easy to use, and they automatically record every change in a document. You can use change tracking with any of the access or consistency features. If you restrict the document by distributing a read-only version or by restricting changes or comments when making an e-mail routing slip, you'll probably foster lots of e-mail messages, marked-up printouts, and phone calls bringing suggestions. These changes will be difficult to consolidate.

- **Plan for consistency** Use Word's master documents, templates, styles, macros, and AutoText entries to ensure consistent word spellings, usage, and document formatting. This will save you lots of reformatting and editing when the documents are returned to you.

Which Word features you end up using will depend on the project you're managing. For each project, the access, change tracking, and consistency issues are often slightly different, so the tools used to address them are implemented or combined in different ways. As you experiment with these tools on various projects, you'll quickly discover which ones work best in different situations.

File conversions are one more task you may need to perform during collaborative projects. To learn about converting files with Word, go on to the next chapter.

Importing, Exporting, and Converting Documents

Microsoft Word, of course, doesn't exist in a vacuum. There are lots of other programs out there. Sometimes you'll need to open files that were created in programs other than Word. Sometimes you'll need to use Word to create files that can be opened by other programs. For these reasons, Word comes with file format converters for many other programs, and even if Word doesn't have a specific converter, you can often access the information created by other programs without one. In this chapter, you'll learn how to open and save files in other formats, along with other techniques you can use to ensure peaceful coexistence between Word and other programs.

Opening NonWord Files

You use the same basic procedure to open a nonWord document as you do to open a Word document, as explained in Chapter 7, "Managing Files." When you open a nonWord document, however, you must select the appropriate file type. To see how this works, let's assume we want to open a Microsoft Excel file called Q299 Sales from the My Documents folder. Here's the procedure:

1　Choose Open from the File menu. Word displays the Open dialog box.

2　Click the My Documents icon in the Places bar to display that folder's contents.

3　Click the arrow button next to the Files Of Type box at the bottom of the Open dialog box. You'll see a list of other file types, as seen in Figure 38-1. The Files Of Type box is normally set to "Word Documents," so the file list shows only standard Word documents (.doc files) along with any folders in the current location. You can't see the Q299 Sales worksheet because it's an Excel worksheet (.xls) file instead of a Word file.

FIGURE 38-1.

The Files Of Type list in the Open dialog box allows you to display and open files from other programs.

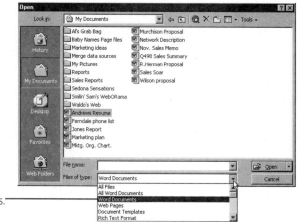

Choose a file type to show only those files.

4　Scroll down the list and select Microsoft Excel Worksheet. The file list above will show only Excel files along with the folders at this location, as shown in Figure 38-2 on the next page.

FIGURE 38-2.

When you select another file type from the Files Of Type list, the file list above shows only files of that type.

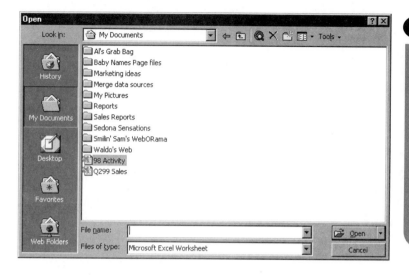

5   Double-click the Excel file to open it. Word needs to know whether you want to open the entire worksheet or a particular sheet and range of cells from it, so it displays the Open orksheet dialog box like this:

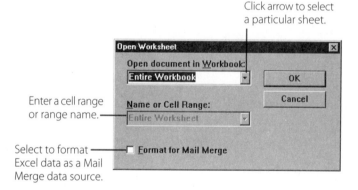

Click arrow to select a particular sheet.

Enter a cell range or range name.

Select to format Excel data as a Mail Merge data source.

If you don't have the Excel file converter installed, you'll be given a chance to install it when you try to open the Excel file.

6   If you like, click the arrow beside the Open Document In Workbook list and select a specific worksheet from the Excel file. Then enter a cell range or range name to limit the amount of data you bring into the new Word file.

7   Click OK. Word opens the worksheet as a table in a new Word document that has the same name as the original Excel Worksheet.

NOTE

In most cases, Word simply opens a file rather than offering you the chance to select specific information from it.

When you select an option from the Files Of Type list, Word uses the file's extension to determine which files to display in the file list. For example, when you choose "Word Documents" in the Files Of Type list, Word displays only files with the .doc extension.

TIP

To view the file extension for any file, right-click it in the Open dialog box, choose Properties from the Shortcut menu, and click the General tab if necessary.

Table 38-1 shows the file types on the Files Of Type list along with notes, if necessary, explaining how the file type affects the file list in the Open dialog box.

TABLE 38-1.   File Formats You Can Open with Word

File Type	Notes
All Files	Shows any file except those marked as Hidden by Microsoft Windows
All Word Documents	Shows Word documents, Web pages, and templates
Word Documents	Word documents only (.doc files)
Web Pages	Any HTML file with the .htm extension
Document Templates	Word templates (.dot files)
Rich Text Format	Files with the .rtf extension (rtf is a special Microsoft format that preserves formatting in a text file.)
Text Files	Text-only files (.txt extension)
Encoded Text Files	Text (.txt) files that contain special encoding, such as Unicode files
Lotus 1-2-3	Files created with this spreadsheet program and saved in its native (.wks, .wk1, .wk3, and .wk4) format

(continued)

TABLE 38-1. *continued*

File Type	Notes
Microsoft Excel Worksheet	Excel worksheet (.xls and .xlw) files
MS-DOS Text With Layout	Text (.asc) files with special MS-DOS characters
Outlook Address Book	An address book from Microsoft Outlook 98 (.olk) or later
Personal Address Book	An address book from older versions of Outlook (.pab)
Recover Text from Any File	Lists all files and extracts text from any file, placing it in a new Word document
Schedule+ Contacts	Contacts files from Microsoft Schedule+ (.scd)
Text with Layout	Text files with extra formatting information(.ans)
Windows Write	Files from the Windows Write accessory program (.wri)
Word 4.0-5.1 for Macintosh	Files from older Macintosh versions of Word (.doc)
Word 6.0/95 for Windows & Macintosh	Files from these older English language versions of Word (.doc)
WordPerfect 5.x, WordPerfect 6.x	Files from these versions of WordPerfect (.wpd, .doc)
Works 4.0 for Windows	Files from this version of Microsoft Works for Windows (.wps)

TIP

The Office Installation CD includes many other conversion filters. *For information about installing them, see the Appendix.*

Opening Files That Word Can't Convert

When you use the All Files option on the Files Of Type list in the Open dialog box, Word lists all the files at the current location that aren't designated as a Hidden file (such as many operating system files) by Windows. Word does not include converters for every known file format, however, and you may try to open a file for which there is no converter. When you try to open such a file, Word either opens the file and displays garbage characters on the screen, or it gives you a chance to salvage the file with the File Conversion dialog box shown in Figure 38-3.

FIGURE 38-3.

When you open a file for which Word doesn't have a converter, you may have a chance to preview it.

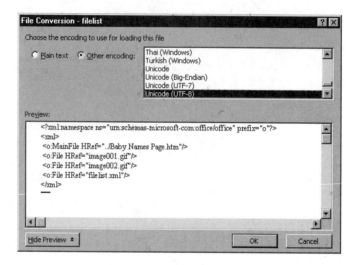

 NOTE

> If the File Conversion feature isn't installed in your copy of Word, you'll see a message asking whether you want to install it. To install the feature, insert the Microsoft Office Installation CD into your CD-ROM drive (unless you can install Office components from a network server) and click the Yes button to install it.

The Preview box at the bottom shows how the file will look in a Word document window. As you can see in Figure 38-3, it's not a pretty sight. However, you may be able to improve the file's appearance by clicking the Other Encoding button, selecting an encoding method from the list at the right, and then clicking OK to display the file in a Word document. If you can't improve the file's appearance, click the Cancel button on the File Conversion dialog box to stop the file-opening process.

TIP

> To use data from a file that Word can't open, open it in its original program and save it in a Word-compatible format like Rich Text Format (.rtf), or copy the data you want and paste it into a Word document.

Alternative Ways to Open Graphics and Database Files

When you use the Open command to open any graphics file, Word will turn it into garbage in the document window. It may do the same with other files from databases or other programs. There are, however, other ways to open and view these files in Word.

■ Even if you don't own any graphics programs, you may be able to open a graphic from the Windows desktop by using one of the programs that comes with Windows. Try double-clicking the file on the Windows desktop. It may open in Microsoft Paint, your Web browser, Adobe Illustrator, or another compatible program on your computer, and you can then select and copy the graphic into a Word document.

Word includes converters for many types of graphics, but you can only make use of them by inserting the graphic as a picture. To do this, choose the Picture command from the Insert menu. *For more information about inserting graphics, see "Inserting Pictures" on page 461.*

■ Word also allows you to insert objects from graphics, multimedia, or other kinds of programs. To do this, choose the Object command from the Insert menu. *For more information on inserting objects, see Chapter 21, "Working with Objects."*

■ You may be able to open records from database files using the Query options in the Mail Merge Helper. *For more information about this, see "Querying a Data File" on page 597.*

■ Finally, you may be able to grab data from a database program file by writing a custom macro that includes the MailMergeOpenDataSource command. *For more information about custom macros, see Chapter 29, "Working with Microsoft Visual Basic."*

Saving Word Documents in Other Formats

Just as you can open files from many different programs with the Open command, you can save files in many different formats with the Save As command. To save a document in another format, do the following:

? **SEE ALSO**

For more information about saving files, see "Saving Documents" on page 137.

1 Choose Save As from the File menu. Word displays the Save As dialog box.

2 Select a location for the file and enter a name for it if necessary.

3 Click the arrow button next to the Save As Type box. Word displays a list of file types like the one shown in Figure 38-1 on page 864.

4 Select a file type from the Save As Type list and click Save to save the file.

> Some other file formats don't support certain Word document features, such as form controls. If you save a Word document in a format that can't store all of the features you used in the document, Word will warn you and you'll have a chance to check the Help window to learn which features can't be converted.

Table 38-2 shows the file types you may find on the Save As Type list and some notes about each type.

TABLE 38-2.   File Formats You Can Save in with Word

File Type	Notes
Word Document	A Word document (.doc file)
Web Page	A file with the .htm extension
Document Template	A Word template (.dot file)
Rich Text Format	A file with the .rtf extension (rtf is a special Microsoft format that preserves formatting in a text file.)
Text Only	A text-only file (.txt extension)
Text Only With Line Breaks	A text (.txt) file with a paragraph marker at the end of each line
MS-DOS Text	A text (.txt) file with special MS-DOS characters
MS-DOS Text With Line Breaks	An MS-DOS text file with a paragraph marker at the end of each line
Encoded Text	A text file with text-based formatting codes embedded in it
MS-DOS Text with Layout	A file in the .ans format, which can store MS-DOS characters and formatting
Text with Layout	A text file (.ans) that includes formatting information
Word 2.x for Windows	A .doc file readable by this older version of Word for Windows
Word 4.0, 5.0, 5.1 for Macintosh versions of Word	A .mcw file readable by these older Macintosh versions of Word

(continued)

TABLE 38-2. *continued*

File Type	Notes
Word 6.0/95	A .doc file readable by these older English language versions of Word
Word 97-2000 and 6.0/95 RTF Converter	An .rtf file compatible with these Word versions
WordPerfect 5.0	A document file for this version of WordPerfect
WordPerfect 5.0 Secondary File	A data file for this version of WordPerfect
WordPerfect 5.1 for DOS	A document file for this DOS-based version of WordPerfect
WordPerfect 5.1 or 5.2 Secondary File	A data file for these versions of WordPerfect
WordPerfect 5.x for Windows	Saves a document file readable by WordPerfect versions 5.x or 6.x
Works 4.0 for Windows	A .wps file readable by this version of Microsoft Works for Windows

Use Text Formats for Maximum Compatibility

If you know in advance precisely which program will be used to open a file, you will naturally want to choose that program's file type from the Save As Type list in the Save As dialog box. But sometimes you don't know which program another person will use to view a document. In that case, it's best to use one of the standard file formats that are supported by most of the programs on the planet.

To save a document that can be opened by any word processing, spreadsheet, or database program, use the Text Only option or the Rich Text Format option. The text may have to be formatted in a certain way to fit properly into spreadsheet cells or database fields, but most spreadsheet and database programs have options for doing that when the file is imported into them. When you use Rich Text format, you preserve italics, boldface, and other formats in a document, while using the Text Only option eliminates all formatting.

The other Text formats on the Save As Type list incorporate additional formatting information in a text file, but you will want to use them for specific situations. For example, if you're saving a text form in which you want each line to end in a specific place, use the Text With Line Breaks option.

Some of the file types listed in Table 38-2 must be installed from the Office Installation CD. *For more information on installing these, see the Appendix.*

Converting Batches of Files

Sometimes you'll receive a whole bunch of files from another user and all of them need to be converted from another format to Word's document format. And in other situations you'll want to convert a lot of Word documents to another format. The procedures covered earlier in this chapter show how to convert documents one at a time, but Word has a Batch Conversion Wizard that can convert whole groups of files at once.

When you use the Batch Conversion Wizard, you select files not by name but by type. You then select the format to which you want to convert those files, along with a location where the converted files will be stored. The wizard makes it easy:

1 Use Windows Explorer or the Desktop to group into one folder all of the files you want to convert. If necessary, create a new folder in which to store the converted files.

2 Choose New from the File menu and click the Other Documents tab.

3 Double-click the Batch Conversion Wizard. The wizard's dialog box opens on your screen.

4 Click the Next button to move to the first step of the wizard, which looks like this:

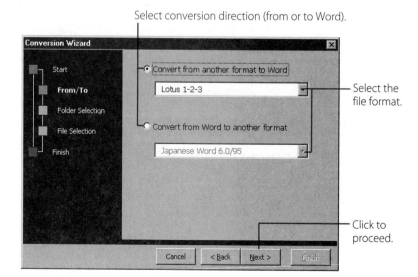

Select conversion direction (from or to Word).

Select the file format.

Click to proceed.

> The Batch Conversion Wizard isn't installed in a typical Word installation, but Word will give you the chance to install it when you first open the wizard.

5 Make sure the proper button is selected to specify whether you want to convert files from Word to another format or from another format to Word.

6 Select the format to which or from which you wish to convert and click the Next button. The wizard then presents two browse buttons so you can select the source and destination folders for the conversion.

7 Click the upper browse button and select the source folder where the files you want to convert are stored, and then click the lower browse button and select a destination folder for the converted files.

8 Click Next. The wizard presents a file selection dialog box like this:

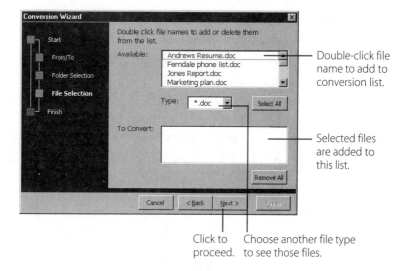

Double-click file name to add to conversion list.

Selected files are added to this list.

Click to proceed.   Choose another file type to see those files.

The Available list shows all of the files that are of the type that is shown in the Type box below.

9 To include a file in the conversion, double-click its name. The file will be added to the To Convert list below. To include all of the files of this type in the source folder, click the Select All button.

10 Click Next when you're finished selecting files, and then click Finish on the new dialog box to convert all of the selected files.

TIP

To clear the To Convert list and begin the file selection again, click the Remove All button. When you have a file selected in the To Convert list, the Remove All button name changes to Remove, and you can click it to remove the selected file.

Adjusting Word's Compatibility Options

Each program has its own way of dealing with things like line spacing, a default font, paragraph indents, and other formatting options. When you use a file converter in Word to open or save another type of file, the converter makes specific changes to the format so the document will look just right when opened. You can set specific compatibility options to control the way Word converts files to or from other formats.

Setting Options for Saving a Document

When you save a Word document as another type of file, Word makes some formatting changes. To set options for these changes, do the following:

1   Choose Options from the Tools menu to open the Options dialog box.

2   Click the Compatibility tab to see the options shown in Figure 38-4.

FIGURE 38-4.

Use the Compatibility tab in the Options dialog box to set specific formatting options for many of Word's file converters.

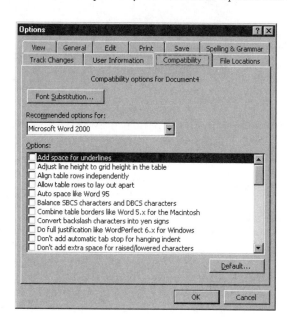

The top of the tab indicates that these options are for the current document only, but you can also set new options and then make them the defaults for all new documents based on Word's Normal template if you like.

3 Select the file type from the Recommended Options For list to display the format options for that file converter in the list below.

4 In the Options list, change the compatibility options by selecting or clearing the check boxes for specific format options. Scroll through the list if necessary to view and change options.

TIP

> Select Custom from the Recommended Options For list and then choose format options for it to create a set of custom file format options for the current document.

5 If you want to make the new options the default for the current document template, click the Default button and then click Yes in the message that appears.

6 Click OK to save the new options.

7 Save the file in the format you modified. For example, if you modified the conversion options for a WordPerfect 5.x file, save the file in that format. Word will convert the document to the new format using the options you specified.

Changing a Substitute Font

When you open a file in another format, Word does its best to convert the file so it looks right in the document window. However, one of the most common problems that occurs when you open files that were created on someone else's computer is that the files contain fonts that aren't available on your computer. These are known as *missing fonts*. When this happens, Word tries to substitute a font that closely resembles the missing font. The substitution Word chooses is temporary, however: if you're not happy with the substitution, you can use Word's compatibility options to substitute a different font for the missing font.

To change the substitute font for a document, follow these steps:

1 Open the document and choose Options from the Tools menu.

2 Click the Compatibility tab and then click the Font Substitution button on it. You'll see the Font Substitution dialog box as shown in Figure 38-5. The dialog box lists all of the fonts in the document that are missing from your computer along with the font that Word has automatically substituted for it.

FIGURE 38-5.

If you don't like the font Word has substituted in a document, you can choose a different one.

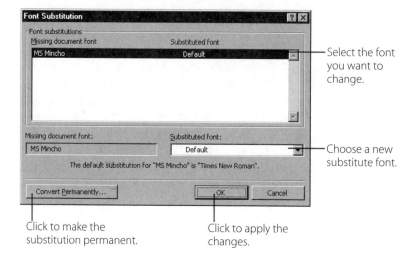

Select the font you want to change.

Choose a new substitute font.

Click to make the substitution permanent.

Click to apply the changes.

3 Select the font you want to change in the list, and then click the arrow button next to the Substituted Font list. The list shows every font available on your computer.

4 Choose a substitute font from the Substituted Font list.

5 If you want to permanently convert the missing font into the substitute font, click the Convert Permanently button and then click the OK button in the alert message that appears. (Otherwise, the change is temporary—the original font remains specified for the document.)

6 Click OK on the Font Substitution dialog box and click OK again in the Options dialog box to apply the change.

Installing and Running Word

Installing and Running Word

M icrosoft Word is distributed as part of Microsoft Office, and you can install Word by using the Installation Wizard on the Office CD-ROM. If you're on a network, you may also be able to install Word from a network file server. You can install all of the Office programs with a couple of mouse clicks or choose custom options to install Word by itself. Once you have Word installed, you can revisit the Installation Wizard at any time to add or remove components.

Hardware and Memory Requirements

To run Word, you need the following:

- A Microsoft Windows 95-compatible computer with an Intel Pentium processor running at least 150 MHz (Pentium II processor recommended)

- A 256-color monitor and video card

- Either Microsoft Windows 95, Windows 98, Windows NT Workstation 4.0 with Service Pack 3, or Windows 2000

- 16 megabytes (MB) of random access memory (RAM) for Windows 95 or 98 systems; 32 MB is required for Windows NT or 2000, and is recommended for every system

- 50 MB of hard disk space (for Word only; around 300 MB for all Office programs and components)

- A CD-ROM drive (if you're installing from a CD)

- A mouse or other pointing device

- An Internet connection (to access World Wide Web features)

In addition to these, you will also need a Web browser program on your computer to preview Web pages or to view Web sites from within Word; a sound card, speakers, or headphones; and a microphone for Word's voice and audio features. All Windows versions come with Microsoft Internet Explorer, and Office offers to upgrade your copy of Internet Explorer to version 5 if you don't already have this version installed.

Using the Installation Wizard

To install, update, or remove Word or any of its components, you use the Installation Wizard. To run the wizard from the Office CD, complete the following steps:

1 Insert the Office CD into your CD-ROM drive. The Installation Wizard should automatically start up after a few seconds. If the wizard doesn't start up after 30 seconds, open the My Computer icon on your Windows desktop and double-click the CD-ROM icon to activate the wizard. The wizard's Welcome dialog box will appear on your screen, as shown as in Figure A-1.

TIP

If you're on a company network, your network administrator will explain how to install Word from a network server.

FIGURE A-1.

You can install, upgrade, or remove Word with the Installation Wizard.

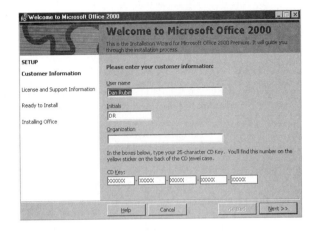

2 Enter your name, your initials, your company name, and the serial number of your copy of Office in the boxes and then click the Next button. The wizard examines your system for previous installations of Office or Word, and then displays the Office license agreement.

3 Click the button labeled I Accept The Terms In The License Agreement, and then click the Next button. You'll see the Ready To Install screen, as shown in Figure A-2.

FIGURE A-2.

You can install a typical collection of Office components by clicking one button or you can select another option to choose which components are installed.

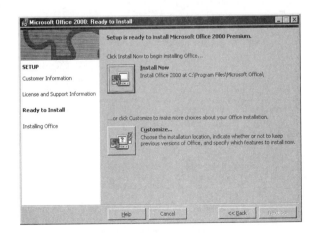

VIII

Appendix

Installing a Typical Office Setup

The Installation Wizard assumes that you want to install all of the Office programs, so it offers a single button on the Ready To Install screen that you can use to perform such an installation, as shown in Figure A-2. To install all of the Office programs with a preselected group of templates and other components at the default location C:\Program Files\Microsoft Office, just click the Install Now button. The Wizard will install the default set of Office programs and components and will let you know when it's done. You'll be asked to restart your computer in order to complete the process.

Customizing an Office Installation

If you want to install Office programs in a different location or you want to select specific components to install, it's easy to customize your installation:

1   Click the Customize button on the Ready To Install screen. The installer will suggest creating a new Microsoft Office folder inside the Program Files folder on your hard disk, as in Figure A-3.

FIGURE A-3.

Before the Installer begins copying files to your hard disk, it shows the location where the files will be copied and allows you to change it.

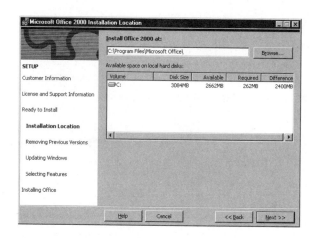

2   Click the Browse button and select a different location, if you like.

3   Click Next. You'll see the Select Features screen shown in Figure A-4. As you can see, the Office components fall into eight categories, each represented by a hard disk icon. The hard disk icon means that some or all of the components in this category will be installed to run from your hard disk. The plus sign next to each icon indicates that you can selectively install individual components in the category.

FIGURE A-4.

When you customize an installation, you can select individual components to install.

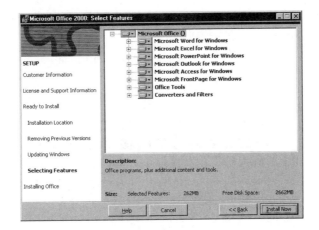

4 Click a category icon to see the components you can select:

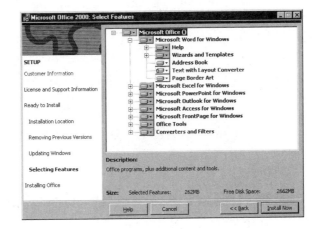

You can open some components to see and select other, more specific components.

5 Click a specific component (an icon without a plus sign next to it). Word displays a menu of options, as shown in Figure A-5.

FIGURE A-5.

You can set one of six different installation and running options for each Office component.

For more information
about each of the
installation options,
see "Installation and
Running Options"
below.

6 Choose an option to specify how you want the component installed.

7 Repeat this procedure with every component you want to install.

8 Click the Install Now button to install the components you selected.

Optional Components You Can Install

During a standard installation, the Installation Wizard installs the Office components you're likely to use, including each of the Office programs and a selection of templates. But there are many more components that you can select and install with a custom installation. You can also use the installation to change how a component runs when you use it in Word.

You can see which additional components you can select in addition to the standard Office components by browsing through the component categories on the Select Features screen, but here are some of the types of components you can add to make Word more powerful:

- Additional templates and wizards

- New Office Assistant characters

- Extra tools such as the Microsoft Equation Editor

- Additional file converters

Installation and Running Options

In addition to adding components, you can also change the way each component runs or installs itself when you select it in Word. The running and installation options are shown in Figure A-5. When you perform a typical Office installation, some of the components that are installed have various running options set. Here's what the options do:

- **Not Available** means the wizard won't install the component. When you try to activate the component from Word, nothing will happen.

- **Run From My Computer** means the wizard will install the component on your hard disk so that it runs immediately when you choose it.

- **Run All From My Computer** means the wizard will install all the components in this category on your hard disk. This option allows you to apply the same installation option to all of the specific components contained within a more general one. For example, choosing Run All From My Computer when you have Microsoft Word For Windows selected will automatically set all of its components (Help, Wizards and Templates, and so on) to be installed on your hard disk.

- **Run From CD** means that the wizard will install the component as a CD-only option. When you choose the component, Word will attempt to run it from your CD-ROM drive. If the Office CD isn't in your CD-ROM drive at the time, you'll see a message saying the component can't be found.

- **Run All From CD** means the wizard will install all the components in this category as CD-only options. This option works only when there are more specific components contained within the component you select. For example, choosing Run All From CD when you have Microsoft Word For Windows selected will automatically set all of its components to be installed as CD-only options.

- **Installed On First Use** means the component won't be installed, but Word will know about it. When you activate the component for the first time, you'll see a message saying it isn't installed, and Word offers an Install button you can click to install the component. If you click the Install button, Word will try to install the component from either your CD-ROM drive or from a network server (depending on where you initially installed it from). If you need to insert the Office CD into your CD-ROM drive, Word will alert you.

Adding, Changing, or Removing Components

Once you have installed Word, you can add more components to it, remove some of the ones you never use, or change the way components run. To do this, complete the following steps:

1 Run the Installation Wizard as explained under "Using the Installation Wizard" on page 880. You'll see the Maintenance Mode screen shown in Figure A-6 on the next page.

2 Click the Add Or Remove Features button. You'll see the Select Features screen much like the one shown in Figure A-4, although the settings for components may be different.

VIII

Appendix

3 Change the installation options to add or remove features or to change the way they run. For example, if a feature is installed, you can choose the Not Available option to remove it. If a feature is installed to run from a CD, you can choose Run From My Computer to install it on your hard disk.

FIGURE A-6.

When you run the Installation Wizard after you have already installed Word, you'll be able to add, change, or remove components in the installation.

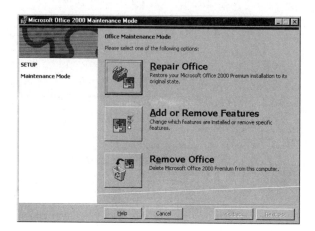

4 Click the Update Now button to install, remove, or change the components. (This button was called Install Now when you first installed Office.)

Repairing Word

Whenever you use programs or files on a computer, small errors can develop in the stored files due to such reasons as small power fluctuations that occur when the computer is reading from or writing to your hard disk. As a result, the Word installation on your hard disk can become damaged. You may notice that a feature doesn't work all the time, for example, or that using some features produces unexpected results. Office 2000 includes some new self-repair features that will keep your copies of Word or other programs running smoothly. You can repair or tune up Office manually by choosing a command or option. In addition, Office sometimes detects problems on its own and automatically launches the Office Tune-Up Wizard to fix them.

If your copy of Word begins doing strange things, there are two ways to resolve the problem. You can use the Detect And Repair command on the Help menu, or you can restore the original Office installation. Unless you experience a severe problem, it's best to try Detect and

Repair first and restore your installation only if Detect and Repair doesn't work. If neither of these remedies solves your problem, you'll want to remove your Office installation and then reinstall it.

Using Detect And Repair

The easiest way to fix minor problems with Word is to use the Detect And Repair command. The Detect And Repair feature examines your entire Office installation, searching for corrupted files. It will then reinstall any problem files it encounters and restore any shortcuts or custom settings you had previously if these were affected by the repair. To use Detect And Repair, do the following:

1 Start Word.

2 Insert the Office CD into your CD-ROM drive (unless you installed Office from a network server).

3 Choose Detect And Repair from the Help menu. Word displays the Detect And Repair dialog box, like this:

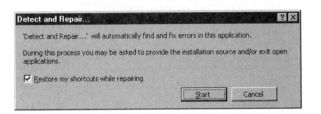

4 Clear the Restore My Shortcuts While Repairing check box if you don't want Detect And Repair to restore your custom settings.

5 Click the Start button to repair your installation.

Restoring Your Installation

To restore an installation to its original state, do the following:

1 Run the Installation Wizard from the Office CD or from your network server. You'll see the Maintenance Mode screen as shown in Figure A-6.

2 Click the Repair Office button. The Installation Wizard will restore your Office installation to its original state, fixing any corrupted files in the process.

Reinstalling Office

If the two repair options don't solve your problem, you'll need to reinstall Office or Word completely. Here's what to do:

1 Run the Installation Wizard from the Office CD or from your network server. You'll see the Maintenance Mode screen as shown in Figure A-6 on page 886.

2 Click the Remove Office button. A message box will ask you to confirm that you want to remove Office.

3 Click the Yes button in the message box. Office will be removed from your computer.

4 Run the Installation Wizard again, and install Word or Office using the techniques described in "Using the Installation Wizard" on page 880.

Network Installation and Administration Tools

If you are installing and running Word on a network, your network administrator has some additional tools that may affect your installation. It's beyond the scope of this book to cover how a network administrator might install and run these options, but as a Word user you should know what they do because they might affect you.

■ **Custom Installation Wizard** This wizard allows a network administrator to customize Office installations for each user. Using the wizard, your administrator can determine which components are installed when you install Word, and he or she can also restrict your customization options when you add or change features later.

■ **System Policy Editor** This tool allows your network administrator to disable certain toolbars or shortcut keys.

■ **Custom Alerts** Your administrator can include customized buttons in many Word and Office alert messages. The buttons link to intranet Web pages where the administrator has posted instructions or other information.

- **Answer Wizard Builder** With this tool your network administrator can create custom Help text that is specific to your company's operations and incorporate it into Word's Help system.

- **Template Manager** This tool allows a network administrator to create a collection of corporate document templates at a certain location on the network and automatically configure your copy of Word so that those templates are easy to locate in the Open dialog box.

- **Office Profile Wizard** Your administrator can give you access to this tool so you can create a profile that stores your custom Word preferences and settings. *For more information about the Office Profile Wizard, see "Running Word from Another Computer" on page 820.*

VIII

Appendix

Index

Note to the reader: Italicized page numbers refer to figures, tables, and illustrations.

O

x-axis (horizontal axis), 498

y-axis (vertical axis), 498

About the Author

Charles Rubin has been writing about computers and software since 1983, when a magazine editor and a literary agent both suggested to him that he could actually get paid for learning about things he found fascinating and explaining them to others. *Running Microsoft Word 2000* will be his 31st computer-related book title; others include multiple editions of *Running Microsoft Works, Guerrilla Marketing Online, Managing Your Business With QuickBooks, The Macintosh Bible Guide to FileMaker Pro,* and *The Macintosh Bible Guide to ClarisWorks.*

> *Running Microsoft Word 2000 will be his 31st computer-related book title.*

Charles also writes technical marketing materials for a variety of clients, including America Online, Apple Computer, Cisco Systems, Compaq, Lotus Development, Microsoft, Veriphone, Visa International, and Xerox. He has also contributed articles to a number of publications including *InfoWorld, Newsweek, PC Week, PC World, Popular Science,* and *The Wall Street Journal.*

When not writing something, Charles can be found either tearing new divots in a local golf course or shredding corners with his motorcycle on a favorite twisty road. He lives in Northern California with his wife and son.

Colophon

The manuscript for this book was prepared and submitted to Microsoft Press in electronic form. Text files were prepared using Microsoft Word 97 for Windows. Pages were composed by nSight, Inc., using Adobe PageMaker 6.5 for Windows, with text in Garamond Light and display type in Myriad Black. Composed pages were delivered to the printer as electronic prepress files.

Cover Designer

Tim Girvin Design, Inc.

Interior Graphics Specialist

Vanessa White

Principal Compositors

Joanna Zito, Angela Montoya

Principal Proofreaders

Janice O'Leary, Rebecca Merz

Indexer

James Minkin

up!Step Step

STEP BY STEP books provide quick and easy self-training—to help you learn to use the powerful word processing, spreadsheet, database, presentation, communication, and Internet components of Microsoft® Office 2000—both individually and together. The easy-to-follow lessons present clear objectives and real-world business examples, with numerous screen shots and illustrations. Put Office 2000 to work today, with STEP BY STEP learning solutions, made by Microsoft.

- MICROSOFT OFFICE PROFESSIONAL 8-IN-1 STEP BY STEP
- MICROSOFT WORD 2000 STEP BY STEP
- MICROSOFT EXCEL 2000 STEP BY STEP
- MICROSOFT POWERPOINT® 2000 STEP BY STEP
- MICROSOFT INTERNET EXPLORER 5 STEP BY STEP
- MICROSOFT PUBLISHER 2000 STEP BY STEP
- MICROSOFT ACCESS 2000 STEP BY STEP
- MICROSOFT FRONTPAGE 2000 STEP BY STEP
- MICROSOFT OUTLOOK 2000 STEP BY STEP

Microsoft Press offers *comprehensive* learning solutions to help new users, power users, and professionals get the most from *Microsoft technology.*

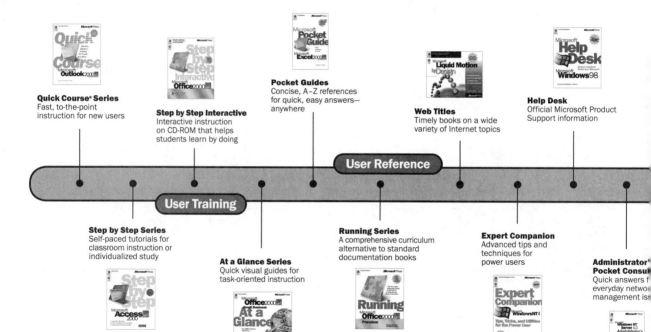

Quick Course® Series
Fast, to-the-point instruction for new users

Step by Step Interactive
Interactive instruction on CD-ROM that helps students learn by doing

Pocket Guides
Concise, A–Z references for quick, easy answers—anywhere

Web Titles
Timely books on a wide variety of Internet topics

Help Desk
Official Microsoft Product Support information

User Reference

User Training

Step by Step Series
Self-paced tutorials for classroom instruction or individualized study

At a Glance Series
Quick visual guides for task-oriented instruction

Running Series
A comprehensive curriculum alternative to standard documentation books

Expert Companion
Advanced tips and techniques for power users

Administrator's Pocket Consul
Quick answers f everyday netwo management iss

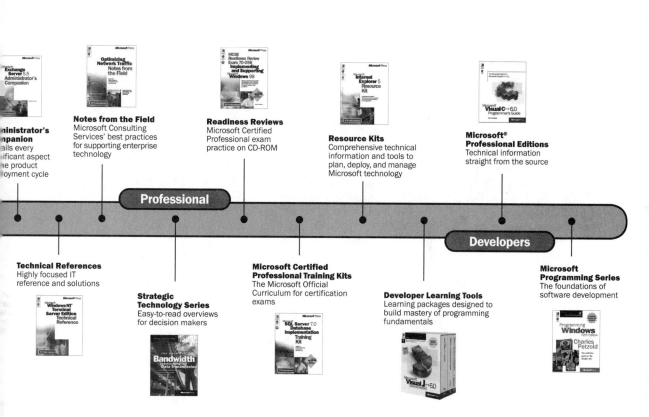

See clearly—
now!

Here's the remarkable, *visual* way to quickly find answers about the powerfully integrated features of the Microsoft® Office 2000 applications. Microsoft Press AT A GLANCE books let you focus on particular tasks and show you, with clear, numbered steps, the easiest way to get them done right now. Put Office 2000 to work today, with AT A GLANCE learning solutions, made by Microsoft.

- MICROSOFT OFFICE 2000 PROFESSIONAL AT A GLANCE
- MICROSOFT WORD 2000 AT A GLANCE
- MICROSOFT EXCEL 2000 AT A GLANCE
- MICROSOFT POWERPOINT® 2000 AT A GLANCE
- MICROSOFT ACCESS 2000 AT A GLANCE
- MICROSOFT FRONTPAGE® 2000 AT A GLANCE
- MICROSOFT PUBLISHER 2000 AT A GLANCE
- MICROSOFT OFFICE 2000 SMALL BUSINESS AT A GLANCE
- MICROSOFT PHOTODRAW® 2000 AT A GLANCE
- MICROSOFT INTERNET EXPLORER 5 AT A GLANCE
- MICROSOFT OUTLOOK® 2000 AT A GLANCE

Microsoft®

mspress.microsoft.com

Register Today!

Return this
Running Microsoft® Word 2000
registration card today

Microsoft® Press
mspress.microsoft.com

OWNER REGISTRATION CARD   1-57231-943-7

Running Microsoft® Word 2000

_____   _____   _____
FIRST NAME   MIDDLE INITIAL   LAST NAME

_____
INSTITUTION OR COMPANY NAME

_____
ADDRESS

_____

_____   _____   _____
CITY   STATE   ZIP

_____   (   )_____
E-MAIL ADDRESS   PHONE NUMBER

U.S. and Canada addresses only. Fill in information above and mail postage-free.
Please mail only the bottom half of this page.

For information about Microsoft Press® *products, visit our Web site at* **mspress.microsoft.com**

Microsoft®*Press*